In the Name of God, the Merc

THE OLD TESTAMENT: AN ISLAMIC PERSPECTIVE

VOLUME 2

FROM MOSES TO ALEXANDER

Revised Edition

A COMPARISON OF THE QURANIC STORIES OF SURABADI WITH THE BIBLE

Being a Comparison of the Stories of the Prophets and Other Personages from the *Quranic Commentary* by Abū Bakr ᶜAtīq Nīshābūrī Sūrābādī (d. 1100 CE) with Those in the *Old Testament*, the *Apocrypha*, *Pseudepigraha*, and Other Relevant Writings of the Ancient and Medieval Worlds
by
Jay R. Crook, Ph.D.

ABC International Group

ii

Library of Congress Cataloging in Publication Data

Bibliographical references.

1. The Bible: An Islamic Perspective: The Old Testament, Volume 2
I. Author. II. Title.
BP137.T331997 297'.1228   77-25941
ISBN 1-56744-727-9

Published by
ABC International Group

Distributed by
KAZI Publications, Inc.
3023 West Belmont Avenue
Chicago, IL 60618
(T) 773-267-7001; (F) 773-267-7002
email: info@kazi.org   online: www.kazi.org

To
Dr. Sayyid Ja'far Shahidi,
Professor of Persian Literature
at Tehran University,
who set me on this journey into the ancient world
and without whose advice, counsel, wisdom, and knowledge
I should have lost my way;
and to
Dr. Laleh Bakhtiar
whose support and encouragement
enabled me to complete this journey
many long years after I had embarked upon it.

Also by Jay R. Crook

The Old Testament: An Islamic Perspective

The entire text and contents of *The Old Testament: An Islamic Perspective* and *The New Testament: An Islamic Perspective* are also available separately in a series format as *The Bible: An Islamic Perspective.* Its constituent volumes are:

Introduction to the Old Testament
From the Creation to the Flood
Abraham
Jacob and Joseph
Moses
From Judges to Monarchy
David and Solomon
From Monarchy to Hellenism
Introduction to the New Testament
Jesus
Paul and Early Christianity
Armageddon (chapter from *Jesus*)

Translations:

The Royal Book of Spiritual Chivalry (Kāshifī)
The Alchemy of Happiness (al-Ghazzālī)

Translations/Adaptations as Muhammad Nur Abdus Salam:
The *Stories for Young Adults* series:

Attar
Kalilah and Dimnah
Rumi
Saadi

TABLE OF CONTENTS

VOLUME 2

PART THREE: THE ERA OF MOSES

I. MOSES

No single figure in later Israel plays the many roles
ascribed to Moses... (Moses, EJ, XII, 388)

A. INTRODUCTORY REMARKS

The most important personality of the Old Testament, the man who shaped Israel, was without doubt Moses. No other leader, no other prophet, no other lawgiver in the Old Testament can even approach the dominating, central position that Moses occupies in Judaism. He is the supreme hero of the Pentateuch, which is in fact the national epic of Israel.[1442]

Traditionally, Moses is credited with promulgating, under divine guidance, the Torah containing the sacred Law to the rebellious, fractious Israelites. He gave them a national identity and a sense of oneness that has sustained them—despite their incessant quarrels, divisions, and disasters—to the present day. The Pentateuch is the written record of this transformation, as viewed retrospectively by men trying to preserve and glorify their national identity as God's Chosen People. Moses is the embodiment of this process. The traditional view is that the entire Pentateuch, except perhaps the last verses of *Deuteronomy* narrating his death and burial, is from the hand of Moses. While the results of modern scholarship no longer support this view, insofar as the present text is concerned, authentic traditions of Moses surely stand behind many of the pericopes, and the text preserves some very ancient material indeed, mostly in songs and incantations.[1443]

[1442] Moses is mentioned more often in the New Testament than any other Old Testament prophet (Moses, EJ, XII, 402).

[1443] The view that Moses actually wrote all or most of the Pentateuch still has its defenders. "Moses had written Genesis out of previously existing documents... His own life and work comprise the subject matter of Exodus, Leviticus, Numbers, and Deuteronomy. He himself wrote these books." (Halley, p. 109) Though that is a popular rather than a scholarly opinion, the view of the Roman Catholic Church was stated in 1906, in a response that warned Catholic exegetes about the Documentary Theory and "required them to maintain the 'substantial' Mosaic authorship of the Pentateuch taken as a whole." In a later letter (1948) however, the Pontifical Biblical Commission took a more lenient view and admitted "a gradual growth of the Mosaic laws and of the historical narratives, a growth due to the social and religious conditions of later times." (JB, p. 7)

As a prophet, it is asserted, Moses spoke directly with God (without an intermediary as in the case of the Prophet of Islam), and in one tradition in *Exodus*, even saw Him.[1444] He is considered the father of the prophets, even though a distinction is sometimes made between Moses and the others because he was in almost continuous communication with God, whilst other prophets received their revelations through dreams, trances, or in states of religious ecstasy. He was also Israel's special intercessor, and he successfully interceded with God on several occasions to save Israel from total destruction by an irate Deity after their behavior had earned His wrath. Later Jewish tradition dwelt lovingly on the figure of Moses. It was said that he was born circumcised;[1445] he surpassed all creation; indeed, he was half man and half God.[1446] He entered Paradise alive;[1447] he emitted a powerful light and his corpse never decayed.[1448] With Aaron (Ar. *Hārūn*), he presides over the first division of Paradise.[1449] As a culmination of this glorification, it was declared that the world had been created for Moses,[1450] as it was created for the Prophet Muhammad in some Islamic traditions. Moreover, Moses, according to the 1st-century CE *Assumption of Moses*, had been prepared to be Israel's mediator with God even before the foundation of the world.[1451]

Jewish tradition also depicted Moses as the king of Israel,[1452] but the Pentateuch does not support the idea that he had the title or paraphernalia of royalty. Such exaltation would doubtless have been repugnant to the fugitives from the despotic government of royal Pharaonic Egypt. Nonetheless, he was a leader of men, as his ability to convince the people to follow him shows. He was able to rally them when they were marching through the harsh, hot aridity of Sinai and Midian. He overcame much murmuring against him, even open rebellion, as they recalled longingly the "comforts" of Egypt in that brutal landscape. He planned military expeditions and organized his people into a proto-nation. He gave the people laws and a kind of social constitution.

[1444] A Muslim, of course, would consider such assertions and claims to be bordering upon blasphemy.

[1445] Nathan, p. 23.

[1446] LJ, III, 480-481. The assertion of demigodhood would be held blasphemous in Islam.

[1447] LJ, V, 96; VI, 161, 162, 166.

[1448] LJ, III, 93.

[1449] LJ, I, 22.

[1450] Moses, EJ, XII, 395.

[1451] Moses, EJ, XII, 392.

[1452] LJ, III, 153-154, etc.

In some fashion, he was the instrument of the introduction of (or rededication to) YHWH-worship among the descendants of Jacob. The problem of Moses and YHWH-worship is perhaps the most discussed and disputed point of religious history to be raised about the Pentateuch.[1453] However, there can be no question but that Moses is regarded as the traditional codifier of the formal aspect of YHWH-worship for Israel. It was often found necessary in later times to attribute virtually all legal and ritual innovations to Moses, in the same way that in the period of uncontrolled of Islamic religious literature, statements were attributed to the Prophet that he could not possibly have uttered. In Islam, these excesses fortunately brought about the scholarly compendia of Traditions edited by al-Bukhari, Muslim, and others, from which spurious Traditions were excluded as much as possible.

Moshe Greenberg writes: "No single figure in later Israel plays the many roles ascribed to Moses... The best analogue to Moses in the history of religions, Muhammad, exhibits the very same multiplicity of roles: oracle, political-military leader, cult founder and lawgiver."[1454] The parallel between the founder of the Israelite nationhood and the founder of Islam is indeed striking. The difference in the results is also striking. The YHWH-worship that Moses introduced or systematized among the Israelites led, in later interpretations at least, to a national religion with exclusivist tendencies based upon the tradition of being the Chosen of God; sentiments Judaism retains to the present day. The evidence, even in the Old Testament, is that YHWH-worship was not always a national club—and we hear of much intermarriage and conversion in the pre-Exilic period, but during the later monarchy and especially after the Exile (invoking the authority of Moses once again), Judaism developed those features of separateness that still characterize it.

Admittedly, if the ancient Jews had not done so, the Jewish nation would probably have disappeared into the Middle Eastern racial melting pot as so many other nationalities had before and after them. It could be argued that during that period, this exclusivity was necessary so that monotheism would not perish from the earth. But with the rise of later monotheistic creeds such as those of some (non-Pauline) Christian sects and Islam, Judaism—no longer possessing a monopoly of this view of God—has had to rely increasingly upon racial criteria to maintain its

---

[1453] See Section E.
[1454] Moses, EJ, XII, 388.

cultural existence.[1455] Even non-observing Jews often hark back to Moses when defending the Jewish experience.

On the other hand, Islam, which considers itself the successor religion, or the logical result of Judaism and Christianity, though it espouses a religious Law (*Sharīᶜah*), rejects any qualifications of birth for total admittance to its fold. Belief and deed are all that are required. It was thus in the beginning. The Arab nationalist reaction to this openness embodied by the Umayyads failed, and a multi-national, color-blind Islam in which race and origin should play no part remains the ideal, although compromised by the divisive ideology of nationalism in recent centuries. Only submission to the Will of God and right action are required to be a Muslim. The social and ritual demands of Islam are predicated upon those foundations.

The Quran attests to the importance of Moses in the prophetic history of Islam. Moses is mentioned twice as frequently as any other Biblical figure (136 times to 69 for Abraham, who is the second). The Moses of the Quran is essentially the Moses of the Old Testament, although there is no interest in the occasional outbursts of primitive anger and impatience attributed to him in the Bible. As the Quranic stories are predicated on the traditions circulating in the Arabia of the Prophet and are not based directly upon the Bible, they afford us additional views of glimpses of Moses taken from other traditions that had become associated with Moses, especially in the accounts of Moses' journey (Q. 18:60-82) and Haman, the vizier of Pharaoh.[1456] There are other differences of detail that will be pointed out and discussed in their appropriate contexts.

References to Moses occur in 34 of the 114 surahs of the Quran. Oddly enough, our basic text, Dr. Mahdavi's edition of the Quranic Stories of Surabadi's Commentary, does not have two of the most important sections, one concerning the Decalogue, the other the Journey of Moses. In view of their importance, we have taken the relative

---

[1455] Large-scale conversions to Judaism by non-Semites in later times, especially that of the Khazars in the 8th century CE who are the principal ancestors, many scholars believe, of the East European Jews and their descendants throughout the world, are minimized or ignored altogether.

[1456] See Section B. The Quran mentions the "leaves" or "pages" of Moses (*Ṣuḥuf Mūsā*) twice, in Q. 53:36 and Q. 87:19, but makes no further comment upon them in those places. It is assumed the references are to the original revelations, not the much-edited Pentateuch we now possess.

passages from *Tarikh-i Bal'ami* as the basis for our comparison of these stories.[1457]

Although most of the principal events of the life of Moses are alluded to in the Quran, they are not in chronological order. It may be useful to give an overview of the Biblical version of the course of Moses' activities for comparison with the Islamic pericopes:

Of the five "Books of Moses," the first, *Genesis*, tells us nothing of Moses. The era of Moses is recorded in the remaining four books: *Exodus*, *Leviticus*, *Numbers*, and *Deuteronomy*. Of these, *Leviticus* is almost entirely concerned with legal matter and offers practically no biographical material. *Deuteronomy* gives a recapitulation of many of the events recorded in *Exodus* and *Numbers*, as the Deuteronomist understood them, but he offers almost new material except the account of Moses' death in the last chapter (34), which itself is a conflation of material from J, E, and P. Thus, our main sources are to be found in *Exodus* and *Numbers*, though both books also contain large sections of a legal character. Virtually the entire Biblical story of Moses is to be found in those two books.

The material in *Exodus* and *Numbers* is from the same three primary sources, but much of it is in a very confused state. Scholars have proposed various reorganizations of verses in key passages in an endeavor to clarify and straighten out the text.[1458] We shall discuss some of these textual problems when they affect our study. In order to prepare a foundation for our comparison, we shall need first an outline the Biblical story of Moses as it unfolds in the Pentateuch, starting with *Exodus*:

A **BIBLICAL LIFE OF MOSES:** Three hundred and twenty years after the death of Joseph, the condition of Jacob's descendants was greatly altered from the honorable state in which they were first held when they their ancestors entered Egypt. Now they were enslaved and impressed into forced labor on the construction projects of a different kind of Pharaoh (Ex. 1:8-22). It was thus when Moses was born in Egypt.

[1457] *Tarikh-i Bal'ami* (Bal'ami's History) is a Persian translation of the Arabic *Universal History* of Tabari (d. 923 CE). Bal'ami began his version 963 CE; it is one of the earliest examples extant of modern Persian prose and antedates Surabadi (d. 1101 CE) by more than a century.

[1458] For example, one passage in *Exodus* relating to the second delivery of the Tables of the Law is reconstructed thus: Ex. 33:1-4a. 17, 12-13. 18-23; 34:6-9; 33: 14-16. (Moses, DB, p. 676.)

After the remarkable circumstances of his birth,[1459] Moses was raised as an Egyptian in Pharaoh's court (Ex. 2:1-10). When he had grown up, he went to see how the Hebrews were faring and while going about, he saw an Egyptian beating a Hebrew. Not seeing anyone around, he killed the Egyptian. The next day, when he tried to intervene in quarrel between two Hebrews, one of them taunted him with the killing of the Egyptian, and Moses knew that his crime had been observed. Fearing retribution from Pharaoh, he fled to Midian (Ex. 2:11-15).[1460] There he aided Reuel's (Jethro's)[1461] daughters and married one of them, Zipporah.[1462] He became a shepherd (Ex. 2:16-22). When Pharaoh died, God appeared to Moses in a burning bush at Horeb and commissioned him to go back to Egypt and lead the Hebrews out of their enslavement (Ex. 3-4:23). During this theophany, God also identified himself to Moses as YHWH, a name by which He had not been previously known.

Moses was awed by the magnitude of the task and felt inadequate to it. He complained that he was not eloquent, and succeeded in altering the conditions of the assignment to include the help of Aaron. Moses was given the signs of the white hand and the rod. On the way, YHWH tried to kill Moses, but He was foiled by Zipporah. (This extraordinary tradition in Ex. 4:24-26 still defies the efforts of exegetes. Many think it is out of place and should precede the theophany and not follow as it does in its present position in the text).[1463]

In Egypt again, after securing the support of the Hebrew elders for their mission, Moses and Aaron went to Pharaoh. He rejected their request to lead the Hebrews out into the desert for a three-day festival. (They secretly planned to use the opportunity of the festival to flee Egypt). Moreover, Pharaoh increased their labors (Ex. 4:27-5:21). The fickle Hebrews reproved Moses and Aaron for their interference as it had only served to make their bondage more difficult. Moses retired for another theophany in which God ordered him to return to Egypt. He did so, and after the contests of the rod and the serpents, the plagues began. At first unyielding, but when faced with the destruction of his own children, Pharaoh agreed to permit the Hebrews to leave Egypt (Ex. 5:22-13:16).[1464]

[1459] See Section C.
[1460] See Section D.
[1461] See Section D for a discussion of the multiplicity of names for Moses' father-in-law.
[1462] Zipporah: Ṣafūrā in Persian.
[1463] See Section E. (Moses, DB, p. 675.)
[1464] See Section F.

The Exodus proper began with God Himself going before Moses and his people, with Pharaoh, who had changed his mind, in hot pursuit.[1465] The Hebrews crossed the sea that had miraculously parted for them, but when Pharaoh and his army tried to follow them, the waters returned, overwhelming them (Ex. 13:17-14:31).

Although much of the text up to this point is confused, the general sequence of events given above may be extracted from it. From the actual Exodus, that is, the departure from Egypt, the chronicler's task becomes more difficult. Apparently, the Hebrews made for Kadesh-Barnea, a well-watered oasis (scholars believe) on the border of Sinai and southern Palestine, but which is here called Horeb. On the way they were treated to the miracles of the water turned sweet, they rested at the twelve springs of Elim, and were fed with manna and quail, a gift of divine providence. This was followed by the provision of water at Massah and Meribah by Moses, who struck the rock with his rod (Ex. 15:22-17:7). The Hebrews defeated the Amalekites in a battle during this time, albeit with divine intervention (Ex. 17:8-16).

All of the above took place within a period of about three months from the departure from Egypt (Ex. 19:1). Now at Sinai, Moses went up the sacred mountain and received the Tables of the Law, and remained there for forty days and nights without food or water (Ex. 19, 24, 31:18). The people waiting for him below grew impatient and persuaded Aaron to fashion a golden calf for them that they proceeded to worship (Ex. 22). When Moses returned, he broke the Tablets of the Law in anger and the people were punished terribly.[1466] Moses then climbed up the mountain again and was given a second set of Tables. After this event, Moses' face was so resplendent that he had to wear a veil (Ex. 33:7-34:35). At this point, the narrative of Moses' acts stops and the remainder of *Exodus* is concerned with Moses' instructions for the making of the Tabernacle in the Wilderness, which later became the prototype for the Temple in Jerusalem.[1467] The next book, *Leviticus*, is a book of ceremonial and

---

[1465] See Section G.

[1466] See Section H.

[1467] The Tabernacle in which the Ark was housed was God's tent, or rather His moveable palace. After YHWH left the mountaintop, He commanded that the Tabernacle be erected as His residence, and the Ark was in some way His throne or footstool, the point of contact between Divinity and man, where Moses would converse with Him and the priests establish ceremonial worship, offering sacrifices to that Presence. As befits a migratory people, these symbols of the Divine Presence—the Ark and the Tabernacle—were portable and could be set up wherever the Israelites made camp. "So they set out from the mount of the Lord three days' journey; and the ark of the covenant of the Lord went before them three days' journey, to seek out a resting place for them. And the cloud

religious laws, most of which is attributed to God Himself, with virtually no narrative, except to link passages.

When *Numbers* picks up the story of Moses again, two years and two months have elapsed since the Exodus. Now back at Kadesh-Barnea we have another account of manna and quails (Num. 11). Next, there was the sedition of Aaron and Miriam who spoke against Moses because of his Cushite wife. This resulted in God's punishing Miriam with leprosy, but Aaron escaped punishment. Fortunately for Miriam, at Aaron and Moses' request, God relented and changed her punishment to a week's confinement (Num. 12).

Spies were sent to Canaan and they returned with mixed reports of a fair land, but with powerful defenders. After an unauthorized battle with Amalekites in which the Israelites were defeated, many of them were disheartened and wished to return to Egypt. For this rebellion, God condemned them to wander in the wilderness for forty years (Num. 13-14). After the rebellion and the punishment of Korah (Num. 16),[1468] and the trial of the twelve rods which asserted the primacy of Aaron (Num. 17:1-11) and, by implication, the later Jerusalem priesthood claiming descent from him, Miriam died and was buried at Kadesh-Barnea (Num. 20:1).

---

of the Lord was over them by day, whenever they set out from the camp. And whenever the ark set out, Moses said, 'Arise, O Lord, and let Thy enemies be scattered; and let them that hate Thee flee before Thee.' And when it rested, he said, 'Return, O Lord, to the ten thousand thousands of Israel.'" (Num. 10:3-36)

From this passage—and it is not unique in the Bible in this respect—we see again that God is not omniscient and had to serve as a scout for the Hebrew horde, preceding them and seeking a place He must locate for them to alight. Primitive stuff indeed! God seems to be an invisible giant with supernatural but limited powers, not the Omnipotent Creator of the Universe. His interests are restricted to the welfare of Israel. There is no indication that any of His activities involve the rest of mankind except insomuch as they are Israel's enemies destined to be conquered, dispossessed, and reduced to servitude; or, occasionally, as a weapon to punish a disobedient or recalcitrant Israel. One gets the sense in much of the early portions of the Old Testament that God was totally preoccupied with the Children of Israel to the neglect of the rest of the world, even residing in their midst. This attitude on the part of God would be consonant with that of a tribal god, but His indifference to the welfare of the rest of mankind, not to mention the rest of the universe, is supremely incongruous for a Supreme Being.

Even after the Israelites had become established in Canaan, YHWH continued to reside in His tent. When David wanted to build a permanent Temple to replace the tent in which the Ark had been kept, God is reported to have come to the prophet Nathan in a dream, telling him: "'Go and tell my servant David, "Thus says the Lord: Wouldst thou build me a house to dwell in? I have not dwelt in a house since the day I brought up the people of Israel from Egypt to this day, but I have been moving about in a tent for my dwelling..."'" (2 Sam. 7:5-6)

[1468] See Section I.

There was still another miracle of water from a rock, this time at Meribah (Num. 20:1-13). Moses sent messengers to the Edomites requesting permission to pass through their lands and thus circle around the Dead Sea to enter Canaan from the east, since they had found that they could not use the more direct northern route blocked by the Amalekites (Num. 20:14-21). The Edomites refused and the Hebrews were forced to make a long detour around the Edomite lands. On the way, at Mount Hor, Aaron died and was buried (Num. 20:22-29).[1469] The people murmured again and were punished by a plague of serpents that Moses brought under control by setting up a copper serpent upon a staff (Num. 21:4-9).

Having made the detour around the Edomites, the Amorites refused passage to the Hebrews. In the ensuing battle, the Israelites were victorious and slew Sihon and Og (Num. 21:21-26, 32-35). The Israelites camped on the Plains of Moab opposite Jericho. Here are inserted the story and oracles of Balaam the seer which apparently do not belong to the Moses cycle, as Moses is not mentioned in them (Num. 22-24).[1470]

There was still another of scene of Israelite apostasy at Beor which was the apparent cause of another plague sent by God (Num. 25). Then God called Moses to a mountain peak east of the Jordan and told him that because of his (Moses') rebellion, he would not be permitted to enter the Promised Land, but would only be allowed to see it. (This prohibition is usually attributed to the incident in which Moses struck the rock for water without first seeking divine permission in Num. 20:10-13.) God also instructed him to nominate Joshua as his successor (Num. 27:12-23).

After Moses returned to his people, there was a battle with the Midianites in which the Israelites were again victorious, and among others, Balaam was slain (Num. 31:1-12). Moses ordered a savage general massacre of the prisoners (the people with whom he had taken refuge when fleeing from Egypt), according to the Priestly text: "Now therefore, kill every male among the little ones, and kill every woman who has known man by lying with him. But all the young girls who have not known man by lying with him, keep alive for yourselves." (Num. 31:17-18)

The Reubenites and the Gadites asked for and received permission from Moses to settle east of the Jordan provided they continued to aid in the conquest on the other side of the Jordan (Num. 32). The biographical information in *Numbers* closes leaving Moses on

---

[1469] See Section N.
[1470] See Section L.

the Plains of Moab opposite Jericho (Num. 33:50). To this, *Deuteronomy* adds the circumstances of the death and burial of Moses (Deut. 34:1-8).

There is no statement in the Pentateuch itself stating that Moses authored the five books which comprise it, although there are references to his writing of the Law.[1471] The Quran confirms the gift of the Torah to Moses, as do Biblical tradition and the later writings in the Bible itself. However, the present Torah, after centuries of redaction and editing—as modern scholarship has shown—cannot be said to be the Law as Moses received it, as is pointed out in the Quran. Behind the Pentateuch we possess, the Torah of Moses undoubtedly lies, but most of the laws incorporated into the present text are demonstrably the product of much later times.[1472]

There are many problems (other than that of the authorship of the Pentateuch) with the above summary that broadly outlines most of what we know of the public life of Moses. The text in both *Exodus* and *Numbers* is extraordinarily confused and difficult, and we again find instances of the same kind of duplication we found in *Genesis*,[1473] There are many ancient traditions inserted into the narrative.[1474] In addition, the Balaam stories do not seem to belong to the story of Moses at all, but were included in *Numbers* by later editors finding their present positioning suitable.

Despite detailed itineraries such as that to be found in Num. 33:1-49, and the summary in the first three chapters of *Deuteronomy*, there is no agreement among scholars about the route of the Exodus and the wanderings of the Israelites in the deserts east of Egypt and south of Canaan. There are many unresolved questions:

Is Sinai/Horeb to be identified with Kadesh? Are Kadesh and Sinai/Horeb located east or west of the Aqabah depression? If Kadesh is to be identified with a site some 50 miles southwest of Beersheba, was that the original goal of the Israelites? Were the forty years of wandering really a settlement of the tribes in this region? Did the twelve tribes travel as a group, or were only the Josephic tribes (Ephraim and

---

[1471] "And Moses wrote this law, and gave it to the priests of the sons of Levi..." (Deut. 31:9) "When Moses had finished writing the words of this law in a book, to the very end..." (Deut. 31:24)

[1472] For a discussion of the probable contents of the original Torah, see Silver, especially chapters 7 and 13.

[1473] E.g., the water from the rock, told twice (Ex. 17:1-7 and Num. 20:2-13); the theophanies in Ex. 3-4 and 5-6.

[1474] Zipporah uses a *flint* to circumcise her son, Ex. 4:25; the sympathetic magic of the copper serpent, Num. 21:4-9.

Manasseh) involved in the Exodus? Was YHWH already known to the Hebrews as the Yahwist seems to imply, or did He reveal Himself to Moses for the first time as the Elohist and Priestly collections state? If the latter is the case, does this account in fact conceal a conversion of Moses to a god already worshipped under the name YHWH by the Kenites into whom he had married? Is there any evidence of the name YHWH before the time of Moses?

At the appropriate places in our investigation of the sources of the Quranic stories of Surabadi's Commentary, we shall attempt to address these questions, but it should be observed that even the formulation of such questions is viewed with disquiet by some Jewish and Christian scholars. There is a tendency to accept the admittedly often tendentious accounts contained in the Bible as *prima facie* evidence in themselves, against any other interpretations which might give primacy in some theological matters to peoples other than the Hebrews, or permit interpretations substantially different from the received ones.

Buber, for example in his book *Moses*, an illuminating work in many respects, is essentially an apologist in the main questions. He rejects the possibility of any connection between the monotheism of Moses and that of Akhenaton, the Kenite theory, or any other proposition that would suggest that YHWH was not the monopoly of Moses and ancient Israel.[1475] Buber may be quite right, but arguing from a text which clearly bears evidence of substantial alterations from its original version or sources to conform with later views of Israel's national and religious origins and current needs, is arguing from a flawed premise. It is just as useless as is the Muslim's arguing his case from the Quran with a person who does not believe that the Quran is God's word. The argument from the Quran becomes valid only after a person has accepted Islam.

As Watts says in discussing a similar question: "It is problematic that most scholars in this field are Jewish and Christian theologians who, liberal as they may try to be, have a special interest in giving temporal priority to the Hebrews in all matters of deep spiritual insight."[1476] That said, the results of their scholarship are impressive, but occasionally marked by reluctance; however, very rarely outright fraud. Overall, they are to be congratulated for their honesty and integrity in presenting the evidence we are now looking at from an Islamic perspective.

What is the extra-Biblical evidence of the events in *Exodus* and *Numbers*? First, let it be stated that there is not a single reference to any of the events of the story of Moses and the Exodus in any Egyptian

---

[1475] See Buber in the Bibliographies.
[1476] Watts-Hands, p. 132.

inscription or document found thus far. No Egyptian monarch or army is reported to have been lost in the manner depicted in *Exodus*, or any circumstance remotely similar to it.[1477] Although Buber would place the Exodus during the reign of Thutmose III (1490-1435 BCE)[1478] and thus safely *before* Akhenaton, thereby eliminating any possibility of the dependence of Moses' monotheism upon that of Akhenaton, most scholars date the Exodus to the XIXth Dynasty (1308-1182 BCE), and therefore *after* Akhenaton.[1479]

The first mention of Israel anywhere is on the stele of Mer-ne-ptah (c. 1230 BCE) recording his conquests: "Israel is laid waste, his seed is not; Hurru is become a widow for Egypt!" The word Israel is accompanied by a hieroglyphic determinative indicating that Israel was a people, not a land; that is, that the Israelites had not yet become established in a definite territory with political institutions. This could also mean that there were already Israelite tribes in the Canaan area, probably east of the Jordan, with whom the tribes led by Joshua after the Exodus could have linked up for the Conquest.[1480] As we have noted above, there is increasing speculation that the Israelites whom Moses led out of Egypt were just the two Josephic tribes. Other tribes already in place on the outskirts of Canaan (such as Reuben and Gad?) were triggered into joining the enterprise that became the Conquest under the military leadership of Joshua. We shall return to this hypothesis later.

The Merneptah stele sheds light on the date of the Conquest, immediately after Moses, in the Biblical time frame. Archeological evidence also supports this period for the arrival of the Israelites in Canaan. Excavations at Bethel, Eglon, Kiriath-sepher (Deber), and Lachish show that these places were violently destroyed during the 13th century BCE, and Lachish more specifically between 1240 and 1230

[1477] Buber, p. 13

[1478] Buber, p. 33.

[1479] See Section G.

[1480] ANE, I, p. 231. The relevant text: "Plundered is the Canaan with every evil; Carried off is Ashkelon; seized upon is Gezer; Yanoam is made as that which does not exist; Israel is laid waste, his seed is not; Hurru is become a widow for Egypt!" The stele boasts of the pharaoh's success in an expedition into the region of Canaan. Though it may be a scribal error, the determinative—if correct—would indicate that the Israelites were not yet a settled people, presumably moving about with flocks or trading caravans.

Bietak writes: "But Israel is mentioned along with Ashkelon, Gezer and Yinoam [Yanoam]. These names follow a progression from the [Mediterranean] coast to the interior (Yinoam is southwest of the Sea of Galilee). The stele may indicate that the people of Israel were still east of the Jordan [River] at this time." (Manfred Bietak, *Israelites Found in Egypt*, BAR, Vol. 28, No. 5, Sep/Oct 2003, p. 82.)

BCE.[1481] Based upon this evidence, the Conquest would appear to have taken place about the middle of the 13th century BCE. Going back a further forty years (the period of the "wandering") we arrive at a date of c. 1290 BCE for the Exodus. If this is approximately correct, then the Pharaoh of the birth story of Moses was Seti I, and the Pharaoh of the Exodus was none other than Rameses II, the Great, (rgd. 1301-1234 BCE), a king who had one of the longest reigns in all history, 67 years. His mummy is preserved in the Egyptian Museum at Cairo and it shows no signs of the violent death ascribed to him in the Bible. We believe that the events depicted in *Exodus* and *Numbers* occurred against the background of the Egypt of the New Empire, and more specifically the XIXth Dynasty.[1482]

It must also be noted that during this time, Canaan was, as it had been for many centuries, under the control of Egypt. Sometimes this meant little more than that Canaan was acknowledged to be in Egypt's sphere of influence, but at other times, there was stronger physical evidence of Egypt's power in the form of armies and officials. This in itself should not be viewed as a contradiction of the Biblical accounts that show little evidence of Egyptian control once the Hebrews had crossed the sea. So long as Egypt felt that her interests were not threatened, tribal movements and wars continued in outlying territories, and petty monarchs battled with each other over land and towns, but the power of Egypt always loomed in the distant background

We do not hear of Israelites treating with Mesopotamian powers at this stage of Israel's history. Such an act would have brought the wrath of Pharaoh upon their heads instantly. Thus, even though Moses and his Israelites had fled Egypt, all of their wandering and their final settlement were conducted in lands in which Egyptian suzerainty or influence prevailed.

We have no independent Egyptian notice of Moses and the events with which he is associated. While naturally the escape from bondage was of the greatest importance to the Israelites, it seems to have been a very minor defection from the Egyptian point of view. If the fleeing Israelites did inflict a defeat upon a pursuing Egyptian force, it was of such minor importance in the grand scheme of things that the Egyptians did not comment upon it in their records. In any event, the Egyptians, in common with other ancient powers, never dwelt upon their defeats or gave them permanence in inscriptions. Disasters were

---

[1481] Israel, DB, p. 432.

[1482] See Section B for more about the problem of the Pharaoh of the Exodus.

reinterpreted favorably. The glass was always half full. *Plus ça change, plus c'est la même chose.*

WHO WAS MOSES? We dismiss arguments out of hand that he is a total fiction. With so much smoke, this time there must be a fire, and a large one at that! The Bible states that his (unnamed) father and mother were both from the tribe of Levi (Ex. 2:1). Gray allots this passage to E;[1483] others admit the possibility of its belonging to J, as it is part of a conflation of J and E. Moses also had an (older) sister. However, the Priestly Document remedies these omissions, telling us in one place that his father was Amram, his mother Jochebed,[1484] and his elder brother was Aaron—no brother is mentioned in the conflated JE story (Ex. 6:20). Miriam, the sister of Moses and Aaron, does not make an appearance by name until the jubilant scene following the Exodus where she is described as "Miriam, the prophetess, the sister of Aaron." (Ex. 15:20) The song attributed to her in the next verse is possibly the oldest poetry to be found in the Bible.[1485]

Quite naturally, modern scholarship has challenged this picture of the sibling relationship Aaron, Moses, and Miriam by suggesting that it was a later device to link these important early figures together, especially Aaron and Moses, in the interests of the Levite and Jerusalem priesthood. Miriam's tomb at Kadesh may have at one time been an important cult center, losing its importance after the establishment of the Israelites in Canaan, but the putative relationship—if it indeed is putative—lingered on in text and tradition.

THE LEVITES: The tribe of Levi is another of the great problems of Biblical research. "How the ancient secular tribe became a priestly tribe is completely unknown."[1486] Much of the Pentateuch is devoted to a delineation of the rights and duties of the priestly caste, the Levites. Not every Levite was a priest, but—in later times at least—to be a priest one had to be a Levite by descent.[1487]

[1483] John Gray, writing in the commentary on *Exodus* in Laymon, p. 34.

[1484] The theophoric name of Moses' mother, with YHWH as an element, is undoubtedly anachronistic, as such names are not found until after the work of Moses, (Moses, EJ, XII, 38.)

[1485] Albright-Ab to Ez, p. 21. The text of the Song of Miriam is:
"*Sing to the Lord, for He has triumphed gloriously;*
the horse and his rider He has thrown into the sea." (Ex. 15:21)

[1486] Levi, DB, p. 578.

[1487] "The Levites had a special relationship to the priestly office and the service of the sanctuary. In Deuteronomy, though the position is not entirely clear, priests and Levites

After the Conquest, the Levites were not given any territory, but a number of cities were assigned to them. A few daring scholars have suggested that the Levites were originally settled at Kadesh-Barnea, but were expelled by the Amalekites until the oasis was reconquered for them by Moses.[1488] Regardless of the merit of that suggestion, Weber points out that "Levi" has no Hebrew etymology (the etymology given in Gen. 29:34[1489] is of course folk etymology) and suggests Minaean associations,[1490] but de Vaux rejects this theory and notes that the name Levi-El has been found in Mari texts.[1491] Weber adds: "All indications point to their [the Levites'] origin in the southern steppe bordering the desert from the oasis of Kadesh to Seir.[1492] A rather early tradition treats the Levites, first, as the quite personal following of Moses who enlisted their support against obstinate and disobedient opponents and secured his authority by a massacre among their near kin."[1493] Weber also doubts that Moses was in fact a Levite.

Be that as it may, the Levites also seem to have had strong Egyptian associations. More than 250 years after the Exodus, we find that the Levite priest Eli has named his two sons Hophni and Phinehas, names of Egyptian origin.[1494] The Bible has played down these Egyptian influences, but they can be detected in the names of many of the principals of the Exodus that have proven to be (or are suspected to be) Egyptian. This should not strike us as unusual. Joseph, we remember, was given an Egyptian name, Zaphenath-paneah (Gen. 41:45), and it is

---

seem to be equated (e.g. Deut. 18:1-5). In the Priestly Source, the specifically priestly functions are reserved for those Levites who are descended from Aaron, whereas the remaining Levites are responsible for other forms of service in the sanctuary (Num. 18:1-7)." (Anderson, p. 78.)

[1488] Buber, p. 11. Buber rejects this hypothesis, probably correctly.

[1489] "Again (Leah) conceived and bore a son, and said, 'Now this time my husband will be joined [Hebrew: *lawah*] to me, because I have borne him three sons'; therefore his name was called Levi." (Gen. 29:34) The two preceding sons were Reuben and Simeon; her fourth son was Judah.

[1490] Weber, p. 170. The Minaeans were an Arabian people, sometimes connected with South Arabia (Yemen) and perhaps preceding the kingdom of Sheba. Other evidence shows them farther north, in north central and western Arabia. (Minaeans, DB, p. 660.)

[1491] de Vaux, Vol. II, pp. 358-359. Mari was one of the most ancient cities in the world, founded by Sumerians on the banks of the upper Euphrates River at the beginning of the 3rd millennium BCE. It was destroyed by Hammurabi c. 1697 BCE. Its ruins, lying in present-day Syria, have yielded the famous Mari archives of more than 20,000 tablets that have been of immense importance in shedding light on the ancient Near East, and especially the age of the patriarchs.

[1492] Seir: a mountainous region in modern southwestern Jordan.

[1493] Weber, p. 170. See section I below for a discussion of this horrific event.

[1494] Albright-Stone Age, p. 282.

not unusual in the history of the world to see people of one nation, or a segment of them (usually those who consider themselves in some way an elite), adopt the clothes, habits, manners, and names of their conquerors; or—as they see it—their cultural superiors. We see the same process today in which much of the non-European world is clothed in European styles and ordering its daily life according to what is perceived to be the European fashion.[1495] In any event, as we proceed we shall see this cultural emulation again in Israelite history, especially during the violent and bloody era of the Hellenization of the Near East, which is discussed at length in *The New Testament: An Islamic Perspective.*

MOSES' NAME: Putting aside the question of the literal truth of the birth story of Moses, there seems to a firm Israelite tradition that Moses grew up at the court of Pharaoh (or more probably, the local court of the representative of Pharaoh at Tanis).[1496] Moses (Ar. *Mūsā*) was educated as an Egyptian "and Moses was instructed in all the wisdom of the Egyptians" (Acts 7:22). Falling out of favor, Moses fled from Egypt, (an act which, as we shall see, has a close parallel in Egyptian literature).[1497] Settled in a new life in the quite different pastoral desert landscape of Midian, Moses experienced a conversion, a religious experience so profound that he either recovered the ancient faith that had lingered in the traditions of his people and which he had half-learned as a child, or was confronted by a completely new realization of God. Whichever it was, he seems to have reacted violently against the way of life he had led amidst the high civilization of Egypt. Yet, there is no evidence that he took the step of changing his name, an act that frequently accompanies conversion, and one that signifies a new spiritual identity and new loyalties. This failure is strange, because he had ever reason to do so, as his name was most probably Egyptian.

Folk etymology, preserved in the text of *Exodus*, tells us that Moses was so called because Pharaoh's daughter "drew him out" of the water, equating "Moses" (*Mushe*) with the Hebrew verb *mashah*, "to draw out" (Ex. 2:10). This is patently absurd, because Pharaoh's

---

[1495] The term "European" here of course includes "American," as America is culturally European. Perhaps, it should be considered a desire to achieve parity with the superior force through some sort of sympathetic magic. The Islamic world is not immune from this social and cultural phenomenon. Few Muslims realize that the necktie (cravat from "Croat") quite possibly originated in the 17th century CE as a stylized cross, used by the Christian Croats to distinguish themselves from the Muslim Turks with whom they were fighting.

[1496] See Sections A and B.

[1497] See Section D.

daughter, an Egyptian, is credited with giving him a *Hebrew* name! In addition, as is well know, the form *Mushe*, could only mean "he who draws out" (active voice), not "he who is drawn out" (passive voice), as the situation would logically require. Scholars now generally agree that the name Moses is Egyptian in origin and means "child."[1498]

Writes the historian Breasted: "It is important to notice that his name, Moses, was Egyptian. It is simply the Egyptian word '*mose*' meaning 'child,' and is an abridgment of a fuller, probably theophoric, form of such names as 'Amenmose' meaning 'Amon-a-child' or 'Ptah-mose,' meaning 'Ptah-a-child'... The father of Moses without doubt prefixed to his son's name that of an Egyptian god like Amon or Ptah, and his divine name was gradually lost in current usage, till the boy was 'Mose.'"[1499] Perhaps it is possible to replace Breasted's suggestion that the theophoric portion of the name simply gradually fell into disuse by the proposition that it was deliberately suppressed, possibly on the authority of Moses himself, and this was his act of name-change. It may be further noted that the supposed Pharaoh of the Exodus himself possessed such a name: Rameses is the Greek form of *Ra-mose*, "Ra-(has given)-a-child.[1500] *Mose* (Moses) by itself simply means "child."[1501]

MOSES AN EGYPTIAN? Although admitting that an Egyptian name is not proof of Moses' being an Egyptian by race, the founder of psychoanalysis, Sigmund Freud, in the last years of his life constructed an ingenious theory that Moses was an Egyptian by race as well as culture; that he was a follower of the monotheistic Aton worship introduced by Akhenaton (rgd. 1370-1353 BCE). After the restoration of Amun-worship that followed the sad end of Akhenaton's reign, Moses fled the repressions of the restored Amun priesthood and sought to convert a group of Semites living on the eastern borders of Egypt to his religion, the Semites who later mixed with his people became the Israelites. At Kadesh, Moses was martyred (this is based upon a dubious interpretation of a passage in *Hosea* suggested by Sellin) and, of course, the whole series of events is given a psychoanalytic interpretation.[1502]

[1498] The Egyptian form is *mes, mesu*. (Moses, DB, p. 675.)

[1499] From *The Dawn of Conscience* by J.H. Breasted (New York: Charles Scribner's Sons, 1934, p. 350, cited by Freud in *Moses and Monotheism*. (Freud, p. 5.)

[1500] Josephus seems to recognize the Egyptian origins of the name "Moses," although he gives us a false etymology based on the Greek form of the word (Moses). He says that it comes from *mou*, Egyptian for "water," and *eses*, "saved," thus, "saved from water." Neat, but incorrect. (Moses, EJ, XII, 379.)

[1501] Ogden Goelet, *Moses' Egyptian Name*, BR, Vol. XIX, No. 3, June 2003, p. 14.

[1502] Freud, p. 42. See also esp. Part II.

The proofs adduced for this theory are rather tenuous considering its larger implications, but nonetheless the suggestion that Moses was an Egyptian deserves more serious consideration than it has heretofore been given.[1503]

Oddly enough, there is some evidence, admittedly capable of more than one interpretation, to support this thesis in the Bible itself. Newly arrived in Midian and having just saved Reuel/Jethro's daughters from the loutish shepherds and aided them in watering their flocks, the girls told their father: "'An Egyptian delivered us out of the hand of the shepherds...'" (Ex. 2:19) Assuredly Moses, in his Egyptian clothes and tonsured in the Egyptian fashion, would have appeared as an Egyptian to them, but the omission of any disclaimer or note of correction, or the establishment of kinship (the Israelites and Midianites were kinfolk) is strange.

There is still something else reported in the Bible that could also be interpreted to support the theory that Moses was an Egyptian, although again it is capable of more than one explanation. In the theophany of the Commission (Ex. 3:1-44:17), one of the principal reasons Moses cites for not being able to undertake God's command to return to Egypt and lead the Israelites out is: "'I am not eloquent, either heretofore or since Thou hast spoken to Thy servant; but I am slow of speech and of tongue.'" (Ex. 4:10) God then told Moses that He would teach him what to say, but Moses still protested, and finally God appointed Aaron to act as Moses' spokesman.

Now, we can accept this at face value—that Moses was not facile with words or perhaps had some sort of speech impediment such as a stutter—or we can continue our enquiries into whether something else lies behind this passage. One very reasonable possibility is that Moses knew the language of the Semites (presumably a dialect of Canaanite) imperfectly as he had been raised in Egypt amongst Egyptians, and perhaps had only learned it after his flight to Midian. In this context, it must be remembered that Moses had a double mission. First, he had to convince the Israelites to follow him, and secondly he had to convince Pharaoh to let them go. Since he had been raised at the Egyptian court, he must have know Egyptian quite well, but how well did he know the Semitic language of his own people—if they were indeed his own people? His lack of Hebrew (or Canaanite) could be explained in two ways: raised at court away from his own people he had not been exposed to it, or... he simply was not a Semite to begin with.

[1503] Such a disruptive, innovative idea is repugnant to most scholars, and especially those who wish to establish and maintain the spiritual precedence of the ancient Hebrews.

There is still another possibility: we can also regard Moses' difficulty with language as a convenient literary device to associate with him his "brother" Aaron, who figured prominently in the later claims of the Jerusalem priesthood.[1504]

This problem did not pass unremarked by the ancient Jews. They offered various explanations of Moses' speech defect, some of which have entered Islamic tradition. With respect to this question, we should remember that the highest authority in Islam, the Holy Quran, nowhere states that Moses was an Israelite; simply that he was sent to the Israelites. Because of tradition (which, however, should not be dismissed lightly) and the religious predispositions of various groups to support one view, there is no reason why we should not consider another explanation. Since the most famous proponent of this theory was the controversial Freud—even worse, he was not a noted scholar in the "field"—the theory has unfortunately become bound up with the acceptance or rejection of some of his more extravagant theories in other fields, and it is not reviewed without some bias.

That Moses was an Egyptian is, of course, simply an hypothesis. It resolves some problems in the life of Moses and creates others. It has little support amongst modern Biblical scholars, although, given their conservatism in such matters, this in itself is no reason to reject the proposition outright. However, the burden of proof is on those who would make Moses an Egyptian, and such proof is not likely to be forthcoming at this late date.[1505]

In this regard, we may argue that in many respects Mosaic Law does not correspond to what we know of Egyptian law. This points to a Semitic provenance for the Mosaic code. The obvious problems created can be considerably reduced when we realize that most of the Law we now have in the Pentateuch was formulated centuries after Moses (see I below). We really do not what the Mosaic Torah contained or would have contained, as the Quran contends.

A direct relationship between Aton-worship and YHWH-worship is usually denied by emphasizing the differences, but there are some striking similarities that suggest some sort of a link, however

---

[1504] See Section E.

[1505] However, many classical writers assumed that Moses was Egyptian by race (Gager, p. 19). Josephus quotes the Egyptian Manetho, who asserted that Moses was a rebellious prince. Manetho says that Moses was a scribe and that his name was originally Egyptian: Tisisthene (*Against Apion*, Josephus, p. 620). Though as quoted by Josephus, the passage does not actually state that Moses was an Egyptian, this can possibly be inferred from the text. Manetho wrote in the 3rd century BCE. From this distance in time there is no way of knowing upon what traditions, if any, he based his material.

obscure. For example, Freud points out that the central feature of Egyptian religion was the cult of the dead and the belief in the afterlife. This was conspicuously absent from Akhenaton's Aton worship that concentrated only upon this life, an attitude it shared with ancient Judaism.[1506]

However, Freud's conclusion that this is a proof of Moses' adherence to the cult of Aton-worship, or at least his being under its influence, can be countered with other equally tenuous explanations. One of these centers around the supposed Asiatic connections of Akhenaton's beautiful wife Nefertiti, who seems to have been the real driving force in the establishment of the monotheistic Aton-cult. As we have noted in other places, the prevailing view in the Fertile Crescent in early antiquity was that the afterlife was a dreary place for everyone, and was not dependent upon the quality or morality of one's earthly existence. It was assumed that wrongs and transgressions would be redressed by gods on earth in the shape of famines, blights, while good behavior would earn good harvests and many children. For the more thoughtful prophets, righteousness was its own reward and there was no expectation of a further transcendent accounting after death.

While we may we may speculate about the figure of the Egyptian noble fleeing to Midian where he married and adopted his in-laws' religion and way of life, finally returning to Egypt to lead some of the Semitic kinfolk of the Midianites out of Egypt, the degree of the Egyptianization reflected in nomenclature is striking when set beside the relative absence of Egyptian influence in Jewish tradition. It would seem that the names were not altered in the general desire to expunge the Egyptian experience from the tribal memory simply because the origins of those names were forgotten in later times. How many English speakers today are aware that James is the Greek form of Jacob or that Jesus is the Greek form of Joshua?

In addition to the name of Moses, we find that the name "Miriam" is also Egyptian; probably a form compounded with *mer*, "love."[1507] Aaron, too, is quite possibly of Egyptian origin, although its

---

[1506] Freud, p. 22.

[1507] Miriam, EJ, XII, 82. The DB suggests another Egyptian derivation, from "beloved of Amun." Miriam is thought to have been older than her brothers Aaron and Moses. (Miriam, DB, p, 666.) Since all three siblings, if indeed they were siblings, probably have Egyptian names, the question of ethnicity arises again. *Micah* credits all three with leading the deliverance from Egypt: "For I brought you up from the land of Egypt, and redeemed you from the house of bondage; and I sent before you Moses, Aaron, and

etymology is still unknown.[1508] Thus, we find that the three principal characters of the Moses saga are likely to have borne Egyptian names. Furthermore, their Levite associations as well as their kinship with each other is also placed in a shadow by modern scholarship.

Although Moses appears to have always been highly regarded as the founder of the Hebrew nation and YHWH-worship, his present preeminence seems to date from the days of the declining monarchy (perhaps as an attempt to placate God) when greater emphasis was placed upon legal and ritual institutions, the foundations of which were ascribed to Moses. Before the crises of that era, Moses was more important in the North than in the South.[1509] With the collapse of the House of David and the transfer of the loyalty formerly given to it to the messianic restoration set in the future, exilic and post-exilic Judaism became even more dependent upon cohesive role of the Law. This, in turn, contributed to the enhancement of the role of Moses in Judaism.

Yet, Moses did not have to be rediscovered. He was too powerful, too potent a figure to be forgotten or dismissed. We can do no better here than to quote the last verses of the Pentateuch as his epitaph: "And there has not arisen a prophet since in Israel like Moses, whom the Lord knew face to face, none like him for all the signs and the wonders which the Lord sent him to do in the land of Egypt, to Pharaoh and to all his servants and to all his land, and for all the mighty power and all the great and terrible deeds which Moses wrought in the sight of all Israel." (Deut. 34:10-12)

B. PHARAOH AND HAMAN

(Haman) said to (Pharaoh): "Where art thou going?"
(Surabadi, p. 296)

Surabadi prefaces his account of the birth of Moses with a legendary history of Pharaoh (Ar. *Fircawn*): Pharaoh's name was originally Walid bin Rayyan, or more commonly Rayyan bin Walid (*Rayyān bin Walīd*)). He lived for 400 years, and claimed to be God.[1510]

Miriam." (Mic. 6:4) She died and was buried at Kadesh. She too was denied entry into Canaan by God.

[1508] Aaron, DB, p. 1.

[1509] Silver, p. ix.

[1510] Other Muslim authorities give different names such as al-Walīd bin Muscab, Muscab bin Rayyām, and Qābūs bin Muscab (the successor of Rayyān bin Walīd?). The Pharaoh at the time of Joseph was said to be Rayyān bin al-Walīd (or Dārim) al-cAmlīqī. Some said that he lived 620 years. According to some, the Pharaoh of the time of Moses was al-

Before he made this claim he was of sound body, but afterwards seventy-two defects appeared in him. It is said that he was originally from Pushanj, a day's journey from Herat.[1511] From there, accompanied by Haman (Ar. *Hāmān*), he traveled until he reached Egypt at the season of the melon harvest. Pharaoh and Haman stopped at a melon field and sought food; they were given a load of melons to take to the city to sell. The people bought them, but did not pay, so the pair returned empty-handed.[1512]

Pharaoh said that the people were lazy, so the two men went to the governor and requested work. They were given the Gate of the Graveyard to guard. Cholera struck and Pharaoh collected a dirham tax on each corpse that was brought out to the graveyard.[1513] Thus, he acquired a large sum of money and by means of bribery gained control of the city. When the governor died, Pharaoh seized power.[1514]

Next, he told Haman that he wanted to claim that he was God. Haman advised him to do it little by little. The people at that time believed in the true religion. Haman advised him to prohibit their learned men from teaching; then the religion would gradually weaken and could be replaced. Any one who taught was to have his tongue cut out. Ultimately, the people accepted Pharaoh's claim of divinity.[1515]

In this odd tale, Surabadi has introduced a number of elements, none of which—beyond the existence of Pharaoh and Haman—can be found in the Bible or the Quran. The account of the migration from Khorasan may be a very, very remote echo of the invasion by the Hyksos and the establishment of non-Egyptians upon the throne of Lower Egypt, told from an Iranian point of view. Though the bulk of the peoples who comprised the Hyksos were Semitic in origin, there were Indo-European elements among them as personal names used by them attest. However,

---

Walīd bin Muṣ'ab. That he was supposed to have reigned the longest period of time is consistent with the assumption that Ramses II was the Pharaoh of Moses. (Pharaoh, Hughes, p. 452; Fir'awn, SEI, pp. 107-108.)

[1511] This would appear to locate Pharaoh's origins in northwestern Afghanistan, a region familiar to Surabadi. Could this be a local tradition?

[1512] Surabadi, pp. 297-298.

[1513] This tax on the dead was actually in the nature of an inheritance tax. Such taxes are attested in the records of Sumeria concerning the middle of the 3rd millennium BCE. "Even death brought no relief from levies and taxes. When a dead man was brought to the cemetery for burial, a number of officials and parasites made it their business to be on hand to relieve the bereaved family of quantities of barley, bread, and beer, and various furnishings." (Kramer-Sumer, p. 48) It would appear that this oppressive and heartless profession is the one Surabadi had envisioned for Pharaoh.

[1514] Surabadi, p. 298.

[1515] Surabadi, p. 298.

that interpretation would be more appropriate to the time of Joseph than of Moses.

There is another possible source, even more remote from Moses: the Persian invasion in 525 BCE. (Egyptian historians considered the rulers of the Persian Empire the XXVIIth Egyptian Dynasty.) The first Persian ruler of Egypt, Cambyses (rgd. as Pharaoh 525-522 BCE), had origins in Fars in southern Iran rather than in Khorasan. The pharaohs of Egypt were accorded a kind of divinity, and they were identified with the Sun god.[1516] Cambyses is said to have offended the Egyptians in a number of ways and to have ultimately gone mad, at least that is what Herodotus and other ancients tell us. Olmstead discounts such stories, saying they have their origin in attempts to justify the "regime change" led by Darius the Great that occurred after Cambyses' death.[1517]

The Bible does not speak of Pharaoh's pretensions of divinity in *Exodus*, but this additional detail is found in the Quran: *And Pharaoh said: O chiefs! I know not that ye have a god other than me... (Q. 28:38)* This is a reference to the divinity that the ancient Egyptians believed to be inherent in their royalty. The claim was not an innovation by the Pharaoh of Moses. Rather it was based upon the most ancient traditions: "...(the Egyptians) believed that they were a divine nation, and that they were ruled by kings who were themselves god incarnate; their earliest kings, they asserted, were actually gods, who did not disdain to live upon earth, and to go up and down through it, and to mingle with men."[1518] "The basic fact of Egyptian religions was the idea that the king was a god. The later ritual of daily service stresses the point that the priest in front of the god's image acted only as the substitute of the king. In festival rites the king represented the gods of his people with the same authority as he represented his people to the gods."[1519]

In discussing the development of this belief, Fairservis writes: "...the gradual development of this concept, of Pharaoh as a god and the development of ceremony for, with, and by this god, is emblematic of the tendency to 'settle in.' The warlike prowess of an individual displayed in the conquering of human enemies seems replaced by the idea that the presence of Pharaoh was the reason for the fertility of the land. Accordingly, Pharaoh was to be worshipped as the 'bringer of good.'"[1520] The stability and prosperity of the state of Egypt was based upon the

---

[1516] Breasted-Religion, pp. 124-125.
[1517] Herodotus, Bk. III, pp. 215-219, and elsewhere; Olmstead, p. 89.
[1518] Budge-Gods, Vol. 1, p. 3.
[1519] Rudolph Anthes, writing in Kramer-Myth, p. 33.
[1520] Fairservis, p. 86.

premise of its ruler's assumed divinity and his special relationship with the gods.

Much has been made of the order by Pharaoh quoted in the Quran, given to Haman: *"So kindle for me (a fire), O Haman, to bake the mud; and set up for me a lofty tower in order that I may survey the god of Moses; and lo! I deem him [Moses] of the liars."* (Q. 28:38) And in another place: *And Pharaoh said: "O Haman! Build for me a tower that haply I may reach the roads, the roads of the heavens, and may look upon the God of Moses, though verily I think him [Moses] a liar." Thus was the evil that he did made fair-seeming unto Pharaoh, and he was barred from the (right) way. The plot of Pharaoh ended but in ruin.* (Q. 40:36-37)

Western scholars cite these as more instances of Quranic "confusion," asserting that the story is derived from the story of the Tower of Babel in *Genesis* and mistakenly intruded into the Islamic Mosaic traditions.

THE TOWER OF BABEL: In view of its importance to this controversy, let us first quote the Biblical story: "Now the whole earth had one language and few words. And as men migrated from the east, they found a plain in the land of Shinar [Lower Mesopotamia, Sumeria] and settled there. And they said to one another, 'Come, let us make bricks, and burn them thoroughly.' And they had brick for stone, and bitumen for mortar.[1521] Then they said, 'Come, let us build ourselves a city, and a tower with its top in the heavens, and let us make a name for ourselves, lest we be scattered abroad upon the face of the whole earth.' (Gen. 11:1-4)

"And the Lord came down to see the city and the tower, which the sons of men had built. And the Lord said, 'Behold, they are one people and they have all one language; and nothing that they propose to do will now be impossible for them. Come, let us go down, and there confuse their language, that they may not understand one another's speech.' So the Lord scattered them abroad from there over the face of all the earth, and they left off building the city. Therefore its name was called Babel, because the Lord confused the language of all the earth;

[1521] This type of construction employing burnt bricks and bitumen as mortar is very ancient. We have inspected vaulted underground chambers—probably tombs—so constructed near the ancient ziggurat of Choga Zambil (in Khuzestan, Iran) of c. 1200 BCE, the largest ziggurat discovered so far in all of Mesopotamia. The temple and the remains of the city around it are roughly contemporaneous with the era of Moses.

and from there the Lord scattered them abroad over the face of all the earth." (Gen. 11:5-9)

The modern reader will be struck by this diminished, anthropomorphic view of God. He is actually fearful of the power of mankind and their plots against them! They are potentially His equal! This is very primitive material indeed, material from a time when gods and men interacted in way which would be as repugnant to later Judaism as it is to Islam, although would not have raised eyebrows in ancient Greece or Rome.

The Tower of Babel pericope, possibly based upon Babylonian sources, is thought to have been added to the work of the First Yahwist by the Second Yahwist.[1522] It seems to have been inspired by one of the great ziggurats of Mesopotamia, perhaps that of Babylon itself. Hooke points out that the story cannot be Mesopotamian in origin, because the tower is to be built to enable mankind to reach heaven. Mesopotamians would have known the real purpose of the tower: a kind of elevated landing place for the god when descending to earth to reside in the temple for a special manifestation. They would not have invented such a story. An attempt to scale it would have been an impiety, and such a narrative an unthinkable blasphemy. Rather, it represents a speculation about such a tower that might be offered by nomads visiting Mesopotamia ignorant of its real purpose. Therefore, the origin of the tale, though it is about Mesopotamia, must be sought elsewhere.[1523]

Furthermore, the story seems to have been suggested by the sight of some specific ruins, because not only is the tower unfinished, but also the city. Jewish tradition linked this story with Nimrod,[1524] although in the Bible it stands by itself. Its main purpose appears to have been aetiological; to explain the origin of the different languages of mankind as a divine effort to block the power that a united mankind would wield. It also explains the invention of brick construction in terms of a people accustomed to use stone in construction (and therefore, it is not from the stoneless alluvial plains of Mesopotamia). It also seems to explain the origin of some particularly spectacular ruins. In addition, the etymology of the name "Babel" (Babel = Babylon) is spurious; the real meaning would have been immediately apparent to any Semite: "Gate of God," or "Divine Gate."

If we assume that the Quranic references are to be ultimately traced to this story, the absence of its principal aetiological features is

---

[1522] IB, I, 446.
[1523] Hooke, pp. 137-138.
[1524] See "Nimrod" in Part III, E.

remarkable. There is no origin of mankind's diverse languages. There is no invention of fired brick construction. There is no name-origin of Babel. Only the building of a tower is shared. The mention in the Quran is an abbreviated reference that seems to imply that the listeners were familiar with the pericope, and its inclusion in the Moses story would suggest that it was already known as a part of the Moses-Pharaoh cycle.

It is also not clear whether the order was carried out by Haman, or was simply a pharaonic boast not intended to be implemented. Perhaps, it is simply a reference by Pharaoh to legends of the Mesopotamia ziggurats (which are thought to have been the pattern for the more famous Egyptian pyramids, some of which were also built of brick). It could also be a reference to the many immense temples still to be found in Egypt that excite the wonder of even the jaded modern traveler. As we have emphasized in many places, there is no real evidence of new invention in these stories in the Quran. They are references and excerpts from stories already in circulation in Arabia, turned to a new purpose.

In any case, there are other possibilities. Although Egypt is famous for its pyramids and temples of stone monuments, we tend to forget that stone was *only* used on a large scale for such religious structures such as temples and tombs, and for other public works for which nothing else would do. The bulk of Egyptian construction was in brick, most of it sun-dried, and thus has not survived. In the Delta region, where there were no handy sources of stone, even the great public buildings such as temples were built largely of brick.

Also, it is important to note that the Arabic word *ṣarḥ* used in the two Quranic verses quoted above and usually translated "tower" (perhaps under the influence of the superficial resemblance to the Tower of Babel pericope in *Genesis*) does not mean "tower" as we think of a tower in English at all. Wehr defines it as "castle, palace, lofty edifice, imposing structure,"[1525] of which Egypt has a surfeit. Such a definition fits very well many of the structures erected by Rameses II, the greatest of all Egyptian builders, and the works of the much earlier Age of Pyramids as well. It is our belief that the similarity is accidental, and the story as it was circulated in the Hejaz was probably connected with tales of the pyramids of Middle Egypt, or the great temples erected throughout the land in which the gods resided, according to Egyptian belief.

In addition, the attitude attributed to Pharaoh in the Quran—his desire to confront the God of Moses—would have been quite plausible in that era. Gods were localized. Travelers from one country to another

---

[1525] Wehr, p. 511.

were at pains to placate the gods of whatever territory they passed through. The worshippers of the god Amun in Egypt did not deny the reality of the god Marduk in Babylonia, or of the gods of India had they known of them. Even today, Hindus accept the reality of the gods of other nations without denying their own gods. Gods were territorial. What probably surprised Pharaoh about the God of Moses was that (1) YHWH was out of His Own territory when invading Egypt, and (2) He was invisible and not to be worshipped in the form of an idol.

PHARAOH'S OPPRESSION OF THE ISRAELITES: In the Quran the exact nature of Pharaoh's oppression is not stated, although we read of the *dreadful torment, slaying your sons and sparing your women...* (Q. 2:49)[1526] Doubtless, the Arabs were familiar with the general context already. The Bible is more specific. The Israelites, prospering by having been attached to the governing class at the time of Joseph, were now — four centuries later — enslaved by the restored native rule. From the Egyptian point of view, they were paying back the hangers-on of the Hyksos interlopers for their own oppression of the Egyptians during their rule.

So, the Hebrews had been put to work on vast public projects:[1527] "therefore they set taskmasters over them to afflict them with heavy burdens; and they built for Pharaoh store-cities, Pithom and Raamses... So they made the people of Israel serve with rigor, and made their lives bitter with hard service, in mortar and brick, and in all kinds of work in the field..." (Ex. 1:11, 13-14) In another place, these tasks are specifically related to brickmaking: "Go now, and work: for no straw shall be given you, yet ye shall deliver the same number of bricks." (Ex. 5:18)

Despite the legendary character of the first chapters of *Exodus*, this accords well with what we know of the building activities of Rameses II, and is more evidence that he was one of the Pharaohs of Moses. The XIXth Dynasty, of which Rameses II was the most important monarch,[1528] was marked by construction projects on a scale even surpassing those of the great Pyramids of the Fourth Dynasty. The dynasty was founded by a military leader descended from an old family

---

[1526] Curiously, Moses is credited with inflicting the same atrocities on the Midianites whom he defeated and in which Balaam was slain. (See sections A above and M below.)

[1527] Not including the pyramids, contrary to popular opinion. The Age of Pyramids had ended some *twelve* centuries earlier. The geographical location of the Israelites, as evidenced by the place names in the Biblical text, was still the northeastern regions of Egypt, that is, the eastern Delta, not the heartland of Egypt on the Nile.

[1528] He reigned 67 of the dynasty's 145 years. (Breasted, p. 502.)

of Upper Egypt upon the collapse of the glorious XVIIIth Dynasty—it had been wrecked by the religious innovations introduced by Akhenaton.

Under Rameses II, the center of power shifted from Thebes (modern Luxor) in the south to the north where he could be nearer his Asiatic conquests. "(Thebes) remained the religious capital of the state and at the greater feasts in its temple calendar the Pharaoh was often present, but his permanent residence was in the north. His constant presence here resulted in a development of the cities of the Delta, such as they had never before enjoyed. Tanis became a great and flourishing city, with a splendid temple... High above its massive pylons towered a monolithic granite colossus of Ramses, over ninety feet in height, weighing 900 tons, and visible across the level country of the surrounding Delta for many miles... (He built) a 'store-city which he called Pithom, or 'House of Atum'... Somewhere in the eastern Delta, he founded a residence city, Per-Ramses, or 'House of Ramses.' Its location is not certain, although it has often been identified with Tanis; but it must have been close to the eastern frontier, for a poet of the time singing of its beauties refers to it as being between Egypt and Syria... Ramses himself was one of the gods of the city."[1529]

This Per-Ramses is almost certainly the Raamses mentioned in *Exodus* in whose construction the Hebrews unwillingly participated, if we may trust the tradition recorded there. In corroboration of the traditions contained in *Exodus*, Egyptian records of the reign of Ramses II mention foreign slaves employed on the royal construction projects. Among them were the 'Apiru, that is Hebrews, a term which could easily have included the descendants of Jacob who still resided at that time in Goshen east of the Delta, a region that was the scene of much building activity inspired by the revived Egyptian Empire's military and strategic needs.[1530]

Rameses II's building efforts went far beyond the normal works calculated to impress and awe his subjects and foreigners; the extent of his operations suggests a positive mania for the perpetuation of his name. He ruthlessly demolished older buildings up and down the Nile, including tombs and temples, in order to secure materials for his own

---

[1529] Breasted, p. 371. Some of his other building projects still stud the face of Egypt from the four colossi at Abu Simbel that had to be moved from the waters backing up behind the High Dam above Aswan to numerous temples in the region of Thebes. "...Surpassing in size all buildings of the ancient or modern world, his architects completed the colossal colonnaded hall of Karnak temple, already begun under the first Ramses, the Pharaoh's grandfather. Few of the great temples of Egypt have not some chamber, hall, colonnade or pylon which bears his name..." (Breasted, p. 372.)

[1530] Exodus, EJ, VI, 1047.

works. The effects of such vast expenditures upon the economy of Egypt, as rich as it was, can scarcely be imagined.

What we know of Rameses II fits very well with the character of Pharaoh as presented in the Quran, where his arrogance is stressed, and to a lesser extent the Pharaoh of the Bible. However, Rameses II was over 90 years old when he died, and he certainly did not perish in a military expedition in pursuit of the Hebrews. If we follow the text of *Exodus*, we must remember that there are *two* Pharaohs to be identified, not just one, because Ex. 2:23 states that while Moses was in Midian, Pharaoh died and was succeeded by a new Pharaoh, the Pharaoh of the Exodus. If we identify Rameses II with the Pharaoh of Moses' birth story, then the Pharaoh of the Exodus must be Merneptah, as he was the son and successor of Rameses II.

There is a problem here because the stele of Merneptah that mentions Israel as being already in Canaan is dated from the fifth year of his reign (c.1231 BCE), hardly enough time for the Exodus and the forty years of wandering. Even if we do not take the period of 40 years to be literal truth, there is still ample evidence in the Biblical text that the Israelites spent a considerable time in the desert and semi-desert between Egypt and Syria before entering Israel in large numbers. Of course, it is possible, as has been suggested, that all of the tribes did not participate in the Exodus, and that there were already Israelite tribes settled in Canaan before the arrival of the group led by Moses and Joshua. This is a view to which we incline, as it would resolve many more historical problems than it would create. This position is upsetting to conservative Biblical scholars who have been brought up to believe that the Exodus was of all twelve tribes of Israel, not just a few. The problem is complex and the final word has hardly been said, although the reign of Rameses II is increasingly favored for some role in the Exodus story.

If we assume that Rameses II is the Pharaoh of the Exodus, then his father Seti I would have been the Pharaoh of the birth narrative. Seti I was also a builder, but not on the scale of his son, though he is credited with the initiation of the building program.[1531] Seti recovered Palestine for the Egyptian Empire and died (c. 1223 BCE) approximately 50 years of age. His mummy is among those on display in the Egyptian Museum at Cairo. Since the building of Per-Rameses, specifically associated with the birth narratives, would appear to be the work of Rameses, not Seti, it

---

[1531] IB, I, 836. See this reference also for a brief discussion of the arguments for and against Seti I-Rameses II or Rameses II-Merneptah as the pharaohs of the birth story and the Exodus.

is difficult to see how Seti could have been the Pharaoh of the birth stories.

This difficulty in chronology is created by the assumption that there were two different Pharaohs. This problem does not exist in the Quranic narratives, where there is no mention of a succession having taken place during the time of Moses. Perhaps the mention of the two Pharaohs in the Bible is an attempt to reconcile the contradictory picture of the Pharaoh of the birth narrative with that of the Pharaoh of the Exodus. The very long reign of Rameses II would suit the Islamic traditions very well, except for the problem of his death.

At this point, it would do well to examine the word "pharaoh" itself. The word is derived from the Egyptian *per a'o* meaning "the Great House" and originally referred to the royal palace, not the person of the king himself. During the Eighteenth Dynasty (1575-1308 BCE) this term became applied as a deferential circumlocution for the king, although not officially. By the time of the Twenty-Second Dynasty (945-730 BCE), it was regularly added to the name of the monarch, but it never seems to have been an official title in Egypt.[1532] Modern parallels to this usage are easily at hand. Americans regularly refer to the president (or at least the institution of the presidency) as the "White House." The British speak of "Downing Street" when they mean the prime minister, and "Buckingham Palace" when they mean the Queen, at least in their official capacities. The Russian government is referred to as the Kremlin, and in Ottoman Turkey, the sultan and his officials were spoken of as the Sublime Porte.

Keeping in mind that in using such terms, the institution described is more in our minds than the individuals holding the power, although both aspects are present, it is not improbable that the "pharaohs" of the Bible and the Quran are representatives of the power of those absolute monarchs rather than the monarchs themselves. That is, high-ranking government officials, governors, military commanders, and the like, attached to the court, or perhaps even a royal prince (Rameses II had fathered an impressive number of princes and princesses), rather than the god-king himself, who probably would not have been involved in such a minor affair as the application of a unimportant group of Semitic sojourners to leave Egypt and return to their homeland, not to speak of a trivial three-day festival. With this proviso, the era of Rameses II would accord very well with the Quranic story of Moses.

Surabadi's statement about the long life of Pharaoh seems to be based upon the tradition of the 430 years that separated the arrival of

---

[1532] Pharaoh, EJ, XIII, 359; Pharaoh, DB, pp. 759-760.

Jacob in Egypt from the Exodus of the Israelites from Egypt. Late Jewish tradition also attributes a remarkable life span to Pharaoh, making the Pharaoh of the oppression one with the Pharaoh of Joseph,[1533] despite the notice of the death of the Joseph's Pharaoh in Ex. 1:8.

With regard to the seventy-two defects in Pharaoh's body mentioned by Surabadi, there is perhaps an echo here of the encounter of a different monarch with Abraham discussed earlier. However, in *Pirke de Rabbi Eliezer* we have: "But just as the leper is unclean and causes uncleanliness, likewise Pharaoh and his people were unclean, and they caused Israel to be unclean."[1534] In the *Exodus Rabbah* this comparison becomes a definite statement that Pharaoh was a leper[1535]: "the latter years of Israel's bondage in Egypt were the worst. To punish Pharaoh for his cruelty toward the children of Israel, God afflicted him with a plague of leprosy, which covered his whole body... (Pharaoh) took counsel with his three advisers, Balaam, Jethro, and Job, how he might be healed of the awful malady that had seized upon him. Balaam spoke, saying, 'Thou canst regain thy health only if thou wilt slaughter Israelitish children and bathe in their blood'... In pursuance of the sanguinary advice given by Balaam, Pharaoh had his bailiffs snatch Israelitish babes from their mothers' breasts, and slaughtered them, and in the blood of these innocents, he bathed. His disease afflicted him for ten years, and every day an Israelitish child was killed for him... It was all in vain; indeed, at the end of the time his leprosy changed into boils, and he suffered more than before."[1536]

Turning from this scene of bloody horror, it may be a relief to read how Moses gave the lie to Pharaoh's claims of divinity. According to the *Exodus Rabbah*: "(Pharaoh) called himself a god, and pretended that he felt no human needs. To keep up the illusion, he would repair to the edge of the river every morning, and ease nature there while alone and unobserved. At such a time it was that Moses appeared before him, and called out to him, 'Is there a god that hath human needs?' 'Verily, I am no god,' replied Pharaoh, 'I only pretend to be one before the Egyptians, who are such idiots, one should consider them asses rather than human beings.'"[1537] This is obviously a little anti-Egyptian ethnic

---

[1533] LJ, II, 78; V, 346.

[1534] PRE, p. 316.

[1535] Pharaoh, EJ, XIII, 360.

[1536] LJ, II, 296. Pharaoh's bathing in blood reminds us of the story of the infamous Hungarian Countess Elizabeth Bathory (d. 1614 CE) who is said to have slaughtered more than 600 virgins in order to renew her youth by bathing in their blood (Bathory, CE, p. 178).

[1537] LJ, II, 347-348.

joke. Nonetheless, the anecdote is interesting for the impression created that Pharaoh did not consider himself an Egyptian. Is this an echo of the tradition in Surabadi of the foreign origin of Pharaoh?

Incidentally, there seems to be some social criticism included by Surabadi related to his own day in the advice Haman gives for corrupting the people and leading them away from the worship of the true God by silencing the learned. The assumption that the people were originally believers, in the Islamic sense, and were later led into idolatry and king-worship is one frequently encountered in Islamic literature and in the Quran itself, where the function of the Prophet is seen as one of restoration rather than religious innovation.

HAMAN, ESTHER, AND AMUN: After our look at Pharaoh, we should now discuss the thorny question of Haman, whose introduction into the Pharaoh-Moses stories in the Quran has been the cause of so much head shaking by Jewish and Christian scholars. In the Quran, he is associated closely with Pharaoh as an opponent of Moses. Later tradition more explicitly makes him the chief henchman and advisor of Pharaoh and, with much elaboration, he is given this role by Surabadi. We have already cited verses of the Quran in which they are linked (see above). Here some others: *(We desired to) show Pharaoh and Haman and their hosts that which they feared from them. (Q. 28:6); Lo! Pharaoh and Haman and their hosts were ever sinning. (Q. 28:8) And Korah, Pharaoh, and Haman! Moses came unto them with clear proofs... (Q. 29:39)*

The only person bearing the name Haman in the Bible and in Jewish tradition is a character in the *Book of Esther*, which shares with *Daniel* the honor of being the latest writing (2nd century BCE) incorporated into the canon of the Old Testament. *Esther*, in its Hebrew version, is unique in being the only book of the Bible in which God is not mentioned, nor indeed even directly referred to! It is an aetiological romance that relates the origin of the Jewish feast of Purim. Its canonicity was disputed by both the Jews and the Christians until the 2nd century CE, when it seems to have finally been admitted into the canon.[1538]

[1538] Esther, DB, p. 269; Trawick-NT, p. 328. For those unfamiliar with the story of Esther, we offer a brief summary here: In the third year of his reign (483 BCE) Ahasuerus (Xerxes) was in residence at his winter capital Susa situated in the Elamite plains [the modern Shush in southwestern Iran]. Giving a banquet that lasted a week, Ahasuerus summoned his wife Vashti, who was entertaining the ladies separately, to his court in order to display her beauty to the people. Her refusal to come when summoned angered the king and he put her away. [Early rabbinic commentators said that the cause of her

In this rather dubious book, the last of the "historical" books of the Old Testament and the least historical of them all, Haman is depicted as a court favorite of the Persian king Ahasuerus (usually identified with the Persian king Xerxes, rgd. 486-465 BCE). He is an enemy of the Jews and in particular Mordecai (who may be a cousin of Esther), and ultimately he meets the fate he had planned for Mordecai. Modern scholars are in general agreement—despite the existence of the supposed tombs of Esther and Mordecai in Hamadan, Iran—that there is absolutely no factual background for the story. Brockington refers to it as an "historical romance."[1539] In other words, *Esther* is a total fiction.[1540]

---

anger was that she was to appear wearing nothing save her crown, Laymon, p. 233.] Maidens were to be brought before the king so that he might select Vashti's replacement.

It happened that there was a Jew in Susa, Mordecai of the tribe of Benjamin, who had been carried away from Jerusalem by Nebuchadnezzar. [This would make Mordecai about 120 years old.] He had brought up Esther, also called Hadassah, the orphaned daughter of his uncle and adopted her as his own daughter. After a year's beauty treatment (all the candidates were subjected to this ordeal), she was brought before the king who chose her and made her his queen, replacing Vashti. The king then chose Haman the Agagite as his vizier. [The Agagites and Benjaminites were enemies; see 1 Sam. 15:7-9.] When Haman passed Mordecai, Mordecai refused to bow to him. This enraged Haman who informed the king that certain people (the Jews) were plotting against him and Haman persuaded him to authorize a pogrom. When Esther heard of this, she decided to intercede. She arranged a dinner for the king to which Haman would be invited. Passing through the king's gate, Mordecai was waiting and did not rise in respect for the vizier as was customary. Haman ordered Mordecai be hanged on the morrow for the insult.

Meanwhile, the king learned that this Mordecai had saved his life (from assault by two of the king's disgruntled eunuchs), but had not been honored. He ordered that this be done. Haman arrived, thinking he was about to be honored, but discovered that the honoree was his enemy Mordecai. In a dramatic scene, Haman was exposed and hanged and Mordecai named vizier in his place. Shedding tears, Esther then persuaded the king to authorize the Jews, instead of being slaughtered, to slaughter their enemies. "In Susa the capital itself the Jews slew and destroyed five hundred men… " (Est. 9:6) This massacre by the Jews was repeated in the other provinces of the Persian Empire, to a total slaughter of 75,000 of the king's subjects (Est. 9:16). To celebrate these bloody events, a joyous holiday on the 14th of Adar (Purim: the feast of the Lots) was instituted.

Modern feminists are rather uncomfortable with the story and tend to be more supportive of Vashti, who refused to be used as a sex object to titillate her husband's guests, than of the scheming sex toy Esther who used her beauty to advance herself and her causes.

[1539] Esther, DB, p. 269. *Esther* is even less historical than the fabulous *Alexander Romance*, about which there will be more in this story (Section L) and in the story of Dhul-Qarnayn in Part Six below.

[1540] Writes Philip L. Essley, Jr. of Tulsa, Oklahoma: "Those who claim the historical accuracy of Esther point to the book's familiarity with Persian customs, laws and the accurate description of the palace in Susa (essentially confirmed by archaeology). Those that deny it is based on history point out that 1) none of the individuals except Xerxes

The similarity in name and position of Haman in *Esther* and Haman in the Quran—they are both confidants and officials of powerful monarchs—has convinced European scholars that they are one and the same character, and that this is another instance of Quranic confusion.[1541] Perhaps; but it is odd indeed that no other aspect of the extremely colorful tale of *Esther* is referred to in the Quran, and only the name of the villain Haman made the trip to the oral tradition of Arabia. In all other respects, the stories and situations are completely dissimilar. Eisenberg says: "…it is remarkable that neither the Quran nor commentary nor the Arab historians know anything of the true Haman of the book of Esther. It must be presumed nevertheless that the story of Haman was not quite unknown in Arabia."[1542] (There is a certain amount of presumption in calling a fictional character in *Esther* the *true* Haman.)

The etymology of the name is Haman is unknown. Since other characters in *Esther* bear the names of deities (Esther = Ishtar,[1543] Vashti

---

(Ahasuerus in the Bible) is named in secular Persian history, 2) Xerxes's queen's name was Amistris, not Vashti or Esther… 3) in the tenth month of the seventh year of Xerxes's reign, when he allegedly married Esther, the king was in fact fleeing from Greece after having watched the Greeks destroy most of his fleet in the battle of Salamis and defeat his army in the battle of Plataea, and 4) other than the Bible, there is no record of the decrees supposedly issued by Xerxes or a revolt or massacres on the 14th day of Adar in any year. Ancient Elam, whose capital was Susa, was a rival of Babylonia and Assyria for centuries. However, in 640 BC Ashurbanipal of Assyria destroyed Elam and Susa (the site of Esther)… In the process, the Babylonian god Marduk (*Merodach* in Persian) and goddess Ishtar (*Esther* in Persian) replaced the Elamic male and female gods Haman and Vashti. Are the similar names a coincidence or literary structure?"

Mr. Essley prefaces these comments with an impressive list of anachronisms found in *Judith*, a romance of the same period that did not make it into the Biblical canon, but is found in the Apocrypha included in many Bibles: "In the story we have seventh-century BC Assyria, under the rule of a sixth-century Chaldean (Babylonian) king, invading a fifth-century restored Judah, with an army led by a fourth-century Persian general (Holofernes was the Persian general under Artaxerxes III in the successful Persian campaign against Egypt in the fourth-century BC). In truth no major attacks were made on Jerusalem while under Persian rule in the fifth and fourth centuries (an unprecedented period of peace for war-weary Canaan)." (Philip L. Essley, Jr., Letter to BR, Vol. XVIII, No. 3, June 2002, p. 6)

[1541] Haman, SEI, p. 130.

[1542] L. Eisenberg, writing in Haman, SEI, p. 130.

[1543] It has been suggested that "Esther" is derived from the Persian for "star" (*sitārah*), but this may be a coincidence. More probably, it is one of the names of the ancient Near Eastern "Great Mother" worshipped in Phrygia and Lydia as Cybele, by the Mesopotamians as Ishtar, by the Syrians and Canaanites as Astarte, by the Egyptians as Isis, etc. Many of her attributes are to be found in the adoration of the Virgin Mary. (Great Mother of the Gods, CE, p. 863.) There is no historical record of a queen Esther for Xerxes, although some hopeful scholars have tried to squeeze "Esther" out of "Stateira," the name of the queen of Artaxerxes II (rgd. 404-358 BCE)

= Mashti,[1544] and Mordecai = Marduk[1545]) it has been proposed that Haman stands in a similar relationship to the Elamite god Human, Humban, or Umman. It has also been related to the sacred drink *haoma* of ancient Aryan religion, and with the Persian name Humayun.[1546] "Such similarity can hardly have come about by accident and may testify to an original Babylonian myth behind the Jewish story."[1547] It has also been proposed that the struggle between Esther and Mordecai (the Semitic Babylonian gods Ishtar and Marduk) on the one hand with Vashti and Haman (the possibly Indo-European Elamite deities Mashti and Human) on the other represents a struggle between Babylonian and Elamite deities.[1548] Of course, all of these equivalencies are admittedly unproven, and since we are dealing with fancy, probably unprovable.

The absence of any reference to the story of Esther in the Quran and Islamic tradition (if we put aside the question of the identity of Haman for the moment) suggests that it may not have been in wide circulation among the Jews of the Hejaz. At first, this may seem remarkable for such a famous story, but it calls to mind an interesting fact about the Dead Sea Scrolls: "All the books of the Old Testament except Esther are represented."[1549] Although this may be fortuitous, the absence of *Esther* among the finds has led some scholars to speculate that the book was rejected by the Qumran community. It could hardly have been unknown to them. This rejection was probably conscious and based upon the secular nature of the book. If this theory be true, and if there was a connection been the Jews of Hejaz and the Qumran Jews who sought sanctuary in Arabia after the catastrophes of the Jewish-Roman wars in Palestine, this curious lacuna in the Jewish lore current in western Arabia would become explicable. At the same time, it would tell us a little more about the kind of Judaism with which the Hejazi Jews had been in contact or had adhered to at some earlier stage in their

---

[1544] Mashti, possibly an Elamite goddess. Historically, the queen of Xerxes was Amestris, not Vashti. Vashti may be a total fiction to introduce Esther into the story. (Harvey, writing in *Vashti*, IDB, Vol. 4, pp. 746-747.)

[1545] Marduk, whose special cult center was in Babylon, was the omniscient king of the pantheon of Babylonian gods and the creator of mankind. (Marduk, CE, p. 1307.)

[1546] Esther, DB, p. 269; Haman, EJ, VII, 1222. The Persian *humāyūn* means, "blessed, sacred, fortunate, august, royal, imperial" (Steingass, p. 1508). However, if the name is derived from the popular Elamite deity, the name would appear to mean "Hum is a creator" (Elamites, ERE, V, 252). See other explanations below in the text. It should be mentioned that the RSV (Note to Est. 1:10-2:4 on p. 603) considers the strange names "attempts to reproduce Persian names."

[1547] Reidar B. Bjornard, writing in the Introduction to *Esther* in BC, Vol. 4, p. 2.

[1548] H. Neil Richardson, writing in Laymon, p. 233; Elamites, ERE, V, 251.

[1549] Dead Sea Scrolls, DB, p. 205.

history in Arabia. Already established Jewish communities in the Hejaz could have been proselytized by the Essenes fleeing from Qumran, after their centers in Palestine had been destroyed. [1550]

While this might explain why there are no references to the colorful tale of Esther and Mordecai in the Quran, it does not explain how Haman came to be mentioned in the Quran. Modern Muslim commentators of course categorically deny the identity of the Haman of Egypt with the Haman of *Esther*, and most of them usually rely upon a homonymic coincidence for defense against the charges of confusion leveled by Western critics. Obviously, simple denial in this situation is not enough. Somewhere we have read the suggestion that the name Haman is connected with the Egyptian god Amun, rather than the Haman of *Esther*. This interesting idea is worth pursuing.

Amun was originally the local god of the city of Thebes (modern Luxor). When Thebes became the capital of Egypt during the Twelfth Dynasty, the god's role in the pantheon began to expand until at the beginning of the Empire period (the XVIIIth Dynasty) Amun's paramountcy was virtually unchallenged in Egypt.[1551] During the Empire, Amun became assimilated with the sun god Ra, and was worshiped under the name Amun-Ra. The supremacy of the Amun-Ra among the Egyptian gods was complete. Except for the short period of heresy under Akhenaton, it remained so for the rest of the Empire period, including the period under our consideration, and a long time thereafter.

The Temple of Karnak at Thebes, by some calculations the largest building in the ancient world, was completed by Rameses II in honor of Amun. During the New Empire, the Temple of Amun became the largest landholder after Pharaoh, and its priesthood became correspondingly powerful. About a century after the period of Moses, during the reign of Rameses III, the temple lands of Amun amounted to 10% of the entire cultivated land of Egypt and employed 86,500 slaves (or serfs). All of the other temple establishments together shared another 5% of the land and some 30,000 slaves.[1552] Inevitably, the High Priest of Amun was the second most powerful man in the land and, in the later Empire, succeeded in making his office hereditary.[1553] Finally, after the death of Rameses XII, in the logical culmination of the process, the High

---

[1550] For a fuller discussion of this possibility, see the section about the Essenes in "Palestine in New Testament Times" in the Introduction to *The New Testament: An Islamic Perspective*.

[1551] Budge-Gods, Vol. 2, pp. 3-4.

[1552] Breasted, pp. 414-415.

[1553] Breasted, p. 384.

Priest of Amun, Hrihor, succeeded in making himself Pharaoh (1090 BCE).[1554] Is the Haman of the Quran the High Priest of Amun?[1555]

In this respect, it is interesting to quote the words of Jeremiah: "The Lord of hosts, the God of Israel, said: 'Behold, I am bringing punishment upon Amon of Thebes, and Pharaoh, Egypt and her gods and her kings, upon Pharaoh and those who trust in him." (Jer. 46:25) Jeremiah's usage of Amun and Pharaoh parallels that in the Quran. Of the six times the name Haman is used in the Quran, in four he is linked with Pharaoh as an opponent of Moses. In two of these four, the name Korah is added. Rather than confusion, this is exceptionally astute: Moses is being opposed in his task by the might of the state and priesthood of Egypt, personified as Pharaoh and Haman.[1556]

The writings of the Roman historian Tacitus establish a link between Pharaoh and Hammon (Amun): "Most authors agree that during a plague in Egypt which disfigured bodies, King Bocchoris consulted the oracle of Hammon in search of a remedy and was instructed to purge the kingdom and to deport this race [the Hebrews], which was hateful to the gods, into other lands. Thus they were sought out, gathered and then abandoned in the desert. While most were overcome with tears, one of the exiles, Moses, exhorted them not to expect any help from gods or men, for they were deserted by both, but rather to rely on themselves and to consider as a heavenly guide whoever should first aid them in overcoming their present difficulties."[1557]

Here we have the disfiguring plague, mentioned by Surabadi, but related to the plagues of Egypt. More importantly, we have the link between Pharaoh and the powerful priesthood of Amun, in this case

---

[1554] Breasted, p. 437.

[1555] The objection that Amun is the name of the god and not the high priest is not an obstacle. Literature offers many examples of individuals' being addressed rhetorically by a term related to their function rather than their proper name. For example, in Shakespeare's *Antony and Cleopatra*, Antony frequently addresses Cleopatra as "Egypt": "I am dying, Egypt, dying; only I here importune death awhile..." (Act IV, Scene 15) We have already observed above the parallel institutional nature of the title-become-name "Pharaoh" itself.

[1556] The other usages of the name Haman in the Quran (Q. 28:38 and 40:36) are connected with the command, perhaps issued sarcastically, to build a tower to challenge the God of Moses. If this Pharaoh is the builder Ramses II, as seems likely, the reference here is singularly apropos: confronted by Moses and his invisible God, Pharaoh turned to the High Priest of Amun to challenge Him, as he had already challenged his own mortality with his frenetic and colossal construction projects. Perhaps this exchange was sharpened by the memory of the chaos and civil strife caused by Akhenaton's failed attempt to convert Egypt to monotheism a century earlier.

[1557] Tacitus, *Histories*, 5.3, quoted by Gager, p. 127.

represented by the famous oracle of Ammon (Amun) situated in the Libyan Desert west of the Nile at the oasis of Siwah, some 300 miles west of Cairo. This oracle was as influential in the ancient world as that of Delphi. Late in the 6th century BCE, the Persian emperor Cambyses lost an army sent to destroy it in a sandstorm. Alexander the Great visited it in 331 BCE to have his right to the throne of Egypt confirmed by his being declared a divinity and the son of Amun.[1558] There would be nothing more natural than for Pharaoh to seek the aid of the High Priest of Amun in a crisis.

How came news of Amun to Arabia? It must be remembered that in addition to the land routes to Egypt via Midian and the Isthmus of Suez, there were also more direct sea routes across the Red Sea from Egypt in use in ancient times. The classical port of Berenice, accessible from Upper Egypt, lies opposite Yanbu' on the Hejaz littoral, and there were other ports as well, both in Egypt and Arabia. It is not at all unlikely that the trading Arabs circulated traditions that linked Pharaoh and Amun, the most powerful figures of Egypt at its apogee of power, and also the still-standing stupendous constructions linked with both names."

There are still other possibilities. There was a Horite clan, located around Mount Seir (now in southwestern Jordan and close to the caravan routes from Makkah to Syria) called Hemanite from an eponymous ancestor Heman (*Hīmān*) (Gen. 36:22). The Chronicler spells his name Homan (*Hūmān*) (1 Ch. 1:39). Jewish tradition mentions an angel Ḥemah, slain by Moses in Midian.[1559] There is also one Heman, a legendary wise man, whose wisdom was excelled by that of Solomon (1 K. 4:31). Nothing other than his name has been preserved. Heman may have been associated with music, and it has been suggested that he was an Edomite.[1560] It is just possible that this is the Haman of the Quran. At one time, he must have been a well-known figure, though now even Jewish tradition offers us little but his name. Perhaps he played some role in the administration of the area where the Semites were settled in Egypt. Being an Edomite would be sufficient reason for later Jews to ignore his story, but his memory may have been preserved in northwestern Arabia.[1561]

[1558] See Dhul-Qarnayn in Part Six below.

[1559] LJ, II, 328. However, the shift from the fricative *Ḥ* to the softer *H* of the Quranic Haman would be difficult to explain. The softer *h* disappears easily in many languages, including English, but not the strong fricative *ḥ* among Semites, rendering the angel an improbable candidate.

[1560] BC, III, 170-171.

[1561] Edom and Midian were neighbors, and to some extent, co-extensive.

In the absence of definite documentary links (although the citation from Tacitus strengthens the already strong hypothesis Haman is High Priest of Amun), the above should suffice to demonstrate that other explanations could be offered other than confusion with the Haman of *Esther* (of whose history all of the sensational details are forgotten) favored by Western critics. It is our belief that Haman is most likely the High Priest of Amun, quite appropriate in the context of the story of Pharaoh and Moses. *And God knows best.*

C. THE BIRTH AND INFANCY OF MOSES

Shall I show you one who will nurse him? (Q. 20:40)

In Surabadi's account of the birth of Moses, we are told first that Pharaoh's astrologers and priests had predicted that his kingdom would be destroyed by the Israelites. However, according to another tradition that Surabadi relates, Pharaoh himself saw a dream in which a fire arose from Jericho and Dar'a[1562] that destroyed his kingdom. The Israelites had been brought to Egypt from Jericho and Dar'a. Pharaoh asked his astrologers and priests who among the Israelites would bring about the downfall of his kingdom. They replied that that person had not yet been born. Pharaoh then ordered that all of their male children should be killed and the females taken into slavery.[1563]

However, the Egyptians were frivolous and only good for war. They discovered that they needed the Israelites for their skills and labor. Consequently, the order was revised so that the slaughter should be carried out every other year. Aaron was born in a year in which there was no slaughter of the male newborn, but Moses was not.[1564]

The above is a considerably embroidered commentary on this verse: *Lo! Pharaoh exalted himself in the land and made its people into factions. A tribe among them he oppressed, killing their sons and sparing their women. Lo! He was of those who work corruption.* (Q. 28:4) In the context of the passage, this is almost certainly a reference to the slaughter of the male children of the Israelites. Except for the matter of

---

[1562] Jericho (*Arīhā*) and Dar'a (*Adhri'ā*). Jericho is located about fifteen miles NW of Jerusalem in the valley of the Jordan in eastern Palestine; Dar'a is located about thirty miles ESE of the Sea of Galilee in southwestern Syria.

[1563] Surabadi, p. 298. In another place (p. 9) Surabadi calls the astrologers and priests Copts. In Islamic times, up to the present, Egyptian Christians have been referred to as Copts, as opposed to the majority Muslim population.

[1564] Surabadi, p. 298.

male infanticide, none of the other details in Surabadi's account is found in the Quran.

Surabadi does not seem to connect the presence of the Israelites in Egypt with the descendants of those who had come to Egypt in the time of Joseph—the Biblical view. Hence, Surabadi has them brought from Palestine and southern Syria, a region historically within the sphere of Egyptian influence in that era.

The first chapter of *Exodus* sets out the circumstances of the descendants of Jacob in Egypt: "Then Joseph died, and all his brothers, and all that generation. But the descendants of Israel were fruitful and increased greatly; they multiplied and grew exceedingly strong; so that the land was filled with them." (Ex. 1:6-7) How much had they multiplied? If we are to accept the traditional interpretation of the census figures given in Num. 1:46, they would have grown to about two millions. In Roman times, the population of Egypt was about 7,000,000, according to Breasted's estimate,[1565] and it must have been considerably less some twelve centuries earlier. If we suggest the not unreasonable figure of 4,000,000 for that earlier period, then the Israelites would have made up half of the population of Egypt![1566]

Of course, we know that that could not have been the case. As we shall see, there are excellent reasons for assuming an Exodus of only 20,000 souls. However, in the region of the eastern Delta, with a local concentration, the number of Israelites (and other Semites) had developed to the point where they had become locally conspicuous and cause for concern on the part of the Egyptian authorities.[1567]

"Now there arose a new king over Egypt, who did not know Joseph. And he said to his people, 'Behold, the people of Israel are too many and too mighty for us. Come, let us deal shrewdly with them, lest they multiply, and, if war befall us, they join our enemies and fight against us and escape from the land.'" (Ex. 1:8-10) The Israelites were enslaved and set to hard tasks (Ex. 1:11-14), probably on the construction projects of Rameses II in the eastern Delta.[1568]

The Biblical phrase quoted above "now there arose a new king over Egypt," can readily be interpreted to mean the direct successor of the Pharaoh of Joseph. Since elsewhere it is stated that about four

---

[1565] Breasted, p. 6.

[1566] McEvedy and Jones propose more conservative estimates of the population of Egypt: about 4,000,000 for the beginning of the Common Era (1 CE) and about 3,000,000 at the time of the New Empire of which the era of Moses is a part (McEvedy, pp. 226-227).

[1567] See Section G below for a more detailed discussion of this problem.

[1568] See previous Section, B.

centuries had elapsed between the time of Joseph and the time of Moses, this ambiguity is probably responsible, in part, for the traditions of Pharaoh's extraordinarily long life.[1569]

The Biblical story quoted above is principally from J, with some glosses by P. The Elohist history is the source of the story of Pharaoh's slaughter of infants and the circumstances of the birth of Moses: "Then the king of Egypt said to the Hebrew midwives, one of whom was named Shiprah and the other Puah,[1570] 'When ye serve as midwife to the Hebrew women, and see them upon the birthstool, if it is a son, ye shall kill him; but if it is a daughter, she shall live.' …Then Pharaoh commanded all his people, 'Every son that is born to the Hebrews ye shall cast into the Nile, but ye shall let every daughter live'" (Ex. 1:15-16, 22) The statement in the Quran obviously follows this tradition of E. The circumstances of Pharaoh's dream or the predictions of the astrologers and priests of *Surabadi* are not found in *Exodus*, nor are they in the Quran.

It has been pointed out that these accounts by J and E are mutually contradictory. If the Israelites were enslaved and used as labor in Egyptian construction schemes, then it would not have been to the Egyptians' advantage to destroy their own labor supply by killing the male children.[1571]

Jewish tradition amplifies the oppression and the slaughter of the male infants considerably.[1572] Although Surabadi speaks of Pharaoh's edict to kill the males as though it continued for a number of years, Jewish tradition gives it a more limited period. The Talmudic tractate *Sotah* mentions one day, the *Book of Jubilees* seven months.[1573] Both of these sources are pre-Islamic. The *Pirke de Rabbi Eliezer* states that three years elapsed between the edict and the birth of Moses.[1574] In Jewish tradition, there is a story that on the day of the birth of Moses, the

---

[1569] See above. As noted above, Rameses II had one of the longest reigns of any monarch in history.

[1570] The text seems to suggest that these two midwives sufficed for the entire population of the Israelites. If that was the case, they could not possibly have provided midwifery services to all of the pregnant women of a population of 2,000,000, as they would have had to deal with some 50 to 60,000 births per year, or 1000 to 1200 per week! Based upon this passage, the Israelites could have numbered only a few thousands.

[1571] Contrary to popular opinion, slaves were a fairly expensive commodity, except when there was a glut of prisoners from wars, as slave prices from ancient times to the end of slavery in the 19th century show. Killing a slave for a trivial reason would have been a bit like running an expensive car off a cliff because the radio would not work.

[1572] One use of the theme, Pharaoh's bathing in their blood, has been cited in the previous section.

[1573] LJ, V, 399-400.

[1574] PRE, p. 378.

astrologers came to Pharaoh saying that they had seen something that they did not understand, but seemed to imply that a danger had been averted. Furthermore, it was said that "on account of the merits of Moses, the 600,000 men children of the Hebrews begotten in the same night with him, and thrown into the water on the same day, were rescued miraculously together with him[1575]..." The numbers here are inflated fantastically. In this pericope, the astrologers appear to call an end to the slaughter rather than precipitating it, as in Surabadi.

In some Jewish traditions, fearing the power of Israel, Pharaoh called his three counselors, Jethro, Job, and Balaam, and asked their advice. (These were same three who had advised Pharaoh to bathe in the blood of the Israelite infants in another tradition related above.) In this story, too, Balaam plays the role of the adversary of Israel and advises the king that nothing would work save: "if it please the king, let him order all the male children that shall be born in Israel from this day forward to be thrown into the water. Thereby canst thou wipe out their name, for neither any of them nor any of their fathers was tried this way."[1576] The purpose of this advice is not given in order to prevent the survival of Moses especially.

Josephus tells us of a warning given to Pharaoh by a sacred scribe that is very similar to that of the astrologers and priests in Surabadi. "One of those sacred scribes, who are very sagacious in foretelling future events truly, told the king that about this time there would be a child born to the Israelites, who, if he were reared, would bring the Egyptian dominion low and would raise the Israelites... Which thing was so feared by the king, that, according to this man's opinion, he commanded that they should cast every male child, which was born to the Israelites, into the river, and destroy it... That if any parents should disobey him, and venture to save their male children alive, they and their families should be destroyed."[1577] In this story, we see that not only were the children threatened, but also their families if they disobeyed, and this was the punishment feared by Moses' mother when she threw him into the oven in Surabadi's account (see below). The tradition reflected in Josephus surely is the same as that which has come to the Muslim commentators.

The Biblical parallel to and a probable source of Surabadi's material about the prophesies of the astrologers and priests may be the birth narrative of Jesus found in *Matthew*: "Now when Jesus was born in

---

[1575] LJ, II, 268-269.
[1576] LJ, II, 254-256.
[1577] Josephus, *Antiquities*, II.9.2, pp. 55-56.

Bethlehem of Judaea in the days of Herod the king, behold, wise men from the East came to Jerusalem, saying, 'Where is he who has been born king of the Jews? For we have seen his star in the East, and have come to worship him.' When Herod the king heard this, he was troubled, and all Jerusalem with him; and assembling all the chief priests and scribes of the people, he inquired of them where the Christ was to be born..." (Mt. 2:1-4)

Herod asked the wise men to report the finding of the child to him, but instead, after finding him and having been apprised of Herod's intentions in a dream, they returned to their own country by a different route. Joseph, also warned in a dream, took his wife and child to safety in Egypt. "Then Herod, when he saw that he had been tricked by the wise men, was in a furious rage, and he sent and killed all the male children in Bethlehem and in all that region who were two years or under, according to the time which he had ascertained from the wise men." (Mt. 2:16)

A closer extra-Biblical parallel has doubtless already occurred to the reader, that with Abraham. His birth had been foretold to Nimrod and was followed by the slaughter of infants, from which Abraham was miraculously spared.[1578] The story in *Matthew* is itself doubtless dependent upon Moses' birth story, with whom Christians liked to compare Jesus.[1579] The 11th-century CE Jewish *Book of Yashar* gives us an account of Nimrod's dream of warning which we may compare with Surabadi's tradition of Pharaoh's dream: One of Nimrod's wise men, Anoqo, interpreted it to mean that the king would lose his life at the hands of a descendant of Abraham, and he was advised to kill Abraham.[1580] However, the most famous royal dream warning of destruction to a kingdom at the hands of an infant is the well-known story concerning Cyrus the Great of Persia, as found in the 5th-century BCE *Histories* of Herodotus.[1581] In the Bible, *Daniel* uses the same

---

[1578] See Part Two, III.B.

[1579] The parallels and sources of the Jesus birth story are discussed at greater length in *The New Testament: An Islamic Perspective* (II.A of the Stories).

[1580] LJ, I, 204-205.

[1581] "(The last Median king) Astyages had a daughter called Mandane, and he dreamed one night that she made water in such enormous quantities that it filled his city and swamped the whole of Asia. He told his dream to the Magi... and was much alarmed by what they said it meant. Consequently, when Mandane was old enough to marry, he did not give her to some Mede of suitable rank, but was induced by his fear of the dream's significance to marry her to a Persian named Cambyses though he considered him much below a Mede even of middle rank. Before Mandane and Cambyses had been married a year, Astyages had another dream. This time it was that a vine grew from his daughter's private parts and spread over Asia. As before, he told the interpreters about this dream, and then sent for his daughter, who was now pregnant.

literary device: Nebuchadnezzar is said to have had two dreams, both successfully interpreted by Daniel, in the first of which the destruction of worldly kingdoms is predicted, heralding the Messianic era, and in the second, the king's insanity (Dan. 2,4).

Returning to Surabadi's story, after listing the twelve marvels of Moses (birth, nursing, upbringing, exile, marriage, shepherding, afflictions, revelation and messengership, proof and miracles, polemic and debate, victory, and prayer and nearness to God), Surabadi proceeds to his version of the birth story: At the time of the birth of Moses all pregnant women gave birth without pain, prisoners were freed, the unfortunate were relieved, a star appeared over Egypt, light shone from Egypt, the palace of Pharaoh shook and his throne fell down and was broken,[1582] and Haman heard a loud sound in his heart.[1583]

Though none of this material is found in the birth narratives of Moses in the Bible or the Quran, some of it may be traced to other writings. Josephus mentions the ease of Moses' birth: "However, the mother's labour was such as afforded a confirmation to what was foretold by God; for it was not known to those that watched her, by the easiness of her pains, and because the throes of delivery did not fall upon her with violence."[1584] The star over Egypt is strikingly reminiscent of the star of Bethlehem that appeared, according to *Matthew*, at the birth of Jesus (Mt. 2:2,7,9,10).[1585] The Talmud (*Sotah*) and Jewish traditions speak of the light that appeared at the time of Moses' birth: "At the

---

"When she arrived, he kept her under strict watch, intending to make away with the child; for the fact was that the Magi had interpreted the dream to mean that his daughter's son would usurp his throne. To guard against this, Astyages, when Cyrus was born, sent for his kinsman Harpagus, the steward of his property, whom he trusted more than anyone..." Astyages told Harpagus to take the child away and kill it. But when he saw the child, his heart softened and he sent the infant away to a herdsman Mitradates who raised the boy as his own. The boy, of course, was Cyrus, destined to become Cyrus the Great, the founder of history's first world empire. He did indeed drive Astyages from the throne, but he "treated him with consideration and kept him at the court until he died." (Herodotus, Bk. I, pp. 85-96.) The same plot device, popular in ancient times, will also be familiar to those who have seen the animated film *Snow White and the Seven Dwarfs*.

[1582] Kisa'i tells of Moses' breaking Pharaoh's throne at a later time: "When Moses was nine, he kicked the legs of the chair Pharaoh was sitting on and it broke. Pharaoh fell and broke his nose, and the blood flowed over his beard. He wanted to kill Moses, but Asiyah said, 'Sire, it would do you no harm to have a son of such strength who could drive away your enemies.'" (Kisa'i, pp. 218-219]

[1583] Surabadi, pp. 298-299.

[1584] Josephus, Antiquities, II.9.4, p. 56.

[1585] See quotation from *Matthew* above.

moment of the child's appearance, the whole house was filled with radiance equal to the splendor of the sun and the moon.[1586]

After Moses was born, according to Surabadi, when the police came to kill him, his mother threw him into an oven, exclaiming: "Letting him burn in the oven is better than his being killed upon my belly by the police of Pharaoh!" The men searched the house but did not find the child. It never occurred to them he could be in the roaring oven. When they left, his mother opened the oven and saw Moses playing with the embers. She knew that this prodigy would not remain a secret in Egypt. After giving him milk, she made a casket waterproof with pitch and, telling herself that the Lord would protect him as He had in the fire, she gave the casket to her daughter Miriam to put in a canal, instructing her to watch what happened to it.

Miriam did this, and she followed the casket until it entered a canal that passed through Pharaoh's garden. Seventy maidens were playing there. They saw the little ark, but were unable to catch it and bring it ashore until one of them pronounced "In the Name of God" (*bismillah*). The casket was brought to Isiyah,[1587] who opened it and was captivated by the beauty of the child's smile.[1588]

Laqitah, the adopted daughter of Pharaoh, was also present. It is said that Pharaoh claimed to have created Laqitah when she was born, and thereafter seventy-two defects had appeared in the infant. When the casket was opened, Moses looked at Isiyah with one eye and Laqitah with the other. Instantly Isiyah gained wisdom and Latiqah shed her defects. All who looked upon him were taken by his grace except Pharaoh, who refused to look and said that the infant was an enemy Israelite child and should be killed. This threat was removed when, one day, the infant Moses said "Baba" to him. After that, Pharaoh became fond of him. That one word had ten rewards: Moses escaped the slaughter, the killing of infants became unlawful and ceased, the king

---

[1586] LJ, II, 264. This light lasted three months, being withdrawn when Moses entered the household of Pharaoh (LJ, V, 397). The 2nd-century Christian apocryphal work, the *Protevangelium*, relates: "And (Joseph and the midwife) stood in the place of the cave: and behold, a bright cloud overshadowing the cave. And the midwife said: My soul is magnified this day, because mine eyes have seen marvellous things; for salvation is born unto Israel. And immediately the cloud withdrew itself out of the cave, and a great light appeared in the cave so that our eyes could not endure it. And by little and little that light withdrew itself until the young child appeared: and it went and took the breast of its mother Mary." (James, pp. 44,46.) Compare also the light that appears in the birth narrative of Abraham. (See Part Two above, III.B.)

[1587] Surabadi writes Isiyah, but Āsiyah is the more common form in Islamic literature.

[1588] Surabadi, pp. 249-250, 299.

held him to his breast, kissed him, and adopted him, Moses was wrapped in silk by the king, a crown was placed upon his head, the sun's eye (a flower) was adorned on his behalf, and the court prostrated themselves before him.[1589]

Forty wet nurses were brought, but Moses would not take their milk. Finally, his sister brought his mother, who found Moses the center of attention at the court, including Pharaoh and Haman. Moses took his mother's breast and began to suck. When Haman saw this, his suspicions apparently aroused, he asked the woman, whose name was Nukhai'dh,[1590] if she were the child's mother in fact. She replied evasively that she wished she were. Thereafter, Moses lived like a prince with 400 servants, etc.[1591]

The incident of Moses' being thrown into the oven by his mother is not found in the Bible or the Quran, nor does it seem to be associated with Moses in Jewish tradition. In the latter, King Manasseh (rgd. 687-642 BCE) was punished by being put in an oven in Babylonia, but the similarity ends there.[1592] The name of Moses' mother, given by Surabadi as Nukha'idh, is doubtless a garbling of the Biblical Jochebed, caused by a misreading of the dots on the letters. (It appears more correctly in other Muslim writings as Yukhabid.) Isiyah is an alternative form of the more usual Asiyah, as Pharaoh's wife is called in Islamic tradition. Pharaoh's wife (or daughter) is not named in the Bible, nor is she in the Quran, contrary to the impression created by Prof. Hirschberg, perhaps inadvertently, in the relevant article in *Encyclopædia Judaica*.[1593]

[1589] Laqitah: Laqīṭah. Surabadi, pp. 299-300.

[1590] Nukha'idh: Nūkhāʾīdh.

[1591] Surabadi, pp. 250-251, 300.

[1592] LJ, IV, 279-280. In the *Pirke de Rabbi Eliezer*, there is a tradition that the Egyptians burnt the children of the Israelites in the furnace of fire, and later writings make this an act of sacrifice to the Egyptian gods (PRE, p. 381). It is possible some such tradition influenced the episode found in Surabadi. It should be pointed out that there is no record that the Egyptians practiced human sacrifice in historical times, although it was practiced in Canaan even into the period of the Israelite monarchy.

[1593] Moses, EJ, XII, 403; Pharaoh, EJ, XIII, 362. In the latter reference, Prof. Hirschberg writes: "Pharaoh of the Koran is the king who oppressed the people of Israel in Egypt; Musa (Moses) and Harun (Aaron) negotiated with him. In accordance with the counsel of his advisors, among them Haman, Pharaoh ordered that all male children be killed (Sura 2:46; 7:137). Asiya, the wife of Pharaoh, adopted Moses, who had been found in an ark (28:9)." The Quranic verse cited does not mention her by name: *And the wife of Pharaoh said: (He will be) a consolation for me and for thee...* (Q. 28:9) Many commentators think that a verse in Surah al-Tahrim (*al-Taḥrīm*) refers to her: *And God cites an example for those who believe: the wife of Pharaoh when she said: My Lord! Build for me a home with thee in Paradise, and deliver me from Pharaoh and his work, and deliver me from the tyrannical people.* (Q. 66:11)

Two passages in the Quran refer to the story of Moses' birth, both focusing on the mother: *And when We inspired in thy mother (O Moses) that which is inspired. Saying: Throw him into the ark and throw it into the river,*[1594] *then the river shall throw it onto the bank, and there an enemy to Me and an enemy to him shall take him. And I endued thee with love from Me that thou might be trained according to My will. When thy sister went and said: Shall I show you one who will nurse him? And We restored thee unto thy mother that her eyes might be refreshed and might not sorrow.* (Q. 20:38-40) In this passage, we have the casting into the river, the intervention of his sister, and his reunion with his mother.

In another place, a fuller version is given: *And We inspired the mother of Moses, saying: Suckle him and, when thou fearest for him, then cast him into the river and do not fear or grieve. Lo! We shall bring him back unto thee and shall make him (one) of Our messengers. And the family of Pharaoh took him up, that he might become for them an enemy and a sorrow. Lo! Pharaoh and Haman and their hosts were ever sinning. And the wife of Pharaoh said: (He will be) a consolation for me and for thee. Kill him not. Perhaps he may be of use to us, or we may choose him for a son. And they perceived not.* (Q. 28:7-9)

And the heart of the mother of Moses became void, and she would have betrayed him if We had not fortified her heart, that she might be of the believers. And she said unto his sister: Trace him. So she observed him from afar, and they perceived not. And We had before forbidden foster-mothers for him, so she said: Shall I show you a household who will rear him for you and take care of him? So We restored him to his mother that she might be comforted and not grieve, and that she might know that the promise of God is true. But most of them know not. (Q. 28:10-13)

These accounts follow the Biblical account remarkably closely, except in a few details: No personal names occur in the Biblical version (Ex. 2:1-10)[1595] save that of Moses at the end: "Now a man from the house of Levi went and took to wife a daughter of Levi. The woman conceived and bore a son; and when she saw that he was a goodly child, she hid him three months." (Ex. 2:1-2) (This implies that Moses was their *first* child.) This period is referred to in the Quran when it speaks of

---

[1594] "river": In this and the following quotation, the word used in the Quran is *yamm*, usually translated as "sea" or "open sea" and not "river." However, the Nile, the largest river in the Near East, is still called in Arabic *Baḥr ul-Nīl*, the "Nile Sea" because of its size and importance.

[1595] Gray assigns this pericope to the Elohist (Laymon, p. 34). It is remarkable how often the Quran uses the traditions of the Elohist as opposed to those of the Yahwist.

Moses' mother nursing her child. "And when she could hide him no longer she took for him a basket made of bulrushes, and daubed it with bitumen and pitch; and she put the child in it and placed it among the reeds at the river's brink. And his sister stood a distance, to know what would be done to him." (Ex. 2:3-4) (Now we learn that Moses had an older sister.)

Up to this point the narratives are virtually the same, except for the greater attention to the workings of Providence and the anguished thoughts of the mother in the Quran, while the Elohist's account in *Exodus*, gives more details about the construction of the ark. Then:

"Now the daughter of Pharaoh came down to bathe at the river, and her maidens walked beside the river; she saw the basket among the reeds and set her maid to fetch it. When she opened it, she saw the child; and lo, the babe was crying. She took pity on him and said, 'This is one of the Hebrews' children.'" (Ex. 2:5-6) In this passage, the differences become stronger. The Elohist states that it was the daughter of Pharaoh who discovered him, while the Quran only mentions the "family of Pharaoh" who rescued the infant Moses from the water. In Surabadi, it was the smile of the child rather than his crying which excited the Egyptian woman's compassion for his plight. At this point Surabadi introduced Laqitah, Pharaoh's daughter who had the seventy-two defects cured by Moses' smile. In Talmudic tradition, Pharaoh's daughter was cured of leprosy as she extended her arm to retrieve the casket.[1596] Josephus calls her Thermuthis;[1597] rabbinic tradition speaks of her as Bithiah, a daughter of Pharaoh who married Mered of the tribe of Judah in another context (1 Ch. 4:17). The Arabic "Asiyah" and Surabadi's "Isiyah" are probably related to this name.

"Then his sister said to Pharaoh's daughter, 'Shall I go and call to thee a nurse from the Hebrew women to nurse the child for thee?' And Pharaoh's daughter said to her, Go.' So the girl went and called the child's mother. And Pharaoh's daughter said to her, 'Take this child away, and nurse him for me, and I will give thee thy wages.' So the woman took the child and nursed him. And the child grew, and she brought him to Pharaoh's daughter, and he became her son; and she named him Moses, for she said, 'Because I drew him out of the water.'" (Ex. 2:7-10)

There are no significant divergences between this and the Quranic version save in the matter of the folk etymology of the name

---

[1596] LJ, II, 267.
[1597] Josephus, Antiquities, II.9.5, p. 56.

Moses[1598] omitted by the Quran and the relationship of Moses' foster mother to Pharaoh. However, in the Biblical account, Moses' nationality is apparently evident to the people of Pharaoh, but no comment is made about sparing him from the threat of death that presumably hung over him, or the suspension of the order to kill the Hebrew children. Surabadi's tradition, recognizing this difficulty, makes Moses' nationality a secret, unknown to or only guessed at by Pharaoh and Haman. Pharaoh at least is won over to him, and Moses' real mother responds cleverly to the question about her relationship to Moses (and therefore his race) without divulging the truth or lying about it.

The Bible does not mention the infant Moses' refusal to take any of the breasts offered him for nursing until his mother was brought to him. His sister simply appears on the spot and offers a wet nurse who is accepted immediately without question. However, Talmudic tradition also contributes this detail of the child's refusal of the milk of the wet nurses. In the Quran, it simply brings about the reunion of mother and child, but in Jewish tradition it is given racial overtones: "(Pharaoh's daughter) ordered an Egyptian woman to be brought, to nurse the child, but the little one refused to take milk from her breasts, as he refused to take it from one after another of the Egyptian women fetched thither. Thus it had been ordained by God, that none of them might boast later on, and say, 'I suckled him that now holds converse with the Shekinah.' Nor was the mouth destined to speak with God to draw nourishment from the unclean body of an Egyptian woman."[1599]

Another tradition, from the much-edited *Deuteronomy Rabbah*, contradicts the Quranic statement that his mother nursed him before he was placed in the ark on the water, but the purpose of this assertion is to show Moses' maturity at birth: "The infant was not yet a day old when he began to walk and speak with his parents, and as though he were an adult, he refused to drink milk from his mother's breast."[1600] This pericope rather obviates the whole point of the reunion of mother and child in the Bible and the Quran.

In sum, the principal difference remaining between the Biblical and Quranic accounts of this story is the identity of the woman who adopted Moses. In the Bible, she is explicitly called Pharaoh's daughter, and the figure of Laqitah, introduced by Surabadi, seems to be a response to Judaeo-Christian insistence on the correctness of this view. Jewish tradition knows of the cure of the foster mother (Pharaoh's daughter)

[1598] See Section A above.
[1599] LJ, II, 267.
[1600] LJ, II, 264.

upon finding Moses. In Surabadi, the person is also Pharaoh's daughter, certainly this is influenced by the Jewish accounts on this point, but the foster mother is Pharaoh' "wife," and therefore a different person.

In respect to this point, it is important to note that the Quranic phrase *imra᾿atu firᶜawn* is somewhat ambiguous. Such an expression could mean "a/the woman of Pharaoh" or "a/the wife of Pharaoh. If we are to regard the Biblical "daughter of Pharaoh" as the definitive version because of its antiquity, the meaning of the Arabic might conceivably include such a relationship, although only in the general sense that Pharaoh's daughter is a woman of his court.

Jewish tradition naturally follows the lead of the Bible here and speaks of Pharaoh's daughter rather than his wife. However, Josephus, though he explicitly states that Thermuthis is Pharaoh's daughter, may also preserve an alternative tradition that corresponds more closely with the Quranic usage. In his version of the arrival of Moses' sister (here called Miriam) and the summoning of his mother to act as wet nurse, he writes: "Now Miriam was by when this happened, not to appear to be there on purpose, but only as staying to see the child; and she said, 'It is in vain that thou, O queen, callest for these women for the nourishing of the child, who are no way of kin to it; but still, if thou wilt order one of the Hebrew women to be brought, perhaps it may admit the breast of one its own nation.' Now since she seemed to speak well, Thermuthis bid her procure such a one, and to bring one of those Hebrew women that gave suck. So when she had such authority given her, she came back and brought the mother, who was known to nobody there. And now the child gladly admitted the breast, and seemed to stick close to it; and so it was, that at the queen's desire, the nursing child was entirely intrusted to the mother."[1601]

It may be notice that in this passage "queen" is not simply an honorific. If it had only occurred in Miriam's statement, it might have been so, but Josephus himself, as narrator, also calls her a queen. In addition to this, the refusal to nurse, also mentioned in the Quran, is found here. Does this tradition in Josephus stand in some sort of relationship to the Arabian tradition found in the Quran? It is our belief that it does.

The Biblical and Quranic versions, if we accept the interpretation that in the Quran the wife of Pharaoh is actually meant, may be reconciled in another somewhat astonishing way. Rameses II, who seems to be the Pharaoh under discussion, like many other of his Egyptian

---

[1601] Josephus, *Antiquities*, II.9.5, p. 57.

predecessors and successors, married his own daughters.[1602] Thus, both the Biblical statements and the Quranic verse could be reconciled, and this could be the situation also reflected in Josephus.

Finally, we may return to the world of Mesopotamia for a legend that may stand behind part of the birth narrative of Moses. A tablet found in the royal library of Nineveh of the 7th Century BCE contains a copy of a much older legend about Sargon of Akkad, the first Semitic king to reign in Mesopotamia, c. 2350-2300 BCE and the founder of the first "world" empire (most of the Fertile Crescent). As we shall see, it has many of the elements of the Moses story:[1603]

> "Sargon, the mighty king, king of Agade, am I.
> My mother was a nun (?); my father I knew not.
> My father's kinsmen lived in the hills.
> My city was Azupiranu, on the banks of the Euphrates.
> When my mother, the nun (?), had conceived me, she bore me
>   in secret.
> She put me in a basket of rushes, with bitumen sealed me in.
> Then she cast me into the river, but the river did not
>   overwhelm me.
> The river bore me up, and carried me to a drawer of water, one
>   Akki.
> As he dipped his ewer, Akki hauled me out.
> He (adopted me and) reared me as his own son.
> He set me to tending his garden.
> While I was so engaged, the goddess Ishtar granted me her
>   love.
> I came to reign over the kingdom for four and ... years.
> The black-headed people I ruled and gov(erned)."[1604]

In this fragment we can see many parallels with the career of Moses: the basket of rushes sealed with bitumen, being set adrift and then rescued, the mean occupation (Moses worked as a shepherd), the theophany, the attainment of power over a great civilization (Egypt for Moses, Sumeria for Sargon). Many of these parallels are perhaps fortuitous, but the incident of the basket cast into the river is suggestive.

[1602] Halley, p. 113.
[1603] Gaster, Vol. I, p. 225; AAWH, Vol. 1, pp. 27, 31.
[1604] Quoted by Gaster (Gaster, Vol. I, pp. 225-226. The black-headed people are the non-Semitic Sumerians who were the first inhabitants of Mesopotamia in historical times. The meaning of the word translated as "nun" is not certain, hence the question marks.

Even closer to the scene of the Moses story, there is an Egyptian legend about the infant god Horus who was concealed among the marsh reeds in order to protect him from the god Seth who sought to destroy him.[1605]

Did either or both of these stories play a part in the formation of the ancient traditions surrounding the birth of Moses? Did one or the other of these legends travel from Mesopotamia or Egypt, as had so many others already noted in *Genesis*, and find a new use in Palestine enhancing the wonder of the story of Moses? Once the story had been absorbed into the Mosaic cycle, it could have easily passed to Arabia where it is used in the Quran as a parable of God's providence.

D. THE FLIGHT TO MIDIAN

And thou didst kill a man and We delivered thee from great distress, and tried thee with a heavy trial. And thou didst tarry some years among the folk of Midian. (Q. 20:40)

The significance of the flight to Midian by Moses and his residence there is undoubtedly of far greater importance that the present text of *Exodus* and *Numbers* suggests. The theological influences to which Moses may have been exposed whilst in Midian, and their consequences still affect a large portion of mankind. That will be discussed in the following section (E).

The Biblical version of the events leading to the flight are to be found in *Exodus*: "One day, when Moses had grown up, he went out to his people and looked on their burdens; and he saw an Egyptian beating a Hebrew, one of his people. He looked this way and that, and seeing no one, he killed the Egyptian and hid him in the sand. When he went out the next day, behold, two Hebrews were struggling together; and he said to the man that did the wrong, 'Why dost thou strike thy fellow?' He answered, 'Who made thee a prince and judge over us? Dost thou mean to kill me as thou didst kill the Egyptian?' Then Moses was afraid, and thought, 'Surely the thing is known.' When Pharaoh heard of it, he sought to kill Moses." (Ex. 2:11-15a)

The principal account of this episode in the Quran is to be found in Surah Qasas (Q. 28). The differences with the Bible are minor: *And when he reached his full strength and was mature, We gave him wisdom and knowledge. Thus do We reward the good. And he entered the city at a time of carelessness of its folk, and he found therein two men fighting, one of his own party* [a Hebrew], *and the other of his enemies* [an

---

[1605] Moses, EJ, XII, 379.

Egyptian]; *and he who was of his party asked him to help against him who was of his enemies. So Moses struck him with his fist and killed him. He said: This is the work of Satan! Lo! He* [Satan] *is an enemy and a plain misleader.* (Q. 28:14-15) The Quran adds the time of day, presumably in the afternoon when people are resting away from the midday heat. (This is Surabadi's understanding; see below.)

Two details about the killing are added: the oppressed Hebrew called for Moses to aid him. This could imply that Moses' national identity was known to him. Secondly, the cause of death was stated: a blow of the fist. In the Bible, the death of the Egyptian was premeditated —Moses looked around to see if anyone were watching before killing the Egyptian—but in the Quran, it is understood to be accidental (killing was not the intended object of the blow; more likely Moses simply wanted to disable the Egyptian or knock him unconscious). The crime was manslaughter, not murder. Moses himself seemed to be astonished at this result of his quick action when he said: *This is the work of Satan!* This is followed by a prayer: *(Moses) said: My Lord! Lo! I have wronged my soul, so forgive me. Then He forgave him. Lo! He is the Forgiving, the Merciful. (Moses) said: My Lord! Forasmuch as Thou hast favored me, I will nevermore be a supporter of the guilty.* (Q. 28:16-17)

Thus, instead of a premeditated murder, the Quran offers an impetuous act by a powerful, but untried, young man who did not yet know his own strength. He was immediately repentant because of the unforeseen death of the Egyptian, and turned to God for forgiveness. God's ready forgiveness would also suggest that the killing was accidental, not intentional. In the Biblical version, Moses expressed no remorse for the death of the Egyptian he had deliberately caused. From the nuances of this Quranic story, we learn that even the killing of one's enemy demands contrition and the acknowledgment of responsibility. Though sanctioned by the state, nevertheless God Himself must be satisfied as to the justice of both the intention and the deed.

The Bible does not tell us how the murder became known. We may surmise that even if there were no spectators to the deed, the Hebrew victim whom Moses had delivered from the Egyptian's cruelty had noised it about. This is the conclusion that later Jewish commentators came to. And though the Bible made no connection between the Hebrew saved by Moses and the two Hebrews fighting the next day, later Jewish tradition does; as does the Quran: *And morning found him in the city, fearing, vigilant, when behold! He who had appealed to him the day before cried out to him for help. Moses said unto him: 'Lo, thou art indeed a plain hothead.' And when he would have fallen upon the man who was an enemy unto them both, he said: 'O Moses! Wouldst thou kill me as thou didst kill a person yesterday? Thou wouldst be nothing but a tyrant in the land, thou wouldst not be of the reformers.'* (Q. 28:18-19)

Since it was the opponent of the man whom he had helped the previous day so addressing him, it was clear to him that the secret had not been kept. The addition of these details is logical and psychologically sound. The man he had helped could not keep the matter to himself, and had talked about it among his family and friends, with the result that when Moses came upon the man quarreling again, he was so taunted by the opponent. (It is possible to interpret this verse to mean that it was a repetition of the incident of the day before, the Hebrew's opponent once again possibly an Egyptian. This is Surabadi's view, see below.) To this the Quran adds another circumstance not found in the Biblical story, although again a natural development of it: *And a man came from the uttermost part of the city, running. He said: O Moses, Lo, the chiefs take counsel against thee to slay thee; therefore, escape. Lo! I am of those who give thee good advice.' So he departed from that place, fearing, vigilant. He said: 'My Lord! Deliver me from the wrongdoing folk.'* (Q. 28:20-21)

The news of the death of the Egyptian had reached the magistrates of the city. A friend of Moses, perhaps from the council or associated with it, rushed to warn Moses to flee the wrath of the Egyptians, his arrival following immediately upon the scene with the two Hebrews.

Surabadi's account seems to strike a balance between the Bible and the Quran: Moses used to go out in the heat of the day in disguise (this seems to be an Islamic addition), when the people were resting, and he would contemplate the people in their error. One day he saw an Egyptian officer, Riqa (*Rīqā*), trying to force an Israelite to carry some straw to a stable. A fight started and when the Israelite sought aid, Moses struck the Egyptian with his fist so forcefully that he died upon the spot, while the Israelite fled. The next day, Moses entered the market apprehensively and came upon the same Israelite fighting with another Egyptian officer. Once again he sought Moses' aid, and when Moses reproved him because of his quarrelsomeness, the Israelite asked sharply whether Moses intended to kill him the way he had killed the Egyptian the previous day. The Egyptian then realized that it was Moses who had killed his comrade on the previous day. Releasing the Israelite, he ran off to tell Pharaoh.[1606]

[1606] Surabadi, pp. 300-301.

This deviates from both the Bible and the Quran. The Bible implies that the two strugglers of the second incident were both Hebrews, not a Hebrew and an Egyptian. Of course, we do not know (from the text of *Exodus*) whether either of the two was the Hebrew of the previous day. On this point, the Quranic text is ambiguous and capable of different interpretations (although the Arabs first hearing it probably knew which was which). Who taunted Moses with the crime, the Hebrew Moses had saved the day before, or the man's opponent? We have given Surabadi's interpretation, and this is also Maulana Muhammad Ali's view.[1607]

Our own inclination is to read the text, as does Yusuf Ali,[1608] to mean that after this reproof Moses made common cause with the man he had saved in a similar situation the day before; that it was the opponent, having heard of the killing, who taunted Moses with it. Although some time could have intervened between the second fight and the arrival of the warning message, the Quranic text seems to read that one followed almost immediately upon the other. In other words, there would have been no need for the device introduced by Surabadi of having the opponent learn who was responsible for the crime of the previous day and rushing off to report the news to Pharaoh.

This would have taken some time, and still more time for the council to convene and discuss the case before arriving at its decision, and then for Moses' friend to warn him. If we assume that the story was already about and the council had already met when Moses came upon the quarreling pair, then the arrival of the messenger upon the scene of the quarrel is not only explicable but also dramatically effective.

In Surabadi's version, after the initial killing, Pharaoh convened a council. One of those present, Kharbil (*Kharbīl*), was a believer, and it was he who rushed to inform Moses of the decision to execute him and who warned him to flee. Apparently, the enhancement of the figure of the "*man who came running,*" or the believer from Pharaoh's people (Q. 40:28), in Islamic tradition is related to the presence of Jethro on Pharaoh's council. He is supposed to have participated in the councils that recommended Pharaoh cure himself of leprosy by washing in the blood of Israelite infants (see above) and recommended the slaughter of the infants to break the might of the Israelites (see above). In both of these traditions, Jethro is depicted as being in opposition to the decisions. We shall have more to say about Jethro below.[1609]

[1607] Quran-MMA, p. 745.

[1608] Quran-Yusuf Ali, p. 1006.

[1609] Surabadi, p. 301. This verse is thought by some to refer to Jethro: *And a believing man of the people of Pharaoh, who hid his faith, said: Would ye kill a man* [Moses]

Jewish tradition gives a different account of the circumstances leading up to the quarrel with the Egyptian: "While Moses abode in Goshen, an incident of great importance occurred. To superintend the service of the children of Israel, an officer from among them was set over every ten, and ten such officers were under the surveillance of an Egyptian taskmaster. One of these Hebrew officers, Dathan by name, had a wife, Shelomith, the daughter of Dibri, of the tribe of Dan, who was of extraordinary beauty, but inclined to be very loquacious. Whenever the Egyptian taskmaster set over her husband came to their house on business connected with his office, she would approach him pleasantly and enter into conversation with him.

"The beautiful Israelitish woman enkindled a mad passion in his breast, and he sought and found a cunning way of satisfying his lustful desire. One day, he appeared at break of dawn at the house of Dathan, roused him from his sleep, and ordered him to hurry his detachment of men to their work. The husband scarcely out of sight, he executed the villainy he had planned, and dishonored the woman, and the fruit of this illicit relation was the blasphemer of the Name [of God; the blasphemer was one Zelophedad] whom Moses ordered to execution on the march through the Desert." A very neat tie-in.

The story continues: "At the moment when the Egyptian slipped out of Shelomith's chamber, Dathan returned home. Vexed that his crime had come to the knowledge of the injured husband, the taskmaster goaded him on to work with excessive vigor, and dealt him blow after blow with the intention to kill him. Young Moses happened to visit the place at which the much-abused and tortured Hebrew was at work. Dathan hastened toward him, and complained of all the wrong and suffering the Egyptian had inflicted upon him. Full of wrath, Moses, whom the holy spirit had acquainted with the injury done the Hebrew officer by the Egyptian taskmaster, cried out to the latter, saying: 'Not enough that thou hast dishonored this man's wife, thou aimest to kill him, too?'

"Neither physical strength nor a weapon was needed to carry to carry out his purpose. He merely pronounced the Name of God, and the Egyptian was a corpse."[1610]

---

because he says: My Lord is God and hath brought you clear proofs from your Lord? If he be lying, then his lie is upon him; and if he be truthful, then some of that with which he threatens you will afflict you. Truly, God guides not one who is prodigal, a liar. (Q. 40:28)

[1610] LJ, II, 279-280.

Jewish tradition also makes the betrayal of the situation to Pharaoh the deliberate act of two Hebrews, Dathan and Abiram.[1611] Betrayed by the man whom he had saved, Moses was condemned to death but saved by the angel Michael who enabled Moses to flee.[1612]

Another parallel to some of the details in which the Quran differs from the Bible may be found in the Hellenistic writer Artapanus (c. 100 CE). He writes that jealousy of Moses by the king, prompted by the success of Moses in an expedition to Ethiopia (see section L below), caused the king to plot against the life of Moses. "Having alienated the Egyptians from Moses, Chenephres [the king] induced Chanethothes to undertake to slay Moses. The plot conspired against him was reported to Moses [as in the Quran], and on the advice of Aaron he sailed across the Nile from Memphis, intending to take refuge in Arabia. Chanethothes, informed of Moses' proposed flight, placed himself in ambush with the intention to kill him. When he saw Moses approach, he drew his sword against him. But Moses seized his hand and slew him with his own hand."[1613] Thus Chanethothes would be the name of the Egyptian slain, the Riqa of Surabadi.

And when he turned his face toward Midian, he said: Perhaps my Lord will guide me in the right road. (Q. 28:22) Surabadi continues his story with the flight of Moses to Midian. In Midian, Moses came upon a well, covered with a stone that required the strength of forty men to lift it. It was supplied with a bucket that required forty men to haul it up. He saw a crowd of men at the well and two girls sitting with their sheep off to one side. Moses asked them about their condition, and they replied that they were the daughters of Shu'ayb,[1614] and that if there were water left after the other shepherds had watered their flocks, they would be allowed to water theirs. Their father was very old. Moses asked the other shepherds why they would not help the girls, but they replied rudely: "If thou art more of a man, draw it thyself!" Thereupon, Moses pushed aside the heavy stone by himself and drew water by himself,

---

[1611] Dathan and Abiram were later involved with Korah in the insurrection against the leadership of Moses related in *Numbers* (Num. 16:1ff); see Section I below. Making them the two Hebrews who exposed Moses is typical of the Talmudic tendency to tie independent incidents together through exegesis and the identification of unnamed characters (and even, sometimes, named characters) with others in another part of the Bible, often creating a tangled web of relationships.

[1612] LJ, II, 281-282.

[1613] Quoted in LJ, V, 407-408.

[1614] Shu'ayb: This identification of the father of the girls with the Midianite prophet Shu'ayb mentioned in Q. 7:83-91, though common in the commentaries, is not universally accepted by Muslim scholars. See below in this section.

giving it to the girls' flocks. Then he continued on his way. He became tired and hungry, and complained to God of being poor and a stranger in this land; that he was ill, sad, and perplexed. God replied that only people without God are so.[1615]

This is a much amplified account based upon the two verses in the Quran: *And when he came to the waters of Midian he found a company of the people there drawing water, and he found, apart from them, two women holding back their flocks. He said, 'What is your business?' They said, 'We may not draw water until the shepherds drive off, and our father is passing old.' So he drew water for them; then he turned away to the shade, and he said, 'O my Lord, surely I have need of whatever good Thou shalt have sent down upon me.'* (Q. 28:23-24)

The Biblical version of these events is part of the conflation of J and E. Gray assigns these verses[1616] to the Yahwist (J): "But Moses fled from Pharaoh, and stayed in the land of Midian; and he sat down by a well. Now the priest of Midian had seven daughters, and they came and drew water, and filled the troughs to water their father's flock. The shepherds came and drove them away; but Moses stood up and helped them, and watered their flock." (Ex. 2:15b-17)

This account differs significantly from the Quran only in the number of daughters (see below) and the Quranic addition of Moses' supplication. A somewhat different sequence of events at the well may be seen, but it does not affect the main flow of the story. Western critics charge that in the story of Moses at the well in Midian, there is still another instance of the confusion in the Quranic account when compared with that of the "true" Biblical account.

In the Bible, there are no less than three stories of a prospective bride being discovered at a well (for that is what was happening above). The first is Rebekah, who was drawing water when the servant of Abraham, sent to bring a wife from among Abraham's kin for Isaac, reached her city. In that incident, she gave him water and watered his camels. Impressed, the servant enquired of her family and eventually she was married to Isaac (Gen. 24).

The second is that concerning Jacob and Rachel, also found in *Genesis*. It is the story which, the critics say, is confused in the Quran with the story of Moses and well in Midian. This is story from *Genesis*: "(Jacob) saw a well in the field, and lo, three flocks of sheep lying beside it; for out of that well the flocks were watered. The stone on the well's mouth was large, and when all the flocks were gathered there, the

---

[1615] Surabadi, pp. 301-302.
[1616] Laymon, p. 34.

shepherds would roll the stone from the mouth of the well, and water the sheep, and put the stone back in its place upon the well.

"Jacob said to them, 'My brothers, where do ye come from?' They said, 'We are from Haran,' He said to them, 'Do ye know Laban the son of Nahor?' They said, 'We know him.' He said to them, 'Is it well with him?' They, 'It is well; and see Rachel his daughter is coming with the sheep!' He said, 'Behold, it is still high day, it is not time for the animals to be gathered together; water the sheep, and go, pasture them.' But they said, 'We cannot until all the flocks are gathered together, and the stone is rolled from the mouth of the well; then we water the sheep.'

"While he was still speaking with them, Rachel came with her father's sheep; for she kept them. Now when Jacob saw Rachel the daughter of Laban his mother's brother, Jacob went up and rolled the stone from the well's mouth, and watered the flock of Laban his mother's brother." (Gen. 29:2-10)

As can be seen, the pericope of Jacob meeting Rachel at the well has clearly influenced Surabadi's story in one point, the matter of the heavy stone covering the mouth of the well. This detail, its most conspicuous feature, is *absent* from the Quranic account. It would surely have been there had it been the basis for the episode of the Quranic story of Moses under consideration. In other respects, the stories are quite different. The shepherds have gathered together with no animosity towards Rachel—indeed they respect her father. (In the Moses story, the shepherds appear to be contemptuous of the women's old, weak father. They would not have behaved so rudely had he been a man of power and influence; the note that he was a priest makes their attitude somewhat perplexing.)

In *Genesis*, they are awaiting the gathering of the flocks to be watered together at a customary time. They appear to be waiting for the others to come, including at the beginning, Rachel. Jacob's rolling aside of the stone seems to be a kind of bravura gesture to impress the beautiful (and rich) Rachel with his physical strength. There is no element of defiance of the other shepherds. None of them had begun watering his flocks.

Because two women are mentioned in the Quranic account of Moses at the well, Western critics assume that Rachel and Leah are meant; yet, it must be noted that there is only one young woman at the well in the Jacob pericope. In fact, the only similarities are the fact of the well, the gathering of the shepherds to water their flocks, a hero (Jacob in one, Moses in the other), and the woman or women. All of these elements are common to both the Biblical and the Quranic versions of the story of Moses at the well in Midian. There is no need to look farther afield for its source. The principal difference is the number of girls at the well: the Bible mentions seven, the Quran two. It is a difference, but not a confusion. However, Surabadi and other commentators must be considered guilty of strengthening the Western critics' hands, as *they* have seemed to confuse the story of Moses with that of Jacob.

The Quranic text continues: *Then there came unto him one of the two women, walking shyly. She said: 'Lo! My father biddeth thee, that he may reward thee with a payment for that thou didst water (the flock) for us. Then, when he came unto him and told him the (whole) story, (Shu'ayb) said: 'Fear not! Thou hast escaped from the wrongdoing folk.' One of the two women said: 'O my father! Hire him! For the best (man) that thou canst hire is the strong, the trustworthy.' He said: 'Lo! I desire to marry thee to one of these two daughters of mine on condition that thou hirest thyself to me for (the term of) eight pilgrimages. Then if thou completest ten it will be of thine own accord, for I would not make it hard for thee. God willing, thou wilt find me of the righteous.' (Moses) said: 'That (is settled) between thee and me. Whichever of the two terms I fulfill, there will be no injustice to me, and God is Surety over what we say.'* (Q. 28:25-28)

Surabadi elaborates the text of the Quran here, relating that the girls returned to their father with their flocks and reported what Moses had done to help them. One of them suggested that he be hired. Shu'ayb proposed instead that Moses marry one of the girls and the dowry (or bride-payment) would be that he would work for him for eight years, or ten years should Moses be gracious. An agreement was reached and Moses became the shepherd of Shu'ayb's flocks.

There is no mention of hire in the Biblical account: "When (the daughters) came to their father Reuel, he said, 'How is it that ye have come so soon today?' They said, 'An Egyptian[1617] delivered us out of the hand of the shepherds, and even drew water for us and watered the flock.' He said to his daughters, 'And where is he? Why have ye left the man? Call him, that he may eat bread.' And Moses was content to dwell with the man, and he gave Moses his daughter Zipporah." (Ex. 2:18-21)

While the dependence of the Quranic scene at the well on that of the Jacob story is more imagined and coincidental than real, there is one real parallel between the Quranic version of Moses' marriage and the Biblical account of Jacob's marriage (See above, Part Two, V.B). The mention of the hire has caught the attention of Western critics and caused

---

[1617] See Introductory Remarks, Section A, above.

them to charge that here is another example of Quranic confusion between the circumstances of Moses' marriage and those of Jacob.

It should be noted that except for the matter of the hire, in every other particular the stories are different. In *Genesis,* Jacob proposes the terms of the contract; whilst in the Quran the father does. In *Genesis,* the wedding is consummated after the contract has been fulfilled; in the Quran, it is at the beginning. In *Genesis,* the term specified is seven years, "a week of years," surely a significant detail that would likely to have been repeated because of the importance of that number to ancient peoples; but in the Quran we read of a vague, eight, possibly ten, years. In *Genesis,* Jacob marries both daughters; in the Quran Moses marries only one. Indeed the "contract" in the Quran is hardly a contract at all,[1618] whilst in *Genesis* the terms of the contract are very rigid, as Jacob finds out to his cost.

The amicable ambiance of the Quran is quite different from the hard bargaining of *Genesis.* The father was impressed by Moses and apparently had no son. He wished to have Moses in his family—and Moses had already proved himself at the well. The father offered to make Moses one of the family, if he would stay and work for him. Furthermore, if he would agree to stay for a considerable period of time, he would make the tie even stronger, by giving one of his daughters to him in marriage. The agreement is informal, and is of a type common to the present day throughout much of the world. As we have seen, the differences between the Quranic episode and the story of Jacob in *Genesis* are far greater than the similarities (aside from the unremarkable existence of a well from which shepherds draw water for their flocks), which can be reduced to two points: the mention of aiding the daughters and the mention of "hire." In all else, the two stories differ. However, this has not prevented Surabadi from falling into the same trap as the critics of the Quran, and he borrows heavily from the Jacob story to fill out his narrative of the years Moses spent in Midian, as we have already seen above, and of which we shall see more below.

The import of the Quranic text is that after the period of eight or ten years had expired, Moses' obligation to the Midianites would be considered fulfilled. It is not stated how long he actually lived in Midian. In Jewish tradition, this is usually said to be 40 years,[1619] although Artapanus makes it 30 years.[1620] In this respect Maulana Muhammad Ali

---

[1618] In a real contract, either eight or ten years would have been specified.

[1619] LJ, II, 301.

[1620] LJ, V, 406. This figure is, of course, artificial and is based upon a rabbinical penchant for symmetry. Thus Moses is supposed to have lived 40 years in Egypt, 40 years in

writes: "According to rabbinical accounts, Moses lived with Jethro [Shu'ayb] for ten years, which corroborates the Quranic story in substance..." and then he proceeds to give an interesting interpretation of the "eight or ten" years: "But what is stated here has really a deeper significance beneath it. In Moses' stay at Midian for ten years, there is a prophetic reference to the ten years of the Prophet's life at Madinah. The mention of eight years has another underlying significance, for it was after eight years that the Prophet came back to Makkah as a conqueror, a clear reference to which is contained further on v. 85: *He Who has made the Quran binding on thee will surely bring thee back to the place of return.* This occurred exactly eight years after his Flight [*Hijrah*]." [1621]

However, according to Surabadi, Moses worked for Shu'ayb eight years and after that, Shu'ayb gave him every lamb that was the same color as its mother (or, in another tradition, every female lamb). Moses touched the staff Shu'ayb had given him to the water the sheep drank, and that year they gave birth only to females. The next year the agreement was changed to males, and Moses did the same thing; as a result, only males were born. The flocks of Moses became greater than those of Shu'ayb. [1622]

This unworthy bit of chicanery and misuse of divine power for personal gain attributed to Moses is another of Surabadi's (that is, his source's) borrowing from the Jacob cycle of *Genesis*, and has absolutely no support in the Quran. The parallel story, found in Gen. 30:25-43, has been summarized in elsewhere. [1623] The criteria for distinguishing the lambs belonging to one or the other are different, but the basic theme is the same and the dependence is obvious. Its inclusion by the commentators in the story of Moses, or that of any other prophet, is to be deplored, as it lends the appearance of divine sanction to such trickery.

THE STAFF OF MOSES: According to Surabadi, the staff mentioned in the pericope as being employed for such an unworthy purpose is the one of myrtle that Adam had carried with him from Paradise. When Shu'ayb hired him, he wanted to give him a staff, but not that one. He sent his daughter to bring a staff, and she brought the one of myrtle. He told her to take it back and bring another. She did so, but it

---

Midian, and 40 years as the leader of the Israelites (Asimov-OT, pp. 129-130), a total of 120 years (Deut. 34:7). Moses was more likely nearer 20 than 40 when he fled to Midian. The *Book of Jubilees* says that he was 21 (LJ, V, 406).

[1621] Quran-MMA, p. 748.

[1622] Surabadi, p. 304.

[1623] See Part Two, V, B.

turned out to be the same one again. This was repeated seven times, until finally Shuʻayb realized that it was destined to be possessed by Moses. He surrendered it to him, saying: "Keep this well and hold it dear so that thou may see wonders."[1624] (We have already seen one in its improper use by Moses in Surabadi's story above.)

This story of the origin of Moses' staff is not found in the Bible or in the Quran; however, it is in Jewish tradition. For example, in the *Pirke de Rabbi Eliezer*: "Rabbi Levi said: That rod which was created in the twilight was delivered to the first man out of the garden of Eden. Adam delivered it to Enoch, and Enoch delivered it to Noah, and Noah (handed it on) to Shem. Shem passed it on to Abraham, Abraham (transmitted it) to Isaac, and Isaac (gave it over) to Jacob, and Jacob brought it down into Egypt and passed in on to his son Joseph, and when Joseph died and they pillaged his household goods, it was placed in the palace of Pharaoh. And Jethro was one of the magicians of Egypt, and he saw the rod and the letters which were upon it, and he desired in his heart (to have it), and he took it and brought it, and planted it in the midst of the garden of his house. No one was able to approach it any more.

"When Moses came to his house he went into the garden of Jethro's house, and saw the rod and read the letters which were upon it, and he put forth his hand and took it. Jethro watched Moses and said: This one in the future will redeem Israel from Egypt. Therefore he gave him Zipporah his daughter to wife..."[1625] In another version, wresting the rod from the garden was a kind of test to which Jethro put Moses before he would allow him to marry Zipporah.[1626] Surabadi mentions that Shuʻayb was blind,[1627] but this does not seem to be supported by any Biblical or traditional text about Jethro.

In connection with the wondrous rod, Surabadi relates to us a story of Moses' killing the dragon that lived in a fertile valley that had been left uninhabited because of the people's fear of the monster. Moses led his flocks into the valley, and when the dragon came forward, he killed it with a blow of his staff.[1628] This particular prodigy has no basis in the Quran or the Bible, and is not mentioned in *Legends of the Jews*. The slaying of the dragon is a popular theme in the mythology legends of the world; numerous parallels are available that require no further comment here: Perseus in Greek mythology, St. George in Christian

---

[1624] Surabadi, p. 303.
[1625] PRE, pp. 312-313.
[1626] LJ, II, 291-295.
[1627] Surabadi, p. 303.
[1628] Surabadi, pp. 303-304.

legend, Daniel in Jewish tradition, Marduk in Mesopotamian mythology, and Baal against the Prince of the Sea in Ugaritic mythology. In central Afghanistan a rock formation is pointed out west of Bamyan that is reputedly the petrified remains of a dragon slain by Ali, the son-in-law of the Prophet.[1629]

The ascription of such a feat to Moses is perhaps suggested by the story that at the court of Pharaoh, the staff itself became a dragon (see below). Other possibilities suggest themselves: in the Bible, a beast, usually depicted as a kind of monstrous crocodile, is used to personify Egypt.[1630] Influenced by this imagery, Moses' defeat of a dragon in Midian would prefigure his defeat of Egypt. Another reptilian parallel that exists in the Biblical story of Moses may be connected with the Surabadi pericope: The incident occurred during the 40 years of wandering. The people were complaining once again against the leadership of Moses (the Israelites do a great of whining in the Exodus): "Then the Lord sent fiery serpents among the people, and they bit the people, so that many of the people of Israel died. And the people came to Moses, and said, 'We have sinned, for we have spoken against the Lord and against thee; pray to the Lord, that He take away the serpents from us.' So Moses prayed for the people. And the Lord said to Moses, 'Make a fiery serpent, and set it on a pole; and every one who is bitten, when he sees it, shall live.' So Moses made a bronze serpent and set it on a pole; and if a serpent bit any man, he would look at the bronze serpent and live." (Num. 21:6-9)

This appears to be an aetiological story to explain the presence of a bronze serpent (by ascribing it to Moses) that was venerated by the Judaeans in YHWH-worship. Called the Nehushtan, it was destroyed by the Judaean king Hezekiah (rgd. 715-687 BCE) as part of his religious reforms (2 K. 18:4).[1631] It is not impossible that a report of this tradition lies behind Surabadi's story.

Surabadi next tells us that after Moses had had two sons by Zipporah, he felt a desire to see his family in Egypt once again. When he left Midian, Zipporah was again pregnant. The Quran has none of these details. In Surabadi's commentary, this is in the nature of an appendix and omits the real reason for Moses' return to Egypt: the command of God to return and liberate the Israelites.[1632] Surabadi attributes to Moses a

---

[1629] See the story of St. George in *The New Testament: An Islamic Perspective*, V.G for more about the dragon.

[1630] Dragon, DB, p. 221.

[1631] Laymon, p. 204; Ark, ERE, Vol. I, 792.

[1632] See next Section.

genuine, natural desire to see his relatives again, but the Bible offers no support for such feelings in Moses. "And Moses was content to dwell with the man [Reuel/Jethro], and he gave Moses his daughter Zipporah. She bore a son, and he called his name Gershom; for he said, 'I have been a sojourner in a foreign land.'" (Ex. 2:21-22)

After the theophany and the divine command to lead Israel out of Egypt to be discussed in the following section: "Moses went back to Jethro his father-in-law and said to him, 'Let me go back, I pray, to my kinsmen in Egypt and see whether they are still alive.' And Jethro said to Moses, 'Go in peace.'... So Moses took his wife and sons and set them on an ass, and went back to the land of Egypt, and in his hand Moses took the rod of God." (Ex. 4:18,20) Moses is using the desire to see his family as a pretext to execute God's command to liberate the Hebrews. In another place, we learn the name of the other son, Eliezer (Ex. 18:4). The Bible speaks only of two sons. If Zipporah was pregnant again, as in Surabadi, then the issue was either a girl (the girls are only mentioned irregularly in Biblical genealogies), or did not survive. The Chronicler also knows only of two sons: "The sons of Moses: Gershom and Eliezer." (1 Ch. 23:15)

IS JETHRO SHU'AYB? The reader not familiar with the vagaries of Biblical text may be a little perplexed by the name of Moses' father-in-law. One time he is called Reuel, and another time Jethro (and many Muslims call him Shu'ayb, if that identification be correct). Many scholars share the reader's perplexity. Apparently in the Northern E tradition he was uniformly referred to as Jethro.[1633] In *Exodus*, the Southern J calls him Reuel (Ex. 2:18). Both sources refer to him as a "priest of Midian,"[1634] which clearly hints at Jethro's (we shall call him Jethro for the sake of simplicity) possessing a religious or possibly a prophetic function.[1635]

However, the question of Jethro's name is further confused by yet another name: Hobab. In *Numbers* we read: "And Moses said to Hobab the son of Reuel the Midianite, Moses' father-in-law..." (Num. 10:29) Depending upon punctuation, this verse can be read to mean that Hobab, the son of Reuel, is Moses' father-in-law, or that Hobab is the son of Moses' father-in-law Reuel, thereby making him his brother-in-law. If this had been the only evidence, then we could safely interpret the passage to mean Moses' brother-in-law. Yet, in *Judges* we find: "Now

---

[1633] Ex. 3:1; 4:18; 18:1; etc.
[1634] Ex. 2:16; 3:1; etc.
[1635] This will be discussed in the following Section.

Heber [not the patriarch Eber of *Genesis*] the Kenite had separated from the Kenites, the descendants of Hobab the father-in-law of Moses..." (Jgs. 4:11)[1636] From this it is clear that there was a third tradition about the name of Moses' father-in-law, and—incidentally—we learn that he was a Kenite, a member of one of the Midianite clans. This may have serious implications, as we shall see in the next section.

Thus we see that Moses' father-in-law, from the Biblical evidence, is known by three different and phonologically unrelated names: Jethro, Reuel, and Hobab. No wonder the Muslim commentators felt free to add a fourth to the list and identify him with Shu'ayb, [1637] although not without reservation, as even Surabadi shows: "He stayed, ten years, among the people of Midian with Shu'ayb; or, they have related, with Jethro[1638] the nephew of Shu'ayb..."[1639] This introduces still another schema of the relationship of Moses with his in-laws and Shu'ayb. The Quran mentions Moses' father-in-law without naming him. The absence of such an identification should give us pause from rashly assuming that Shu'ayb and Moses' father-in-law are the same person. In the Quran, Shu'ayb was not old and feeble as was Jethro, and he was sent to Midian (Q. 7:85; 11: 84), in particular to a section of them called the "people of thicket" (Q. 26:176). Ignoring Shu'ayb's warning to reform their lives, they were destroyed, presumably be an earthquake (Q. 11:94).

Although the religious character of Jethro has been established by both the Biblical text and Jewish tradition, which generally show him a righteous man, no mission of warning seems to have been associated with his name. "In the city of Midian, named thus for a son of Abraham

---

[1636] The problem created by Num. 10:29, which states that Hobab is the son of Reuel, still defies all attempts at rationalization. To make matters worse, that verse is assigned to the Yahwist (J), and—were it not for the statement in *Judges*—probably would be interpreted to mean that Hobab was Moses' brother-in-law. This would make J internally consistent. The passage in *Judges* might be dependent upon an error in the transmission of oral tradition, but it is odd that redactor of J did not see the contradiction. After the conflation with E and P, this no longer stood out and so was left in the text as one of the many lesser and greater inconsistencies of the Bible. For his part, the Elohist was firmly and consistently behind the Jethro tradition.

[1637] The Elohist (E) knows the father-in-law of Moses as Jethro. The Yahwist (J) calls him Reuel in *Exodus* but refers to him as Hobab in *Numbers* (Num. 10:29). McNeile, writing in the article on "Hobab" (Heb: Ḥobāb) in the DB (p. 387), speculates that the Arabic Shu'ayb (who in Islamic tradition is the father-in-law of Moses) is in some manner related to Hobab, but the extreme shift from the Hebrew hard guttural *H* to Arabic *Sh* and the middle consonant from Hebrew *B* to Arabic *'Ayn* would be unusual between the sister Semitic languages. The form Shu'ayb is an Arabic diminutive from the root *sh-'-b*, which has a range of meanings: among them are "people, branch, and dividing."

[1638] Surabadi uses the form Yathrun (*Yathrūn*) or Yathrawn (*Yathrawn*).

[1639] Surabadi, p. 251.

by Keturah, the man Jethro had lived for many years doing a priest's service before the idols. As time went on, he grew increasingly convinced of the vanity of idol worship. His priesthood became repugnant to him, and he resolved to give up his charge."[1640] Although the tradition speaks of a city, Midian was a largely pastoral region principally east of the Gulf of Aqabah.

Whereas the impression created in the Bible makes Midian rather remote from Egyptian power (it was 200 miles to the east of the Nile over difficult arid and mountainous territory), Jewish tradition depicts it as more closely attached to Egypt and involves Jethro himself in the councils of Pharaoh. In the absence of any more explicit confirmation in the Quran in places where it might be expected, we can only regard the identification of Shu'ayb with Jethro as highly speculative. The tradition of the prophet Shu'ayb in Midian seems to be another of those that passed down into Arabia without entering the mainstream of Biblical and Jewish tradition. A clue doubtless lies in the phrase "people of the thicket," but it has not been deciphered as of yet, though it must have been understood by Arabs of the Prophet's time.

MIDIAN AND MOUNT SEIR: As our focus is now upon Midian, it may be appropriate to look at the area for a moment. The Midianites were, in the Biblical paradigm of racial relationships, descendants of Abraham by Keturah (Gen. 25:1-2), who is probably also Hagar,[1641] and therefore close kin of the Ishmaelites. Indeed the terms, when used in a general sense, were probably roughly co-extensive.[1642] The extent of their territory seems to have varied, depending upon their own prosperity and the amount of pressure their neighbors were able to bear upon them. However, the core of their lands was east of the line of the Gulf of Aqabah and the Arabah valley, the southwestern region of modern Jordan and the northwestern corner of Saudi Arabia. The names of the five sons of Midian (Ephah, Epher, Hanoch, Abida, and Eldaah) given in a genealogical table (Gen. 25:4) aid us in fixing their territory more precisely, at least at the time of the Yahwist (c. 1000 BCE) who is responsible for the passage. The "sons" were doubtless eponymous ancestors of Midianite clans.

[1640] LJ, II, 289.
[1641] See III, G in Part Two.
[1642] Asimov-OT, p. 92.

Ephah has been associated with the modern oasis town of Tabuk in northwestern Arabia.[1643] A Hanoch is also listed as a son of Reuben (Gen. 46:9), and while it may be simply a case of two individuals bearing the same name, it could also represent an adoption of the Midianite clan by the Reubenites. (Hanoch the Midianite is from J; Hanoch the Reubenite is from the later P. The tribe of Reuben was settled east of the Jordan, north of Midian.) This might indicate a distribution of Midianites from east of the Dead Sea to the northern Hejaz, a distance of some 250 miles. A conspicuous absence from the list of clans is mention of the Kenites who are definitely stated to be Midianites,[1644] and to which clan Moses' father-in-law belonged. Therefore, the Kenites were detached (except in the passages cited above) from the Midianites of whom the Israelites disapproved. The possible significance of this will be discussed in the next Section.

The Midianites appear to have been an originally semi-nomadic people who gradually became nomadic, perhaps as the result of desertification. In addition to their herding, they seem to have also been traders and raiders. In the absence of a firm basis of archeological work in the region, we have little extra-Biblical evidence about their history.[1645] They seem to have entered the land of Midian roughly during the period in which the Abrahamites moved into Canaan and were an intermittent power in the lands south and east of Palestine until they received a crushing defeat at the hands of Gideon and the Israelites about the 12th century BCE. After this, they were no longer a political or military factor in the region.[1646] In general, the territory of the Midianites was semi-desert and desert. There are a number water holes and oases and some small districts that could be called "thickets."

One of the most conspicuous features of this region is Mount Seir, or as it is sometimes known, Mount Esau. It is a mountainous chain that stretches about 100 miles from north to south, lying east of the Arabah-Aqabah rift valley. It seems to have been shared by Edom (in the north) and Midian (in the south. This is presumably the region to which Moses fled. Even today, the memory of Moses is preserved in the small town of Wadi Musa (Ar. *Wādī Mūsā*, Valley of Moses) about midway in

---

[1643] OBA, p. 67. The author of this work spent several years as a teacher in Tabuk, an important agricultural region.

[1644] Jgs. 1:16; 4:11; Num. 10:29. See also "Jethro, EJ, X, 18-19.

[1645] How slow Muslims are to explore their own historical and archeological roots before the evidence is bulldozed away in "development" and "modernization"!

[1646] Midian, EJ, XI, 1505-1506; Midian, DB, p. 658.

the length of the mountain, and this tradition is not unreasonable, as we shall see.

"(Mount Seir) attains a general elevation of 4,000 to 5,000 feet above sea level, far higher than the heights of Hauran, the Gilead, or Moab..." It is actually the highest elevation along the Great Rift Valley between Mt. Hermon west of Damascus (9,232 ft.) and Shifa in northwestern Saudi Arabia (8,461 ft.) "...which gives it in parts a different climate and aspect... Almost treeless on its slopes to the desert the mount bears on its back and west flanks plentiful timber, groves of the evergreen oak and the *butm* or terebinth, and stretches of juniper, a conifer with a trunk often a foot in diameter, which fetches a good price in Kerak or Ma'an. Poplar and willow are frequent along Wady Hesa and found elsewhere on the limestone. Below 3,000 feet flourish laurels, oleanders and tamarisks, tarfa. Pasture abounds—'the greatest sheep flocks which I have seen of the Arabs were in the rocky coomb-land between Shobek and Petra'"[1647]

This should convince the most reluctant reader that the conditions associated in the Quran with the "people of the thicket" who dwelt in Midian do indeed exist in that region. Even though Shu'ayb may not be the Jethro of Moses, he was probably a prophet in the same region in which the Biblical Jethro lived. This will be seen to be of considerable importance when we come to consider the Kenite Hypothesis in the next Section.

THE TALE OF SINUHE: Finally, it is interesting to compare the story of the flight of Moses with still another parallel to the Bible to be found in ancient literature, this time Egyptian. It is the *Story of Sinuhe*; the earliest manuscripts of this tale (which may be based upon fact) date from about 1800 BCE, clearing antedating Moses by at least 500 years and manuscript evidence of Moses' flight to and residence in Midian by several hundred years more.[1648] Sinuhe writes that he was a court official and he styles himself "the hereditary prince and count, judge and District Overseer of the domains of the Sovereign in the land of the Asiatics, real acquaintance of the king, his beloved, the Attendant Sinuhe..." These seem to be his titles after his restoration to favor; originally he "was an attendant who followed his lord, a servant of the royal harem (and of) the hereditary Princess, the great of favor, the wife of King Sen-Usert in (the pyramid town) Khenem-sut, the daughter of King Amen-em-het in (the

---

[1647] Geo HL, p. 362, 363, 364. The quotation is from Doughty.
[1648] ANE, I, p. 5.

pyramid town Qa-nefru, Nefru, the lady of reverence."[1649] Here we see that Sinuhe was an attendant of the king's daughter Nefru; compare this with Moses and the daughter of Pharaoh in *Exodus*.

The XIIth Dynasty king Amen-em-het died c. 1960 BCE, and for some reason which the text does not give, Sinuhe fell out of favor with the new king Sen-Usert I (rgd. 1971-1928 BCE)—the old king shared his reign with his son in his last years. He (Sinuhe) apparently overheard a royal conversation in which his death or severe punishment was discussed. "While I was standing (near by) I heard his voice as he was speaking and I was distraught, my arms spread out (in dismay), trembling fell upon my limbs. I removed myself by leaps and bounds to seek a hiding place for myself. I placed myself between two bushes, in order to cut (myself) off from the road and its travel."[1650]

Sinuhe then fled past the "Mistress of the Red Mountain" (still called "Red Mountain" today in Arabic, Jabal al-Ahmar, east of Cairo) and then crossed the line of defenses, "the Wall of the Ruler," across the Isthmus of Suez "made to oppose the Asiatics and to crush the Sand-crossers. I took a crouching position in a bush, for fear lest the watchmen upon the wall where their day's (duty) was might see me." Then he speaks of his trek across the waterless wastes of Sinai: "I set out at evening time, and when day broke, I reached Peten. I halted at the Island of Kem-wer. An attack of thirst overtook me. I was parched, and my throat was dusty. I said: 'This is the taste of death!' (But then) I lifted up my heart and collected myself, for I heard the sound of the lowing of cattle, and I spied Asiatics. The shaikh among them, who had been in Egypt, recognized me. Then he gave me water while he boiled milk for me. I went with him to his tribe. What they did (for me) was good."[1651]

He seems to have settled in the pasturage on the western side of the Syrian desert. About his life there he writes: "He set me at the head of his children. He married me to his eldest daughter. He let me choose for myself of his country, of the choicest of that which was with him on his frontier with another country... He made me ruler of a tribe of the choicest of his country. Bread was made for me as daily fare, wine as daily provision, cooked meat and roast fowl, beside the wild beasts of the desert, for they hunted for me and laid before me, beside the catch of my (own) hound...

"I spent many years, and my children grew up to be strong men, each man as the restrainer of his (own) tribe. The messenger who went

---

[1649] ANE, I, p. 5.
[1650] ANE, I, p. 6.
[1651] ANE, I, p. 7.

north or who went south to the Residence City [that is, the residence of Pharaoh in Egypt] stopped over with me, (for) I used to make everybody stop over. I gave water to the thirsty. I put him who had strayed (back) on the road. I rescued him who had been robbed..."[1652] Sinuhe became very prosperous in his adopted land. Eventually he was cleared of the charges against him in Egypt, whatever they were, and returned to Egypt in triumph.

This story, as the numerous manuscripts of it show, was an extremely popular one in ancient Egypt, and therefore was most likely known to the Semites (the Asiatics) dwelling on the steppes of Goshen east of the Delta. Whether it played any role in the development of the Moses story can only be speculated upon, although there are some potentially embarrassing parallels. There are indications in the text that Sinuhe's flight was not unique (he appears to speak of other Egyptian exiles living in the regions beyond Egypt's frontiers).[1653] The tradition of Moses' taking refuge in Midian, which was about the nearest habitable region not directly under Egyptian control during that period, need not be dependent upon Sinuhe's fascinating glimpse of life in Egypt 3700 years ago. It could reflect a fairly common circumstance in ancient Egypt.

E. THE REVELATION AND THE COMMISSION

"I AM WHO I AM" (Ex. 3:14)

In the preceding material, we have frequently mentioned the difference between the Yahwist and the Elohist (with the Priestly Document following the Elohist in this respect) concerning the use of the divine name YHWH. After the events to be discussed in this section that particular Biblical distinction will disappear, but a difference in theological approach remains that helps scholars to separate the different strands of the text.

To recapitulate, the Southern (Judahite) Yahwist (J) tradition seems to assume that YHWH-worship existed from the very beginning of history. Though other titles for God may have been used by the patriarchs, He was also known to them as YHWH. This position has its parallel in Islam, which holds that God had revealed Himself to the prophets and messengers from the very beginning of human history, beginning with Adam. Though the commonalty of mankind have often ignored or retreated from this basic truth of the unseen, ineffable, one

---

[1652] ANE, I. P. 7-8.
[1653] ANE, I, p. 7, note 2.

Supreme Being, lapsing into the easier worship of idols, natural objects, animals, and even mortal humans, the central fact of the Most High One looming behind everything was known or suspected. This crucial and eternal truth has been preached in a continuing tradition of prophets, from Adam to the time of last, Muhammad, peace be upon them all.

For the Yahwist, the significance of the theophany, the central event of this section, lies in the commission given to Moses to lead Israel out of Egypt; that is, it is an act of salvation. For the Yahwist it did not represent the commencement of the special relationship between YHWH and Israel, but rather was a crucial sign of His favor.

The Northern (Josephic) Elohist (E) tradition takes quite a different view. While the patriarchs may have been granted a special knowledge of God intuitively, they had not received the benefit of the revelation of His true nature, as represented by His personal name YHWH. The knowledge of this name established the people who knew it, the Israelites, in a special relationship with God as His Chosen People. The significance of the knowledge of one's personal name, be it of man or god, is a well-known feature of Semitic religion.[1654]

Thus, in the Elohist view (and P follows E in this), the name (and true nature) of YHWH was unknown to the ancient Hebrews (and, by implication, the rest of mankind) until its revelation to Moses in a scene of supernatural terror and awe on the Holy Mountain. Until that moment, E always referred to the Deity as *Elohim*, a word plural in form but almost always used in a singular sense in the Bible when referring to God.[1655] It is only with the revelation of the Divine Name to Moses that E

[1654] Anderson, p. 32; de Vaux, p. 327.

[1655] *Elohim*: the singular would be *Eloah*, a cognate of the Arabic *Ilāh* "god" (the Arabic plural is *ālihah* "gods"), seems to be a vestige of a time when the plurality of gods was accepted. In later times, probably with the growth of monotheism in ancient Israel, the meaning shifted and came to mean the one god of Israel, although it still retained its plural meaning when referring to the polytheistic beliefs of other peoples. (In Persian, the literary word *yazdān* meaning God is also a plural derived from the singular *yazd*. See note in Burhan, Vol. 4, p. 2432.) Phipps opines: "Elohim, the name that is used for deity some twenty-five hundred times in the Hebrew Bible, may have developed via the merging of the names of the two primordial deities and the addition of the plural *-im* ending. Walter Eichrodt explains that the plural Elohim was used 'to express the higher unity subsuming the individual gods and combining in one concept the whole pantheon.'" [Walter Eichrodt, *Theology of the Old Testament* (Philadelphia: Westminster, 1961) p. 185.] (Phipps, p. 20.)

Originally, each Israelite shrine seems to have possessed its own tutelary god. With the introduction of YHWH-worship, YHWH absorbed, assimilated, or displaced, these local deities. (Albright-Ab to Ez, p. 18) Probably at the same time, He absorbed the usage to Himself of the term *elohim* when referring to the totality of the gods (of Canaan), and thus the word came to be uniformly construed as a grammatical singular.

begins to use that name in his text to refer to God. For him, the real religious history of Israel begins at this moment.[1656] It is important to keep these distinctions between the Yahwist and the Elohist-Priestly views in mind when examining the traditions of Moses, and especially the material of this section.

It is at this point that the figure of Aaron is introduced into the Biblical story for the first time. The first two chapters of *Exodus* make no mention of a brother, although a sister (to be later identified with the prophetess Miriam) was mentioned. Aaron is brought into the narrative ostensibly to serve as Moses' spokesman because of some problem with Moses' speech (Ex. 4:10-16). The appearance of Aaron in the story of Moses presents problems. His Biblical role seems to have been moulded by the rival claims of various clans of hereditary priests in the periods of the monarchy and the post-Exilic religious establishment. The reconstruction of these events is difficult, but in monarchical times, the priesthood at Jerusalem was in the hands of the Zadokites of Levite descent, while the Aaronites were associated with other sanctuaries in Palestine. Apparently, their strongest connections were with the Northern sanctuaries. There are compelling reasons to believe that the Aaronites were not originally considered Levites,[1657] as Moses was probably not, notwithstanding E's assertions at the beginning of ch. 2 of *Exodus*.

This odd usage of a plural noun with a singular verb probably did not originate with the Hebrews. Akkadian records of the 14th century BCE found in Egypt have *ilani*, "gods," also construed as a singular when referring to a single Deity. (God, DB, p. 334) *Elohim*, when meant to indicate the pantheon of gods, would be a grammatical plural, but when used to designate the abstract aspect of their divinity, which all the gods shared in common, it became a singular. It was this usage which passed into Hebrew. There are parallels in British English in the usage of collective words such as "government," "cabinet," and "team" that can be singular or plural depending upon whether the group as a unit or the individuals who constitute it is intended. "News" is an example of a plural noun being construed as a singular.

It should also be noted that though YHWH-worship was monotheistic, it originally did not deny the reality of other gods worshipped by other peoples, as we shall see. Israel's special god was One, and therefore Israel worshipped one God and was monotheistic; furthermore He was invisible and not to be depicted. In these respects, Israel's monotheism differed from the polytheism of their more civilized neighbors, all of whom worshipped national pantheons. But originally Israel' monotheism was not a denial of the reality of the gods of Egypt, Canaan, Babylonia, etc. (Anderson, p. 34), but was instead henotheism. Universal monotheism came much later in Israel's religious history. The monotheism of Moses, according to the Biblical record, was national. Evidence in support of this proposition will be cited in the relevant contexts when appropriate.

[1656] As we have observed, the lapse of this distinction in usage between the Elohist and the Yahwist makes the task of separating the two sources more difficult henceforth. See the Introduction, III.

[1657] Aaron, EJ, II, 19.

With the destruction of the Solomon's Temple at Jerusalem 586 BCE by the Babylonian Nebuchadnezzar, the Zadokite priesthood seems to have lapsed, or had been carried off to Babylon during the Exile. During this traumatic period for the Jews, the Aaronites became the primary priesthood of YHWH worship in Palestine. It is thought that the destruction of Jerusalem allowed the Northern shrines to revive or increase their influence. As these were probably already in the hands of the Aaronites, the rebuilding of the Jerusalem Temple and the re-institution of the Zadokite priesthood as its functionaries by Nehemiah and Ezra must have precipitated an inter-priestly crisis. This crisis seems to have been resolved by ascribing Aaronite descent to the Zadokites and Levite descent to the Aaronites.[1658]

With this in mind, the minor role (or as some scholars suppose, total absence) of Aaron in the J account is understandable; J's was the view of the non-Aaronite Zadokite priesthood. Aaron's more prominent

---

[1658] Aaron, DB, pp. 1-2; Aaron, EJ, II, 18-20. The situation was considerably more complex than the above remarks might indicate, but this summary will suffice for our purposes to show the broad outlines of the problem. It should be remembered that priesthood in Judaism was hereditary and dependent upon lineage. Descendants of other tribes could officiate in other capacities, but the all-important sacrifices had to be carried out by the priestly caste.

Jerusalem was the latest of the shrines of YHWH-worship to be founded in Palestine. It was originally a Jebusite city that contained a shrine dedicated to El-'Elyon, a Canaanite deity who is known from other ancient sources. When David conquered Jerusalem, he brought the Ark there and established YHWH-worship, with some thought towards making the city his new capital and a national center as well, since it was his personal conquest and had no particular association with the Israelite tribes. Accordingly, one Zadok was established as high priest of the new YHWH-worship. (Although this office appears to have been initially shared, Solomon seems to have made it hereditary in the Zadokite clan.)

Because the local El-'Elyon was absorbed by YHWH and El-'Elyon become one of His titles, it has been suggested that the Zadokite priesthood were originally in the service of the Canaanite deity, and that David invited Zadok to lead the new YHWH-worship. Zadok is not heard of before the conquest of Jerusalem. The meeting between Abraham and the king-priest of Salem (Jerusalem), Melchizedek, recorded in Gen. 14:18-20 is thought to be an attempt to further sanctity both the shrine at Jerusalem and the Zadokite priesthood by associating it with Abraham.

Note the element *zedek* in the priest's name; the only other king-priest of pre-Davidic Jerusalem whose name remains to us is also compounded with *zedek*: Adonizedek. (Jgs. 19:1). It is thought that the use of *zedek* may have been part of the title of the Jerusalem king-priest of which Zedek may have the last example before converting to YHWH-worship. The theory of the Canaanite origin of the Jerusalem priesthood, though attractive, cannot be considered proven, though it has gained fairly wide acceptance among some circles of scholars. (See de Vaux, pp. 311, 372-374; Melchizedek, DB, p. 642; Zadok, DB, p. 1050; rebuttal of Canaanite theory in Priests and Levites, DB, p. 794; God, Names of, EJ, VII, 675.)

role in E's material is thus explicable by the influence of the Aaronites in the Northern sanctuaries and among the laity. In a later layer, great concern is shown by the Priestly Writer (P) to trace the privileges of the Levite priesthood, and especially the Jerusalem (Zadokite) priesthood, to Aaron. The great enhancement of his role in the narrative portions of *Exodus* speaks of a period in which the compromise had been achieved: the priesthood at Jerusalem was now associated with all the Aaronite priests in Palestine, though in a paramount position, echoing the paramountcy of Jerusalem as the royal city. All now traced their ancestry to Aaron, who had become a Levite. Finally, during the same period, with its concentration upon the Law, the authority of Moses was called upon to sanctify all the minutiae of Jewish religious law. The anomaly of the towering figure of Moses as the founder of Israel's religious institutions lacking any prominent role in the priesthood, who were now Aaronite Levites, was resolved by stressing that Aaron was Moses' elder brother (and therefore the presumed inheritor of priestly functions), even though *Exodus* makes Moses his parents' firstborn (male). Of course, Moses himself became a Levite in the process.[1659]

THE FIRST THEOPHANY: Surabadi's account of the theophany begins with Moses and his family, together with their flocks, lost in the desert on a cold winter night while returning from a visit to Shu'ayb. They were all miserable and Moses tried to make a fire, but the spark would not catch. In anger, Moses struck the flint, and it broke into speech: "'O Moses! Give not rein to thy anger; for, not only I, but no other iron and flint has permission to give forth fire this night.' Moses was astonished. He asked: 'Why not?' It replied: 'Because the light of prophethood and messengerhood has been brought to a shepherd.'" Then Moses saw a fire in the distance. He told his people to wait while he went to get some embers and directions from the persons who, he presumed, had lit the fire.[1660]

This is an elaboration of the circumstances implied in the Quran: *When (Moses) saw a fire and said unto the people of his household:*

[1659] There was an hereditary priesthood at the sanctuary of Dan in northern Israel claiming descent from Moses, but it was regarded with the most profound disapproval by the redactors of the Bible with their Aaronite associations. The most scurrilous tales were told about its founding in an effort to combat the popularity it retained up to the Assyrian conquest of 721 BCE. (See below for the story.) (De Vaux, p. 308; also Jgs. 17-18; 1 K. 12:29-30.)

[1660] Surabadi, p. 243.

'Wait! Lo, I see a fire afar off. Perhaps I may bring you a brand therefrom or may find guidance at the fire. (Q. 20:10)[1661]

The comparable Biblical passage narrating what is called the First Theophany,[1662] mentions neither the need for fire nor the accompanying family: "Now Moses was keeping the flock of his father-in-law, Jethro, the priest of Midian; and he led his flock to the west side of the wilderness, and came to Horeb, the mountain of God. And the angel of the Lord appeared to him in a flame of fire..." (Ex. 3:1-2a) Thus begins the much-edited account of the first theophany, combining elements from J and E. The Biblical narrative continues: "And the angel of the Lord appeared to him in a flame of fire out of the midst of a bush; and he looked, and lo, the bush was burning, yet it was not consumed. And Moses said, 'I will turn aside and see this great sight, why the bush is not burnt.'" (Ex. 3:2-3)

Mention of the angel here is a later redactor's[1663] attempt to increase the distance between man and God by interposing one of the heavenly court, as we have see in the case of the theophany vouchsafed to Abraham.[1664] As the passage shows, it is quite clear that no angel is speaking on God's behalf; it is He Himself addressing Moses from the burning bush. *Exodus* makes no mention of any others with Moses in this incident, but Jewish tradition, in the *Exodus Rabbah*,[1665] describes Moses with other shepherds. The vision of the burning bush is vouchsafed to Moses alone, remaining unseen by the others, as in the Quran. In both the Quran and the Bible, Moses is attracted to the fire by curiosity, but the causes appear to be different: in the Quran, Moses seems to need fire and directions, whereas in the Bible, it is solely curiosity. Jewish tradition prefaces this incident with an account emphasizing Moses' trustworthiness as a shepherd, influenced of course by the parallel of

---

[1661] Q. 27:7 and 28:29 have substantially the same account: Q. 27:7: *When Moses said unto the people of his household: 'Lo, I spy afar off a fire; I will bring you tidings thence, or bring to you a borrowed flame that ye may warm yourselves.* Q. 28:29: *Then, when Moses had fulfilled the term, and was travelling with the people of his household, he saw in the distance a fire and said unto his people: 'Bide ye (here)! Lo, I see in the distance a fire; perhaps I shall bring you tidings thence, or a brand from the fire that ye may warm yourselves.* The attentive reader will surely have noticed the minor differences among the three passages, further evidence that the thrust of the story was being adapted to the point of its repetition rather than the recounting of rehearsed historical chronicles. The point of the stories of the prophets alluded to in the Quran is illustrative and inspirational, not a recitation of historical data.

[1662] The Second Theophany will be discussed in the succeeding Section (F).

[1663] Probably the Second Yahwist.

[1664] See Part Two, III, G.

[1665] LJ, II, 304-305.

Moses and the Israelites with the shepherd and his sheep. It is an image that Christians later used with Christ.[1666]

THE MOUNTAIN OF GOD: In the Biblical passage quoted above, the Mountain of God is identified with the mountain called Horeb, thus marking the verse as from the Northern Elohist. The mountain is more famous under its other name Sinai (if, indeed, the two traditions speak of the same mountain), now usually thought to be Jabal Musa (Ar. *Jabal Mūsā*, "Mountain of Moses") in the triangular peninsula between the Gulfs of Suez and Aqabah. This tradition of the location of the mountain is of Christian origin and cannot be attested earlier than the 4th century CE. Aside from the extraordinary difficulty of the country (what good shepherd would lead his flocks from the rich pastures of Mount Seir to the wastes of Jabal Musa?), we last saw Moses in Midian that lies *east* of that conspicuous gash in the earth's surface, the Wadi Arabah. The western side of the wilderness probably means the western side of Seir. In addition, as we shall see later, "… in spite of efforts to disprove it, the phenomena connected with the theophany at Sinai/Horeb are clearly volcanic, and geological evidence has shown that there are no signs of volcanic activity in the southwest corner of the [Sinai] peninsula, but there is abundant evidence of such activity in the region to the south of Edom"[1667]

The Biblical directions for locating Mount Sinai/Horeb are not very helpful. Elijah took 40 days and 40 nights to reach Horeb from Beersheba (1 K. 19:8). (He could have reached Makkah in that time.) The Deuteronomist (who also, with E, calls the mountain Horeb) writes: "It is eleven days journey from Horeb by the way of Mount Seir to Kadesh-Barnea." (Deut. 1:2) This appears to make Mount Seir between Kadesh and Horeb, which would eliminate a location in the Egyptian Sinai, and would suggest Midian once again, perhaps one of the peaks such as Jabal al-Lawz in northwestern Saudi Arabia, an idea once scoffed at but now gaining more advocates. However, some peak of Mount Seir may be meant, and perhaps we should not take the "eleven days" too literally. The specific coupling of Seir and Horeb is noteworthy. The very ancient "Song of Deborah" (before c. 1000 BCE) also associated YHWH with Seir: "Lord, when Thou didst go forth from Seir, when Thou didst march from the region of Edom…" (Jgs. 5:4) Also, in 10th-

---

[1666] Cf. Jn. 10:11, in which Jesus is depicted as saying, "I am the good shepherd. The good shepherd lays down his life for his sheep."
[1667] Sinai, DB, p. 923; see also Anderson, p. 24.

century BCE "Blessing of Moses": "The Lord came from Sinai, and dawned from Seir upon us..." (Deut. 33:2)

Once again, there is no unanimity of opinion on this problem, but the Seir identification is gaining supporters, particularly when coupled with another theory also attracting scholars: that the traditions of the Exodus and the Holy Mountain were originally separate. Sites in the Sinai Peninsula are largely determined upon the fact that the Biblical text, as it stands today, links the two traditions, so that the Holy Mount must, of necessity, have lain on a possible route from Egypt to Kadesh. This makes the identification with Seir awkward. Gray, writing Laymon, acknowledges the volcanic activity in the Seir region in historical times, but objects to locating the Mountain of God there.[1668] However, separating the two traditions eliminates the necessity for locating Sinai/Horeb in Sinai. This theory also appears to be gaining acceptance.[1669] More will be said about the question below.

Surabadi continues: Moses came to a tree that appeared to be on fire, but its branches were green. Moses placed some brush at the end of his staff to get fire, but the fire went to another side. Though he could not see anyone, he heard a voice, saying: "O Moses, I am thy Lord. Remove thy shoes." Surabadi observes that the shoes were made of the hide of a dead ass, or some say a camel. Moses had been barefoot when he left Shu'ayb and had made slippers from the skin of the dead animal along the way. Moses was told to remove his shoes so that the blessedness of that earth upon which the prophets had walked would be received by him. In another tradition, the reason was that he should not concern himself with his family for God would take care of them. He should prepare himself for revelation. It is also said that as soon as Moses left his family, a son was born who grew instantly into manhood and took charge of the family's flocks, leading them back to Midian.

Surabadi also informs us that when departing, Moses was told by Zipporah (Ar. *Ṣafūrā*, *Ṣiffūrah*) that he should not go at that time because of the snakes and scorpions in the wilderness of Tuwa (Ar. *Ṭūwā*). Moses replied that he could protect himself with his staff against the snakes and against the scorpions with the shoes. Since he had relied upon them rather than God, he was told take the shoes off. They immediately became scorpions and the staff became a snake, a precursor of the miracle that would occur later in the course of the theophany.

[1668] Laymon, p. 39.
[1669] Sinai, DB, p. 923; Mount Sinai, EJ, XIV, 1599.

As usual, Surabadi has gone considerably beyond the Quranic text, and most of his additions do not seem to be found in the earlier Jewish traditions, although some were used by later Jewish writers. The Quran appears to name the site of the burning bush the blessed valley of Tuwa, although some commentators have taken the word to mean "Twice": *And when he reached it, he was called by name: 'O Moses! Lo! I, even I, am thy Lord. So take off thy shoes, for lo, thou art in the holy valley of Tuwa.* (Q. 20:11-12)

In another place a more vivid description is given of the scene of the fire: *And when he reached it, he was called from the right side of the valley in the blessed field, from the [burning] tree: 'O Moses! Draw near and fear not. Lo, I, even, I am God, the Lord of the Worlds.'* (Q. 28:30) This description is so particularized, it suggests that a strong tradition is reflected in the text of the Quran, some place or shrine which had been pointed out to the Hejazi caravaneers on their way to and from Syria, on a route which would have taken them by Mount Seir. Furthermore, in two places (Q. 19:52 and Q. 20:80), the Quran refers explicitly to the "right side of the Mount" (*jānib al-ṭūr al-ayman*) in connection with Moses' theophany. Yet, in still another place (Q. 28:44), the site is identified as being on "the western side" (*jānib al-gharbī*) of the Mount. These statements can be reconciled if one assumes we are viewing the mountain from the north. Could the Prophet himself have seen this site? Is this too a bit of evidence in support of the identification of one of the peaks of Mount Seir or Jabal al-Lawz with Horeb?

The Bible, too, mentions the command to remove the shoes: "When the Lord saw he that turned aside to see, God called unto him out of the bush,[1670] 'Moses! Moses!' And he said, 'Here am I.' Then He said, 'Do not come near' put off thy shoes from thy feet, for the place upon which thou are standing is holy ground.' And He said, 'I am the God of thy father, the God of Abraham, the God of Isaac, and the God of Jacob.' And Moses hid his face, for he was afraid to look at God." (Ex. 3:4-6)

In both the Quran and the Bible God is manifesting himself to Moses in the fire. Both the Quran and the Bible seem to imply that the site of the burning bush was already sacred.[1671] Indeed, we probably have here another example of a shrine associated with a tree.[1672] In this respect,

---

[1670] Note that in this version God is the speaker, not an angel.

[1671] In support of this, we may cite the epithet of God "(He) that dwelt in the bush" found in the 10th century BCE "Blessing of Moses." (Deut. 33:16, Moses, EJ, XII, 380.)

[1672] Cf. the Oak of Shechem (Gen. 35:4; the Palm of Deborah (Jgs. 4:5); the Oak of Mamre (Gen. 13:19) etc. See de Vaux, pp. 278-279; Smith, pp. 185, 191-195. This miraculous appearance of the Divinity in the burning bush is not without ancient parallels. "At Aphaca at the annual feast the goddess appeared in the form of a fiery

the evidence of the Quran is extremely important, as it supports the Biblical text and even adds details that seem to be based upon observation or the reports of a local tradition otherwise lost.

There is a greater distance between man and God in the Quranic version than in the Biblical account, in which Moses hides his face, seemingly able to view the form of God that is some manner disclosed in the fire. That is why the Second Yahwist (J2) thought it necessary to create the impression that it was not God Himself in the bush; rather it was an angel of God. It is also why such a device was not necessary in the Quran where God is not localized in the fire, itself merely a device to draw Moses to the sacred spot, and also to put him into the appropriate state in which to receive his first divine revelation. Noteworthy, too, is God's identification of Himself. In the Bible, He says that He is the God of the Israelites and their patriarchal ancestors, Abraham, Isaac, and Jacob—a relatively small portion of mankind. However, in the Quran, God is the Lord of everything that is: *Lo, I, even I, am God, the Lord of the Worlds.'* (Q. 28:30) We have progressed from national to universal monotheism

In the Quran, this is followed by the commissioning of Moses as a messenger: *Verily I Myself have chosen thee, so hearken unto that which is inspired. Lo! I, even I, am God. There is no God save Me. So serve Me and establish worship for My remembrance. Lo, the Hour is surely coming. But I shall keep it hidden, that every soul may be rewarded for that which it strives (to accomplish). Therefore, let not him turn thee aside from it who believes not therein, but follows his own desire, lest thou perish.'* (Q. 20:13-16) At this point, Surabadi abandons artifice and lets an unadorned translation of these magnificent verses into Persian resound grandly.

The address of God to Moses in the Bible is quite different and restricted to the Israelites. "Then the Lord said, 'I have seen the affliction of My people who are in Egypt, and have heard their cry because of their taskmasters; I know their sufferings, and I have come down to deliver them out of the hand of the Egyptians, and to bring them up out of that land to a good and broad land, a land flowing with milk and honey [Canaan]...'" (Ex. 3:7-8)

---

meteor, which descended from the mountain-top and plunged into the water, while according to another account fire played about the temple, presumably... in the tree-tops of the sacred grove. Similarly, it was believed that fire played about the branches of the sacred olive tree between the Ambrosian rocks at Tyre, without scorching its leaves... The same phenomenon, according to Africanus and Eustathius, was seen at the terebinth of Mamre; the whole tree seemed to be aflame, but when the fire sank again remained unharmed..." (Smith, p. 193.)

Moses protested: "'Who am I that I should go to Pharaoh, and bring the sons of Israel out of Egypt?' (God) said, 'But I will be with thee; and this shall be the sign for thee, that I have sent thee: when thou hast brought forth the people out of Egypt, thou shalt serve God on this mountain.'" (Ex. 3:11-12) The first quotation is from J and the second is from E. Already we can see what appears to be a difference in destination. For J, Canaan (Palestine) is the object of the Israelites after they are liberated; but E seems to plan a future in which the Israelites will be led to the Holy Mountain where Moses (and his descendants) will serve as priests.

The next two verses of *Exodus* describe the occurrence that is, for E and P, the most important event in the history of Israel: the revelation of the divine name to Moses. "Then Moses said to God, 'If I come to the people of Israel and say to them, "The God of your fathers has sent me to you," and they ask me, "What is His name?" what shall I say unto them?' God said to Moses, 'I AM WHO I AM.' And He said, 'Say this to the people of Israel, "I AM has sent me to you."'" (Ex. 3:13-14) Thus, YHWH disclosed His Name to man for the first time, as He would later be known to His chosen people, Israel.[1673]

YHWH, the name of God, has caused much discussion in the world of Biblical scholarship and a considerable literature has grown up concerning its etymology, meaning, correct pronunciation, and ritual use. The etymology given in the verse quoted above is considered folk etymology. Yahweh would mean "he is." The vowelization of the word has been preserved by Greek transliterations,[1674] so we know that the correct form is *Yahweh*, even though in later times the Jews regarded the name with such awe that while writing the consonants YHWH, they substituted the vowels of *Adonai* ("my Lord"), thereby creating the written form *Yehowah*, but reading this hybrid as *Adonai*. This practice led to the regular, though erroneous, usage in Europe (among Gentiles) of *Jehovah*, still current in English. In time, it seems the actual voweling of YHWH was forgotten and had to be recovered from the Greeks. Prof.

[1673] However, in the Yahwist/Deuteronomist view, and the Islamic view paralleling it, God had made His true identity known to mankind from the very beginning, but people were continually being diverted from His pure worship and His law through indifference, laziness, the machinations of evil, lust, greed, etc., necessitating the periodic renewal and reminder of the message throughout history.

[1674] The pronunciation of Hebrew short vowels was not indicated in the Old Testament until the invention of the diacritics possibly in the 8th century CE, centuries after the consonantal texts had been stabilized. See "The Text of the Old Testament" in Introduction, III.D.

Meek believes that the name YHWH was foreign to the Hebrews and was in fact of *Arabic* origin, "from the Arabic root *hwy*, 'to blow'"[1675]

Although there is still hardly unanimity on the etymology of the word, the view of Albright and others seems to be prevailing, that *Yahweh* is the third person singular of a causative form of the verb *H-W-Y* meaning "to fall, become, or come into existence." Perhaps it was originally part of a sentence formula, as some ancient names were: *Yahweh asher yihweh* "he brings into existence whatever exists."[1676]

Did the patriarchs before the time of Moses worship a god named YHWH? We do not know and opinion is divided. It is quite possible that the Northern (Josephic) tribes did not know of YHWH until He was introduced to them by Moses. The Elohist text certainly indicates that Moses did not know this name of God (and hence this God) until the theophany, and he did not expect that the Israelites living in Egypt (the Josephites?) would recognize it. The editor apparently also felt this way, and the verse of the revelation of the Divine Name was followed immediately by an explanation drawn from the Yahwist, telling us who this YHWH was: "God also said unto Moses, 'Say this to the people of Israel, 'The Lord, the God of your fathers, the God of Abraham, the God of Isaac, and God of Jacob, has sent me to you': this is My Name for ever, and thus I am to be remembered throughout all generations.'" (Ex. 3:15) Is this a declaration of the assimilation of three separate deities?

In the next verse, also ascribed to the Yahwist, the same triple formula is repeated: "'Go and gather the elders of Israel together, and say to them, 'The Lord, the God of your fathers, the God of Abraham, the God of Isaac, the God of Jacob, has appeared to me...'" (Ex. 3:16) The tradition of the Southern Yahwist suggests that YHWH was not new to him and his people, but we cannot be sure that the ancestors of the Southerners worshipped God under that name. However, they may have

---

[1675] God, DB, p. 334; Names of God, EJ, VII, 680.

[1676] Albright-Stone Age, pp. 15-16; Names of God, EJ, VII, 680. Another form of Yahweh is attested in names formed with a theophoric element: *Yahu*. It has been suggested that this has a parallel in the Arabic usage *Ya Huwa!* (O He!) in religious, especially ecstatic liturgy. It is now believed the *yahu* is a jussive form of *yahwiyu*, YHW. Of course, the form *huwa* and the verb *HWY* are quite probably related as cognates anyway. (Albright-Stone Age, p. 16; God, EB, p. 334.) Joseph Campbell quotes Meek's argument that the confusion about the meaning of the name indicates that the stem HWY was foreign to the Hebrews; however, it is still represented in modern Arabic which is a close relative or development of the language spoken by the Kenite/Midianites. "The most probable [origin of the name] in our opinion is... from the Arabic root *hwy*, 'to blow.'" (Campbell, III, 132-133.)

learned of YHWH from their despised neighbors to the south, the Midianites.[1677]

THE KENITE HYPOTHESIS: This brings us to the Kenite Hypothesis (some call it "Midianite"): "The fact that J and E locate Moses' first encounter with Yhwh during his residence among his Midianite in-laws, and the fact that J speaks of Yahwism long before Moses, while E and P claim the name Yhwh was first revealed at Sinai (Horeb), spawned a thesis in the 19th century that Yhwh was a Kenite or Midianite deity."[1678] In 1862, F.W. Ghillany (using a pseudonym at the time) first suggested that Moses not only learned the name of YHWH from the Kenite clan to which his Midianite father-in-law, Jethro, belonged, but many aspects of the cult and social institutions associated with YHWH-worship as well.[1679] In other words, YHWH had revealed Himself to the Midianites *before* He had revealed Himself to the Israelites! The implications of this thesis are stunning. It would make a section of the close kin of the Arabs, the Midianites—whom the later Israelites strove to vilify and obliterate, perhaps because of this secret knowledge—the earliest receivers of the primitive revelation of the invisible One God Who would gradually disclose Himself to mankind as the sole Lord of the Universe. For the Muslim, this process culminates in the revelation of the Quran.

We have already noted that the Kenites were on friendly terms with Israel (in distinction to the bulk of the Midianites who appear as Israel's implacable enemies in the Bible). The Kenites appear to have ultimately been absorbed by the Judahites, as apparently were many other Canaanite clans. It has been suggested that these Kenites were a nomadic tribe of smiths, and this is reinforced by their association with Midian where there were copper mines.[1680] It has been proposed that their god was YHWH, probably worshipped without an idol, and that he was particularly associated with a mountain in Midian[1681] that had exhibited

---

[1677] Anderson, p. 39.

[1678] Baruch Halpern, Kenites, ABD, Vol. IV, p. 20.

[1679] Baruch Halpern, Kenites, ABD, Vol. IV, p. 20; Kenites, EJ, X, 906-907. The EJ article minimizes this possibility.

[1680] Kenites, DB, p. 548.

[1681] Further evidence of the mountain origin of YHWH may be adduced from one of His epithets, *El Shaddai* (Almighty), which was "most likely directly related to the Assyrian 'shadu' (mountain) and the original connotation was 'God of the mountain' rather than 'God Almighty.'" (BC, I, 342; also see God, DB, p. 335; also Gray, writing in Laymon, p. 41.) This ties in well with what we know of worship at "high places" in Canaan and

volcanic activity at some time within the period of the residence of the Kenites in that region. For example: "And Mount Sinai was wrapped in smoke, because the Lord descended upon it in fire; and the smoke of it went up like the smoke of a kiln, and the whole mountain quaked greatly." (Ex. 19:18) The Yahwist is clearly describing the phenomena of a volcanic eruption.

Jethro, the Kenite/Midianite father-in-law of Moses, was also a priest. Was he a priest of YHWH? The events related in Exodus 18 seem to suggest so. After the successful escape from Egypt, Moses and the Israelites camped by the Mountain of God. There Jethro, bringing Moses' family, came to visit him. Moses described the escape to Jethro who rejoiced "for all the good that the Lord had done to Israel." (Ex. 18:9) Jethro's God is the God of Moses.

"And Jethro said, 'Blessed be the Lord, who has delivered you out of the hand of the Egyptians and out of the hand of Pharaoh. Now I know that the Lord is greater than all gods, because He delivered the people from under the hand of the Egyptians, when they dealt arrogantly with them. [This is from the Yahwist. Notice that the reality of other gods is not denied; only the Lord's being stronger than they is asserted.] And Jethro, Moses' father-in-law, offered a burnt offering and sacrifices to God; and Aaron came with all the elders of Israel to eat bread with Moses' father-in-law before God." (Ex. 18:10-12; the last sentence is from E.)

Thus, in this conflated account, Jethro is associated with YHWH, and in the last (Elohist) verse, he is shown conducting the ritual sacrifice to Him. The absence of Moses from the feast has been interpreted to show that since Moses had already been received into YHWH-worship formally during his earlier stay with Jethro, his participation was unnecessary. The ceremony was the initiation of Aaron and the elders into the cult of YHWH-worship. Furthermore, in the following verses Jethro gave administrative and organizational advice to Moses and taught him judicial procedure: all of which were aspects of the cult in ancient times (Ex. 18:13-26).[1682]

Naturally, this hypothesis has not been very attractive to those who wish to support the primacy of Israel in all things monotheistic and the uniqueness of Israel's religious experience. Nevertheless, the ascription of the founding of these institutions to a clan of the hated Midianites argues for the authenticity of the tradition. It was too well

---

Israel before their suppression in favor of the centralized cult at Jerusalem under David and Solomon.

[1682] See IB, I, 13-26.

known to be denied. We also see that the monotheism of the Pentateuch is not absolute; it is in fact henotheism. Monotheism was the way YHWH was worshipped—He ruled alone, without a pantheon of lesser gods to assist Him, but His worship was not yet considered incumbent upon other peoples who were not of the elect. As the story of Moses proceeds, we shall increasingly see how anthropomorphic and territorial was the concept of God in the Pentateuch. Already we have seen that God has told Moses that He will accompany him to Egypt. This should be read quite literally, as subsequent events will show. YHWH is invading Egypt and challenging His peers, the gods of Egypt. This alone would justify questioning whether Moses' revelation was fully understood by his contemporaries and their early descendants.

Is there any extra-Biblical evidence to support the Kenite Hypothesis? As a matter of fact, there is. Two Egyptian texts of about 1400 BCE, thus antedating the period of Moses by more than a century, mention a "land of Yahweh Bedouins." The region referred to lay east of Egypt, the very region of Midian.[1683] There is also archeological evidence: "The excavations at biblical Timna, just (north) of Eilat [Eilath], uncovered a 12th-century BCE temple. This temple was characterized by what archaeologists call 'Midianite' pottery. And, it was apparently a tent-shrine, much like the tabernacle in the biblical tradition. Inside it, the excavators uncovered a copper snake...

"Curiously, the only zoomorphic icon associated with Moses in any source earlier than P is a copper snake called Nehushtan (2 K. 18:4; Num. 21:9). The tent-shrine, if that indeed is what it is was, is not altogether unexpected on the desert fringe, but it may be that Israel's notions of its early cult were in part shaped by Midian-Kenite models. Snakes, too, were common icons in the Mediterranean basin..."[1684] There is also the more tenuous evidence that the Exodus and the Israelite Conquest from the east followed Midian trading routes.

This is, of course, circumstantial evidence, but it lends support to the Kenite Hypothesis if one does not assume that God restricted His revelation to just one people. If one can suspend one's preconceived certainties inherited from centuries of assumptions based upon flawed documents and flawed history, one may glimpse a completely different picture of the emergence of monotheism. There is no reason we must assume the late Biblical genealogies absorbing Moses and Aaron into the

---

[1683] Wolff, pp. 17-18; Moses, EJ, XII, 381.
[1684] Baruch Halpern, *Kenites*, ABD, Vol. IV, 20. For Nehushtan, see "The Staff of Moses" in the preceding section D.

Hebrews are any more historically accurate than much else of what we have been examining.

All of this strengthens the theory that the area in which Moses took refuge already knew of YHWH and that he learned of YHWH and His worship during his sojourn there. In other words, Egyptian, Israelite, or a mixture of both, Moses may have been a convert to YHWHism. It should not shock our sensibilities to entertain the *possibility* that God revealed himself to a messenger or messengers in Arab Midian before He did so in Israel, and that Moses embraced the truth at the hands of Jethro, his Midianite father-in-law.

The tradition of Shu'ayb, the prophet of Midian, to be found in Arabia and in the Quran can also be enlisted in support of this theory. We have already discussed the tentative identification of Jethro with Shu'ayb, and the reasons for its probable rejection.[1685] In our opinion, Shu'ayb may well antedate the era of Moses by a period of unknown length. The circumstances of Shu'ayb could be involved with some development of the tradition of YHWH-worship in Midian, which Moses found already there (if the Kenite Hypothesis be correct). The prophet Shu'ayb of Midian, whose existence was forgotten or suppressed by the ancient Israelites (it is also possible that he was never known to them), was remembered by the Midianites and their successors the Ishmaelites in that region. The tradition like others, moved south down the Hejaz until it was enshrined in the text of the Quran. Today, we might enlist that memory in support of the theory that monotheism, perhaps not yet the absolute monotheism of later Judaism, but a localized monotheism, existed in Midian before it was adopted or co-opted by Israel.

It may, therefore, be one of the supreme ironies of history that the sacred name of God amongst the Israelites, YHWH, is of Midianite (Arab) origin, and they may very well have learned of Him from the desert Arabs. The basis of the national identity of this people, that is YHWH-worship, would thus become a borrowing from Arabia. The God of Israel was not the God of Isaac and Jacob at all, but rather the God of Ishmael and Esau. As Joseph Campbell reluctantly expresses it: "Hence we are forced, to some extent, to agree with Mohammad's startling claim that the people of his own Semitic stock were the first worshippers of the God proclaimed in the Bible."[1686]

The course of events in the story of the Exodus and the sojourn in the wilderness may shed more light on the problem.

[1685] See in preceding Section above.
[1686] Campbell, III, pp. 430-431.

THE STAFF: *"And what is that in thy right hand, O Moses?"* He said: *"This is my staff whereon I lean, and wherewith I beat down branches for my sheep, and wherein I find other uses."* (Q. 20:17-18) To this, Surabadi adds that Moses was asked this in the way a child is asked, to bluff him, or to have him certify that it was a staff before it was turned into a snake.

He said: "Cast it down, O Moses!" So he cast it down, and lo, it was a serpent, gliding. He said: "Grasp it and fear not. We shall return it to its former state." Q. 20:19-20) Surabadi interpreted these verses to mean that God had told Moses to cast down the staff because he relied too much upon it, or more obviously, so that God might show His power by turning it into a snake, and to teach Moses not be frightened when the miracle was performed before Pharaoh. After it had become a snake, he had been told to seize it again, which he did with trepidation. It became a staff again in his hand.[1687]

The Quranic version is less elaborate than Surabadi's commentary. In another place, there is a longer version of the speech, delivered by God after Moses has approached the fire: *"O Moses! Lo, it is I, God, the Mighty, the Wise: And throw down thy staff!" But when he saw it writhing as it were a demon, he turned to flee headlong: (but God said:) "O Moses! Fear not! Lo, the emissaries fear not in My presence, save him who has done wrong and afterward has changed evil for good. And lo! I am Forgiving, Merciful."* (Q. 27:9-11)[1688] Comforting words for the imperfect believer; he has nothing to fear before his compassionate Creator. The "evil" referred to in the verse is taken to be a reference to Moses' crime of manslaughter in Egypt, later redeemed by his good behavior in Midian.

In the Bible, the miracle of the staff is preceded by a speech attributed to God in which He gives directions on how to act when delivering the message. It also gives a precognition of the miracles and plagues that will occur in Egypt. And finally God is depicted (by E) as instructing Moses to have the Israelites loot the defeated Egyptians: "'And I will give this people favor in the sight of the Egyptians; and when ye go, ye shall not go empty, but each woman shall ask of her neighbor, and of her who sojourns in her house, jewelry of silver and

---

[1687] Surabadi, pp. 245-246.

[1688] These internal differences within passages touching upon the same incident or person suggest to us that the speeches are not to be taken as the literal words of the speaker (after all Moses, did not speak classical Arabic), but as types and gists. The point is the message itself, not the words in which it is couched. The verse gives hope to an imperfect man, Moses, and by extension, gives hope to all of us with all of our imperfections that we may enjoy God's mercy and forgiveness, *inshāllāh*.

gold, and clothing, and ye shall put them on your sons and on your daughters; thus ye shall despoil the Egyptians.'" (Ex. 3:21-22) Rather unexpected instructions from the Creator of the Universe.

We arrive now at the Biblical passage (from the Yahwist) paralleling the Islamic versions quoted above: "then Moses answered, But behold, they will not believe me or listen to my voice, for they will say, "The Lord did not appear to thee,"' The Lord said to him, 'What is that in thy hand?' He said, 'A rod.' And he said, 'Cast it on the ground.' So he cast it on the ground, and it became a serpent; and Moses fled from it. But the Lord said to Moses, 'Put out thy hand, and take it by the tail'—so he put out his hand and caught it, and it became a rod in his hand—'that they may believe that the Lord, the God of their fathers, the God of Abraham, the God of Isaac, and the God of Jacob, has appeared unto thee.'" (Ex. 4:1-5)[1689]

The difference between this passage from *Exodus* and the verse quoted above from the Quran is negligible: only Moses' explanation of his use of his staff is added to the Quranic version. However, both Jewish and Islamic traditions have developed the theme of the Rod of Moses with competing imaginings. We have already met it as the rod which Adam carried with him from Paradise and passed on to his sons, and then handed down the ages from generation to generation until it came to Jethro, who surrendered it to Moses. More will be said its properties below.[1690]

In the Biblical account, Moses keeps putting forth objections to the mission God has set before him. This has led to some rabbinic criticism of Moses' behavior. For example in the medieval (11th century CE) *Abkir Midrash*, quoted in *Yalkut*, we have: "And the Lord said unto him, 'What is that in thine hand?' And (Moses) said, 'A rod." And the Lord said: 'Thou deservest to be castigated with it. If thou didst not intend to take My mission upon thyself, thou shouldst have said so in the beginning. Instead, thou didst hold back with thy refusal, until I revealed to thee the great secret of the Ineffable Name, that thou mightest know it if the children of Israel should ask thee concerning it. And now thou sayest, I will not go. Now, therefore, if thou wilt not execute My charge

---

[1689] Note that in these formulae God does not use the inclusive "your fathers" instead of "their fathers." Does it mean, as it appears to, that He is not the god of Moses' fathers? Another indication that Moses was an Egyptian whose father worshipped idols?

[1690] It is interesting that these traditions put the rod in the custody of a Midianite, notwithstanding the device of his obtaining it from the household of Pharaoh. More support for Midianites being in the main stream of YHWH-worship?

to thee, it will be executed by this rod. It was My wish to distinguish thee and make thee My instrument for doing many miracles.'"[1691] Though the tradition is a late, its hectoring tone owes nothing to Islamic tradition.

After the miracle of the staff at the theophany, Surabadi tells us that there was another sign. Moses was told to draw his hand from under the other and it shone with a white light brighter than the sun. Then he was told to go to Pharaoh and call him to God. Moses then requested that God open his breast to prophethood and messengership and banish the rashness and haste in it, for messengership was difficult, and bringing the message to Pharaoh and disputing with him was difficult. "And untie my tongue so that they understand my speech."

In an explanation of this problem with Moses' speech, Surabadi offers the following story: When Moses was a two-year old, while he was being held by Pharaoh, he tugged at Pharaoh's bejeweled beard. Pharaoh became angry and said that the child was an enemy, but Isiyah asked, what could a child know? To test him, two trays were brought in, one of coals, and the other of oleaster. Moses wanted to reach for the oleaster,[1692] but Gabriel directed him to the coals. He seized a handful and put them in his mouth, thereby burning his tongue. This was the cause of Moses' speech defect. The reason his hand was not burned was that it had been toughened on the beard of Pharaoh. However, his tongue had flattered him by calling him "baba," and therefore it was susceptible to being burnt. He cites another (contradictory) tradition, in which it was said that the hand did not burn because it was the source of light, and fire could not affect it, as fire could not affect the heart of a believer.[1693] The Quran does not attribute luminosity to Moses' hand.

Moses then asked God to make his brother Aaron his counsellor and aide. This petition was granted. Moses was forty when he received the revelation and was sent with his brother to call Pharaoh to God.[1694] Finally, in a typical medieval Islamic development of the story, Surabadi adds: When Moses was sent to Pharaoh, the angels protested that Moses was not adequately fitted out. In response, he was given the clothing of purity, the steed of divine grace, the sword of proof, the aid of continence, and the army of God's help.[1695]

[1691] Quoted in LJ, II, pp. 320-321.
[1692] "oleaster": the wild olive.
[1693] Surabadi, pp. 247-248.
[1694] Surabadi, pp. 248-249, 251.
[1695] Surabadi, 251-252.

THE WHITE HAND: The miracle of the white hand of Moses is mentioned in both the Quran and the Bible. *"And thrust thy hand within thine armpit, it will come forth white without harm. Another sign that We show thee from Our great signs."* (Q. 20:22-23) And in the Bible, the Yahwist tells us: "Again, the Lord said to him, 'put thy hand into thy bosom'; and he put his hand into his bosom; and when he took it out, behold! his hand was leprous, as white as snow. Then God said, 'Put thy hand back into thy bosom.' So he put his hand back into his bosom; and when he took it out, behold! it was restored like the rest of his flesh. 'If they will not believe thee,' God said, 'or heed the first sign, they may believe the latter sign...'" (Ex. 4:6-8)

In this, God Himself does not seem to know whether the Israelites (for they are the object of this passage, not Pharaoh, as in the Quran) will be impressed by these miracles to the point of believing in Moses' mission and following him. In the event that they are not, God proposes still a third sign, turning the water from the Nile into blood (Ex. 4:90).

The miracle of the white hand of Moses is not specifically mentioned again in the Biblical text although presumably it was included among the signs shown to the Israelites when Moses and Aaron successfully enlisted their support in the project to leave Egypt (Ex. 4:30). It must be emphasized that there is a fundamental difference between the approach of the Quran and that of the Bible in the nature of Moses' mission. In the Bible, Moses is sent to the Israelites only, to lead them out of bondage in Egypt into Canaan and to establish their rituals and institutions, that is, the Law. There is no Biblical record of Moses' inviting Pharaoh to worship the One Universal God, or even the more limited God of the Israelites, YHWH. The Biblical mission of Moses is national.

However, in the Quran, it has become universal. It does not refer to the necessity of his convincing the Israelites to accept his leadership. That is assumed. Moses' mission was to invite the Egyptians, as represented by Pharaoh and his court, to the true religion of the One Invisible God, Whom he calls the Lord of the Worlds; and secondly, to lead the Israelites out of Egypt in a bid for the free worship of the One God.[1696] Another difference is the addition in the Quran of the phrase "without harm" to God's command to Moses to withdraw his hand from his armpit, which could be taken as a denial of the Biblical statement that Moses' hand had become leprous. Jewish rabbinical tradition has offered many explanations about the hand: "The Lord now bade Moses put his

---

[1696] Q. 7:104-105; 20:46-48; 26:15-17; 44:18.

hand into his bosom and take it out again, and when he took it out, behold, his hand was leprous, as white as snow. And God bade him put his hand into his bosom again, and it turned again as his other flesh. Beside being a chastisement for his hasty words, the plague on his hand was to teach him that as the leper defiles, so the Egyptians defiled Israel, and as Moses was healed of his uncleanness, so God would cleanse the children of Israel of the pollution the Egyptians had brought upon them."[1697]

However, Josephus refrains from using the term "leprous" in describing Moses' hand in his account: "After this God bid Moses to put his right hand into his bosom; he obeyed, and when he took it out it was white, and in color like to chalk, but afterwards it returned to its wonted color again."[1698]

MOSES' SPEECH: The Quran also notes Moses' reservation about his ability to speak eloquently: *(Moses) said: "My Lord! Relieve my mind and ease my task for me; and loose a knot from my tongue, that they may understand my speech. Appoint for me an aide from my folk, Aaron, my brother. Confirm my strength with him and let him share my task, that we may glorify Thee much..."* (Q. 20:25-33) *(Moses) said: "My Lord! Lo, I fear that they will deny me. And I shall be embarrassed, and my tongue will not speak plainly, therefore send for Aaron..."* (Q. 26:12-13) And Moses expresses another fear: *"And they have a crime (counted) against me, so I fear they will kill me."* (Q. 26:14) This was a reference to the manslaughter Moses had committed and which had prompted him to flee from Egypt.[1699]

In the above, though we see Moses pleading for more assistance, both divine and human, the underlying assumption is that he has tacitly accepted the task God has given to him. However, the parallel Biblical passage has a quite different tone: "But Moses said to the Lord, 'Oh, my Lord, I am not eloquent, either heretofore or since Thou hast spoken to Thy servant; but I am slow of speech and of tongue.' Then the Lord said to him, 'Who has made man's mouth? Who makes him dumb, or deaf, or seeing, or blind? Is it not I, the Lord? Now therefore go, and I will be with thy mouth and teach thee what thou shalt speak.' But he said, 'Oh,

---

[1697] LJ, II, 321. Lepers were ritually unclean. No less than two whole chapters of *Leviticus* (13 and 14; more than one eighth of the whole) are devoted to the regulations concerning the treatment and cleansing of lepers.

[1698] Josephus, Antiquities, II.12.3, p. 59.

[1699] That in the Quran Aaron is called Moses' brother is not necessarily an obstacle to an absence of a blood kinship, as it is quite common to address a comrade or close friend as "brother," especially in the Middle East.

my Lord, send, I pray, some other person.' Then the anger of the Lord was kindled against Moses and he said, 'Is there not Aaron, thy brother, the Levite? I know that he can speak well; and behold, he is coming out to meet thee, and when he sees thee he will be glad in his heart. And thou shalt speak to him and put the words in his mouth; and I will be with thy mouth and his mouth, and will teach thee what thou shalt do. He shall speak for thee to the people; and he shall be a mouth for thee, and thou shalt be to him as God. And thou shalt take in thy hand this rod, with which thou shalt do the signs.'" (Ex. 4:10-17)

Moses then returned to Jethro and, dissimulating somewhat as described above in section D, told him that he wanted to go back to Egypt to see his kinsfolk. Jethro told him: "'Go in peace.' And the Lord said to Moses in Midian, 'Go back to Egypt; for all the men who were seeking thy life are dead.' So Moses took his wife and his sons and set on an ass, and went back to the land of Egypt; and in his hand Moses took the rod of God." (Ex. 4:19-20)

We have already noted above the problem of Moses' language difficulties as a possible indication that he did not know the Semitic language of the Israelites adequately for the purposes of his mission (see above, section A); the assumption is that Moses was fluent in Egyptian, but not the Hebrew dialect of Canaanite. In this respect, Jewish tradition, as represented in the *Tanhuma*, also associates Moses' objection about his speech with his lack of Hebrew. God granted him the knowledge of seventy languages to remove this objection of his.[1700] In another Jewish tradition, it is said that Moses prophesied in seventy-one languages.[1701]

One of the possible explanations of the problem (discussed above) would be that Moses was actually an Egyptian who had taken refuge with the Semitic Midianites, married among them, learned their language in an imperfect manner, and had become a convert to their unique religion of single invisible God. The residence of God was conceived to be on a mountain with which volcanic phenomena were associated, and Whose worship included sacrifices, but no idols. To our way of thinking, this would not diminish Moses in the least, as his race is of no concern, but Jews would be understandably upset, just as many Englishmen would be if it were asserted that Shakespeare was actually a Russian.

Of course, this is speculation, and could be entirely or partly incorrect. Nevertheless, the circumstantial evidence for such a chain of events is both strong and plausible. In the Bible, Moses' problem with

---

[1700] LJ, II, 322-323.
[1701] LJ, II, 322; VI, 225.

speech may be simply a device to introduce Aaron into the narrative, and perhaps the tradition has no more significance than that, except for the stubborn insistence upon the point. The Quran also recognizes the connection between Moses' lack of eloquence and the appointment of Aaron, but the phrases *"knot upon my tongue"* and *"that they may understand my speech"* suggest problems of communication greater than mere ineloquence.

In any event, Surabadi's pericope about Moses and the coals is also found in the *Exodus Rabbah* (9th and 10th centuries CE) in virtually the same form, possibly under Islamic influence.[1702] The *Exodus Rabbah* makes the test the suggestion of Jethro and instead of oleaster, the other tray has gold (in another version, onyx), but the results are the same thanks to the intervention of Gabriel, as in the Islamic story.[1703] Tabari also mentions the story, substituting pearls for Surabadi's oleaster.[1704] *Pirke de Rabbi Eliezer* does not refer to the story, nor does Josephus.

Surabadi notes that Moses was forty years old when he received his first revelation, obviously influenced by the strong tradition of the Prophet's receiving his first revelation at that age. Jewish tradition, cited earlier, makes Moses eighty years old.

Finally, it may be noted that at the point where Moses, in the Quran, asks God to "open his breast," medieval Jewish tradition inserts an account of the ascension of Moses, which is very similar to Muslim accounts of the Night Journey of the Prophet.[1705] There is no justification for this insertion in the Biblical text, but perhaps here Jewish tradition was influenced by the Islamic development of the story and the mystical interpretations given to the phrase used several times in the Quran.

F. MOSES AND PHARAOH

Here is a dramatic story... (Trawick-NT, p. 65)

Then, after them, We sent Moses with Our signs unto Pharaoh and his council, but they abused them. Now, see the nature of the consequence for the workers of corruption! Moses said: "O Pharaoh!

[1702] Compare also the vision of Isaiah in which he sees the heavenly court and bewails his unclean lips. "Then flew one of the seraphim to me, having in his hand a burning coal which he had taken with tongs from the altar. And he touched my mouth and said: 'Behold, this has touched thy lips; thy guilt is taken away, and thy sin forgiven.'" (Is. 6:6-7.)

[1703] LJ, II, 174; V, 402.

[1704] Tabari, I, 303.

[1705] LJ, II, 309-316.

Lo, I am messenger from the Lord of the Worlds [not just the God of the Patriarchs], *approved upon the condition that I speak nothing but the truth concerning God. I come unto you (lords of Egypt) with a clear proof from your Lord* [not *our* Lord]. *So let the Children of Israel go with me." (Pharaoh) said: "If Thou comest with a sign, then produce it, if thou art of those who speak the truth." Then (Moses) flung down his staff and, behold! it was a serpent manifest! And he drew forth his hand, and lo! it was white for the beholders! The elders of Pharaoh's people said: "Lo! This is some knowledgeable sorcerer who would expel you from your land. Now what do ye advise?" They said (unto Pharaoh): Put him off—him and his brother—and send summoners into the cities to bring every knowledgeable sorcerer unto thee."* (Q. 7:103-112)

In another place, the Quran expands this first encounter between Moses as a messenger of God and Pharaoh. After Moses has asked the monarch to let the Children of Israel depart from Egypt, Pharaoh replies with an accusation: *Did we not rear thee among us as a child? And thou dwelt amongst many years of thy life. And thou didst that which thou didst, and thou wast one of the ingrates!* (Q. 26:18-19) [According to the Bible (Ex. 7:7), Moses was eighty years old when he commenced his mission of liberation.]

Moses admits his fault: *I did it them, when I was of the ones who err.* (Q. 26:20) [This refers to the killing of the Egyptian.] *Then I fled from you when I feared you. Then my Lord gave me a command and made me one of those who are sent. And this is the past favor of which thou remindest me, that thou hast enslaved the Children of Israel.* (Q. 26:21-22)

Pharaoh said: Then, what is this Lord of the Worlds? (Q. 26:23)

(Moses) said: The Lord of the heavens and the earth and all that is between them, if ye would be sure. (Q. 26:24)

Pharaoh is shocked at Moses' presumption and threatens him. This leads to threats and the demonstration of the signs.

In Surah Ta Ha, to which Surabadi is linking his commentary in this section, Moses, in obedience to the command: *"And speak unto him a gentle word, that mayhap he may heed or fear"* (Q. 20:50-55), also addresses Pharaoh, calling him to God. Pharaoh must accept God of his own free will. He may accept or refuse Islam (Submission to God); his is the choice. Note also that the day of the festival will be appointed for the trial with the Egyptian sorcerers: *(Moses) said: "Your rendezvous shall be the day of the festival, and let the people assemble when the sun has risen high."* (Q. 20:59)

Surabadi amplifies his account by including the figure of Haman:[1706] Pharaoh had been convinced by Moses' speech, but Haman dissuaded him, pointing out that he (Pharaoh) was a king and a god, and could not agree to serve another god. Then Pharaoh accused Moses of trying to force him from his kingdom through magic and said that he would have his magicians challenge him. The date for the contest was set, as in the Quran. Thus we have the following sequence of events: the audience in which Moses, with Aaron, shows Pharaoh the signs (the rod and the white hand); the call to Pharaoh to submit to God; a delay while the Egyptians summon their sorcerers for a public contest to be held on a festival day; and the contest itself.[1707]

In the Biblical account, Aaron had come out of Egypt to meet Moses by the Mountain of God. They then traveled first to the Israelites in Egypt, to whom Moses showed the signs and convinced the people to accept his leadership. Then: "Moses and Aaron went to Pharaoh and said, 'Thus says the Lord, the God of Israel, "Let My people go, that they may hold a feast to Me in the wilderness."' But Pharaoh said, 'Who is the Lord, that I should heed His voice and let Israel go? I did not know the Lord, and moreover I will not let Israel go.' Then they said, 'The God of the Hebrews has met with us; let us go, we pray, a three days' journey into the wilderness, and sacrifice to the Lord out God, lest He fall upon us with pestilence or with the sword.' But the king of Egypt said to them, 'Moses and Aaron, why do ye take the people away from their work? Get to your burdens.'" (Ex. 5:1-4) Then Pharaoh commanded that the labor of the Israelites be increased.

In this first encounter (from JE), there is no record of Moses' showing his signs to Pharaoh, as he had already done to the Israelites. Instead, in its aftermath, the Israelites, their burden of labor now increased, repudiated Moses and Aaron (Ex. 5:20-21). Note also that the Lord (YHWH) is not known in Egypt and that He seems to be restricted to being the God of the Israelites. Furthermore, He is neither omnipotent nor omniscient, for He resorts to a deception (the pretext of the feast in the wilderness) to get His people out of Egypt. This is not the Lord of the Worlds, Who merely utters "Be!" and it is. Instead, we are at an early stage of the evolution of the monotheistic idea from a tribal god to the One God, the Creator of all that is in the universe.

[1706] The *Proverbs Midrash* introduces Balaam in much the same role as Surabadi's Haman, counseling Pharaoh against Moses and Aaron, and suggesting the contest with the magicians.

[1707] Surabadi, pp. 252-253.

THE "SECOND" THEOPHANY: As the text of the *Exodus* stands today, this encounter is followed by the so-called Second Theophany (Ex. 5:22-7:7). In it, Moses is first once again instructed in His Name: "And God said to Moses, 'I am the Lord. I appeared to Abraham, to Isaac, and to Jacob, as God Almighty,[1708] but by My name the Lord [YHWH] I did not make Myself known to them. I also established My covenant with them, to give them the land of Canaan, the land in which they dwelt as sojourners." God tells Moses to expound upon His concern for the Israelites and seems to be almost pleading to be accepted as their God. After promising to deliver them out of Egypt, He is represented as telling Moses to say on His behalf: "I will redeem you with an outstretched arm and with great acts of judgment, and I will take you for my people, and I will be your God; and ye shall know that I am the Lord your God, who has brought you out from under the burdens of the Egyptians. And I will bring you into the land which I swore to give to Abraham, to Isaac, and to Jacob; I will give it to you for a possession. I am the Lord.'" (Ex. 6:6b-8)

The people did not heed this declaration by YHWH, so Moses complained to Him when He ordered him to go to Pharaoh to obtain the release of the unwilling Israelites: "But Moses said to the Lord, 'Behold, the people of Israel have not listened to me; how then shall Pharaoh listen to me, who am a man of uncircumcised lips?' But the Lord spoke to Aaron, and gave them a charge to the people of Israel and to Pharaoh king of Egypt to bring the people of Israel out of the land of Egypt." (Ex. 6:12-13) Note that Aaron has also been included in this version of the theophany, a circumstance unreported in the earlier text. P (5th century BCE or later) is at work exalting his priestly caste among the post-Exilic Israelites.

This exaltation of Aaron continues when P summarizes: "These are the Aaron and Moses to whom the Lord said: 'Bring out the people of Israel from the land of Egypt by their hosts.' It was they who spoke to Pharaoh king of Egypt about bringing out the people of Israel from Egypt, this Moses and this Aaron. On the day when the Lord spoke to Moses in the land of Egypt, the Lord said to Moses, 'I am the Lord; tell Pharaoh king of Egypt all that I say unto thee.' But Moses said to the Lord, 'Behold, I am of uncircumcised lips; how then shall Pharaoh listen to me?' and the Lord said to Moses, 'See, I make thee as God to Pharaoh; and Aaron thy brother shall be thy prophet [*naby*]. Thou shalt speak all that I command thee; And Aaron thy brother shall tell Pharaoh to let the people of Israel go out of his land...' Now Moses was eighty

---

[1708] Or: God of the Mountain. See Note 1681 above.

years old, and Aaron eighty-three years old, when they spoke to Pharaoh." (Ex. 6:26-7:2,7)

Aaron is now the equal of Moses in position (in the Priestly Writer's account) and his elder brother to boot! The implications of this have been discussed above. Once more, the problem of Moses' difficulty with language is the prime cause of Aaron's role as Moses' interpreter. Did Moses stutter? Was it a language problem?[1709]

Scholars now realize that this Second Theophany is the really the 5th-century BCE or later Priestly (P) version of the First Theophany on the Holy Mountain which we discussed in the previous section. P had the conflated account of J and E to draw upon in Ex. and 4. In the light of modern scholarship, the Quran correctly refers to only one theophany, that is, the call symbolized by the fire. In the older JE version, the pericope of the plagues directly followed the complaints of the overburdened Israelites against Moses.

In Surabadi's story, on the day of the contest, amid a scene of great splendor, Moses and Aaron appeared in simple dress, provoking laughter from the Egyptians. The sorcerers said that if Moses were victorious, it would be because of his God and faith, but if they themselves were, it would be because of Pharaoh's great wealth. *And the sorcerers came to Pharaoh, saying: "Surely there will be a reward for us if we are victors."* (Q. 7:113)

Surabadi records that it was said that there were 70,000 sorcerers with a like number of staffs, (in another tradition) that they had 70 assloads of staffs and ropes, and they were 70 chosen from among the 70,000. The sorcerers made their staffs in the form of snakes, and filled them with mercury. They painted them and leather ropes in the same manner. They were on a height. When they cast down their "staffs," they all made for Moses. Moses was frightened, but then cast down his own staff. It became a dragon and consumed all the sorcerers' snakes, and then made for the pavilion of Pharaoh to consume him as well. Pharaoh pleaded for a respite, and Moses seized the tail of the dragon and it immediately changed back into a wooden staff. The Egyptian sorcerers prostrated themselves and said that they were convinced. Pharaoh was furious [despite just having been rescued from the dragon] and threatened them for believing in Moses and his God without his

---

[1709] Gray notes that "uncircumcised lips" may signify "defective lips." A harelip comes to mind. He also dismisses P's remarks about the ages of Moses and Aaron as "artificial." (Laymon, pp. 41-42.)

permission. But Moses and Aaron persisted, and Pharaoh told Moses to take the slaves out of Egypt.[1710]

This contest is narrated in the Quran in several places. Taking the narrative from Surah Ta Ha, which is the basis of Surabadi's commentary in this section, we read: *(The sorcerers) said: "O Moses! Wilt thou throw first, or let us be the first to throw?" He said: "Nay, do ye throw! Then lo, their cords and their staves, by their magic appeared to him as though they ran. And Moses conceived a fear in his mind. We said: "Fear not! Lo, thou art the higher. Throw that which is in thy right hand! It will eat up that which they have made. Verily, that which they have made is but a sorcerer's artifice, and a sorcerer shall not be successful to whatever point (of skill) he may attain." Then the sorcerers were flung down prostrate, crying: "We believe in the Lord of Aaron and Moses."* (Q. 20:65-70) This is followed by Pharaoh's anger against his sorcerers as in Surabadi.

At this point, the Egyptians appear to have judged the God invoked by Moses superior to their own gods. They had not yet realized that the God of Moses was the One God, the only God. Incidentally, the Quranic text regards the tricks of the Egyptians as illusions and unreal, just as their gods were unreal. By contrast, in the Biblical text, the snakes brought to life by the Egyptian magicians are depicted as quite real, as we shall see. Even the relatively late Priestly Writer who tells the story in *Exodus* is either as yet untouched by God's universality, did not notice the inconsistency, or is simply recounting a well-established primitive tradition.

Let us turn to the Biblical version of the contest. In it, the gods of Egypt are real. They had powers of magic and could work miracles, but the miracles wrought by YHWH were more powerful. In the Quran, there is no provisional acceptance of the divinity of the gods of ancient Egypt. Above, we have seen how the Quran speaks of God as the God of Pharaoh as well. There is no parallel to this in *Exodus*, where Moses consistently refers to the Lord as the God of the Hebrews.

"So Moses and Aaron went to Pharaoh and did as the Lord commanded; Aaron cast down his rod before Pharaoh and his servants, and it became a serpent. Then Pharaoh summoned the wise men and the sorcerers; and they also, the magicians of Egypt, did the same by their secret arts. For every man cast down his rod, and they became serpents. But Aaron's rod swallowed up their rods. Still Pharaoh's heart was hardened, and he would not listen to them; as the Lord had said." (Ex. 7:10-13)

[1710] Surabadi, pp. 252-255.

All of this is usually thought of as having occurred at one audience, although it would be logical to assume that it would have taken some time to summon the wise men and the sorcerers, as in the Quran. The reader will have noticed that in this account by P, the rod has become Aaron's instead of Moses'. In the earlier sources the rod clearly belongs to Moses, but in the Priestly concern for the enhancement of the role of Aaron and the Aaronid priesthood in the foundation-story of Israel's religion and national identity, the rod has now been placed in the hand of Aaron.

As in the Quran (Q. 7:127-129), so in the Bible this contest did not settle the issue and Pharaoh was not persuaded to release the Israelites. Further signs were necessary before Pharaoh would finally give his permission.

The *Tanhuma* (perhaps under Islamic influence) also makes the occasion of the contest some kind of festival day, in this case the birthday of Pharaoh.[1711] Later Jewish tradition, too, paints a scene of great magnificence: Pharaoh's palace was surrounded by an army. It had 400 entrances, each one guarded by 60,000 troops; all this to enhance the feat of Moses and Aaron in securing an audience at all, for they finally had to enter Pharaoh's presence by miraculous means.[1712] And in the *Exodus Rabbah*, Balaam dismissed the marvel of Aaron's rod-turned-snake's devouring those created by the magicians with superb cheek, saying: "There is nothing marvelous or astonishing in this feat. Your serpent has but devoured our serpents, which is in accordance with a law of nature, one living being devours another. If thou wishest us to acknowledge that the spirit of God worketh in thee, then cast thy rod to the earth, and if, being wood, it swallows up our rods of wood, then we shall acknowledge that the spirit of God is in thee." This was done, causing Pharaoh to fear whether this wonderful rod of Aaron might not swallow up him and his throne also.[1713]

THE TEN PLAGUES: *And they said: "Whatever portent thou (O Moses) bringest wherewith to bewitch us, we shall not put faith in thee. So We sent them widespread death*[1714] *and the locusts and the vermin and*

[1711] LJ, II, 331.

[1712] LJ, II, 331-332.

[1713] LJ, II, 335-336.

[1714] *"widespread death"* (Ar. *ṭūfān*): The Arabic word is used more commonly to mean a "destructive storm." Noah's Flood is referred to as Noah's *ṭūfān*. However, it is used metaphorically to describe a widespread calamity, usually with considerable death, such as an epidemic. Both Yusuf Ali and Maulana Muhammad Ali take it in that sense. The Arabic root implies circular motion (Quran-Yusuf Ali, p. 378; Quran-MMA, p. 345;

the frogs and the blood—a succession of clear signs. But they were arrogant and became guilty. (Q. 7:133)

Our edition of the *Stories of the Prophets* drawn from Surabadi's Commentary does not include the material paralleling the Ten Plagues that were sent upon Egypt to convince the Pharaoh to let Israel go after the miracle of the rod had failed to secure the Hebrews their freedom. Surabadi refers to the last plague, that of the death of the firstborn, when he relates how Moses led the people out of Egypt on the pretext of a celebration, an echo of the device used in *Exodus* commented upon above. As it happened, the eldest born of each house died and so the Egyptians were all in mourning for three days and three nights. The opportunity was seized by Moses to flee Egypt.[1715]

In two places in the Quran the number of signs given to Moses is said to be nine, and this indicates there must have been a strong tradition about that particular number: *And We gave unto Moses nine signs, clear proofs.* (Q. 17:101) *And put thy hand into the bosom of thy robe, it will come forth white but unhurt, (a sign) among nine signs unto Pharaoh and his people. Verily, they were ever an ever-evil folk.* (Q. 27:12)

This figure probably includes the rod and certainly the white hand, as well as those listed above in Q. 7:133. The full list of nine, according to Yusuf Ali, is: the rod, the radiant hand, years of drought (Q. 7:130); failed crops (Q. 7:130); epidemics; locusts, lice, frogs, and water turning to blood.[1716] How this compares with the Biblical list we shall see below. But before beginning, we should note that the Quran speaks of "signs" (*āyāt*), not plagues. That said; let us look at the Biblical plagues:

The story of the plagues is given at rather great length in *Exodus*, from Ex. 7:14 to 12:32. It is also a composite of material from J, E, and P, plus glosses by the Deuteronomist, together with other editorial additions. This is not the place to go into a detailed study of the plagues themselves, but several points about the narrative should be made. For the most part, they are amplified natural phenomena: unusual numbers and concentrations of pests, animals, diseases, and storms. The darkness is probably meant to suggest some sort of sandstorm. Only the first (the turning of the water of the Nile into blood) and the last (the death of the firstborn) require a more elaborate explanation, or greater reliance upon

---

Wehr, pp. 573-574). Arberry and Pickthall translate the word as "flood" (Quran-Arberry, p. 158; Quran-Pickthall, p. 158). If the word is taken to mean death, it would refer to the last of the Biblical plagues, but if it refers to a storm, it could be the ninth: darkness.

[1715] Surabadi, pp. 9-10.

[1716] Quran-Yusuf Ali, p. 378.

the miraculous, that is, the supernatural. For all of the others, the miracle lies in the timing and size of its occurrence.

Though most scholars are reluctant to put it so, the plagues represent the battles between YHWH, Who has invaded Egypt purposing to bring out His chosen people, and the ancient Egytian gods. Their opposing human proxies are Moses and Aaron on one side and the Egyptian magicians on the other.[1717] The power of these gods of Egypt is real, as it was in the contest with the rods, but the point of the narrative is that YHWH was victorious over them on their own terrain. After two more contests, the gods of Egypt seem to retreat from the field and leave it entirely to YHWH, Who continues afflicting the Egyptians until finally Pharaoh agrees to let the Israelites go. (Why he was ready to endure such a series of catastrophes and humiliations to keep his slaves may be something of a mystery to the modern mind.) However, Pharaoh was not so overwhelmed by these miracles so as not to change his mind and take off in pursuit of Moses and his followers shortly after the last one.

In the Bible, the first of the ten plagues is that of blood. "Moses and Aaron did as the Lord commanded; in the sight of Pharaoh and in the sight of his servants, he lifted up the rod and struck the water that was in the Nile, and all the water that was in the Nile turned to blood. And the fish in the Nile died; and the Nile became foul, so that the Egyptians could not drink water from the Nile; and there was blood throughout all the land of Egypt. But the magicians of Egypt did the same by their secret arts; so Pharaoh's heart remained hardened..." (Ex. 7:20-22a)

This involves an obvious impossibility. If the river had already been turned into blood, how could the magicians have done the same thing? Perhaps originally the miracle was more local and involved canals or different branches of the river in the Delta rather than the whole river. In this contest, we see that YHWH and the gods of Egypt are tied.

Apropos of this plague, there is an even more ancient parallel: In Sumerian texts, we read of the goddess Inanna who, having been taken advantage of by a mortal male whilst asleep in a garden, sent three plagues upon Sumer. In the first, all the wells of the land became filled with blood, so that the palm groves and vineyards were all saturated with blood. The second plague was destructive winds and storms (the

---

[1717] One must not underestimate the power of Egyptian magic. It was famous in the ancient world, and it was even suggested by the pagan critics of Christianity that Jesus had come to Egypt and learned to perform his miracles from Egyptian sorcerers. See *The New Testament: An Islamic Perspective.*

darkness of *Exodus*?). The nature of the third is unknown, as the text is fragmentary.[1718]

The second plague, that of the frogs, ended in the same way, with the Egyptians equaling the feats of Moses and Aaron (Ex. 8:1-15). It is only at the third plague, that of the gnats, that the gods of Egypt prove themselves impotent: "The magicians tried by their secret arts to bring forth gnats, but they could not... And the magicians said to Pharaoh, 'This is the finger of God.' But Pharaoh's heart was hardened, and he would not listen to them; as the Lord had said." (Ex. 8:18-19) And the Egyptian sorcerers remained just as helpless in the subsequent seven plagues.

The exact nature of the some of the plagues is in doubt, as in the case of the third plague. The Quran refers to it as *qummal* or "lice." The Hebrew word used is *ken*, the exact meaning of which is unknown, but supposed to be "gnat." The LXX translated the Hebrew word with the Greek *skniphes*, a small insect which pierced the skin and set up itching. This would be more suggestive of mosquitoes or lice than of gnats. The King James translators call them lice, the New English Bible maggots, the *Jerusalem Bible* gadflies, and the RSV gnats. Since these insects infested man and beast, their activities are more suggestive of lice than any of the other possibilities.

The agents of the fourth plague, not mentioned in the Quran, are even more doubtful. The Hebrew word is *'arob*, meaning "mixture" or "swarm." The RSV calls them "flies," and suggests in a note that the fourth plague is simply a variant of the third plague.[1719] Some rabbinic commentators have also thought that the word refers to wild beasts, especially lions and leopards. However, advocates of a plague of flying insects appear to have a stronger case.[1720]

The Quran refers to drought and famine. These events are not specifically mentioned in the Biblical narrative, although they would be natural consequences, in whole or part, of some of the Biblical plagues,

---

[1718] Kramer-Sumer, p. 71.

[1719] RSV, p. 76. The JB calls them "gadflies." (JB, p. 87.) Roy Honeycutt, Jr., writing in the Broadman Commentary, notes an ingenious "rational" explanation of the plagues: "Some suggest that there was a direct causal relationship between each of the plagues. Finegan, for example, indicates that the pollution of the Nile [plague 1] killed great numbers of fish... which in turn drove the frogs [plague 2] ashore. The masses of dead fish were points of origination for the spread of... (anthrax), which is carried by insects [plague 3]. The insects, especially the files of the fourth plague spread the disease, spread the disease from the dead frogs, causing the plague of cattle and the boils of plagues 5 and 6." (BC, Vol. 1, p. 355.)

[1720] Rendsburg, Gary A. "Beasts or Bugs?" BR, Vol. XIX, No. 2; April 2003; pp. 18-23.

especially those of the blood (in Jewish tradition this is depicted as causing a severe water shortage, thirst, and drought), the pestilence that afflicted the animals, the hail (destructive of standing crops), and the locusts (which consume them).[1721] It may be useful to compare the Biblical and Quranic plagues in a table:

Biblical Plague and Textual Reference	Biblical Source	Quranic Order (Q. 7:133)
1. Blood (Ex. 7:14-24)	JEP	5
2. Frogs (Ex. 7:25-8:15)	J and/or P	4
3. Lice (Ex. 8:16-19)	J and/or P	3
4. Flies (Ex. 8:20-32)	J	-
5. Murrain (Ex. 9:1-7)	J	-
6. Boils (Ex. 9:8-12)	P	-
7. Hail (Ex. 9:13-26)	JE	-
8. Locusts (Ex. 10:3-20)	JE	2
9. Darkness (Ex. 10:21-23)	E	-
10. Death (Ex. 11:1-12:32)	JEP	1

Thus Yahwist material is found in seven, possibly eight, of the plagues; Elohist material in only five, and Priestly in from three to five. This does not mean that the original forms of these sources were limited to the numbers given above, but rather that the conflated material has come down to us in this form. In these accounts, later editors could have selected one version over another or eliminated passages of extensive duplication. The selection of the plagues (as opposed to the signs) listed in Quran seems to follow the Yahwist, however, in reverse order. This may be a coincidence. Although the present text of *Exodus* gives us ten plagues, the nine signs in the Quran may be an allusion to another tradition of nine signs, perhaps roughly corresponding to the Yahwist's list. The only sign specifically included among the nine in the Quran is, however, that of the white hand, which is not one of the plagues.

Perhaps we should examine the question from another angle. If we accept the proposition that the rod and the white hand are two of the nine signs mentioned in the Quran, then we should look for a list of seven more signs, probably including the five mentioned in Q. 7:133. These would be among the plagues, although there are possibilities such as the crossing of the sea, water from the rock, etc. Returning to the plagues, is there evidence of such a list of seven plagues?

[1721] At the time of Moses' abandonment by his mother, Jewish tradition says that Egypt was afflicted with scorching heat, leprosy, and boils. (LJ, II, 266.)

Actually there is, once again remarkably corroborating the Quran. Scholars have suggested a first version of the plagues in which there were six items: blood, frogs, lice, boils (?), darkness, and the death of the firstborn. It is thought that the second version of the plagues extended the number to seven: blood, frogs, insects, animal murrain, hail with fire, locusts, and finally the death of the firstborn. This would appear to be the original Yahwist-Elohist (JE) conflated version.[1722] All of the plagues in Q. 7:133 are to be found on this list. It should also be remembered that Quranic verse does not claim to be exhaustive, but is rather in the nature of giving examples of a genre.

Furthermore, there are other references to the plagues to be found in the Bible. Two psalms each give a list of seven items. In Psalm 78 from the time of David[1723] we read:

"He (God) turned their rivers to blood,
        so that they could not drink of their streams. (1)
He sent among them swarms of flies, which devoured them,
        and frogs, which destroyed them. (2)
He gave their crops to the caterpillar,
        and the fruit of their labor to the locust. (3)
He destroyed their vines with hail,
        and their sycamores with frost. (4)
He gave their cattle to the hail,
        and their flocks to the thunderbolts (5)
He let loose on them his fierce anger,
        wrath, indignation, and distress,
        a company of destroying angels. (6)
He made a path for his anger;
        but he did not spare them from death,
        but gave their lives over to the plague.
He smote all the firstborn of Egypt,
        the first issue of their strength in the tents of Ham. (7)
(Ps. 78:44-51)

In this hymn we have seven items, some arranged in parallels, a favorite device of Hebrew poetry: (1) blood, (2) flies/frogs, (3) caterpillars/locusts, (4) hail/frost, (5) hail/lightning, (6) death by pestilence, and (7) the death of the firstborn. The doublets are different

---

[1722] Plagues of Egypt, EJ, XIII, 610-611.
[1723] Lawrence E. Toombs, writing in Laymon, p. 284. This psalm would appear to be a century earlier than the work of the Yahwist and two centuries earlier than the Elohist.

aspects of the plagues; thus, the flies and frogs assaulted Egypt together and were counted as one by the psalmist.

In Psalm 105 there is still another list of seven plagues: (1) darkness, (2) blood causing the fish to die, (3) frogs, (4) flies and gnats, (5) hail and lightning, (6) locusts, and (7) the death of the firstborn (Ps. 105:28-36). The items mentioned in the Quranic verse appear on both of these lists. Incidentally, neither of these two sources (nor the Quran) mentions the plague of boils that seems to have originated with the Priestly Document.

Therefore, in all likelihood the original tradition was of seven plagues and, with the rod and the white hand, we arrive at the Quranic figure of nine signs (*not* plagues). The differences between the two lists suggest that an "official" version had not yet coalesced during the early monarchic period. The expansion to ten separate plagues is doubtless a later development achieved by dividing some of the plagues (that is, flies from the frogs, or gnats, etc.) and probably by the addition of the plague of boils by a later redactor from the Priestly circle.[1724]

The most decisive of the plagues was the last one, and it is the only one to which Surabadi gives much space. In the Bible, after the plague of darkness that lasted three days, Pharaoh agreed to let the Israelites go, but their flocks and herds would have to remain behind in Egypt. Moses would not agree to these terms, so once again Pharaoh's heart was hardened and he refused to allow the people to go. From the Elohist:

"The Lord said unto Moses, 'Yet one plague more I will bring upon Pharaoh and upon Egypt; afterwards he will let you go hence; when he lets you go, he will drive you away completely.'" (Ex. 11:1) Then the Yahwist takes up the tale: "And Moses said, 'Thus says the Lord: About midnight I will go forth in the midst of Egypt; and all the firstborn in the land of Egypt shall die, from the firstborn of Pharaoh who sits upon his throne, even to the firstborn of the maidservant who is behind the mill; and the firstborn of the cattle. And there shall be a great cry throughout all the land of Egypt, such as there has never been, nor ever shall be again. But against any of the people of Israel, either man or beast, not a

---

[1724] Like 7 and 12, 10 was also a favorite schematic number of ancient and later Jewish writers. In addition to the ten plagues and the ten commandments, we have the ten temptations of Abraham, the ten curses, the ten pious ones, the ten cosmocrators, the ten words of Creation, the ten punishments, the ten revelations, the wages of Jacob charged ten times, the ten classes of angels, the ten candlesticks, the ten mysteries, the ten attributes of God, a schema of the ten heavens, etc. (See LJ, VII, 467-468.)

dog shall growl; that ye may know that the Lord makes a distinction between the Egyptians and Israel..."'" (Ex. 11:4-7)

Then God, almost in the character of a night-demon, is reputed to have said, "'For I will pass through the land of Egypt that night, and I will smite all the firstborn in the land of Egypt, both man and beast; and on all the gods of Egypt I will execute judgments: I am the Lord. The blood shall be a sign for you, upon the houses where you are; and when I see the blood, I will pass over you, and no plague shall fall upon you to destroy you, when I smite the land of Egypt.'" (Ex. 12:12-13)

While perhaps delighting the hearts of the Israelites, these primitive verses depict a God—certainly not the Universal God of Mercy—who discriminates between races, favoring one over another. Innocent animals are also to suffer, as are the other slaves and captives held by the Egyptians in Egypt. Not only that, He is not omniscient and requires the sign of the blood to inform Him of the presence of His favored folk. Even worse, from the point of view of absolute monotheism, He even takes vengeance on the defeated gods of Egypt. If they were non-existent, why would He waste words upon them?

Let us return to the Biblical story: The Israelites followed these instructions. "At midnight the Lord smote all the firstborn in the land of Egypt, from the firstborn of Pharaoh who sat on his throne to the firstborn of the captive who was in the dungeon, and all the firstborn of the cattle. And Pharaoh rose up in the night, he, and all his servants, and all the Egyptians; and there was a great cry in Egypt, for there was not a house where one was not dead. And he summoned Moses and Aaron by night, and said, 'Rise up, go forth from among my people, both ye and the people of Israel; and go, serve the Lord, as ye have said. Take your flocks and your herds, as ye have said, and be gone, and bless me also.'" (Ex. 12:29-32)

While for the Muslim this episode is a demonstration of the power of God, the final disaster which He had let loose upon the Egyptians, prompting them to let the Hebrews free in accordance with God's plan; for the Jew this plague has an even greater importance. Jews from ancient times to the present find the origins of their Paschal Feast, or the Passover in this story. Many modern scholars, however, no longer believe that the feast originated with this plague, as the Biblical text would have it. More likely than not, they believe, it originated among pasturing folk who offered the firstborn of their flocks in the springtime to whatever deity or spirit they worshipped and then consumed the animal ritually in one night, so that nothing of it remained in the morning. The blood was smeared on tent posts to ward off demons.

Among the settled Jews this pastoral origin of the Paschal Feast seems to have been forgotten or suppressed in favor of a later association with Moses and the Exodus from Egypt.[1725] Perhaps some ancestral memories of human sacrifice have also influenced the form of the story. *And God knows best.*

G. THE EXODUS

Then Moses led Israel onward from the Red Sea. (Ex. 15:22)

Although the selection from Surabadi describing the Exodus comes from his commentary of Surah Baqarah (Q. 2), the Quranic reports are fuller in other places, and we shall turn to one of them: *And We revealed to Moses, "Go with My servants by night; surely ye will be pursued." Then Pharaoh sent into the cities summoners, (saying), "Lo, these indeed are but a small band, and indeed they are offenders against us. And lo, we are a host on guard." So We expelled them from gardens and fountains, and treasures, and a noble state. Thus, they followed (the Israelites) at sunrise; and when the two hosts saw each other, those with Moses said, "Lo, we are indeed overtaken!" Said he, "Nay, for lo, my Lord is with me. He will guide me." Then We revealed to Moses, "Strike the sea with thy staff." And it parted, and each part was as a great mountain. And there We brought near the others to that place, and We saved Moses and those with him, everyone; then We drowned the others.* (Q. 26:52-66)

In his narrative of these events, Surabadi explains that Moses led the Israelites out of Egypt on the pretext of holding a festival. They sought ornaments and robes, put them on, and departed towards the sea. As it happened, from each Egyptian household a dear one had died and the Egyptians were in mourning for three days. At the end of the period, Pharaoh collected an immense army, while Moses had only 300,000 fighting men [this despite the fact that the Quran in the above quotation refers to the small number of the Israelites; see below]. The vanguard of Pharaoh's army had 1,000,000 horsemen and a right wing, a left wing, a van, and a center with like numbers. There were 12,000 piebald horses at the front of the army.[1726]

The departure of the Israelites by night alluded to in the Quran is confirmed by events as depicted in the Bible. After the full horror of the tenth and final plague had become apparent, during that same night

---

[1725] Schauss, pp. 38-40; Buber, p. 70.
[1726] Surabadi, p. 10.

Pharaoh, defeated, summoned Moses and Aaron and told them to leave Egypt with their people and their flocks (Ex. 12:31-32; quoted in the previous section). Then: "And the Egyptians were urgent with the people, to send them out of the land in haste; for they said, 'We are all dead men.' So the people took their dough before it was leavened, their kneading bowls being bound up in their mantles on their shoulders." (Ex. 12:33-34) This passage from the Yahwist, a picture of haste and forcible expulsion, contrasts with the looting of the defeated and mourning Egyptians described with evident approval by the Elohist immediately thereafter: "The people of Israel had also done as Moses told them, for they had asked of the Egyptians jewelry of silver and gold, and clothing; and the Lord had given the people favor in the sight of the Egyptians, so that they let them have what they asked. Thus they despoiled the Egyptians." (Ex. 12:35-36)

This is a completely different picture. The passage harks back to Ex. 3:21-22 (quoted above in section E) and is perhaps a continuation or consequence of it. The Israelites had (treacherously as it turns out) ingratiated themselves with the Egyptians to borrow their finery and then flee Egypt with it. For the Yahwist, the Israelites were being terrorized as the Egyptians responded to the death that YHWH through Moses had brought upon them. Instead of looting, they were forced into a hasty departure; that is, they were in full flight. For the Elohist, this is another opportunity for an Israelite leader to turn the tables on his perceived oppressors by means of trickery. With YHWH's approval—for though He had defeated the gods of Egypt, they are not yet dead—the Israelites left Egypt after borrowing everything of value they could convince the generous Egyptians to lend them on the excuse that they were going to hold a festival of YHWH-worship in the desert. Once again, the Biblical text appears parochial and morally dubious, tainting the episode with deception and lying. The Israelites are depicted as decamping in the night like thieves.

The unleavened dough mentioned above is an aetiological addition, explaining, retrospectively, the origin of the unleavened bread eaten in commemoration of an event that had not yet occurred, the hasty flight before the women had had time to bake their bread. Jewish custom seems to have dictated that the participants in the Passover feast not leave the house until morning (and thus they remained under the protection of the sign of the blood). In the Bible, Moses and Aaron were summoned by Pharaoh (and therefore had left the site of the feast), but in

Jewish tradition, to remove this obvious problem, Pharaoh was depicted coming to Moses as a supplicant![1727]

While the text of *Exodus* suggests that the triumphant Hebrews extorted wealth from the Egyptians, many ancient Jewish authorities make the Egyptians voluntary contributors to their own despoilment. Josephus says "they also honored the Hebrews with gifts; some in order to get them to depart quickly, and others on account of their neighborhood, and the friendship they had with them."[1728] This, a mixture of bribery and goodwill, is an attempt to correct the unfavorable impression created by the Biblical text.

In the Quran, Pharaoh refers to the departing Hebrews contemptuously as a "small band" (*shirdhimah qalīlūn*). Surabadi would have been better advised to follow that cue instead of honoring the vast numbers attributed to the Israelites in the Bible: "And the people of Israel journeyed from Rameses[1729] to Succoth, about six hundred thousand men on foot, besides women and children. A mixed multitude also went up with them, and very many cattle, both flocks and herds." (Ex. 12:37-38)[1730] "The time that the people of Israel dwelt in Egypt was four hundred and thirty years. And at the end of four hundred and thirty years, on that very day, all the hosts of the Lord went out of the land of Egypt. It was a night of watching by the Lord, to bring them out of the land of Egypt; so this same night is a night of watching kept to the Lord by all the people of Israel throughout their generations." (Ex. 12:40-42) The last quotation is the explanation of the origin of the Feast of the Passover.

What was the mixed multitude? Scholars have thought this to be a reference to the non-Hebrews, perhaps other Semites or even Egyptians, who accompanied the Hebrews on their flight from Egypt. This addition has a ring of authenticity to it, for it goes against the ethnocentric ideas that developed later in post-Exilic times. Whilst it probably does not, of itself, justify the interpretation Freud gave to it, that the band fleeing Egypt was actually composed of a remnant of Aton-worshippers (the monotheistic Egyptian faith established by Akhenaton which had failed a century earlier), it does seem to imply that Moses' followers were not homogeneous. This did not concern the writer of this

---

[1727] LJ, II, 370.

[1728] Josephus, Antiquities, II.14.6, p. 62.

[1729] Rameses the city, identified with Tanis in the eastern Delta of the Nile. It was also known as Zoan. (ABL, p. B-7.

[1730] Verse 37, giving the figure of 600,000, is a much later Priestly gloss inserted into the Yahwist text.

passage (J or E) as it concerned the Jews who had experienced the dispersals of the Exile. Despite all of the editing and additions that put so many injunctions towards ethnic purity in the mouth of Moses in the Pentateuch, at this time YHWH-worship was still open to all believers regardless of origin. However, its principal recruiting grounds were among the Semitic clans of southern Syria (Palestine and Jordan).

THE CENSUS: Both the Biblical figure of 600,000 men and Surabadi's more modest 300,000 are grossly overstated. The population of Egypt in Pharaonic times is not known from any census records, but in the Roman era, according to Diodorus, it was about 7,000,000.[1731] (McEvedy and Jones give a more conservative figure of 4 millions for the Roman period.) During the time of Rameses II of the XIXth Dynasty, that is, the era of Moses (c. 1300 BCE), the population of Egypt is estimated by McEvedy and Jones to have been about 3,000,000. This may be too conservative, but given the state of agricultural technology, it could not have been much greater by any significant factor.[1732]

The Biblical figure of 600,000 men would imply a general Israelite population of 2,000,000; not counting the mixed multitude presumably not included in this figure. In other words, a majority of the inhabitants of Egypt were fleeing the country! This is already about two and one-half times the estimated population of all Palestine at the height of its prosperity under David and Solomon (c. 1000 BCE).[1733] Except for the credulous, the idea of such a multitude surviving for 40 weeks, much less 40 years, in the arid mountains and small oases of Sinai and northwestern Arabia is unthinkable. As we have seen, the Quran eschews such figures.

There is Biblical evidence for a more realistic appraisal of the size of the group fleeing Egypt. In the first chapter of *Exodus* (Ex. 1:15-21), as we have noted above, it is stated that there were only two midwives for the Israelites and their names are given. Just two midwives would suggest a community of several thousands, not 2,000,000.[1734] It

---

[1731] Breasted, p. 6.

[1732] McEvedy, pp. 226-277. The same authorities estimate that the population of the entire world in the time of Moses to have been no more than 50,000,000. (McEvedy, pp. 342-343.) The population figures in Surabadi and the Pentateuch are fantastically exaggerated.

[1733] This comparison is based on Albright's estimate of 800,000 (Albright-Ab to Ez, p. 56). McEvedy and Jones believe that the land of Palestine had a much lower population of about a quarter of a million during the period of the Egyptian Empire. (McEvedy, p. 141.)

[1734] See Section C above.

has also been suggested that the Hebrew word *eleph*, which has been translated as "thousand," in giving the above figures really means "clan," perhaps in a military sense, as the figures are always concerned with fighting men. The passage would then be rendered 600 clans, instead of 600,000 men.[1735]

The first chapter of *Numbers* gives the alleged results of a census of men capable of bearing arms undertaken in the second year of the wandering. The passage is from the Priestly Document. It gives us a total of 603,550 fighting men. The usual translation of the census passages that leads to these grossly inflated figures is thus, using Benjamin as an example: "Of the people of Benjamin, their generations, by their families, by their fathers' houses, according to the number of names, from twenty years old and upward, every man able to go forth to war: the number of the tribe of Benjamin was thirty-five thousand four hundred." (Num. 1:36-37) These are the census figures by tribe:

Reuben	46,500	Ephraim	40,500
Simeon	59,300	Manasseh	32,200
Gad	45,650	Benjamin	35,400
Judah	74,600	Dan	62,700
Issachar	54,400	Asher	41,500
Zebulon	57,400	Naphtali	53,400

Of course these figures actually represent the point of view of a much later era, that of the Priestly Writer. Note that Levites, who had not yet been designated as the priestly tribe and thus exempted from military service, are not included in the census, although the Levites are specifically mentioned as participating in bloodshed and mayhem later on in *Numbers*. Some think that only the Josephic tribes (Manasseh and Ephraim) participated in the Exodus and that the confederation of twelve tribes was a post-Conquest development.

If we take the word translated as "thousand" to mean "clan" as has been suggested, the final clause would read: "the number of the tribe of Benjamin was 35 clans; 400 (men)." In support of this interpretation, it should be noted that the hundreds tend to be larger or smaller in accordance with the thousands, with the single exception of Simeon, whose large figure may be a scribal error, because the tribe of Simeon was early absorbed by the tribe of Judah. By this calculation, the total

---

[1735] BC, I, 365-367. The Arabic cognate for the Hebrew *eleph* is *alf. Ilf*, from the same root, means "friend, confidant" in Arabic, but there is no suggestion of "clan," though the root also means "assemble," "compose," and "unite."

would be a more realistic 5,550 men. This would imply a total horde of some 15 to 20,000 people, much more in accord with the more recent population estimates we have already noted, much less if were only composed of the Josephic tribes.[1736]

Let us digress a moment about size of populations and armies in the ancient world. Our notions of these have been greatly distorted by the exaggerations of transmitters of tradition and historians. Though the Bible is rife with such exaggeration, the Greeks were no strangers to this tendency. Witness the immense figures Herodotus attributes to the Persian army invading Greece, inflated by a factor of at least ten, to several million![1737] An example may be cited which is very relevant to this topic as it refers to ancient Egypt during the era we are discussing: the largest Egyptian army assembled in Pharaonic times of which we have record was that of Rameses II (the same Pharaoh whom we believe to be connected with the events of the Exodus), used in the battle of Kadesh, Syria, 1288 BCE. It had only four divisions totaling 20,000 men.[1738] The Hebrew men-at-arms (not to mention the mixed multitude) would have outnumbered Rameses' grandest army 30 to 1! This historical figure is also quite different from Surabadi's 5,000,000 — which would have exceeded the total population of Egypt at that time.

The *Mekilta Beshallah* also tells us of the huge forces the Egyptians had mustered against the Israelites, more than their (the Israelites') total number including women and children, that is to say an Egyptian army of more than two millions.[1739] The medieval *Zohar* gives us figures even more fantastic that those of Surabadi: It was said that the Egyptians outnumbered the Israelites 300 to 1; assuming that only Israel's 600,000 fighting men are to be counted, that would mean a force of some 180,000,000 Egyptian soldiers![1740]

Surabadi, in this place, mentions the three-day celebration for which, according to the Bible, Moses had requested permission during his first interview with Pharaoh (Ex. 5:3). However, late Jewish tradition

---

[1736] "According to scripture the Israelites were numbered at something over 2m. Ten thousand would be a better figure..." (McEvedy, p. 141.) This estimate is more conservative than our calculations based on reinterpreting the Biblical data, but probably closer to the truth.

[1737] Herodotus, Bk. 7, pp. 459-461.

[1738] Breasted, p. 355.

[1739] LJ, III, 13.

[1740] The total of all the armies engaged in World War I on both sides was about 65,000,000 men; while in World War II, the figure was about 70,000,000. (World Almanac, 1968, p. 735.)

(the *Mekilta Beshallah*) also states that Pharaoh was under the impression the Hebrews were going away for only a three days' journey into the wilderness to offer sacrifices.[1741] The Biblical text can be read to support this idea.

Surabadi continues, when the Egyptians approached the encampment of Moses, it was dark and Pharaoh decided to wait until the morning. The Israelites were very frightened. Then God sent a white cloud which descended between the two armies, so that they could not see each other.[1742]

According to the Bible, the Israelites left Rameses (Tanis) and made for Succoth (Ex. 12:37), with God Personally leading them: "When Pharaoh let the people go, God did not lead them by the way of the land of the Philistines, although that was near; for God said, 'Lest the people repent when they see war, and return to Egypt.' But God led the people round by the way of the wilderness toward the Red Sea. And the people of Israel went up out of the land of Egypt equipped for battle. And Moses took the bones of Joseph with him; for Joseph had solemnly sworn the people of Israel, saying, 'God will visit you; then ye must carry my bones with you from here.' And they moved on from Succoth, and encamped at Etham, on the edge of the wilderness." (Ex. 13:17-20)

"And the Lord went before them by day in a pillar of cloud to lead them along the way, and by night in a pillar of fire to give them light, that they might travel by day and by night; the pillar of cloud by day and the pillar of fire by night did not depart from before the people." (Ex. 13:21-22)

The pillar of cloud may be explained by a natural phenomenon occurring in dry, dusty lands, the whirlwind or "dust devil." Urbanites rarely see them but they are common in the Middle East, and we have seen many of them, some quite impressive, like tornadoes of dust. This explanation does not diminish the miracle; as we have said, it is often the timing—not necessarily the event itself—that is miraculous.

Except for the notes on the itinerary that are from the P, the passage is a conflation of the J and E accounts. The spectacle is magnificent, though perhaps primitive. YHWH, Who has come from His mountain home in Midian with Moses to bring His chosen people out of Egypt, is personally conducting the multitude out of Egypt. God's caution about leading His people along the shorter and easier shore route to Canaan is anachronistic, as the Philistines (that is, the Sea People) did not attack this corner of the Mediterranean until the 11th century BCE,

---

[1741] LJ, III, 9.
[1742] Surabadi, p. 10.

two centuries after the Exodus and after the Hebrews had become established in Canaan. One wonders where a band of slaves found all that military armament; weapons are not usually put in the hands of recalcitrant or rebellious slaves.

God then directed Moses to lead the people back to a place opposite Pi-hahiroth, between Migdol and the sea, in front of Baal-zephon, and to camp there by the sea (Ex. 14:1-2).

Thus, we see that the people, led by God, were force-marched day and night out of the cultivated regions of Egypt. It took some time (three days according to Surabadi and Jewish tradition) for the forces of Pharaoh to catch up to them. Despite the series of disasters Egypt had suffered, Pharaoh had once again changed his mind and was now in pursuit of his fleeing serfs. This is explicable only if we admit that the plagues were not as widespread and devastating as later tradition has made them out to be.

When considering these accounts we must remind ourselves, that no matter how significant they are in Jewish and later Christian and Islamic religious literature, there is no explicit reference to any of these events in contemporary Egyptian records. The only alternative to denying the historicity of these events (subject of course to the possibility that in the future some confirmation will be discovered) is to recognize that this was a local or, at most, a provincial affair on the fringe of an empire, involving hundreds or perhaps several thousands of people rather millions. The impact of these events upon later Jewish literature is sufficient to convince us that real events lay behind these stories. However, in the Biblical narrative they have been blown out of proportion and are shrouded in the many veils of hyperbole and wishful thinking woven by later generations anxious to increase the wonder of it all.

So Pharaoh, who had previously ordered Moses to take his followers out of Egypt post haste (Ex. 13:31-32), had changed his mind: "When the king of Egypt was told that the people had fled, the mind of Pharaoh and his servants was changed toward the people, and they said, 'What is this we have done, that we have let Israel go from serving us?'" (Ex. 14:5) Thereupon Pharaoh with 600 chariots took off in pursuit. "The Egyptians pursued them, all Pharaoh's horses and chariots and his horsemen and his army, and overtook them encamped at the sea, by Pi-hahiroth, in front of Baal-zephon." (Ex. 14:9)

As the Quran and Surabadi reflect, when the Israelites saw the Egyptian army, they were greatly frightened: "And the people of Israel cried out to the Lord; and they said to Moses, 'Is it because there are no

graves in Egypt that thou hast taken us away to die in the wilderness?...
For it would have been better for us to serve the Egyptians than to die in
the wilderness.'" (Ex. 14:10b-11a,12b) Moses reassured the people and
told them to remain calm; God would fight for them. With the two
hostile camps facing each other, a cloud descended and separated the
forces, as in Surabadi: "The angel of God[1743] who went before the host of
Israel moved and went behind them; and the pillar of cloud moved from
before them and stood behind them, coming between the host of Egypt
and the host of Israel. And there was the cloud and the darkness; and the
night passed without one coming near the other all night." (Ex. 14:19-20)
A rationalist would deem this to mean that a dense sea fog had come
ashore and immobilized the camps, but in the mind of the Yahwist, it
was God Himself, manifested in the cloud, Who kept the two forces
apart.

CROSSING THE SEA: With morning, Surabadi tells us, Gabriel
told Moses to command the people to cross the sea in safety. The people
were afraid. Joshua was commanded to cross the surface of the water on
a horse. When this was done, the querulous Israelites objected that
Joshua had special qualities they did not have. Then Moses was
commanded by Gabriel to strike the water, but while he was receiving
the message, Aaron took the staff and struck the sea, as he wanted the
honor of parting the waters. But the sea reproved him. Ashamed, Aaron
returned the staff to Moses who struck the sea with it. It still did not part.
Gabriel told Moses to address the sea by its proper title. Moses struck it
again, calling, "Father of the Immortal, divide by God's permission."
Still it would not part. Then Gabriel told him to praise the Last of the
Prophets [Muhammad]. Moses uttered ten greetings of praise to him and
then struck the sea, "and the sea split asunder."

Now the Israelites complained that the way was too narrow.
Moses struck the sea and twelve paths appeared, one for each tribe. The
people protested that they would not be able to see each other and know
the fate of the other tribes. Moses (who must have possessed a truly
divine capacity for patience) struck the sea again and the sea formed a
vast arch. Then they were afraid of the mud of the sea bottom. In
response to the plea of Moses, a wind arose and dried the sea bottom.
Moses struck the ground and dust arose. Only then would the people
consent to pass to their salvation.[1744]

[1743] Here the Elohist has an angel intervene rather than God Himself as the Yahwist has it.
[1744] Surabadi, pp. 10-11.

This trying scene in Surabadi's Commentary is represented by only a few verses in the Bible: "Then Moses stretched out his hand over the sea; and the Lord drove the sea back by a strong east wind all night, and made the sea dry land, and the waters were divided. And the people of Israel went into the midst of the sea on dry ground, the waters being a wall to them on their right hand and on their left." (Ex. 14:21-22)

The Psalmist describes the same scene:

> "He divided the sea and let them pass through it,
>   and made the waters stand like a heap." (Ps. 78:13)

Jewish tradition also speaks of the refusal of the sea to obey Moses' command at first. In the 11th-century CE Midrash *Wa Yosha'*, God orders Moses, "Take the rod that I gave unto thee, and get to the sea upon Mine errand, and speak thus: 'I am the messenger sent by the Creator of the world! Uncover thy paths, O sea, for My children, that they may go through the midst of thee on dry ground.'

"Moses spoke to the sea as God had bidden him, but it replied, I will not do according to thy words, for thou art only a man born of woman, and, besides, I am three days older than thou, O man, for I was brought forth on the third day of creation, and thou on the sixth. Moses lost no time, but carried back to God the words the sea had spoken, and the Lord said: 'Moses, what does a master to with an intractable servant?' 'He beats him with a rod,' said Moses. 'Do thus!' ordered God. 'Lift up thy rod, and stretch thine hand over the sea, and divide it.'"[1745]

The earlier *Targum Yerushalmi* describes the rod: "thereupon Moses raised up his rod—the rod that had been created at the very beginning of the world, on which were graven in plain letters the great and exalted Name, the names of the ten plagues inflicted upon the Egyptians, and the twelve tribes of Jacob. This rod he lifted up, and stretched it out over the seas."[1746] The involvement of Gabriel in the events of the crossing is also attested in Jewish tradition.[1747]

The refusal of the Israelites to cross the sea once it had parted for them is found in Talmudic literature. In the pre-Islamic (3rd or 4th century CE) *Fathers According to Rabbi Nathan*, there is an extensive account of this dialogue between Moses and the Israelites: "When our ancestors stood at the Red Sea, Moses said to them: 'Rise, go across!'

[1745] LJ, III, 18-19.
[1746] LJ, III, 19.
[1747] LJ, III, 20.

"'We shall not go across,' they declared, 'until tunnels are made in the sea.'

"Moses took his rod and smote the sea, and tunnels were made in it [the arches of Surabadi?]. Then Moses said to them: 'Rise, go across!'

"'We shall not go across,' they declared, 'until the sea is turned into a valley before us.'

"Moses took the rod and smote the sea, and it became a valley before them... Said Moses to them: Rise, go across!'

"'We shall not go across,' they declared, 'until it is cut asunder before us.' Moses took the rod and smote the sea, and it was cut asunder before them... Said Moses to them: 'Rise, go across!'[1748]

"'We shall not go across,' they declared, 'until it is turned into clay for our benefit.' Moses took the rod and smote the sea, and it became clay... Said Moses to them: 'Rise, go across!'

(Once again, one marvels at Moses' self-control in this scene. At other times, he was not so patient.)

"'We shall not go across,' they declared, 'until it is made into a wilderness before us.' Moses took the rod and smote the sea, and it became a wilderness... Said Moses to them: 'rise, go across!'

"'We shall not go across,' they declared, 'until it is broken into many pieces before us.' Moses took the rod and smote the sea, and it turned into rocks... Said Moses to them: 'Rise, go across!'

"'We shall not go across,' they declared, 'unless it is turned into walls before us.' Moses took the rod and smote the sea, and it turned into walls Said Moses to them: 'Rise, go across!'

"'We shall not go across,' they declared, 'unless it is turned flaskshaped before us.' Moses took the rod and smote the sea, and it turned flaskshaped... As for the waters between the sundered paths, a fire came down and lapped them..."[1749]

In the above, many of the elements of Surabadi's catalog of Israelite protests can be found, including the twelve paths and the final elimination of the waters separating the paths. Earlier Jewish writers such as Philo and Josephus conceived of the path between the divided waters as a road.[1750] Josephus writes: "When Moses had thus addressed himself to God, he smote the sea with his rod, which parted asunder at the stroke, and receiving those waters into itself, left the ground dry, a road and a place of flight for the Hebrews. Now when Moses saw this appearance of God, and that the sea went out of its own place and left dry

---

[1748] This is the miracle of the 12 paths to which Surabadi refers. See note, ARN, p. 206.
[1749] ARN, pp. 133-135. Most of our omissions are Biblical citations.
[1750] LJ, VU, 6-7.

land, he went first of all into it, and bid the Hebrews to follow him along that divine road, and to rejoice at the danger their enemies that followed them were in: and gave thanks to God for this so surprising a deliverance which appeared from Him."[1751]

Above, we saw that Surabadi has introduced the character of Joshua into the narrative of the crossing of the sea. In the Bible, Joshua does not appear in the story of the crossing. He makes his first appearance in the story of the battle with the Amalekites in Exodus 17. Joshua is not mentioned by name in the Quran, and there is no figure in the Quranic narrative of Moses in Egypt with whom he could be identified, just as there is not in the Bible. In *Exodus,* Aaron is also conspicuously absent from the account of the crossing of the sea.

Surabadi continues: After the Israelites had begun the crossing, the fog lifted and the Egyptians saw the Israelites in the midst of the sea. Pharaoh boasted that the waters had parted out of fear of him and started to follow. Haman reminded him that they were still the same persons who had left Pushanj,[1752] and that they had not reached that degree of genuine divinity. He cautioned Pharaoh that the waters had parted because of Moses' prayer, and said: "Let us return or we shall be destroyed." Pharaoh recognized the truth of what Haman was saying and wanted to turn back, but Gabriel came to them on a mare (in heat), and the stallions of Pharaoh and Haman ran after her. Pharaoh could not dismount, and he was ashamed to call for help, for could a god not control a horse? (Gabriel had previously come to Pharaoh and asked him what should be done with a servant who usurped the position of the master. Pharaoh had replied that he should be cast into the Red Sea.) [1753]

On that day, Pharaoh saw his own judgment written in his own hand. The sea fell back on itself and Pharaoh and the Egyptian forces were destroyed just as the last of the Israelites reached the safety of the opposite shore. At that moment, Pharaoh wanted to recite the Declaration of Faith[1754] and be saved, but Gabriel threw a fistful of mud into his mouth, preventing him, and he was destroyed.[1755]

This last is inspired by a passage found in Surah Yunus: *And We brought the Children of Israel across the sea, and Pharaoh with his hosts pursued them in rebellion and transgression, till, when the drowning*

[1751] Josephus, Antiquities, II.16.3, p. 63.

[1752] Pūshang, to be identified with Pūshanj (in Khorasan) mentioned in Section B by Surabadi as the original home of Pharaoh and Haman.

[1753] Compare this with the quotation from *Wa Yosha'* cited in the text above.

[1754] "Declaration of Faith": Ar. *Shahādah.* "I testify that there is no god but God, (He is) One; He has no partner, and I testify that Muhammad is His servant and His Messenger."

[1755] Surabadi, pp. 11-12.

overtook him, he exclaimed: 'I believe that there is no god save Him in Whom the Children of Israel believe, and I am of the believers!' What? Now? When hitherto thou hast rebelled and been of the wrongdoers? But this day We save thee in thy body that thou mayest be a portent for those after thee. Lo, most of mankind are heedless of Our portents. (Q. 10:90-92)

In his account of the destruction of the Egyptian forces, Surabadi has reintroduced the figure of Haman. The Quran does not indicate that Haman was with Pharaoh in the final scenes. The import of the above passages seems to be that as death was coming upon Pharaoh, he repented, but it was too late. The preservation of his body would be a reference to the well-known Egyptian custom of embalming and mummifying their dead. Many Pharaonic mummies are housed in the Egyptian Museum, Cairo, including that of Rameses II. However, we must remind ourselves that historically no Egyptian monarch is known to have perished in the manner described in the Bible and the Quran. If we are concerned with historicity, we can only assume that Pharaoh in this passage describes Pharaoh's representative or governor, as discussed above.

The Bible describes the scene thus: "The Egyptians pursued, and went in after them into the midst of the sea, all Pharaoh's horse, his chariots, and his horseman. And in the morning watch, the Lord in the pillar of fire and of cloud looked down upon the host of the Egyptians, clogging their chariot wheels so that they drove heavily; and the Egyptians said, 'Let us flee from before Israel; for the Lord fights for them against the Egyptians.' (Ex. 14:23-25)

"Then the Lord said to Moses, 'Stretch out thy hand over the sea, that the water may come back upon the Egyptians, upon their chariots, and upon their horsemen.' So Moses stretched forth his hand over the sea and the sea returned to its wonted flow when the morning appeared; and the Egyptians fled into it, and the Lord routed the Egyptians in the midst of the sea. The waters returned and covered the chariots and the horsemen and all the host of Pharaoh that had followed them into the sea; not so much as one of them remained. But the people of Israel walked on dry ground through the sea, the waters being a wall to them on their right and on their left. Thus the Lord saved Israel that day from the hand of the Egyptians; and Israel saw the Egyptians dead upon the seashore." (Ex. 14:26-30)

It will be noted in the above verses from *Exodus* that there is no specific notice of Pharaoh's death, although it can be inferred—and this is the usual interpretation. However, in old sources there was a difference of opinion about his fate. According to some, he was destroyed with his forces; according to others, he survived so that he could see the power of God. The last Quranic verse quoted above (Q. 10:92) could support such an interpretation, were it not for explicit references to his drowning elsewhere.[1756] In the *Pirke de Rabbi Eliezer* there is a reference to the tradition that Pharaoh repented and was saved to become the ruler of Nineveh (near Mosul in modern Iraq), where, at the behest of Jonah, he led the people in repentance for their evil behavior.[1757]

A composite version of this tradition is found in the *Legends of the Jews*: "Thus all the Egyptians were drowned. Only one was spared— Pharaoh himself. When the children of Israel raised their voices to sing a song of praise to God at the shores of the Red Sea, Pharaoh heard it as he was jostled hither and thither by the billows, and he pointed his finger heavenward, and called out: 'I believe in Thee, O God! Thou art righteous, and I and my people are wicked, and I acknowledge now that there is no god in the world beside Thee.' Without a moment's delay, Gabriel descended and laid an iron chain about Pharaoh's neck, and holding him securely, he addressed him thus: 'Villain! Yesterday thou didst say, "Who is the Lord that I should hearken to His voice?" and now thou sayest, "The Lord is righteous."' With that he let him drop into the depths of the sea, and there he tortured him for fifty days, to make the power of God known to him. At the end of the time he installed him as king of the great city of Nineveh..."[1758] This version would seem to owe something to Islamic stories, as we are sure the Muslim reader will appreciate, however none are cited by Ginzberg as direct sources.

The text of Ex. 14:21-30 is a conflation of J and P. In general, J is less supernatural than the much later P. J explicitly states that the waters were parted by an east wind: "Then Moses stretched out his hand over the sea; and the Lord drove the sea back by a strong east wind all night, and made the sea dry land, and the waters were divided." (Ex. 14:21) However, P envisions walls of water standing on either side of the

---

[1756] For example: *(Moses) said: "In truth thou knowest that none sent down these (signs) save the Lord of the heavens and the earth as proofs, and lo, I deem thee lost, O Pharaoh." And (Pharaoh) wished to frighten them from the land, but We drowned him and those with him, all together.* (Q. 17:102-103) The destruction of "the people of Pharaoh" is referred to a number of times in the Quran, and such a term could be interpreted to exclude Pharaoh himself, but the verses just cited exclude that possibility. If we are to reconcile this judgment on Pharaoh with history, as we know it now, we must look for another explanation of the form the tradition assumed in Arabia, perhaps the use of Pharaoh as an office rather than an individual, as has been discussed above.

[1757] PRE, pp. 341-343.

[1758] LJ, III, 29.

road made through the sea for the Israelites (Ex. 14:22, 29). Again, in the destruction of the Egyptians, J sees them mired in mud as the waters rise around them (Ex. 14:25), whereas to P, the walls of water collapsed upon the Egyptians in an overwhelming flood (Ex. 14:28). The Quranic description reflects traditions nearer to P than J in this section.

Although we can simply consider the events at the Red Sea to have been a miracle, inexplicable in terms of natural phenomena, are there possible natural explanations? Josephus reminds his readers about a similar story concerning Alexander the Great: "While, for the sake of those that accompanied Alexander, king of Macedonia, who lived, comparatively but a little while ago,[1759] the Pamphylian Sea[1760] returned and afforded them a passage through itself, when they had no other way to go."[1761] Arrian also describes this episode: "Alexander now left Phaselis. Part of his forces he dispatched over the mountains towards Perga, along the tracks made for him by the Thracians to facilitate what was otherwise a long and difficult journey. He himself marched with his picked troops along the coast, a route that is practicable only in northerly winds—during southerlies the beach is impassable. It had been blowing hard from the south before he started; but (by the grace of God, as both he and his staff felt) the wind went round into the north and made the passage quick and easy."[1762] This is very similar to the Yahwist's explanation of what happened in Egypt for Moses. Is such a natural phenomenon possible in Egypt too?

Part of the problem is geographical. The sea referred to in the Bible is popularly thought to be the Red Sea, but in these passages the Hebrew text of the Bible speaks of the Sea of Reeds, not the Red Sea. The tradition that it was the Red Sea itself arose much later. Some Biblical passages that speak of the Sea of Reeds clearly mean the Red Sea, that its northeastern arm called the Gulf of Aqabah (Num. 14:25; 21:4; 1 K. 9:26) while other uses are considerably vaguer.[1763] It has been noted that reeds do not grow around the Red Sea, but they do in the lagoons by the Mediterranean such as Lake Manzalah.[1764]

Five place names are given in *Exodus* in the account of the flight of the Israelites from the city of Rameses (or Tanis, Ex. 13:20; 14:2,9): Succoth, Etham, Pi-hahiroth, Migdol, and Baal-zephon. All of these are

---

[1759] Josephus was writing c. 93-94 CE. Alexander the Great (356-323 BCE) lived some three and one-half centuries earlier.
[1760] The modern Gulf of Antalya, off southern Turkey.
[1761] Josephus, Antiquities, II.16.5, pp. 64-65.
[1762] Arrian, p. 94.
[1763] BC, I, 380.
[1764] Keller, p. 126.

from P. In Ex. 12:37 where he says simply that Israelites went from Rameses to Succoth, the Yahwist seems to imply a flight in a southerly direction. Of the five place names, only Succoth seems to have been identified with reasonable certainty as Tell el-Mashkāṭah some 10 miles west of Lake Timsah.[1765] Baal-zephon has been located at Tell Defneh,[1766] Migdol means "tower" and may simply refer to a watchtower that the Israelites passed by. In any case, its site is still unknown, as are the sites of Etham (perhaps in the Wādī Ṭumilāt) and Pi-hahiroth. [1767]

If the Priestly tradition of Baal-zephon be reliable, then the crossing of the "sea" probably occurred across the southern extension of Lake Manzalah, about 6 to 9 miles northwest of modern Al-Qantarah on the Suez Canal.[1768] This is the view of the editors of the *Oxford Bible Atlas*.[1769] With regard to Lake Manzalah, "it is related... by an eye witness that on one occasion the waters of Lake Manzalah at the entrance to the Suez Canal were driven back by the east wind as much as seven miles."[1770]

It is quite possible that some such occurrence, probably at Lake Manzalah, in which the Israelites were able to take advantage of a temporary land passage created by the unusual winds driving off the salt waters of the lake, lies behind the Biblical story. The cessation of those winds trapped their pursuers and their heavy chariots in the mud of the lake bottom and a returning sea. The Hebrews may also have had prior knowledge of the phenomenon, as they were resident near the lagoons of the eastern Delta. In support of this, we may mention the tradition recorded by Artapanus that Moses knew the area of the crossing well and waited to take advantage of the ebb tide.[1771] If so, then this escape would

---

[1765] Succoth, DB, pp. 941-942.

[1766] BC, I, 381.

[1767] Etham, DB, p. 270; Migdol, DB, p. 658; Pi-hahiroth, DB, p. 771.

[1768] The excavation of the Suez Canal in the 19th century has, of course, considerably altered the topography and hydrology of the region.

[1769] OBA, pp. 58-59.

[1770] Gaster, I, p. 240. The same source also mentions similar phenomena elsewhere: "In 1485, for example, and again in 1645, a strong wind drove back the waters of the Rhone into the Lake of Geneva for a distance of about a quarter of a league [nearly a mile]. 'It looked,' says the record, 'like a wall of water'—words strikingly reminiscent of those used in the Scriptural narrative (Ex. 14:22). 'The inhabitants would go down on dry ground between the bridges and pass from one bank to the other. So too in 1738 when the Russians were fighting the Turks, they were able to enter the Crimea at the Isthmus of Perekop only because a strong wind suddenly blew upon the waters of the Putrid Sea, a the northwest corner of the Sea of Azov, causing them to recede and permit passage."

[1771] Moses, EJ, XII, 391. Prof. Hans Goedicke has proposed that the miracle of the parting of the sea and the drowning of the Egyptian army occurred nearly two centuries earlier than the generally accepted date of c. 1290 BCE. The cause, he suggests in an article in

nonetheless have been interpreted as an act of God, and most of us would certainly have agreed with their assessment in such a dire situation.[1772]

H. IN THE WILDERNESS

...the land will surely be forbidden them for forty years that they will wander in the earth... (Q. 5:26)

With the departure of the Israelites from Egypt, the setting of the Biblical drama shifts back towards the southwestern end of the Fertile Crescent and the neighboring steppes and deserts, where it remains for the rest of the Old Testament's historical books.[1773] As we have remarked before, the narrative portions of *Exodus* and *Numbers* are frequently in great disorder, much more so than the stories in *Genesis*. The fact that the historical narratives of these books are interrupted by longer and shorter legal and ritual codes has had the effect of masking this disjointedness, enabling the casual reader to miss the inconsistencies, duplications, and patching.

What we now have in the Pentateuch is a view of Moses' life assembled some eight or nine centuries after the fact, during the final post-exilic redacting processes. It is a retrospective view of Moses, designed to provide Israel with a unifying ethos to carry it through the difficulties and attacks on the concept of Israel as God's chosen people that assailed the latter-day Jews (for they had become Jews, the northern non-Judahic tribes having disappeared from history) by the immensely more powerful nations and empires among whom they found themselves.

BAR, was a tidal wave generated by a catastrophic volcanic eruption of the Island of Thera in the Aegean Sea in 1477 BCE, during the reign of Pharaoh (Queen) Hatshepsut of the XVIIIth Dynasty. The wave swept across the marshes and wetlands of the northeastern Delta, destroying the Egyptians. This is not a technical impossibility, but it would have to be a very discriminating tidal wave to make a distinction between the pursuers and the pursued in such circumstances. This problem was solved by having the Israelites' swing south around the marshland thereby avoiding the impact of the tidal wave. However, no such wave is reported in Egyptian annals. That aside, the date does not fit in with other evidence. Writes Charles Krahmalkov at the end of his critique of the proposal: "We may never know what really happened, but we may be sure that it did not happen on a spring day in 1477 B.C. on or near the shores of Lake Manzaleh." (Hershel Shanks, *The Exodus and the Crossing of the Red Sea, According to Hans Goedicke*, BAR, Vol. VII, No. 5, Sept/Oct 1981, pp 42-50; Charles Richard Krahmalkov, *A Critique of Professor Goedicke's Exodus Theories*, BAR, Ibid., p. 54.)

[1772] One is reminded of the story of the natural, but providential, flight of sea birds hundreds of miles from the sea, which saved the Mormons in Utah in the 19th century.

[1773] Being romances and fantasies, we do not count *Esther* and *Daniel*, with their exotic locations, among the historical books.

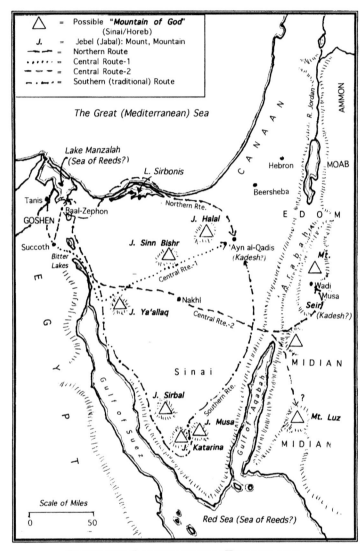

PROPOSED ROUTES OF THE EXODUS AND
SITES OF THE HOLY MOUNTAIN[1774]

[1774] Map based upon *Exodus*, EJ, VI, pp. 1043-1044; OBA, pp. 58-59; ABL, p. 7;
National Geographic Map of Bible Lands, Dec. 1956.

Scholars face enormous difficulties when trying to reconstruct the course of events in the crucial "wandering" between and Egypt and Canaan. They have had to exercise considerable ingenuity in their efforts to establish a chronology and an itinerary that reconciles all of the contradictions and inconsistencies of the patchwork text. It is no wonder, considering the confused state of the material with which they are working, that nothing approaching unanimity of opinion about the course of events has been achieved.

We have already mentioned that it is increasingly felt that only a part of what became the later twelve tribes of Israel were actually involved in the Exodus experience, perhaps just the Josephic tribes, Manasseh and Ephraim.[1775] Another reconstruction is that Moses was associated with the Judahites and Joshua with the Josephites, and that the Israelites left Egypt in at least two separate groups. The link between the Exodus and Sinai has also been questioned. There has been voluminous debate over virtually every aspect of the route from Egypt to Canaan and the exact nature of the Conquest of Canaan which followed, the very historicity of which is challenged by some authorities. It has been suggested that the forty years in the Wilderness was a period of settlement and residence, rather than aimless wandering, before a move was made towards Canaan, perhaps prompted by pressure from other tribes sharing the sparse resources of the region.

While these questions are extremely interesting—and in some respects fundamental—to the student of religious history, they are for the most part beyond the scope of this work. We shall touch upon them only as they concern the relationship between the stories in the Quran and Surabadi's Commentary on the one side and those in the Bible and other Judaeo-Christian traditional material on the other.

Having described how Moses led his mixed multitude of followers across a body of water in circumstances that could be considered miraculous, we must now look at the route to Canaan. Later editors resolved the contradictions and ambiguities by attributing the change of direction of Moses' caravan at Succoth to a stratagem to confuse the pursuing Egyptians.[1776] In general, the Yahwist seems to support a view of the crossing of the sea in the region of the Bitter Lakes, whereas the later view was that Lake Manzalah had been the scene of the crossing. It should be also kept in mind that the entire region of the Sinai and Lower Syria, including Canaan, the scene of the Exodus and the

---

[1775] Silver, p. ix.

[1776] The passage mentioning this (Ex. 14:1-2) is from P.

wanderings, was in fact still under Egyptian control, however loosely it may have been exercised. That there is no reference to encountering Egyptian troops or even emissaries is curious, perhaps the result of editing or, more likely, Egyptian indifference to tribal affairs in the eastern steppes and deserts unless they represented a threat to the homeland. This has the effect of minimizing the historical importance of the Exodus from the Egyptian point of view.

In any event, from this point in the narrative there is even more confusion and uncertainty, leading various scholars, in their efforts to reconstruct the route of the Israelites and fit the events of the Biblical narrative into it, to propose at least three different routes (see map). The most direct route (if Canaan was really the objective) would have been what was later called the Way of the Land of the Philistines along the Mediterranean coast; but *Exodus* specifically rules that route out (Ex. 13:17, quoted above). So, with what are we left?

The traditional reconstruction is the southerly one, via what is now Jabal Musa in the southern triangle of the peninsula formed by the Gulfs of Suez and Aqabah. However, this is dictated by the comparatively late location of Mount Sinai/Horeb there by 4th-century CE Christians. In addition to Jabal Musa, at least two other peaks in that region, Jabal Katerina and Jabal Serbal, have been proposed as the Holy Mountain.[1777] An eastward identification of Sinai/Horeb with Mount Seir, or even Jabal Halal, has also been proposed. This would also eliminate much of the raison d'être for the southerly route.

In the proposed northern route, Moses and his followers crossed at Lake Manzalah (or perhaps Lake Sirbonis) and then followed the Brook of Egypt inland to Kadesh-barnea. Mount Sinai would be Jabal Halal.[1778]

The central route has at least two variations, one of which leads southward from Goshen and follows the eastern shore of the Gulf of Suez for about 20 miles before turning inland towards Kadesh. Mount Sinai could be Jabal Sinn Bishr or Jabal Ya'allaq, in this view. The second central route follows the (Muslim) Pilgrims Road from Egypt to the Hejaz after crossing the Bitter Lakes and passing the vicinity of modern Aqabah. The Holy Mountain would be in Seir, and Kadesh somewhere in Edom (Wadi Musa?).[1779] The second central route would also have been the most likely for Moses to take when he fled to Midian after killing the Egyptian, and so has the added argument that he would

---

[1777] OBA, pp. 58-59; Exodus, EJ, VI, 1049-1410; Exodus, DB, p. 279.

[1778] Exodus, EJ, VI, 1049.

[1779] Exodus, EJ, VI, 1049; OBA, pp. 58-59. (We personally are inclined to this view.)

have been familiar with it. More than one of these proposed routes may have been used by the Israelites if, as many scholars feel the present account is really a composite of the experience of at least two separate groups leaving Egypt, perhaps at different times and under different leadership.

References to these events, especially after the crossing of the sea, are scattered and episodic in the Quran. It is difficult to construct a Quranic "history" of the wandering of the Israelites because the Quran is not interested in retelling history, except insofar as it illuminates the general condition of man. Since in the Quranic view, Truth has always been available to men through either revelation or intuition, the establishment of Israel is not seen as a necessary prototype for the universal community of all human social groupings that is Islam. Rather, it was simply one more step in the process of calling mankind to self-evident truth. The Israelites are more noteworthy for their stubborn backsliding and custodial lapses while producing great prophets.[1780]

In addition to the major historical and theological changes that occurred during the "forty years in the wilderness," there were other incidents and miracles as well, some of them alluded to in the Quran and the Quranic commentaries, such as that of Surabadi. He compares the Wilderness of Tih to a prison. The Israelites wandered there for 40 years, though it was a tract of land seven leagues in extent.[1781] A horseman riding from morning to night would find himself back at his own bedroll.[1782]

The forty years of wandering are referred to in the Quran, after several verses that are doubtless related to the sending of the spies into Canaan from Kadesh, and the disheartening report that they brought about the strength of its inhabitants (Num. 13:17-14:3). This led to considerable murmuring against the leadership of Moses (perhaps referred to in Surah al-Saff, Q. 61:5[1783]). As a result, according to P (the source for this), God decreed that none of those who left Egypt should live to see Canaan, and that they should remain in the wilderness forty

---

[1780] This is a theme repeated constantly by the later Israelite prophets as well, although their criticisms were grounded on the firm belief that Israel was God's Chosen People, and thereby differentiated from the rest of mankind.

[1781] About 21 miles.

[1782] Surabadi, pp. 56-57.

[1783] *And when Moses said unto his people: O my people! Why persecute ye me, when ye well know that I am God's messenger unto you? So when they went astray God sent their hearts astray. And God guideth not the evil-living folk.* (Q. 61:5)

years to implement this punishment (Num. 14:26-35).[1784] As we read in the Quran: *(God) said: "For this the land will surely be forbidden them for forty years that they will wander in the earth, bewildered. So grieve not over the sinful."* (Q. 5:26)

Surabadi also writes that the people cried for sustenance. In answer to Moses' prayer, manna and quail were sent to them. They needed water and Moses struck the rock with his staff and water burst forth from it. They needed clothing and whoever was born, was born with clothing that grew with him and served at death as his shroud. When they complained of the heat, a cloud was sent to give them shade. When they complained of the darkness, a pillar of light lit the night for them.[1785]

THE TWELVE SPRINGS: The Quran does not mention the miraculous clothing, nor the miraculous nighttime illumination. However, the other miracles are referred to: *And We caused the white cloud to overshadow you and sent down on you the manna and quails, (saying): "Eat of the good things wherewith We have provided you—We wronged them not, but they did wrong themselves... And when Moses asked for water for his people, We said: "Smite with thy staff the rock. And there gushed out therefrom twelve springs (so that) each tribe knew their drinking-place. Eat and drink of that which God has provided, and do not act corruptly, making mischief in the earth.* (Q. 2:57, 60) The cloud mentioned in the passage need not have shaded the Israelites throughout the entire period of their wanderings, but is probably a single incident when the burning sun was blocked at a particularly critical time by a thick layer of cloud. Such things happen naturally. Again, a miracle is often a question of timing. For the sufferer, any unexpected relief is miraculous.

Leading his thousands through a largely barren land, Moses encountered severe food and water shortages which, according to the Biblical account, were alleviated by means of divine assistance. There are several incidents of water problems. The first occurred three days after the rejoicing caused by the successful escape from Egypt: "When they came to Marah, they could not drink the water of Marah because it was bitter; therefore it was named Marah (*bitter*). And the people murmured against Moses, saying, 'What shall we drink?' And he cried to the Lord; and the Lord showed him a tree, and he threw it into the water, and the water became sweet." (Ex. 15:23-25a) Advocates of the southern

---

[1784] Since Joshua, for example, did enter Canaan, does this mean that he did not leave Egypt with Moses? Was he born during the Wandering?
[1785] Surabadi, p. 57.

route identify Marah with 'Ayn Hawarah.[1786] This miracle shares none of the features mentioned in the Quran about the provision of water.

"Then they came to Elim, where there were twelve springs of water and seventy palm trees; and they encamped there by the water." (Ex. 15:27) Although in this watering there is no miracle mentioned, it does possess the twelve springs mentioned in the Quranic verse. This has caused critics to charge another instance of Quranic confusion. More will be said about this below.

The Priestly account of the manna and quails (see below) intervenes between the watering at Elim (from J) and the E version of the water from the rock, is quoted here: "But the people thirsted there[1787] for water, and the people murmured against Moses, and said, 'Why didst thou bring us up out of Egypt, to kill us and our children and our cattle with thirst? So Moses cried unto the Lord, 'What shall I do with this people? They are almost ready to stone me!' And the Lord said to Moses, 'Pass on before the people, taking with thee some of the elders of Israel; and take in thy hand the rod with which thou didst strike the Nile, and go. Behold, I will stand before thee there on the rock at Horeb; and thou shalt strike the rock, and water shall come out of it, that the people may drink.'" (Ex. 17:3-6)

To this a Yahwist note is appended: "and he called the name of the place Massah and Meribah,[1788] because of the faultfinding of the children of Israel, and because they put thee Lord to proof by saying, 'Is the Lord among us or not?'" (Ex. 17:7) In this version, the site of the miracle seems to be associated with Horeb, the sacred mountain. It is perhaps pertinent to ask here, are we in Seir again?

There is still another account of water from the rock, a pericope paralleling the one just quoted. In this instance, the scene is Kadesh, and the figure of Aaron is introduced. Once again, the Israelites were complaining (did they never cease?), but this time against Moses *and* Aaron (Num. 20:2). "Then Moses and Aaron went from the presence of the assembly to the door of the Tent of Meeting, and fell upon their faces. And the glory of the Lord appeared to them, and the Lord said to Moses, 'Take the rod and assemble the congregation, thou and Aaron thy brother, and tell ye the rock before their eyes to yield its water; so thou shalt bring water out of the rock for them; so thou shalt give drink to the

---

[1786] Marah, DB, p. 618.
[1787] At a place called Rephidim (Ex. 17:8). This is traditionally located near Mount Sinai, but that is based upon the assumption that Sinai is the Mountain of God.
[1788] Massah means "proof" and Meribah "contention."

congregation and their cattle.' And Moses took the rod from before the Lord, as he commanded him." (Num. 20:6-9)

This and the following is a conflation of J and E. Note how Aaron is introduced and then omitted, a detail obscured in the RSV translation which eschews differentiating between the 2nd-person singular "thou/thee/thy" and the 2nd-person plural "ye/you/your." In part of the passage, Aaron and Moses are on their faces before God as equals, but then the source changes, and only Moses is to take the rod, a task that Aaron often performed in Egypt. We have discussed the reasons behind these intrusions of Aaron above.

"And Moses and Aaron [together again!] gathered the assembly together before the rock, and he [Moses? Aaron?] said to them, 'Hear now, ye rebels; shall we bring forth water for you out of this rock?' And Moses lifted up his hand struck the rock with his rod twice; and water came forth abundantly, and the congregation drank, and their cattle." (Num. 20:10-11)

By this act, Moses and Aaron in some manner provoked the wrath of God. Explanations by Bible commentators are admittedly educated guesses and vary considerably.[1789] *Numbers* continues: "And the Lord said to Moses and Aaron, 'Because ye did not believe in me, to sanctify me in the eyes of the people of Israel, therefore ye shall not bring this assembly into the land which I have given them.'" (Num. 20:12) This appears to be an alternative explanation, albeit obscure, for the forty years of wandering in the wilderness and the reason that neither Moses nor Aaron ever entered the Promised Land. The passage ends with a topographical note: "These are the waters of Meribah where the people of Israel contended with the Lord, and He showed Himself holy among them." (Num. 20:13)

In *Exodus* (Ex. 17:3-7), the waters are named Massah and Meribah, and in the *Numbers* pericope (Num. 20:2-13), they are called Meribah. It should be obvious that the two passages are about the same place, and most probably the same event. They are simply another example of duplicate accounts, the like of which we have encountered before. The repetition in *Numbers* would seem to be made to account for the Wandering and for God's refusal to allow either Moses or Aaron to enter the Promise Land. The Quran refers only to one such miracle, and

---

[1789] Among those offered in the *Broadman Bible Commentary* are: Did Moses' question "shall we bring forth water for you?" imply some doubt of God's power? Was Moses' striking the rock twice instead of once a display of anger? Was God's anger at the constant complaining of the Israelites directed at Moses as their leader? The text is silent as to the specific cause. (BC, I, 136.)

since it does not associate Aaron or the consequences stated in *Numbers* with it, we may say that it parallels the *Exodus* account; except for the mention of the twelve springs, which has given rise to another charge of confusion.

However, George Sale, not noted as an apologist for Islam, wrote: "Marracci thinks this circumstance [the twelve springs mentioned in the Quran] looks like a Rabbinical fiction, or else that Mohammed confounds the water of the rock at Horeb with the twelve wells at Elim [Ex. 15:27; Num. 33:9] for he says that several who have been on the spot affirm there are but three orifices whence the water issued.[1790] But it is to be presumed that Mohammed had better means of information in this respect than to fall into such a mistake; for the rock stands within the borders of Arabia, and some of his countrymen must needs have seen it, if he himself did not, as it is most probable that he did. In effect, he seems to be in the right. For one who went into those parts in the end of the fifteenth century[1791] tells us expressly that the water issued from twelve places of the rock. According to the number of the tribes of Israel... A late curious traveller observes that there are twenty-four holes in the stone, which may be easily counted—that is to say, twelve on the flat side, and as many on the opposite round side, every one being a foot deep and an inch wide; and he adds, that the holes on the side do not communicate with those on the other, which a less accurate spectator not perceiving (for they are placed horizontally, within two feet of the top of the rock) might conclude they pierce quite through the stone, and so reckon them to be but twelve."[1792]

Jewish tradition, too, speaks of streams (in the plural) gushing from the rock that Moses struck.[1793] In the old Jewish tradition of Miriam's Well, the well that accompanied the Israelites in their wanderings through the desert, there is mention of separate streams of water that went to different parts of the camp, itself arranged by tribes.[1794] This traveling well is even mentioned by Paul in the New Testament: "...and (the Israelites) all drank the same supernatural drink. For they

---

[1790] Sale inserts a reference here: "Marracc. Prodr. Part IV, p.80."

[1791] Sale's 15th-century authority here is Breydenbach. The following "late curious traveler" was Sicard.

[1792] Quran-Sale, pp. 9-10. Yusuf Ali also refers to this passage by Sale, and describes the rock thus: "huge mass of granite, twelve feet high and about fifty feet in circumference, where European travellers... saw abundant springs of water twelve in number." (Quran-Yusuf Ali, p. 32.)

[1793] LJ, III, 312.

[1794] LJ, III, 53.

drank from the supernatural Rock which followed them, and the Rock was Christ." (1 Cor. 10:4)

Remarkably, the miracle of the water from the rock may also have a natural explanation, and has been duplicated in the same region. Major C.S. Jarvis who was the British governor of the Sinai in the 1930's actually witnessed such an occurrence: "Several men of the Sinai Camel Corps had halted in a dry wadi and were in the process of digging about in the rough sand that had accumulated at the foot of a rockface. They were trying to get at the water that was trickling slowly out of the limestone rock. The men were taking their time about it and Bash Shawish, the colored sergeant, said: 'Here, give it to me! He took the spade of one of the men and began digging furiously... One of his violent blows hit the rock by mistake. The smooth hard crust which always forms on the weathered limestone split open and fell away. The soft stone underneath was thereby exposed and out its apertures shot a powerful stream of water...",[1795]

With all this evidence, we believe that the passage in the Quran reflects a strong local tradition of the caravaneers who trekked past such sites as these, which were already associated with Moses, either on the land route to Egypt across the Sinai, or the more frequented route from Makkah to Damascus. Tradition reports that the Prophet accompanied caravans to Syria. He could easily have become acquainted with the traditions of Moses and the twelve springs, as the caravan route to Syria passed close to Petra and other sites of the Wandering of the Israelites. Such stories brought back to Makkah had entered the corpus of oral tradition current there by the time of the Prophet.

MANNA: The providential feeding of the Israelites in the desert was considered a special sign of their favor in the eyes of God. In later times, this became an important proof supporting Israel's claim to be the "chosen people." And in Christianity, the manna given by God became a metaphor for Christ. "Jesus said to them, 'Verily, verily, I say unto you, it was not Moses who gave the bread from heaven, my Father gives you the true bread from heaven. For the bread of God is that which comes down from heaven, and gives life to the world.' They said to him, 'Lord, give us this bread always.' Jesus said to them, 'I am the bread of life; he who comes to me shall not hunger...'" (Jn. 6:32-35a)

Regardless of how the provision of manna was perceived in later times, during the wandering it became still another source of Israelite complaint and ingratitude. In *Exodus*, we find the Israelites murmuring

---

[1795] Quoted in Keller, p. 142.

against Moses and Aaron, after just having had their thirst miraculously assuaged, because they were now hungry: "the Lord said to Moses, 'Behold I will rain bread from heaven for you; and the people shall go out and gather a day's portion every day, that I may prove them, whether they walk in My law or not.'" (Ex. 16:4) Although there was no mention of the quails in God's speech, Moses and Aaron inform the grumbling people that in the evening they will be provided with flesh to eat and on the following morning bread.

"In the evening quails came up and covered the camp; and in the morning dew lay round about the camp. And when the dew had gone up, there was on the face of the wilderness a fine, flake-like thing, fine as hoarfrost on the ground. When the people of Israel saw it, they said to one another, 'What is it?' For they did not know what it was. And Moses said to them, 'It is the bread which the Lord has given you to eat...'" (Ex. 16:13-15)

The people were enjoined to gather as much of it as they could eat but not keep any until morning, as it would spoil during the night. However, (contradicting this injunction) on the sixth day, they were to gather twice as much, and the manna was not provided on Saturday, the day of rest.[1796]

"Now the house of Israel called its name manna; it was like coriander seed, white, and the taste of it was like wafers made with honey... And the people of Israel ate the manna forty years, till they came to a habitable land; they ate the manna till they came to the border of the land of Canaan..." (Ex. 16:31,35) The provision of the manna is also described (in another duplication) in *Numbers*: "Now the manna was like coriander seed, and its appearance like that of bdellium. The people went about and gathered it, and ground it in mills or beat it in mortars, and boiled it in pots, and made cakes of it; and the taste of it was like the taste of cakes baked with oil. When the dew fell upon the camp in the night, the manna fell with it." (Num. 11:7-9)

There has been considerable research into the question of the nature of the manna. It may have been an edible lichen or a sweet sap exuded in early summer by the *Tamarix gallica mannifera* (the tamarisk), which grows in Sinai and elsewhere. The sap would appear during the night but melt in sunlight. Insects may have played a role in its production.[1797] This identification seems quite reasonable. To the Israelites coming from Egypt who had never heard of it, its appearance

---

[1796] This last condition is from the Priestly Document, as always concerned with ritual, in this case the sanctity of the Sabbath.

[1797] BC, II, 115-116; Manna, DB, p. 617; Gaster, p. 242.

would have seemed quite miraculous; however, since Moses had already traveled and lived in this region, he probably knew of its existence. It still occurs today: "In a good year the Bedouins of Sinai can today collect four pounds each in a morning, a considerable quantity, which is quite sufficient to satisfy a grown man... the Bedouins knead the globules of manna into a puree which they consume as a welcome and nourishing addition to their often monotonous diet. Manna is indeed an exportable commodity, and if carefully preserved, it forms an ideal 'iron ration,' since it keeps indefinitely... Tamarisks with manna still grow in Sinai and along the Wadi al Arabah right up to the Dead Sea."[1798]

However the faultfinding Israelites tired of the diet of manna (the quails had only been provided once at that point) and complained wistfully: "'O that we had meat to eat! We remember the fish we ate in Egypt for nothing, the cucumbers, the melons, the leeks, the onions, the garlic; but now our strength is dried up, and there is nothing at all but this manna to look at.'" (Num. 11:4-6)[1799] Once again, God sent them quails in vast numbers, and as the Israelites ate flesh again, a killing plague swept the camp, as punishment (deserved, some might say) for their constant grumbling (Num. 11:31-35).

The presence of quail in the Sinai region is also a well-attested seasonal occurrence. The quail migrate from the south during the spring, following the Red Sea, on their way to their summer grounds in Europe. They usually alight in the northern Sinai and on the Mediterranean coast to rest before crossing the great expanse of the sea. Josephus also recognized the seasonal nature of the phenomenon: "Accordingly a little after came a vast number of quails, which is a bird more plentiful in the Arabian Gulf[1800] than anywhere else, flying over the sea, and hovered over them, till wearied with their laborious flight, and indeed, as usual, flying very near to the earth, they fell down upon the Hebrews, who caught them and satisfied their hunger with them, and supposed that this was the method whereby God meant to supply them with food. Upon which Moses returned thanks to God for affording them His assistance so suddenly, and sooner than He had promised them."[1801]

[1798] Keller, pp. 133. 135.

[1799] Cf. *And when ye said: "O Moses! We are weary of one kind of food; so call upon thy Lord for us that He bring forth for us that which the earth grows—of its herbs and its cucumbers and its corn and its lentils and its onions." (Q. 2:61)*

[1800] This mention of the Arabian Gulf in reference to the Red Sea, found also in medieval Arabic literature, supports the Iranian position that the Persian Gulf should be called just that, as the Arabian Gulf already exists in the form of the Red Sea.

[1801] Josephus, Antiquities, III.1.5, p. 66.

"Even today the Bedouins of this area catch the exhausted quails in spring and autumn by hand."[1802] Both the quail and the manna are associated with spring, the season during which the Israelites left Egypt. However, the mention of quail seems argues a northerly route for the Israelites across Sinai, as the quail alight near the Mediterranean in large numbers, but are not common in the southern Sinai.[1803]

Joshua states that after crossing the Jordan River, and entering Canaan, the Israelites camped at Gilgal a mile or two from Jericho. "And the manna ceased on the morrow, when they ate of the produce of the land; and the people of Israel had manna no more, but ate of the fruit of the land of Canaan that year." (Josh. 5:12)

Neither the Bible nor the Quran mentions the miraculous provision of clothing described by Surabadi. However, this does exist in Jewish tradition, which can be attested at least back to the time of Justin in the 2nd century CE: "During their forty years' march they had no need of change of raiment. The robe of purple with which the angels clothed each one among them at their exodus from Egypt remained ever new; and as a snail's shell grow with it, so did their garments, and though they wore the same things throughout the forty years, still they were not annoyed by vermin, yes, even the corpses of this generation were spared worms."[1804]

Such durable clothing is known in other mythologies as well. For example, in the *Epic of Gilgamesh*, when the hero has reached the Spring of Youth, Utnaphistim [the Mesopotamian Noah] says: "... he shall throw off his skins and let the sea carry them away, and the beauty of his body shall be shown, the fillet on his forehead shall be renewed, and he shall be given clothes to cover his nakedness. Till he reaches his own city and his journey is accomplished, these clothes will show no sign of age, they will wear like a new garment.'"[1805]

Paul also referred to the miracles of the wandering, although he gave them his own Christological interpretation: "I want you to know, brethren, that our fathers were all under the cloud, and all passed through the sea, and all were baptized into Moses in the cloud and in the sea, all ate the same supernatural food and all drank the same supernatural drink. For they drank from the supernatural Rock which followed them [the

---

[1802] Keller, p. 130.
[1803] Arden, *In the Steps of Moses*, National Geographic, Vol. 140, No. 1 (Jan. 1976), p. 21.
[1804] LJ, III, 237, from a medieval version of the tale (LJ, VI, 83.).
[1805] Gilgamesh, p. 112.

Well of Miriam], and the Rock was Christ. Nevertheless with most of them God was not pleased; for they were overthrown in the wilderness." (1 Cor. 10:1-5)

We have already quoted the verse from *Exodus* that described the Lord leading the Israelites in a pillar of cloud by day and a pillar of fire by night (Ex. 13:21-22). Even when God had taken up residence in the Tabernacle built for Him, we read: "For throughout all their journeys the cloud of the Lord was upon the tabernacle by day, and the fire was in it by night, in the sight of all the house of Israel." (Ex. 40:38)

There are numerous Jewish traditions concerning the cloud, mentioned also by the Quran, which protected them from the sun during the forty years in the wilderness. Because Abraham had bade the angels who visited him seek shade under a tree, God had spread a cloud over Israel in the wilderness.[1806] In the further elaboration of this tradition, the cloud had other properties as well. It shed sunlight by day and moonlight by night, so that Israel who were surrounded by clouds, might distinguish between night and day. It also served as armor; the missiles of their enemies could not penetrate it. The cloud disappeared at the death of Aaron although it later reappeared and remained until the death of Moses when it departed forever.[1807]

I. THE TABLES OF MOSES AND THE GOLDEN CALF

(Moses) threw down the tables... and broke them... (Ex. 32:19)

We read of the delivery of the tablets in Surah Al-A'raf: *And when We did deliver you from the people of Pharaoh who were afflicting you with dreadful torment, slaughtering your sons and sparing your women. That was a tremendous trial from your Lord. And when We did appoint for Moses thirty nights (of solitude), and added to them ten, and he completed the whole time appointed by his Lord of forty nights; and Moses said unto his brother: "Take my place among the people. Do right, and follow not the way of the corrupters. And when Moses came for Our appointed meeting and his Lord had spoken unto him, he said: "My Lord! Show (Thyself) to me that I may look upon Thee." He said: "Thou wilt not see Me, but look upon the mountain! If it stand still in its place, then thou wilt see Me."*

And when his Lord revealed (His) glory to the mountain, He sent it crashing down. And Moses fell down senseless. And when he woke, he

---

[1806] LJ, III, 43. In the *Exodus Rabbah*.
[1807] LJ, III, 49, 235.

said: "Glory unto Thee! I turn unto Thee repentant, and I am the first of the believers." Said He: "O Moses! I have preferred thee above mankind by My messages and by My speaking (unto thee). So hold that which I have given thee, and be among the thankful." And We wrote for him upon the tablets [the Arabic is plural, not dual] the lesson to be drawn from all things and the explanation of all things, then (said): "So hold it fast and command thy people: 'Take the better therein.' I shall show thee the abode of the sinful." (Q. 7:142-145)[1808]

In the Quran, this is followed by the incident of the worship of the Golden Calf by the Israelites in Moses' absence. Then: *And Moses chose of his people seventy men for Our appointed time and, when the trembling came on them, he said: "My Lord, if thou hadst willed Thou hadst destroyed them long before, and me with them. Wilt thou destroy us for that which the foolish among us did?"* (Q. 7:155) In the Biblical narrative, as we shall see, the order of events is different.

As the edition of Surabadi we are using as the basis of this study does not include the story of Moses' receiving the Law and the story of the worship of the Golden Calf by the Israelites, we use Bal'ami's version of these stories for our comparison with the Biblical version.[1809] Bal'ami expands the Quranic narrative considerably, both in detail and interpretation: In the beginning, an angel is introduced as the summoning agent who informs Moses that he is to go to Mount Sinai (*Ṭūr Sīnā*) and fast for thirty days so that his body will become like that of an angel; obedience will overcome his natural earthly passions.

In the Muslim commentators and historians, we see the same process of increasing the distance between God and man by means of the insertion of angelic mediators that we find in the later redactions of the Bible. In this instance, the relevant Quranic text shows God communicating directly with Moses, but Bal'ami makes an angel the actual bearer of the words of God. We have already noted several instances of this in the Bible, among them: Abraham and God before the events at Sodom; Hagar and God; Jacob's wrestling with God; and God's leading the Israelites before the pursuing Egyptians. In all of these stories, the original form, as the text still betrays, was of God dealing directly with man, but later redactors, regarding this as unseemly, interposed angels acting on God's behalf. In the present example from Quran, there is no mention of an angel in the Quranic text, but Bal'ami and his fellows have thought it proper to insert one.

[1808] Surah Baqarah also mentions the "forty nights" Moses spent in separation from his people (Q. 2:51).
[1809] Bal'ami, I, pp. 427-450.

Bal'ami's narrative is influenced by Christian and Jewish tradition in another way. He locates the Mountain of God in Sinai. As we have seen this is a relatively late Christian tradition, though now espoused uncritically by most Jews, Christians, and Muslims. Bal'ami's reference to Moses' body becoming like an angel's may be an echo of the Priestly ending of the events concerning Moses and the giving of the Law: "When Moses came down from Mount Sinai, with two tablets of the testimony in his hand as he came down from the mountain, Moses did not know that the skin of his face shone because he had been talking with God." (Ex. 34:29) [No angel here.]

"And when Aaron and all of the people of Israel saw Moses, behold, the skin of his face shone, and they were afraid to come near him... And when Moses had finished speaking with them, he put a veil on his face; but whenever Moses went in before the Lord to speak with Him, he took the veil off, until he came out... the people of Israel saw the face of Moses, that the skin of Moses' face shone; and Moses would put the veil upon his face again, until he went in to speak with him. (Ex. 34:30,33-34a, 35)[1810]

According to Bal'ami, Moses informed the Israelites that he would be absent on Mount Sinai for thirty days in order to receive the Law. He appointed Aaron to rule the people in his stead. The Israelites suggested to Moses that seventy righteous elders be selected to accompany him in order to be witnesses to the event. Moses agreed, but al-Samiri,[1811] upon hearing this request, realized how foolish the Israelites were. [He apparently interpreted their request as an indication of doubt.] Bal'ami notes that the interval between the destruction of the Egyptians in the sea on the 10th of Muharram and the call of Moses at the beginning of Dhul-Qa'dah was eleven months.[1812]

[1810] This rather confused and repetitious passage is quoted here partly as a good example of the awkwardness in combining divergent sources (vv. 29-33 are attributed to P, 34 and 35 to J), as well as for its content. The veil Moses used to conceal the peculiarity of his face recalls to mind Muqanna', the famous false prophet who disturbed the peace of Khorasan in the c. AH159/776CE and whose lively career fills several pages of the *History of Bukhara*. He was called Muqanna' "because he always veiled his head and face." According to the hostile historian, this was because he was so ugly, but perhaps he adopted this device as a conscious attempt to increase his remoteness, mystery, and majesty. (Bukhara, p. 90 ff.)

[1811] "al-Samiri" ("the Samaritan"): more about him, his name, and his identity below.

[1812] Bal'ami, I, p. 430. It would actually have been nine months, twenty days. Here Bal'ami is referring to the Pilgrimage season, which would make it a full eleven months. Such traditions would appear to be pious additions to increase the sanctity of important dates in the Islamic calendar by linking them with the ancient prophets, as we have seen Jewish tradition and exegesis link originally unrelated Biblical material.

According to the Biblical text (from P), the Israelites set out from Rameses on the 15th day of the first month (Num. 33:3), and crossed the sea a few days later. The events of this section commenced on the third new moon after that (Ex. 19:1), or after an interval of about two and one-half months. Since the Hebrew calendar was (and is) lunar with the addition of an intercalary month every several years to bring it more or less in line with the solar calendar, an exact modern equivalent cannot be given; however, the Exodus began approximately in April and the Giving of the Law occurred in June. (The provision of manna and quail also supports these dates.[1813])

It will be noticed that Bal'ami has already introduced the seventy elders before the worship of the golden calf. In the Quran, the seventy elders are mentioned after the golden calf, although considering the scattered nature of the allusions in the Quran, it cannot be asserted with certainty that a chronological sequence is intended. Indeed, Q. 7:154 seems to close the pericope of the Golden Calf, and Q. 7:155 with its mention of the seventy may commence a new parable. In any case, in the Bible: "the narratives attached to the delivery of the laws at Sinai are in an extraordinarily confused state,"[1814] and the relevant chapters (Ex. 19,24,32,33, and 34) are a patchwork of different layers of the Yahwists, (J1 & J2) the Elohist (E), the Priestly Writer or Writers (P), with Deuteronomist (D) additions.

These are broad outlines of the Biblical narrative after this process of conflation and reaction: The Israelites agreed to accept YHWH as their God and Moses went up the Holy Mountain where he was given the Ten Commandments and the Book of the Covenant, the book to be found in *Exodus*, chs. 20-23. Sacrifices were made and the seventy elders were permitted to see God. Then Moses went up the mountain by himself and stayed for forty days and forty nights while he received the instructions concerning the establishment of the ritual of worship and the design of the sanctuary. (These instructions, Ex. chs. 25-31, are by the much later P.)

Tiring and thinking that Moses would not return, the people persuaded Aaron to make a golden calf for them to worship. When Moses returned and saw this, he was angered by the spectacle and threw down the tablets upon which God had written, breaking them. He destroyed the calf and the Levites were enlisted to slaughter the apostates. Then Moses hewed two more tablets of stone and went back up the mountain where the revelation was (obligingly) renewed by God.

[1813] See previous Section.

[1814] Moses, DB, p. 675.

When Moses came down from the mountain, again after forty days and nights, he brought the tablets with him and his face shone, so that henceforth he had to veil it from the people in ordinary intercourse.

This is how the story now appears as given shape in the Bible several centuries before the Christian era. The work of separating out the original Yahwist and Elohist strands from each other and from the accretions and additions of ancient editing and revising is by no means finished in detail, and there is disagreement over the order of the text and its interpretation. However, it is useful to try to reconstruct the original Yahwist and Elohist accounts, remembering of course that these accounts themselves are composites of various traditions and do not have so simple a history as the terms *Yahwist* and *Elohist*—suggesting a single author for each—might imply.

THE YAHWIST'S ACCOUNT: According to the reconstructed Yahwist: "Then Moses told the words of the people to the Lord." (Ex. 19:9b) "And Mount Sinai was wrapped in smoke, because the Lord descended upon it in fire: and the smoke of it went up like the smoke of a kiln, and the whole mountain quaked greatly." (Ex. 19:18) "And the Lord came down upon Mount Sinai, to the top of the mountain; and the Lord called Moses to the top of the mountain, and Moses went up. And the Lord said to Moses, 'Go down and warn the people, lest they break through to the Lord to gaze and many of them perish. And also let the priests who come near to the Lord consecrate themselves lest the Lord break out upon them.'" (Ex. 19:20-22) "And the Lord said to him, 'Go down, and come up bringing Aaron with thee; but do not let the priests and the people break through to come up to the Lord, lest He break out against them.'" (Ex. 19:24) [Moses here relates what God has told him], then: "'... for on the third day the Lord will come down upon Mount Sinai in the sight of all the people. And thou shalt set bounds for the people round about, saying, "Take heed that ye do not go up into the Mountain or touch the border of it; whoever touches the mountain shall be put to death; no hand shall touch Him but he shall be stoned or shot; whether beast or man, he shall not live." When the trumpet sounds a long blast, they shall come up to the mountain." (Ex. 19:11b-13) "So Moses went down to the people and told them." (Ex. 19:25)

By noting the verse references, the reader may see how out of order the text of chapter 19 is. Dr. McNiele's reconstructed order is vv. 9-10, 18, 20-22, 11b-13, 25.[1815] Verse 23 (not quoted here) is a later

---

[1815] The reconstruction in this section is based on the analysis of Dr. A.H. McNiele in "Moses, DB, pp. 675-676.

addition caused by the displacement of vv. 11b-13. The volcanic character of the phenomena associated with the Mountain of God is obvious and cannot be easily explained in any other away. The Mountain of God is a sacred place,[1816] forbidden to ordinary people upon pain of death. Not even the priests can approach it. The Yahwist account, as preserved to us, continues:

"The Lord said to Moses, 'Cut two tables of stone... and I will write upon the tables... Be ready in the morning, and come up in the morning to Mount Sinai, and present thyself there to me on the top of the mountain. No man shall come up with thee, and let no man be seen throughout all the mountain; let no flocks or herds feed before that mountain.' So Moses cut two tables of stone... and he rose early in the morning and went up on Mount Sinai, as the Lord commanded him, and took in his hand two tables of stone. And the Lord descended in the cloud and stood with him there, and proclaimed the name of the Lord." (Ex. 34:1-5)

"And he was there with the Lord forty days and forty nights; he neither ate bread nor drank water." (Ex. 324:28a) [This is followed by a section of law from the Yahwist, incompletely preserved in Ex. 34:10-26.] Then: "And the Lord said to Moses, Write these words; in accordance with these words I have made a covenant with thee and with Israel." (Ex .34:27) "And he wrote upon the tables the words of the covenant, the ten commandments." (Ex. 34:28b)

The phrase "ten commandments," it can now be seen, does not refer to the famous ten prohibitions of Ex. 20:2-17 (which are from the Elohist history), but to the laws preserved by the Yahwist in Ex. 34:10-26. These commandments focus more on sacrifices and rituals and do not appear concerned with social and ethical matters. What we have quoted above is the Yahwist report of the theophany. This seems to be followed by the incident of the seventy elders referred to in Q. 7:155:

"And He said to Moses, 'Come up to the Lord, thou and Aaron, Nadab, and Abihu, and seventy of the elders of Israel, and worship afar off. Moses alone shall come near to the Lord; but the others shall not come near, and the people shall not come up with him.'" (Ex. 24:1-2) "Then Moses and Aaron, Nadab, and Abihu, and seventy of the elders of Israel went up, and they saw the God of Israel; and there was under His feet as it were a pavement of sapphire stone, like the very heaven for clearness. And He did not lay His hand on the chief men of the people of Israel; they beheld God, and ate and drank." (Ex. 24:9-11)

[1816] Similar to the precincts of the great mosques (*ḥarāmayn*) of Makkah and Madinah.

In addition to the anthropomorphic and primitive character of this meeting,[1817] we learn that God has Feet and His guests even celebrate a meal in His presence. An indication of the age of this material is the prominence given to the two elder sons of Aaron, Nadab and Abihu. Later on, we learn that they died without issue, and the third and fourth sons, Eleazar and Ithamar became the ancestors of the Jerusalem priesthood (Num. 3:2-4). A later text would have included at least the name of Eleazar in an event of such national and religious significance.

After this, something happened to arouse the anger of God. In the present edition of *Exodus*, the worship of the golden calf is the cause, but that is from E. We do not know whether J offered this reason or some other, but it seems to have been more in the nature of a civil rebellion judging by his account of the measures taken to quell it: "And when Moses saw that the people had broken loose (for Aaron had let them break loose, to their shame among their enemies), then Moses stood in the gate of the camp, and said, 'Who is on the Lord's side? Come to me.' And all the sons of Levi gathered themselves together to him. And he said to them, 'Thus says the Lord God of Israel, "Put every man his sword on his side, and go to and from gate to gate throughout the camp, and slay every man his brother, and every man his companion, and every man his neighbor."' And the sons of Levi did according to the word of Moses; and there fell of the people that day about three thousand men. And Moses said, 'Today ye have ordained yourselves for the service of the Lord, each one at the cost of his son and of his brother, that He may bestow a blessing upon you this day.'" (Ex. 32:25-29)

There seems to be an aetiological aspect to the above horrific account, an explanation of the status of the priestly tribe of Levites. Here they seem to have been a kind private militia for Moses.[1818] The brutal slaughter of their own relatives by the Levites has been interpreted as a trial to demonstrate that their loyalty to God was stronger than human ties of kinship. The only crime of the victims, according to the version we have here, was their kinship. It is surely one of the most disturbing incidents in the entire Bible.

"The Lord said to Moses, 'Depart, go up hence, thou and the people whom thou hast brought up out of the land of Egypt, to the land

---

[1817] One is reminded of Michelangelo's famous painting of God, the Creator of the Universe, in the form of a bearded man, an image itself based upon Greek and Roman depictions of their supreme god Zeus-Jupiter.

[1818] Gray disagrees with the ascription of this passage to the Yahwist: "The loose connection of the passage with its context suggests that it represents an independent tradition..." Certain features make him think that it is a Northern tradition and therefore E is a more probable source (writing in Laymon, p. 64).

of which I swore to Abraham, Isaac, and Jacob, saying, "To thy seed I will give it." And I will send an angel before thee, and I will drive out the Canaanites, the Amorites, the Hittites, the Perizzites, the Hivites, and the Jebusites. Go up to a land flowing with milk and honey; but I will not go up among thee, lest I consume thee, for thou art a stiff-necked people.' When the people heard these evil tidings, they mourned…" (Ex. 33:1-4a)

Evidence of the confused state of the text may be plainly seen in the odd reaction of the Israelites to God's promise to give them what later came to be called Palestine. The news is referred to as "evil-tidings"! Why? There does not seem to be a consensus about the answer to this question. In this passage, God appears to be saying that He will remain on His mountain and not move to the land of Canaan with His people; or perhaps, that He is rejecting them as the Chosen People, though He will keep His promise to give them Canaan. The preceding bloodshed does not seem to have assuaged God's anger and it persisted.

The last portion of the Yahwist's account of these events deals with the sight of God which He vouchsafed Moses and His acceptance of Moses' prayer that Israel be forgiven [for which offense?]: "Moses said to the Lord, 'See, Thou sayest to me, "Bring up this people"; but Thou hast not let me know whom Thou wilt sent with me. Yet Thou hast said, "I know thee by name, and thou hast also found favor in My sight." Now therefore, I pray Thee, if I have found favor in Thy sight, show me now Thy ways, that I may know Thee and find favor in Thy sight. Consider too that this nation is Thy people.' (Ex. 33:12-13)

"And the Lord said to Moses, 'This very thing that thou hast spoken I will do; for thou hast found favor in My sight, and I know thee by name.' Moses said, 'I pray Thee, show me Thy glory,' And He said, "I will make all My goodness pass before thee, and will proclaim before thee My name "The Lord" [YHWH]; and I will be gracious to whom I will be gracious, and will show mercy on whom I will show mercy. But, 'He said, 'Thou canst not see My face; for man shall not see Me and live.' And the Lord said, 'Behold, there is a place by Me where thou shalt stand upon the rock; and while My glory passes by I will put thee in a cleft of the rock, and I will cover thee with My hand until I have passed by. Then I will take away My hand, and thou shalt see My back; but My face shall not be seen.'" (Ex. 33:17-23)

"The Lord passed before him, and proclaimed, 'The Lord, the Lord, a God merciful and gracious, slow to anger, and abounding in steadfast love and faithfulness, keeping steadfast love for thousands, forgiving iniquity and transgression and sin, but Who will by no means clear the guilty, visiting the iniquity of the fathers upon the children and the children's children, to the third and fourth generation.' And Moses made haste to bow his head toward the earth and worshipped. And he said, 'If now I have found favor in Thy sight, O Lord, let the Lord, I pray thee, go in the midst of us, although it is a stiff-necked people; and pardon our iniquity and our sin, take us for Thy inheritance.'" (Ex. 34:6-9)

"And He said, 'My presence will go with thee, and I will give thee rest.' And he said to Him, 'If Thy presence will not go with me, do not carry us from here. For how shall it be known that I have found favor in Thy sight, I and Thy people? Is it not in Thy going with us, so that we are distinct, I and Thy people, from all other people that are upon the face of the earth?'" (Ex. 33:14-16)

This reconstruction of the original Yahwist account is, of course, not necessarily definitive or complete. Subsequent editing and conflation with other documents caused the loss of portions of the Yahwist's history, as for example the cause for God's anger now drawn from the Elohist. The extent of the losses and dislocations may be easily appreciated from the above version.

THE ELOHIST'S ACCOUNT: The Elohist's version is similarly disconnected, as its reconstruction shows: "And there Israel encamped before the mountain. And Moses went up to God." (Ex. 19:2b-3a) "And the Lord said to Moses, 'Lo, I am coming to thee in a thick cloud, that the people may hear when I speak to thee, and may also believe thee for ever.'" (Ex. 19:9a) "And the Lord said to Moses, 'Go to the people and consecrate them today and tomorrow, and let them wash garments, and be ready by the third day...'"(Ex. 19:10-11a)

"So Moses went down from the mountain to the people and consecrated the people; and they washed their garments. And he said to the people, 'Be ready by the third day; do not go near a woman.' On the morning of the third day there were thunders and lightnings, and a thick cloud upon the mountain, and a very loud trumpet blast, so that all the people who were in the camp trembled. Then Moses brought the people out of the camp to meet God; and they took their stand at the foot of the mountain. And as the sound of the trumpet grew louder and louder, Moses spoke, and God answered him in thunder." (Ex. 19:14-17,19) Note the resemblance of the restrictions and preparations to some of those Muslims observe for the Pilgrimage to Makkah. Both sets of rules probably reflect general ancient Semitic practice when visiting important shrines and holy places and are not to be thought of as consecratory innovations in either case.

"Now when all the people perceived the thunderings and the lightnings and the sound of the trumpet and the mountains smoking, the people were afraid and trembled; and they stood afar off, and said to Moses, 'Speak thou to us, and we will hear; but let not God speak to us, lest we die.' And Moses said to the people, 'Fear not; for God has come to prove you, and that the fear of Him may be before your eyes, that you may not sin.' And the people stood afar off while Moses drew near to the thick darkness where God was." (Ex: 20:18-21)

"Moses came and told the people all the words of the Lord and all the ordinances; and all the people answered with one voice, and said, 'All the words which the Lord has spoken we will do.' And Moses wrote all the words of their Lord. And he rose early in the morning, and built an altar at the foot of the mountain, and twelve pillars, according to the twelve tribes of Israel. And he sent young men of the people of Israel, who offered burnt offerings and sacrificed peace offerings of oxen to the Lord. And Moses took half of the blood and put it in basins, and half of the blood he threw against the altar. Then he took the book of the covenant, and read it in the hearing of the people; and they said, 'All that the Lord has spoken we will do, and we will be obedient.' And Moses took the blood and threw it upon the people, and said, 'Behold the blood of the covenant which the Lord has made with you in accordance with all these words.'" (Ex. 24:3-8) This use of blood has no parallel in Muslim rituals.

Later on, we learn something more about the ritual life of the camp and the immediacy of God: "Now Moses used to take the tent and pitch it outside the camp, far from the camp; and he called it the Tent of Meeting. And every one who sought the Lord would go out to the Tent of the Meeting, which was outside the camp. Whenever Moses went out to the tent, all the people rose up, and every man stood at his tent door, and looked after Moses, until he had gone into the tent. When Moses entered the tent, the pillar of cloud would descend and stand at the door of the tent, and the Lord would speak with Moses. And when all the people saw the pillar of cloud standing at the door of the tent, all the people would rise and worship, every man at his tent door. Thus the Lord used to speak to Moses fate to face, as a man speaks to his friend. When Moses turned again into the camp, his servant Joshua the son of Nun, a young man, did not depart from the tent." (Ex. 33:7-11)

After reading these accounts, one realizes that multitudes of hundreds of thousands are simply not involved. One is left with the impression of a camp of at most a few thousand. The picture of God is more remote than that of J, and the phenomena associated with Him are more atmospheric than geological.

THE DECALOGUE: It is at this point that a later Elohist redactor inserted the familiar Ten Commandments (as they are now called) of Northern provenance, now found in Ex. 20:1-17. These were followed by verses now found in the previous chapter: "So Moses came and called the elders of the people, and set before them all these words which the Lord commanded him. And all the people answered together and said, 'All that the Lord has spoken we will do.' And Moses reported the words of the people to the Lord." (Ex. 19:7-8)

"The Lord said to Moses, 'Come up to me on the mountain, and wait there; and I will give thee the tables of stone, with the law and the commandment, which I have written for their instruction.' So Moses rose with his servant Joshua, and Moses went up into the Mountain of God. And he said to the elders, 'Tarry here for us, until we come to you again; and, behold, Aaron and Hur are with you; whoever has a cause, let him go to them.' Then Moses went up on the mountain, and the cloud covered the mountain." (Ex. 24:12-15) "And He gave to Moses... the two tables of stone, written with the finger of God." (Ex. 31:18)

Thus begins the Elohist's account of the gift of the tables of the Law to Moses. As in Bal'ami, Moses appointed Aaron (here with Hur[1819]) to act in his absence, although he does not specify how long he will be gone.

E's account then continues with the story of the Golden Calf that will be discussed below. We need only point out here that the breaking of the tables in the course of that story is a later editorial device in order to harmonize the inclusion of *two* accounts of the giving of the tables, since without the destruction of one set, we would have been left with two sets of tables. If we separate the two strains, we can better compare the two versions.

The Yahwist does not mention Aaron as Moses' representative, whilst E has Moses nominate him to act in his absence (as does Bal'ami). J mentions that Moses stayed forty days upon the mountain, as do the Quran and Bal'ami, but the portions of the text of E that have survived leave us only the notice that he was delayed a long time. In the J version, at one place Moses is to prepare the stones and God is to write upon them, at another God tells Moses to write the words He dictates to him

---

[1819] Hur is an attendant bearing still another probably Egyptian name who, with Aaron, held up Moses' hands in the battle with the Amalekites so that Israel might prevail. (Hur, DB, p. 407.)

upon them (Ex. 34:27). In E, they are apparently already prepared on the sacred mountain.

Both accounts associate unusual natural phenomena with the sacred mountain, and emphasize the necessity of approaching it with caution. The concept of God in both versions, though monotheistic in a general sense, is primitive and anthropomorphic, J the more so. He tells us of the seventy elders who are permitted to see God, and also of the permission granted Moses to look upon God, while in E, we see God coming to the tent of the meeting in the form of a pillar of cloud visible to all, where He converses with Moses "face to face." E mentions Joshua (destined to lead the Hebrews into Canaan), while J does not. E gives us the classical form of the Ten Commandments (the Decalogue), while those laws called the Ten Commandments by the Yahwist are largely different. Finally, the Elohist also tells of the apostasy of the Golden calf, about which the Yahwist is silent.

In the present edition of *Exodus*, with its duplicate grantings of the Law to Moses in the form of stone tables, neither version associates those tables with the famous Ten Commandments![1820] In their present position, the first set seems to follow the Elohist *Book of the Covenant* (Ex. 20:21-23:33), or more probably the elaborate instructions from P about the construction of the Tabernacle and the ritual of service to be established therein (Ex. 24-31:17). It is after that passage that the tables are given to Moses (Ex. 31:18), only to be broken in the following chapter (Ex. 32:19). The second set of tables are granted after the notice of the J's commandments in Ex. 34:27-28, and they are *not* the famous ten.

The term "ten commandments" is connected to the second (J's) version in the text of *Exodus*. It is only in the Deuteronomist's preface to the older *Book of the Law* which forms the core of the present *Deuteronomy*,[1821] that we find an unequivocal linking of the Decalogue to

---

[1820] The Ten Commandments are: 1. Thou shalt have no other gods before Me; 2. Thou shalt not make unto thee an idol; thou shalt not bow down to them or worship them; 3. Thou shalt not take the name of the Lord thy God in vain; 4. Remember the Sabbath day, to keep it holy; 5. Honor thy father and thy mother; 6. Thou shalt not kill; 7. Thou shalt not commit adultery; 8. Thou shalt not steal; 9. Thou shalt not bear false witness against thy neighbor; 10. Thou shalt not covet the neighbor's house, thou shalt not covet thy neighbor's wife, nor his maidservant, nor his ox, nor his ass, nor any thing that is thy neighbor's. (From Ex. 20: 3-17) Of course, it is not as simple as that. The version we have given here is roughly the Judaic version. Various Christian denominations split and count them differently, though always ending up with ten. (See the chart in Robert Youngblood's article, *Counting the Ten Commandments*, BR, Vol. X, No. 6, Dec. 1994, pp. 34-35.)
[1821] See Introduction.

the Tables Moses received from God: "And ye came near and stood at the foot of the mountain, while the mountain burned with fire to the heart of heaven, wrapped in darkness, cloud, and gloom. Then the Lord spoke to you out of the midst of the fire; ye heard the sound of words, but saw no form; there was only a voice. And He declared to you His covenant, which he commanded you to perform, that is, the ten commandments; and he wrote them upon tables of stone." (Deut. 4:11-13) After repeating the commandments of Exodus 20 in Deut. 5:6-21 (taken from E), D continues: "These words the Lord spoke to all your assembly at the mountain out of the midst of the fire, the cloud, and the thick darkness with a loud voice; and He added no more. And He wrote them upon two tables of stone and gave them to me." (Deut. 5:22) That is what the later Israelites made of the confused accounts contained in *Exodus*.

THE SEVENTY ELDERS: Returning to the question of the difference in the order of the events of this section between the Bible and the Quran, we have seen that in the present edition of *Exodus*, the visit of the seventy elders to the mountain of God stands *before* the granting of the tables, but in the reconstruction of the Yahwist account, this episode *follows* that incident as it does in the Quran (if its position there is an indication of sequence; it may not be). In the Quran, it also follows the apostasy of Israel and the worship of the Golden Calf, but as this story is from the Elohist, its relationship to the incident of the seventy elders, if any, cannot be easily ascertained now.

The seventy elders[1822] seem to have been a group whose existence can be attested before and after the affair of the theophany. Moses spoke to the elders (their number unspecified here) when he returned to Egypt in order to secure their assent to his plan to lead the Israelites out of bondage (Ex. 3:16, 18, from J). The elders are mentioned again in connection with the instructions concerning the Passover and the last plague (Ex. 12:21, from JE). At the miracle of the turning of the bitter water to sweet on the march out of Egypt, God specifically told Moses to involve the elders (Ex. 17:5, from E). They participated in the sacrificial meal of Jethro (Ex. 18:12, from E), and may have been given judicial powers (Ex. 18:25-26, from E) upon Jethro's advice. They

---

[1822] The seventy elders should not be confused with the seventy scholars who translated the Hebrew Bible into Greek c. 2nd century BCE (the *Septuagint*), and indicated in our text by Roman numeral LXX.

accepted the Covenant on behalf of the people (Ex. 19:7-8, from D).[1823] In none of the foregoing is their number specified.

In the theophany, which seems to have included a ritual meal, their number is specified as seventy (Ex. 24:1-2, 9-11, from J). If this be the incident to which the Quran refers, the atmosphere is quite different. The Biblical text give us no hint of the reaction felt by the elders when they actually saw God, while this is the main point of the Quranic reference: the awe and fear inspired by the apperception of the presence of God. The Quranic text seems to speak of a fear of divine retribution upon the elders for some crime that Israel had committed. Since it follows the Quranic story of the Golden Calf in Q. 7, it is usually assumed that this is intention of the verses. However, this is by no means certain, as we have pointed out before, and penance had already been done for that sin. There were already plenty of causes to be found in the ample catalog of complaint and lack of faith in divine providence displayed by the Israelites on their march from Egypt to provoke the divine wrath against Israel before the incident of the Golden Calf.

The seventy elders reappear in *Numbers*, when they are again summoned by God to be consecrated to share in the responsibility of governing the Israelites (Num. 11:16-17, 24-25, from JE). This was done in the midst of grumbling by the Israelites because of the food. The miracle of the quails was repeated, but followed immediately by a retaliatory plague. Although our text of *Numbers* does not mention it, this would have been an appropriate time for the elders to disassociate themselves from the behavior of the people, as mentioned in the Quran.

Jewish tradition further involves the seventy elders in the story of the Wandering. They officiated at the sacrifice mentioned by the Elohist (see above) because the (Levite) priesthood had not yet been established.[1824] They tried to prevent Moses from breaking the first set of tablets, but were unsuccessful because he was physically stronger than all of them put together.[1825] Some traditions say that the original seventy elders were destroyed by celestial fire at Taberah (Num. 11:1-4) and had to be replaced for the consecration mentioned above (in Num. 11:16-17, 24-25).[1826] The celestial fire was still another divine punishment inflicted upon the Israelites for their ingratitude.

[1823] As J indicates the Yahwist, E the Elohist, JE the conflated Yahwist and Elohist sources, and P the Priestly Document, so D indicates the Deuteronomist.

[1824] LJ, III, 88.

[1825] LJ, III, 129.

[1826] LJ, III, 248.

In sum, we see there are already ample circumstances for the elders to suffer for the iniquities of the Israelites in the extant text. Others may have been omitted. The Quranic passage need not be bound to the story of the Golden Calf for want of other provocations.

ANOTHER THEOPHANY: *And when his Lord revealed (His) glory to the mountain He sent it crashing down.* (Q. 7:143) The vision of God granted to Moses in answer to his request to see Him differs in the Biblical and Islamic traditions. In the Bible, Moses is covered by the hand of God and he sees His back, for seeing His face would have caused Moses' destruction (see above). This primitive scene in which God appears to be a physical being—a much enlarged man, albeit supernatural, not unlike the pagan gods of Mesopotamia or Greece— becomes in the Quran a demonstration of the *effect* of God, that is, a demonstration of His power: the pulverization of a mountain, an act incidentally suggestive of a violent volcanic eruption, if a natural explanation be required.

In Bal'ami, this is somewhat expanded: Moses was told to look at the mountain. If the mountain could withstand the power of the immanence of God, then Moses would be able to see Him. But when the power of God was displayed, the mountain disintegrated and Moses swooned without seeing actually Him. Bal'ami adds that the mountain flew into six parts, three of which landed in Hejaz and three in Madinah.[1827]

Jewish tradition records a contest among various mountains for the honor of being the site of the granting of the Torah.[1828] Early sources tell us that Mount Sinai was originally part of Mount Moriah (supposed to be the present Haram and the site of the Temple of Solomon in Jerusalem), but had separated itself at the time of the sacrifice of Isaac. In the future, it will return to its original home.[1829] Another tradition asserts that God's words "break mountains into pieces."[1830]

Bal'ami also tells us that when Moses was on the mountain praying, a white cloud would envelop him.[1831] The seventy elders were to

---

[1827] Is this an echo of a local Arab tradition that sacred mount, the Mountain of God, was located in Arabia, that is, Midian, or the northwestern Hejaz?

[1828] LJ, III, 82-85.

[1829] LJ, III, 84; VI, 32.

[1830] LJ, II, 333; V, 425.

[1831] This detail is absent from the Quranic account, but is found in the Bible: "Then Moses went upon the mountain, and the cloud covered the mountain. The glory of the Lord settled on Mount Sinai, and the cloud covered it six days; and on the seventh day He called to Moses out of the midst of the cloud. Now the appearance of the glory of the

have been witnesses to these events, but even they could be grumblers. For after Moses recovered from his swoon at the manifestation of the power of God, and he had taken up the Tables of the Law, the cloud left him and he became visible again to the seventy. They complained (!) that they had been sent to bear witness to the speech between God and Moses, but had heard nothing. Moses asked God to let them hear Him speak, so God agreed and sent the cloud to cover all of them and spoke again with Moses so that they might hear. The seventy were so struck with terror that they died of fright. Moses prayed for them. God forgave them for their doubt, and they were revived. Then Moses picked up the Tables and descended the mountain with them.[1832]

Part of this can also be traced to a Biblical source. After the Deuteronomic version of the Ten Commandments, Moses is made to say: "'And He wrote them upon two tables of stone, and gave them to me. And when ye heard the voice out of the midst of the darkness, while the mountain was burning with fire, ye came near to me, all the heads of your tribes, and your elders; and ye said, "Behold, the Lord our God has shown us His glory and greatness, and we have heard His voice out of the midst of the fire; and we have this day seen God speak with man and man still live."'" (Deut. 5:22b-24)[1833]

Paralleling another episode in Bal'ami's story, the Talmudic tractate *Sanhedrin* tells us that the seventy elders died upon hearing the divine voice (in the thunder), but that the Law itself made intercession for them and they were restored to life.[1834] It is interesting to note that in Bal'ami, the reason for the fear of punishment felt by the seventy is their own doubt and it is not connected with the Golden Calf. Bal'ami also cites traditions about the tables: they were made of gold and seven in number, or of ruby and emerald.

This ignores the Biblical traditions, that they were two and made of stone, but we caution the reader that the Quran always uses the *plural* (three or more) when referring to the tables, not the *dual* (two). There is a

---

Lord was like a devouring fire on the top of the mountain in the sight of the people of Israel. And Moses entered the cloud, and went up on the mountain." (Ex. 24:15-18a, from P.) As in Bal'ami, this incident refers to the receiving of the Tables of the Law and the revelation of the Torah to Moses. Notice once again the volcanic character of the phenomena associated with the mountain. Could the fumes from the bowels of the earth have played some part in Moses' visions, as they did with the Oracle of Delphi? Or, was the observed phenomenon a forest fire, caused by man or lightning?

[1832] Bal'ami, pp. 433-435, 39-40.

[1833] See also from Ex. 24:1-2, 9-11 quoted above.

[1834] Cited in Tisdall, p. 114.

Jewish tradition that the Tables were made of sapphire,[1835] but, after all, a sapphire is also a stone. There are many more Jewish traditions about these events, but they do not add much to our discussion of the relationship of the Islamic versions to those of the Bible.

THE GOLDEN CALF: We turn now to the story of the worship of the Golden Calf. The principal Biblical source for this is *Exodus*, and it is usually attributed to the Northern Elohist, There are, as we shall see, substantial differences between the E and the Quranic accounts. In its present position in the Bible, it comes between the two versions of the theophany and the promulgation of the Law. In its original context, it followed the Elohist account of the theophany, as it does in the Quran, where it follows the *single* granting of the Law to Moses. The story opens with Moses still on the mountain:

"When the people saw that Moses delayed to come down from the mountain, the people gathered themselves together to Aaron, and said to him, 'Up, make us gods, who shall go before us; and as for this Moses, the man who brought us out of Egypt, we do not know what has become of him.'" (Ex. 32:1) This request is referred to in the Quran: *And We caused the Children of Israel to cross the sea. Then they came upon a people who had given themselves up to their idols. (The Israelites) said: O Moses, make for us a god as they have a gods. He said: Verily, ye are a people who are ignorant!* (Q. 7:138) [This situation strongly suggests that the Israelites were accustomed to worshipping idols and had not preserved the purity of the monotheistic traditions imputed to their ancestors. In other words, they were latent idolators. Moses had come to convert them (back?) to the worship of one God, promising them freedom from bondage, if they followed him.[1836] That bondage, apparently, was not so onerous that they did not wish to return to it in Egypt on a number of occasions before settling in Canaan.]

"And Aaron said to them, 'Take off the rings of gold which are in the ears of your wives, your sons, and your daughters, and bring them to me.'" (Ex. 32:2). "So all the people took off the rings of gold which were in their ears, and brought them to Aaron. And he received the gold at their hand, and fashioned it with a graving tool, and made a molten calf; and they said, 'These are thy gods, O Israel, who brought thee out of the land of Egypt!' When Aaron saw this, he built an altar before it; and Aaron made a proclamation and said, 'Tomorrow shall be a feast to the Lord.' And they rose up early on the morrow, and offered burnt

---

[1835] LJ, III, 119; VI, 40.

[1836] Or, one might say: "bribing them with freedom from bondage."

offerings and brought peace offerings; and the people sat down to eat and drink, and rose up to play." (Ex. 32:3-6) Was Aaron in fact an Egyptian or a Canaanite priest? Here he does not hesitate to shrug off YHWH and lead the people in their older, idolatrous forms of worship. Not only that, the ancestor of the priesthood of YHWH actually sculpted their idol for them.

Although the story of the worship of the calf is alluded to in several places in the Quran, it is related at length in only two places. In Surah al-A'raf we read: *And the people of Moses, after (he had left them), chose a calf (made) out of their ornaments, an (empty) body which gave forth a lowing sound. Did they not see that it spoke not to them, nor did it guide them in the way?* [Creating sounds from idols and causing them to appear to speak was a well-known art in ancient Egypt. Bull worship was common in many societies of the ancient world, including Egyptian.] *They chose it and became oppressors (of themselves). And when they feared the consequences thereof and saw that they had gone astray, they said: "Unless our Lord have mercy upon us and forgive us, truly we are of the lost!"* (Q. 7:148-149)

In this place, no mention is made of al-Samiri or of Aaron. The text seems to indicate that after the calf had been made, the people realized their error, before the return of Moses in the next verse (Q. 7:150). Maulana Muhammad Ali points out that "the order here is not historical, but one connecting the repentance with the sin, mentioning the events which brought about that repentance afterwards."[1837] It would be reasonable to attribute this repentance to the efforts of Aaron who, though Moses castigates him for poor stewardship of the people in his absence, is specifically exonerated of the charge of having made the idol (Q. 20:92-93), as the Biblical text would have it. Another difference here is the Quran states that the calf lowed; this detail is not mentioned in *Exodus*, but see below.

In Surah Ta Ha (*Tā Hā*), the story of the Golden Calf is referred to at greater length. It is here that we find the figure of al-Samiri (*al-Sāmirī*): Moses was away from his people, in communication with God. [This would correspond to his receiving the Tables of the Law in the Elohist history discussed above.] God informed Moses that his people had gone astray in his absence. *"What is it that has caused thee to hasten from thy people, O Moses?" He said: "They are close upon my track. I hastened unto Thee that Thou mightest be well pleased."* [If this be taken to mean that Moses had rushed ahead of the people who were following

---

[1837] Quran-MMA, p. 349.

him, then it differs from the Biblical version in which the people are waiting below while Moses goes up the Holy Mountain to receive the Law. However, in Surah al-A'raf, Moses has just been described as receiving the Law. In Surah Ta Ha, too, Moses returns to his people, which would imply that they were encamped rather than in motion. Therefore, the verse is best read to mean that Moses was under the impression that they were following him, whilst in fact, they had apostatized.] *(God) said: "Lo. We have tried the people in thine absence, and al-Samiri*[1838] *has misled them."* (Q. 20:83-85)

Bal'ami substantially repeats the Quranic story, although he adds that the Israelites were worshipping by the waterside, probably because, later on, the ash of the Golden Calf is thrown into the water, which Bal'ami and other commentators have taken to mean the sea. Considering the disagreement over the actual site of these events, it is not clear which body of water is meant. Most of the proposed sites for this story are situated inland at some distance from any large bodies of water such as the Red Sea, or its arms, or even the Dead Sea. More probably, a large stream or pool is meant, since the Israelites were camped by a large spring. Bal'ami also adds that God told Moses that al-Samiri had made the calf and caused it to low. Moses demurred and said that, if the calf lowed, it was by the permission of God, not the work of al-Samiri, and was therefore a test of the people. God agreed with this interpretation and said that al-Samiri had led the people in error.[1839]

The parallel passage in the Bible states: "and the Lord said to Moses, 'Go down, for thy people, whom thou didst bring up out of the land of Egypt have corrupted themselves; they have turned aside quickly out of the way which I commanded them; they have made for themselves a molten calf, and have worshipped it and sacrificed to it, and said, 'These are thy gods, O Israel, who brought thee up out of the land of Egypt!'''" (Ex. 32:7-8) Note the singular here; Israel is being addressed as a unit. The tone of these verses is similar to that of the Quranic passage quoted above; however, the omission of a reference to Aaron, while not conclusive evidence that Aaron is a later addition to the Biblical text (Ex. 32:1-6, quoted above), is nonetheless striking.

In this passage, the people have made the golden calf, whilst in the former it was Aaron; another contradiction. About this, the Quran states that the instigator was al-Samiri. This assertion has two sides to it; on the one hand, it can be taken to exonerate the prophet Aaron of such a blasphemy and on the other, it names the culprit as "al-Samiri." This

---

[1838] See below for the discussion of al-Samiri.
[1839] Bal'ami, pp. 432-433.

would appear to represent a strong tradition about al-Samiri and the worship of the golden calf current in the Hejaz during the time of the Prophet; otherwise, there would not have been any need to introduce this figure into the text. More will be said about this below.

Bal'ami's version of these events is, as might be expected, much fuller, although in some places he differs slightly from the course of the story in the Quran. After thirty days had passed, he relates, the Israelites worriedly approached Aaron. (Thus Bal'ami seems to explain the thirty days plus ten mentioned in the Quran, Q. 7:142.) Al-Samiri seized the opportunity to say that he knew why Moses had not returned; it was because of the unclean gold and silver that the Israelites had seized as plunder from the vanquished Egyptians. He said that Moses had separated himself and the righteous elders[1840] from the rest of the people so that they would not share in the imminent vengeance of God. Al-Samiri suggested that a well be dug into which the offending wealth would be buried. When Moses returned, he could decide what should be done with it. If Moses said that it was lawful, then they could dig it up again; if not, then it could be destroyed by fire.

The Israelites agreed to this proposal and Aaron had the well dug. The plunder was thrown in and the well filled up. Now, al-Samiri had recognized the angel Gabriel when he had come to summon Moses to the Mountain of God, because he himself had been brought up by Gabriel. He had picked up a handful of dust from the spot where Gabriel had stood (or some say where his horse had stood) and preserved it.

When thirty days passed and Moses had not returned, al-Samiri told the people that Moses would never return until the gold and silver were burned. He told them to dig it up so that it could be destroyed by fire. Instead of destroying it, Samiri fashioned from it the calf and threw the dust which he had picked from where Gabriel had stood upon the idol, and the calf lowed. Bal'ami mentions that some add that the calf continued to low and graze like a real living animal, whilst others say that it remained metal and only lowed once. Al-Samiri told them that this was their god. Moses had gone looking for God, while he was here all the time! At al-Samiri's command, the Israelites prostrated themselves before the calf.

Aaron tried to call the people away from the idol worship to the worship of the true God, but the Israelites said that they would persist until Moses returned, and they threatened to kill Aaron if he did not

---

[1840] Bal'ami seems to put the incident of the seventy elders here, perhaps under the influence of the received form of the story in the Bible, where this incident precedes the revelation of the Decalogue. See above.

remain silent. They also accused Aaron of sending Moses away so that he could seize the prophethood for himself. Aaron wanted to separate himself and the 12,000 steadfast Israelites from the idol worshippers, but he was afraid that Moses, upon his return, would accuse him of dispersing his people.[1841]

In the defense the Israelites made for their behavior to Moses when he returned, much of the above has Quranic support. They said: *"We broke not our appointment with thee of our own will, but we were laden with burdens of the people's ornaments, then cast them (in the fire), for thus al-Samiri proposed." Then he produced for them a calf, a mere body that gave forth a lowing sound. And they cried: "This is your god, and the god of Moses, whom he has forgotten." What? Did they not see that thing returned no speech unto them and possessed naught by which to hurt or benefit (them)? And Aaron indeed had told them before hand: "O my people! Ye are but being seduced by it, for truly your Lord is the Merciful, so follow and obey my order." They said: "We shall not cease to be its votaries until Moses returns to us."* (Q. 20:87-91)

And when Moses demanded an explanation from al-Samiri for his behavior, the latter replied: *"I perceived what they perceived not, so I seized a handful from the footsteps of the messenger, and then threw it in. Thus my self commended me.* (Q. 20:96) While the tradition repeated by Bal'ami—that the footsteps were those of Gabriel or his steed—is widely circulated, Maulana Muhammad Ali rejects it, stating instead that they were those of Moses himself. Yusuf Ali mentions both versions.[1842]

Thus we see that the Quran contradicts the Biblical (Elohist) statement that Aaron was directly involved in the making of the idol; indeed, he tried to dissuade the Israelites from doing so, although he seems to have taken no action other than to warn them. Yet, in another place, there is an allusion that presupposes an intervening misunderstanding between Moses and Aaron: *And when Moses returned unto his people, angry and grieved* [because he had learned of their lapse into idolatry], *he said: "Evil is that which ye took after I had left you. Would ye hasten on the judgment of your Lord?" And he cast down the tablets, and he seized his brother* [Aaron] *by the head, dragging him toward him. (Aaron) said: "Son of my mother! Lo, the people did judge me weak and almost killed me. Oh, make not mine enemies to triumph over me and place me not among the oppressors!"* (Q. 7:150)

The literature of Jewish traditions about the golden calf is quite extensive. The Egyptian gold and silver were too highly regarded to be

---

[1841] Bal'ami, pp. 430-433.
[1842] Quran-MMA, p. 620; Quran-Yusuf Ali, p. 810.

considered unclean in the mainstream of Jewish tradition, as Bal'ami would have it. Even though the explicit Biblical statements about Aaron's role in the making of the calf served to constrain the apologists, nonetheless, excuses were found for Aaron's behavior—after all, he was an ancestor of the priestly caste. Indeed, several others were declared the actual fabricators of the calf. One version, based on earlier sources, is given in the *Pirke de Rabbi Eliezer*: "When Israel received the commandments they forgot their God after forty days, and they said to Aaron: The Egyptians were carrying their god, and they were singing and uttering hymns before it, and they saw it before them. Make unto us a god like the gods of the Egyptians, and let us see it before us…" [The ancient Egyptians religious processions and liturgy must have been spectacular indeed. Even today, their depictions on the walls of tombs and temples astonish the traveler who visits Egypt.]

"They betook themselves to the one who carried out the words of Moses, to Aaron his brother, and Hur, the son of his sister… But since Hur was of the tribe of Judah, and one of the magnates of the generation, he began to reprove Israel with harsh words, and the plunderers who were in Israel arose against him, and slew him.

"Aaron arose and saw that Hur, the son of his sister, was slain; and he built for them an altar… Aaron argued with himself, saying: If I say to Israel, Give ye to me gold and silver, they will bring it immediately; but behold, I will say to them, Give ye to me the earrings of your wives, and of your sons, and forthwith the matter will fail… The women heard this, but they were unwilling to give their earrings to their husbands, but they said to them: Ye desire to make a graven image and a molten image without any power in it …" [This tradition makes Aaron's evident cooperation a stratagem to defeat their purpose.]

"The men saw that the women would not consent to give their earrings to their husbands. What did they do? Until that hour, the earrings were also in their own ears, after the fashion of the Egyptians, and after the fashion of the Arabs. They broke off their earrings which were in their ears, and they gave them to Aaron… Aaron found among the earrings one plate of gold upon which the Holy Name was written, and engraven thereon was the figure of a calf, and that plate alone did he cast into the fiery furnace… The calf came out lowing, and the Israelites saw it, and they went astray after it."

[This is a reference to Aaron's self-defense in *Exodus*: "'And I said to them, "Let any who have gold take it off"; so they gave it to me, and I threw it into the fire, and there came out this calf.'" (Ex. 32:24) as though he were surprised by it.]

"Rabbi Jehudah said: Sammael [the devil][1843] entered into it, and he was lowing to mislead Israel, as it is said, 'The ox knows its owner.'"[1844]

Bal'ami's tradition of the calf's behaving like a living animal is also found in older Jewish tradition: "The Egyptian magicians made the calf move about as if it were alive."[1845] The later Jews frequently put the blame for making the golden calf and its worship on the Egyptians who were in the "mixed multitude," although the Biblical text does not support this. The Egyptian magicians referred to are probably Jannes and Jambres. These brothers are not mentioned in the Old Testament, but in Jewish tradition, they are the sons of Balaam who took refuge in Egypt and became magicians at Pharaoh's court, and were involved in the contest with Moses.[1846] They were present when Pharaoh's army was drowned in the crossing of the sea, and they made themselves wings and tried to fly away to escape.[1847] However, in one version, the angel Michael caught them and dashed them against the rocks in the sea, killing them;[1848] in other versions, they survived this event and accompanied the Israelites out of Egypt as part of the mixed multitude, where they became the instigators of the making of the Golden Calf.[1849]

Bal'ami's tradition that al-Samiri had been raised by Gabriel may be related to the Jewish tradition, mentioned in the 2nd-century CE *Zadokite Fragment*, that Belial (the tempting spirit) had raised Johannan (Jannes) and his brother.[1850] Much has been written, by Muslim and Western scholars, about the exact significance of al-Samiri's picking up a handful of dust from the messenger's footprints and casting it into the calf. Among other things, Bal'ami's statement suggests that the calf was hollow, and al-Samiri cast something into it which made it ring, accounting for the "lowing." However, the tradition of the commentators, that al-Samiri saw the angel who had come to summon Moses and had picked up some earth from his footprints, may in some way be related to a Jewish tradition attested in the 11th-century CE *Lekah* (which does not seem to have been commented upon in this connection), that the Israelites had noticed the feet of angels were like those of calves and thus were inspired to make the image of the calf.

[1843] See below.
[1844] PRE, pp. 352-355; also LJ, III, 121-122; VI, 51.
[1845] From the 6th-century CE *Song of Songs Rabbah*, quoted in LJ, VI, 52.
[1846] LJ, II, 283, 287, 334.
[1847] Like Daedalus and Icarus in Greek mythology.
[1848] LJ, III, 28-29.
[1849] LJ, III, 120.
[1850] LJ, VI, 293.

In a medieval Jewish commentary, this tradition is given in a different version: The Israelites had noticed the imprints of the angels (who had come to fight the Egyptians at the Exodus) left in the sand of the shore of the sea were like those of calves; therefore they adopted the form of a calf as their idol.[1851] Although these references are several centuries later than the Quran, they may represent an older tradition connected with the Quranic allusion. In the *Psalms,* a verse can be read to mean that the Golden Calf was actually alive:

> "They made a calf in Horeb and worshipped a molten image.
> "They exchanged the glory of God
> > for the image of an ox that eats grass."
> >   (Ps. 106:19-20)

If the phrase "that eats grass" be taken to modify *image* rather than *ox,* it would suggest that that is what the idol did. The poet probably did not mean that; but some such interpretation could later have given rise to the tradition found in both Jewish and Islamic written and oral literature.

Another Jewish tradition names still another man as the actual fabricator of the calf: Micah. Although in the Bible, he lived during the period of the Judges, after the Conquest and before the Monarchy, in the Midrashim, Micah was also alive at the time of Moses. In these traditions, Micah was the son of Delilah[1852] and would have been used as building material had not Moses rescued him. (According to a Jewish tradition, Israelite children were used as building material by the Egyptians.[1853]) However, he was not worthy of this honor and he made idols, including the Golden Calf. Later, during the time of David and Solomon, he reformed and became a pious man; therefore, he would have lived some three hundred years.[1854] He is counted among the Minor Prophets and is the reputed author of the Biblical book *Micah.* Here, however, we are concerned with Micah in his idolatrous period.

[1851] LJ, VI, 52.

[1852] The Delilah who betrayed Samson. See Part Four, I. These traditions are full of anachronisms.

[1853] This gruesome accusation against the Egyptians may have been inspired by the very real infanticide that was practiced in Canaan (or transferred to them). Infant remains have been found in the foundations of structures, apparently placed there as sacrifices to the gods. As we have already noted, there is no record of ritual human sacrifice in Egypt in the historical era, although there is recent evidence that it may have occurred in the shadowy First Dynasty (c. 3000 BCE). (Galvin, pp. 106-121.)

[1854] LJ, IV, 49-53.

MICAH'S GOLDEN CALF: Let us digress here and consider the story of Micah, as it is found in the Bible, for the light it will shed on the question of how the accusation of Aaron's participation in the incident of the golden calf found its way into scripture. Micah's story is told in *Judges*, chs. 17 and 18. These chapters do not seem to have been part of the original Deuteronomic recension of *Judges*, but were added a century or so later, probably by P.[1855] They represent traditions of the Danites, one of the twelve tribes, in their present form, turned into attacks against the supposed practices of the Danite shrine at Dan at the northern end of Palestine, near the foot of Mount Hermon, and indeed upon its right to exist. This was accomplished by giving the shrine—a potential rival to Jerusalem's Temple—a scurrilous origin. Clearly, the chapters were included by editors whose interests were identified with the primacy of the Jerusalem sanctuary. They tried to diminish its rivals, and at the same time advance the interests of the centralizing monarchical (Davidic) party, by implying that under the strong hand of a king (the story takes place during the period of the Judges, before the establishment of the monarchy) such a scandalous shrine could not have come into existence.

According to the foundation story in *Judges*, Micah was an Ephraimite (therefore a descendant of Joseph) who stole 1,100 pieces of silver from his mother. Frightened by his mother's curse, he returned the money to his mother who said: "'I consecrate the silver to the Lord from my hand for my son, to make a graven image and a molten image; now therefore, I will restore it to you.'" So his mother took 200 pieces of silver and had the images made and placed in Micah's house. Micah installed one of his sons (being a Ephraimite, he was therefore a non-Levite) as the priest of this idol. Thus, we see in this hostile story that the idol had its origin in theft and was ministered to blasphemously by a non-priest (Jgs. 17:1-6).[1856]

Then a young Levite happened to stop at the house of Micah, and Micah hired him to be priest (Jgs. 17:7-13). A little later, the Danites, who had had difficulty in claiming their original inheritance in lands inhabited by the Philistines (the region southeast of modern Jaffa), sent five scouts to find another homeland for themselves. On the way, they made the acquaintance of the young Levite priest (Jgs. 18:1-6). The scouts went on and decided to recommend the region of Laish to the Danites for their new home.[1857] When the war party of 600 Danites set out to attack Laish, they passed by way of Micah's house, and the five

---

[1855] BC, II, 451; Laymon, p. 136.
[1856] Under later Jewish law, only Levites could be priests.
[1857] Laish, in northern Palestine, was renamed Dan by the Danites.

scouts told their brethren of the shrine and its furniture there. They decided to loot it and take the furniture to establish a new shrine at Laish after they had captured it:

"And they turned aside thither, and came to the house of the young Levite, at the home of Micah, and asked him of his welfare. Now six hundred men of the Danites, armed with their weapons of war, stood by the entrance of the gate; and five men who had gone to spy out the land went up, and entered and took the graven image, the ephod, the teraphim and the molten image, while the priest stood by the entrance of the gate with the six hundred men armed with weapons of war. And when these went into Micah's house and took the graven image, the ephod, the teraphim, and the molten image,[1858] the priest said to them, 'What are ye doing?' And they said to him, 'Keep quiet, put thy hand upon thy mouth, and come with us, and be to us a father and a priest. Is it better for thee to be priest to the house of one man, or to be priest to a tribe and family in Israel?' And the priest's heart was glad; he took the ephod, and teraphim, and the graven image, and went in the midst of the people." (Jgs. 18:15-20)

When Micah saw what they had done, he pursued them, crying for the Danites to return his idols and his priest, but the Danites, who were much more powerful, threatened to kill him, so he desisted (Jgs. 18:21-26). After capturing Laish and massacring the inhabitants, the Danites renamed the place Dan and established the sanctuary. "And the Danites set up the graven image for themselves; and Jonathan the son of Gershom, son of Moses, and his sons were priests to the tribe of the Danites until the day of the captivity of the land." (Jgs. 18:30)

Now, whatever the foundation story of the shrine was, this travesty cannot have been it. "Its origin was, you could say, just about as unlawful as possible... It is a false sanctuary served by a false priest— which is exactly the impression the redactor wanted to produce by telling this story. His plea is that the first sanctuary of Dan was worthless, and was a fitting predecessor of the sanctuary into which Jeroboam I [the first king of the Northern kingdom of Israel, rgd. 931-910 BCE] brought the second golden calf."[1859]

The fact that the priesthood at Dan claimed Mosaic descent (through Gershom) did not make them immune from the attacks of the Jerusalem (Aaronite-Levite) priesthood. The story itself seems to have been inspired by the secession of the ten Northern tribes after the break up of Solomon's Empire under his incompetent son Rehoboam and

---

[1858] See Glossary.
[1859] de Vaux, II, pp. 307-308.

Jeroboam's attempt to upgrade two sanctuaries (Dan and Bethel) within his own kingdom (Israel). As part of this effort: "So the king took counsel, and made two calves of gold. And he said to the people, 'Ye have gone up to Jerusalem long enough. Behold thy gods, O Israel, who brought you up out of the land of Egypt.'[1860] And he set one in Bethel, and the other he put in Dan. And this thing became a sin, for the people went to the one at Bethel and the other one at Dan. He also made houses on high places, and appointed priests from among all the people, who were not Levites." (1 K. 12:28-31)

Now, we know that the Danite priesthood claimed Mosaic origin. Does *1 Kings* then preserve a tradition that Moses himself was *not* a Levite, contradicting the statement of Ex. 2:1? Quite possibly. We have seen how Jewish tradition linked the story of Micah's idol with the incident of the Golden Calf at Horeb. Scholars have suggested that the link between the two stories is genuine, and the original inclusion of the story in *Exodus* has more than a little to do with the rivalry between Jeroboam's sanctuaries and the Jerusalem Temple establishment in the sister kingdom of Judah.

In order to understand the symbolism of these incidents, it is important to realize that both the priesthood and especially the prophets of Israel regarded the establishment of YHWH-worship in Canaan under constant threat from the earlier, but still covertly popular, local Baal-worship. Jeroboam's bulls were probably meant to be the pedestals upon which the presence of the invisible YHWH was supported, but the bulls themselves were not idols to be worshipped. This motif of a god supported by an animal is a common one in ancient Near Eastern art. Though the parallel of the worship of the sacred bull Apis in Egypt is an attractive one, neither the incident of the golden calf nor Jeroboam's bulls seem to be related to it. Rather, the symbolism is drawn from Semitic religion. The bull was the symbol of the Canaanite gods Baal and El, in their capacity as gods of fertility, as the Ras Shamra finds have shown us.

During the process of the establishment of YHWH-worship, YHWH was frequently given the attributes and titles of the gods He displaced. Equating YHWH with El, YHWH-worship probably was influenced by the bull-symbol of El. Therefore, when the Israelites worshipped the golden calf, they probably thought of the calf as the symbol of El-YHWH. The incorporation of this calf as an object of

---

[1860] This is a deliberate reference to Ex. 32:4, using the same language in order to equate Jeroboam's calves with Israel's lapse into idolatry in the Wandering. That the king would have made such a statement is almost certainly a Southern fabrication.

worship created a strong reaction among those Israelites who were believers in the invisible YHWH, because it compromised the purity of their concept of Him. Hence, the anger of Moses, and the shock and horror of the writer of the passage in *1 Kings* quoted above.

When Jeroboam set up the images of calves in his shrines, it is not clear whether he meant them to be thrones or symbols of YHWH.[1861] However, in addition to the threat to the supremacy of the Jerusalem Temple, many saw the danger of the associations with the earlier Canaanite gods and the idolatrous practices linked to their worship that still lingered on in the land.[1862]

Against this background, Jewish tradition made a bridge between the bulls of Jeroboam and the Golden Calf of the Israelites at Horeb. Even without that, the quotation from the story in *Exodus* inserted into the account of Jeroboam's making of the calves in *1 Kings* shows that such a parallel was implicit, though perhaps spurious.

Just as we have seen that scurrilous foundation story was invented by the enemies of the Danite shrine, whatever their motivation, the inclusion of Aaron in the story of the Golden Calf in *Exodus* can probably be attributed to some similar hostility directed by the redactor towards the Aaronites. This appears to reflect the period after the exile, when the Zadokite priesthood of the Temple was trying to reestablish its primacy in Judah and engaged in a propaganda war against the local Aaronites who resisted their claims.[1863] By the time the compromise had been achieved in which the Zadokites became Aaronites and the Aaronites Levites, the additions to the text of the Elohist account of the apostasy of Israel at Horeb had already acquired the sanctity of the surrounding material and later scribes did not dare to excise them.

It is also possible that Aaron's role in this story may be attributed to some other hostility directed at the Aaronites from some other phase of Israel's religious history. Our reconstruction of that history is incomplete, but the method of the *ad hominem* attack, by impugning the character of a supposed ancestor of an institution or social group, has many parallels in the Bible, such as the origin of the Danite shrine discussed above, also the origins of the Moabites, the Hamites in *Genesis*, etc. The gratuitous nature of such vicious attacks is often self-

---

[1861] It may be going to far to say, with Kapelrud, that Jeroboam had identified YHWH with Baal-Hadad whose symbol was the bull. However, it would certainly have suggested such an identification (or the approval of it) to many of the more syncretizing Northerners. (Kapelrud, p. 76.)

[1862] Calf, DB, p. 119; Kapelrud, pp. 37-38, 57, 76; de Vaux, II, pp. 333-335.

[1863] See above in Section E.

evident. Therefore, we need feel no reservations about commending the story of Aaron's actually making the calf to the same category of maliciously inspired fabrications.[1864] The rejection by the Quran of the story of Aaron's apostasy is perfectly sound in the light of the directions of modern research. More will be said about this below when we discuss the problem of the identity of al-Samiri.

As we have seen, the Jewish defense that Aaron felt threatened by the Israelites, while itself not exactly redeeming, is also reflected in Bal'ami. In the Quran, Aaron's fear is not for himself but for the division of the people: *(Moses) said (upon returning from the Mountain of God): "O Aaron! What held thee back when thou didst see them gone astray, that thou didst not follow me? Hast thou then disobeyed my order?" (Aaron) said: "O son of my mother! Clutch not my beard nor my head! I feared lest thou shouldst say: 'Thou hast caused division among the Children of Israel, and has not waited for my word.'"* (Q. 20:92-94)

This summarizes Aaron's role (in the Quranic view) in the incident: that he preached against the worship of the calf, but took no further steps, fearing the disintegration of the Israelite community. He recognized his own limitations, and knew that a greater man of action than he, that is Moses, would have to remedy the situation, so he played for time. He is guilty, perhaps, of timidity, but not—in the Quranic view—of the apostasy portrayed in the Bible.

[1864] The argument often put forth supporting the authenticity of this tradition on the grounds that no one would have dared to invent such a tale about one of his ancestors can be discounted for several reasons. One is the conservative nature of the transmission of the texts. Once a story had found its way into writing, however secular, it acquired the sanctity of age and was to some extent, in the Pentateuch, protected by the later assertion of Mosaic authorship, whilst additions were still made both deliberately and accidentally by a copyist's incorporating notes and glosses into a text, outright suppression—an audacious move—was less frequent.

The original motivation for recording many of these stories, some of them quite damaging, was forgotten (as the difficulties faced by modern scholars trying to reconstruct these events show) and later generations were perplexed and disturbed by them, but—having retained them—were often quite ingenious in devising explanations that more or less obviated the plain unpleasantness of the pericope. Too, since authenticity of lineage and descent were more important to the post-Exilic Jews than the moral characters of their progenitors, such stories were probably not so disturbing to them as they are to the modern readers who care little for the veneration of remote ancestors but a great deal about the moral reputations of their religious teachers. In proof of this attitude, in addition to the story of Aaron's apostasy, we can cite many others: the deceitful behavior of Abraham, Isaac, and especially Jacob; Noah's drunkenness; Samson's violations of his Nazirite vows (Part Four, I), and unfavorable stories about Reuben, Levi, and Judah, David and Bathsheba, etc.

Bal'ami's report of 12,000 steadfast Israelites, as well as giving support to a potential civil war among the ranks of the Israelites, seems to be an "enhanced" reference to the Levites mentioned above (Ex. 32:25-29) who massacred 3,000 of the apostates, thereby proving their own loyalty to YHWH. The connection of the passage to the worship of the Golden Calf is somewhat obscure (some scholars deny any connection), but in its present context, this blood bath was precipitated by the crisis of the Golden Calf. Jewish tradition comes down firmly in support of this view.[1865] Yet, in the Bible (Ex. 32:1-8, 15-24, 35), there is no hint of popular opposition to the worship. The Quran can be read to imply that the repentance by the apostates had already begun before the return of Moses: *And when they feared the consequences thereof and saw that they had gone astray, they said: "Unless our Lord have mercy upon us and forgive us, truly we are of the lost!"* (Q. 7:149)

After being informed by God about the apostasy of his people: "...Moses turned, and went down from the mountain with the two tables of the testimony in his hands, tables that were written on both sides; on the one side and on the other side were they written. And the tables were the work of God, and the writing was the writing of God, graven upon the tables. When Joshua[1866] heard the noise of the people as they shouted, he said to Moses, 'there is a noise of war in the camp.' But he said, 'It is not the sound of shouting for victory, or the sound of the cry of defeat, but the sound of singing that I hear.' And as soon as he came near the camp and saw the calf and the dancing, Moses' anger burned hot, and he threw the tables out of his hands and broke them at the foot of the mountain. And he took the calf which they had made, and burnt it with fire, and ground it to powder, and scattered it upon the water, and made the people of Israel drink it." (Ex. 32:15-20)

"And Moses said to Aaron, 'What did this people do to thee that thou hast brought a great sin upon them? And Aaron said, 'Let not the anger of my Lord burn hot; thou knowest the people, that they are set on evil. For they said to me, "Make us gods, who shall go before us; as for Moses, the man who brought us up out of the land of Egypt, we do not know what has become of him." And I said to them, "let any who have

---

[1865] LJ, III, 94, 130, 170, 211, 404.

[1866] According to the Elohist, Joshua alone had accompanied Moses up the mountain when the latter went to receive the Tables of the Law (Ex. 24:13, see above in text). This is interpreted to mean that the elders accompanied Joshua and Moses part of the way and were told to wait until the pair returned.

gold take it off"; so they gave it to me, and I threw it into the fire, and there came out this calf.'" (Ex. 32:21-24)

In the original version, the story was probably completed by: "And the Lord sent a plague upon the people, because they made the calf which Aaron made." (Ex. 32:35) This is plainly a syntactically awkward sentence, and it suggests the heavy-handed effort of a later redactor who added the phrase "which Aaron made" to complete his work of indicting the Aaronites. In the original version, the plague was probably the punishment, but as the chapter is now constituted, the massacre by the Levites inserted between vv. 24 and 35 appears to be the punishment of the people for their lapse into idol worship.

Paralleling this, in the Quran we read: *And when Moses returned unto his people, angry and grieved, he said: "Evil is that (course) which ye took after I had left you. Would ye hasten on the judgment of your Lord? And he cast down the tablets, and he seized his brother by the head, pulling him toward him. (Aaron) said: "Son of my mother! Lo, the people did judge me weak and almost killed me. Oh, make not mine enemies to triumph over me and place me not among the oppressors!" (Moses) said: "My Lord! Have mercy on me and on my brother; bring us into Thy mercy, Thou the Most Merciful of all who show mercy."* (Q. 7:150-151) Surah Ta Ha (Q. 20:92-94) quoted above has a slightly different exchange on the same theme. Aaron's warning to the people while Moses was away (Q. 20:90-91) has also been quoted above.

The differences between the Biblical and Quranic accounts once again are about the role of Aaron and the nature of his response to the people's demand to make the idol. In the Bible, he is the instigator, whilst in the Quran he is reproved for not taking strong enough action to stamp out the idolatry, in the other words, a lack of leadership. He is the object of Moses' wrath in both accounts.

In the Bible, Moses' simple reproof for the enormity of Aaron's own lapse into idolatry thereby encouraging that of the people seems strikingly inadequate. In one version of the punishment, 3,000 were slaughtered, and in another, the people were struck down by a plague. However, strangely, Aaron who, in the Biblical account as it stands at present, was the author of the idolatry and himself the manufacturer of the calf—acts which ought to have made him of all people the most culpable and subject to the righteous anger of both Moses and God— escapes scot-free after his plea not to be humiliated before the people!

What sort of justice is that? That Aaron could have directed and participated in the apostasy and afterwards not only be forgiven and unpunished for this blasphemy, but also be credited with the founding of the line of Temple priests, as related in *Exodus*, is incomprehensible. There would seem to be a grave imbalance in the scales of divine justice in this case, if we accept the veracity of the Biblical story. Fortunately, with a little understanding of the how scripture was utilized by one faction against another as a tool of propaganda during the formative period of the text (before it came to be regarded as Holy Writ), we do not have to do so.

With regard to the fate of the tables, the Quran does not support *Exodus* where it states they were broken, though it mentions that Moses cast them down (Q. 7:150). They were picked up by him unbroken (see below). The Biblical words in: "and (he) broke them at the foot of the mountain" (Ex. 32:19) are probably the addition of the redactor who was conflating the J and E accounts and making their duplicated theophany two separate granting of the tables. In order to do this, the redactor was forced to dispose of one set, and he did this by having Moses not only dash the tables down on the ground, but also break them as well. The considerable blasphemy attendant upon this action — remember that it was emphasized the God himself had inscribed these tables with His Own Hand (Ex. 32:16) — did not seem to disturb the redactor.

Since, we believe, the Quran correctly speaks of only one granting of the Tables of the Law, after he had set them down in exasperation at the behavior of the people whom he was trying to enlighten, we read: *And then when the anger of Moses abated, he took up the tablets, and in their inscription there was guidance and mercy for all those who fear their Lord.* (Q. 7:154) Before the conflation of J and E, the Elohist version probably only spoke of Moses' setting down of the tables. However, later Muslim commentators, once again misled by the weight of Jewish opinion on the subject (and without the benefit of the higher criticism) also mention the breaking of the tables,[1867] even though the Quran itself does not.

There are other minor differences. In the Bible, Moses grinds up the calf and throws the dust into the water and makes the Israelites drink of it. In the Quran, the fate of the calf is described thus: *(Moses said): "Now look upon thy god of which thou has remained a votary. Verily we will burn it and will scatter it dust over the sea."* (Q. 20:97) In this, the Quran has Biblical support in the words of the Deuteronomist (who also refrained from repeating that Aaron actually made and worshipped the calf): "Then I [Moses] took the sinful thing which ye had made, and burned it with fire and crushed it, grinding it very small, until it was as

---

[1867] Bal'ami, p. 442.

fine as dust; and I threw the dust of it into the brook that descended out of the mountain." (Deut. 9:21)

Some commentators interpret the words in Surah Baqarah *and they drank the calf into their hearts with their unbelief* (Q. 2:93) to mean that Israelites had to drink the ashes of the calf literally, as in *Exodus*, whilst others interpret the passage metaphorically. If it is taken literally, it is not a contradiction of the speech of Moses in Surah Ta Ha (Q. 20:97) quoted above, in which he said what the intended to do with the idol. Scattering the ashes in the river does not preclude the symbolic penance by the Hebrews of drinking of the water so tainted. With regard to the punishment, Bal'ami, taking his cue form the pericope of the slaughter of the 3,000 by the Levites, relates that God would only accept the repentance on behalf of the 12,000 who had not joined in the idol worship. They were commanded to take up their swords and slaughter those who had done so. In typical medieval exaggeration, the Bible's 3,000 became the 70,000 dead in Bal'ami, of the 360,000 who, he records, had participated in the worship.[1868]

Next, in Bal'ami's narrative, Moses read the Torah to the surviving Israelites. After he had finished, they commented that it would have been easier to worship the calf and be killed than to follow that which Moses had brought them.[1869] This seems to parallel the reaction to the reading of the Law to the people by the 5th-century BCE prophet Ezra: "For all the people wept when they heard the words of the law... So the Levites stilled all the people saying, 'Be quiet, for this day is holy; do not be grieved.'" (Neh. 8:9, 11)

Finally, Bal'ami tells us, stronger measures had to be taken in order to coerce the reluctant Israelites to accept the provisions of the Law. The Holy Mountain was raised up over their heads and Moses threatened that if they did not accept the Torah, they would be crushed beneath it. The Israelites tried to flee, but the mountain kept pace with them. At length they accepted the Law. However, they pleaded with Moses to pray to have the Law lightened, and God responded favorably.[1870]

Bal'ami's raising of the mountain over the people of Israel is based upon a literal interpretation of the Quranic text: *And We made a covenant with you and caused the Mount to tower above you...* (Q. 2:63,

---

[1868] Bal'ami, pp. 446-448.

[1869] Bal'ami, p. 448.

[1870] Bal'ami, pp. 449-350. This reminds us of the tradition of the imposition of the numerous obligatory prayers which were reduced by God to five through the intercession of the Prophet.

93) and another text: *And when We shook the Mount above them as it were a covering, and they supposed that it was going to fall upon them...* (Q. 7:171) We have already discussed the traditions of the volcanic nature of the Mountain of God, with its towering columns of smoke, explosions of dust, fire, and rocks, etc., also echoed in the Quran. The explicit tradition is found in the Talmud and other Jewish writings: "It was not indeed quite of their own free will that Israel declared themselves ready to accept the Torah, for when the whole nation, in two divisions, men and women, approached Sinai, God lifted up this mountain and held it over the heads of the people like a basket, saying to them: 'If you accept the Torah, it is well, otherwise you will find your grave under this mountain.' They all burst into tears and poured out their heart in contrition before God, and then said: 'All that the Lord hath said, will we do, and be obedient.'"[1871]

AL-SAMIRI: Before concluding this section of the story of Moses, we must return to the question of al-Samiri (*al-Sāmirī*). We have already pointed out the dubious nature of the Biblical text which makes Aaron responsible for the actual making of the Golden Calf, and we have also discussed some of the Jewish traditions which attempted either to exonerate him by showing him coerced, or foiled in his own strategy to prevent the Israelites from relapsing into idolatry. Other individuals were accused of either stirring up the people (such as Jannes and Jambres), or actually making an idol, as did Micah.

Although some of this material may shed some light on the question of the tradition of al-Samiri, because the Bible has already accepted the guilt of Aaron, we must not expect to find much direct support for the Quranic al-Samiri in Jewish and Christian writings. We advise the reader that in the absence of external documentary evidence, much about the reference in the Quran, based upon oral tradition, remains obscure and we can only lay out what we possess, together with some speculations.

To begin, the use of the definite article tells us that al-Samiri is probably not a given personal name; it is rather in the nature of an epithet or nickname. The Arabic root *s-m-r* is associated with "spending or passing an evening," with the implication of entertainment and pleasantry. Sāmir (an active participle) is a general term for one enjoying himself this way and is not necessarily a proper name. For example if Ahmad is watching some entertainment, we say he is a

---

[1871] LJ, III, 92; VI, 36.

"spectator," but that is not Ahmad's personal name; rather it is a word describing what he is doing at the moment. In the Quran, the word (in the accusative form) is used once with the meaning of "(someone) passing the night" (Q. 23:67). The final *i*, the *y* of relationship (*nisbah*), could mean some one associated with such an evening of entertainment. If the source of the epithet is to be found among these definitions, then we can probably pursue the question no further, for lack of relevant documentary support.

Before turning to the usual interpretation, the Samaritan, a different similar name may be considered. We have seen how, according to some Jewish traditions, Satan (called Sammael or Samael in these traditions) entered the calf and caused it to low. Both the Quranic and the Jewish traditions may be oblique references to the well-known deception practiced in some ancient shrines by which an idol was made to speak by various means. One of these was the concealment of a priest either in the hollow of an idol (metal idols of any size were usually hollow because, if they had been solid, they would have been immovably heavy), or somewhere nearby so that the voice would seem—to a gullible public— to be proceeding from the mouth of the idol itself. That is not an aspect of the report which we wish to consider here. By a well-known linguistic rule, the frequent interchange of *l* and *r*, Samael could become Samaer. It is just possible that this tradition of Samael and the calf was known in Arabia, but with the fallen angel's name transformed from Samael to Samaer, or Samir. The Samiri would be a follower of Samir/Samael. There is no documentary evidence to support such an hypothesis, and it can only remain a possible avenue for further investigation.[1872] Some have suggested that al-Samari in the Quran is actually Aaron himself, but on balance, this seems improbable.

Following the common translation of al-Samiri, the Samaritan, Western critics have made the usual charges of Quranic confusion: firstly, on the ground that the Bible clearly states that Aaron made the calf and any other suggestion must *ipso facto* be wrong, the certainty of which we have challenged above; and secondly, on the ground that the use of the word *Samaritan* itself is anachronistic (never mind all of the

---

[1872] Tisdall has also pointed out the possibility of a connection between Samael and the Samiri (Tisdall, p. 113), although his conclusion that Samiri is a mistake for Samael is not justified by the Arabic form of al-Samiri. It could not mean Samael himself, but rather a follower or adherent of Samael, or one who possessed his attributes, parallels of which would be on the lines of al-Mūsawī (a follower of Moses), al-ᶜĪsawī (a follower of Jesus), etc.

Biblical anachronisms), because the Samaritans had not yet (at the time of Moses) come into existence as a people.

Who were the Samaritans? The question is better phrased: "Who *are* the Samaritans?" for a remnant the Samaritan community numbering several hundred souls still survives in central Palestine. They represent a schismatic group of YHWH-worshippers, dissenters who have never accepted the primacy of the Jerusalem cult, nor many of the other principally Exilic and post-Exilic developments of official Judaism.[1873]

We have noted frequently that throughout most of Israelite history a strand of rivalry (and frequently hostility) may be detected between the Northern tribes under the leadership of the Josephic tribes, especially Ephraim, and the Southern tribes led by Judah. To some extent, it is an accident of history that the Judahites have survived to the present day, giving their name to Judaism, while the Northerners, the "Samaritans," are represented only by a few hundred survivors. (It must also be remembered that the Old Testament we have today is a product of the South.) Although the threat from the Northern rivals has long since passed, during the formative period of Judaism and the scriptures, the competition between two groups of YHWH-worshippers was a very real and often acrimonious one, and the outcome by no means certain. In these circumstances, there are many direct and indirect references to this hostility, some of which we have already pointed out. The Southerners were not above using the sacred word attributed to YHWH Himself as a weapon against their Northern rivals. The picture of the North in the Bible is often a biased and negative one.[1874]

Politically, this rivalry was reflected in the fact that all of YHWH-worshippers of Palestine were united only under their first three kings: Saul, David, and Solomon (although the extent of Saul's domain was not that comprehensive). After the accession of Solomon's son Rehoboam in c. 931 BCE, the North broke away and established it own line of the kings of Israel, while the South—called Judah, later Judaea—continued under the Davidic line. According to *Kings*, composed in the South, every one of the 19 monarchs of the North (c. 931 to 721 BCE)

[1873] Material from this section, including what follows, about the Samaritan comes from: Samaritans, EJ, XIV, 725-732; Gerizim, DB, p. 325; Samaria, DB, p. 879; Samaritans, DB, p. 880; Cambridge, Vol. 1, pp. 185-190.

[1874] If the bitter enmity of these two tiny groups of YHWH worshippers that acknowledged kinship with each other seems a trifle ridiculous today, one may recall the bitter and bloody centuries of war and slaughter—on a much grander and sadder scale—between the world's principal adherents of the Prince of Peace, the Protestants and the Catholics, in Europe following the Protestant Reformation. I need not remind Muslim readers of the damage disputing Islamic factions have inflicted upon one another.

was a villainous oppressor of his people and an enemy of God. In general, we are given an unfavorable view of most things Northern, religious or political, from the historical books of the Bible, all of which (not coincidentally) of are Southern redaction.

It was during this period of the Northern monarchy of Israel that about 880 BCE one of their kings, Omri, decided to build a new capital. "He bought the hill of Samaria from Shemer for two talents of silver; and he fortified the hill, and called the name of the city which he built, Samaria, after the name of Shemer, the owner of the hill." (1 K. 16:24) From the name of this city, the central hill country of Palestine, primarily inhabited by the Josephic tribes of Ephraim and Manasseh, came to be called Samaria. This was the name applied to the region in Roman times, with Galilee to the north and Judaea to the south.

In 721 BCE, after a three-year siege, Samaria fell to the Assyrians and the kingdom of Israel became a province of their empire. The inhabitants, according to the Southern record, were transported to other parts of the Assyrian Empire, and were replaced by non-Israelite colonizers, who corrupted the purity of YHWH-worship in the North (2 K. 17:32-41). For centuries, this passage condemning the Samaritans on the grounds of impure race (mixed origins!) and impure religious practices has been the starting point for assessments of these schismatics. However, the passage is almost certainly post-Exilic[1875] and is another salvo in the long war of propaganda between the North and the South that resumed with the Return of the Southerners and the rebuilding of the Temple in Jerusalem, after Judah had suffered the same fate as Israel at the hands of the Babylonians in 586 BCE. There is no *a priori* reason to believe that the Samaritans were any more ethnically mixed than the Judahites, and their still-surviving religion is uncompromisingly monotheistic, contradicting the accusations found in *2 Kings.*[1876]

As has been remarked above, the claims of the Jerusalem cult gradually evolved from primacy to exclusivity. Jerusalem was the latest

---

[1875] BC, III, 269-271.

[1876] Sargon of Assyria, in his own records of the event, claims to have transported 27,290 Israelites into captivity. (Albright-Ab to Ez, p. 73.) This does not support the Bible's assertion than the entire population of the ten tribes of Northern Israel was carried off. The population of Israel must have been considerably more than 27 thousand, probably closer to 200,000. Sargon may simply have carried of the people of the city of Samaria and its environs, and the Biblical statement is simply another slanderous attack on the Northerners, making them the descendants of non-Israelites. Though there was considerable depopulation, doubtless many, if not most, of the villages where the bulk of the people lived were relatively untouched. After all, cultivators and herders would pay taxes to whoever was in charge. It would not have served Assyria to lose such potential revenue.

of the YHWH-shrines to be established (by David after 1000 BCE), but in the period before and during the United Monarchy of David and Solomon a number of YHWH-sanctuaries had already been established much earlier: Dan, Shechem, Bethel, Shiloh, Hebron, Beersheba, etc. The Jerusalem, sanctuary, though the youngest, enjoyed royal patronage and the considerable prestige of possessing important national relics such as the Ark of the Covenant and the Tables of the Law given to Moses. From its beginnings, therefore, Jerusalem enjoyed certain advantages none of the others could claim, but as long as the sanctity of the older shrines was recognized, regardless of political conditions, there was a feeling of community among YHWH worshippers, both Northern and Southern.

The collapse of the Northern kingdom in 721 BCE changed matters. Simultaneously in the Southern kingdom, the exclusivist claims of the Jerusalem shrine gained royal support, especially under Hezekiah (716-687 BCE) and later Josiah (640-609 BCE). Judah was now the sole political representative of the YHWH cult, and steps were taken to suppress rival sanctuaries throughout the land and to completely centralize the sacrificial and ritual aspects of YHWH-worship at Jerusalem. Whenever circumstances permitted, the Judahites extended this policy of suppression of rival shrines to the lands of the former kingdom of Israel, that is, Samaria.[1877]

With the destruction of Jerusalem and the Temple by the Babylonians in 586 BCE, the situation was reversed. Sanctuaries at Shechem and other places flourished freely while the Jerusalem Temple lay in ruins, its leadership and its priesthood carried off in captivity (the Exile) to Babylonia. Despite the impression created in the Bible, the depopulation of Judah by the Babylonians—Judah was after all half the size of its former rival, the kingdom of Israel—was much more sweeping than that of Israel by the Assyrians a century and a half earlier.

When the Persian king Cyrus, history's first world emperor, generously permitted the exiles to return and rebuild the Temple at Jerusalem, the priesthood was determined to reassert its exclusivity and primacy in all Palestine—North and South—with the renewal of its interpretation of the YHWH cult. This resulted in a series of political and priestly squabbles that eventually led to a rejection of the legitimacy of the priesthoods of the (primarily) Northern sanctuaries by the Southerner Ezra in the middle of the 5th century BCE. Schism between the two rival cults was inevitable, just as the division of Solomon's kingdom had

---

[1877] As under Josiah. (See 2 K. 23:15, 19; 23 Ch. 34:6.7.)

become inevitable through Rehoboam's mismanagement nearly five centuries earlier. (This rivalry goes back even further, to the ancient competition between the southern Judahic and northern Josephic tribes for domination in Canaan.)

For their part, the Northerners rejected the claims of the Jerusalem cult and completely focused their attention upon the ancient sanctuary at Shechem and the sacred mountain of Gerizim. Henceforth, it became their religious center, as it has remained to the present day for the Samaritans, the descendants of those Northerners of ancient times. That the claims of the Samaritans had considerable validity is shown by the degree of the hostility directed at them by the (Southern) Jews. The Samaritans rejected all scripture save the Torah (the Pentateuch). Their own version has numerous minor and major readings that differ from the received Massoretic text of the Old Testament that was finally established c.700 CE[1878] (a date *later* than the establishment of the received text of the Quran).

The Samaritans' claim that Gerizim (in the heart of Ephraim, the dominant Josephic tribe) was the mountain of the Lord, rather than the upstart Mount Moriah at Jerusalem, seems also to be well-grounded in the present text of the Old Testament, despite several alterations and the probable deliberate suppression of the role of Shechem. The great national covenant after the Conquest is set at Shechem (Josh. 24:1-28). Joseph was buried there, and the shrine has Jacobite associations. When Solomon's kingdom split up under his son, "Rehoboam went to Shechem, for all Israel had come to Shechem to make him king."[1879] (1 K. 12:1) Shechem was also the first capital of Israel (1 K. 12:25). More importantly, the Samaritan Pentateuch makes Mount Gerizim the scene of the sacrifice by Abraham.

The Samaritans built a temple on Mount Gerizim that was destroyed by the (Southern) Maccabean John Hyrcanus in 126 BCE. Nonetheless, the Samaritans survived and towards the end of the 2nd century CE, some 300,000 were living in their central Palestinian homeland.[1880] During the Christian and Islamic periods, their numbers gradually dwindled to the remnant remaining today.

Mainstream Jews regarded them as a pariah people. Their origins, their customs, and religious practices were cruelly

---

[1878] Text of the Old Testament, DB, p. 972.

[1879] His purpose was to prevent his rival Jeroboam, who was away in Egypt, from establishing a secessionist Northern kingdom of Israel. Rehoboam failed in this and Jeroboam became the first king of Israel.

[1880] Samaritans, EJ, XIV, 731.

misrepresented. However, Ackroyd writes: "There is nothing to suggest that they were involved in alien religious practices or belief as some of the stories about them state. Such stories are part of a propagandist tradition in some Jewish circles... All this suggests the possibility that the Samaritan community was in origin a conservative protest against Jerusalem practice."[1881]

More than a hint of this animosity between the Jews and the Samaritans during New Testament times can be gained from the encounter between the Jew Jesus and the Samaritan woman at the well: "There came a woman of Samaria to draw water. Jesus said to her, 'Give me drink.' For his disciples had gone away into the city to buy food. The Samaritan woman said to him, 'How is it that thou, a Jew, askest a drink of me, a woman of Samaria?' For Jews have no dealings with Samaritans...'" (Jn. 4:7-9)

This relationship between the Jews and the Samaritans has led Golziher and others to interpret the statement of Moses in the Quran to al-Samiri: *"Then go! And lo, in this it is easy for thee to say: Touch me not! And lo, there is for thee an appointment thou canst not break..."* (Q. 20:97) as a reference to the pariah status of the Samaritans (and hence as further proof of the anachronism involved in the figure of Quranic al-Samari).[1882] This is an attractive and facile view. However, a little consideration will show that there are problems in our accepting it. Schismatics, even with the heritage of enmity that the Samaritans and the Jews felt for each other, do not go around warning their opponents to avoid pollution (literally or figuratively) by crying out "Touch me not!" The story of Jesus and the woman at the well, quoted above, shows that though the Jews regarded the Samaritans as ritually impure, as were *all* non-Jews (Romans, Greeks, Egyptians, etc.), the feeling was not so strongly reciprocated by the Samaritans, at least this woman expressed no concern about becoming ritually impure through contact with a Jew.

There is, however, a class of people who from ancient times until comparatively recently were obliged by law and custom to warn people of their approach and who were isolated from society: lepers. It would seem that al-Samiri's punishment in this life was leprosy. There are numerous traditions of leprosy associated with Moses. When Miriam, his sister, criticized him, she was afflicted with leprosy that was only cured through her brother's prayer (Num. 12). The white hand of Moses and his shining face both have leprous connotations (see above). Others connected with the story of Moses who were supposed to have been

---

[1881] Ackroyd, p. 170.
[1882] Samiri, SEI, 501-502.

afflicted with leprosy at one time or another include Aaron, Bithiah, the Egyptians at the time of the birth of Moses, Job, Pharaoh, *and* Samael.[1883] Jewish tradition also makes Moses capable of inflicting leprosy (on the Egyptians)[1884] as well as knowing how to cure it.[1885] While this explanation helps us to understand the possible implication of the Quranic verse in question, it does not advance our enquiry into the identity of al-Samiri in any particular direction, save perhaps that of Samael. However, in Jewish tradition, his leprosy will occur at the last judgment,[1886] so perhaps too much should not be made of that aspect of the connection in this life, although a different tradition about him may have been circulating in the Hejaz.

Returning to the meaning of "Samiri," the evidence of the Samaritan community in this regard is important. The Samaritans called themselves *Shamerim*, meaning "keepers or observers" (of the truth). They do not derive their name from the city or country of Samaria which they call *Shomron*, and its people *Shomronim*. This name is, according to the passage from *2 Kings* cited above, derived from the former owner of the site of the city, one Shemer, whose name, from the same root as *shamer*, is taken to mean "guardian."[1887] (The Hebrew root *sh-m-r* is the cognate of the Arabic root *s-m-r*.)

The Samaritan priesthood claimed descent from Phinehas, the son of Eleazar, the son of Aaron, and the line survived until the 17th century CE.[1888] Phinehas bears an Egyptian name and became high priest after Eleazar.[1889] *Chronicles* preserves a tradition associating Phinehas with Korah: "And Phinehas the son of Eleazar was the ruler over them [the Korahites] in time past; the Lord was with him." (1 Ch .9:20) Both Eleazar and Phinehas were buried at Gibeah, in the hill country of (Josephic) Ephraim, that was later called Samaria (Josh. 24:33).[1890]

[1883] LJ, VII, 283.

[1884] LJ, II, 354.

[1885] LJ, III, 260.

[1886] LJ, V, 101.

[1887] Samaritans, EJ, XIV, 728.

[1888] Samaritans, EJ, XIV, 727.

[1889] Phinehas, DB, 768. Yusuf Ali also speculates that "Samiri" could be of Egyptian derivation, from *shemer* meaning "stranger, foreigner." (Quran-Yusuf Ali, p. 807, Note 2605.) As a given name used by Israelites, it appears in both *Kings* and *Chronicles*, though no one of that name is associated in the Bible with the events of the Exodus or the Wandering. Perhaps he was an Egyptian in the "mixed multitude."

[1890] Gibeah was actually in the territory of the other Rachel tribe (Joseph was also Jacob's son by Rachel) Benjamin. This tradition may reflect a time before the Benjaminites had become established there. In the Biblical text cited (Josh. 24:33), it is specifically said that Gibeah was "in the hill country of Ephraim." It is thought that the Benjaminites, a

Neither Eleazar not Phinehas figured in any rebellious activity against Moses in the Pentateuch; indeed, the oldest sources, the Yahwist and the Elohist, hardly mention them.

There is an old Jewish tradition of an abortive attempt by the Ephraimites to leave Egypt under the leadership of one Ganon or, as he was also called, Jair. The leader is depicted as a false prophet, and the expedition ended in disaster.[1891] However, if he is to be identified with Jair, there is nothing else unfavorable about him. Aaron had two other sons, Nadab and Abihu, both of whom were reported accompanying Moses to the top of Mount Sinai (Ex. 24:1) and being made priests (Ex. 28:1). However, they were guilty of making a sacrifice with "unholy fire" "and fire came forth from the presence of the Lord and devoured them, and they died before the Lord." (Lev. 10:2) They are not mentioned in the story of the Golden Calf and one can only speculate about whether one of their names was originally in place of that of Aaron, or the phrase "son of Aaron" in place of "Aaron." In any case, such speculation does not explain the use of the Quranic term al-Samiri.

Trying to solve the problem by resorting to the North-South controversy is difficult. If, as is supposed, the Mosaic tradition really originated with the South, Moses was certainly honored in the North. Indeed, the only priestly line claiming Mosaic descent was to be found there (at Dan). As an aspect of the Levite/Aaronite competition, the Levites rallied to Moses after the incident of the Golden Calf, whilst on the other hand, the Levite Korah opposed him—although the Korahites may originally have been (despised) Edomites and not Levites (or even Hebrews) at all![1892]

If we are to regard *al-Samiri* as a reference to someone in the Northern tradition of YHWH-worship, as opposed to the Southern tradition represented by Moses, not enough seems to be found in the Biblical data to help us make a positive identification. The weight of the role of the Aaron, however spurious, has obscured any other traditions of leadership in the affair of the Golden Calf. That the term Samiri, if it is to be equated with either *shamerim*, the keepers, or *shomronim*, the Samaritans, is an anachronism in this situation is not a serious obstacle. A representative of the Northern tradition that became the *shamerim*

---

small tribe, were late in seizing the territory in Canaan allotted to them, as has been discussed in the text above.

[1891] LJ, III, 899; VI, 2,3.

[1892] Korahites, DB, p. 560.

would be meant.[1893] This is supported by the evidence of the persistence of calf worship in the North (Jeroboam's calves) and some leader of the (Northern) Josephic tribes whose name has been lost to us may have led the opposition to Moses and proposed the construction of the idol along familiar Egyptian lines. The story would then reflect the tensions between the Judahic and Josephic tribes before they settled in Palestine. The Samiri's seizure of the dust could be interpreted to mean that he was imitating the acts of Moses and had set himself up as a rival leader. Moses rallied his Levites and crushed the rebellion. In later times for other reasons, the name of the leader was replaced by that of Aaron.

On the other hand, equating al-Samiri with the Samaritans or the Samarians may be a false lead. Perhaps we should look to the meaning of the word. Perhaps al-Samiri was in some way connected with keeping the watch (mixing the Hebrew and Arabic meanings of the word); or it was connected with an earlier corruption of one of the names of the Hebrew Satan, Samael. From this distance, we can only offer these lines of investigation. However, it is necessary to remark again, the use of the term "al-Samiri" in this Quranic text is very firm and unhesitating, reflecting a well-known tradition among its auditors. The accusation made by Westerners that it is an echo of Jewish hostility towards the Samaritans learned by Muhammad is obviated by the fact that the term never occurs in the Quran in any context other than the story of the Golden Calf, and there are no important Jewish traditions associating that story with the later Samaritans. (The bulls installed by Jeroboam belong to a time before the term Samaritan had come into use.) However, in the 8th century BCE, Hosea wrote:

> "The inhabitants of Samaria tremble
> > for the calf of Bethaven. [Bethel?]
> Its people shall mourn for it,
> > and its idolatrous priests shall wail over it,
> > over its glory which has departed from it.
> Yea, the thing itself shall be carried to Assyria,
> > as a tribute to the great king.
> Ephraim shall be put to shame,
> > and Israel shall be ashamed of his idol."
>
> (Hos. 10:5-6)

[1893] We commonly speak of Judaism as including the periods of David and Solomon, or even Abraham, when the history of the term properly begins with the Exile. A person of English descent in the United States considers himself an American, not an Englishman.

Nonetheless, in later times there does not seem to have been any stress on the association of the Samaritans with the worship of the golden calves, because the schism occurred long after the disappearance of those idols and they do not figure prominently in the polemics the two rivals directed against each other.

For the present, the story of al-Samiri, like those of Hud, Shu'ayb, and others whose names would have recalled a network of associations familiar to the first audience of the Quran but now lost, is unfinished. It remains clothed in ambiguity because in varying degrees the context of the oral tradition has vanished, pending any new discoveries. So, who was al-Samiri? Samael? We do not yet have a definitive answer. We do not, or no longer, know. We have no reason to doubt that, based upon other parts of our examination of the stories, the people of the Prophet knew. *And God knows best.*

J. KORAH

"I don't want the treasure of Qarun!" (Persian song)

Now Korah (Ar. Qārūn) was of the people of Moses, but he oppressed them; and We gave him so much treasure that his keys[1894] *thereof would truly have been a burden for a number of strong men. When his own people said unto him: "Exult not! God loves not the exultant. Rather seek the abode of the Hereafter in that which God has given thee and neglect not thy portion of the world, and be thou kind even as God has been kind to them and seek not corruption; lo, God loves not the corrupters." He said: "I have been given it only on account of a knowledge which I possess."*

Did he not know that God had destroyed generations of men before him, mightier than he in strength and more numerous? And the guilty are not to be questioned about their sins! Then he went forth before his people in his finery. Those who desired the present life said,

---

[1894] *keys*: some translate the Arabic word here, *mafātīh*, as "hoards." The Arabic word is a plural of either *maftah* or *miftāh*, the former meaning "hoard," "stores"; the latter meaning "key." As the great number of keys for Korah's treasure is referred to in older Jewish writings, it is the preferred reading here. The attached possessive pronoun is masculine singular and cannot refer to "treasure" (*kunūz*), which is a broken plural and grammatically feminine. Consequently it refers to Korah, and is translated "his." In the Islamic world Korah is known as *Qārūn*. We feel that the exaggeration here is deliberate, emphasizing the parabolic nature of the passage, an illustration of the proverb from *Proverbs* that "pride goeth before destruction, and an haughty spirit before a fall." (Prbs. 41:18)

"Would that we had what Korah has been given! Truly he is a man of great fortune!"

So We caused the earth to swallow him and his dwelling. Then he had no host to help him, save God, nor was he of those who can save themselves. And in the morning those who had longed to be in his place were saying: "Ah! God spreads out and narrows His provision for whom He will of His servants. If God had not been gracious to us, He would have caused us to be swallowed up (too). Ah! The unbelievers never prosper!" (Q. 28:76-82)

This is the principal Quranic text of the parable of Korah. He is mentioned in two other places (Q. 29:39; 40:24), along with Pharaoh and Haman, as an opponent of Moses. In the Quran, his story is a cautionary tale rehearsed for the benefit of the Prophet's contemporaries and for future generations concerning the arrogant futility of amassing great wealth and the delusions of temporal power, as the references to the afterlife indicate — not a prominent consideration in the era of Moses.

Once again, the later Muslim commentators have laden the Quranic story with more details and incidents, some of them quite out of harmony with the moral of the pericope. In Surabadi's expansion, Korah was very wealthy, and — it is said — the treasurer of Pharaoh. His wealth was derived from Pharaoh's treasury. When he saw all the honor the Israelites were giving Moses, he became jealous. He approached Moses and asked him what was left for him (Korah), as Moses had been given the honor of prophethood, and Aaron chieftainship. Moses replied that the giving belonged to God. Korah was displeased and became a hypocrite.[1895] Moses told him to bring him his staff. Korah brought the staffs of 360 Israelite nobles, and they were placed in Moses' leather tent. The next day the staffs of Moses and Aaron were found to have grown and sprouted branches. Korah accused Moses of sorcery, and Moses, angered, prayed that the earth would swallow Korah up.[1896]

This seems to make Korah's destruction the result of a fit of pique by Moses. The incident of the staffs was doubtless ultimately dependent upon the tradition of the staffs found in Num. 17:1-11, wherein a similar contest is described with twelve staffs, one for each tribe, with Aaron's staff representing the tribe of Levi. It is meant as the assertion of the rights of the priestly tribe of Levi represented by Aaron. "The Lord said to Moses, 'Speak to the people of Israel, and get from them rods, one for each fathers' house... twelve rods. Write each man's

---

[1895] The use of the word "hypocrite" by the Surabadi is a strong condemnation, because of its association with the opponents of the Prophet during his mission.

[1896] Surabadi, pp. 306-307.

name upon his rod, and write Aaron's name upon the rod of Levi. Then thou shalt deposit them in the tent of the meeting before the testimony, where I meet with you. And the rod of the man whom I choose shall sprout..." (Num. 17:1-5)

This was done. As in Surabadi: "and on the morrow Moses went into the tent of the testimony; and behold, the rod of Aaron for the house of Levi had sprouted and put forth buds, and produced blossoms, and it bore ripe almonds..." (Num. 17:8) This device has been used in other places by both Muslim[1897] and Jewish commentators. In the Bible, this test immediately follows the account of the destruction of Korah and his party, so Surabadi's use of the incident is not out of place.

In the description Surabadi gives us of Korah's wealth, he says that Korah's treasure was 400,000 dirhams, carried by 40 men whom he kept with him always. When Moses came down from the Holy Mountain and found them worshipping the Golden Calf, he threw down the tables (of the Law) and broke them. Then God commanded him to fashion two tablets of gold to replace them.[1898] Moses asked where he could get so much gold. Then Gabriel taught him about three plants which, when mixed with iron, copper, and tin, would turn those metals into gold.

Moses then fashioned the tablets and separately disclosed the secret of one plant each to Korah, Aaron, and to Miriam, who was married to Korah. Aaron gave his secret to Korah, and Korah got Miriam's so that he (now possessing the knowledge of all three plants) could then make as much gold as he wished. While Moses went without food for three days, Korah paraded about in worldly splendor. It is also said that there was never such rejoicing as at the birth of Korah because of his great fortune, and never such sorrow as at the birth of Jesus.[1899]

Josephus also speaks of Korah's great wealth and his envy of Moses: "Korah, a Hebrew of principal account, both by his family and his wealth, one that was also able to speak well, and one that could easily persuade the people by his speeches, saw that Moses was in an exceeding great dignity, and was uneasy at it, and envied him on that account, (he was of the same tribe with Moses, and of kin to him,) and was particularly grieved, because he thought he better deserved that

---

[1897] See Joseph, Part Two, VI.B.

[1898] This contradicts the Quranic silence on the breaking of the tables of the law by Moses, but it entered the commentaries anyway; perhaps it was too good a story to pass over. The conflated nature of the accounts in the Pentateuch was of course unknown when Surabadi was writing. In this instance, two separate, somewhat different, versions of the same story found their way into *Exodus*, creating the erroneous impression that there were two deliveries of the tables of the law to Moses.

[1899] Surabadi, pp. 308-309.

honorable post on account of his great riches, and not inferior to him in birth."[1900]

In Talmudic tradition, Korah's wealth was given the following origin: "(Korah) had been the treasurer of Pharaoh [as in Surabadi], and possessed treasures so vast that he employed three hundred white mules to carry the keys of his treasures... when Joseph, during the lean years, through the sale of grain amassed great treasures, he erected three great buildings, one hundred cubits wide, one hundred cubits long, and one hundred cubits high, filled them with money and delivered them to Pharaoh, being too honest to leave even five silver shekels of this money to his children. Korah discovered one of these three treasuries."[1901] Korah was the richest man who ever lived.[1902]

The discovery of Joseph's treasure is the usual explanation given as the origin of Korah's immense wealth in Jewish tradition, and alchemy does not seem to be connected with it, as Surabadi would have it, but then Surabadi lived in a world preoccupied with the transformation of base metals to gold. If they had been successful, it would paradoxically have immediately made gold almost worthless. There is also mention of Miriam's husband in the Bible. In Jewish tradition, he was not Korah. She is sometimes said to have been the wife of Caleb of the tribe of Judah, or the clan of Kenizzites, thought to have been absorbed by Judah.[1903]

The Quran uses the story of Korah, in its popular form well known to the Prophet and his contemporaries, as a parable on the folly of the arrogance of wealth and man's reliance upon the material. Its lesson is eternal, and we should avoid taking the story too literally. The Biblical purpose of the story was quite different, and is connected with the rather unedifying struggles between the Levites and Aaronites for supremacy in the Israelite priesthood, as is so much else in the extant Biblical version of the story of Moses.

Scholarly analysis of Num. 16 has identified two separate stories of rebellion in three different strata.[1904] The oldest, from the JE conflated history, deals with the rebellion of Dathan and Abiram of the tribe of Reuben against the civil authority of Moses.[1905] Impatient with the delay in reaching the land of milk and honey promised to them, they rebelled

---

[1900] Josephus, Antiquities, IV.2.2, p. 85.

[1901] LJ, III, 286.

[1902] LJ, IV, 393.

[1903] LJ, II, 253. In this view, Miriam and Caleb were counted among the ancestors of the house of David.

[1904] Korah, DB, p. 560.

[1905] It is to be found fragmented into Num. 16:1b-2a, 12-15, 25-26, 27b-32a, 33-34.

against Moses. Angered, Moses isolated them from the rest of Israel and prayed that they be swallowed up by the earth: "And as he finished speaking all these words, the ground under them split asunder; and the earth opened its mouth and swallowed them up..." (Num. 16:31-32a) "So they and all that belonged to them went down alive into Sheol; and the earth closed over them, and they perished from the midst of the assembly. And all Israel that were round about them fled at their cry; for they said, 'Lest the earth swallow us up!'" (Num. 16:33-34) Thus, in the original version, Dathan and Abiram, and their families, were punished by being swallowed up for their rebellion against Moses' authority.

The story of Korah in this chapter is in two strata, both from the Priestly tradition.[1906] In the first version, when the story probably stood independently, Korah and 250 leaders of the people contested the priestly authority of the Levites. They agreed to a trial by censers. Each man of the 250 plus Aaron and Moses appeared at the tent of the meeting with incense in his censer. "And the Lord said to Moses and Aaron, 'Separate yourselves from among this congregation, that I may consume them in a moment.' ...And the fire came forth form the Lord, and consumed the two hundred and fifty men offering the incense.'" (Num. 16:20-21,35) In a sequel to this, a plague struck the people killing 14,700 (Num. 16:49). The superiority of the Aaronites was further demonstrated in the story of the rods (correctly introduced into the narrative of Korah by Surabadi, but in the wrong place) in which Aaron's rod sprouted branches (Num. 17).

Thus, the original version reflects a challenge to the special status of the Levites as the only priests acceptable to YHWH. In that version, Korah was destroyed by fire at the tent of meeting. The next step was the conflation of these two accounts of rebellion into one by another redactor of the Priestly school. In the process, he made certain additions.[1907] In the resulting account, Korah became a co-conspirator with Dathan and Abiram at the head of 250 Levites against the religious monopoly of the Aaronites; or perhaps it was an intercollegiate struggle between the Zadokites and the Korahites who, despite this story of their progenitor, were in the Temple service in later times. In this edited version, Korah shared the fate of Dathan and Abiram and was swallowed up by the earth, while the 250 rebel Levites were consumed by fire. Num. 16 is an interesting example of the process that shaped the present text of the Bible. Although the Bible mentions the men and goods that belonged to Korah (Num. 16:32b), there is no emphasis upon his wealth.

[1906] It is to be found in Num. 16:1a, 2b-7a, 18-24, 27a, 32a, 35, 41-50, and ch. 17.
[1907] Num. 16:7-11, 16-17, 36-40.

That was a later development of Jewish tradition. In this conflated form, it entered Arab oral tradition and supplied a parable for the Quran.

Surabadi mentions another incident leading up to the destruction of Korah. Prompted by his envy of Moses, Korah bribed a woman to stand up in the assembly and accuse Moses of having had carnal intercourse with her. However, when she attended the assembly, she regretted this arrangement, and instead of accusing Moses, she related Korah's proposal to the congregation. Moses complained to God that he could not tolerate this. God granted him power over the earth. Moses went to Korah, who had surrounded himself with all of his servants and dependents, and ordered the earth to swallow them up. When Korah had sunk to his head, Aaron rushed up and tried to save him as he was a relative, but Moses threatened him as well. Aaron turned aside, and Korah disappeared under the earth.[1908]

This pericope seems to be in some way connected with the story of the sedition of Miriam and Aaron against a marriage of Moses: "Miriam and Aaron spoke against Moses because of the Cushite woman whom he had married, for he had married a Cushite woman..." (Num. 12:1) Why this act aroused such anger—other than that Cush was in Africa and we may presume that the woman was black or dark—we do not know. The punishment meted out to Miriam (she became leprous) seems unduly harsh if this was all there was to the story. (As usual Aaron escaped without any punishment.) As a result of Moses' prayer, she was cured after seven days (Num. 12:13-15).

Who was the Cushite woman? Some have proposed that she is the same as Zipporah, a Midianite. However, this identification meets this criticism: Why had not Miriam and Aaron objected to her earlier? There is a possibility that the Cushite is an error for Cushanite because Cushan (not Cush) was a tribe in Midian, but the obvious meaning that would have first occurred to the reader was that she was a woman of Cush; that is, Ethiopia.[1909] More will be said about this in the Section L below.

Many of the developments in the story of Korah appear to be Islamic additions, as the story caught the imagination of the Muslim public from early times and his wealth became proverbial, as has the wealth of Croesus in the West. The differences between the Talmudic and Islamic traditions suggest that this embellishment took place without a great deal of dependence upon the form the Jewish traditions took, as the stories borrowed from or suggested by other Biblical passages

---

[1908] Surabadi, pp. 307-308.
[1909] BC, II, 1180119; Cush, Cushan, Cushite, DB, pp. 194-195.

indicate. The exaggerations of medieval Muslim exegetes have, to some extent, obscured the point of the Quranic parable.

K. THE ISRAELITES AND THE COW

God commands you that ye sacrifice a cow. (Q. 2:67)

In this section, Surabadi relates at some length the story of an unsolved murder. During the time of Moses, there was a rich Israelite named 'Amil(Ar. *ᶜĀmīl*) who had a daughter whom his nephew desired to marry. 'Amil would not agree to the match, as the lad was poor. The nephew developed a hatred for his uncle and plotted to kill him, seize his wealth, and then marry his daughter. By means of a ruse, telling his uncle that there was a merchant in a neighboring town who had received a large quantity of goods for sale, the nephew enticed 'Amil out of his own town where he killed him on the road. He then returned to town displaying the signs of mourning. No one was able to discover the killer. The people swore to accept blood money[1910] and the people of both towns quarreled over the matter. Finally, they approached Moses and asked that he intercede with God so that He might reveal the culprit. In reply, God said that they must find a cow which fitted a certain description, slaughter it, and strike the meat on the corpse of 'Amil, who would revive and reveal the identity of his murderer.[1911]

Surabadi offers several versions of the purchase of the cow. In one, the only animal fitting the description belonged to a jewel merchant. The merchant was asleep and his son refused to awaken him. Finally, the Israelites were forced to agree to pay for the cow by filling its hide with gold. In another version, the same price had to be paid to a woman who had lost all of her herds to an epidemic, except one, which fitted the divine description. In still another version, the cow was the last remaining property of a widow with one pious son. She told him one day to go and bring the cow in, telling him that no one was to sit upon it. The boy found the cow and the animal invited him to ride her, but he remembered his mother's injunction and refused. Then Iblis came along feigning illness and asked to ride the cow, but once again, the boy refused. An angel came and tested him by trying to get him to sell the cow without his mother's consent. Again, he refused. Then the angel told

---

[1910] That is, they agreed that they would not demand that the murderer be executed and would accept the blood money, or indemnity, for the crime. This was done in the hope that the murderer, fearing retribution, would confess and indemnify the victim's family.

[1911] Surabadi, pp. 12-13.

him the Israelites would come and offer its hide filled with gold. And so it happened the next day.[1912]

After securing the cow, they slaughtered it and struck the corpse of 'Amil with its flesh. He revived, as did the cow, and named his murderer. The cow confirmed his statement, and they both expired again.[1913]

This story is offered by the Muslim commentators in explanation of the passage in Surah Baqarah[1914] that gives the surah its name. It has two parts. This is the first part:

And when Moses said unto his people: "Lo, God commands you that ye sacrifice a cow." They said: "Dost thou make game of us?" He answered: "God forbid that I should be among the foolish!" they said: "Pray for us unto thy Lord that He make clear to us what (cow) she is." (Moses) said: "Lo, He says that she is a cow, neither with calf, nor immature; between the two conditions. So do that which ye are commanded." They said: "Pray thou for us unto thy Lord that He make clear to us of what color she is." (Moses) said: "Lo, He says that she is a yellow cow. Bright is her color, gladdening beholders." They said: "Pray thou for us unto thy Lord that He make clear what (cow) she is. Lo, cows are much alike to us; and lo, if God wills, we may be led aright." (Moses) said: "Lo, He says that she is a cow unyoked; she ploughs not the soil, nor waters the tilth. Whole and without any mark." They said: "Now thou bringest the truth." So they sacrificed her, though they almost did not. (Q. 2:67-91)

Taken by itself, the passage is so similar to the sacrifice of the red heifer in *Numbers* that it is most likely connected with it. In that passage (from P), God told Moses and Aaron: "'This is the statute of the law which the Lord has commanded: Tell the people of Israel to bring thee a red heifer without defect, in which there is no blemish, and upon which a yoke has never come. And ye shall give her to Eleazar the priest, and she shall be taken outside the camp and slaughtered before him; and Eleazar the priest shall take some of her blood with his finger, and sprinkle some of her blood toward the front of the tent of meeting seven times. And the heifer shall be burned in his sight; her skin, her flesh, and her blood, with her dung, shall be burned; and the priest shall take cedarwood and hyssop and scarlet stuff, and cast them into the midst of the burning of the heifer.'" (Num. 19:2-6)

[1912] Surabadi, pp. 13-15.

[1913] Surabadi, pp. 15-16.

[1914] *Baqarah* means *cow*.

There follow some instructions about the ritual purification of those involved in the slaughter of the heifer, then: "'And a man who is clean shall gather up the ashes of the heifer, and deposit them outside the camp in a clean place; and they shall be kept for the congregation of the people of Israel for the water of impurity, for the removal of sin.'" (Num. 19:9)

The remainder of the chapter explains the use of this "water of impurity" (it is to be prepared by mixing the ashes of the heifer with running water). Its purpose is to remove the ritual uncleanness caused by contact with the dead. "But the man who is unclean and does not cleanse himself, that person shall be cut off from the midst of the assembly, since he has defiled the sanctuary of the Lord; because the water of impurity has not been thrown upon him, he is unclean." (Num. 19:20)[1915]

As they stand in the Quranic text, the verses quoted above (Q. 2:67-71) form a complete unit. The purpose of the text, considered as a self-contained unit, would then become a perhaps wry criticism of the excessive nit-picking of rabbinical writings, of which the red heifer is cited as an example. A tractate of the Talmud (*Parah* of the *Order Tohorot*) is devoted to the Red Heifer, and its qualifications were so elaborated by the rabbis that, according to Rabbi Nisin, no one had been able to find such a cow since the days of Moses.[1916] In the pestering questions of the Israelites in their dialogue with Moses, there is more than a hint of satire, as the Israelites keep trying to find an excuse for not making the sacrifice.

In order to tie the above into Surabadi's story of murder, one most read the following two verses with them: *And (remember) when ye slew a man and disagreed concerning it and God brought forth that which ye were hiding. And We said: "Smite him with some of it. Thus, God brings the dead to life and shows you His portents so that ye may understand.* (Q. 2:72-73)

[1915] Jewish tradition gives further details about the use of the red heifer's ashes and the practice was continued throughout the ages: "Although, beside this one, a number of other red heifers were provided in future generations, this one was distinguished by having its ashes kept forever, which, mingled with the ashes of other red heifers, were always used for the purification of Israel." *Mishna Parah* also states that from the time of Moses until the Second Temple nine such heifers were furnished. The tenth will be supplied by the Messiah. (LJ, III, 216; VI, 79.)

The late 1st century or early 2nd century pseudepigraphic *Epistle of Barnabas* considers the red heifer a "type of Christ," a prefiguration of the incidents in the passion of Jesus, represented by the calf. It also holds that Christians, not Jews, are the true heirs of the Covenant. (Fathers, pp. 114-115, 124-125.)

[1916] Cited by MMA, Quran-MMA, and p. 33.

These verses are extraordinarily difficult. How the story of 'Amil developed from them is easy to see. Nevertheless, the verses do not necessarily support the interpretation of the commentators. The order of events is: 1, a murder committed by three or more persons[1917]; 2, a dispute concerning the crime, not necessarily over the identity of the murderer; 3, a parenthetical expression stating that God is the revealer of what they had concealed; 4, the divine order to strike something (the corpse?) with something (a part of the cow?); 5, a general statement (that may be allegorical) that God resurrects the dead (plural).

A passage in the Bible cited in connection with these two verses is found in *Deuteronomy*. It describes the rites of absolution in the case of finding a person whose slayer is unknown. "'If in the land which Lord God gives thee to possess, any one is found slain, lying in the open country, and it is not known who killed him, then thy elders and thy judges shall come forth, and they shall measure the distance to the cities which are around him that is slain; and the elders of the city which is nearest to the slain man shall take a heifer which has never worked and which has not pulled the yoke. And the elders of that city shall bring the heifer down to a valley with running water, which is neither ploughed nor sown, and shall break the heifer's neck there in the valley." (Deut. 21:1-4)

"And the priests of the sons of Levi shall come forward, for the Lord thy God has chosen them to minister to Him and to bless in the name of the Lord, and by their word every dispute and every assault shall be settled. And all the elders of that city nearest to the slain man shall wash their hands over the heifer whose neck was broken in the valley; and they shall testify, 'Our hands did not shed this blood, neither did our eyes see it shed. Forgive, O lord, Thy people Israel, whom Thou hast redeemed, and set not the guilt of innocent blood in the midst of Thy people Israel; but let the guilt of blood be forgiven them.' So thou shall purge the guilt of innocent blood from your midst, when thou shalt do what is right in the sight of the Lord." (Deut. 21:5-9)

Q. 2:72-73 seems to refer to a story well known among the Hejazi Arabs. Is it the story that Surabadi has given us, linking both passages of the Quran? If it is unconnected with the preceding verses, it is not even certain that the addressees are Israelites. Maulana Muhammad Ali denies any connection between the two parts, but Surabadi and other commentators plainly thought there was such a link, as the story of 'Amil shows. Indeed, if one interprets the verses about the killing to mean an unsolved crime, then the dependence is certain. The

---

[1917] The Quran uses the plural "ye slew."

Quran, in the first part, makes no reference to the rites of burning the heifer and mixing the ashes with water to make the "water of impurity," as in *Numbers*.

On the other hand, no color is specified in the case of the unsolved murder, whilst it is in the case of the heifer whose ashes are to be used to remove ritual uncleanness. In this respect, the passage is closer to *Deuteronomy* than *Numbers*. Maulana Muhammad Ali denies a connection and suggests that Q. 2:72-73 is a reference to the attempted crucifixion of Jesus.[1918] He makes the feminine pronoun *hā*, translated here as "it" in the phrase "some of it," a reference to the act of killing rather than the cow. Not very many have followed him in this explanation. He denies any relationship between these verses and the Biblical passages in *Numbers* in *Deuteronomy*.

It is conceivable that the two Quranic verses refer to this aspect of the sacrifice, that is, as a dispute over the purification procedure after a killing and the resultant uncleanness therewith created. *Thus God brings the dead to life* would therefore be a metaphor for the removal of the uncleanness and rejoining the community. Against this interpretation is the fact that the object of "smite" appears to be the corpse, not the perpetrators of the crime. (*Jalalayn* says that it was struck with the tongue or tail of a cow, bringing the corpse to life to identify his assassins.[1919]) The passage seems to be a reference to some well-known circumstance, now lost. Again, it may be completely independent of the preceding parable of the heifer and simply deriding extremes of scrupulousness. Whatever the basis of the second part, its point seems to be a parable of resurrection and the omniscience of God, not just the disclosure of a murderer.

It must also be noted that neither Biblical passage is concerned with the solution of an unsolved murder. *Numbers* is only concerned with the removal of ritual impurity caused by contact with the dead, while *Deuteronomy* is concerned with the removal of bloodguilt from a community created by an unknown killer. In the Quran, the same people who were responsible for the death are told to perform the action of striking the corpse (?) with something, and the whole is seen as a proof of God's ability to resurrect the dead, perhaps in this case for the slain man to name his killers, as Surabadi would have it. In the Quran, they are known to God, but not to man. Indeed, the circumstances may not be homicide, but an accidental death and some expiatory ritual connected with it. The problem remains unresolved. *And God knows best.*

[1918] Quran-MMA, pp. 33-35.
[1919] Jalalayn, p. 11.

L. THE JOURNEY OF MOSES

*"I will not give up until I reach the point
where the two seas meet..."* (Q. 18:60)

Our edition of the Quranic Stories from the *Commentary of Surabadi* does not include an account of Moses' journey to the "meeting of the two seas." In view of its importance in the story of Moses and the considerable controversy that surrounds it, we feel obliged to examine it, however briefly. Although it probably relates to his youth in Egypt, before the flight to Midian, we place it here as a kind of appendix, so as not to interrupt the traditional, Biblical sequence of events. We shall begin with Quranic version. This is found in Surah al-Kahf and belongs to the Makkan period. Other details for the amplified Islamic version will be drawn from Bal'ami's account.[1920] Some commentators, as Bal'ami notes, have suggested that this story is not about the Moses of the Exodus, but another, one Moses the son of Manasseh the son of Joseph, but this is not the prevailing view.[1921] In his history, Bal'ami places this story after the destruction of the Egyptians in the Red Sea and before the rebellion of Korah.

The story in the Quran begins thus: *And when Moses said unto his servant: "I will not give up until I reach the point where the two seas meet, though I march on for ages."* (Q. 18:60)[1922] Bal'ami explains that his companion was Joshua the son of Nun and the place of the meeting of the two seas was three days journey from Egypt. The geographical directions he gives seem to point to some place in the Gulf of Oman or the Arabian Sea.[1923]

And when they reached the point where the two met, they forgot their fish, and it took its way into the waters, being free. And when they had gone further, he said to the servant: "Bring us our breakfast. We have truly found fatigue in this our journey." (Q. 18:61-62) In Bal'ami,

---

[1920] Bal'ami, I, pp. 461-477. Because of the extensive elaboration of this story in Islamic tradition, which would entail a separate volume in itself to do the material justice, we shall generally confine ourselves to the parallels and sources of the Quranic version, supplementing it only with details from Bal'ami that are closely related to the original Quranic text.

[1921] Bal'ami, I, p. 462. There is no Moses among the sons of Manasseh listed in the Bible. The closest to "Moses" in form, and not very close at that, would be Machir, who settled east of the Jordan.

[1922] This verse always reminds us of Alfred Lord Tennyson's *Ulysses*: "I cannot rest from travel; I will drink life to the lees...To sail beyond the sunset... To strive, to seek, to find, and not to yield."

[1923] Bal'ami, I, pp. 467-468.

the fish had swum away and the waters parted, leaving land in the middle upon which the fish sat.[1924] The sudden introduction of the fish (see below) in this passage, without preamble, is proof that the story that forms the basis of the parable was already well known to its early 7th-century CE Arab audience.

He said: "Didst thou see, when we took refuge on the rock, and I forgot the fish—none but Satan caused me to forget to mention it—it took its way into the waters by a marvel." He said: "This is that which we have been seeking." So they retraced their steps again. (Q. 18:63-64) Bal'ami says that Moses and Joshua followed the fish back to the rock.[1925]

They found one of Our servants, unto whom We had given mercy from Us, and had taught him knowledge from Our presence. (Q. 18:65) Bal'ami identifies this servant as Khidr.[1926]

Moses said unto him: "May I follow thee, to the end that thou mayest teach me right conduct of that which thou hast been taught?" Said he: "Lo, thou canst not bear with me patiently. How canst thou bear with that whereof thou hast never encompassed in thy knowledge?" (Moses) said: "Thou shalt find me, God willing, patient and I shall not rebel against thee in anything." Said he: "Well, if thou go with me, ask me not concerning anything till I myself mention it unto thee." (Q. 18:66-70)

From this point on Moses and the "servant of God" seem to be by themselves; no further mention is made of Moses' traveling companion, and the verbs in the Quranic text are dual.[1927] We are left to speculate as to whether he was with them or not. The nature of the following events and the absence of any response or comment by the former companion suggest that he was not a participant in them. The first of the mysterious incidents to follow the servant of God's agreement to let Moses accompany him was his holing of the boat in which they had set out (Q. 18:71-73). Moses was astonished. Forgetting his promise not to question anything the servant of God did, he asked about it. *(The servant of God) said: "Did I not say unto thee that thou couldst never bear with me?"* (Q. 18:72)

[1924] Bal'ami, I, p. 468.

[1925] Bal'ami, I, p. 470.

[1926] Bal'ami, I, p. 470.

[1927] We remind the reader that classical Arabic has three "numbers": singular, dual, and plural (three or more). This is reflected in the conjugations of verbs and the declensions of nouns and adjectives.

They went on and met a boy whom the servant of God slew (Q. 74-76). Once again, Moses forgot his promise and asked, using words of condemnation, the meaning of the act. *He said: "Did I not say unto thee that thou couldst never bear with me?"*

Nevertheless, he accepted Moses' renewed promise that he would not repeat his behavior. They went on until they reached a town that refused them hospitality. Nonetheless, the servant of God stopped to repair a wall that was on the point of collapsing. Once again, Moses forgot his promise and commented upon the servant of God's action (Q. 18:77). *Said (the servant of God): This is the parting between me and thee! Now I shall tell thee the interpretation of that thou couldst not bear with patience. As for the ship, it belonged to poor people working on the sea, and I wished to mar it, for there was a king behind them who was taking every ship by force."* (Q. 18:78-79) Bal'ami relates that the king was Mandal bin Khaland al-Azdi of Antioch in Syria.[1928]

"As for the lad, his parents were believers and we feared lest he should oppress them by rebellion and disbelief. And we intended that their Lord should change him for them for one better in purity and nearer to mercy." (Q. 18:80) Bal'ami observes that the boy was a secret idolator.[1929]

"As for the wall, it belonged to two orphan boys in the city, and there was beneath it a treasure belonging to them, and their father had been righteous, and thy Lord intended that they should come to their full strength and should bring forth their treasure as a mercy from their Lord. I did it not at my (own) bidding. Such is the interpretation of that wherewith thou couldst not bear." (Q. 18:81-82)

Bal'ami adds that the treasure was a golden tablet upon which were written five lines in the manner of Wisdom: "I wonder at him who is certain to die and rejoices. I wonder at him who is certain of merit and is lazy. I wonder at him who is certain of retribution yet disobeys. I wonder at him who is certain of sustenance yet seeks it. I wonder at him who is certain of the world and its perishing, yet relies upon it." After Khidr [for Bal'ami identifies him as Khidr, see below] had finished speaking, he vanished and Moses and Joshua (who has rejoined Moses) returned to the Israelites.[1930]

This is the Quranic version of this story with the comparatively restrained additions of a reputable commentator. The elaborations seem

---

[1928] Bal'ami, I, pp. 474-475. The word translated as "sea" (*bahr*) could also mean "large river" in some situations.

[1929] Bal'ami, I, p. 475.

[1930] Bal'ami, I, pp. 476-477.

to be in the direction of treating the parables as history rather than as moral lessons that emphasize the necessity of trusting in the plan of God in preference to our own shortsightedness. "The Lord moves in mysterious ways his purposes to accomplish" is the spirit of this passage. In the Quranic story, no personal names are used except that of Moses, and that but twice. Treating it as literal history, explaining everything, giving the characters names, and introducing extraneous figures and events, as the commentators were wont to do, detracts from the deceptive simplicity and directness which harbor many layers of lessons for believers.

However, there is nothing in the Biblical story of Moses that even closely resembles this. It has a visionary quality, but it does not seem to be related to any of the several accounts of ascensions by Moses to heaven or the revelations of the workings of the universe in the apocalyptic spectacles to be found in later Judaeo-Christian religious writings. But, as we shall see, some of the material for the framework of the story in this episode has an ancestry that once again takes us back to ancient Babylonia. How that became part of the oral tradition of the Hejazi Arabs in the 6th and 7th centuries CE is uncertain; possibly it coalesced earlier with another tradition about the expedition of Moses to Ethiopia not found in the Bible, but attested in Hellenistic literature as early as Artapanus, writing in the 1st century BCE. This story seems to have been an alternative explanation of the cause of Moses' flight to Midian; at least it precedes it in those versions.

Artapanus, tells us: "Chenephres,[1931] the husband of Moses' foster-mother, became envious of Moses, and sought to slay him on some plausible pretext. And so, when the Ethiopians invaded Egypt, Chenephres sent Moses in command of a force against them, and enrolled a body of husbandmen for him, hoping that through the weakness of his troops, Moses would be easily destroyed by the enemy. Moses, however, was victorious in his campaign that lasted ten years, and on account of his excellence even the Ethiopians became so fond of him that they learned from him the custom of circumcision. Moses built a city as quarters for his vast army, and therein he consecrated the ibis, because this bird destroys the animals that are noxious to man. When Moses returned to Egypt, he was welcomed by Chenephres, who in reality continued to plot against him."

[1931] Chenephres is called the king of Memphis (LJ, V, 398), a longtime capital of Egypt, situated about fifteen miles south of Cairo, on the left bank of the Nile.

This narrative is followed by the circumstances leading to Moses' seeking refuge in Midian.[1932] So, here we have the tradition of Moses' making an expedition, the frame of the Quranic story, already well established.

In Josephus, too, Moses' expedition to Ethiopia takes place in his youth, before his flight to Midian. The circumstances leading up to the participation of Moses in the expedition are somewhat different. In Josephus' account, the Ethiopians had invaded Egypt from the south and proceeded as far north as Memphis and in places had even reached the (Mediterranean) sea. The Egyptian forces were crushed and the priests consulted their oracles for divine advice. The oracles, directed by God, answered that the Egyptians were to put Moses in command of the army. Moses had been protected from his enemies at the court of Pharaoh by his foster-mother, the princess Thermuthis. When approached by the leaders of Egypt to let them have Moses, she refused to release him until they swore to do him no harm.

"So Moses, at the persuasion both of Thermuthis and the King himself, cheerfully undertook the business: and the sacred scribes of both nations were glad: those of the Egyptians, that they should at once overcome their enemies by his valour, and that by the same piece of management Moses would be slain; but those of the Hebrews, that they should escape from the Egyptians, because Moses was to be their general; but Moses prevented the enemies, and took and led his army before those enemies were apprised of his attacking them, for he did not march by the river, but by land...

"When he had therefore proceeded thus on his journey, he came upon the Ethiopians before they expected him; and, joining battle with them, he beat them and deprived them of the hopes they had of success against the Egyptians, and went on in overthrowing their cities, and indeed made a great slaughter of the Ethiopians."

Victory heartened the Egyptians and Josephus describes further success under Moses' generalship: "Now when the Egyptian army had once tasted of this prosperous success, by the means of Moses, they did not slacken their diligence, insomuch that the Ethiopians were in danger of being reduced to slavery, and all sorts of destruction; and at length they retired to Saba, which was the royal city of Ethiopia, which Cambyses[1933] afterwards named Meroe,[1934] after the name of his own sister.

[1932] Quoted in LJ, V, 407.
[1933] Cambyses, the Persian king who conquered Egypt c. 525 BCE.

"The place was to be besieged with very great difficulty, since it was both encompassed by the Nile quite round, and the other rivers, Astapus and Astaboras, made it a very difficult thing for such as attempted to pass over them: for the city was situate in a retired place, and was inhabited after the manner of an island, being encompassed with a strong wall, and having the rivers to guard them from their enemies, and having great ramparts between the wall and the rivers, insomuch, that when the waters come with the greatest violence it can never be drowned; which ramparts make it next to impossible for even such as are gotten over the rivers to take the city."[1935]

Where arms will not succeed, passion often does, as Josephus continues the story: "However, while Moses was uneasy at the army's lying idle, (for the enemies durst not come to battle,) this accident happened:—Tharbis was the daughter of the king of the Ethiopians: she happened to see Moses as he led the army near the walls, and fought with great courage; and admiring the subtlety of his undertakings, and believing him to be the author of the Egyptians' success, when they had before despaired of recovering their liberty, and to be the occasion of the great danger the Ethiopians were in, when they had before boasted of their great achievements, she fell deeply in love with him; and upon the prevalency of that passion, sent to him the most faithful of all her servants to discourse with him about marriage. He thereupon accepted the offer, on condition she would procure the delivering up of the city, and gave her the assurance of an oath to taker her to his wife; and that when he had once taken possession of the city, he would not break his oath to her. No sooner was the agreement made, but it took effect immediately; and when Moses had cut off the Ethiopians, he gave thanks to god, and consummated his marriage, and led the Egyptians back to their own land."[1936]

This is all that Josephus tells us about the matter, but in it he adds to Artapanus' notice about Moses' leading an expedition up the Nile into Cush/Ethiopia, and he puts Moses in the vicinity of the confluence of two great rivers. Josephus' geographical details seem to be based upon Diodorus, who also describes Meroe as an island and attributes its founding to Cambyses. The legend of the Island of Meroe

---

[1934] Meroe was the Nubian capital located on the Nile between the 5th and 6th cataracts, some 40 miles south of Atbara in Sudan.

[1935] The rivers mentioned flow from Ethiopia, the Astapus into the Astaboras (the modern Atbara) and then into the Nile 40 miles above Meroe. No perennial rivers flow into the Nile after the Atbara. See text below.

[1936] Josephus, Antiquities, II.10.2, p. 58.

seems to be derived from the fact that the region of Nubia, of which Meroe is the center, is bounded by southwest by the Blue Nile, on the northwest by the Nile and on the northeast by the Atbara, the Astaboras of Josephus.[1937]

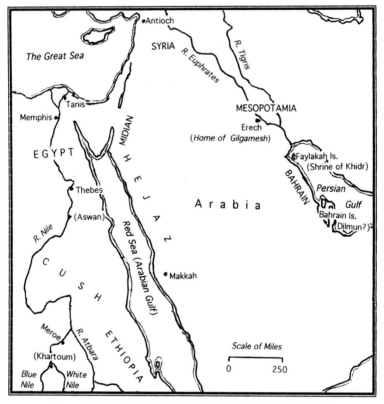

PLACES MENTIONED IN THE *JOURNEY OF MOSES*

There are two major junctions of rivers in the Sudan, that of the Blue and White Niles at modern Khartoum, the other being the meeting of the Nile and the Atbara at Atbara. One of these junctions may lie behind the tradition of Moses and the meeting of the seas (large rivers). If, indeed, Josephus' story be related to it at all, it would be no great stretch to suppose that Moses traversed the entire country, as far as these confluences, of which the locals would surely have informed him.

In Artapanus and Josephus, the expedition of Moses to Ethiopia is the first major incident of his adult life, unmentioned in the Bible.

[1937] Shinnie, p. 16.

Josephus' more detailed version, though later than Artapanus', presupposes a much longer history of transmission, as he did not invent stories for his *Antiquities*, but preserved many extra-Biblical traditions that would other wise have been lost, much as the Quran preserves and refers to otherwise lost Arab lore.

Some of the characteristics of the story can also be found in the Quranic pericope: the idea of the journey itself, the meeting of the two waters, and the youth of Moses. The Quranic story is redolent of youth, but focuses more upon the incipient prophet being taught the ways of God. The noisy military setting with its armies and battles is completely absent.

The Talmud ignores Moses' journey, and the earliest notice in rabbinic literature is in the *Targum Yerushalmi* of the 7th and 8th centuries CE. Because of its conflict with the text of the Pentateuch, it does not seem to have received much attention until medieval times, when it attracted considerable elaboration (perhaps prompted by Muslim interest in the Quranic story): After the death of the king of Ethiopia Quqanos, Moses was crowned king and married the widow of the former king, Adoniah. (Artapanus made no mention of a wife, though Josephus did.) However, because it was not seemly for a Jew to cohabit with a non-Jewish woman, he refrained from having sexual relations with her (contradicting Josephus who explicitly says that Moses consummated the marriage). Eventually, after forty years, she complained of this, and the Ethiopians selected another king in his place and sent him away with presents.[1938]

As have already noted, the Bible knows nothing of this episode in the life of Moses, but then it is silent about Moses' "lost years" as an Egyptian princeling until he killed the Egyptian, an act which precipitated his flight to Midian. However, the complaint of Aaron and Miriam about the Cushite woman whom Moses had married may have a connection with this story: "Miriam and Aaron spoke against Moses because of the Cushite woman whom he had married, for he had married a Cushite woman." (Num. 12:1) This sedition resulted in Miriam's leprosy.[1939] The presence of this Cushite woman that excited this protest is one of the mysteries of the Bible. This tradition may be its solution.

To the ancient Egyptians, Cush meant the territory south of the first cataract of the Nile, at modern Aswan, and though the name is usually translated as Ethiopia, Nubia (the modern northern Sudan), with a general extension to the Horn of Africa, would be a better equivalent.

[1938] LJ, II, 286-289.
[1939] See Section J above.

This is the usual meaning of Cush in the Bible, but the Table of Nations appears to locate the descendants of Cush in southern and central Arabia, a possible confusion with the Kassites or Cossaeans. In one place, a tribe called Cushan is associated with Midian (Hab. 3:7). It is also known that there were Cushite slaves in both Egypt and Palestine.[1940]

Jewish tradition frequently identifies this Cushite woman with Zipporah, the daughter of Jethro whom Moses married during his first stay in Midian, but modern scholars favor the view that they were not identical, and that the Cushite was probably of Nubian/Sudanese origin.[1941] We do not know whether the story of Moses' journey was suggested by the verse in *Numbers*, or whether both are related to some tradition of Moses' participation in an Egyptian military expedition to the south. Such expeditions were not uncommon during the period of the Egyptian New Empire, although the Ethiopians did not invade Egypt successfully until the middle of the 8th century BCE (more than five centuries after the time of Moses) when they founded the XXVth Dynasty that ruled the country for about half a century. The Cushite woman may have been married by Moses in some other circumstance.

Could Moses have made such a journey? Certainly. Such travel was possible in his era. Is there evidence that he did? Just the Arab tradition remembered in the Quran, and the tantalizing paragraphs of Artapanus and Josephus. As it was feasible and could have occurred while he was in Midian, we may choose to believe that he did—or we may read the story as a parable. There is no evidence, other than the Bible, that Abraham lived and journeyed from Ur to Canaan, but most of us accept his reality. For our purposes, the historicity of Moses' expedition is perhaps not so important as is the question: How did these traditions travel to Arabia? In the centuries between Josephus' evidence and that of the Quran, there was ample opportunity for the creative aspect of oral transmission to do its work and for other traditions to coalesce about a basic tradition of Moses' journey to a distant and somewhat mysterious land, where the two seas met.

In Arabia at least, other traditions, this time from Mesopotamia and the Persian Gulf also collected about Moses in pre-Islamic times, as the nature of the necklace of parables in the Quran demonstrates. The text of the Bible itself proves that traditions of great antiquity have survived in oral transmission. Generally, there is a subtle process of editing; oral tradition is a growing organism until frozen into writing.

[1940] Cush, DB, pp. 194-195; Cushite, DB, p. 195.
[1941] Ethiopian Woman, DB, p. 273.

Something of this sort may have occurred in Arabia with the reputation of Moses. The Hejazi Jews had probably heard of the journey of Moses, though in the absence of strong confirmation this can only be a supposition. Moses himself was not unknown in the Arabian Peninsula, and none of the varied ingredients in the story of Moses' journey appear to have been startling or new, though of course as with any old story, some may have been hearing if for the first time in its Quranic version. The journey itself does not seem to have been unfamiliar, as gaps and leaps in the narrative indicate. There was already a tradition in circulation linking Moses with the meeting of the seas.

However, in the Arabian version, there is perhaps the tradition of another powerful figure from the past became mingled with that of Moses. This conflated version may have become the basis for the parables in the Quran. The tradition was that of the young Moses on his way to becoming a prophet; the journey, a mystical excursion with its lessons about the obscure manner in which divine providence fulfills its aims. It fitted into the period when Moses was in Egypt, before the Exodus and his taking up the burden of leading the fractious and often unwilling Israelites out of captivity and delivering the Law that turned them into the people of YHWH. In the Quran, too, in this story, Moses seems to be a young man; he has the impatient curiosity of youth. There are the three elements in common between the Quranic story and that of Josephus: the journey itself, the confluence of the waters, and youth.

Where do the other elements come from? The reader may recall references to and excerpts from the ancient *Epic of Gilgamesh* in the story of the Creation and that of Noah and the Flood. This epic assumed literary shape in Sumerian times and, in its (Semitic) Akkadian recensions, achieved wide circulation in the ancient Near East, contributing directly and indirectly to what later became the Yahwist and Priestly histories of the world before Moses, as found in the *Genesis*.

Much of the *Epic of Gilgamesh* has to do with search and wandering. Gilgamesh and his companion Enki traveled westward in search of adventure. When they returned to Erech,[1942] the goddess Ishtar attempted unsuccessfully to seduce the hero Gilgamesh. Furious, she persuaded another god to create the Bull of Heaven, which was supposed to wreak havoc upon Gilgamesh's people. Instead, Gilgamesh killed it, and the gods decided that for this act Enki [not Gilgamesh!] must die. Struck by the reality of death for the first time, Gilgamesh set out alone

---

[1942] Erech, or Uruk (the modern Warka), lies about 150 miles NW of Basrah (Iraq) near the Euphrates River. Once the largest city in Mesopotamia (and probably the entire world), it was founded in the 5th millennium BCE. (Erech, CE, p. 666; et al.)

to find his ancestor Utnapishtim [the Mesopotamian Noah], the only mortal who had been granted immortality. After many more adventures, Gilgamesh found him in a place called Dilmun [Eden?]. Utnapishtim taught him how to find the plant at the bottom of the sea that bestowed immortality.[1943]

Although there are other epics involving travel and wandering in ancient literature, Homer's *Odyssey* perhaps the most famous, this one seems to stand in some sort of a relationship to the story of Moses in the Quran and the "immortal" man. In addition to the theme of the journey, we also have a traveling companion (Enki = Joshua in Bal'ami?) for part of the story, though missing in much of it.[1944] There is also the figure of the wise man. In the Quran, he and Moses travel together for a while (during the three "lessons"), whilst in the *Epic of Gilgamesh*, he is the goal of Gilgamesh's quest. There is an atmosphere of the marvelous in both stories, and the goal of the journey is knowledge, but in the Quran, it is the knowledge of the workings of God, while for Gilgamesh it is the secret of eternal life to be found in Dilmun.

And Dilmun is believed to be Bahrain.[1945] The Arabic name, *Baḥrayn*, meaning "two seas," has always been a bit of a mystery. The ancient Mesopotamians believed that there were two seas: one sweet, the other salt, and the sweet water underlay the salt water. Their separation was the first step in creation, which the Babylonians conceived to have been the replacement of chaos by order.[1946] We have also seen how the Babylonian paradise at first possessed everything except sweet water, which the sun god Utu provided by causing it to well up from under the earth.[1947] This still occurs in a startling fashion around Bahrain. The undersea freshwater springs were for centuries the principle source of drinking water for the island.

Bahrain—the name originally applied to the adjacent coastal region of modern Saudi Arabia as well, as its waters shared the same characteristics—does not stand at the junction of any geographical bodies of water as a glance at a map of the Persian Gulf will show. Yet, Bahrain, according to a belief of the greatest antiquity, was located at the

---

[1943] Hooke, pp. 36, 37, 49-55.

[1944] Wensinck, writing in SEI, has apparently forgotten about Enki when he states: "The figure of the travelling companion is not connected with the Gilgamesh Epic." (Khadir, SEI, p. 232.) It is true that Gilgamesh was not along in this part of the epic, but he was very much present in the Sumerian hero's earlier adventures, and it was his death that prompted Gilgamesh to go upon his quest.

[1945] See Part One, II, C.

[1946] See Part One, I.

[1947] See Part One, II, C.

junction of two seas: the salt sea on the surface and the sweet sea that lay beneath earth. The sweet sea came to the surface around that fortunate island, and mingled, or "met": the "meeting of the two seas." There is probably no need to look further for the source of the Quranic phrase.[1948]

Whether this meeting of the branches of the Nile in the story of Moses and the meeting of the two "seas" at Dilmun/Bahrain in the *Epic of Gilgamesh* are related is not easy to say. Probably, the Arabic Bahrain is the latest translation of a name meaning "two seas" that has been applied to the area from ancient times. Geoffrey Bibby also speculates that the word Dilmun itself may have originally meant "two seas."[1949]

The distance from Lower Egypt (if that is taken as the starting point for Moses' journey) to the region of Bahrain is shorter than the distance up the Nile to the confluence of the Atbara and the Nile. If the journey is associated with his religious conversion in Midian and began there, it would be even shorter. Such journeys were not unusual and the Midians were experienced traders, traveling throughout the region. If such a trip lies behind the tradition of the journey, then it would be another point of contact between Moses and the Prophet, who is reported to have accompanied caravans to Syria in his youth, broadening his own experience thereby and, perhaps, personally visiting some of the sites associated with Moses and other ancient prophets discussed in this study.

All of this is striking enough, but there is another point of contact: the Quranic figure of the "servant of God" with whom Moses traveled in search of knowledge. This servant is identified with the mysterious figure of Khidr by the strongest Muslim tradition. Khidr is not mentioned in the Quran by name; this may indicate that he was not meant to be an historical figure per se. In any case, in popular tradition, Khidr is immortal.[1950] In the *Epic of Gilgamesh*, Utnapishtim is immortal. Utnapishtim is associated with Dilmun-Bahrain and the saint Khidr has a shrine of unknown age (though presumably Islamic in its present form) on the small island of Faylakah off the coast of Kuwait, at the northern end of the classical Bahrain.[1951] According to local traditions, Khidr was the companion of Moses. He normally resides at Karbala,[1952] but on Tuesdays, he flies to the Island of Faylakah where he spends the night.

[1948] See Bibby-Dilmun, p. 236-238.

[1949] Bibby-Dilmun, p. 238.

[1950] Khidr, or perhaps more properly *Khaḍir*, means "green," the color signifying eternal life.

[1951] Bibby-Dilmun, p. 238.

[1952] Karbala is located by the Euphrates River, about 120 miles NW of the site of Gilgamesh's home city of Erech.

Petitioners often spend that night at the shrine.[1953] In the *Epic of Gilgamesh*, Utnapishtim is called "Exceeding Wise."[1954] Is this not reminiscent of the Quranic description (Q. 18:65) of the servant as one to whom "God had taught knowledge"?

The incident of fish is a still bit of a puzzlement. Besides Bal'ami's story, some commentators have also allegorized it. There is a suggestion that it may be traced to the *Alexander Romance*, which is itself indebted to the *Epic of Gilgamesh*, substituting Alexander for Gilgamesh, and considerably elaborating the story of Alexander's quest for the spring of eternal life, but the connection with the Quranic fish is tenuous.[1955]

That the quest for eternal life, the theme of the latter part of the *Epic of Gilgamesh* as well as the *Alexander Romance*, is not hinted at in the Quranic version is further evidence of a selective union of the features of one story or another in the fashioning of the extended parable. One may adduce a story circulating before the time of the Prophet with the features of the pericope in the Quran, but probably without the three tests. Clearly, at some point in pre-Islamic times, the traditions drawn from those that went into the Gilgamesh and Alexander stories became conflated with the tradition of the journey of Moses. However, if the story as it was known in the Hejaz had simply contained these elements, it would not have earned notice in the Quran. They are interesting, but their entertainment value far exceeds their moral value.

The reason for the story's inclusion in the Quran is the unique twist given to it as a parable in patience and trust in the wisdom of God; that is, the episode of the three tests. We now return to Jewish literature. There is a fable about one Joshua ben Levi who accompanied the prophet Elijah on a trip in which there were incidents similar to these in the Quran. There are four tests instead of the three in the Quran. It is worthwhile to quote the story in full:

"Among the many and various teachings dispensed by Elijah to his friends, there are none so important as his theodicy, the teachings vindicating God's justice in the administration of earthly affairs. He used many an opportunity to demonstrate it by precept and example. Once he granted his friend Rabbi Joshua ben Levi the fulfillment of any wish he

---

[1953] Bibby-Dilmun, p. 195.

[1954] ANE, I, p. 71.

[1955] Khadir, SEI, p. 232. On the fantastic journey Alexander came upon a river: "And there were... many kinds of fish which were cooked not by fire but rather by cold spring water. For one of the soldiers washed one in cold water, put it in a pan and left it, and then he found the fish cooked in the pan. And an hour after he had tried this, he showed it to the others." (PseudoCal, p. 114.)

might express, and all the Rabbi asked for was, that he might be permitted to accompany Elijah on his wanderings through the world. Elijah was prepared to gratify this wish. He only imposed the condition, that, however odd the Rabbi might think Elijah's actions, he was not to ask any explanation of them. If ever he demanded why, they would have to part company."

As in the Quran, in this story we find the condition of trust imposed upon the accompanier.

"So Elijah and the Rabbi fared forth together, and they journeyed on until the reached the house of a poor man, whose only earthly possession was a cow. The man and his wife were thorough good-hearted people, and the received the two wanderers with a cordial welcome. They invited the strangers into their house, set before them food and drink of the best they had, and made up a comfortable couch for them for the night."

"When Elijah and the Rabbi were ready to continue their journey on the following day, Elijah prayed that the cow belonging to his host might die. Before they left the house, the animal had expired. Rabbi Joshua was so shocked by the misfortune that had befallen the good people, he almost lost consciousness. He thought: 'Is that to be the poor man's reward for all his kind services to us?'

"And he could not refrain from putting the question to Elijah. But Elijah reminded him of the condition imposed and accepted at the beginning of their journey, and they travelled on, the Rabbi's curiosity unappeased." This test is not found in the Quranic story.

"That night they reached the house of a wealthy man, who did not pay his guests the courtesy of looking them in the face. Though they passed the night under his roof, he did not offer them food or drink. This rich man was desirous of having a wall repaired that had tumbled down. There was no need for him to take any steps to have it rebuilt, for, when Elijah left the house, he prayed that the wall might erect itself, and lo! it stood upright. Rabbi Joshua was greatly amazed, but true to his promise he suppressed the question that rose to his lips." This, of course, resembles the third test in the Quranic pericope.

"So the two travelled on again, until they reached an ornate synagogue, the seats in which were made of silver and gold. But the worshippers did not correspond in character to the magnificence of the building, for when it came to the point of satisfying the needs of the way-worn pilgrims, one of those present said: 'There is no dearth of water and bread, and the strange travellers can stay in the synagogue, whither these refreshments can be brought to them.'

"Early the next morning, when they were departing, Elijah wished those present in the synagogue in which they had lodged, that God might raise them all to 'heads.' Rabbi Joshua again had to exercise great self-restraint, and not put into the words the question that troubled him profoundly." This has no equivalent in the Quranic story.

"In the next town, they were received with great affability, and served abundantly with all their tired bodies craved. On these kind hosts Elijah, on leaving, bestowed the wish that God might give them but a single head. Now the Rabbi could not hold himself in check any longer, and he demanded an explanation of Elijah's freakish actions. Elijah consented to clear up his conduct for Joshua before they separated from each other. He spoke as follows:

"'The poor man's cow was killed, because I knew that on the same day the death of his wife had been ordained in heaven, and I prayed to god to accept the loss of the poor man's property as a substitute for the poor man's wife.

"'As for the rich man, there was a treasure hidden under the dilapidated wall, and, if he had rebuilt it, he would have found the gold; hence I set up the wall miraculously in order to deprive the curmudgeon of the valuable find.

"'I wished that the inhospitable people assembled in the synagogue might have many heads, for a place of numerous leaders is bound to be ruined by reason of the multiplicity of counsel and disputes.

"'To the inhabitants of our last sojourning place, on the other hand, I wished a "single head," for with one to guide a town, success will attend all its undertakings.

"'Know, then, that if thou seest an evil-doer prosper, it is not always unto his advantage, and if a righteous man suffers need and distress, think not God is unjust.' After there words Elijah and Rabbi Joshua separated from each other, and each went his own way."[1956]

The resemblance of this story to that of Moses the servant of God in the Quran is readily apparent. Elijah plays the same role as the "servant of God" (Khidr?),[1957] and Rabbi Joshua ben Levi that of Moses. Wensinck, in the SEI, and Ginzberg, in the *Legends of the Jews*, assert the dependence of the Quranic pericope account upon this story.[1958] There is clearly some sort of dependency, but it is not immediately clear which is dependent upon which; for, as far as written evidence goes—

[1956] LJ, IV, 223-226.
[1957] Surabadi identifies or links Elijah with the Khidr, by which link Elijah is also thought to be immortal. (See Elijah in Part Six below, I.)
[1958] Khadir, SEI, p. 232; LJ, VI, 334.

according to Ginzberg, the Quranic story's appearance is earlier by several centuries than its appearance in Jewish literature. The text we have just quote is from the medieval *Hibbur Yafeh*; it also appears in the *Ma'asiyot*.[1959] If this be taken as an Islamic borrowing from the Joshua ben Levi cycle, it would be the only one in Islamic tradition.[1960]

Only one of the acts of Elijah has a parallel in the Quranic story; that of the collapsing wall, and even in that the denouement is quite different and, in many respects, more satisfying. If there were a close connection, surely one of the others would also have been echoed in the Quran. But that is not the case. Perhaps both the Jewish and the Quranic stories were influenced by older oral traditions of which the written evidence—if such ever existed—has been lost. Such traditions may have been associated with some one else. They bear the stamp of folk wisdom. Ginzberg's argument that the story is of Jewish origin because Elijah appears in pre-Islamic Haggadah as the vindicator of God's justice is hardly conclusive. Such a theme can scarcely be said to have been a monopoly of Elijah in ancient literature. And the fact of the greater antiquity of the Quranic text remains. There is certainly a relationship, but it may be one of a common source from which both the Jewish and Arabian versions took form in pre-Islamic times, one associated with Elijah and the other with the Moses, who was better known among the Arabs.

It is reasonably clear that the Quranic story represents a cluster of traditions that must have developed over a considerable time. We have identified here at least three strands woven together in its development: the journey of Gilgamesh in search of the secret of eternal life, the expedition of Moses to the regions of Cush/Ethiopia cited in Artapanus and Josephus, and the tradition of the tests of patience by a mysterious figure endowed with supernatural prescience (Utnapishtim/servant of God-Khidr/Elijah) represented in Sumerian, Islamic, and Jewish versions, possibly from an even earlier source. The principal elements of the story were apparently well known among the Arabs (the journey, the fish, the two seas); the tests, perhaps less so as they are related more fully.

The result in the Quran is a quest for knowledge that may be understood by all of us, who are each on our own journeys, at many levels of spirituality. We are taught patience and to look beyond the obvious. We are taught that things are not always as they seem. We must

---

[1959] LJ, VI, 334. The composition of the *Ma'asiyot* last from the 7th to 11 centuries CE and cannot be necessarily free of Islamic influence.
[1960] Khadir, SEI, p. 232.

trust in the providence of God with its corollary of hope, and we must persevere in adversity.

The secret of everlasting life that Gilgamesh sought is found here in trust in the wisdom of God. The search for everlasting life is not a wrong one. Gilgamesh was simply looking in the wrong place. It is a long quest, but success does not lie on a mountaintop or beneath the sea. In fact, the secret of immortality is found in each one of us, in the soul and in the heart. And perhaps the final lesson to be derived from these few verses describing the journey of Moses is one of humility: even a prophet and lawgiver as great as Moses had to learn before he could teach.[1961]

M. BALAAM

"What have I done unto thee, that thou hast smitten me three times?"
(Num. 22:28)

Several verses in Surah Al-A'raf are taken by many commentators, among them Surabadi, to refer to Balaam (Ar. *Bal'am*), a seer mentioned in the Bible: *And recite unto them the tale of him to whom We gave Our revelations, but he sloughed them off, so Satan overtook him and he became of those who lead astray. And had We willed, We could have raised him by their means, but he clung to the earth and followed his own lust. Therefore, his likeness is as the likeness of a dog; if thou attackest him, he panteth with his tongue out, and if thou leavest him, he panteth with his tongue out...* (Q. 7:175-176)

This identification with the Biblical Balaam of *Numbers* is by no means certain, but once again, the Quran seems to be alluding to a story familiar to its initial audience. Whoever the person may be, in the Quran his story has become a parable condemning those who would cling to the world rather than climb the precipitous heights of spirituality.

According to Surabadi, the protagonist of the Quranic verses is Balaam the son of Beor, the religious leader of Jericho. He lived during the time of Moses. When Moses made to attack Jericho,[1962] he was opposed by Og the son of Anak.[1963] Og was so huge that he could pluck a

---

[1961] In the Quran, this story is followed immediately by the story of Dhul-Qarnayn with which it shares many features, including possible associations with Alexander. See Part Six, V, below.

[1962] According to the Bible, Moses never crossed the Jordan into Palestine; therefore, he never attacked Jericho. Joshua was responsible for that (Josh. 6).

[1963] The Arabic form of these names: Beor, *Bā'ūrā*; Og, *'Ūj* (or, according to some, *'Awj*) and Anak, *'Unuq*.

fish from the bottom of the sea and fry it on the sun. During the Flood, when all the mountains were covered by at least forty cubits (c. 60 ft.) of water, the waters only reached his knees. When he went to a city the people had to prepare an immense amount of food for him, or he would destroy them.

During the fight between Og and Moses, Og tore up a mountain of granite one parasang square[1964] and carried it up to drop on the camp of Moses. God ordered a hoopoe with a diamond beak to chip away at the rock. Gabriel came to Moses and told him to fight Og, whom he would defeat with one blow. When Moses went out to fight him, the hoopoe had carved a hole in the mountain Og was carrying, and it slipped down upon his neck. Moses, who was twelve cubits (c. 18 ft.) tall and his staff the same, leaped the same distance and struck Og's ankle with the head of his staff and killed him. Thus Surabadi.[1965]

The Biblical Og was the king of Bashan, and his defeat by the Israelites under Moses seems to have made a particularly deep impression upon them. There are scattered references to Og and his defeat in the books of *Numbers, Joshua,* and *Psalms* (135 and 136), which add little information to the principal narrative found in *Deuteronomy* (Deut. 3:1-13).[1966]

The Israelites, having defeated the Amorite king Sihon, turned north and defeated Og, king of Bashan, at the battle of Edrei (modern Der'a in Syria). Before the battle, the Israelites were afraid of the strength of Og, but God promised them victory. "So the Lord our God gave into our hand Og also, the king of Bashan, and all his people; and we smote him until no survivor was left to him. And we took all his cities at that time—there was not a city which we did not take from them—sixty cities, the whole region of Argob, the kingdom of Og of Bashan. All these were cities fortified with high walls, gates, and bars, besides very many unwalled villages. And we utterly destroyed them, as we did to Sihon the king of Heshbon, destroying every city, men women, and children. But all the cattle and the spoil of the cities we took as our booty." In this manner, Moses is said to have described the defeat of Og (Deut. 3:3-7). The genocidal massacre of the defeated was in accordance with the divine commandment about dealing with the vanquished peoples whose lands the Israelites were seizing: "And when the Lord thy God gives them over to thee, and thou defeatest them; then thou must

---

[1964] "a parasang square": about 3 miles square, or 9 square miles.

[1965] Surabadi, pp. 88-89. This resembles the story of the Greek hero Achilles. See below.

[1966] In a reversal of the usual pattern, the passage in *Numbers* is thought to have been borrowed from *Deuteronomy*, not the reverse. (BC, II, 141.)

utterly destroy them and show no mercy." (Deut. 7:2)[1967] No comment is needed about the barbarity of these scenes, and the knavery of ascribing them to God in a war of conquest.

Og's kingdom, Bashan, was located east of the Sea of Galilee and the Jordan valley, in the southwestern portion of modern Syria, extending as far as modern Salkhad (Biblical Salecah) in the east and almost reaching Damascus in the north. The capital was probably Ashtaroth. Bashan became the inheritance of the eastern half of the tribe of Manasseh. Its cattle were famous for their quality in Biblical times. Quite possibly, it was one of the last remaining Hyksos principalities in the region of Canaan.[1968]

Deuteronomy also notes Og's gigantic stature, or at least the size of his tomb: "For only Og the king of Bashan was left of the remnant of the Rephaim; behold, his bedstead of iron[1969]; is it not in Rabbah of the

---

[1967] For the Mosaic Law about holy war we may quote from the 20th chapter of *Deuteronomy*: "When thou drawest near to a city to fight against it, offer terms of peace to it. And if its answer to thee is peace and it opens to thee, then all the people who are found in it shall do forced labor for thee and shall serve thee. But if it makes no peace with thee, but makes war against thee, then thou shalt besiege it; and when the Lord thy God gives it into thy hand thou shalt put all its males to the sword, but the women and the little ones, the cattle, and everything else in the city, all its spoil, thou shalt take as booty for thyself; and thou shalt enjoy the soil of thy enemies, which the Lord has given thee. Thus thou shalt do to all the cities which are very far from thee, which are not cities of the nations here.

"But in the cities of these people that the Lord thy God gives thee for an inheritance, thou shalt save alive nothing that breathes, but thou shalt utterly destroy them, the Hittites and the Amorites, the Canaanites and the Perizzites, the Hivites and Jebusites, as the Lord thy God has commanded; that they may not teach thee to do according to all their abominable practices which they have done in the service of their gods, and so to sin against the Lord thy God." (Deut. 20:10-18)

When discussing the treatment of the Jewish Qurayzah after they had acted treacherously to the Muslims of Madinah at the time of war, Phipps argues that according to the Mosaic Law those who surrendered should not have been executed, just enslaved, and that therefore Muslim apologists are ignoring that provision of the (Mosaic) Law. But he ignores the two-tier approach of the Mosaic Law, or rather twists it on its head: clemency in surrender for those outside of 'inheritance of Israel,' but annihilation for those within the 'inheritance.' (Phipps, p. 89.) By that criterion, Madinah lay within the Islamic 'inheritance,' and the annihilation of the Jews without any provocation or cause would have been justified, whether they had acted treacherously or not. According to this interpretation of the Mosaic dictum, they should simply have been slaughtered in any case. In wartime Madinah, however, it was their own treason that brought this fate upon themselves; moreover, the arbiter of their fate was not a Muslim, but one of their own Jewish chiefs, Sa'd bin Mu'adh.

[1968] Bashan, DB, p. 91; Og, EJ, XII, 1341; ABL, p. 6.

[1969] At that time, before the development of high-temperature smelting techniques, iron was a precious metal and used decoratively as gold, silver, and ivory were. The bed was

Ammonites? Nine cubits was its length, and four cubits its breadth, according to the common cubit." (Deut. 3:11) This verse seems to imply that something called Og's bedstead could still be seen in the day of the writer. The Rephaim were a pre-Israelite people living east of the Jordan: "The Emim formerly lived there, a people great and many, and tall as the Anakim; like the Anakim they are also known as Rephaim, but the Moabites call them Emim." (Deut. 2:10-11) The Rephaim appear, from this passage, to be inclusive of the Anakim and Emim.

Not a great deal is known about these peoples who appear in the Bible as opponents of the occupation of their lands by the incoming Israelites. They were all defeated, and the scope of these victories was magnified by making them of gigantic stature, somewhat as a precursor to the David vs. Goliath tradition. This interchangeability of tribal names also includes the Nephilim.[1970] In Num. 13, spies sent out to survey Canaan before the Conquest reported: "the land... is a land that devours its inhabitants; and all the people that we saw in it are men of great stature. And there we saw the Nephilim (the sons of Anak, who come from the Nephilim); and we seemed to ourselves like grasshoppers, and so we seemed to them." (Num. 13:32-33, from P and JE) Thus, the demigod Nephilim of *Genesis* (Gen. 6:4) are related to the Anakim who are, in turn, related to the Rephaim and Og.

Since Surabadi uses the phrase "'Uj (Og) son of 'Unuq," let us consider the word *'Unuq* for a moment. The father (or ancestor) of Og would appear to be one 'Unuq, the Anak of *Joshua*: "According to the commandment of the Lord to Joshua, he gave Caleb the son of Jephunneh a portion among the people of Judah, Kiriath-arba, that is Hebron (Arba was the father of Anak), and Caleb drove out from there the three sons of Anak, Sheshai and Ahiman and Talmai, the descendants of Anak." (Josh. 15:13-14) Thus, Anak was associated with Hebron. His father Arba was said to be the founder of Hebron, whilst Anak was the father of the three clans of Anakim. However, this genealogy is not given much credence by scholars.[1971]

In the Biblical context, these traditions are connected with southern Palestine (Judah) and not with Bashan, some 120 miles to the northeast. However, another passage in *Joshua* (Josh. 11:21-22)[1972]

---

probably decorated with iron, not made of solid iron. (See Alan R. Millard's article, *King Og's Bed—Fact or Fancy?* BR, Vol. VI, No. 3, April 1990, pp. 16-21, especially p. 20.) The Biblical measurements would indicate a bed 14.5 ft. in length, and 6 ft. wide.

[1970] See Part One, IV, "Harut and Marut."

[1971] Kiriath-arba means "village of Arba." (Anak, DB, p. 30; Arba, DB, p. 49.)

[1972] "And Joshua came at that time and wiped out the Anakim from the hill country, from Hebron, from Debir, from Anab, and from all the hill country of Judah, and from all the

suggests that the Anakim were far more widespread than Josh. 15:13-14 indicates. The name itself (Ar. *'unuq*, a cognate of Hebrew *'anāq*, both associated with the neck) would imply that there was something significant about the necks of these people. They may have been "long-necked" or tattooed on their necks, or perhaps they wore conspicuous necklaces. The passages cited above indicate a relationship between the Anakim of the Hebron region and Og of Bashan, but it is probably one of kinship rather than direct descent, as Surabadi asserts.

The most noteworthy feature of these peoples: the Nephilim, the Anakim, and the Rephaim—according to their Israelite enemies who perhaps interested in magnifying their victories over them and the glory of their extermination—was their gigantic size and strength. The dimensions of Og's bed make it about five yards long. Commentators have suggested that this was in reality a reference of a prehistoric dolmen in the neighborhood of Rabbah, the modern Amman, capital of Jordan. This would seem to be based upon the idea that the Biblical writer, who was referring to a well-known relic, did not know the difference between iron and stone. In any event, the text makes about 14 ft. the upward limit of Og's height.

Jewish tradition joins Surabadi in the exaggeration of Og's stature. In the Talmud, it is said that his thighbone was three leagues long (nine miles!).[1973] He was born either before the Flood or before Abraham and lived either 800 or 500 years until killed by Moses.[1974] He consumed one thousand oxen a day or an equal quantity of other animals,[1975] and his death is described in the Talmud in the following fashion: "When he discovered that Israel's camp was three parasangs [9 miles] in circumference, he said: 'I shall now tear off a mountain of three parasangs, and cast it upon Israel's camp, and crush them.' He did as he had planned, pulled up a mountain of three parasangs, laid it upon his head, and came marching in the direction of the Israelite camp, to hurl it upon them. But what did God do? He caused ants to perforate the mountain, so that it slipped from Og's head down upon his neck, and when he attempted to shake it off, his teeth pushed out and extended to left and right, and did not let the mountain pass, so that he now stood there with the mountain, unable to throw it from him. When Moses saw

---

hill country of Israel; Joshua utterly destroyed them with their cities. There was none of the Anakim left in the land of the people of Israel; only in Gaza, in Gath, and in Ashdod, did some remain." (Jgs. 11:21-22)

[1973] LJ, III, 344; VI, 119.
[1974] LJ, III, 343; VU, 120.
[1975] LJ, III, 344.

this, he took an axe twelve cubits [18 ft.] long, leaped ten cubits [15 ft.] into the air, and dealt a blow to Og's ankle, which caused the giant's death."[1976]

The dependence of Surabadi's story upon this legend is obvious. Later Jewish Midrashim have a version in which birds, the hoopoe (as in Surabadi) or the raven, are substituted for the ants, perhaps under Islamic influence.[1977] Og's manner of death, killed by a wound in the ankle, is reminiscent of the death of Achilles in Greek legend — quite possibly the inspiration of both the Jewish and Islamic versions — who was killed by an arrow shot into his heel, the only vulnerable part of his body.[1978] In one Jewish tradition Og (and his brother Sihon) are represented as being so tall that the Flood did not reach to their ankles, as in Surabadi.[1979] However, in another place, Og saved himself by riding on the Ark.[1980]

Now Balaam makes his appearance. According to Surabadi, after the people of Jericho learned of the death of Og, they were frightened and they approached Balaam who was a learned man and whose prayers were answered. They asked him to pray against Moses. Balaam replied that Moses was a prophet and that they should submit themselves to him. The Jerichoans, knowing that the greatest man can be deceived by a woman, decided to offer a treasure to Balaam's wife to persuade her husband to pray against Moses. She agreed and approached her husband. At first Balaam would not agree to do so, but finally he did. He left for his retreat outside the city. On the road, he came to a sea that had never been there before. Taking it as a sign, he returned home, but his wife sent him out again. The second time the road was blocked by a high wall. Again he returned home and again his wife persuaded him to start out again. The third time, a lion blocked his way. In this fashion, he was obstructed seventy times, until at least he reached the retreat and was able to pray against Moses.[1981]

[1976] LJ, III, 245-246; VI, 120.

[1977] LJ, VI, 120.

[1978] Graves, Vol. 2, p. 316. According to the myth, his mother Thetis dipped the infant Achilles into the River Styx in order to make him invulnerable. But the waters did not touch the heel by which she was holding him, and that was his only vulnerable spot.

[1979] LJ, III, 469.

[1980] LJ, I, 160.

[1981] Surabadi notes that some say Balaam was to pray against Joshua rather than Moses. This perhaps is an indication of some confusion about the identity of the prophet involved in this story. Moses is not recorded as having proceeded north into the Bashan, so presumably Joshua was the commander in that war, or more probably it was fought independently by the Israelite tribes trying to wrest the land from its occupants.

When Moses found himself and his people lost in the wilderness, he asked who had caused it. The answer came that Balaam had done this. Moses prayed that the best thing Balaam had been given be taken away from him. So, when Balaam was praying to the Muslim qiblah with his wife behind him, he stood up and became an infidel, something that he should have done seventy years earlier. It is said that a white bird flew out of his throat, and that that was his "light of spiritual knowledge"[1982]; and a black bird flew in to replace it. It is also said that God took away from him His Greatest Name (or the Torah, or the Books of the Prophets, or His miraculous power (*karāmat*). He was likened to a dog whose tongue is extended in love of the world unnecessarily (compare Q. 7:176 quoted above).

When they saw that a man such as Balaam, who had been so near to God, had fallen into error, 70,000 Jewish scholars gathered to discuss the matter. They decided that the loss of divine knowledge came from four things: irresolution, dishonor, boldness, and neglect. If Balaam had prayed: *Our Lord, make not our hearts to swerve after Thou hast guided us,* (Q. 3:8) he would have avoided ruin.[1983]

In the Bible, the story of Balaam has nothing to do with the fall of Jericho; that story is associated with Joshua (Josh. 6). Nor is Balaam associated with Jericho itself, although the main source for his story, (Num. 22-24), begins with a statement that Israel was encamped in the plains of Moab beyond the Jordan at Jericho. This verse (Num. 22:1) is from P and is designed to tie the next three chapters about Balaam and his oracles to the events of the Conquest. Moses is not mentioned once during the three chapters, nor is his lieutenant Joshua. A redactor has simply inserted in this place the independent tradition of Balak and Balaam, as it is sometimes called. It is a conflation of accounts from J and E, in which are embedded several oracles in poetic form from another source, probably of greater antiquity.[1984] It is only in the Priestly material of Num. 31 that a link between Moses and Balaam is provided.[1985]

There is little in the Balak-Balaam chapters to justify the abhorrence in which Balaam was held by later writers such as John in the New Testament *Revelation*. In that book, the last in the Christian Biblical canon, we read (Jesus is the putative speaker): "'But I have a few things

---

[1982] "light of spiritual knowledge": Per. *nūr-i maᶜrifat.*
[1983] Surabadi, pp. 89-92.
[1984] Albright suggests that the oracles date from the 13th or 12th centuries BCE in an oral form. (Balaam, DB, p. 85.)
[1985] However, see the description of Balaam's death below.

against thee: thou hast some there who hold to the teaching of Balaam, who taught Balak to put a stumbling block before the sons of Israel, that they might eat food sacrificed to idols and practice immorality.'" (Rev. 2:14) And in *Jude*: "Woe to them! For they walk in the way of Cain, and abandon themselves for the sake of gain to Balaam's error, and perish in Korah's rebellion." (Jude 11)

In the Priestly tradition of Num. 19, it was the counsel of Balaam that was responsible for leading the Israelite men into a disaster which cost them 24,000 lives. Although the principal narrative is concerned with Moab (east of the southern half of the Dead Sea), in this chapter the scene is the aftermath of a battle with Midian farther to the south in which the Israelites were victorious: "They slew the kings of Midian... and they also slew Balaam the son of Beor with the sword." (Num. 31:8) The reason is made clear a little further on: "Moses said to them, 'Have ye saved all the women alive? Behold, these caused the people of Israel, by the counsel of Balaam, to act treacherously against the Lord in the matter of Peor, and so the plague came among the congregation of the Lord. Now therefore, kill every male among the little ones, and kill every woman who has known man by lying with him. But all the young girls who have not known man by lying with him, keep alive for yourselves.'" (Num. 31:15-18) This brutal, sanguinary reprisal wreaked by the Biblical Moses, extending even to male children, was in response to the defeated people's having followed the counsel of Balaam "in the matter of Peor."

But what was Peor? Peor should not be confused with Beor, Balaam's father. Peor was a mountain in the neighborhood of Mount Nebo east of the Jordan, where Baal-worship was long established.[1986] So, what was the affair of Peor? "While Israel dwelt in Shittim the people began to play the harlot with the daughters of Moab. These invited the people to the sacrifices of their gods, and the people ate, and bowed down to their gods. So Israel yoked himself to Baal of Peor." (Num. 25:1-3) In Jewish tradition, the explanation given is that this was a deliberate seduction by the Moabite women upon the advice of Balaam. However, in this passage, Balaam is not mentioned at all, and the women are Moabites, not Midianites as in Num. 31, where Balaam is mentioned. Though neighbors, the Moabites and Midianites were distinct peoples. Why was Moses wreaking vengeance upon the Midianites for the alleged crime of the Moabites? In any case, the result was that the Lord, angered by still another example of Israel's easy apostasy, sent a plague that took 24,000 lives.

[1986] See also the Story of Job, Part Three, II, which follows the Story of Moses.

Following these Biblical hints, many unfavorable notices about Balaam are to be found in Jewish tradition, associating him with the hated Pharaoh and the oppression of the Hebrews in Egypt.[1987] He incited nations against Israel,[1988] and counseled the Israelites to immorality.[1989]

In the Bible, as in Surabadi, a victory precedes the appeal to Balaam. The role played by the people of Jericho in Surabadi is instead assigned to the Moabites and their king Balak. The Israelites had just defeated the Ammonites under Sihon and the Bashanites under Og. The Moabites were terrified and their king, Balak, son of Zippor, sent messengers to bring Balaam, son of Beor, from his home at Pethor[1990] to come and curse the Israelites. It was believed that such a curse would aid in the defense of Moab. "God said to Balaam, 'Thou shalt not go with them; thou shalt not curse the people, for they are blessed.'" (Num. 22:12) The messengers returned to Moab without Balaam.

Balak sent another embassy, this time consisting of more important personages, and with offers of greater rewards. Balaam replied to their entreaties: "'Though Balak were to give me his house full of silver and gold, I could not go beyond the command of the Lord my God, to do less or more.'" (Num. 22:18) Balaam entertained the emissaries for the night and during the night God told Balaam to go with them, but to do only what He instructed him to do. "So Balaam rose in the morning, and saddled his ass, and went with the princes of Moab." (Num. 22:21)

In another of those improbable contradictions that are a commonplace in portions of the Bible, after just having been commanded by God to go with the Moabites, we read: "but God's anger was kindled because he went; and the angel of the Lord took his stand in the way as his adversary. Now he was riding on the ass, and his two servants were with him." (Num. 22:22) The princes of Moab have vanished from the narrative and have been replaced by two servants! This is caused by the awkward (and careless) joining of the Elohist source to Yahwist source in v. 22.

Visible only to the ass, the angel stood with a drawn sword at three points on the road. Not knowing the cause for the animal's stopping, on each occasion Balaam abused the beast until on the third halt it was given the power of speech. The ass reproached him, saying:

[1987] LJ, II, 255-256.

[1988] LJ, III, 354, 411.

[1989] LJ, III, 355, 362, 410, 411, etc.

[1990] Pethor: probably a town on the upper Euphrates south of Carchemish (Pethor, DB, p. 759). That would make Balaam a man of the same region, Harran, from which Abraham and his clan had set out for Canaan several centuries earlier.

"'What have I done to thee, that thou hast struck me these three times?'" (Num. 22:28) Showing no amazement at the prodigy of a talking ass, Balaam threatened to kill the animal in the short dialogue that ensued. "Then the Lord opened the eyes of Balaam, and he saw the angel of the Lord standing in the way, with his drawn sword in his hand; and he bowed his head, and fell on his face." (Num. 22:31)

Excusing himself for not understanding the behavior of the ass as a sign, Balaam offered to turn back. "And the angel of the Lord said to Balaam, 'Go with the men; but only the word which I bid thee, that shalt thou speak.' So Balaam went on with the princes of Balak." (Num. 22:35)

Thanks to a quick change from J to E, the princes have reappeared! The point of including this episode would appear to be to emphasize that the oracles and prophecies that Balaam will soon be called upon to utter in the text have come from God, and perhaps secondarily to justify his death because of the unsanctioned advice he is reported to have given the Midianites (not the Moabites) in chapter 31, although that episode belongs to a redaction several centuries later than the chapters we are now considering.

Balak honored Balaam by greeting him on the boundary of his territories. After making animal sacrifices and building altars, Balak asked Balaam to pronounce the curses. But instead of a curse, God made Balaam pronounce a blessing upon Israel. Balak and Balaam tried three different places, but in each, the result was the same. [In other words Balaam had actually come to curse Israel as in the original story, despite the divine instructions received in the incident of the balky ass. Could Balaam have forgotten his promise to God so quickly?]

Exasperated, Balak "struck his hands together; and... said to Balaam, 'I called thee to curse mine enemies, and behold, thou hast blessed them these three times. Therefore now flee to thy place; I said, "I will certainly honor thee," but the Lord has held thee back from honor.' And Balaam said to Balak, 'Did I not tell thy messengers whom thou didst sent to me, "If Balak should give me his house full of silver and gold, I would not be able to go beyond the word of the Lord, to do either good or bad of my own will; what the Lord speaks, that will I speak"?'" (Num. 24:10-13)

With several more dire predictions by Balaam concerning the fate of Israel's enemies, the Balak-Balaam chapters end somewhat ambiguously. The reader is left with the impression that Balaam is not firmly on the side of the Lord. If the Quranic verses cited at the beginning of this section do indeed refer to Balaam, then they are based upon the edition of the story in which Balaam later acts against Israel and Moses. As we have seen in the above, these chapters are associated with neither Moses nor Joshua. It is only in the late account of Balaam's death (by P, quoted above) that a connection is made.

Albright suggests that though the Priestly context of the defection and slaying of Balaam is late, it represents an oral tradition going back to the same period as that of the material in Num. 22-24. This is not unreasonable and would account for the strength the Jewish tradition that, though he was originally favored by God with prophetic powers, he later apostatized.[1991]

The Balaam stories quite probably are related to a real historical personality. The name Balaam is Northwest-Semitic, and was originally *Yabil-'ammu*, probably meaning, "May the clan lead." Similarly, the name of his father Beor is probably a shortened form of a name such as *Ba'al-ram*, "Baal is exalted."[1992] His country, Pethor in the land of the 'Amau, is also attested in 15th century BCE Egyptian inscriptions.[1993]

Many of the elements of Surabadi's story are obviously Islamic, such as the mention of Balaam's praying in the direction of the Muslim direction of prayer (*qiblah*). Indeed, there is considerable evidence that Surabadi's story of Balaam is only inspired in a vague way by the Biblical and later Jewish versions. Because the story is given in considerable (albeit confused) detail in *Numbers*, later Jews could not stray too far from the general outline. Perhaps the most conspicuous feature of the Biblical story and the later developments of it in Jewish traditions is the talking ass, but that is not even mentioned by Surabadi. The angel blocking Balaam's way is also absent from Surabadi. On the other hand, neither the Bible nor Jewish tradition assigns a role to Balaam's wife.

In Jewish tradition, it is Balaam's own avarice which leads him on.[1994] There is no mention of a sea or a lion as obstacles; however, there is a point of similarity in the matter of the wall. The Bible relates: "Then the angel of the Lord stood in a narrow path between the vineyards, with a wall on either side. And when the ass saw the angel of the Lord, she pushed against the wall, and pressed Balaam's foot against the wall; so he struck her again." (Num. 22:24-25) This similarity may be an accident rather than dependence, in view of the wide range of differences throughout the rest of the narrative. Jewish tradition also lists three faults

---

[1991] Balaam, EJ, IV, 121.
[1992] Balaam, EJ, IV, 122.
[1993] Balaam, EJ, IV, 122.
[1994] LJ, III, 361.

of Balaam's character that led to his downfall: a jealous eye, a haughty spirit, and a greedy soul. This may be compared with the list of four causes attributed to the 70,000 Jewish scholars in Surabadi.

The Islamic tradition of Balaam, as found in Surabadi, seems to be dependent upon the Biblical and rabbinic accounts in only its broadest outlines. The reader may not be satisfied that the Quranic passage refers to Balaam at all, but perhaps to someone else. Most of the detail does not seem to owe much to the material in available sources. This contrasts with other stories also suggested by brief Quranic references that correspond much more closely to their Biblical or later counterparts, as the following section will demonstrate. *And God knows best.*

N. THE DEATH OF AARON

And Aaron died there on top of the mountain. (Num. 20:28)

The Quran does not comment upon the death of Aaron, but Surabadi in his Commentary describes it: When the time for his death had come, instead of his going to Moses as he was wont to do each morning, "Moses, peace be upon him, came to him and took his hand and said: 'Come, let us enter this mountain and admire the wonders of the handiwork of God Most High.' They went in, taking Eleazar[1995] the son of Aaron with them. Upon entering the mountain, a luxuriant garden appeared in the midst of which was a mansion. Atop the mansion was a copula, and upon it, there was an adorned couch. Aaron said: 'Behold, what a pleasant place to sleep!' Moses, peace be upon him, said: 'If thou dost wish it, sleep on that couch.' Aaron removed his clothing and lay upon the couch. God Most High took his soul. Moses and Eleazar returned."[1996]

The Israelites preferred Aaron to Moses and they accused Moses of killing him out of jealousy because of Aaron's popularity and eloquence. Moses denied that he could slay his own brother. When the Israelites threatened to kill Moses, "God Most High commanded the angels to take Aaron's couch and bring it to the Children of Israel. It is said that God revived Aaron. Until the return of Moses [who had gone off to pray to God for His aid in this difficulty] Aaron chastised the Children of Israel, saying: 'Why do ye accuse Moses, the Word of God, of killing me? Nay, rather I died as was my destiny.' Having spoken

---

[1995] Surabadi calls him ᶜĀzar.
[1996] Surabadi, p. 57.

thus, Aaron died again and was returned to his place. Then the Children of Israel believed Moses and they mourned Aaron for many years."[1997]

The Biblical narrative of the death of Aaron makes no such accusation against Moses: "And they journeyed from Kadesh, and the people of Israel, the whole congregation, came to Mount Hor. And the Lord said to Moses and Aaron at Mount Hor, on the border of the land of Edom, 'Aaron shall be gathered to his people; for he shall not enter the land which I have given unto the people of Israel, because ye rebelled against My command at the waters of Meribah [see following section]. Take Aaron and Eleazar his son, and bring them up to Mount Hor; and strip Aaron of his garments and put them on Eleazar his son; and Aaron shall be gathered to his people and shall die there.'

"Moses did as the Lord commanded and they went up Mount Hor in the sight of all the congregation. And Moses stripped Aaron of his garments, and put them upon Eleazar his son; and Aaron died there on the top of the mountain. Then Moses and Eleazar came down from the mountain. And when all the congregation saw that Aaron was dead, all the house of Israel wept for Aaron for thirty days." (Num. 20:22-29)

The transfer of the garments symbolized, of course, the transfer of the office of the high priest of Israel from Aaron to his son Eleazar, thereby strengthening the claims of that branch of the Temple priesthood centuries later. (Not surprisingly, this passage—of doubtful historicity—is from the hand of the Priestly Writer.) Surabadi's account mentions the same three at the final scene: Moses, Aaron himself, and his son, but does not appear to know the reason for Eleazar's presence.[1998]

The scene of Aaron's death in the Bible is Mount Hor. Since the time of Josephus at least, Mount Hor has been identified with Jabal Harun, a peak in Mount Seir, above the fabled ruins of Petra in western Jordan. A tomb there is still pointed out to the traveler as that of Aaron.[1999] Josephus writes: "And when he came to a place which the Arabians esteem as their metropolis, which was formerly called Arce, but has now the [Greek] name of Petra, at this place, which was encompassed with high mountains, Aaron went up one of them in the sight of the whole army, Moses having before told him that he was to die, for this place was over against them. He put off his pontifical

---

[1997] Surabadi, pp. 57-58. The reader may be reminded of the murder of 'Amil in Section K above where 'Amil was also revived, albeit not to exonerate, but rather to accuse.

[1998] Aaron had four sons: Nadab, Abihu, Eleazar, and Ithamar. The first two died without issue after being struck down for some ritual offense against YHWH (Lev. 10:1-2; Num. 3:2-4). Therefore Eleazar, now the eldest, was Aaron's successor. See Section I above.

[1999] Hor, DB, p. 396. We have also seen the peak where Aaron reputedly rests.

garments, and delivered them to Eleazar his son, to whom the high priesthood belonged because he was the elder brother; and died while the multitude looked upon him."[2000]

In the Biblical account, Aaron's death is announced to Moses and Aaron together, but in Josephus, Moses knows of it before Aaron. This also seems to be also the assumption of Surabadi. A version of Aaron's death found in the 8th-century CE Midrash *Petirat Aharon* seems to stand behind Surabadi's story. In the *Petirat Aharon*, God asks Moses to prepare Aaron for death. "Ascend thou also with them, and there speak with thy brother, sweet and gentle words, the burden of which will, however, prepare him for what awaits him...[2001]

"Now it had been customary during the forty years' march through the desert for the people daily to gather, first before the seventy elders, then under their guidance before the princes of the tribes, then for all of them to appear before Eleazar and Aaron, and with these to go to Moses to present him their morning greeting. On this day, however, Moses made a change in this custom, and after having wept through the night, at the cock's crow summoned Eleazar before him and said to him: 'Go and call to me the elders and the princes, for I have to convey to them a commission from the Lord.' Accompanied by these men, Moses now betook himself to Aaron who, seeing Moses when he arose, asked: 'Why hast thou made a change in the usual custom?'"[2002]

Moses persuaded Aaron to go up the mountain with him in his priestly robes. On the mountain a cave opened up and they both entered it. Aaron divested himself of his clothes, though he still did not know that death awaited him, and Eleazar put them on. Gradually Aaron came to understand that his end was near. He lay down upon the "adorned couch in the cave and God received his soul." Then Moses left the cave, and it immediately disappeared.

"When the people saw Moses and Eleazar return without Aaron, they were not at all in the mood to lend faith to the communication of Aaron's death... Some declared that Moses had killed Aaron because he was jealous of his popularity; some thought Eleazar had killed his father to become his successor as high priest; and there were also some who declared that he had been removed from the earth to be translated to heaven. Satan had so incited the people against Moses and Eleazar that they wanted to stone them.

[2000] Josephus, Antiquities, IV.4.7, p. 89.
[2001] LJ, III, 321.
[2002] LJ, III, 322.

"Moses hereupon prayed to God, saying: 'Deliver me and Eleazar from this unmerited suspicion, and also show to the people Aaron's bier, that they may not believe him to be still alive, for in their boundless admiration of him they may even make a God of him.' [This is an oblique criticism of the Christian deification of Jesus.]

"God then said to the angels: 'Lift up on high the bier upon which lies My friend Aaron, so that Israel may know he is dead and may not lay hands upon Moses and Eleazar.' The angels did as they were bidden, and Israel then saw Aaron's bier floating in the air, while God before it and the angels behind intoned a funeral song for Aaron."[2003]

Jewish tradition describes the mourning for Aaron as even greater than that for Moses. In the *Fathers According to Rabbi Nathan* we read: "Why did all Israel weep for Aaron thirty days while for Moses only the men wept? Because Moses rendered judgment strictly according to the truth; but Aaron never said to a man, 'Thou hast acted offensively,' or to a woman, 'Thou hast acted offensively.' That is why it is said, 'And all the house of Israel wept for him.' But of Moses, who reproved them with strong words, it is said, 'And the men of Israel wept for Moses.' (Deut. 34:8) Moreover how many thousands there were in Israel named Aaron! For had it not been for Aaron these children would not have come into the world."[2004]

The same source shows Moses overwhelmed by the splendor of Aaron's death: "At that time Moses begged for a death like Aaron's death; for he saw Aaron's bier laid out with great honor, and bands and bands of ministering angels mourning him."[2005] The correspondence between these traditions and the story of Surabadi is quite close, contrasting strongly with his story of Balaam in the previous section that is a much freer in its adaptation.

A final point: this exaltation of Aaron, even over Moses, must strike the reader as curious. Had Aaron not been accused in the Bible of abetting apostasy and rebellion against the pure worship of YHWH? Clearly, there is a contradiction here which probably originates in a much more benign popular view of Aaron, possibly encouraged by the Aaronite priesthood, in contrast to the negative traditions hostile to him preserved in *Exodus* and *Numbers*.

[2003] LJ, III, 324-327.
[2004] ARN, p. 64.
[2005] ARN, p. 65.

O. THE DEATH OF MOSES

And there hath not arisen a prophet since in Israel like Moses...
(Deut. 34:10)

As in the case of Aaron, the Quran gives no special notice of the death of Moses, but Surabadi gives us an elaborate account of the event: When Moses' time had come, the Angel of Death accosted him on the road. Moses protested that he had requested that he be given a warning of his death. The angel replied that each grey hair and the weakening of his body were warnings. Moses asked permission to bless his family; his request was granted. He returned home and knocked on his door. When the people in the house asked who it was, Moses replied that it was he. They said it could not be Moses, because he had gone for three days of meditation and was not yet due back. Moses replied that he had returned with the Angel of Death. The inhabitants began to weep and mourn.

Moses asked Gabriel what would be the fate of his three children after his death.[2006] Gabriel told him to go to the seashore and strike the sea with his staff. He did and saw a stone at the bottom of the sea. He was told to strike the stone; when he did, it split apart revealing a red worm with a green leaf in its mouth. Gabriel said that if God had provided for this worm, how would He not provide for the children of His friends?

Moses returned and appointed Joshua son of Nun as his successor. Then he went with the Angel of Death to the place appointed for his death. Moses asked from what part of the body his life would be taken, that which had spoken with God, or the eyes which had beheld Him, or the hand which had grasped the Tables of the Law, or the feet which had gone to the Place of Prayer? The angel remarked that Moses did not want to die and commanded him to sigh. When he did so, the angel seized his soul.

In another version, Surabadi relates that when the Angel of Death came to Moses, the angel said that it was not proper that he take Moses' life without his agreement, and (the angel) retired to await that. Then Moses passed four angels in human form digging a grave. He learned it was for a friend of God, and the scent of Paradise rose out of it. Moses entered the grave and lay down, saying that he wished it were his own grave. He sought death and he died.[2007]

[2006] The Bible mentions only two of his children, his sons Gershom and Eliezer. (Ex. 18:3-4.)
[2007] Surabadi, pp. 58-59.

These stories have little in common with the Biblical version of Moses' death, although both share an atmosphere of the miraculous. In the Biblical account, Moses, when his time came, went willingly to the place appointed for his death. Like the rest of his generation, he was prohibited from entering the Promised Land. *Deuteronomy*, which is chief our source for the last days of Moses, gives the reason for this prohibition: God told Moses: "'Ascend this mountain of Abarim, Mount Nebo, which is in the land of Moab, opposite Jericho; and view the land of Canaan, which I give to the people of Israel for a possession; and die on the mountain which thou ascendest, and be gathered to thy people, as Aaron thy brother died in Mount Hor and was gathered to his people; because thou didst break faith with Me in the midst of the People of Israel at the waters of Meribah-kadesh, in the wilderness of Zin; because thou didst not revere Me as holy in the midst of the people of Israel. For thou shalt see the land before thee; but thou shalt not go there, into the land which I give unto the people of Israel.'" (Deut. 32:49-52)

It is presumed that this offense was the striking of the rock and producing water without first securing God's permission for the performance of this miracle. The punishment, considering some of the barbarous activities attributed to Moses in the Bible, seems rather disproportionate, and suggests that it is an interpretation of these events invented in a later time to explain how it was that a prophet and leader as favored by God as Moses had never set foot in Canaan.

JOSHUA: As Surabadi reports, so in the Bible Joshua was appointed Moses' successor. The book immediately following the Pentateuch is called by his name, and belongs to the same literary tradition as the five preceding books. Hence, the six books taken together are often spoken of as the *Hexateuch*.[2008] They relate the history of Israel from the beginning of the world to the Conquest of Canaan under Joshua.

Joshua (Ar. *Yūshaᶜ*, *Yushaᶜ*) is first mentioned at the battle with the Amalekites (Ex. 17:8-14). His name, according to the Priestly tradition to be found in *Numbers*, was originally Hoshea ("salvation"), and under that name he was one of the spies sent out to Canaan to survey the strength of its defenses: "from the tribe of Ephraim, Hoshea the son of Nun." (Num. 13:7) Later on, by adding the Name of God, Moses changed his name to Joshua, meaning "YHWH is salvation": "And Moses called Hosea the son of Nun Joshua" (Num. 13:16), still another Biblical name change. The mention of Ephraim shows that Joshua was of

---

[2008] As Pentateuch is from the Greek and means "Five Books," so Hexateuch means "Six Books."

the Josephic tribes, and the tradition is probably a Northern one. Joshua was also expressly exempted by God (as was Caleb of Judah) from the punishing prohibition against the entrance into Canaan of all Israelites over twenty that had prevented Moses and Aaron from doing so (Num. 14:28-20).

Joshua is not mentioned by name in the Quran, but he is probably one of the two men referred to in Surah al-Ma'idah: *Then two of the men who feared (God) unto whom God had been gracious spoke out: "Enter in upon them by the gate, for if ye enter by it, lo, ye will be victorious. So put your trust (in God) if ye are indeed believers.* (Q. 5:23) The other man, if this identification be correct, would be Caleb, and the incident would be their attempt to give heart to the Israelites who had been disheartened by the reports of the strength of the inhabitants of Canaan: "And Joshua the son of Nun and Caleb the son of Jephunneh, who were among those who had spied out the land, rent their clothes, and said to all the congregation of the people of Israel, 'The land, which we passed through to spy it out, is an exceedingly good land. If the Lord delights in us, He will bring us into this land and give it to us, a land which flows with milk and honey. Only do not rebel against the Lord; and do not fear the people of the land, for they are bread for us; their protection is removed from them, and the Lord is with us; do not fear them.' But all the congregation said to stone them with stones." (Num. 14:6-10)

But Joshua and Caleb were not stoned, and later, at the command of God, Moses appointed Joshua his successor: "And the Lord said to Moses, 'Take Joshua the son of Nun, a man in whom is the spirit, and lay thy hand upon him; cause him to stand before Eleazar the priest and all the congregation, and thou shalt commission him in their sight. Thou shalt invest him with some of thy authority, that all the congregation of the people of Israel may obey...' And Moses did as the Lord commanded him; he took Joshua and caused him to stand before Eleazar the priest and the whole congregation, and he laid his hands upon him, commissioned him as the Lord directed through Moses." (Num. 27:18-20, 22-23) A charismatic leader, Joshua went on to lead the Israelites into Canaan, invading from the far (eastern) side of the Jordan where the Israelites had been camped. Significantly, when the Israelites, carrying the Ark of the Covenant, reached the east bank of the river, they paused at Joshua's command. The River Jordan ceased flowing and the Israelites were able to cross to Canaan on the west bank on dry land as their parents had crossed the Red Sea under Moses (Josh. 3:14-17). He then ordered the Israelite males be circumcised, as circumcision had lapsed during the forty years of wandering in the wilderness under the supervision of Moses (Josh. 5:2-9).

The first city captured by Joshua, Jericho, was the scene of an horrific carnage: "then they utterly destroyed the city, both men and women, young and old, oxen, sheep, and asses, with the edge of the sword." (Josh. 621) Only a harlot who had betrayed her people survived the holocaust. The slaughter also reminds of some of Moses' acts. The most famous "miracle" associated with Joshua occurred when, in answer to his prayers, the sun stood still in its course thereby prolonging the day and enabling him and his forces to complete their victory over the Amorites: "the sun stayed in the midst of heaven, and did not hasten to go down for about a whole day." (Josh. 10:13b)

Although the military prowess attributed to him in the Bible may be exaggerated, there is little doubt that he was a real person. He was buried in the territory of the Ephraimites. As he does not figure prominently in Islamic tradition, we shall content ourselves with this much about him.

In the final scenes of Moses' life, after blessing the tribes of Israel in fulfillment of the command cited earlier: "...(he) went up from the plains of Moab to Mount Nebo, to the top of Pisgah, which is opposite Jericho. And the Lord showed him all the land, Gilead as far as Dan, all Naphtali, the land of Ephraim and Manasseh, all the land of Judah as far as the Western Sea [the Mediterranean], the Negeb, and the Plain, that is the valley of Jericho the city of palm trees, as far as Zoar. And the Lord said to him, 'This is the land of which I swore to Abraham, to Isaac, and to Jacob, "I will give it unto thy seed." I have let thee see it with thy eyes, but thou shalt not go over there.'" (Deut. 34:1-4)

"So Moses the servant of the Lord died there in the land of Moab, according to the word of the Lord, and He buried him in the valley in the land of Moab opposite Beth-peor; but no man knows the place of his burial to this day. Moses was a hundred and twenty years old when he died; his eye was not dim, nor his natural force abated. And the people of Israel wept for Moses thirty days; then the days of weeping and mourning for Moses were ended... And there has not arisen a prophet since in Israel like Moses, whom the Lord knew face to face, none like him for all the signs and the wonders which the Lord sent him to do in the land of Egypt, to Pharaoh and to all his servants and to all his land, and all the mighty power and all the great and terrible deeds which Moses wrought in the sight of all Israel." (Deut: 34:5-8, 10-12)

This is the Biblical account of the death of Moses and its summary of his accomplishments; his epitaph by the Elohist. He was buried by God Himself, the bible tells us, in an unknown place in Moab, in what later became the territory of the tribe of Reuben. Mount Nebo is traditionally identified with Jabal al-Naba, about fifteen miles southwest of Amman, the capital of Jordan.[2009] It rises 3907 ft. above the surface of the Dead Sea, the northern end of which lies less than ten miles due west of its peak. On a clear day, the view can be as described in the passage above from the northern end of Palestine to the Negeb, although the Mediterranean Sea is not visible from any point in the region.

Beth-peor has been identified with Baal-peor, the modern Khirbat al-Shaykh Jāyil, about three miles northwest of Mount Nebo.[2010] If the Deuteronomic tradition be correct, the grave of Moses would have been located in the valley that lies to the north of Mount Nebo. (The Talmud says that Moses' grave can never be discovered, because from the top of the mountain it looks as though it were in the valley, but from the valley it looks as though it were on the top of the mountain.[2011]) No Muslim shrine in the area seems to be associated with Moses, although there is one called Nabī Mūsā in a valley east of the Jordan, visible from the road between Jericho and Jerusalem.

The traditions in Surabadi about the death of Moses show greater independence of the Bible and Jewish literature than do those of Aaron cited in the previous section, although Surabadi's anecdotes about Moses' evasiveness when his hour had come are confirmed by Jewish tradition, much of it stemming upon Moses' great desire to live a few more years and enter the Promised Land. When Moses prayed for this, God told the angel Akrazaiel to lock all the gates of heaven so that Moses' prayer could not ascend into it.[2012] God tried to comfort Moses concerning his death,[2013] but he would not be comforted and he pleaded with the Earth, the Heavens, the Sun and the Moon, the Stars and the Planets, the Hills and the Mountains, Mount Sinai, the Rivers, the Deserts and all the Elements of Nature, and even the Great Sea to intercede with God on his behalf, but they all refused.[2014] He then approached Joshua, Eleazar, and Caleb, but also in vain,[2015] and ultimately the Angel of the Face, who told him: "'Why, Moses dost thou

---

[2009] Nebo, DB, p. 693.
[2010] OBA, pp. 63, 69; Beth-peor, DB, p. 101.
[2011] Moses, EJ, XII, 398.
[2012] LJ, III, 418-419.
[2013] LJ, III, 428-431.
[2014] LJ, III, 431-433.
[2015] LJ, III, 433-435.

exert thyself in vain? Standing behind the curtain that is drawn before the Lord, I heard that thy prayer in this instance is not to be answered.' Moses now laid his hand upon his head and wept bitterly, saying, 'To whom shall I not go, that he might implore God's mercy for me?'"[2016]

All of this is rather undignified and inconsistent with Moses' role as the founder of a nation and a religion. Of course, it is partly to be explained by a desire to show Moses' concern for his people who settled in the Promised Land after his death, and his burial outside of it seemed to orphan them.

Another view is reflected in *Deuteronomy Rabbah*. In this passage, Moses actually seems to fear death at the hands of the Angel of Death: "A voice from heaven resounded, saying, 'Why, Moses, dost thou strive in vain? Thy last second is at hand.' Moses instantly stood up for prayer, and said. 'Lord of the world! Be mindful of the day on which Thou didst reveal Thyself to me in the bush of thorns, and be mindful also of the day which I ascended into heaven and during forty days partook of neither food nor drink. Thou, Gracious and Merciful, deliver me not into the hand of Samael." God replied, 'I have heard thy prayer. I Myself shall attend to thee and bury thee.'

"Moses now sanctified himself as do the Seraphim that surround the Divine Majesty, whereupon God from the highest heavens revealed Himself to receive Moses' soul. When Moses beheld the Holy One, blessed be His Name, he fell upon his face and said, 'Lord of the world! In love didst Thou create the world, and in love Thou guidest it. Treat me also with love, and deliver me not into the hands of the Angel of Death." A heavenly voice sounded and said, 'Moses, be not afraid. "Thy righteousness shall go before thee; the glory of the Lord shall be thy reward.'"

"With God descended from heaven three angels, Michael, Gabriel, and Zagzagel. Gabriel arranged Moses' couch, Michael spread upon it a purple garment, and Zagzagel laid down a woolen pillow. God stationed Himself over Moses' head, Michael to his right, Gabriel to his left, and Zagzagel at his feet, whereupon God addressed Moses, 'Cross thy feet,' and Moses did so. He then said, 'Fold thy hands and lay them upon thy breast,' and Moses did so. Then God said, 'Close thine eyes,' and Moses did so. Then God spoke to Moses' soul, 'My daughter, one hundred and twenty years had I decreed that thou shouldst dwell in this righteous man's body, but hesitate not now to leave it, for thy time is

---

[2016] LJ, III, 435. The Angel of the Face is one of a select group of angels also called the Angels of the Presence. In rabbinic lore there were about a dozen of them. They were also referred to as angels of sanctification or glory (Davidson, p. 28).

run.'"[2017] (The soul is addressed as "daughter" because the word is feminine.)

The soul pleaded to remain in Moses, but "when Moses saw that his soul refused to heave him, he said to her, 'Is this because the Angel of Death wishes to show his power over thee?' the soul replied, 'Nay, God doth not wish to deliver me into the hands of death.' Moses: 'Wilt thou, perchance, weep when the others will weep at my departure?' The soul: 'The Lord "hath delivered mine eyes from tears.'"; Moses: 'Wilt thou, perchance, go into Hell when I am dead?' The soul: 'I will walk before the Lord in the land of the living.' When Moses heard these words, he permitted his soul to leave him, saying to her, 'Return unto thy rest, O my soul; for the Lord had dealt bountifully with thee.'"[2018] Another source, the Talmudic tractate *Baba Batra*, adds that God took Moses' soul by kissing him on the mouth.[2019]

As may be seen, Surabadi's traditions have little in common in detail with these Jewish traditions. Ginzberg records a version from the Falashas (of Ethiopia) very similar to Surabadi's account, but can find no pre-Islamic source for it.[2020] In the Talmud, the Angel of Death also has to resort to trickery in order to claim the soul of David,[2021] but the parallel ends there.

While the Bible makes Moses' death a solitary affair, away from the eyes of men, Josephus gives us a different version in which the people, who knew that Moses was going to die as he had told them so, were weeping and lamenting. Then, with the elders, Eleazar, and Joshua, Moses ascended the mountain. "He dismissed the senate [the elders]; and as he was going to embrace Eleazar and Joshua, and was still discoursing with them. A cloud stood over him on the sudden, and he disappeared in a certain valley, although he wrote in the holy books that he died, which was done out of fear, lest they should venture to say that, because of his extraordinary virtue, he went to God."[2022] That is how Moses came to be credited with writing the passage in *Deuteronomy* describing his own death and the subsequent mourning—although modern scholars consider the last chapter to be a pastiche with verses from all three of the principal sources of the Pentateuch: J, E, and P.

[2017] LJ, III, 471-472.
[2018] LJ, III, 472-473.
[2019] LJ, III, 473.
[2020] LJ, VI, 162-163.
[2021] LJ, IV, 113-114.
[2022] Josephus, Antiquities, IV.8.48, p. 103.

Thus died one of the most influential men who ever lived. His life, acts, and teachings have directly affected half of modern mankind: the Jews, the Christians, and the Muslims. Though some critics have doubted the reality of his existence because of the legendary nature of much of the material about him in the Bible, it would be as easy to doubt the historicity of Alexander simply because of the development of the Alexander romances of a later era. No, Moses was a real man, physically strong and impressive, yet meek (Num. 12:3); a leader who could rise to tremendous anger and passion when he saw his people violating their covenant with God. And in some manner, he was touched by God.

We have already quoted the Deuteronomist's judgment that "there has not arisen a prophet since in Israel like Moses." Josephus also commented upon his life: "He was one that exceeded all men that ever were in understanding, and made the best use of what that understanding suggested to him. He had a very graceful way of speaking and addressing himself to the multitude: and as to his other qualifications, he had such a full command of his passions, as if he had hardly any such in his soul, and only knew them by their names, as rather perceiving them in other men than in himself. He was also such a general of an army as is seldom seen, as well as such a prophet as was never known, and this to such a degree, that whatsoever he pronounced, you would think you heard the voice of God himself."[2023]

Is it any wonder then that Muslims, when reflecting upon the life of the Prophet Muhammad, have so often seen in Moses his prefigurement?

[2023] Josephus, Antiquities, IV.8.49, p. 103.

II. JOB

...we, too, like Job, are living precariously between the times.
(Laymon, p. 241)

The patience of Job (Ar. *Ayyūb*) has become proverbial among every people that have been reached by the Bible and the Quran. Surabadi also praises Job's patience, although in the stories of the prophets we have from his hand, the patience of Jacob is perhaps more perfect than that of the Biblical Job. However, that aside, for much of the world Job is the exemplar of pious patience. Does he deserve that reputation?

Job seems to be the only "Arab" to have been given a favorable report in the Bible; of course this "base" origin has been somewhat disguised and the story of Job is set in a kind of never-never land. Nonetheless, the Arabian origin of *Job* has been deduced from its language and geographical references. Its language differs substantially from classical Hebrew by using many words and idioms in their "Arabic" rather than in their Hebrew sense. The absence of a genealogy or the identification of Job with Israel and its tribal system is another significant indication that he was not a Hebrew. All of this points to an Edomite origin for the book.[2024] Indeed, Surabadi cites a tradition that asserts that Job was a son of Esau.[2025] This is probably more on target than many of his other traditions about Biblical ancestors.

The Biblical story of Job is contained in *Job*, the 18th book of the Old Testament in the standard Protestant Christian editions. It follows the fictional romance of *Esther* and precedes the *Psalms*. The fact that it follows *Esther*, set in the 5th- or 4th-century BCE Achaemenian period, and all of the historical books from *Genesis* to *Nehemiah* must not be taken as indication of the time period of Job's story, but rather the nature of its contents and, perhaps, the date of its recension.

Job was doubtless already a legendary figure when a 6th- or 5th-century BCE compiler took the existing prose legend about him and reworked it, inserting three cycles of speeches in poetry (the Dialogue),

---

[2024] Gaster, II, p. 784. Defenders of the Jewish origin of the book claim that these features are a conscious exoticism (Job, EJ, X, 120).

[2025] Surabadi, p. 136: "(Isaac) prayed that (Esau's) sons and their children be given great wealth [as compensation for the loss the prophethood and the rights of primogeniture out of which Esau had been tricked by Jacob] and no prophet came from his (line), except in a rare narrative that Job the Patient was one of his children (or descendants)."

and the Divine Intervention—if our compiler is the author of that section too.[2026] At a later date, at least two major additions were made to this text: the Hymn to Wisdom (ch. 28) and the Elihu Section (chs. 32-37). The way *Job* has been stitched together is a fascinating study of Bible-formation at work. The result is a complex composite, "divine inspiration" at its most incongruous. The source breakdown of the 42 chapters of *Job*, according to this theory, looks like this:

1. The Prologue in prose, probably based upon more ancient non-Hebraic texts and traditions (Babylonian, Edomite, Moabite, proto-Arabic?): Chs. 1 and 2.

2. The Dialogue in poetry, chs. 3-27, 29-31, the principle work of the first compiler, with the exception of ch. 28, the Hymn to Wisdom, added by a later redactor. The linguistic evidence suggests that the author was not in the mainstream of Jewish culture; indeed, the absence of specific references to Jewish religious custom and thought implies that he very well may not have been a Jew at all, but possibly an Edomite.

3. The Elihu Section, in poetry, Chapters 32-37. Almost certainly a later interpolation, though Gaster denies this.[2027] Job 2:11 mentions three friends of Job, the speakers of the Dialogue: Eliphaz of Temen, Bildad of Shuah, and Zophar of Naamah, who engage Job in a long discussion of the question of the suffering of the righteous. Elihu is not mentioned as being present at all. Suddenly in ch. 32, in a brief prose introduction, Elihu son of Barakel the Buzite of the family of Ram[2028] is introduced because "when he saw that there was no answer in the mouth of these three men, he became angry." (Job 32:5) Before this passage, there is no mention of him.

Scholars have noticed that the Dialogue is divided into three cycles of speeches, each cycle containing a speech by each of the three friends and a response to each speech by Job, a total of six speeches in each cycle. If this scheme had been followed to the end of the section, there would have been eighteen speeches. However, in the present text, the Dialogue breaks off after the second speaker in the third cycle and Zophar's speech (if there was one) is omitted. In view of the plan of the Dialogue, many scholars feel that in the original book there was such a speech, but it was excised, perhaps for theological reasons. The Elihu insertion would represent the effort by a later redactor (between 400 and

---

[2026] Trawick-OT, p. 274.

[2027] Gaster, II, pp. 784-785.

[2028] Elihu appears to have more Hebraic associations than Job's other three friends, but if "Ram" is a scribal error for "Aram," he would be from Job's own group. In any case, at this late date it can only be speculation (BC, Vol. 4, p. 120).

200 BCE) to correct the preceding theological debate in terms of later Jewish thinking.

4. The Divine Intervention, ch. 39-42:6, in poetry, which is a dialogue between God and Job, in which Job comes to realize that his sin has been that of questioning the purposes of God.

5. The Epilogue in prose, Job 42:7-43, like the Prologue based upon older material.

If this analysis be correct or nearly so, we have at least three levels of composition in the *Book of Job*: the original legend of a righteous man who is supremely patient in the face of great affliction, earning him his right to the epithet "patient" (the ensuing dialogues would not). It was not Hebraic in origin but probably current in the oral tradition of a wide section of the Fertile Crescent and, the evidence of the Quran suggests, in northwestern Arabia as well. The cosmology outlined in chs. 38, 39, and 41 is a further indication of the non-Hebraic origin of the original source of the story. This portion also shows signs of internal development: the character of Satan may belong to a later stratum [Edomite?].[2029] The Job mentioned by the writer of *Ezekiel* (Ezek. 14:14,20) along with Noah and Daniel as exemplary righteous men seems to be this Job the Patient of the *original* prose legend.

About 400 BCE, in the second stage, a writer, who may have been familiar with the forms of Greek tragedy, took the legend and made it the basis for a lofty dialogue concerning the human moral dilemma and in particular the question of the suffering of the innocent and righteous. In this, the patient Job of the original legend is converted into the impatient, questioning, rebellious Job of the Dialogue.

The reader will recall that the promise of Heaven and Hell does not play a prominent part in the Old Testament, and the condition of the soul after death was not the subject of much speculation until later times, presumably after contact with Persian thought. In general, it was believed that punishment and reward for actions were received in this life. Without the concept of reward in Heaven or punishment in hell in a kind of sentient afterlife, people were faced with dilemma: it was an observable fact (as it is to us today) that the righteous and innocent frequently suffer undeservedly whilst the evil-doers frequently go to their graves not only unpunished but with the undeserved rewards and honors that ought to have belonged to the righteous.

This is the problem addressed in *Job*. In reality, despite the fine speeches and the lofty poetry (some of the finest in the Bible), no answer

---

[2029] Job, EJ, X, 119-120.

is given; for to say that Job had sinned in questioning God's divine plan and therefore deserved his punishment, as much of the argument of the book holds, is no answer at all, since his punishment *preceded* his "crime." There is a hint, however, that in *Job* we see the Persian idea of judgment in the afterlife entering Semitic thought.[2030] In one place, Job, in replying to Bildad, says: "'For I know that my Redeemer liveth, and at last he will stand upon the earth; and after my skin has been thus destroyed, then from my flesh I shall see God, whom I shall see on my side, and my eyes shall behold, and not another.'" (Job 19:25-27)[2031]

Thus, *Job* represents an articulation of this problem for the first time in the Old Testament, and perhaps it is an indication that the moral climate was being readied for the acceptance of the revelation of the Judgment after death that was soon to enter Jewish thinking, probably stimulated by Persian beliefs. The irruption of the Iranians upon the Fertile Crescent in the 6th century BCE introduced new ideas of the duality of Good and Evil, Heaven and Hell, and the Judgment of the Dead which began working their way into the mainstream of Jewish and, later, Christian thought and writing.

In the third stage, some time between 400 and 200 BCE, the book was edited and added to, this time definitely by Jewish hands, for it came to be included among the Sacred Writings. At this stage, the Hymn to Wisdom was inserted at the end of *Job*'s reply to the second speech of

---

[2030] This concept of course reached a great refinement much earlier among the Egyptians, but for some reasons still not adequately explained, the Semites were not greatly influenced by Egyptian beliefs save, perhaps, an elite group who became Egyptianized in the same way other groups were to become Hellenized or Romanized later on. The Egyptians saw that the soul was answerable for the deeds of the body in this world, but was rewarded in a material fashion in the afterlife which was in some way dependent upon the good will of the living. For the people of the Fertile Crescent, as reflected in extant Sumerian, Babylonian, Assyrian, Syrian, and Hebrew literature, though the soul was believed to survive death, it went to an unpleasant place called by the Hebrews Sheol, mentioned above several times, regardless of the type of life led by its possessor on earth. Why this idea was, for the Hebrews, unacceptable from the Egyptians, but acceptable from the Persians is perhaps because the vastness of the Persian Empire and its comparative tolerance impressed the Jews favorably.

[2031] In these verses Christians have long seen a reference to Christ. In the 18th century CE, G.F. Handel set them to music in a magnificent aria in his oratorio, *Messiah* (at the beginning of Part Three). However, the text has many problems and probably does not refer to either a Jewish or a Christian Messiah. "Vindicator" may be a better translation than "redeemer" and may hark back to Sumerian cosmological ideas. It may not reflect belief in a resurrection and the "redeemer" may be a family member, not a spiritual being. "The Hebrew word refers to the next of kin who has the duty of avenging the blood of a brother or protecting his title to property after his death." (Laymon, pp. 246-7; BC, Vol. 4, pp. 82-4.)

the third cycle of the Dialogue and the possibly unsuitable speech of Zophar was removed from the third cycle of the Dialogue, assuming there was such a speech. The Elihu section was included to balance the book according to the Jewish editor's views of appropriateness.

It is in *Job* that we have the first appearance of Satan as a distinct personality in the Bible. In the scenes in heaven in which God is surrounded by His "sons," Satan is among them (Job 1:6).[2032] He is a member of the court of heaven and inflicts the calamities upon Job only with the permission of God. Indeed, the whole atmosphere of these brief scenes in heaven is redolent of ancient Middle Eastern images of the celestial court. The resemblance to certain graphic passages in the Quran (Q. 2:30; 115:28-29, for example) coming from the same tradition is not accidental, once again demonstrating the continuity of religious evolution.

Another point to be noted is that the present text of *Job* is in great disorder, a condition we have encountered in other Biblical texts before this. Modern scholars and editors have made a number of changes in the order of verses in various chapters, an indication of the gross corruption of the text. For example, in the *New English Bible*, the first six verses of ch. 41 are now placed after ch. 39 and before ch. 40; in ch. 34, v. 25 is transposed to follow v. 23. In ch. 24, the following verse order is now observed: 1,2,6,3,9,4,5,7,8,10,11,12, etc. Altogether, there are two dozen such transpositions in the recent emendation of the text.[2033]

Various etymologies have been proposes for the name Job, a name that is attested in inscriptions as early as the 14th century BCE. In its Hebrew form *ʾyybh*, it resembles a verb meaning: "to bear ill-will, or to be an enemy."[2034] Another derivation proposed is: *ay* ("where?") plus *ab* ("father") = "Where is (my) father?" "Object of enmity" and "the Assailed" have also been suggested.[2035] Ezekiel's linking of Job with Noah and Daniel, who are both drawn from non-Hebraic traditions, suggests that Job also was a saint of foreign origin, and the text of *Job*, as noted above, also supports this theory.

Returning to the Biblical story itself, the first verse of *Job* tells us that Job lived in the land of Uz (*ʿŪdh*). There are two lines of tradition about this, one pointing to the region of Hauran south of Damascus; another, stronger, to Edom south of Palestine or even

---

[2032] Eve's tempter in the Garden of Eden is a serpent and not called Satan, which in Hebrew means "adversary."

[2033] NEB, pp. 565-8, 560, 551.

[2034] Job, DB, p. 502; Job, EJ, X, 111.

[2035] BC, IV, 35.

northwestern Arabia.[2036] Edom was famous in the ancient world for its wisdom (Jer. 49:7; Bar. 3:22-23; Ob. 8). Glaser has placed Uz northwest of Madinah in the Hejaz.[2037] Tur-Sinai has suggested that a tribe called the Uz once lived in Edom but migrated to the Hauran.[2038] One is led to speculate about a possible connection between the 'Uz and the 'Ad of Arabian and Quranic tradition.[2039]

The question of the date of the original story of Job, the frame for the entire book, is also a vexed one. There is little in the book in the way of references to historical persons or events to help us, although the setting is the patriarchal, almost primeval, past.[2040] Jewish tradition associated Job with the Pharaoh of Moses, although there were other views pointing to the times of Abraham, Jacob, the Queen of Sheba, or even Esther! But the most widespread traditional view associates him with the era of Moses—though he is unmentioned in the Pentateuch—and for that reason we have included his story in this Part.[2041]

There are several parallels to various aspects and themes of the *Job* in ancient Near Eastern literature. From Egypt there is the *Dispute Over Suicide* found in a Middle Kingdom papyrus (2000-1740 BCE), but probably several centuries older. In it, a weary man tries to convince his soul of the desirability of suicide. The debate it contains has parallels in the Dialogue of *Job*, but since the Egyptian believes in an afterlife, and is looking forward to it, the flavor of the piece is quite different. It raises a different question, not dealt with in *Job*: Why live on when a better existence awaits us after death?[2042] There is nothing to suggest a dependence of the Biblical *Job* upon this text.

From the Babylonian Akkadian texts there is a closer parallel that has earned it the name "the Babylonian Job," dated between 1600 and 1200 BCE.[2043] Its relationship to the Biblical *Job* is more of a possibility. In this poem, the unnamed sufferer has been brought low

---

[2036] Uz, DB, p. 1021; BC, IV, 35.

[2037] Uz, DB, p. 1021.

[2038] Uz, EJ, XVI, 38. Hauran is a large district some 30 miles east of the Sea of Galilee, now in Syria.

[2039] The Hebrew 'Uz and Arabic 'Ad, despite their difference in English, have a good possible resemblance. Consonants are stronger and more persistent than vowels in Semitic languages, and both words share the same initial letter, a central long vowel, and closely related final letters: Heb. 'Ayn + long u + dh; Ar. 'Ayn + long a + d.

[2040] Job, DB, p. 501.

[2041] Job, EJ, X, 124.

[2042] Thomas, pp. 162-167. Of course, at that time the idea of an afterlife, the quality of which was tied to the moral conduct of this earthly life was not current among the Israelites.

[2043] BC, IV, 27.

from a high position and afflicted with loathsome physical ailments. He bears his suffering with less protest than the Biblical Job (or at least the Impatient Job of the dialogue). Eventually the god Marduk answers his pleas, healing and restoring him.[2044] All in all, he seems to have more in common with the Job of Surabadi and Islamic tradition than the composite picture in the Bible, as we shall see.

Another Akkadian poem, the *Babylonian Theodicy* of c. 1000 BCE is cast in the form of a dialogue between a sufferer and his friend. It has so much in common with the Biblical Dialogue between Job and his friends that the influence of this Babylonian poem upon the Biblical *Job* cannot be easily dismissed.[2045] However, as the dialogue does not figure in Surabadi's account, nor in the Job of the Quran, we shall not quote from it extensively here.

Other literary parallels exist, both in Near Eastern writings and in Greek literature, especially the great tragedies of Aeschylus (c. 525-456 BCE), Sophocles (496-406 BCE), and Euripides (486-406? BCE). However, the suggestion that there were links more direct than the similarity of the theodictic theme that seemed to be exercising men in much of the civilized world at that time, as shown in the wisdom literature then in vogue, is rather tenuous, but not impossible.

Job is mentioned in the Quran in four surahs, but his story is nowhere told in full in the sacred text. All we have are allusions listing him among the prophets (Q. 4:163) or as a guided man (Q. 6:85), and two somewhat fuller references to his story: *And Job, when he cried unto his Lord, saying: "Lo! Adversity afflicts me, and Thou are Most Merciful of all who show mercy." Then We heard his prayer and removed that adversity from which he suffered, and We gave him his household (that he had lost) and the like thereof along with them, a mercy from Our store, and a remembrance for the worshippers.* (Q. 21:83-84)

This is clearly a reference to the form of the story as it was known before the "Impatient Job" had become added to it. In Surah Sad, there are more allusions to details of the story as it must have been current among the Arabs: *And remember Our servant Job, when he cried unto his Lord (saying): "Lo, Satan doth afflict me with distress and torment." (And it was said to him): "Strike the ground with thy foot. This (spring) is a cool bath and a refreshing drink." And We bestowed on him (again) his household and therewith the life thereof, a mercy from Us, and a reminder unto men of understanding. And (it was said unto him): "Take in thy hand a branch and smite therewith, and break not thine*

[2044] BC, IV, 27; ANE, II, 148-160.
[2045] BC, IV, 27: ANE, II, 160-167; Thomas, pp. 97-103.

oath. Lo, We found him steadfast, how excellent a servant! Lo, he was ever penitent. (Q. 38:41-44)

This is the sum of what the Quran tells us about Job. Oddly, two of these rather specific traditions about him mentioned in the Quran are not found in the Biblical text of Job. Ignoring the possibility of local traditions of Job that might differ from or supplement the received text of the Bible, Jeffrey, writing in the *Encyclopædia of Islam*,[2046] quotes the suggestion that the two incidents mentioned in Surah Sad (Q. 38, quoted above) were suggested by two passages in *2 Kings*.

The incident of spring, in this view, was suggested by Naaman's cure of leprosy in *2 Kings*: "So Naaman came with his horses and chariots, and halted at the door of Elisha's house.[2047] And Elisha [Ar. *Alīsha*ᶜ] sent a messenger to him, saying, 'Go and wash in the Jordan seven times, and thy flesh shall be restored, and thou shalt be clean.' But Naaman was angry, and went away, saying, 'Behold, I thought that he would surely come out to me, and stand, and call on the name of the Lord his God, and wave his hand over the place, and cure the leper. Are not Abana and Pharpar, the rivers of Damascus, better than all the waters of Israel? Could I not wash in them, and be clean?' So he turned and went away in a rage. But his servant came near and said to him, 'My father, if the prophet had commanded thee to do some great thing, wouldst thou not have done it? How much rather, then, when he says to thee, "Wash, and be clean"?' So he went down and dipped himself seven times in the Jordan, according to the word of the man of God; and his flesh was restored like the flesh of a little child, and he was clean." (2 K. 5:9-14)

There is no stamping of the foot to apparently produce a spring, an event that more resembles the springs produced by Moses striking the rock with his staff in the Exodus. However, there is a resemblance to the report of the cure of the blind man by Jesus: "(Jesus) spat on the ground and made clay of the spittle and anointed the man's eyes with the clay, saying to him, "Go, wash in the pool of Siloam"... So he went and washed and came back seeing." (Jn. 9:6-7) Then there is the tradition of the appearance of Zamzam at Makkah, but it is not necessary to resort to such parallels. Bathing to relieve physical and mental stress is hardly an unusual circumstance in daily life. It is not necessary to postulate a direct Biblical antecedent for everything in the Quran.

[2046] Job, EI, I, 795-796.
[2047] Naaman was the commander of the army of the king of Syria (2 K. 5:1). Elisha was a 9th century BCE Israelite prophet, the successor of Elijah.

As for the bundle of rushes, this passage is offered as its origin: "Now when Elisha had fallen sick with the illness of which he was to die, Joash king of Israel[2048] went down to him, and wept before him, crying, 'My father, my father! The Chariots of Israel and its horsemen!' And Elisha said to him, 'Take a bow and arrows'; so he took a bow and arrows. Then he said to the king of Israel, 'Draw the bow'; and he drew it. And Elisha laid his hands upon the king's hands. And he said, 'Open the window eastward'; and he opened it. Then Elisha said, 'Shoot': and he shot. And he said, 'The Lord's arrow of victory, the arrow of victory over Syria! For thou shalt fight the Syrians in Aphek until thou hast made an end of them.' And he said, 'Take the arrows'; and he took them. And he said to the king of Israel, 'Strike the ground with them'; and he struck three times, and stopped. Then the man of God was angry with him, and said, 'Thou shouldest have struck five or six times; then thou wouldst have struck down Syria until thou hadst made an end of it, but now thou wilt strike down Syria only three times.'" (2 K. 13:14-19)

However, Muslim commentators explained the Quranic reference as the fulfillment of a vow Job had made to punish his virtuous wife Rahmah. (See below.)

Turning to what our exemplar commentator Surabadi did with the story of Job, he begins by observing that no one had ever received more bounty than Solomon or more trials than Job, and he was patient in the face of them. The devil (Iblis) was envious of Job, whose obedience to God was greater than that of all mankind. Iblis told God that Job's obedience was due to his wealth and health. God rejected this, saying that it was because of His divine grace, and He gave Iblis permission to tamper with Job's prosperity. According to the traditions cited by Surabadi, Job had large herds of camels, cattle, sheep, and donkeys; he employed no less than 4,000 shepherds.[2049]

The Bible, too, makes Job rich in flocks and herds (the coin of wealth in that distant time), but not so great as Surabadi's figure of 4,000 shepherds would suggest: "He had seven thousand sheep, three thousand camels, five hundred yoke of oxen, and five hundred she-asses, and very many servants; so that this was the greatest of all the people of the east." (Job 1:3) Mention of the east here reminds us of Cain's taking refuge "east of Eden." (Gen: 4:16) Both references have the flavor of lands unknown at that time.

[2048] Joash (or Jehoash), king of Israel, rgd. 798-782 BCE.
[2049] Surabadi, p. 370.

Despite the very specific Biblical figures, the 1st-century BCE pseudepigraphical *Testament of Job* [2050] has already inflated the figures of Job's wealth along the lines that the medieval Muslim commentators were to follow: "Of sheep he had no less than 130,000, and he required 800 dogs to keep guard over them, not to mention the 200 dogs needed to secure the safety of his house. Besides, his herds consisted of 340,000 asses and 3,500 pairs of oxen."[2051] In addition to all this, according to Talmudic tradition, Job was blessed with a foretaste of the messianic era, and harvest followed close upon the ploughing of his fields. "No sooner were the seeds strewn in the furrows than they sprouted and grew and ripened produce... His sheep killed wolves, but were themselves never harmed by wild beasts."[2052]

The Quran mentions Satan's role in Job's afflictions, and in Surabadi the scene leading up to this is pictured much as it is in this Biblical description: "Now there was a day when the sons of God came to present themselves before the Lord, and Satan also came among them.[2053] The Lord said to Satan, 'Whence hast thou come?' Satan answered the Lord, 'From going to and fro on the earth, and from walking up and down on it.' And the Lord said to Satan, 'Hast thou considered My servant Job, that there is none like him on the earth, a blameless and upright man, who fears God and turns away from evil?' Then Satan answered the Lord, 'Doth Job fear God for naught? Hast Thou not put a hedge about him and his house and all that he has, on every side? Thou hast blessed the work of his hands, and his possessions have increased in the land. But put forth thy hand now, and touch all that he has, and he will curse Thee to Thy face.' And the Lord said to Satan, 'Behold, all that he has is in thy power; only upon himself do not put forth thy hand.' So Satan went forth from the presence of the Lord." (Job 1:6-12)

In the Biblical text, this is followed immediately by the swift loss or destruction of all of Job's folk and property: "And there came a messenger to Job, and said, 'The oxen were ploughing and the asses feeding beside them; and the Sabeans [?, Chaldeans? spoilers?] fell upon them and took them, and slew the servants with the edge of the sword;

[2050] Known only in Greek. Job, Testament of, EJ, X, 129.

[2051] This is Ginzberg's summary in LJ, II, 229. The edition by Kraft has a more extensive list of Job's property including 9000 camels, fifty bakeries, etc. Kraft changes Ginzberg's figure of 800 sheep dogs to 80 (Test Job, pp. 31-37), although considering the size of Job's flocks, more than 80 ought to have been employed.

[2052] LJ, II, 228-229.

[2053] This passage shows the great antiquity of the tradition. A later work would almost certainly have referred to angels rather than the "sons of God."

and I alone have escaped to tell thee.' While he was yet speaking, there came another, and said, 'The fire of God fell from heaven and burned up the sheep and the servants, and consumed them; and I alone have escaped to tell thee.' While he was yet speaking, there came another, and said, 'The Chaldeans formed three companies, and made a raid upon the camels and took them, and slew the servants with the edge of the sword; and I alone have escaped to tell thee.' While he was yet speaking, there came another, and said, 'Thy sons and daughter were eating and drinking wine in their eldest brother's house; and behold, a great wind came across the wilderness, and struck the four corners of the house, and it fell upon the young people, and they are dead; and I alone have escaped to tell thee.'" (Job 1:14-19)

What a cascade of misfortunes! Surabadi divides this litany of unremitting disaster into two parts by inserting another dialogue between God and Satan after the destruction of Job's wealth and before the destruction of his children, in which Satan told God that Job's strength lay in his offspring, for Job had seven sons and three daughters.[2054] God gave Satan permission to try Job [in a morally debatable fashion], and while the (presumably innocent) children were sitting at the foot of their teacher, the column supporting the roof of the house was wrenched away and the ceiling collapsed, crushing to death all the children. Then Satan, assuming the appearance of the teacher, reported the disaster to Job. Job replied that God takes away that which He has given; if the teacher had been a good person, he would have perished also. Then Job returned to his worship.[2055]

The reaction of the Biblical Job to this string of catastrophes is phrased in similar terms, although there is no hint that the bearer of the bad news was Satan himself: "Then Job arose, and rent his robe, and shaved his head, and fell upon the ground, and worshipped. And he said, 'Naked came I out of my mother's womb, and naked shall I return thither; the Lord gave, and the Lord hath taken away; blessed be the name of the Lord.'" (Job 1:20-21)

The *Testament of Job* gives us a somewhat different version of the fate of Job's children, although the role of the instigator is assigned to Satan, as in Surabadi. "Satan disguised himself as the king of Persia, besieged the city of Job's residence, took it, and spoke to the inhabitants, saying: 'This man Job hath appropriated all the goods in the world, leaving naught for others, and he hath also torn down the temple of our

---

[2054] The Bible agrees with Surabadi: "There were born to (Job) seven sons and three daughters." (Job 1:2)

[2055] Surabadi, pp. 370-371.

god, and now I will pay him back for his wicked deeds. Come with me and let us pillage his house.' At first the people refused to hearken to the words of Satan. They feared that the sons and daughters of Job might rise up against them later, and avenge their father's wrongs. But after Satan had pulled down the house wherein the children of Job were assembled, and they lay dead in the ruins, the people did as he bade them, and sacked the house of Job."[2056]

In this version (as in the Islamic versions), Satan is assigned a much more prominent role. The Satan of the *Book of Job* is not the enemy of God, but rather a kind of inspector who attacks God's confidence in Job by a not unreasonable logic. The pitting of Satan against God, as we see in the *Testament of Job*, the New Testament, the Quran, and Islamic tradition, is a later development, to a greater or lesser extent under Iranian influence. Satan in the Biblical *Job* represents a stage in the acceptance of this idea into Jewish thought.[2057]

After failing to turn Job away from the worship of God, narrates Surabadi, Satan returned to God saying that Job's obedience was due to his good health. With God's permission, he afflicted Job with a loathsome disease whilst he was at prayer. It is said that Satan breathed into Job' nostrils, or, in another tradition, attacked his feet.[2058]

In the Bible, the illness is prefaced by the second scene at the heavenly court in which God chides Satan for his failure to weaken Job's faith. "Then Satan answered the Lord, 'Skin for skin! All that a man has he will give for his life. But put forth Thy hand now, and touch his bone and his flesh, and he will curse Thee to Thy face.' And the Lord said to Satan, 'Behold, he is in thy power; only spare his life.' So Satan went forth from the presence of the Lord, and afflicted Job with loathsome sores from the sole of his foot to the crown of his head. And he took a potsherd with which to scrape himself, and sat among the ashes." (Job 2:4-8)

The *Testament of Job* adds more details: "Satan now caused a terrific storm to burst over the house of Job. He was cast from his throne by the reverberations and he lay upon the floor for three hours. Then Satan smote his body with leprosy from the sole of his foot unto his crown. This plague forced Job to leave the city, and sit down outside upon an ash-heap... His body swarmed with vermin, but if one of the little creatures attempted to crawl away from him, he forced it back, saying, 'Remain on the place whither thou wast sent, until God assigns

---

[2056] LJ, II, 234; see also Test Job, pp. 39-41.
[2057] Albright-Stone Age, pp. 361-362.
[2058] Surabadi, p. 371.

another unto thee.'"[2059] The unnamed sufferer in the much older *Babylonian Job* described his affliction in even more graphic terms,[2060] but the connection of that poem with the Biblical Job is uncertain and may just be a coincidence of theme.

After Job becomes diseased, his wife joins the *dramatis personae* for the first time, both in Surabadi and the Bible. In the Bible her appearance is not a happy one, for she suggests to her husband that he end his suffering by means of suicide: "Then his wife said to him, 'Dost thou still hold fast thy integrity? Curse God, and die.' But he said to her, 'Thou speakest as one of the foolish women would speak. Shall we receive good at the hand of God, and shall we not receive evil?' In all this Job did not sin with his lips." (Job 2:9-10)

This is the only mention of Job's wife in the *Job*. As reflected in Islamic tradition and Surabadi, she is a more sympathetic character.

[2059] Cited in LJ, II, 234-235; see also Test Job, p. 43.

[2060] Said the Babylonian Job:

> "As for me, exhausted, a windstorm is driving me on!
> Debilitating Disease is let loose upon me:
> An Evil Wind has blown from the horizon.
> Headache has sprung up from the surface of the underworld.
> An Evil Cough has left its *Apsu*,
> The Irresistible Demon has left *Ekur*...
> They all joined in and came on me together.
> They struck my head, they enveloped my skull;
> My face is gloomy, my eyes flow.
> They have wrenched my neck muscles and made my neck limp.
> They struck my chest, beat my breast.
> They affected my flesh and made me shake,
> In my epigastrium [stomach, gut] they kindled a fire.
> They churned up my bowels
> Causing the discharge of phlegm, they tired out my lungs.
> They tired out my limbs and made my fat quake.
> My upright stance they knocked down like a wall,
> My robust figure they laid down like a rush,...
> My eyes stare straight ahead, but cannot see,
> My ears are open, but cannot hear,
> Feebleness has overcome my whole body,
> An attack of illness has fallen upon my flesh...
> And at night he does not let me breathe easily for a minute.
> Through twisting my joints are parted,
> My limbs are splayed and knocked apart.
> I spent the night in my dung like an ox,
> And wallowed in my excrement like a sheep.
> My symptoms are beyond the exorcist,
> And my omens have confused the diviner." (ANE, II, 152, 153, 154.)

Rahmah,[2061] Job's wife, had carried him to a shelter made of branches outside the city because the people could not endure seeing his misery in the town. She worked in the houses of the townsfolk in order to earn enough to provide for them both. Once, when she had no money, she sold her hair for bread. In the form of an old man, Iblis rushed to Job and told him that his wife had committed adultery and her hair had been cut off as punishment. When she returned to Job, he touched her head and found that her hair was gone. His anger flared and he swore to beat her with 100 strokes. Rahmah was so saddened by this false accusation that God Himself (or by means of Gabriel) told Job of her innocence and that he should honor his vow by striking his wife lightly with a sheaf of 100 blades of grass. Gabriel told him that the old man had been Iblis who, after taking away Job's wealth and children, was now after his faith.[2062]

Although the Bible does not tell us very much about Job's wife, other than the rather negative speech quoted above, she is more prominent in the *Testament of Job*, and her story there is in contact with the Islamic (ancient Arabian orally transmitted?) tradition. "Her lot was bitter, indeed, for she had had to take service as water-carrier with a common churl, and when her master learnt that she shared her bread with Job, he dismissed her. To keep her husband from starving, she cut off her hair, and purchased bread with it. It was all she had to pay the price charged by the bread merchant, none other than Satan himself, who wanted to put her to the test. He said to her, 'Hadst thou not deserved this great misery of thine, it had not come upon thee.' This speech was more than the poor woman could bear. Then it was that she came to her husband. Amid tears and groans she urged him to renounce God and die. Job, however, was not perturbed by her words, because he divined at once that Satan stood behind his wife, and seduced her to speak thus. Turning to the tempter, he said: 'Why dost thou not meet me frankly? Give up thy underhand ways, thou wretch.' Thereupon Satan appeared before Job, admitted that he had been vanquished, and went away abashed."[2063]

It is clear that this story lies behind part of Surabadi's narrative, although neither the incident of the oath nor the accusation of adultery occur in it. At this distance, it is difficult to determine whether the commentator's explanation of the Quranic verse about the oath of Job is based upon a divergent Arabian tradition about her or not. In lieu of any

---

[2061] Rahmah: her name means "mercy" (Ar. *Raḥmah*). In Islamic tradition, she was the daughter of one of the sons of Joseph. (Ayyub, EI, Vol. I, pp. 795-796.)

[2062] Surabadi, pp. 371-373.

[2063] LJ, II, 235-236; see also Test Job, pp. 43-53.

other reasonable suggestion (the Biblical "parallel" in *2 Kings* cited above can hardly be taken seriously), we may consider that it possibly reflects an older tradition current in Arabia, which was the context of the Quranic verses. Nevertheless, there will always remain a suspicion that the original oral tradition was lost or distorted and the later Muslim commentators, unable to retrieve it, adapted the story of Job's wife from the later Jewish Job cycle to meet their exegetic needs.

While the Bible makes no mention of the fate of Job's wife Zitidos,[2064] in the *Testament of Job* she died during the years of the trial of Job, and when he had recovered, he married Dinah, the daughter of Jacob.[2065] This tradition of the death of Job's first wife is not reflected in Surabadi, but Dr. Mahdavi, in a footnote, cites a tradition of Kisa'i to the effect that Rahmah (Zitidos) was the daughter of Ephraim, the son of Joseph.[2066] By this "convenient" discovery, the revered Job was now a son-in-law of the Israelites and he became linked with Jewish tradition, despite the silence of the Bible on the existence of such a tie.

The Quran knows only the Patient Job (Q. 21:83-84, quoted above).[2067] However, Surabadi and the commentators, displaying again the strength of the influence of the Jewish development of the tradition as found in the present Biblical book, also speak of the Impatient Job. There is no indication in the Quran (or in the original Biblical frame story) that Job begged for relief from his afflictions, however, several instances of this are quoted by Surabadi. In one version, Job is shown asking for relief when Rahmah was returning to him and Iblis encountered her on the way and told her that the reason for her husband's misfortunes was that he had not worshipped the god of the earth and only worshipped the god of the sky. Rahmah had not heard of the god of the earth and asked where he might be found. Iblis answered that he was at a certain high

---

[2064] Zitidos, in Ginzberg's spelling. In the Kraft edition of the *Testament of Job* she is named Sitidos. The EJ writes that she was called Sitis (Job, Testament of, EJ, X, 29).

[2065] LJ, II, 241.

[2066] Surabadi, p. 370.

[2067] Compare also the acceptance of his suffering by the Babylonian Job:

"What is good for oneself may be offense to one's god,
What in one's own heart seems despicable may be proper to one's god.
Who can know the will of the gods of heaven?
Who can understand the plans of the underworld gods?
Where have humans learned the way of a god?...
When full they oppose their god.
In good times they speak of scaling heaven,
When they are troubled they talk of going down to hell.
I am perplexed at these things; I have not been able to understand their
   significance..." (ANE, II, 152.)

place. He showed it to her with himself enthroned and surrounded by demons in the guise of angels. Rahmah believed him and told Job that he should worship the god of earth. When he heard that, he begged relief from God, because Satan was attacking his faith.[2068]

This does not have a close parallel in the Bible or the Jewish traditions cited by Ginzberg. However, in the *Testament of Job*, before Job's tribulations begin, the God-fearing life led by Job had excited the hatred of Satan. "Near Job's house there was an idol worshipped by the people. Suddenly doubts assailed the heart of Job, and he asked himself: 'Is this idol really the creator of heaven and earth? How can I find out the truth about it?' In the following night he perceived a voice calling: "Jobab! Jobab![2069] Arise, and I will tell thee who he is whom thou desirest to know. This one to whom the people offer sacrifices is not God, he is the handiwork of the tempter, wherewith he deceives men.' When he heard the voice, Job threw himself on the ground, and said: 'O Lord, if this idol is the handiwork of the tempter, then grant that I may destroy it. None can hinder me, for I am the king of this land.'"[2070] And calling fifty men, Job did just that, thereby earning the enmity of Satan who thereafter proposed to God that Job be tested in his faith. Perhaps this pericope of Job's doubts is related to the tradition in Surabadi.

The next cause given was that his students of the days in which he had been whole had come to visit him: One day one of them said that God never punished anyone unless he deserved it [the empirically incorrect assumption that forms the main theme of *Job*]. Job could not bear this imputation and so he sought relief from God.[2071] This would seem to be based on the visit of the three (later four) interlocutors who commiserate with Job. Their conversation, the Dialogue (Job 3-31), occupies the bulk of the Biblical *Book of Job* (as it now stands) and represents Job, as we have noted above, as being Impatient and protesting against the injustice of his fate. This is quite the opposite of the older form of the story reflected in the Quran and the prose passages of the Biblical book (chs. 1,2, 42:7-17).

In the Bible, their visit begins as an act of sympathy: "Now when Job's three friends heard of all this evil that had come upon him, they came each from his own place, Eliphaz the Temanite, Bildad the Shuhite,

---

[2068] Surabadi, p. 373.
[2069] Jobab is an alternative form of Job.
[2070] LJ, II, 231; see also Test Job, 23-25.
[2071] Surabadi, p. 373.

and Zophar the Naamathite.[2072] They made an appointment together to come to condole with him and comfort him. And when they saw him from afar, they did not recognize him: and they raised their voices and wept; and they rent their robes and sprinkled dust upon their head toward heaven. And they sat with him on the ground seven days and seven nights, and no one spoke a word to him, for they saw that his suffering was very great." (Job 2:11-13)

However, in the great debate—the Dialogue—everything is changed. It begins with Job's cry against his fate: "Let the day perish wherein I was born, and the night which said, 'A man-child is conceived.'" (Job 3:3) This is the opening challenge of the debate. The theodictic argument about divine justice commences, with Job the questioner and the three friends defending its reality. The first speaker accuses Job, saying that some sin of his must have brought about all this retribution (an accusation to which Surabadi has referred). Eliphaz beings with a reference to Job's role as a teacher: "If one ventures a word with thee, wilt thou be offended? Yet who can keep from speaking? Behold, thou hast instructed many, and thou hast strengthened the weak hands...'" (Job 4:2-3) But this is shortly after followed by the accusation: "'Think now, who that was innocent ever perished? Or where were the upright cut off?'" (Job 4:7)

In a later passage, Eliphaz accuses Job of all sorts of possible crimes that could earned such punishment: "'Is not thy wickedness great? There is no end to thy iniquities. For thou hast exacted pledges of thy brothers for nothing, and stripped the naked of their clothing. Thou hast given no water to the weary to drink, and thou hast withheld bread from the hungry. The man with power possessed the land, and the favored man dwelt in it. Thou hast sent widows away empty, and the arms of the fatherless were crushed. Therefore snares are round about thee, and sudden terror overwhelms thee; thy light is darkened, so that thou canst not see, and a flood of water covers thee.'" (Job 22:5-11) The darkness and the flood of water are metaphors for death.[2073]

It is not suggested (or is it?) that Job actually committed all those crimes;[2074] but in his friend's (!) view Job must have done some grievous sinning to merit his present condition. This passage is followed, as in the

---

[2072] Eliphaz was from Teman, a major part of Edom, in southern Jordan (Teman, DB, p. 961). Bildad the Shuhite's tribal home was on the steppes of the right bank of the Euphrates (Shuah, DB, p. 913). The location of Zophar's Naamah is not certain, but the commentators in the BC suggest northwestern Arabia (Naamah, DB, p. 684; BC, Vol. 4, p. 43). All three appear to belong to non-Israelite Semites, especially Arabs.

[2073] BC, IV, 91.

[2074] The *Testament of Job* explicitly repudiates the accusations. (LJ, II, 229-302, 242.)

case of all the other speeches, by Job's protesting his innocence and declaring the injustice of his suffering. Perhaps Job's feelings were those of the sufferer in the *Babylonian Theodicy* of 1000 BCE:

> "Just one word would I put before you.
> Those who neglect the god go the way of prosperity,
> While those who pray to the goddess are impoverished and dispossessed.
> In my youth I sought the will of my god;
> With prostration and prayer I followed my goddess.
> But I was bearing a profitless corvée as a yoke.
> My god decreed, instead of wealth, destitution.
> A cripple is the man over me; a lunatic is the man in front of me.
> The rogue has been promoted, but I have been brought low."[2075]

The modern reader will perhaps sympathize with the sufferer's observations about the world as it really is. Many suffer unjustly and many thrive unjustly. There was much law but little justice in ancient times, as is much the case today. True justice awaits us somewhere else.

Surabadi cites other traditions about Job's request for relief: A worm had started to eat his heart and a little worm his tongue, and he said that if they ate him, he would not be able to remember God in his heart and praise him with his tongue. God promised that nothing would afflict those two members. This may be related to the statement in the *Testament of Job* that had limited Satan's power to Job's body; his soul Satan could not touch.[2076] This tradition in turn is based upon the divine command to Satan: "Behold he is in thy power; only spare his life." (Job 2:6)

And still another tradition from Surabadi: After seven years of suffering, Gabriel came to Job and told him to complain to God, and not to be so patient, as God loves the request of His servant as He does his patience.[2077] This refinement also does not seem to appear in Jewish literature.

Surabadi tells us that Job's illness lasted seven years, seven months, seven days, and seven hours.[2078] As in the Quran, Job was

---

[2075] Thomas, p. 100.

[2076] LJ, II, 234.

[2077] Surabadi, p. 374.

[2078] In perhaps another version of the same tradition, Surabadi says that after Job had been afflicted seven years, Rahmah came to him and told him to pray to God, because his prayer would be accepted. Job said that he had lived 70 years in God's favor, and until he

commanded to strike the earth with his foot. A spring of warm water appeared in which he was commanded to bathe. His exterior was healed but internally he still suffered. He was commanded to strike the earth again; another spring appeared from which he was to drink. He did so and he was healed.[2079] As we have noted above, this incident has no Biblical equivalent and cannot be found in any pre-Islamic Job narratives. Jewish tradition gives varying periods of time for the length of Job's illness: seven years, thirty years, or one year.[2080]

There was a spring outside Damascus reported to be the spring of Job. Perhaps the tradition of it antedates Islam and was brought to the Hejaz by Arab caravaneers who had seen it. The Prophet himself may have seen it. Thus, it came to be mentioned in the Quran.

In the *Babylonian Job*, the sufferer's restoration to health is described vividly:

> "And in the dream I had at night
> A remarkable priest (was...)
> Holding in his hand a piece of purifying tamarisk wood.
> 'Laluralimma, resident of Nippur,
> Has sent me to purify you.'
> The water he was carrying he poured over me,
> Recited the life-restoring incantation, and massaged (my body).
> A third time I had a dream,
> And in the dream I had at night
> A remarkable young woman of shining countenance...
> ...equal to a god.
> A queen of the peoples ...
> She entered and (sat down...):
> She said, 'Be delivered from your very wretched state,
> Whoever has had a vision during the night.'
> [Then an exorcist came and said:]
> 'Marduk has sent me.
> To Shubshi-meshre-Shakkan I have brought prosperity,...'
> My illness was quickly over..."[2081]

---

had suffered 70 years, he would have no right to pray for relief. (Surabadi, p. 374) This tradition also belongs to the characterization of Job as the Patient.
[2079] Surabadi, p. 371.
[2080] LJ, II, 240; V, 388.
[2081] ANE, Vol. II, pp. 155-156.

Does this cure by means of water in ancient Babylonia have anything to do with the Arabian tradition reflected in the Quran? Folk memory of tradition is a very long one, and there is no *a priori* reason to dismiss its entering Arabian oral literature.

The Bible does not tell us how Job's afflictions were alleviated, although it seems to be connected with a sacrifice offered on his behalf by the three friends (Job 42:7-9). In the *Testament of Job*, "God appeared to Job once more, and gave him a sash composed of three ribands, and he bade him tie it around his waist. Hardly had he put it on when all his pain disappeared, his very recollection of it vanished, and more than this, God made him to see all that ever was and all that shall ever be."[2082]

Surabadi tells us that when Rahmah returned to Job's place on the ash heap, she did not find him, and she feared that he was dead. She began running about looking for him and calling his name. When she found him now healed and seated on a throne with Gabriel, she did not recognize him until he smiled and identified himself.[2083] Since in the *Testament of Job*, Zitidos had already died, there is no equivalent scene there. We prefer Surabadi here.

Next, he describes the restoration of Job's wealth: God caused locusts of gold to fall from heaven. When Job rushed to collect them, Gabriel observed that Job was in reality not an ascetic if he collected gold with such relish. Job replied that they were the bounty of God, and he would never tire of the bounty of God.[2084]

The Biblical resolution is achieved by a kind of levy on Job's family and friends: "And the Lord restored the fortunes of Job, when he had prayed for his friends; and the Lord gave Job twice as much as he had before. Then came to him all his brothers and his sisters and all who had known him before, and ate bread with him in his house; and they showed him sympathy and comforted him for all the evil that the Lord had brought upon him;[2085] and each of them gave him a piece of money and a ring of gold. And the Lord blessed the latter days of Job more than his beginning; and he had fourteen thousand sheep, six thousand camels, a thousand yoke of oxen, and a thousand she-asses. He also had seven sons and three daughters. And he called the name of the first Jemima; and the name of the second Keziah; and the name of the third

---

[2082] LJ, II, 240.

[2083] Surabadi, p. 374.

[2084] Surabadi, p. 374.

[2085] In the original version, it will be remembered, Satan did not appear, and the evil that had afflicted Job therefore was caused directly by God, and not by means of the machinations of Satan. See above.

Kerenhappuch. And in all the land, there were no women so fair as Job's daughters; and their father gave them inheritance among their brothers.[2086] And after this Job lived a hundred and forty years, and saw his sons, and his sons' sons, four generations. And Job died, an old man, and full of days." (Job 42:10-17) Al-Mas'udi mentions the Tomb of Job at a place called Nawa, near Damascus.[2087]

If we compare the Biblical figures given above, Job's wealth was exactly doubled, although he was given the same number of children as before. Tradition says that Job was 70 years old when the afflictions began, as in Surabadi.[2088]

Thus, we see that the Biblical solution offered, in keeping with the view that the afterlife was not a place of justice or connected with the morality of the deeds of this life, is the traditional one of the Old Testament. Job is amply rewarded materially in this life and given a long life span. (Nothing is said about redeeming all the innocent lives lost in this cosmic experiment.) That was all that could be hoped for before the moral and religious evolution reached the point where Jesus could ask us: "For what shall it profit a man, if he shall gain the whole world, and lose his own soul?" (Mk. 8:36)

[2086] It is interesting that contrary to the usual Biblical practice, here only Job's daughters (of the second lot) are named. Their names mean "Turtle-dove," "Cassia," and "Mascara" respectively. (JB, p. 778) We can only guess at what traditions these verses hint.
[2087] EI, Vol. I, pp. 795-796.
[2088] BC, IV, 151.

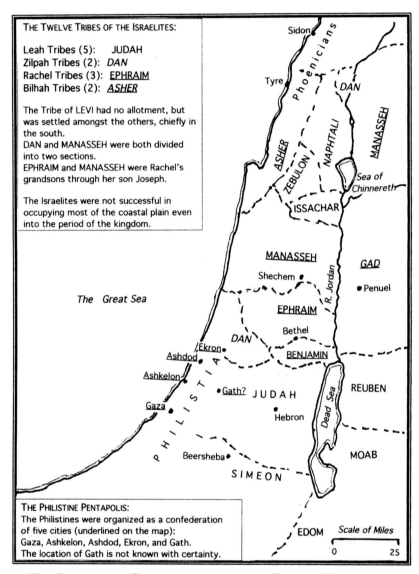

THE TWELVE TRIBES OF THE ISRAELITES:

Leah Tribes (5):   JUDAH
Zilpah Tribes (2): *DAN*
Rachel Tribes (3): EPHRAIM
Bilhah Tribes (2): *ASHER*

The Tribe of LEVI had no allotment, but was settled amongst the others, chiefly in the south.
DAN and MANASSEH were both divided into two sections.
EPHRAIM and MANASSEH were Rachel's grandsons through her son Joseph.

The Israelites were not successful in occupying most of the coastal plain even into the period of the kingdom.

THE PHILISTINE PENTAPOLIS:
The Philistines were organized as a confederation of five cities (underlined on the map): Gaza, Ashkelon, Ashdod, Ekron, and Gath. The location of Gath is not known with certainty.

THE DIVISION OF CANAAN AMONGST THE TWELVE TRIBES AND
THE PHILISTINES

PART FOUR: FROM JUDGES TO MONARCHY

I. SAMSON

He loved a woman... whose name was Delilah. (Jgs. 16:4)

After the establishment of the Israelites in Canaan, either by military conquest (the view of the later Israelites) or peaceful infiltration (or both), during the two-century interval between Joshua's invasion and the establishment of the monarchy under Saul (c. 1020 BCE), the tribes were ruled by a series of "judges." The principal Biblical sources for this period are *Judges* and *1 Samuel*, the latter chiefly concerned with the transition from the rule of judges to the rule of anointed kings.

Judges purports to cover the period from the death of Joshua to a point just before the birth of the prophet Samuel. The bulk of the present book[2089] is in the form given to it by the editors of the Deuteronomic circle. For the most part, they limited themselves to arranging the various heterogeneous stories and traditions in a semblance of order and providing connecting passages. The chronological notices scattered throughout the book give a total of 410 years for the period,[2090] but the "judges" were not active in succession with an authority over all or most of the tribes as the present text implies. Instead, for the most part they were local authorities dependent upon their personal leadership and charismatic qualities. Consequently, the periods of activity of many of the judges overlapped and were sometimes contemporaneous. As a result, this period can be shortened considerably. Modern scholars suggest a period of about 180 years between the first of the judges mentioned (Othniel) and the rise of Saul; that is, from c. 1200 to c. 1020 BCE.[2091]

The sources that the Deuteronomic editors used to assemble this book were probably both oral and written, and they represent a variety of local and tribal traditions. There are also doublets within the narratives, as was the case with many of the "historical" books of the Bible. The story of Samson, our present subject, is to be found in the narratives found in chs. 13-16 of *Judges*. They seem to be from a Samson-cycle of

---

[2089] Jgs. 2:6-16:31. The rest of the book (1:1-2:5; 17-21) consists of the additions from later editors. (BC, II, 380, and other places.)
[2090] BC, II, 380.
[2091] IB, II, 682; BC, II, 380.

the Danites (the tribe of Dan). It is possible that Samson was the central figure in other stories that have been lost or never transcribed.[2092]

The "judges" of *Judges*, at least the major ones, were in reality charismatic heroes rather than judicial officials. Most of the exploits recorded of them are of a military nature. For the most part, they functioned as popular leaders when the Israelites, or some portion of them, were severely threatened by some external enemy. They normally are only of interest to the editors during the crisis; after that they recede into the background.[2093] At least one of them appears to have made an abortive attempt to establish a royal dynasty (see below). Amongst all these heroes, Samson (Ar. *Shamsūn* or *Shamshūn*) is the strangest. His rise was in no way an answer to a military threat and his exploits involved no leadership of Israel, but were prompted entirely by personal motives. In fact, his character and his deeds remind one more of the Greek heroes, especially Herakles (Hercules). Myers suggests that Samson was active about 1100 BCE.[2094]

Scholars have proposed affinities between Samson and the Mesopotamian hero Gilgamesh, and a relationship between Samson and the cult of sun-worship—his name is derived from *shemesh*, "sun."[2095]— However, there is really no need for such postulates, nor is there much supportive evidence for them, as the principal elements of the stories could easily have developed locally, and indeed are imbued with a high degree of local color.[2096]

Samson is not mentioned in the Quran, directly or indirectly. Surabadi takes an Islamic tradition about the significance of the Night of Power in Surah al-Qadr (Q. 97) as the cue to give his version of the story of Samson: *Lo! We revealed it on the Night of Power. Ah, what will convey unto thee what the Night of Power is? The Night of Power is better than a thousand months.* (Q. 97:1-3)

[2092] Samson, DB, p. 881.

[2093] Judges, DB, p. 538; BC, II, 377; Judges, Book of, EJ, X, 442.

[2094] Myers, writing in IB, II, 682.

[2095] Samson, EJ, XIV, 771. "Samson" means "sun man" and his birthplace was not far from Beth-shemesh, "house of the sun." (Samson, DB, p. 880; see also next story about Saul.) This might indicate a tradition of pre-Israelite sun worship in Samson's home region. In addition, in ancient mythology, the sun was often depicted as a round face with hair in the form of long locks standing out from it symbolizing the rays of the sun. As there is nothing other than the statement in his story that he was a Nazirite—his acts and unbridled passions had nothing of the ascetic about them—and if we choose to disregard that, then there may very well be some ancient motif of sun worship underlying the Israelite face put upon the story.

[2096] Samson, EJ, XIV, 773; Samson, DB, p. 881.

What is the connection between these verses and the story of Samson? Surabadi tells us: "Some have said that the revelation of this surah was occasioned one day when the Messenger (S) was relating the story of Samson the Israelite. He said to his Companions that Samson was an ascetic, worshipful, warrior (in the cause of God) of the Children of Israel." According to this tradition, Samson lived a thousand months in fasting by day and prayer by night. He lived a league (3 miles) from a city of the unbelievers. Samson called them to God, but they fought against him.[2097]

Rabbinic tradition, while conceding that God's spirit rested upon Samson, generally does not regard him as a prophet.[2098] However, Josephus seems to have thought that he was: "So the child grew apace: and it appeared evident that he would be a prophet, both by the moderation of his diet, and the permission of his hair to grow."[2099]

In the Biblical version, Samson was born in the answer to the prayer of yet another childless couple, this time of Manoah of Zorah and his barren wife. The angel[2100] who announced the impending conception of Samson said that he was to be dedicated as a Nazirite (Jgs. 13:5). Indeed, he is the first to be called a Nazirite in the Bible. A Nazirite was one who was consecrated or dedicated to God, either for a stated period, or for life. In Samson's case, it was to be for life. Among the rules of their order, they had to abstain from wine and strong drink, leave their hair uncut, avoid contact with the dead, and avoid all unclean food.[2101] We shall soon see just how faithful Samson was to his Nazirite vows.

Samson grew up in the region of Zorah and Eshtaol in the valley of Sorek, about fifteen miles west of modern Jerusalem.[2102] Samson's adult life shows little of the asceticism attributed to it by Surabadi. He is presented in the Bible as a God-fearing man, though willful, vengeful, and imprudent. There is no indication in the Biblical record that Samson ever called upon the Philistines[2103] to become believers. However,

---

[2097] Surabadi, p. 455. If the tradition of the occasion of the revelation be a sound one, it would show that not all of the Prophet's parables have been preserved in the Quran, the distinction being that they were not related under divine inspiration.

[2098] LJ, VI, 207.

[2099] Josephus, Antiquities, V.8.4, p. 119.

[2100] This angel seems to be a later redactor's substitution for YHWH Himself. (See Jgs. 13:22-23.)

[2101] Nazirite, DB, p. 691. The custom survived for centuries and figures in the New Testament as well. (See *The New Testament: An Islamic Perspective*.)

[2102] Jgs. 13:25; OBA, p. 63.

[2103] Samson's (and the Israelites') opponents were the Philistines who gave their name to Palestine and who had recently occupied the plain and lower hills between the central and

according to Surabadi, a Philistine city responded to Samson's preaching by coming out to fight against him. He fought them off for three days with nothing more than the jawbone of a camel (set in iron) from which he also drew nourishment when hungry or thirsty,[2104] reminding us of Moses drawing nourishment from his fingers.

In the Bible, this fight was the result of his unfortunate marriage with a Philistine woman. Samson had married this woman of Timnah, some four miles down the valley, against the wishes of his parents. [He should have listened to his parents.] The marriage was of a type modern scholars call ṣadīqah meaning that the husband became part of the wife's clan, rather than the other way around.[2105] However, the Philistines' relations with him do not seem to have been very cordial. During the wedding festivities, Samson gave them a riddle to solve, and wagered thirty linen and thirty festal garments that they could not solve it: "Out of the eater came something to eat. Out of the strong came something sweet." (Jgs. 14:14) This had been suggested to him by his stopping to scoop some honey from the carcass of a dead lion on his way to see his intended bride before the wedding. (Touching the carcass was also a violation of his Nazirite code.)

The Philistines were unable to solve the riddle and finally persuaded Samson's wife to extract the solution from him. She did so and they were able to reply: "What is sweeter than honey? What is stronger than a lion?" (Jgs. 13:18) Samson realized what had happened and: "he went down to Ashkelon and killed thirty men of the town, and took their spoil and gave the festal garments to those who had told the riddle." (Jgs. 14:19) When Samson returned to Timnah, he found that his father-in-law had given his wife-to-be to "his companion, who had been his best man." (Jgs. 14:20)

Understandably incensed at this affront, Samson decided to take revenge indirectly: "So Samson went and caught three hundred foxes, and took torches; and he turned them tail to tail, and put a torch between each pair of tails. And when he had set fire to the torches, he let the foxes go into the standing grain of the Philistines, and burned up the shocks and the standing grain, as well as the olive orchards. Then the Philistines said, 'Who has done this?' And they said, 'Samson, the son-in-law of the Timnite, because he has taken his wife and given her to his companion.' And the Philistines came up and burned her and her father with fire. And

---

southern Palestinian highlands and the Mediterranean Sea. (See Story of Saul below for a fuller discussion of them.)

[2104] Surabadi, pp. 455-456.

[2105] Marriage, DB, p. 623.

Samson said to them, 'If this is what ye do, I swear I will be avenged upon you, after that I will quit.' And he smote them hip and thigh with great slaughter; and he went down and stayed in the cleft of the rock of Etam." (Jgs. 15:4-8)

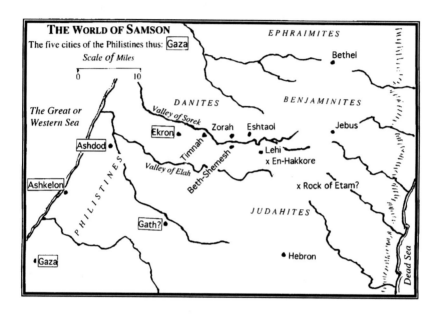

The Philistines then threatened the Judahites in whose territory was the rock of Etam where Samson had taken refuge. Three thousand Judahites came up to him and after promising not to kill him, they were able to bind him and hand him over to the Philistines. But when the Philistines went to take him, "the Spirit of the Lord came mightily upon him, and the ropes which were on his arms became as flax that has caught fire, and his bonds melted off his hands. And he found a fresh jawbone of an ass, and put out his hand and seized it, and with it he slew a thousand men." (Jgs. 15:14-15)

From the above, it will be plain to the reader that Surabadi's jawbone of a camel is obviously an echo of the Biblical jawbone of an ass; but the differences between the events leading up to this fight are far greater. There is no hint of Surabadi's pious devotee in the Biblical story.

In the Biblical story, this is immediately followed by the miraculous quenching of Samson's thirst in a manner reminiscent of Moses: "And God split open the hollow place that is at Lehi, and there came water from it; and he drank, his spirit returned and revived.

Therefore the name of if was called En-hakkore; it is at Lehi to this day."
(Jgs. 15:19) This is obviously an aetiological tale connected with a spring
that was still in existence at the time of the recording of the Samson
traditions, as the text indicates.[2106]

The name given to the spring itself means "Spring of the
Partridge"; while Lehi means "Jawbone." The tradition is obviously
based upon the double use of Lehi, as a place name, and a weapon.
Samson killed the thousand men with a jawbone (*lehi*) and it was at Lehi
that the spring appeared. Taken literally, it would mean that the spring
had appeared at Jawbone. Surabadi's note that Samson took nourishment
from the jawbone is not unsupported in Jewish literature, Talmudic and
Midrashic: "God said, 'He likes that which is unclean (Philistine
women), and his life shall be saved by the water coming from an unclean
thing (the jawbone of an ass)."[2107] A tradition even more miraculous is
mentioned in the *Genesis Rabbah*, where the water is reported to have
flowed from Samson's own mouth.[2108]

Samson's encounters with the women of Philistia were doomed
to end in disaster. In the Bible, after the horrible fate of his first consort
and the slaughter that the events of his marriage had precipitated,
Samson's next contact nearly ended in his own death: "Samson went to
Gaza, and there he saw a harlot, and he went in to her. The Gazites were
told, 'Samson has come here.' And they surrounded the place and lay in
wait for him all night at the gate of the city. They kept quiet all night,
saying, 'Let us wait till the light of the morning; then we will kill him.'
But Samson lay till midnight, and at midnight he arose and took hold of
the doors of the gate of the city and the two posts, and pulled them, bar
and all, and put them on his shoulders and carried them to the top of the
hill that is before Hebron." (Jgs. 16:1-3) This was quite a feat, as Hebron
is situated some 40 miles due east of Gaza.

Discreetly, Surabadi does not refer to this exploit. The incident
he recounts is based upon Samson's third encounter with a Philistine
woman in the Bible, the famous—or infamous—Delilah:[2109]

Sagely observing that great men can be humbled by women,
Surabadi tells us that the Philistines bribed a woman to bring Samson to

---

[2106] Lehi was located about five miles southeast of Zorah, if the identification with Beit
'Atab be correct. (OBA, p. 63; Lehi, DB, p. 575.)

[2107] LJ, VI, 207.

[2108] LJ, IV, 48.

[2109] Some scholars have seen the Hebrew word for "night" (*lilah*) in Delilah's name, and
thus make the story a myth of night overcoming the sun (Samson). (Asimov-OT, p. 251.)
This is of course a false etymology, neat as it is. The word means "worshipper" or
"devotee" and has nothing to do with night. (Samson, DB, p. 881.)

them. He was a heavy sleeper and she tied his hands with a stout rope. When he awoke, he asked her why she had done so. She said to test his strength. Samson broke the ropes. The next time she bound him with chains, with the same result. Finally, she asked wherein his strength lay. He replied that it was in his hair. When he was asleep, she cut his hair and bound two fingers together. When he awoke, he could not free himself.[2110]

The Biblical version of this humiliation: "After this he loved a woman in the valley of Sorek, whose name was Delilah. And the lords of the Philistines came to her and said to her, 'Entice him, and see wherein his great strength lies, and by what means we may overpower him, that we may bind him to subdue him; and we will each give thee eleven hundred pieces of silver.' And Delilah said unto Samson, 'Please tell me wherein thy great strength lies, and how thou couldst be bound, that one might subdue thee.' Samson said to her, 'If they bind me with seven fresh bowstrings which have not been dried, then I shall become weak, and be like any other man.'

"Then the lords of the Philistines brought her seven fresh bowstrings which had not been dried, and she bound him with them. Now she had men lying in wait in an inner chamber. And she said to him, 'The Philistines are upon thee, Samson!' But he snapped the bowstrings, as a string of tow snaps when it touches the fire. So the secret of his strength was not known." (Jgs. 16:4-9)

In the Bible, the first binding was with bowstrings, whilst in Surabadi it was with rope. Rope, however, is used in Delilah's second attempt: "And Delilah said to Samson, 'Behold, thou hast mocked me, and told me lies; please tell me how thou mightest be bound.' And he said to her, 'If they bind me with new ropes that have not been used, then I shall become weak, and be like any other man.' So Delilah took new ropes and bound him with them, and said to him, 'The Philistines are upon thee, Samson!' And the men lying in wait were in an inner chamber. But he snapped the ropes off his arms like a thread." (Jgs. 16:10-12)

In the Bible, chains were not used. The next attempt has no equivalent in Surabadi: "And Delilah said to Samson, 'Until now thou hast mocked me, and told me lies; tell me how thou mightest be bound.' And he said to her, 'If thou weavest the seven locks of my head with the web and make it tight with the pin, then I shall become weak, and be like any other man.' So while he slept, Delilah took the seven locks of his head and wove them into the web. And she made them tight with the pin,

---

[2110] Surabadi, p. 456.

and said to him, 'The Philistines are upon thee, Samson!' But he awoke from his sleep, and pulled away the pin, the loom, and the web." (Jgs. 16:13014)

It is said that love is blind. Abundantly proving the adage and apparently still suspecting nothing (how unperceptive can one be?), Samson submitted to still another test. "And she said to him, 'How canst thou say, "I love thee." when thy heart is not with me? Thou hast mocked me these three times, and thou has not told me wherein thy great strength lies.' And when she pressed him hard with her words, day after day, and urged him, his soul was vexed to death. And he told her all his mind, and said to her, 'A razor has never come upon my head; for I have been a Nazirite to God from my mother's womb. If I be shaved, then my strength will leave me, and I shall become weak, and be like other men.'

"When Delilah saw that he had told her all his mind, she sent and called the lords of the Philistines, saying, 'Come up this once, for he has told me all his mind.' Then the lords of the Philistines came up to her, and brought the money in their hands. She made him sleep upon her knees; and she called a man, and had him shave off the seven locks of his head. Then she began to torment him, and his strength had left him. And she said, 'The Philistines are upon thee, Samson!' And he awoke from his sleep, and said, 'I will go out as at other times, and shake myself free.' And he did not know that the Lord had left him. And the Philistines seized him and gouged out his eyes, and brought him down to Gaza, and bound him with bronze fetters; and he ground at the mill in the prison." (Jgs. 16:18-21) Note the use of bronze fetters. Iron had not yet been introduced on a large scale into the Near East.[2111]

Thus ended, in *Judges*, Samson's third encounter with a Philistine woman; he had been reduced to the condition of a blind slave forced to work like an animal turning a millstone. However, he had become an ordinary man, not Surabadi's weakling who could be subdued by binding two of his fingers together. In the Bible, there is considerable emphasis on Samson's sensual nature. Jewish tradition further elaborates on this theme and tells us that the Philistines, after they had captured him, continued to encourage him in this behavior in the hope that he would produce for them strong descendants.[2112] In light of the Jewish concern for racial purity, the loss of his eyes, which had betrayed

---

[2111] For more about iron and David's connection with it, see Part Five, I.

[2112] LJ, IV, 48-49. According to one legend, Samson was an ancestor (or the father) of Goliath, the Philistine giant whom David slew (see Part Five, I). (LJ, VI, 250.

Samson by causing him to lust after foreign (unclean) women, was considered appropriate by later generations.[2113]

Surabadi gives us a somewhat different version of Samson's downfall at the hands of the Philistines. The people mocked him and insulted him. His nose, ears, and feet were cut off and they planned to torture him to death. Then he prayed to God and an angel came down and beat his wings at him and Samson became whole again. He pulled down the pillar which supported the court and all perished, except Samson, who escaped.[2114]

These events in Surabadi seem to follow in rapid succession upon Samson's capture. Samson's escape at the end seems to be an Islamic contribution, made in the belief that Samson was a prophet, and that such a fate as the Bible describes for him would have been unseemly for a prophet of God. Jewish tradition says that Samson was maimed in both feet and lame, but that this was a birth defect (unremarked in the Bible) and not the result of his capture by the Philistines.[2115]

In the Biblical narrative, there is a lapse of time between Samson's capture and the climax of the story at the festival of Dagon, a Semitic agricultural deity adopted by the Philistines upon their settlement in Canaan (peoples moved but the gods stayed put).[2116] "But the hair of his head began to grow again after it had been shaved." (Jgs. 16:22) Thus, Samson's supernatural strength began to return. "Now the lords of the Philistines gathered to offer a great sacrifice to Dagon their god, and to rejoice; for they said, 'Our god has given Samson our enemy into our hand.' And when the people saw him, they praised their god; for they said, 'Our god has given our enemy into our hand, the ravager of our country, who has slain many of us.'" (Jgs. 16:23-24) It is only at this point in the Bible that Samson's quarrels with the Philistines begin to assume a larger dimension and become a demonstration of the power of God, and those consecrated to Him, over the uncircumcised Philistines and their deities. YHWH is invading Philistia as He had done to Egypt.

"And when their hearts were merry, they said, 'Call Samson, that he may make sport for us.' So they called Samson out of the prison, and he made sport before them." (Jgs. 16:25) [This is found in Surabadi too, as the prelude to the disaster that was about to befall Gaza.] "They made him stand between the pillars; and Samson said to the lad who held him by the hand, 'Let me feel the pillars on which the house rests, that I may

---

[2113] LJ, VI, 208.
[2114] Surabadi, pp. 456-457.
[2115] LJ, IV, 47.
[2116] Dagon, DB, pp. 197-198.

lean against them.' Now the house was full of men and women; all the lords of the Philistines were there, and on the roof there were about three thousand men and women, who looked on while Samson made sport." (Jgs. 16:25-27) The "house" was, of course, the temple of Dagon.[2117]

"Then Samson called to the Lord and said, 'O Lord God, remember me, I pray thee, and strengthen me, I pray thee, only this once, O God, that I may be avenged upon the Philistines for one of my two eyes.' [Again Samson sees these events from the viewpoint of exacting personal vengeance.] And Samson grasped the two middle pillars upon which the house rested, and he leaned his weight upon them, his right hand on the one and his left hand on the other. And Samson said, 'Let me die with the Philistines.' Then he bowed with all his might; and the house fell upon the lords and upon all the people that were in it. So the dead whom he slew at his death were more than those whom he had slain during his life. Then his brothers and all his family came down and took him and brought him up and buried him between Zorah and Eshtaol in the tomb of Manoah his father. He had judged Israel twenty years." (Jgs. 16:28-31)

What are we to make of this unedifying tale? If he was a judge, he did not show much good judgment. In any event, it is plain that there is a considerable gap between the Danite hero, who had a light regard for his Nazirite vows and an unfortunate taste in women, and the idealized prophet-hero Samson that Surabadi describes. Samson the prophet is a product of Islamic religious optimism. Jewish tradition does not make Samson a prophet. That supreme apologist, Josephus, takes a positive view of Samson's character and deeds, but is forced to qualify it: "But as for his being ensnared by a woman, that is to be ascribed to human nature, which is too weak to resist the temptations to that sin; but we ought to bear him witness, that in all other respects, he was one of extraordinary virtue."[2118]

[2117] BC, II, 450.
[2118] Josephus, *Antiquities*, V.8.12, p. 121.

II. SAUL

And when Saul set out with an army... (Q. 2:249)

Surabadi's narrative of the story of Saul is based upon some verses in the Quran (Q. 2:246-248) that are a series of references to the establishment of the Israelite monarchy, first under Saul, and then—after Saul had proved inadequate to the task—under David. In Surabadi's story, there are scattered references to events from the time of Moses to the time of David.

The "official" (Biblical) history of this transformation of a loose tribal confederation with popularly acknowledged leaders ("judges"), such as the last of them, Samuel, into a typical Near Eastern kingdom—that is, from amphictyony to monarchy—is to be found principally in the *Books of Samuel.* There is much evidence in these two books of a conservative opposition to this political revolution. Though Samuel is not mentioned by name in the Quran, there can be little doubt but that he is the prophet referred to in these verses in connection with the anointing of Saul as king.

Samuel, Saul, and David are each very important personalities in their own right in the Bible; taken together they played crucial roles in the establishment of the monarchy. However, *Samuel* is rife with textual problems, and in addition to these, there are problems of historicity, the causes of the change, the political and religious environment, questions of cult and ritual, and the evolution of Israelite religion, each of which has been the subject of voluminous scholarly research and debate. In so vast a field, we shall confine ourselves to an examination of points raised by the text of the Quran and by Surabadi's narrative.

It is important to remind ourselves once again that the Quran is not a textbook of history. The sketchy references to Israelite history here and elsewhere should not be taken as purporting to be a chronological account of events. Though the Biblical record is much closer both geographically and in time to the underlying historical realities, we have already seen how research over the past two centuries has led scholars to the reluctant conclusion that we cannot unquestioningly take Biblical statements at face value. We must remind ourselves that whilst the Bible is giving us a spiritualized national history of the Children of Israel, the Quran is relating selected illustrative moral parables from that history (and other sources) for the nascent Islamic community and the future world religion.

THE ARK OF THE COVENANT: Surabadi begins his story of Saul with an account of the Ark: After the death of Moses, the Israelites fought hard with the pagans. The Israelites would win because of the Ark which Moses and Aaron had left them. The Ark was made of boxwood within which were preserved the staff of Moses, the Tables of Moses, the turban of Aaron,[2119] the Golden Tub in which was kept a measure of manna, and the Holy Presence, which was a figure with the head of a cat, the face of a man, and two wings. When the Israelites went out to fight, they would bring the Ark forward and a roar would come out from the Holy Presence and terrify the enemy.[2120]

The Quran only mentions the Ark (Ar. *tābūt*) as a sign in which there is *a tranquility* (Ar. sakīnah) *from your Lord, and a remnant of that which the house of Moses and the house of Aaron left behind, the angels bearing it.* (Q. 2:248) It gives no further details about its contents. This is certainly a reference to the Ark of the Covenant that the Israelites were supposed to have had with them in their wanderings after the Exodus, during the Conquest and thereafter,[2121] and to the Divine Presence (the Shekinah) associated with it, translated as "tranquility" in the Quranic context. The Biblical accounts of its origins are relatively late and therefore their reliability is open to question. The principal account is given by P in *Exodus*. In this version, when God took up residence with the migrating Israelites, He instructed Moses: "'Let them make Me a sanctuary [the Tabernacle], that I may dwell in their midst.'" (Ex. 25:8) The most important of the furnishings of this Tabernacle was the Ark of the Covenant.

[2119] This reference to Aaron's turban must be to Aaron's priestly ephod and the vestments worn for service in the Tabernacle. They are elaborately described in Ex. 28 & 29: "And he made the ephod of gold, blue, and purple and scarlet stuff, and fine twisted linen. And gold leaf was hammered out and cut into threads to work into the blue and purple and the scarlet stuff, and into the fine twined linen, in skilled design." (Ex. 39:2-3) It had carefully worked shoulder-pieces and a breastplate with twelve stones, each bearing the name of a tribe of Israel, as well as other robes and decorations. Aaron's turban is thus described: "And they made the plate of the holy crown of pure gold, and wrote upon it an inscription, like the engraving of a signet. 'Holy to the Lord.' And they tied to it a lace of blue, to fasten it on the turban above; as the Lord commanded Moses.'" (Ex. 39:30-31) This passage belongs to the late Priestly Document and is probably a description of the attire of the high priest in that Post-Exilic period. In order to give the garments sanctity and authority, they were ascribed to the period of Moses and Aaron. Report of these traditions about the vestments of the high priest and their connection with Aaron account for the note here by Surabadi. They certainly were held in great sanctity by later Jews during the Second Temple, as their memory after the destruction of the Temple and the lapse of the office of high priest in 70 CE attests.

[2120] Surabadi, p. 19. See also below about the Ark.

[2121] Num. 10:33; 14:44; Josh. 3:3-6, 6:6, 9, etc.

Its construction is described in detail by the same Priestly Document in *Exodus*: "They shall make an ark of acacia wood; two cubits and a half shall be its length, a cubit and a half its breadth, and a cubit and half its height.[2122] And thou [Moses] shalt overlay it with pure gold, within and without, and thou shalt make a moulding of gold round about. And thou shalt cast four rings of gold for it and put them on its four feet, two rings on the one side of it, and two rings on the other side of it. Thou shalt make poles of acacia wood, and overlay them with gold. And thou shalt put the poles into the rings on the sides of the ark, to carry the ark by them. The poles shall remain in the rings of the ark; they shall not be taken from it. And thou shalt put into the ark the testimony which I shall give thee." (Ex. 25:10-16)

Since writer of this passage had almost certainly never laid eyes upon this Ark, as it had disappeared—at the latest—with the fall of Jerusalem in 586 BCE, and probably much earlier,[2123] we do not know how closely this description corresponded to the original object. From this passage, we see that it was remembered as a gilded wooden chest of easily portable and unspectacular dimensions to which rings were attached for carrying poles, in the manner of a litter. In it was contained the "testimony"; that is, the stone Tables of the Law. However, the construction of the Ark was not completed with the addition of the poles:

"Then thou shalt make a mercy seat of pure gold; two cubits and a half shall be its length, and a cubit and a half its breadth. And thou shalt make two cherubim of gold; of hammered work thou shalt make them, on the two ends of the mercy seat. Make one cherub on the one end, and one cherub on the other end; of one piece with the mercy seat shalt thou make the cherubim on its two ends. The cherubim shall spread out their wings above, overshadowing the mercy seat with their wings, and their faces one to another; toward the mercy seat shall the faces of the cherubim be. And thou shalt put the mercy seat on the top of the ark; and in the ark thou shalt put the testimony that I shall give thee. There I will meet with thee, and from above the mercy seat. From between the two cherubim that are upon the ark of the testimony, I will speak with thee of all that I will give thee in commandment for the people of Israel." (Ex. 25:17-22)

This mercy seat seems to have been a kind of stand or throne for the invisible presence of YHWH, where He could be approached under certain conditions. De Vaux feels that this mercy seat was a later

---

[2122] If we assume that a cubit is equal to 1.5 ft., the dimensions of this box would have been approximately 3'9" x 2'3" x 2'3"; not a very large object.

[2123] Ark, DB, p. 53.

substitute for the Ark itself, after it had disappeared.[2124] Be that as it may, in the Pentateuch it is linked with the Ark and the Divine Presence, an aspect of which was later to become the "Shekinah."

Though the Quran does not specifically refer to the mercy seat itself, the phrase *the angels bearing it* (Q. 2:148)—though it may be taken figuratively—more probably is a reference to a tradition of the cherubim made of one piece with the mercy seat. Yet, although *Exodus* commands that there be two cherubim, in the ideal Temple of *Ezekiel* there were to be four, each with two faces, that of a man and a lion (Ezek. 41:18), or four faces, those of a man, a lion [Surabadi's cat?], an ox, and an eagle (Ezek. 10:14). However, these seem to have been conceived of as freestanding, and not the small cherubim of the mercy seat.

In the description of the furnishings of Solomon's Temple, we read that Solomon caused two cherubim to be made of olivewood, "each ten cubits [15 ft.] high. Five cubits [7.5 ft.] was the length of one wing of the cherub; and it was ten cubits [15 ft.] from the tip of one wing to the tip of the other... And he overlaid the cherubim with gold." (1 K. 6:23-24, 28) These cherubim would thus have been of considerable size. Figures of the cherubim also decorated the walls of the interior of the Temple (1 K. 6:29).

What were the cherubim? Most scholars now agree that the cherubim were of Assyrian origin. "The Akkadian word *karibu* means "one who prays," that is, an intercessor. This was the function of secondary gods called *lamassu* and *shedu* who are represented as winged creatures with human faces. They guarded the entrances to temples and palaces (and can be seen in many books and museums), and were commissioned to intercede for men. These, or similar representations, may well have fired the imagination of the Hebrew writers."[2125] In Iran, the direct descendants of those Assyrian cherubim may be seen on the Gate of Xerxes still guarding the entrance to the ruined palace of Persepolis.

There is no hint of the intercessory character of these Assyrian *karibu* in the Biblical cherubim. The Hebrews, at least at the time of the compilation of the books mentioning them, seemed to think of them as emblems or guardians of the Divine Majesty. They also bore the Throne of God or His Chariot: "... And at the east of the garden of Eden He placed the cherubim... to guard the way to the tree of life." (Gen. 3:24) "...So I cast thee as a profane thing from the mountain of God, and the

---

[2124] de Vaux, p. 300.
[2125] Cherubim, DB, p. 133.

guardian cherub drove thee out..." (Ezek. 28:16) "He rode on a cherub, and flew; He was seen upon the wings of the wind." (2 Sam. 22:11)[2126] "...Also (David's) plan for the golden chariot of the cherubim that spread their wings and covered the ark of the covenant of the Lord." (1 Ch. 28:18)

In Ezekiel's vision (6th-century BCE), the cherubim are shown carrying God: "Then the glory of the Lord went forth from the threshold of the house, and stood over the cherubim. And the cherubim lifted up their wings and mounted up from the earth in my sight as they went forth, with the wheels beside them; and they stood at the east gate of the house of the Lord; and the glory of the God of Israel was over them." (Ezek. 10:18-19) "This conception of the throne of Yahweh carried by the (two) winged creatures became conventionalized in the representation of the Ark in the inner sanctuary surmounted by its covering (mercy-seat) and guarded by the cherubim, at the very heart of the sanctuary, the abode of Yahweh."[2127]

Before the building of the Temple at Jerusalem by Solomon, the primary focus of YHWH-worship was centered upon the Ark. YHWH was thought to either use it as His throne,[2128] or to be actually *inside* the Ark.[2129] Consider also the following passage based upon the Midrash *Yelammedenu*: "as often as they broke camp or pitched camp Moses would say to them: 'Do what the Shekinah within the Ark bids you do.' But they would not believe Moses that the Shekinah dwelt among them unless he spoke the words: 'Rise up, Lord, and let Thine enemies be scattered; and let them that hate Thee flee before Thee,' whereupon the Ark would begin to move, and they were convinced of the presence of the Shekinah."[2130]

The Ark is mentioned in an older tradition, from the pre-Exilic Deuteronomist, and may attest to the existence of the Ark during that writer's lifetime. He narrates that Moses was commanded to return to the mountain and receive a second set of stone tablets to replace the set broken in the incident of the Golden Calf, as the conflated text of *Exodus*, upon which he based his summary, would have it. As part of the preparations, Moses was told to prepare the stones and to make an Ark of wood (Deut. 10:2). After receiving the second set of tables, Moses is

---

[2126] Pictorial representations of the marvelous steed Buraq will inevitably come to the mind of the Muslim reader.

[2127] Cherubim, DB, p. 133.

[2128] Cherubim, DB, p. 133; Weber, p. 91.

[2129] Ark, DB, p. 53. (See 1 Sam. 6:19-20; 2 Sam. 6:6-9.)

[2130] LJ, III, 243.

made to say: "'Then I turned and came down from the mountain, and put the tables in the ark which I had made; *and there they are* [our italics], the Lord commanded me.'" (Deut. 10:5) In this version, Moses seems to have constructed the Ark himself, whilst in the later Priestly Document, Bezalel is the carpenter.[2131] The phrase "and there they are" indicates that Moses is displaying the objects about which he has been speaking to the assembled multitude, but it may also carry the implication there were still extant at the time of the Deuteronomist.

Surabadi speaks of a number of objects contained in Ark. If the tradition of its rather small size is correct, as we suppose it to have been since it was portable, it could not be thought to have contained an object so long as, say, the staff of Moses. According to the Bible, the only material objects it contained were the Tables of the Law. In the description of the dedication ceremonies of the Temple of Solomon, it is stated that: "There was nothing in the ark except the two tables of stone which Moses put there at Horeb, where the Lord made a covenant with the people of Israel, when they came out of the land of Egypt." (1 K. 8:9)

The Talmudic tractate *Yoma* mentions a number of items preserved in the Temple that were hidden by King Josiah (rgd. 640-609 BCE). Among them were the Ark, the vessel with the manna, the rod of Aaron (not Moses; the rod of Aaron was more prominent than that of Moses in Jewish tradition). Aaron's headgear (mentioned by Surabadi) or other priestly vestments do not appear to have been preserved in it.

Surabadi may have conceived of the Sakinah (Ar. *Sakīnah*) as a material object of some veneration, perhaps the mercy seat described above. The Quranic verse does not justify this assumption, and seems to use the term in a general way meaning the tranquility of assurance that the Ark's presence gave the Israelites. The Hebrew equivalent *Shekinah* does not occur in the Old Testament, although it is frequently encountered in extra-Biblical Jewish literature where it appears to mean Divine Glory or Presence, particularly in connection with the localization of God in the moveable Tabernacle and later in the fixed Temple.[2132]

That this Divine Presence was connected with the Ark is shown by the statement that it was only after the Ark had been placed inside Solomon's newly constructed Temple that God entered it to dwell therein: "And when the priests came out of the holy place [of the Temple], a cloud filled the house of the Lord, so that the priests could not stand to minister because of the cloud; for the glory of the Lord filled the

---

[2131] See Ex. 37:1-9.

[2132] See the Introduction to the Story of Moses above (Part Three, I.A) for more about the Tabernacle, especially the notes.

house of the Lord." Then Solomon said: 'The Lord has set the sun in the heavens, but has said that He would dwell in thick darkness. I have built Thee an exalted house, a place for Thee to dwell in for ever.'" (1 K. 8:10-13) By not using the definite article "the," the Quran avoids this restriction of God's universal presence, but at the same time accepts the reality of the psychological security that the Israelites derived from their beliefs about it at that state of their religious development.[2133]

However, Israelite ideas about the Ark were not static. In the early stages, it is certain that they thought that God's presence was connected with it.[2134] Parallels to this concept exist outside the Jewish experience. Pre-Islamic Arabs transported their tribal gods in a special chest covered with a tent on camelback,[2135] and their gods were thought to accompany them into battles, as was the case with the early Israelites.[2136] The important sacred Egyptian text, the *Book of the Dead*, was supposed to have been found in an ark that was the pedestal of the god Khnum.[2137];

After his description of the Ark, Surabadi relates that the Israelites became corrupt and the Ark fell in the hands of the enemy who insulted it and cast it upon a dunghill. Immediately, all the people in the neighborhood became ill with hemorrhoids. The Ark was placed on the back of an ox and driven out of the city. The ox brought it to the door of Saul's house. Saul was a leather worker. He took the Ark and hid it.[2138]

This capture of the Ark is recorded in the Bible, although the Biblical story differs somewhat in detail from that of Surabadi. As proof of the Divine Presence, the Ark was not always effective. Apparently, YHWH did not always feel obliged to manifest His power from this throne. In a battle with the Philistines during the time of Samuel, the Ark was brought out from the shrine at Shiloh[2139] in order to strengthen the Israelites. Despite an initial surge of courage demonstrated by the soldiers upon its arrival, the Philistine enemy was ultimately victorious and even carried off the Ark itself.

[2133] Therefore Maulana Muhammad Ali's translation "that there shall come to you the *heart* in which there is tranquility" and his explanatory note for this curious evasion of the obvious meaning of *tābūt* (ark, box, coffin, coffer) is unnecessary. (See Quran-MMA, p. 107.)

[2134] Anderson, pp. 39-40.

[2135] Hooke, p. 151.

[2136] Smith, p. 37.

[2137] de Vaux, p. 301.

[2138] Surabadi, p. 19.

[2139] The Tabernacle had given way to a permanent structure, it would seem, despite YHWH's protest to David that He preferred to live in a tent when David wanted to build a temple for Him (2 Sam. 7:6).

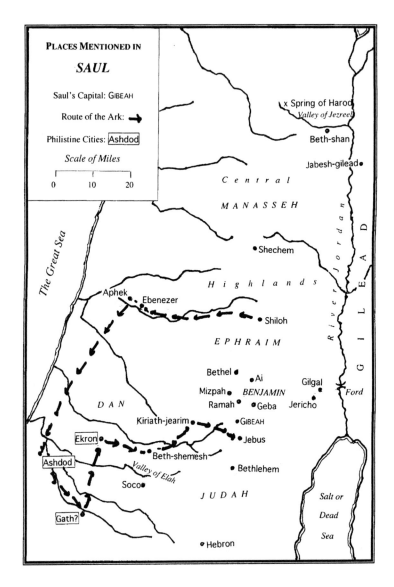

PLACES MENTIONED IN

SAUL

Saul's Capital: GIBEAH

Route of the Ark: ➡

Philistine Cities: Ashdod

Scale of Miles

0   10   20

This humiliation occurred at the battle of Aphek (before c. 1020 BCE). The Ark had been kept at Shiloh since the days of Joshua. Therefore, Shiloh, in the territory of the Josephic Ephraimites was the original "Temple," or at least its prototype, to be replaced by Jerusalem during the reign of David.[2140] After suffering the loss of 4,000 men on the first day of the battle (Aphek was also in Ephraim), the elders decided to "'bring the ark of the covenant of the Lord here from Shiloh, that He may come among us and save us from the power of our enemies.' So the people sent to Shiloh, and brought from there the ark of the covenant of the Lord of Hosts, Who is enthroned on the cherubim; and the two sons of Eli, Hophni and Phinehas, were there with the ark of covenant of God." (1 Sam. 4:3-4) Clearly, the expectation was that YHWH would in some way accompany His throne and give the Israelites victory. In fact, YHWH is here depicted as a war god.[2141]

"When the ark of the covenant of the Lord came into the camp [at Ebenezer, east of the Philistine camp at Aphek], all Israel gave a mighty shout, so that the earth resounded." (1 Sam. 4:5) The Philistines were frightened when they heard that "a god has come into the camp" (1 Sam. 4:7), but rallied and defeated the Israelites, slaughtering 30,000 of their number (surely an exaggeration). "And the ark of God was captured; and the two sons of Eli [the high priest at Shiloh], were slain." (1 Sam. 4:11)

A Benjaminite ran to Shiloh with the terrible news; when Eli heard of the disaster, he died on the spot. It was not the news of the death of his sons which had killed him, but when the messenger "mentioned the ark of God, Eli fell over backward from his seat by the side of the gate; and his neck was broken and he died, for he was an old man, and heavy." (1 Sam. 4:18)

The Philistines carried off the Ark to Ashdod[2142] where they set it up in the temple of their god Dagon. The following morning they found the statue of Dagon thrown down. They set it up again, but the next day, it was not only thrown down, and shattered as well (1 Sam. 5:1-5). Then the people of Ashdod were afflicted with "tumors" (1 Sam. 5:6).[2143]

[2140] But see Jgs. 20:27 where it is stated that the Ark was at Bethel, originally assigned to Benjamin, but later occupied by the Ephraimites. Bethel was also a religious sanctuary of great antiquity with Jacobite and Abrahamic associations. (Bethel, DB, p. 99.)

[2141] As He is in other places in the Bible, for example: "The Lord is a man of war; the Lord is His name." (Ex. 15:3)

[2142] Ashdod, located near the Mediterranean Sea about 35 miles due west of Bethlehem, was one of the five cities of the Philistine confederacy. Lest this give the impression that Philistia was a large country, it was a strip of coastal plain less than 20 miles wide, east to west, and about 60 miles long, north to south; about the size of the land area of the State of Rhode Island. (See text below.)

[2143] The exact nature of the disease is uncertain; some have suggested bubonic plague, but the Massoretes read "hemorrhoids" in agreement with Surabadi. (BC, III, 25.) Josephus describes the plague visited upon the Philistines thus: "At length God sent a very destructive disease upon the city and country of Ashdod, for they died of dysentery and

Frightened, the people of Ashdod sent the Ark to Gath and Ekron with the same results in those cities. Finally, the Philistines decided to return it to the Israelites. [All of this may have been a fiction to glorify the Israelites and their God. The Israelites may have ransomed the Ark, or perhaps it was returned as part of some sort of a settlement.]

There is no indication in the Biblical text that, as Surabadi asserts, the Philistines dishonored the Ark. In fact, by putting it in their temple they probably thought they were showing it great respect as a valuable trophy of war by offering it to the view of their own god. "The ark of the Lord was in the country of the Philistines seven months." (1 Sam. 6:1) After these plagues, the priests and diviners consulted and told the Philistines to "'take and prepare a new cart and two milch cows upon which there has never come a yoke, and yoke the cows to the cart, but take their calves home, away from them... Then sent it off, and let it go its way.'" (1 Sam. 6:7.8) If the cows ignored their own calves and pulled the cart towards Beth-shemesh, then this was a sign that the God of the Israelites had indeed been responsible for their maladies.[2144]

"Now the people of Beth-shemesh [who were Israelites] were reaping their wheat harvest in the valley; and when they lifted up their eyes and saw the ark, they rejoiced to see it. The cart came into the field of Joshua of Beth-shemesh and stopped there... and the men of Beth-shemesh offered burnt offerings and sacrificed sacrifices on that day to the Lord. And when the five lords of the Philistines[2145] saw it, they returned that day to Ekron." (1 Sam. 6:13-14,15-16.)

---

flux, a sore distemper, that brought death upon them very suddenly; for before the soul could, as usual in easy deaths, be well loosed from the body, they brought up their entrails, and vomited up what they had eaten, and what was entirely corrupted by disease. And as to the fruits of their country, a great multitude of mice arose out of the earth, and hurt them, and spared neither plants nor the fruits." (Josephus, Antiquities, VI.1.1, p. 123.) Pseudo-Philo tells us that the plague destroyed 75,000 women with child, 65,000 nursing infants, 55, 000 of those nursing, plus 24,000 men. (Cited in LJ, VI, 224.) Such figures, a total of nearly 220,000 dead, are patently preposterous, as the Philistines probably never numbered more than 50,000; more likely they were considerably fewer. A later Jewish text says that the plague consisted of "mice crawling forth out of the earth, and jerking the entrails out of the bodies of the Philistines while they eased nature." (LJ, IV, 62-63.)

[2144] In the meantime, the sanctuary and Shiloh had probably been destroyed by the Philistines, accounting for its being returned to Beth-shemesh (Ark of the Covenant, EJ, III, 463). The name means "House/Temple of the Sun," suggesting some connection with pre-Israelite sun-worship. It lay in Judah and had associations with Samson though he was a Danite. His birthplace, Zorah, was but two miles away. (Beth-shemesh, DB, p. 101; Beth-shemesh, EJ, IV, 773-774; Asimov-OT, p. 250.)

[2145] "the five lords of the Philistines": they were the chiefs (or rulers) of the five cities of the Philistine confederacy.

However, this return of the Ark to the Israelites was not without its unfortunate consequences: "And (God) slew some of the men of Beth-shemesh because they looked into the ark of the Lord; He slew 70 men of them, and the people mourned because of the great slaughter among the people." (1 Sam. 6:19)[2146]

Such was YHWH's homecoming, turning the Israelites' joy into mourning. The people of Beth-shemesh, who had so welcomed the Ark were now as anxious to be rid of it as the Philistines had been: "So they sent messengers to the inhabitants of Kiriath-jearim, saying, 'The Philistines have returned the ark of the Lord. Come down and take it up to you.' And the men of Kiriath-jearim came and took up the ark of the Lord, and brought it to the house of Abinadab on the hill." (1 Sam. 6:21-7:1)[2147]

The official version, reflected in the Bible, would be that the Ark remained at Kiriath-jearim until the time of David, when it was brought to the newly conquered Jerusalem. Although Saul's harboring of the Ark (as Surabadi says) is not supported by either the Bible or Jewish tradition, there is one bit of tantalizing evidence implying a closer connection of the Ark with Saul (as in Q. 2:248). In the war of independence from the Philistines, Saul's capital was at Gibeah, about three miles north of Jerusalem (then still in the hands of its non-Israelite Jebusite population) in the territory of Benjamin. Whilst in a difficult military situation at Gibeah, "Saul said to Ahijah, 'Bring hither the ark of God.' For the ark of God went at that time with the people of Israel." (1 Sam. 14:18)

This contradicts other statements that it was kept at Kiriath-jearim during the time of Saul's career. Quite probably, this tradition of Saul's using the Ark as a palladium is true, but was ignored in order to give the honor of reinstituting the Ark ritual to David, thereby serving to enhance the role of the founder of the House of David, from among whose descendants, in later belief, the Messiah would arise. This was accomplished by showing the Ark as relatively ignored until he brought

---

[2146] The Hebrew text makes the number of slaughtered Israelites on this occasion 50,700 men, another impossible figure. As the Ark seems to have been a cause of death for both friend and foe, one may be forgiven if one suspects that some sort of contagious disease had in some manner contaminated the Ark.

[2147] This pericope seems to be an attempt to account for, or accommodate, a tradition of the Ark's being lodged at Kiriath-jearim, besides the tradition of Shiloh. Kiriath-jearim "Town of the Woods," was also in Judah, but occupied by Danites. A connection with Saul is suggested by the fact that it was a Gibeonite town and Gibeon was in Benjamin, the tribe to which Saul belonged. Kiriath-jearim probably possessed a high place. One of Saul's sons was named Abinabab. (Kiriath-jearim, DB, p. 557; Abinadab, DB, p. 4.)

it up to Jerusalem. Hence, the official version (anti-Saulic, pro-Davidic propaganda) that the ill-starred Saul had ignored the Ark left at Kiriath-jearim.

Saul's career was judged unsuccessful (by unfriendly writers supporting the claims of the House of David) in terms of founding a dynasty and accomplishing the union of all the Israelites.[2148] This was contrasted with the much-glorified career of David as a further reason to disassociate Saul from the Ark. It was important—at least at that stage of Israelite history—that the Ark, the symbol of God's presence in Israel, be linked with the successful establishment and preservation of the House of David. If it had conferred similar benefits upon a defeated rival, that special relationship would have been weakened. Similarly, if the Ark had been connected with Saul's abortive effort to found a dynasty, then the prestige of the Ark and, by inference, that of YHWH could have been compromised.

The solution achieved by the pro-Davidic writer of this portion of *Samuel* would appear to have been to be silent about any connection linking Saul with the Ark. The verse quoted above seems to have been preserved because it makes Saul show disrespect to the Ark, as he did not wait for the completion of the oracle being sought from it before rushing into battle (1 Sam. 14:19-20).

The truth would appear to be quite the opposite: Samuel seems to have been involved in a controversy in which he sought to replace the Elide (Levitical) priesthood—which, among other things, was associated with the rituals and institutions of the Ark—with a non-Levitical priesthood of ecstatic prophets. Despite the later assertion of the Chronicler (1 Ch. 6:16-43), Samuel himself was *not* a Levite but an Ephraimite (see 1 Sam. 1:1). In this religious power struggle, it is not likely that Saul ignored the Ark. In fact, it was Samuel who ignored the Ark, as the Biblical text plainly shows. Despite the deliberate silence of the Bible with regard to Saul's attitude toward the Ark, and the assigning of the honor of the revival of its cult to David, the fact that it was lodged in the sanctuary at Kiriath-jearim on the borders of Benjamin, only seven or eight miles west of Saul's capital at Gibeah, cannot be without significance. The Quranic association of the Ark with Saul would appear to be quite justified.

[2148] "Saul's early kingdom probably consisted of [the tribal territories of Ephraim and Benjamin]. In other words, he initially ruled only over the central hill country, the region just north of Jerusalem, and not over all Israel." (Marsha White, *Searching for Saul*, BR, Vol. XVII, No. 3, April 2002, p. 27.) It is not entirely clear how much larger his kingdom was when he died.

Before proceeding with our discussion of Surabadi's text, the importance of the Ark in Israelite history and its mention in the Quran warrant a short digression about its later fate. After David captured Jerusalem and made it his capital, the Ark was brought "out of the house of Abinadab which was on the hill" at Baal-Judah [Kiriath-jearim] and conveyed in a joyous procession to Jerusalem. The sons of Abinadab, Uzzah and Ahiom, drove the oxen hauling the cart carrying the Ark. However, before it reached the city, the oxen stumbled. Uzzah, trying to prevent the Ark from falling to the ground, touched it. He was not thanked for his effort: "And the anger of the Lord was kindled against Uzzah; and God smote him there because he put forth his hand to the ark; and he died there beside the ark of God." (2 Sam. 6:7)

In view of this bad omen and having witnessed the touchiness of YHWH, David prudently halted the procession and left the Ark with a Philistine (!) who had a house near the spot where this tragedy had occurred.[2149] The Ark remained with the Philistine—one Obed-edom[2150]—for three months. When disaster did not overtake him, David ordered that the procession be organized again. This time the Ark came to rest in Jerusalem without further mishap. (2 Sam: 24-26)

After Solomon completed the Temple of Jerusalem, the Ark was ceremoniously brought out of the City of David (just south of the Temple precinct) where it seems to have been housed in a tent sanctuary modeled upon the wilderness Tabernacle of Moses, and installed in the sanctuary of the Temple, the Holy of Holies, as described above. With the installation of His throne or pedestal, YHWH took up residence in the Temple.[2151]

However, not five years after the death of Solomon, Shishak[2152] the pharaoh of Egypt plundered Jerusalem and "took away the treasures

---

[2149] Once again, notice how God is some manner considered to be resident within the Ark.

[2150] Scholars are not agreed as to whether Obed-edom was a Philistine or an Israelite. He is called a Gittite, meaning from Gath, one of the five cities of Philistia, but that word means "mill." He may simply have been a miller. There are other places named Gath, and he may have been a native of Gath-Rimmon rather than the Philistine Gath. (Gath-Rimmon, EJ, III, 464; Grierson, p. 464.) Naturally, there is considerable pressure to make him an Israelite, but the entry in the DB considers him a Philistine. (Obed-edom, DB, p.708.)

[2151] Compare this with the description of YHWH entering the completed Tabernacle in the Wilderness: "then the cloud covered the tent of the meeting, and the glory of the Lord filled the tabernacle." (Ex. 40:3-35) This, too, followed the installation of the Ark in the tent (Ex. 40:20-21).

[2152] Shishak: Sheshonq I, the founder of the XIInd Dynasty, the Libyan Dynasty. He reigned c. 940-919 BCE, and may have been one of Solomon's fathers-in-law. His capital was at Bubastis in the eastern Delta. (Shishak, DB, p. 911.)

of the house of the Lord..." (1 K. 14:25) It is not known whether the Ark was carried away with the other treasures. It may have disappeared from the view of history at that point (928 BCE) or remained until the destruction of Jerusalem and the Temple of Solomon by Nebuchadnezzar in 586 BCE. Neither *Kings* (2 K. 25:13-17) nor *Jeremiah* (Jer. 52:17-23) mentions the Ark in the inventories of the treasures and furniture carried away to Babylon. Since these lists appear to be concerned with items of intrinsic value, their silence in the matter of the Ark cannot be considered conclusive evidence that it was not in existence at that time. *Chronicles*, which is a relatively late text, mentions the Ark as being in existence during the reign of Josiah (2 Ch. 35:3), but the parallel passage in *Kings* (2 K. 23:21-23) is silent on the matter, and the unsupported statement of the Chronicler cannot be considered definitive. The fate of the Ark and the fate of the Tables of the Law written by the Hand of God and placed in the Ark by the hand of Moses (Ex. 40:20) remain mysteries to this day. Some believe that the Ark is now housed in Ethiopia.

SAMUEL: Surabadi continues the story, telling us that Samuel (Ar. *Samūʾīl, Ashmuwīl*) prayed that a king would be found for Israel. Gabriel came with a reed and said that whenever it stood erect above an Israelite's head, that man would be king. Samuel tested everyone he could until he found Saul and the reed stood erect. Saul was proclaimed king. Saul said that he had the Ark. The Israelites objected that royalty belonged in the tribe of Judah, and Saul was not of that tribe. Samuel replied that possession of the Ark was a sufficient sign.

In this account, Surabadi seems to be trying to achieve a compromise between the Jewish and Quranic accounts. The objection that Saul was not of the tribe of Judah is of course a reflection of the much later Jewish belief in the legitimacy of the Judahite House of David from which—an important corollary—the Messiah was to arise.[2153] Surabadi's assertion of the actual possession of the Ark by Saul was suggested by its mention as a sign in the Quran. In this passage, the Quranic notice is considerably closer to the Biblical text than is Surabadi:

Hast thou not seen the leaders of the Children of Israel after Moses, how they said unto a prophet whom they had: "Set up for us a king and we will fight in God's way." He said: "Would ye then refrain from fighting if fighting were prescribed for you?" They said: "Why

---

[2153] This is the reason the conflicting New Testament genealogies for the Galilean Jesus (Mt. 1:1-17; Lk. 3:23-38) agree upon making him a descendant of David and therefore an eligible candidate for the Jewish Messiahship.

should we not fight in God's way when we have been driven from our dwellings with our children?" Yet when fight was prescribed for them, they turned away, all save a few of them. God is Aware of the evildoers. (Q. 2:246)

Their prophet said unto them: "Lo! God has raised up Saul to be a king for you." They said: "How can he have kingdom over us when we are more deserving of the kingdom than he is, since he has not been given ample wealth?" He said: "Lo! God has increased him abundantly in knowledge and stature. God bestows His sovereignty on whom He will. God is All-Embracing, All-Knowing." (Q. 2:247)

And their prophet said unto them: "Lo, the token of his kingdom is that there shall come unto you the Ark wherein is a tranquility from your Lord, and a remnant of that which the house of Moses and the house of Aaron left behind, the angels bearing it. Lo, herein shall be a token for you if ye are believers." (Q. 2:248)

There is no question but that the unnamed prophet in the above passage is correctly identified by Surabadi as the prophet Samuel, probably the greatest figure in Israelite history between Joshua and David. Despite a late Levite attempt to co-opt him, Samuel was an Ephraimite who followed Eli as the charismatic judge and seer of Israel, after Eli's untimely demise upon hearing of the capture of the Israel's most sacred relic, the Ark, by the Philistines.

Samuel was born in answer to the prayers of another barren woman, Hannah, a co-wife of Elkanah, whose other wife had borne him children; a situation recalling Abraham and his wives and Jacob and his. In this period, Shiloh, deep inside the tribal allotment of Ephraim, was the religious center of the Israelite confederation, or perhaps more properly, the Israelite amphictyony. The tent tabernacle had probably become, at least in part, a permanent structure in which was kept the Ark and other sacred relics. Eli was the chief priest there.

Whilst on one of her annual pilgrimages to Shiloh, Hannah vowed to dedicate her son to the Lord if she conceived. God answered Hannah's prayers, and in accordance with her vow, Samuel was dedicated to God as a Nazirite,[2154] and sent as a young boy to serve in the

---

[2154] Samuel, EJ, XIV, 780. Note the parallel with the story of Samson we have just looked at in the preceding story. That Samuel was a Nazirite is not explicitly mentioned in our present Biblical texts, but is found in one of the early recensions of *1 Samuel* found among the Dead Sea Scrolls at Qumran, and also in a Hebrew recension of *Ecclesiastes* found in Cairo. (Albright-Ab to Ez, p. 43.) As an example of the changes that have occurred to the Biblical test, we may compare the Qumran version of 1 Sam. 1:22-23a with that in the *Revised Standard Version* (RSV):

temple (at Shiloh) under Eli's tutelage (1 Sam. 1:24-28). Gradually, through revelation and visions, it became clear that God had selected Samuel to succeed Eli rather than one of his sons (1 Sam. 2-3). After the return of the Ark from its Philistine captivity, Samuel led the Israelites in a religious revival and persuaded the people to put away the foreign gods (Israel had fallen into idolatry once again) and serve YHWH alone. "So Israel put away the Baals and the Ashtaroth, and they served the Lord only." (1 Sam. 7:4)

Then Samuel summoned the Israelites to Mizpah, an ancient assembly place,[2155] to repent their sins. The Philistines heard of the assembly and thought it would an opportune moment to attack them. The terrified Israelites asked Samuel to intercede with God for them. "So Samuel took a suckling lamb and offered it as a whole burnt offering to the Lord; and Samuel cried to the Lord for Israel, and the Lord answered him. As Samuel was offering up the burnt offering, the Philistines drew near to attack Israel; but the Lord thundered with a mighty voice that day against the Philistines and threw them into confusion; and they were routed before Israel." (1 Sam. 7:9-11)

Though the presence of the Ark is not mentioned in this passage, the affair of the sacrifice and the presence of YHWH Himself associated with the Ark in those days would suggest that it had been brought there. This passage is probably the origin of Surabadi's reference to the roar from the Ark that frightened the enemies.

The Bible then tells us that: "Samuel judged Israel all the days of his life. And he went on a circuit year by year to Bethel, Gilgal, and Mizpah; and he judged Israel in all these places. Then he would come back to Ramah, for his home was there, and there also he administered justice to Israel. And he built there an altar to the Lord." (1 Sam. 7:15-17) But, as was the case with Eli, Samuel's sons were not worthy of succeeding him. They "turned aside after gain; they took bribes and perverted justice." (1 Sam. 8:3)

RSV: "But Hannah did not go up, for she said to her husband, 'As soon as he child is weaned, I will bring him, that he may appear in the presence of the Lord and abide there for ever.' Elkanah her husband said to her, 'Do what seems best to thee...'"

Qumran: "But Hannah went not up with him: for she said unto her husband, 'I will not go until the child goes up when I have weaned him that he may appear before the Lord, and there abide before the Lord for ever, and I shall give him for a Nazirite for ever, all the days of his life.' And Elkanah her husband said unto her, 'Do what seemeth thee good...'" (Cited in Allegro-Scrolls, p. 59.) As Albright says there is good reason to believe that the Qumran version represents the original text and the statement that Samuel was a Nazirite was dropped by later editors.

[2155] Either at Nabi Samwil 4 or 5 miles NW of Jerusalem or Tell en-Nasbeh, 8 miles north of Jerusalem. (Mizpah, DB, p, 667.)

This, then, was the cause of the approach to the prophet mentioned in the Quran (Q. 2:246) and the Bible: "then all the elders of Israel gathered together and came to Samuel at Ramah, and said to him, 'Behold, thou art old and thy sons do not walk in thy ways; now appoint for us a king to govern us like all the nations.' But the thing displeased Samuel when they said, 'Give us a king to govern us.' And Samuel prayed to the Lord." (1 Sam. 8:4-6) Although this request by the Israelites is mentioned in the Quran, it is not reported by Surabadi who apparently has Samuel taking the initiative.

After being warned of the burdens that a monarch would impose upon the people, as God had told Samuel to do, the people persisted in their request. In Surabadi, we find Samuel using a kind of divining rod to select the king. Saul was a Benjaminite from Gibeah, the son of Kish. The Bible does not tell us what his occupation was, but it does say in one place that Kish was a man of wealth (1 Sam. 9:1), although it later contradicts itself and suggests that his material circumstances were quite ordinary. The Quranic reference to Saul's lack of wealth though supported by the Biblical text (see below), may be relative and an allusion to the weakness of his power base, the tribe of Benjamin. Benjamin was the smallest of the tribes and perhaps of comparatively recent acceptance into the Israelite confederation. Whilst the Quran cites both Saul's physical and mental excellences—*God has increased him abundantly in wisdom and stature* (Q. 2:247)—his Biblical introduction remarks only about his physical qualities: "...and (Kish) had a son whose name was Saul, a handsome young man. There was not a man among the people of Israel more handsome than he; from his shoulders upward he was taller than any of the people." (1 Sam. 9:2)

This reference to Saul's height is thought to account for his Quranic name *Ṭālūt* from the Arabic root *ṭ-w-l* "to be tall or long."[2156] Since there is no documentary evidence of the occurrence of the name before the Quran, Jeffrey assumes that it is a "formation of Muhammad himself from *Shawul*, a name which he may not have heard correctly and formed probably under the influence of *ṭāla* to rhyme with *Jālūt*, "itself a "garbled version of *Jlyt* (for Goliath).[2157]

Setting aside Jeffrey's assumptions about the composition of the Quran, the derivation of *Ṭālūt* from *ṭāla* would seem to have a much higher degree of probability than the Prophet's mishearing *Shawul* (Saul) as *Ṭālūt*. Because its first documentary appearance is in the Quran there is no reason to assume, as Jeffrey does, that the Prophet snatched the

---

[2156] Talut, SEI, 571.
[2157] Jeffrey, pp. 204, 97.

name out of thin air. Jeffrey ignores the history of oral tradition that we may surmise lies behind the name. The name is not given any special attention in the Quran (new or strange terms are frequently explained) and presumably was already known to the Hejazis. *Ṭālūt* would appear to have nothing to do with *Shawul* (a mix-up between *sh* and *ṭ* is remarkable, as they are quite distinct in Semitic languages). However, an independent Arabic formation, a nickname based on a tradition of his most conspicuous and well-known physical feature (his height) may very well have originated among the Arabic-speaking Jews settled in the Hejaz who would have been aware of the connotation.[2158] If it were a nickname and not a proper name, it would not have been given to anyone and would be absent in inscriptions. Perhaps, it would be better to translate the word as "the Tall One" or "Longneck" instead of "Saul."

After the above comments about Saul's physical appearance, the Biblical story of his selection as king begins: "Now the asses of Kish, Saul's father, were lost. So Kish said to Saul his son, 'Take one of the servants with thee, and arise, go and look for the asses.'" (1 Sam. 9:3) After searching for a considerable time with no luck, Saul and his servant arrived at a town in which Samuel happened to be present. Saul decided to seek the prophet's help in finding the lost animals.

"Now the day before Saul came, the Lord had revealed to Samuel: 'Tomorrow about this time I will sent to thee a man from the land of Benjamin, and thou shalt anoint him to be prince over my people Israel. He shall save my people from the hand of the Philistines...'" When Samuel saw Saul, the Lord told him, "'Here is the man of whom I spoke to thee! He it is who shall rule over my people.'" (1 Sam. 9:15-17)[2159]

Before Saul had a chance to speak, Samuel invited him to eat with him and told him that the asses had been found. Saul was disconcerted by Samuel's hospitality and warmth, and protested: "'Am I not a Benjaminite, from the least of the tribes of Israel? And is not my family the humblest of all the families of the tribe of Benjamin? Why then hast thou spoken to me in this way?'" (1 Sam. 9:21) This statement seems to be more than just humility and though in agreement with the Quran's lack of "ample wealth" (Q. 2:247), conflicts with the earlier Biblical statement that Saul's father was a man of wealth. Saul's protest has the ring of truth to it.

[2158] The writer of these lines has heard several times particularly tall students addressed humorously as *Yā Ṭawīl* (O Tall One!) in Saudi Arabia.

[2159] The divine revelation of the previous day was apparently not adequate identification. One wonders why the Almighty did not simply give Samuel Saul's name.

In any case, Saul passed the night with Samuel. On the following morning: "as they were going down to the outskirts of the city, Samuel said to Saul, 'Tell the servant to pass on before us, and when he has passed on, stop here thyself for a while that I may make known to thee the word of God.' Then Samuel took a vial of oil and poured it on his head, and kissed him and said, 'Hath not the Lord anointed thee to be prince over His people Israel? And thou shalt reign over the people of the Lord and thou wilt save them from the hand of their enemies round about. And this shall be the sign to thee that the Lord has anointed thee to be prince over His heritage.'" (1 Sam. 9:27-10:1)

In addition to this consecration by anointment, several other signs were given to Saul, including the spirit of prophecy, but none of which could form the basis for the Surabadi's story of selection by divining rod. As is so often the case in the Bible, we are given an alternative version of the selection, unrelated to the first. It involves a lottery and probably provides the basis of Surabadi's pericope:

Saul's first selection had not been made public. Samuel called an assembly of Israel at Mizpah, in which the people clamored for a king. The selection of a king was to be made by lots. This is clearly a different second tradition from another source about the selection of Saul. Among the tribes, the lot fell to Benjamin; among the families of Benjamin, the lot fell to the Matrites; among the Matrites, the lot fell to Saul, son of Kish. "But when they sought him, he could not be found" because he had hidden himself. Eventually he was discovered and presented by Samuel to the people. "...And when he stood among the people, he was taller than any of the people from his shoulders upward. And Samuel said to all the people, 'Do ye see him whom the Lord has chosen? There is none like him among all the people.' And all the people shouted, 'Long live the king!'" (1 Sam. 10:20-23)

After instructing the people in the rights and duties of kingship, Samuel sent them home. "Saul also went to his home at Gibeah, and with him went men of valor whose hearts God had touched. But some worthless fellows said, 'How can this man save us?' And they despised him, and brought him no present. But he held his peace." (1 Sam. 10:26-27)

Despite the considerable authority and sanction of Samuel (not to mention divine appointment), the imposition of the monarchy was not accomplished without opposition. This is hinted at in the Biblical passage cited above and stated more explicitly in the Quran: *They said: "How can he have kingdom over us when we are more deserving of the kingdom than he is, since he has not been given ample wealth?"* (Q. 2:247), that is, a power base.

Part of this opposition appears to have been directed at Saul himself. Doubtless, the protest he made to Samuel when the matter was broached (in the first story of his accession) contains the gist of the personal attacks he expected to hinder him. The Benjaminites were apparently not well regarded by other Hebrews. One of the few occasions in the period of the judges when the Israelites acted in relative unity was an inter-tribal war in which the Benjaminites were nearly exterminated in revenge for the commission of a particularly heinous crime by some of their young men (see *Judges*, chs. 19-21).[2160] In addition, the prophecy about the tribe put in the mouth of Jacob was not very reassuring: "Benjamin is a ravenous wolf, in the morning devouring the prey, and at evening dividing the spoil." (Gen. 49:27) But they had a bellicose reputation, and perhaps that was what Israel needed at that time to deal with the Philistines.

The rise of the Israelite monarchy is a complicated subject with scholarly disagreement over many of its aspects, both in the broad course of its development and in its details. We shall content ourselves here with only a few remarks about it to establish the context for the Quranic references and Surabadi's stories. In the time of the judges, Israel was perhaps in theory a theocratic amphictyony, in the name of which the judges exercised their various degrees of authority, but in practice the tribes were independent of each, united in a loose confederation of tribal cantons.[2161] They got along together with varying degrees of amity and enmity. The tribal units themselves were not organized uniformly. In fact, their leadership was charismatic rather than formal. At the same time there were the regulatory claims of the Levitical priesthood, at some times coinciding with the aims and policies of the judges, and at other times not. The Levites were a powerful force in the priesthood and they managed various shrines, but they did not monopolize all sacerdotal offices at this stage, as the story of the non-Levite Samuel demonstrates.

[2160] The serial rape of the Levite's concubine. Several hundred years earlier (19th-18th centuries BCE) the Benjaminites (*Banu-yamina*) are mentioned in the Mari texts as marauders, or brigands. (Anderson, p. 17) Their relationship to the Benjaminites of the Bible, if any, has not been established. (See *The Tribe of Benjamin* in Part Two above, V.B.)

[2161] Much like, though even less formal a union than, the confederation of independent American states that preceded the establishment of a much stronger central government by the current Constitution of the United States.

And, of course, the shrines were rivals to one other in their efforts to attract worshippers, pilgrims, and donations.

There existed other religious tensions as well, for the worship of YHWH—despite the picture of triumph given to us at the end of the Hexateuch—had by no means completely ousted earlier competing religious ideas (and gods), just as the Israelite settlement had not expelled all of the Canaanites, who had formerly been its principal occupants. Indeed, Canaanite religious practices and ideas were long a threat to the purity of the worship of the Israelites themselves. They often lapsed back to pagan rites, such as infanticide, throughout the period of the monarchy, especially in the North (Israel).

There was also the rivalry between the Northern (Josephic) and Southern (Judahic) tribes that we have had many occasions to note above. It probably originated before the Israelite settlement in Canaan had achieved the distribution it had in the period of the judges. The tribe of Benjamin was likely the last to enter Canaan (according to many scholars) and to settle its "allotted territory."[2162] This was located between these two rival groups of Northern and Southern tribes, and it contained a rather disproportionate number of holy places within its restricted borders: Bethel, Mizpah, Gilgal, Geba, Kiriath-jearim, and the still unconquered Jebus (Jerusalem).

Although geographically well located to administer Palestine, the Benjaminites were a warrior people not well liked by the other tribes. A cloud seems to have remained over their legitimacy as Israelites. The selection of a man (Saul) from this tribe may be regarded as a compromise between the Northern and Southern tribes, each resentful and fearful that a king from the other grouping who would favor his own kinsmen and oppress the other group. Given these conditions, Saul—a compromise candidate with a weak base—would have had to tread very carefully indeed in order to establish a strong, centralized monarchy and to found a dynasty. That he managed to survive twenty years in this nest of rivalries and jealousies is ample justification for the Quranic statement that *God has increased him abundantly in knowledge...* (Q. 2:247) The knowledge here is statecraft and survival. In this situation, Saul could only count on the loyalty of his own Benjaminites, and the "men of valor whose hearts God had touched" (1 Sam. 10:26).

We remind the reader that in the above Biblical material we have *two* versions of the selection of Saul.[2163] The gathering at Mizpah (1 Sam. 10:17-27) would logically follow 1 Sam. 8, where the people ask Samuel

---

[2162] Benjamin, DB, p. 97.
[2163] Anderson, p. 51.

to appoint a king. Note also that in the meeting at Mizpah, Saul was elected by lottery, whilst in the other version he was selected by God Himself Who had revealed His intentions to Samuel. At Mizpah, Samuel gave no indication that he had met Saul before. While that could be attributed to Samuel's political discretion, more likely we have another Biblical conflation, this time of two different accounts of Saul's accession to the throne.

And there is still a *third* probable version of the beginning of the monarchy: Ch. 11 of *1 Samuel* narrates the defeat of the Ammonites by Saul at Jabesh-gilead, east of the Jordan River. If we assume that this chapter is indeed another proclamation narrative, and not a sequel to the events at Mizpah, as would seem to be the case, Saul appears as a tribal leader of the Benjaminites who summons other tribes to come to the aid of the people of Jabesh-gilead besieged by the Ammonites. Under Saul's generalship, the Ammonites were utterly routed.

"Then the people said to Samuel, 'Who is it that said, "Shall Saul reign over us?" Bring the men, that we may put them to death.' But Saul said, 'Not a man shall be put to death this day, for today the Lord has wrought deliverance in Israel.' Then Samuel said to the people, 'Come, let us go to Gilgal and there renew the kingdom." So all the people went to Gilgal, and there they made Saul king before the Lord in Gilgal..." (1 Sam. 11:11-15)

As the text stands today, Samuel's invitation to "renew the kingdom" is strange. There is no indication that between Mizpah and Gilgal the monarchy had lapsed. Instead, the proclamation of Saul as king would be a logical result of this heroic achievement at Jabesh-gilead. Throughout history, many dynasties have been founded in similar circumstances. Before the battle, by inviting cooperation from the other tribes rather than summoning them, Saul was behaving more like a local lord than an acknowledged king to whom fealty was due. He invoked no monarchical privileges until after Jabesh-gilead.

Thus, it would appear that we have no fewer that *three* proclamation traditions associated with three different places about the enthronement of Saul: one at Samuel's home Ramah (or Bethel), another at Mizpah, and most likely a third from Gilgal. All three places were sacred sites within or adjacent to the territory of Benjamin, quite probably rivals for attracting pilgrims. Saul's capital as king was at Gibeah in Benjamin where Albright has uncovered the foundations of Saul's "palace." It is a modest affair, a simple rectangular fortified compound enclosing a courtyard of about 100 ft. by 60 ft.[2164]

[2164] Albright-Pal, pp. 120-122; Keller, p. 196.

It may be surmised that conservative opposition to the establishment of the monarchy was considerably stronger than the present text of *Samuel* suggests. In part, it seemed to be a rejection of the rule of YHWH and was therefore critical of that institution, a view which Samuel himself is represented as holding: "And the Lord said to Samuel, 'Hearken to the voice of the people in all that they say unto thee; for they have not rejected thee, but they have rejected Me from being king over them.'" (1 Sam. 8:7)[2165] *Samuel* is a complex quilt of traditions representing opposing and contradictory points of view: pro- and anti-monarchical, pro- and anti-Saulic, and pro- and anti-Davidic.

The remainder of the Quranic passage dealing with these events at the beginning of the monarchy is centered about Goliath and the struggle against him and his fellow Philistine warriors: *And when Saul set out with the army, he said: "Lo! God will try you with a river. Whosoever therefore drinks thereof he is not of me, and whosoever tastes it not he is of me, save him who takes (thereof) in the hollow of his hand. But they drank thereof, all save a few of them. And after he had crossed (the river), he and those who had believed with him, they said: "We have no power this day against Goliath and his hosts. But those who knew that they would meet their Lord exclaimed: "How many a little company has overcome a mighty host by God's permission! God is with the steadfast."* (Q. 2:249)

And when they went into the field against Goliath and his hosts, they said: "Our Lord! Bestow on us endurance, make our foothold sure, and give us help against the disbelieving folk. (Q. 2:250)

So they routed them by God's permission and David slew Goliath; and God gave him of that which He wills. And if God had not repelled some men by others, the earth would have been corrupted. But God is the Lord of Kindness to (all) creatures. (Q. 2:251)

This is, as we shall see, a considerably telescoped account of the struggle between the Israelites under Saul and later David with the Philistines. The purpose of the verse is to encourage the believer in the face of an apparently stronger opposition, be it military, economic, social, or individual. The first verse in the passage quoted above (Q. 2:249) has spawned numerous charges of confusion and inaccuracy by Western critics of the Quran. At issue this time is the matter of the water test.

[2165] Anderson, p. 51; Saggs, p. 343.

THE WATER TEST: The Biblical text that most closely resembles this incident is part of the story of Gideon, one of the pre-monarchical judges. In the Quran, it is part of the story of Saul. Surabadi elaborates the circumstances, and his version further confuses the issue: When the Philistines came out under the leadership of Goliath with 100,000 horsemen to attack the Israelites, Saul brought a large army to oppose them. Samuel told Saul that they were entering the desert and there was a stream. Whoever drank a large amount of water from it would not reach the objective; while whoever drank a little would do so.[2166] Surabadi has here introduced Samuel, who is not involved either in the Biblical story of Gideon, nor in the parts of the Biblical story of Saul we shall consider. In addition, Surabadi seems to regard the water test as one of continence; those who drank to excess would not reach the objective; those who drank but a little would.

There is no Biblical record of Saul's applying such a test to his army. The closest parallel is that of Gideon: "Then Jerubbaal (that is, Gideon) and all the people who were with him rose early and encamped beside the spring of Harod; and the camp of Midian was north of them, by the hill of Moreh, in the valley." (Jgs. 7:1) Gideon was probably active about 1100 BCE.[2167] In this battle, the Midianites were the enemy, not the Philistines, and it was fought in northern Palestine some nine miles west-northwest of modern Beit Shean. Gideon himself was from the Northern Josephic tribe of Manasseh (Jgs. 6:15).

"The Lord said to Gideon, 'The people with thee are too many for Me to give the Midianites into their hand, lest Israel vaunt themselves against Me, saying, "My own hand has delivered me." Now therefore proclaim in the ears of the people, saying, "Whosoever is fearful and trembling, let him return home."' [YHWH seems to fear being rejected or ignored by Israel.] And Gideon tested them; twenty-two thousand returned, and ten thousand remained." (Jgs. 7:2-3)

"And the Lord said to Gideon, 'The people are still too many; take them down to the water and I will test them for thee there; and he of whom I say unto thee, "This man shall go with thee," shall go with thee; and any of whom I say unto thee, "This man shall not go with thee," shall not go.' So he brought the people down to the water; and the Lord said to Gideon, 'Every one that laps the water with his tongue, as a dog laps, thou shalt set by himself; likewise every one that kneels down to drink.' And the number of those that lapped, putting their hands to their mouths, was three hundred men; but all the rest of the people knelt down

---

[2166] Surabadi, p. 20.
[2167] IB, II, 682.

to drink water. And the Lord said to Gideon, 'With the three hundred men that lapped I will deliver thee, and give the Midianites into thy hand; and let all the others go every man to his home.' So he took the jars of the people from their hands, and their trumpets; and he sent all the rest of Israel every man to his tent, but retained the three hundred men; and the camp of Midian was below him in the valley." (Jgs. 7:4-8)

Virtually all that we know about Gideon is to be found in the "obviously composite"[2168] narrative of chapters 3-6 of *Judges*. Once again there are duplications, this time in the account of Gideon's call to leadership (Jgs. 6:11-24 and Jgs. 6:25-32) and double-naming in the two names given to the Israelite hero: Gideon and Jerubbaal. An ancient fragment about the Ephraimites (Jgs. 7:24-8:3) is inserted into its present position between two other episodes of the war with the Midianites. And while considering the story of Gideon, the story of Abimelech, his son, told in Jgs. 9 should also be taken into account:

Abimelech was proclaimed king in Shechem in the territory of Western Manasseh after the death of his father. In the course of the chapter, his father's name is given nine times, and it is always Jerubbaal. Not once is he called Gideon. The matter is further confused by *Samuel* which names Abimelech's father as Jurebbeseth (2 Sam. 11:21), but this is doubtless a variant created for theological reasons; that is, the desire to excise the name of Baal, YHWH's rival, from the theophoric form "Jerubbaal."[2169]

The last verses of the second account of Gideon's call (Jgs. 6:31-32) purport to narrate the origin of the name Jerubbaal, but the etymology is false, and it follows that the story around it might be false as well. At least, it renders suspect the conclusion that Gideon and Jerubbaal are indeed the same person, rather than the conflation of traditions about two separate individuals. Although recognizing the false etymology of Jerubbaal and the conflation of at least three traditions present in the text, many Biblical commentators are generally content to accept the identification of Gideon with Jerubbaal.[2170] Not to do so would only increase the historical chaos. Smith, however, thinks that Jerubbaal and Gideon may indeed have been two different heroes.[2171]

It may also be noted that Abimelech, the son of Jerubbaal/Gideon is the first Israelite to be proclaimed king (Jgs. 9:6), not Saul. Of course, Saul became king of all, or at least (perhaps) most of

---

[2168] Gideon, DB, p. 328.

[2169] Jerubbaal, DB, p. 471.

[2170] Gideon, DB, pp. 328-329; BC, II, 417.

[2171] Robert Houston Smith, writing in the Commentary on Judges, Laymon, p.142

Israel, whilst Abimelech's authority was probably confined to north-central Palestine. Gideon himself was offered the kingship after his defeat of the Midianites, but he rejected it for himself and his son (Jgs. 8:22-23). This is curious, as we find Abimelech a king in the following chapter, and it probably indicates that the verse of Gideon's renunciation is a criticism of Abimelech inserted by a hostile editor rather than a report of a real event. In any case, with or without the title, Gideon functioned as a king.[2172] Despite some Biblical criticism of his religious activities, Gideon was highly regarded by later Jews.[2173]

Turning to the water test itself, a careful reading of the text does not make the nature of the test itself clear. Those who lapped water like dogs were to be separated from those who knelt to drink. Dalglish, commenting on this passage, interprets this to mean that the lappers "used their hands to bring water to their mouths as a dog uses his tongue. Others kneeled down to drink the water."[2174] This is not a satisfactory distinction. Another scholar admits: "the nature of the test is not quite clear in the Massoretic Text."[2175]

Lapping water with the tongue like a dog would imply a prone position, unnatural in most human beings unless driven by extreme thirst, and in that position one would be more likely so suck the water into the mouth rather than lap it with the tongue. There is no reason to suppose (from the text) that the army was experiencing a shortage of water, for there was ample water in the region. The ancient editor revising these passages saw the difficulty and rejected the obvious meaning by adding "putting their hands to their mouths" in the following verse. But people who drink from a pool or river using their hands would normally squat, kneel, or bend over to reach down. In this case, the distinction between the two groups is not clear. Presumably, all were drinking by hand as no vessels are mentioned.

Dalglish gives the following analysis of the test: "Another paradoxical order of Yahweh further diminished the army. And the

---

[2172] Asimov feels that Gideon did in fact rule as a king, at least in Manasseh, and the crisis was created not by Gideon's royal prerogatives, but by the question of whether his kingship was to be hereditary or not. (Asimov-OT, p. 244.) In this view, the kingship was initially hereditary, for Abimelech then succeeded his father. But for reasons not clearly preserved in the Bible, there was a reaction against him, and he was ignominiously killed by a woman (Jgs. 9:53-54). Gideon's renunciation would then have been fabricated at a later time to prevent other members of his house from laying claim to the vacant throne.

[2173] LJ, VI, 201.

[2174] Edward R. Dalglish, writing in "Judges," BC, II, 419.

[2175] Guthrie, p. 264.

selection or rejection of the soldiers was based not upon physique, or experience, or age, or military prowess, but upon the way they drank water! Some of the soldiers lapped the water with their tongues, as a dog does; that is, they used their hands to bring the water to their mouths as a dog uses his tongue. Others kneeled down to drink the water. The divine test appears to indicate that the former had an alertness and preparedness which the latter lacked."[2176] Perhaps.

As far as the physical motions are concerned, the attempt to reconcile the irreconcilable is not entirely successful. The simple fact is that vv. 5 and 6 contradict each other, where the former speaks of the tongue, the latter speaks of the hand. V. 6 is certainly a later gloss to v. 5. Interpreted another way, instead of being a test of alertness, it might rather have been a test of confidence; the 300 who were fearless went down (unnaturally) on all fours to drink the water were demonstrating their faith in God's watchfulness.

This is the opposite of the interpretation Josephus gives the incident. It suggests that his Biblical text may have differed from the present received Massoretic Text, which is later than Josephus by several centuries. He shows God [somewhat jealously] concerned that the impending victory over the Midianites might be ascribed to the large Israelite army rather than to Himself, so He orders the test to reduce the size of the army in order to demonstrate His power. Disregarding the theological implications of this portrait of God, we may continue with Josephus' narrative: "(God) advised (Gideon) to bring the army about noon, in the violence of the heat, to the river, and to esteem those that bent their knees and so drank to be men of courage; for those that drank tumultuously, that he should esteem them to do it out of fear, and as in dread of their enemies...[2177] When he had done as God had suggested to him, there were found 300 men that took the water with their hands tumultuously; so God bid him take these men [that is, the fearful] and attack the enemy."[2178]

These contrary conclusions demonstrate that as a test of faith and courage, the manner in which one drinks water is not infallible. It is possible, perhaps even probable, that this water test should not be considered a test of courage or alertness at all, but rather as a kind of divinely sanctioned lottery.[2179] Indeed, this is all the test justifies, and

---

[2176] BC, II, 419.

[2177] Cf. Surabadi above. This element of Surabadi's tradition is doubtless related to the tradition represented by Josephus.

[2178] Josephus, Antiquities, V.6.3, p. 115.

[2179] See note to RSV, pp. 302-303.

trying to read other motives into the text may be an unprofitable exercise, particularly in view of the spliced nature of the text. Water tests have been used throughout history. Suspected criminals (or witches) were dunked in ponds. If the individual drowned or collapsed under the treatment, he (or she) was guilty of the accusation. Here too, Providence was considered the actual agent of determining the suspect's guilt or innocence; that is, his ability to survive the test.

Now, as we have stated above, there is no water test associated with Saul in the Bible. This has led Western critics to pounce upon the Quranic verse with charges of confusion, in this case a confusion of Gideon with Saul.[2180] Though the strength and integrity of the Biblical account is weakened because itself it is a product of editing and conflation, this is not an adequate rebuttal to this charge.

Muslim commentators—Surabadi among them—relying upon the veracity of revelation, tend to ignore the connection of this incident with Gideon, although they are clearly influenced by the details of his story as recorded in *Judges*. Looking closely at the Biblical story of Gideon, the water test pericope may be analyzed as follows:

1. The reduction of the size of the army commanded by God so that He can demonstrate His strength (and thereby win back defecting worshippers to His worship).

2. God speaks directly to Gideon, and for the second reduction, orders the water test.

3. The test is based upon the manner in which the men drink the water, though the significance of the distinction and the actual differences of drinking are obscure.

4. The men are ignorant of the test being applied to them.

5. Of the original 32000, and the 10,000 left after the first winnowing; the final 300 are selected by the water test.

The Quranic version:

1. The reduction is to eliminate the less faithful and courageous. (A parallel may be found in the first reduction of Gideon's army whereby 22,000 were allowed to return home.)

2. A trial is ordered by Saul at a river. (This may represent a frontier.)

[2180] For example: Sale in a note to Surah Baqarah, writes: "It seems that Mohammed has here confused Saul with Gideon, who by divine direction took with him against the Midianites such of his army only as lapped water out with their hands, which were 300 men." (Quran-Sale, p. 36.)

3. The sign of adherence to Saul's leadership is the gesture of either refraining from drinking or moderation; that is, the quantity of water drunk.

4. Since they have already informed of the criterion in an address by Saul, they are aware of the significance of their behavior at the river.

5. Only Saul and *those who had believed with him* (Q. 2:249) crossed the river. They are few.

Though the Quranic text does not associate Samuel with this, Surabadi does. The Quranic silence is in accordance with the Bible. Samuel had already broken with Saul by the time of the confrontation with Goliath (1.Sam. 13:13-14).

Despite the apparent similarity of the Quranic pericope to the water test of Gideon, reflection on the points of the above analysis will show that there are fundamental differences, sufficient to justify at least the reconsideration of the conventional assumptions. Many commentators, aware of the problem, contented themselves with a statement to the effect that the Quranic tradition reflects a tradition of an incident in the career of Saul that had some points of resemblance to the Gideon water test, but had not been incorporated into the present text of the Bible.[2181] From what we have already seen of the sometimes haphazard survival of material through the sifting of editors with theological, national, and tribal prejudices, we could let the matter rest here with that not improbable conclusion.

Putting aside the parallels with the Gideon story, let us look at the Quranic verse independently of it. The scene may be reconstructed thus: When reaching a river which represents a point of no return (a frontier or a boundary of influence) on the way to an impending battle with the Philistines, Saul allowed the weak-hearted in his army to leave. The test was one of loyalty to the leadership of Saul, and no divine lottery was invoked. The army was assembled on the riverbank and Saul addressed them, telling them that those who did not want to continue with in this perilous enterprise were free to water themselves and their animals and return home. Those who would continue with him were to drink in moderation, or not drink at all; on guard to protect those were watering and preparing to return. When that was done Saul and his loyal troops would cross the river. Perhaps this was done with a conscious symbolic reference to the surely well-known story of Gideon in the minds of Saul and his soldiers. Only a few did not let their fear of the

---

[2181] For example: Quran-MMA, p. 108; Quran-Yusuf Ali, p. 99; Quran-Maududi, I, 179.

iron-armed Philistines[2182] and their gigantic leader Goliath overwhelm them. Those few stayed and watched the majority depart for home.

The above is not a farfetched reconstruction of the story contained in the Quranic verse. The test was an opportunity for those did not have the stomach to face the Philistines to leave.[2183] Bal'ami makes it a test of obedience: "And Saul [Talut] thus had said to himself, that if these people obey me and cross the river without drinking, then they will also obey me in war..." Of an army of 76,000, only 4,000 accompanied Saul across the river.[2184] Nasafi is clearly under the influence of the Gideon story, although in order to harmonize it with the Quranic verse, he reverses the Biblical interpretation of the signs: "God most High will try you by a stream; whosoever lies on his stomach and drinks water with his mouth, he is not of my army; and whosoever does not drink in this way, but takes water from his hand, he is of my army... and they were 313 men..."[2185] An even older commentary from the 10th century CE gives the same figure of 313.[2186]

The scene of Gideon's water test was the "Well of Harod," or more accurately, the spring of Harod in the valley of Jezreel, about nine miles northeast of Jenin in modern north-central Palestine. "The water rises in a natural cavern and spreads itself out into a considerable pool, partially artificial, before descending the valley."[2187] Its Arabic name, ʿAyn Jālūt (Spring of Goliath), suggests once again the influence of the Gideon story and the confusion caused by it, by associating the Quranic water test of Saul with that of Gideon, thereby transferring the battle of Goliath from the more arid areas of western Judah on the edge of Philistia, to this site with its Gideonite connects in northern Palestine.

Returning to the reconstruction of events that we have proposed above, it is reasonable to ask whether any of the other ingredients of the Quranic verse are present in the Biblical story of Saul. If it is assumed that the battle referred to is the one in which David killed Goliath, then—according to the Bible—that fight took place in the valley of Elah which contains a non-perennial stream now called the Ha'ela, lying between the

---

[2182] In this period, iron was just being introduced into Palestine and the Philistines had a monopoly of it. See the story of David for about the introduction of iron into the Near East, Part Five, I.

[2183] Compare with Husayn at Karbala, who permitted those of his army who wished to abandon the camp before the inevitable slaughter by Yazid's army to leave during the darkness of night.

[2184] Bal'ami, I, p. 540.

[2185] Nasafi, I, p. 63.

[2186] Kuhan, p. 110.

[2187] Harod, DB, p. 365.

two armies (1 Sam. 15:2-3). That this could contain water if the battle occurred during the autumn, winter, or spring, requires no strain upon one's credulity. However, none of the other ingredients is present in the Biblical text: there is no reduction of forces; there is despondency, but the leadership is not being questioned.

The battle of Elah took place after David had been introduced into the Bible narrative (1 Sam. 16:12-13); from that point onward, the (Judahite) Biblical view of Saul was far from favorable. Prior to the break with Samuel, he had been regarded as a hero and the savior of Israel. Saul's earlier favorable reputation was built upon his success in freeing the Israelites from the domination by the Philistines. At the beginning of this War of Liberation, *Samuel* states: "Saul chose 3,000 men of Israel; the rest of the people he sent home, every man to his tent." (1 Sam. 13:2) This is clearly an instance of a selection process, but we are given no details about the criteria used in the process, nor its manner. Is the Quranic pericope related to this?

Further on we read that after suffering a defeat at the hands of Saul and his son Jonathan: "...the Philistines mustered to fight with Israel, 30,000 chariots, and 6,000 horsemen, and troops like the sand on the seashore in multitude; they came up and encamped at Michmash, to the east of Beth-aven.[2188] When the men of Israel saw that they were in straits... the people hid themselves in caves and in holes and in rocks and in tombs and in cisterns, or crossed the fords of the Jordan to the land of Gad and Gilead. Saul was still at Gilgal, and all the people following him were trembling." (1 Sam. 13:5-7) "And Saul numbered the people who were with him, about six hundred men." (1 Sam. 13:15) Does the Quranic pericope refer to this?

In this Biblical passage we have all the circumstances of Q. 2:249: the vast host of a threatening enemy, a fearful Israelite army, fleeing across the River Jordan, and a small number of followers who are questioning their ability to confront the superior Philistines. At this point, for our purposes, the documentary evidence of the Bible ceases and we can only speculate. Saul was at Gilgal impatiently awaiting Samuel while the Philistines were encamped at Bethel thirteen miles to the west in the central Palestinian highlands. (Goliath had not yet been slain by David, so it is rather likely that the Philistine champion—though unmentioned here—would not have wanted to miss an opportunity to fight the frightened Israelites; see below.) Gilgal itself was located[2189] only five miles from an important ford of the Jordan, almost certainly the one used

---

[2188] According to the OBA, Beth-aven = Bethel. (OBA, p. 63.)

[2189] If the identification of Gilgal with Kirbat Mafjar be correct. (Gilgal, DB, p. 330-331.)

by the fleeing Israelites. Though there is no Biblical statement to support this, it is completely possible that Saul himself forded the Jordan during the seven days he waited for Samuel (1 Sam. 13:8), and tried to rally support among the deserters. Those who followed him would have crossed back to the west bank of the Jordan by that ford and the army assembly point at Gilgal would be those men mentioned in the Quran.

In the career of David, there is another parallel to the Quranic description. In this incident, the Amalekites had raided Ziklag and captured David's two wives amongst others, and much booty. "So David set out, and the six hundred men who were with him, and they came to the brook Besor, where those stayed who were left behind. But David went on with the pursuit, he and four hundred men; two hundred stayed behind, who were too exhausted to cross the brook Besor." (1 Sam. 30:9-10) We do not suggest that this incident is connected with the Quranic account of Saul, but rather cite it to show that the symbolic crossing water (witness Moses crossing the Red Sea), or the mention of a river at some crucial point in an expedition, is not so unique in the Bible as one might think.

Another aspect of the relationship of the Quranic verses to the Bible should be considered. The Quran seems to associate these events with a battle in which Goliath personally participated. It is not necessary to assume that it was the battle in which David slew Goliath at Elah, as that statement can be read parenthetically without doing any injustice to the text. On the other hand, there is no Biblical mention of Goliath except in connection with that battle. The Philistine giant and champion appears on the battlefield with no previous Biblical history. However, Saul is reported to have said to David, when trying to dissuade him from accepting Goliath's challenge: "'Thou art not able to go against the Philistine to fight with him; for thou art but a youth, and he [Goliath] *has been a man of war from his youth.*'" (1 Sam. 17:33; our italics) Despite the previous Biblical silence about him, Goliath was already a renowned, experienced soldier. It is highly unlikely, considering the reputation Saul attributes to him, that he had not participated—as a leader of the Philistine army of Gath—in other battles with the Israelites, though there is not explicit Biblical statement to that effect.

Such a man, it would be logical to assume, would have been included in any general Philistine muster, including those cited above. Jewish tradition confirms this assumption. Goliath is reported as having fought the Israelites at Aphek when the Ark was captured and he had killed the sons of Eli, Hophni and Phinehas.[2190] Jewish tradition also

---

[2190] LJ, IV, 87: VI, 223.

reports a confrontation between Goliath and Saul, establishing a link between the two men: "For Goliath was intent upon doing away with Saul. His grievance against him was that once, when, in a skirmish between the Philistines and the Israelites, Goliath had succeeded in capturing the holy tables of the Law, Saul had wrested them from the giant."[2191]

Therefore, it is entirely possible, even in the absence of Biblical confirmation, that Goliath and his fierce reputation would have been in the minds of the frightened Israelites who had deserted Saul and taken refuge east of the Jordan, leaving Saul at Gilgal with a small number of loyal supporters. Incidentally, the immediate outcome of this confrontation at Michmash was Saul's victory over the Philistines.[2192]

If this speculation be accepted as *possible*, then we may press it further by making the words *"How many a little company has overcome a mighty host by God's permission! God is with the steadfast"* (Q. 2:249) a reference to the battle at Michmash in which Saul would have taken part, but was not slain and in which David did not take part. Q. 2:251 (see above) would be an account of Goliath's subsequent fate at the hands of David at Elah, a kind of gloss suggested by the mention of him in the preceding verse. The paucity of extra-Biblical literary survivals from the period make it difficult to proceed beyond what we have laid out here. The reader may consider the matter for himself and come to his own conclusions. In any event, the Quranic verses reflect the form of the story, as it was known in the Hejaz of the Prophet. *And God knows best.*

THE PHILISTINES: The Quran does not name the enemy, but Surabadi unhesitatingly identifies them as the Philistines. This is in agreement with what we know of Saul's career and the history of the period, both from the Bible and from other sources. We know that the "Conquest" of Canaan was even less complete than the Bible would imply. Pockets of Canaanite resistance remained until the time of David, and Canaanite religious ideas persisted despite the triumph of the official YHWH worship, as later prophets would constantly bemoan. In the highlands, the Canaanites ceased to be a major military concern after

---

[2191] LJ, IV, 86. This reference to an earlier encounter was related in connection with Saul's allowing David to battle the giant. Jewish tradition also says that Goliath had three brothers as big as he (LJ, IV, 86).

[2192] Perhaps Goliath was not mentioned in these accounts of Philistine defeats in order to enhance David's feat of killing him by giving Goliath an aura of invincibility. Reporting Goliath's participation in a battle in which the Philistines lost would have diminished the magnitude of David's victory over him, and glorifying David was a major preoccupation of some redactors of the Old Testament.

their defeat at Hazor in the late 13th century BCE, although sometimes they came to the aid of the Hebrews' external enemies. Nonetheless, the Israelites were still barely a majority of the inhabitants of the area of Palestine.

Though God (in the present text of the Bible) promised Abraham and the other patriarchs the entire land of Canaan, the Israelites were unable to dislodge all the peoples they found therein, especially in the lowlands by the Mediterranean Sea: the Semite Phoenicians in the north and the non-Semite Philistines in the south. The Philistines themselves were latecomers, and the Hebrews' conquest or settlement had begun at least a century before the arrival of the Philistines from across the sea.

The origin of the Philistines has long been the subject of debate. Even now, we must confess that we do not know a great deal about them. Most scholars today believe that their arrival on the shores of the eastern Mediterranean was connected with the collapse of Minoan civilization on the island of Crete. The prophet Amos has God say: "...Did I not bring up Israel from the land of Egypt, and the Philistines from Caphtor?..." (Amos 9:7) Caphtor is usually identified with Crete.[2193] In this view, the Philistine migration to Palestine was part of the displacement of peoples caused by movements of other peoples from the north (the Balkans and eastern Europe) into Greece and the Near East.

Presumably, this was one phase of the expansion of the Indo-Europeans peoples from their homeland in southern Russia for causes still unknown. During this period, Aryan invaders continued to penetrate the Iranian plateau (and probably destroyed the ancient Indus Valley civilization in Pakistan as well). Waves of fugitives moved south before these hardy and warlike invaders.[2194] As the "Sea Peoples," the displaced peoples brought about the destruction of the Hittite Empire (c. 1200 BCE), but were defeated by Rameses II about 1188 BCE when they tried to invade Egypt. However, they successfully occupied the coast of Palestine where the northern groups were called the Tjikal and the southern the Philistines.

These Sea Peoples came from the Aegean region and were probably either part of the Dorian migration (1200-1000 BCE) or, more likely, fleeing in front of it. Philistine pottery shows affinities with Mycenaean pottery in Greece, and the Mycenaeans were overwhelmed by the Dorian tribes. Since similar pottery has been found in eastern Cyprus, a reasonable conclusion might be that the Philistines were

---

[2193] Caphtor, DB, p. 127.

[2194] The expansion of the Vikings in Europe had the same effect on older populations from the 9th to the 11th centuries CE.

Mycenaeans who had been forced out by the invading Dorian Greeks and who came to Philistia via Crete and Cyprus.[2195] Further support for this theory is the linking of the Philistines and the Cretans in passages of *Samuel* about David's foreign bodyguard who were composed of men from those peoples.[2196]

The fact that the Philistines were in possession of iron tools and weapons connects them with the Dorians who introduced the use of iron on a large scale to the Aegean area.[2197] Of course, the migrating Mycenaeans could have acquired the necessary techniques from their conquerors before becoming the Sea Peoples attacking the eastern Mediterranean. These migrations were not as one group but rather in waves; the Philistines seem to have been part of the second wave.[2198]

A further clue to the origin of the Philistines is provided by their name. The Greeks called the non-Greek indigenous people of Greece "Pelasgians," and this term seems to have included the Mycenaeans, even though they were related to the Greeks. The similarity of the names "Pelasgian" and "Philistine" has long been noted. The Egyptians called the Philistines "Peleset."[2199] And "the proof brought by J. Berard and V. Georgiev in 1950-1 that the name Philistine is identical with Pelasgian confirms the evidence of pottery, that they came from the Aegean basin."[2200] All of this strengthens the theory that they were displaced Mycenaeans.

The Philistines retained their identity as a people, but they gradually adopted the religion (the resident gods again) and the material culture of the Canaanites, and probably their language as well.[2201] In

---

[2195] Albright-Pal, pp. 112-117. If this theory be correct, then it would seem that the Philistines blazed the trail for future invaders of Palestine, such as the medieval Christian Crusaders and the 20th-century European Zionists, both of whom also used Cyprus as a staging place for the final assault on Palestine.

Some scholars have suggested that the Philistines arrived by land rather than by ship, although considering the seafaring nature of the Mycenaeans and Greeks, ships would have been adequate to transport the migrators, whose number probably did not exceed 25,000 and may have been much, much lower. (See the debate between Dr. Tristan Barako and Assaf Yasur-Landau, *One if by Sea...*, on the question on the merits of the sea route vis-à-vis the land route in BAR, Vol. 29, No, 2, March April, 2003, p. 24ff.)

[2196] 2 Sam. 8:18; 15:18, etc., in which they are called the Cherethites and Pelethites, perhaps to hide the connection with the hated Philistines.

[2197] See 1 Sam. 13:19-22.

[2198] Philistines, EJ, XIII, 399.

[2199] Breasted, p. 401. Note the similarity to Surabadi's word for the Philistines: *Palashtāʾīyān*.

[2200] Albright-Pal, p. 185.

[2201] Philistines, DB, p. 765.

other words, they became Semiticized, but not to the point of adopting circumcision.[2202] They also seem to have retained Mycenaean burial practices.[2203]

Since the Philistines did not enter Canaan until the 12th century BCE, any Biblical references to them in earlier times—such as in *Genesis* (Gen. 21:32,34)—are anachronistic and erroneous. Though the Israelite occupation preceded their arrival, there is no indication that the Philistines had any difficult in establishing themselves in the southern part of the coastal plain. Apparently, they were organized into a confederacy of five principal cities: Gaza, Ashkelon, Ashdod, Ekron, and Gath. Despite their relatively small home territory (perhaps 600 square miles, less than half the size of Rhode Island), the Israelites were never able to totally subdue them militarily. For most of the period of the monarchy, they were independent and became a threat during the periods of Israelite dynastic disorder and weakness.

After Assyrian times, the Philistines seem to have disappeared as a distinct people, probably absorbed by the dominant Semitic population, although not before bequeathing their name to the coastland and eventually the whole of Canaan. The stubborn later history of some of the former Philistine cities suggests that warlike Philistine elements persisted there even in later times. Necho of Egypt, Cambyses the Persian, Alexander of Macedon, and the Maccabees all met with heroic resistance when they conducted siege operations at Gaza. In the 7th century BCE, Ashdod held out against Pharaoh Pstamik I of Egypt for 29 years![2204] Ten thousand Gazite defenders lost their lives in Alexander's two-month siege of 332 BCE. Arrian describes the inhabitants at that time as Arabs.[2205]

It was to this warlike race Goliath belonged.[2206] Surabadi tells us that his forehead was twelve hands wide, and his armor weighed 600 lbs., his helmet weighed 300 lbs., and his club weighed 400 lbs. The Biblical description is only slightly more modest: "And there came out from the camp of the Philistines a champion named Goliath, of Gath, whose height was six cubits and a span [9'9"]. He had a helmet of bronze

---

[2202] Jgs. 14:3,15:18; 1 Sam. 17:26; 18:25.

[2203] Philistines, EJ, XIII, 400.

[2204] "Gaza and Askelon, which offered resistance were taken and punished..." (Breasted, p. 485.)

[2205] Arrian, pp. 144-147. Josephus says that the siege lasted a year and resulted in the city's being razed to the ground. (Josephus, antiquities, XIII.13.3, p. 284.

[2206] Other places in the Bible state that Goliath was descended from the race of giants, the pre-Canaanite Rephaim, or the Anakim. (2 Sam. 21:19-20; 1 Ch. 20:8; Goliath, EJ, VII, 756; Goliath, DB, p. 339.

on his head, and he was armed with a coat of mail, and the weight of the coat was five thousand shekels of bronze [c. 220 lbs.].[2207] And he had greaves of bronze upon his legs, and a javelin of bronze slung between his shoulders. And the shaft of his spear was like a weaver's beam, and his spear's head weight six hundred shekels of iron [c. 26 lbs.]..." (1 Sam. 17:4-7) Such was the man who had terrorized Israel.

DAVID'S RISE TO PROMINENCE: According to Surabadi, after the army had been selected, Saul brought out a coat of mail Samuel had given him, telling him that whomever it fitted would defeat Goliath. The only person it fitted was David. David was the youngest of Jesse's seven sons (more ultimogeniture). Six went to war and when Jesse heard that Saul's army had dispersed after drinking the water, David went to find out what had happened to his brothers. While traveling in the desert, a stone spoke to him, saying that David should pick it up, as it would prove useful. When David reached the army and saw the host of Goliath opposed to the discouraged Israelites, he asked why they were not fighting. They replied that they had not found a champion to challenge Goliath. Saul's spirits revived when the mail fit David. The king promised him his daughter and half his kingdom should David be victorious. However, David said that he could not fight in mail, and he threw it off and made for Goliath, armed only with his slingshot. David and Goliath exchanged names. Then, David shot the stone he had picked up at the giant. In the air, the stone separated into three parts; one part killed Goliath, the second Goliath's horse, and the third shattered into fine pieces and destroyed the Philistine army. Goliath was wearing three coats of mail that day.[2208]

By this time, we should not be surprised to find that in the Bible the *Book of Samuel* gives us not one, but *three* stories of David's rise to prominence, perhaps paralleling the three stories of Saul's ascendancy. They were all originally separate traditions, but have now been strung together in an attempt to make a comprehensive account of David's early days before he became king. The first of these has to do with David's selection by God as His anointed, and the other two are traditions of David's introduction to Saul's court. Each one of these stories focuses upon an important feature of David as he was remembered in later times: the anointed of God and the founder of the House of David (and by extension the Messiahship), David the poet and singer, and David the

---

[2207] Weights and Measures, DB, p. 1036.
[2208] Surabadi, pp. 20-21.

warrior. Surabadi uses the first and third of these pericopes in constructing his version of David's rise.

In the first of these Biblical stories, Saul is not directly involved, but his estrangement from Samuel is the immediate cause. Earlier, Saul had been God's anointed one, but after the break with Samuel, the divine commission seems to have been withdrawn, although how this was done is not clear. If Saul had been guilty of some sacrilege, so were several other later monarchs in the House of David, and the condition of their anointment persisted in their line nonetheless.[2209] In any event, the

---

[2209] There are two phases in the break between Samuel and Saul, or possibly, we have once again two separate accounts. In the first, Saul was to wait for Samuel to come to Gilgal and perform certain sacrifices. After seven days had elapsed without Samuel's appearance, Saul gave the order that the sacrifices be performed without him. "As soon as he had finished offering the burnt offering, behold, Samuel came; and Saul went out to meet him and salute him. Samuel said, 'What hast thou done?' And Saul said, 'When I saw that the people were scattering from me, and that thou hadst not come within the days appointed, and the Philistines had mustered at Michmash, I said, "Now the Philistines will come down upon me at Gilgal, and I have not entreated the favor of the Lord"; so I forced myself, and offered the burnt offering.' And Samuel said to Saul, 'Thou hast done foolishly; thou hast not kept the commandment of the Lord thy God, which He commanded thee; for now the Lord would have established thy kingdom over Israel for ever. But now thy kingdom shall not continue; the Lord has sought out a man after His Own heart; and the Lord has appointed him to be prince over his people, because thou hast not kept what the Lord commanded thee.' And Samuel arose, and went up from Gilgal to Gibeah of Benjamin." (1. Sam: 13:10-15a)

Whatever lies behind this incident (see text above), in its present form, with Samuel's parting prediction of another prince—obviously David—it is a piece of Davidic anti-Saulic propaganda.

The other occasion occurred after the defeat of the Amalekites, and its primitive viciousness is redolent of authenticity. Saul had spared Agag the king and the best of the animals that had fallen into the hands of the Israelites. The word of God came to Samuel and told him that all the Amalekites and their animals had not been destroyed according to the divine command. "And Samuel said, 'What then is this bleating of the sheep in my ears, and the lowing of the oxen which I hear?' Saul said, 'They have brought them from the Amalekites; for the people spared the best of the sheep and of the oxen, to sacrifice to the Lord thy God; and the rest we have utterly destroyed.'" (1 Sam. 15:14-15) Samuel told Saul that he was rejected as king for not having destroyed everything and everyone as he had been commanded. Samuel turned to leave, but Saul entreated him to stay. Uttering another allusion to David (surely an interpolation), Samuel agreed to remain and offer sacrifice with Saul.

"Then Samuel said, 'Bring here to me Agag the king of the Amalekites. And Agag came to him cheerfully. Agag said, 'Surely the bitterness of death is past.' And Samuel said. 'As thy sword has made women childless, so shall thy mother be childless among women.' And Samuel hewed Agag in pieces before the Lord at Gilgal." (1 Sam. 15:32-33) Turning his back upon the gore (Agag may have actually been a human sacrifice to YHWH, although the idea is too shocking for most Biblical scholars to entertain), Samuel left his home at Ramah and never saw Saul again. In this pericope,

episode opens with Samuel grieving for Saul. "The Lord said to Samuel, 'How long wilt thou grieve over Saul, seeing I have rejected him from being king over Israel? Fill thy horn with oil, and go; I will sent thee to Jesse the Bethlehemite, for I have provided for Myself a king among his sons.'... Samuel did what the Lord commanded, and came to Bethlehem... And he consecrated Jesse and his sons, and invited them to sacrifice." (1 Sam. 16:1,4,5)

"And Jesse made seven of his sons pass before Samuel. And Samuel said to Jesse, 'The Lord has not chosen these.' And Samuel said to Jesse, 'Are all thy sons here?' And he said, 'There remains yet the youngest, but behold, he is keeping the sheep.'[2210] And Samuel said to Jesse, 'Send and fetch him; for we will not sit down till he comes here.' And he sent and brought him in. Now he was ruddy, and had beautiful eyes, and was handsome. And the Lord said, 'Arise, anoint him; for this is he.' Then Samuel took the horn of oil, and anointed him in the midst of his brothers; and the Spirit of the Lord[2211] came mightily upon David from that day forward." (1 Sam. 16:10-13)

Surabadi does not refer to this anointment story, which in any case may be a later invention to strengthen the legitimacy of the House of David. There is a minor difference in the number of Jesse's sons; in the Bible they total eight, while Surabadi says they were seven.

The second story of David's rise to prominence is concerned with him as a musician. Surabadi does not refer to this talent of David here, but he does in another place. However, as there is mention of armor in it, it may have an indirect connection with the "Cinderella" motif of the trial by fitting a garment introduced by Surabadi. In the Biblical story, Saul was depressed and melancholy. "And Saul's servants said to him, 'Behold now, an evil spirit from God is tormenting thee. Let our lord now command thy servants who are before thee, to seek out a man who is skillful in playing the lyre; and when the evil spirit from God is upon thee, he will play it and thou wilt be well.' So Saul said to his

---

Saul may be said to have lost God's favor because he was merciful and tried to save his honorable opponent Agag.

[2210] Still another example of the "youngest son" motif found throughout the Bible.

[2211] The "Spirit from (or, of) the Lord" is apparently the same as the Holy Spirit of the Christian Trinity, although not yet a separate entity, but rather a manifestation of the power of God. In these passages, the Spirit represents God sanctifying or "commissioning" the Israelite kings. The idea is repeated in the New Testament at the baptism and "commissioning" of Jesus as the Christ (Messiah), q.v. in *The New Testament: An Islamic Perspective* (Stories, II).

servants, 'Provide for me a man who can play well, and bring him to me.'

"One of the young men answered, 'Behold, I have seen a son of Jesse, the Bethlehemite, who is skillful in playing, a man of valor, a man of war, prudent in speech, and a man of good presence, and the Lord is with him.' Therefore Saul sent messengers to Jesse, and said 'Send me David thy son, who is with the sheep.' And Jesse took an ass laden with bread, and a skin of wine and a kid, and sent them by David his son to Saul. And David came to Saul, and entered his service. And Saul loved him greatly, and he became his armor-bearer. And Saul sent to Jesse, saying, 'Let David remain in my service, for he has found favor in my sight.' And whenever the evil spirit from God was upon Saul, David took the lyre and played it with his hand; so Saul was refreshed, and was well, and the evil spirit departed from him." (1 Sam. 16:15-23)

This too is a proclamation story, introducing David to Israel. However, it is not the principal account that goes into Surabadi's story. That is based primarily on the most spectacular and most familiar of the three introductions, that of David as warrior and giant-killer:

The Philistines had gathered at Soco[2212] in Judah in order to fight the Israelites. The camps of the Philistines and the Israelites were separated by the river Elah. Goliath came out of the camp of the Philistines and challenged the Israelites. "He stood and shouted to the ranks of Israel, 'Why have ye come out to draw up for battle? Am I not a Philistine, and are ye not servants of Saul? Choose a man for yourselves, and let him come down to me. If he is able to fight with me and kill me, then we will be your servants; but if I prevail against him and kill him, then ye shall be our servants and serve us.' ...When Saul and all Israel heard these words of the Philistine, they were dismayed and greatly afraid." (1 Sam. 17:8-9,11)

The scene shifts to Bethlehem. For the third time David is introduced as though he had not been mentioned before: "Now David was the son of an Ephrathite of Bethlehem in Judah, named Jesse who had eight sons... The three eldest sons of Jesse had followed Saul to the battle..." (1 Sam. 17:12,113) In Surabadi, all of the sons save David were already in the army.

The stalemate at Elah continued for forty days (1 Sam. 17:16). Jesse sent David to bring food to his brothers in the Israelite camp. "And David left the things in charge of the keeper of the baggage, and ran to

---

[2212] Soco, a fortified town located about fifteen miles west of Bethlehem on the then frontier with Philistia. (Soco, DB, p.928)

the ranks, and went and greeted his brothers. As he talked with them, behold, the champion, the Philistine of Gath, Goliath by name, came up out of the ranks of the Philistines, and spoke the same words as before. And David heard him." (1 Sam. 17:22-23)

Despite the anger of his brothers at what they considered to be David's presumption, "David said to Saul, 'Let no man's heart fail because of him; thy servant will go and fight with this Philistine.' And Saul said to David, 'Thou art not able to go against this Philistine to fight with him; for thou art but a youth, and he has been a man of war from his youth.'" (1 Sam. 17:32-33) However, David persuaded Saul to let him challenge Goliath.

"Then Saul clothed David with his armor; he put a helmet of bronze on his head and clothed him with a coat of mail. And David girded his sword over his armor, and he tried in vain to go, for he was not used to them. Then David said to Saul, 'I cannot go with these; for I am not used to them.' And David put them off. Then he took his staff in his hand, and chose five smooth stones from the brook, and put them in his shepherd's bag or wallet; his sling was in his hand, and he drew near to the Philistine." (1 Sam. 17:38-40)

Surabadi has followed this part of the story quite closely except in the matter of the stones. The Biblical story continues with an exchange of insults and oaths (Surabadi's more gentlemanly exchange of names). Then the combat begins: "When the Philistine arose and came and drew near to meet David, David ran quickly toward the battle line to meet the Philistine. And David put his hand into his bag and took out a stone, and slung it, and struck the Philistine on his forehead, and he fell on his face to the ground. So David prevailed over the Philistine with a sling and with a stone, and struck the Philistine, and killed him; there was no sword in the hand of David." (1 Sam. 17:48-50) Seizing Goliath's sword, he cut off Goliath's head and brought it as a trophy to Jerusalem.[2213]

There is another tradition that apparently denies David the honor of slaying Goliath. Despite the strength of the tradition of David's role in this contest, in *2 Samuel* one Elhanan also a Bethlehemite, is named as Goliath's killer: "and Elhanan the son of Jaareoregim, the Bethlehemite, slew Goliath the Gittite, the shaft of whose spear was like a weaver's beam" (2 Sam. 21:19). In *Chronicles* this is corrected to: "and Elhanan the son of Jair slew Lahmi the brother of Goliath the Gittite..." (1 Ch. 20:5), but this may be a later attempt to harmonize the apparent discrepancy rather than an authentic tradition. The problem is serious.

[2213] This is an anachronism and it weakens the authority of the account. Jerusalem, at that time, was still in the hands of the non-Israelite Jebusites.

The annotator of the RSV notes the strange circumstance that Saul does not know David and suggests that the whole pericope is a conflation of two sources. Taking into consideration the statement in 2 Sam. 21:19 naming the slayer as one Elhanan, he writes: "It may be supposed that this name (Goliath) became erroneously attached to David's victim, whose name was unknown."[2214]

But is this really an adequate rebuttal? The claims of Elhanan have been largely ignored or dismissed by Biblical commentators (as has so much else when it does not suit the *du jour* exegesis), but this glaring fragment remains in the text, seriously challenging the credibility of the David and Goliath pericope. Is it just more Davidic propaganda? The much later statement in *Chronicles* is of little value in this situation. Still another Biblical mystery?

Several theories have been advanced to resolve this problem, including one that Elhanan was the actual slayer in the original tradition, but later this incident was absorbed by the Davidic legend. Another explanation is that David's real name was Elhanan and that David was his throne name, the name he assumed at the commencement of this reign, in accordance with ancient Near Eastern practice. It has also been suggested that David is not a proper name at all, but rather a title meaning general or commander, and therefore a reference to his military role. This is based upon the interpretation of certain Mari texts where the word *dūvīdum* is supposedly used in this sense.[2215]

Parallels can be cited from other traditions, such as the transformation of the family name Caesar into a title in ancient Rome, or the transformation of the title Messiah "Christ" into a proper name Jesus Christ among Christians where the literal meaning of Christ (Messiah) is ignored or subordinated, and Christ is thought to be part of Jesus' name. British monarchs frequently ascended the throne with a name different from that which they use in private (Edward VIII was known to his intimates as Bertie, a nickname not derived from Edward). With a high degree of probability, either Elhanan is an editorial mistake, or there was a name change by the man who became David upon his assumption of prominence and power. It is as David that the slayer of Goliath is known to history. *So they routed them by God's permission and David slew Goliath...* (Q. 2:251)

Surabadi's principal addition to this story of David and Goliath is the incident of the miraculous stone, which does not seem to be found

---

[2214] RSV, pp. 3562-353.
[2215] Keller, p. 212.

in any major Jewish tradition.[2216] That Goliath was wearing several suits of armor is mentioned in Jewish writings.[2217] There is also an account of the stone that killed Goliath miraculously penetrating Goliath's helmet.[2218] Although the boon offered by Saul to a potential victor over Goliath did not include half his kingdom, as Surabadi states, it did include great riches, his daughter, and the freedom of the king's house (1 Sam. 17:25). Instead of the total destruction of the Philistines recorded by Surabadi, in the Bible, the Philistines are reported to have fled to Ekron and Gath, leaving their camp to be plundered by the Israelites (1 Sam. 17:51-53).

One last remark about the confusion of these texts concerning the traditions of David's rise to prominence: if we read the text consecutively, though David had been introduced to Saul as a musician (1 Sam. 16:14-23) and Saul had given David his armor when he was going out to fight Goliath (1 Sam. 17:31-39), when David went out to fight Goliath, Saul had to ask Abner, his commander: "'Abner, whose son is this youth?' And Abner said, 'As thy soul lives, O king, I cannot tell.' And the king said, 'Inquire whose son the stripling is.' And as David returned from the slaughter of Goliath, Abner took him, and brought him before Saul with the head of the Philistine in his hand. And Saul said to him, 'Whose son art thou, young man?' And David answered, 'I am the son of thy servant Jesse the Bethlehemite.'" (1 Sam. 17:55-58) In this passage, it is clear that Saul did not know David despite two previous introductions. It is plain evidence of the patchwork nature of the text of *Samuel*. As Caird says: "The Hebrew text of *Samuel* shares with that of *Ezekiel* the doubtful honor of being the most corrupt in the Old Testament."[2219]

[2216] At least it is not cited in Ginzberg's encyclopedic work, the *Legends of the Jews* nor have we encountered it anywhere else in our research.

[2217] LJ, IV, 88.

[2218] LJ, VI, 251.

[2219] Caird writing in the Introduction to *Samuel*, IB, II, 855.

PART FIVE: THE UNITED MONARCHY

I. DAVID

The Lord is my light and my salvation; whom shall I fear?
(Ps. 27: 1, a psalm of David)

A. INTRODUCTORY REMARKS

Neither the Quran nor Surabadi in his Commentary gives us a connected historical account of the reign of David (Ar. *Dāwud* or *Dāwūd*), or for that matter of any other Israelite monarch. The Quran contents itself with a few references to God's favor for David, David's merit, and short notes from the David legend to illustrate those points. However, in order to give those scattered references an historical context, it may be useful to first summarize David's career, according to the Biblical record. The primary source for the biographical information about David in the Bible is *Samuel* and the first two chapters of *Kings* (1 Sam. 16:1 through 1 K. 2:12), This is augmented by the much later parallel account of the Chronicler (1 Ch. 10:14-29:30), and references to David in other Biblical books, especially *Psalms*.

In the previous section,[2220] we described the three stories accounting for the rise of David to prominence: the anointment story linking David with the last of the judges and the first of the major prophets (in the later Biblical sense) Samuel, thus legitimizing the ascendancy of the House of David; the invitation to Saul's court because of the fame of his musicianship, a story making use of the strong traditions associating David with many of the psalms and thereby the Temple ritual in which they were used; and the story of David the warrior, his heroism and prowess in battle exemplified by the killing of the Philistine giant Goliath that earned him the favor of Saul the king.

It also earned him the friendship of Saul's son Jonathan: "When he had finished speaking to Saul, the soul of Jonathan was knit to the soul of David, and Jonathan loved him as his own soul. And Saul took him that day, and would not let him return to his father's house. Then Jonathan made a covenant with David, because he loved him as his own soul. And Jonathan stripped himself of the robe that was upon him, and gave it to David, and his armor, and even his sword and his bow and his

---

[2220] The story of Saul, Part 4, III.

girdle." (1 Sam. 18:1-4) Although this may be based upon a true tradition of friendship between David and Jonathan, it also has its propaganda aspects: since Jonathan was Saul's heir apparent, the passage could also be interpreted as a resignation of the succession to David. The adoptive brotherhood Jonathan and David would make the transfer of legitimacy from the House of Saul to the House of David in some manner a continuity rather than a disruption.

We do not mean to imply that all of these three traditions of David's early years are necessarily self-serving fictions; they may have arisen retrospectively, based upon well-established features of David's deeds and character in his later years. David's connections with music and poetry are too strong to be discounted out of hand, as is his prowess as a warrior. Though there is a cloud over the tale of David's defeat of Goliath, he most likely did defeat the Philistine champion in some spectacular fashion, a feat that quite probably contributed to his reputation as a warrior.[2221] There is no reason to suspect the sincerity of David's friendship with Jonathan.

From the appearance of David in the Bible history—and the break between Saul and Samuel may be considered a prelude to the Davidic history and a part of it—Saul is cast in an unfavorable light. This reflects a struggle for legitimacy between the Houses of Saul and David, of which we have little more than the account from the supporters of the House of David. After all, "history is written by the victors." We have no Saulic account to balance this favorable view of David's rise to power, involving war and rebellion, not all of it redounding to David's good reputation, though the redactors of the Old Testament have put as good a face on it as they could. In reading the Biblical story of David, we must keep its generally pro-Davidic bias in mind.

According to the Biblical version of events, the honor accorded by Saul to David quickly turned to jealousy, though not so quickly as the present text would suggest. The verses relating Saul's attempt to murder David (1 Sam. 18:10-11) are out of place,[2222] and should perhaps be put after 1 Sam. 19:10. That David was very popular is attested by an ancient couplet quoted in the text: "Saul has slain his thousands and David his ten thousands." (1 Sam. 19:7)

Nevertheless, Saul, perhaps in an attempt to bind David in loyalty to himself, offered his daughter Merab to David, but something seems to have upset the negotiations, and David was given another daughter of Saul, Michal, instead. This betrothal was contingent upon

---

[2221] See David, DB, p. 201.
[2222] David, DB, p. 203.

David's bringing back the foreskins of 100 slain Philistines[2223] as the bride-price. Saul privately hoped that David would be slain in the process of collecting them (according to the pro-Davidic text), but David discharged his obligation successfully. David thus won Michal and continued to gain fame in more battles with the Philistines. Finally, Saul sought assassins to murder David. Jonathan learned of the plot and arranged a peace between his father and David, which, however, did not last long, as Saul himself (we are told) tried to slay his son-in-law. At that, David fled and took refuge with Samuel. Jonathan visited David in exile and renewed their friendship.

After this, David became a fugitive. He sent his parents to the king of Moab east of the Jordan, where they were given asylum. He himself gathered a band of followers and lived the life of an outlaw captain in Judah, first fighting the Philistines, then allied with them against Saul! Saul continued the pursuit of the rebel intermittently and, in one encounter, David (according to the partisan Biblical account) came upon the sleeping king and spared his life. While at Ziklag, the city that the Philistines had given him, David learned that Jonathan had been killed and Saul had committed suicide during a battle with the Philistines at Mount Gilboa.

David, then aged thirty, was proclaimed king over Judah (the South), while a rival Saulic (Ishbosheth, a son of Saul) set up a kingdom in the North, the precursor of the later kingdom of Israel. A civil war began between the North and the South that ended in defeat of Ishbosheth who was treacherously slain while taking his noonday rest. David punished the murderers for their efforts on his behalf, a crisis with the Philistines apparently helping his cause. For the next seven and a half years, he reigned from his capital at Hebron deep inside Judah.

Realizing the disadvantages of trying to rule all of Israel from a base so far south, David cast his eyes upon the strategically located, but still unconquered, city of Jebus (the fortress of which was called Zion) roughly on the border between the North (Israel) and the South (Judah). He took Jebus and renamed it Jerusalem —not many details of this important event are found in the Bible—and established his court there, c. 1000 BCE.[2224] The Ark of the Covenant was brought up to the city and

---

[2223] Somewhat akin to the scalping that prevailed North America during the Indian wars, when monetary rewards for paid for the evidence of the kills, that is, the scalp.

[2224] Jerusalem, DB, p. 472; Zion, DB, p. 1058. David did not invent the name Jerusalem. It is referred to by the equivalent of that name in the 14th-century BCE Tel Amarnah tablets of Egypt (Thomas, p. 42ff.) It was also called Salem, but site of the City of David is better known as Zion, the name of its Jebusite citadel. Christians long misidentified Zion with the higher hill to the west, across the Valley of the Cheesemakers.

the special link between the House of David and YHWH-worship begun. The shift from Hebron to Jerusalem probably stimulated literary activity at Hebron, in an effort to preserve the importance of the Hebron sanctuary, but Jerusalem quickly became the most important shrine in all Palestine. David made Jerusalem his capital about 994 BCE, and he reigned thirty-three more years. It remained the capital of the United Kingdom of Israel and Judah until Israel seceded about 925 BCE. Jerusalem continued as the capital of the Southern kingdom of Judah until taken by Nebuchadnezzar in 586 BCE.[2225] It has remained the focus of Judaism ever since.

For the rest of his life, David conducted an active foreign policy with several foreign wars. He strengthened his power through administrative innovations,[2226] perhaps modeled upon Egyptian practice,[2227] and implemented a re-organization of his army that included a special band of exceptional ability and loyalty called the Thirty, together with a mercenary bodyguard of Philistines and Cretans.[2228] Nevertheless, David faced considerable opposition and he had to quell no less than three rebellions, the first, and most serious, led by his own son Absalom. This rebellion was preceded, according to the text of *Samuel*, by his affair with Bathsheba. The last passages in *Samuel* connect David with the site upon which Solomon, his son by Bathsheba, was to build the Temple. At the end of his life, David named Solomon his successor. David was buried in the City of David (Jerusalem).

Such is the outline of the Biblical account of David. Most of the *Book of Samuel*, and much later Biblical literature as well, was composed or edited by partisans of the House of David, as the abrupt change in the portrait of Saul upon the entry of David into the story shows. In addition to this dynastic conflict between the two royal houses reflected in *Samuel*, there is another conflict as well, a conflict between the strong monarch and the conservative reaction to the growing centralization and the burdens imposed by a monarchy. David's opponents envisioned the *ideal* of Israel, not the reality of the worldly Israel of the House of David (and especially Solomon). They longed for a return to the loosely organized Israel of the judges and decentralized YHWH-worship.

[2225] See story of Nebuchadnezzar in Part Six, III.

[2226] He conducted a census, deemed an "infringement upon the prerogatives of God" and therefore a sin. The results recorded in 2 Sam. 20:9 (800,000 in Israel and 500,000 in Judah) are proportionate, but impossibly high. (RSV, note, p. 411.)

[2227] David, DB, p. 202.

[2228] Keller, p. 212.

Despite the point of view of most of the writers and editors of the Biblical text, there are preserved here and there passages that hint at quite a different state of affairs from the picture given us by *Samuel*. These political and religious grievances replaced the tensions between the rival houses of Saul and David and increased in strength during the reign of Solomon. While the relatively homogeneous South was content with a monarch of a native (Southern) dynasty that gave it special privileges and patronage, the more heterogeneous North chafed under it. It would eventually break off to pursue a separate existence of its own, characterized by repeated palace revolutions, assassinations, and intrigue until the Assyrians finally called a halt to the whole sordid history by annihilating the Northern kingdom of Israel some two centuries after it had been founded.

The Quranic picture of David concentrates upon his spiritual qualities. Although David is recognized as a warrior (Q. 2:251), his role as a prophet and recipient of revelation (the Psalms) is stressed more (Q. 4:163; 6:85) than it is in the Bible. Other traditions about him are noted, such as David's connection with metallurgy (Q. 21:80; 34:10). These references do not make a connected history, but refer to aspects of David as he was known to 7th-century Arabs. Later commentators fleshed out the account considerably, borrowing heavily from the Bible and Jewish traditions.

B. DAVID THE MUSICIAN AND THE PSALMS

And We gave unto David the Psalms. (Q. 4:163)

According to Surabadi, the excellence of David over others was in his voice, which caused the mountains and their inhabitants, the sea and its inhabitants, and the birds of the air to die of pleasure.[2229] He also refers to the well-known association of David with the Psalms by depicting him sitting his chamber with them by his side.[2230] And in the Quran we read: *And with David We subdued the mountains to give praise, and the birds; We were the doers.* (Q. 21:79) *and with (David) We subjected the mountains to give glory at evening and sunrise, and the birds, duly mustered, all turning unto Him!* (Q. 38:18-19) These beautiful images have too often been taken literally by the commentators who offer us fantastic spectacles of mountains and birds literally singing

---

[2229] Surabadi, pp. 343-344.
[2230] Surabadi, p. 364.

or swooning at David's voice, leading some critics to charge that that was the way the verses were understood by the Prophet himself. The verses are, as we shall see, references to the Psalms.

In his triple role as warrior, the anointed of God, and musician, David is one of the most important figures of the Old Testament. The kingdom and conquests of the warrior have, of course, long since perished. As the anointed of God and founder of the House of David, David became—probably unwittingly—the progenitor of the messianic expectations of later ages which form the background of the rise of Christianity and still animate large sections of world Jewry and evangelical Christianity. As a musician and singer, David is considered responsible for a large part of one of the most beautiful works of ancient literature preserved for us: the Psalms. David's mellifluous voice is still, the House of David is dust, but the Psalms survive. Muslims hold that the authentic Davidic Psalms are a part of the corpus of divine revelation.

The story of David's reputation as musician and singer leading to his entrance into Saul's court where he is brought to use his talents to soothe the troubled monarch during fits of melancholy and depression has already been discussed above:[2231] "And whenever the evil spirit from God was upon Saul, David took the lyre and played it with his hand; so Saul was refreshed, and was well, and the evil spirit departed from him." (1 Sam. 16:23) Indeed, he is credited with the invention of musical instruments by the 8th-Century BCE prophet Amos: "... and like David invent for themselves instruments of music." (Amos 6:5)

It may be noted that in Amos' account, David is introduced as musician rather than as a poet, although the two talents are frequently linked in musical history. Furthermore, there is nothing incongruous about David's being both a skilled warrior and a skilled musician. Those familiar with Arab history will be reminded of 'Antarah; Europeans will recall the fighting troubadours, such as François Villon.[2232] In *Samuel*, he is credited with elegies on Saul, Jonathan, and Abner, a magnificent song of deliverance, and an oracle in poetic form. *Samuel* was probably put into approximately its present form by 700 BCE,[2233] more than two and one-half centuries after the events described, although much of it may date from the reign of Solomon. In *Chronicles*, written much later, we find another hymn attributed to David, commemorating the bringing of the Ark to Jerusalem. However, in its present form, it cannot be possibly

---

[2231] See preceding Section: Part Four, II.

[2232] Frederick the Great of Prussia composed symphonies. Henry VIII of England is also credited with musical compositions.

[2233] Samuel, Books of, DB, p. 884.

a composition of David. Instead, it is composed of elements found in the Psalter, and even post-Exilic aspirations for the Return:

"Deliver us, O God of Salvation,
        and gather and save us from among the nations,
    that we may give thanks to Thy holy name
        and glory in Thy praise." (1 Ch. 16:35)

It is as the prophet-king to whom the Psalms are given that David is important in Quranic and Islamic imagery. This is not the place to enter into the controversy concerning the meaning of the word translated as "Psalms" (*Zabūr*), however, the Quran explicitly states that David received revelation and refers to that revelation as "Zabur." David is not really accorded prophetic status in the Bible, but the Talmud includes him among the prophets,[2234] as does Islam. In one place, the Quran quotes (or paraphrases) a verse from the Psalms: *We have written in the Psalms, after remembrance, "The earth, My righteous servants shall inherit it."* (Q. 21:105) This may be compared with "The righteous shall possess the land, and dwell upon it for ever." (Ps. 37:29). It is from a psalm ascribed to David.

The present *Psalms* (also called the Psalter), the longest book of the Bible, achieved its final shape in the first half of the 2nd century BCE.[2235] It is not claimed in the Bible that the entire Psalter, as we have it, is the work of David. Of the present collection of 150 psalms, some are obviously quite late, but others are very ancient. There is considerable skepticism among modern scholars about David's role as a poet. Trawick, for example, writes: "The Psalms were the products of numerous poets. By tradition seventy-three are ascribed to David... However, most modern scholars doubt the accuracy of the ancient attributions or authorship. It seems exceedingly unlikely that Moses or Solomon wrote the Psalms ascribed to them. As for David, it is possible that he wrote some; certainly, he had the reputation of being a musician... But few critics today believe that he wrote very many of the seventy-three Psalms attributed to him..." No single psalm can be identified with absolute certainty as the work of David.[2236] The centuries-long process of editing and redaction has obscured Biblical certainty.

Toombs opines: "...it is probable that the original of almost every (psalm) was composed in preexilic times for use in public worship

---

[2234] LJ, VI, 249-250.
[2235] Trawick-OT, p. 242.
[2236] Trawick-OT, pp. 241-242.

during the period of the monarchy. Once introduced into worship, however, a psalm would naturally be adapted and revised to make it appropriate to changing circumstances."[2237] The period of the monarchy would of course include the period of David. However, the custodians of these works did not regard them highly enough to safeguard their integrity, another corroboration of the Quranic assertion that the text of Scriptures has been compromised.

The author of the Introduction to the *Psalms* in the *Jerusalem Bible* writes: "Not all the psalms of the Davidic collection are by him, no doubt, but the collection must have had a few of these for nucleus. It is difficult, however, to be more definite than this."[2238] This seems to be about as far as modern scholarship will go in admitting Davidic authorship. Of course, it represents an improvement over the 19th-century view that the entire Psalter was a creation of the Second Temple, and the possible Davidic authorship of any part of them was denied out of hand.[2239]

Archeological discoveries of the last centuries have revealed a very ancient tradition of psalm-composition for liturgical use in Near Eastern cultures such as those of Babylonia, Egypt, Canaan, and Assyria. The Hebrews did not invent psalms; rather, they were using a common form.[2240] Without manuscript evidence, there is no way we can prove that David composed anything, but in the face of such a strong tradition, there is every reason to give him the benefit of the doubt for the authorship of the original forms of a number of psalms in the present Psalter, whatever their current state.

Rabbinic tradition regarded the entire Psalter the work of David, despite the superscriptions on many of them contradicting that position.[2241] A scroll found at Qumran credits David with 3600 psalms and 450 songs.[2242] This would appear to represent the opposite pole of David's literary output, equally extreme. The Muslim would probably take the position that David did receive a book of hymns (the Zabur), but as in the case of the books of Moses and Jesus, they have been either inadvertently or deliberately corrupted, or, as a result of poor stewardship, have been lost either wholly or in part. In the case of the

---

[2237] Lawrence E. Toombs, writing in the Introduction to the commentary on the *Psalms* in Laymon, p. 253.

[2238] JB, p. 784.

[2239] Psalms, EJ, XIII, 1311.

[2240] Laymon, 253.

[2241] In addition to the 73 ascribed to David, 12 are attributed to Asaph, 11 to the "sons of Korah," 2 to Solomon, etc. Forty-nine have no superscriptions. (Trawick-OT, p. 241.)

[2242] Psalms, EJ, XIII, 1313.

Psalms, the first part of this judgment might be unnecessarily harsh, and though poor stewardship could be charged, it must be remembered that the Jews did not regard the *Psalms* as prophetic literature, referring to them instead as Writings, a lower category.[2243]

How did the present collection of *Psalms* come into being? The history of the book is not a simple one, and it went through several stages before reaching its present form. The oldest portion is to be found in the First Book, Pss. 3-32, 34-41, all of which are ascribed to David, including that which contains the parallel of the Quranic verse quoted above.[2244] Three more books, ascribed to David, to Asaph (Asaph being the name of a guild of singers: Ezra 2:41), and to the "sons of Korah" (also probably a guild of singers; cf. 2 Ch. 20:19) were revised by an editor who substituted the Hebrew word *elohim* for YHWH and produced an edition called the "Elohist Psalter," (Pss. 42-83).[2245] This was further enlarged at another time by the addition of Pss. 84-89.[2246] To this was added still another book, the Book of Ascents (Pss. 120-134). Another Davidic collection provided Pss. 101,103,108-110,138-145.[2247] Other individual psalms, added at other places to older collections, brought the collection up to its present total of 150 psalms.

The psalms vary considerably in character and length. There are hymns praising God, communal and individual laments, communal and individual songs of thanksgiving, royal psalms, oracular psalms, and wisdom psalms.[2248] Despite the uncertainties surrounding their authorship, date, and the circumstances of their composition, they comprise one of the great treasures of the world's poetic literature.

Returning to the question of David's role as an author or—as a Muslim might put it—the recipient of poetic revelation, despite the skepticism of scholars, the tradition of David as a poet and musician is a very ancient one. *Amos*, perhaps the most ancient of the prophetic books (c. 750 BCE), refers to this tradition: "Woe to those... who sing idle songs to the sound of the harp, and like David invent for themselves instruments of music." (Amos 6:4,5) Even older traditions in *Samuel* expressly mention him as the composer of laments (2 Sam. 1:17; 3:33). And Josephus reflects for us the traditions about David in his day (1st

---

[2243] Psalms, EJ XIII, 1305.
[2244] Psalms, DB, pp. 815-816; Psalms, EJ, XIII, 1309.
[2245] Psalms, DB, pp. 815-816; Psalms, EJ, XIII, 1309.
[2246] Psalms, DB, p. 816.
[2247] Psalms, EJ, XIII, 1310.
[2248] Psalms, DB, p. 818.

century CE): "And now David being freed from wars and dangers, and enjoying for the future a profound peace, composed songs and hymns to God, of several sorts of meter; some of those which he made were trimeters, and some were pentameters. He also made instruments of music, and taught the Levites to sing hymns to God, both on that called the Sabbath-day, and on other festivals."[2249] Jewish tradition also adds that the strings of David's harp were made of the gut of the ram sacrificed by Abraham.[2250]

Can we identify more closely the psalms of David in the present *Book of Psalms*? With scholarly approval, we can only limit the possibilities to those which bear the superscription "of David," recognizing that that term itself is ambiguous and can either mean "by David" or "for David."[2251] Presumably, David's psalms must be found among these and, if the identification of the Davidic Psalter with the *Zabur* of the Quran is correct, therefore possible fragments of God's revelation to David. The Davidic Psalms are: 3-32 (including 10 which is a part of 9), 34-41, 51-65, 68-70, 86, 101, 103, 108-110, 122, 124, 131, 138-145.

A theme that is frequently found in the Quran is that nature gives continuing evidence of the power and glory of God. Several verses from the Quran utilizing this type of imagery in a special reference to David's voice and praises were quoted at the beginning of this section. We find this theme in the Davidic Psalms of as well:

> "The heavens are telling the glory of God;
> and the firmament proclaims His handiwork.
> Day to day pours forth speech,
> and night to night declares knowledge.
> There is no speech, nor are there words;
> their voice is not heard;
> yet their voice goes through all the earth,
> and their words to the end of the world." (Ps. 19:1-4)

> "When I look at Thy heavens, the work of Thy fingers,
> the moon and the stars which Thou hast established;
> what is man that Thou are mindful of him,
> and the son of man that Thou dost care for him?" (Ps. 8:3-4)

[2249] Josephus, *Antiquities*, VII.12.3, p. 165.
[2250] LJ, IV, 101.
[2251] Psalms, EJ, XIII, 1313; Psalms, DB, p. 819.

"The pastures of the wilderness drip,
the hills gird themselves with joy,
the meadows clothe themselves with flocks,
the valleys deck themselves with grain,
they shout and sing together for joy." (Ps. 65:12-13)

And in one of the unassigned psalms we have a very close parallel to Quranic themes:

"Praise the Lord from the earth,
ye sea monsters and all deeps,
fire and hail, snow and frost,
stormy wind fulfilling His command!
Mountains and all hills,
fruit trees and all cedars!
Beasts and all cattle,
creeping things and flying birds!" (Ps. 148:7-10)

Jewish tradition too speaks of the praises of God sung by the sun, the moon, the stars, the clouds, the winds, the lightning, and the dew. On earth every plant has a song of praise, as do the birds, the beasts, the fishes, and even the "contemptible" reptiles.[2252], About David's relationship with the birds, it is said that when David died, eagles shaded the corpse with their outspread wings.[2253]

C. DAVID, IRON, AND THE INVENTION OF MAIL

And We made iron supple unto him... (Q. 34:10)

Surabadi tells us that David could make iron soft and shape armor out of it for his people in their fight against the powerful Philistines.[2254] This is based upon the traditions referred to in the Quranic verse: *And We taught (David) the art of garments (of mail) for you to protect you from your terror; are ye then thankful?* (Q. 21:80) *And We had given David grace from Us... And We made the iron supple unto him, (saying): "Make thou loose-fitting (garments of mail), and measure the links thereof, and do ye right; verily, I am the Perceiver of what ye do."* (Q. 34:10-11) There are interpretations to the effect that David

---

[2252] LJ, I, 44-46; V, 60-62.
[2253] LJ, IV, 114.
[2254] Surabadi, p. 344.

invented chain mail. That is not necessarily what the Quran says: God taught David (that is, enabled him to learn the secret of) working iron and fashioning protective body armor from it. The importance of this distinction will become clear shortly.

On the basis of these verses, Bal'ami, for example, depicts David as a blacksmith.[2255] The traditions linking David with iron and armor were certainly current in Arabia before the advent of Islam, as the brief notices in the Quran imply. If we could not infer that from the Quran, we have the evidence of the pre-Islamic poets, such as Tarafah (Ar. *Tarafah*) (c. 538-564 CE) and Labid (Ar. *Labīd*) (c. 560-661 CE).

> And (the women) stripped from David the finest of his work
> It was strong and pliable
> He made it of iron to protect himself from piercing
> So that he would obtain a long life... (Labid)

Though current in Arabia, these traditions seem to have no close parallels in either the Bible or Talmudic and rabbinical literature.

In the Bible, smithery is associated with Cain and the Kenites. In the Talmud there is a reference to David's making himself as hard as steel: "And these are the names of the mighty David: Josheb-basshebeth a Tahchemonite, (etc.) (2 Sam. 23:8). Tahchemon Rab explained: The Holy One, blessed be He, said to (David), 'Since you humbled yourself you shall be like Me (that is), that I made a decree and you (may) annul it." *Chief of the Captains* (that is) you be chief next to the three Fathers. *He is Adino the Eznite* (that is) when he was sitting engaged in the (study of the) Torah he rendered himself pliant as a worm, but when he went marching out to (wage) war he hardened himself like a lance."[2256]

Perhaps this tradition is a link in an otherwise lost cycle of traditions connected with this skill of David, attested by the existence of the story in pre-Islamic Arabia. The tradition may also have a connection with Iranian legends about Jamshid, who is credited with the invention of armor and chain mail in Firdawsi's *Shahnamah*. Of course, the form in which Firdawsi puts his tradition may itself have been influenced the Quran. In any event, the tradition had been absorbed by the Arabian Davidic cycle—if the Iranian tradition is in any way related—before the period of the Prophet, and was associated by the pre-Islamic Arabs with David, not Jamshid, whose name they probably did not know. However,

---

[2255] Bal'ami, I, p. 556.
[2256] Lazarus, pp. 104-105.

it may be that the Arab traditions have quite a different origin, relating to the history of the introduction of iron into Palestine.

In very ancient times, the only iron known was of meteoric origin. Beads made from such material have been found in Egyptians tombs belonging to the 4th millennium BCE.[2257] Although vastly more abundant than copper or tin on earth, iron remained a precious metal throughout much of antiquity because of the great difficulty the ancients found in working it. The oldest known iron object is a wrought-iron dagger found in Egypt dated c. 1350 BCE. The main obstacle to the spread of the use of iron was the problem of achieving the very high temperatures needed to smelt it. A process for doing this was finally discovered by the Hittites in Asia Minor (modern central Turkey) before 1300 BCE, and it was probably a Hittite technological monopoly until the destruction of the Hittite Empire about 1200 BCE. Shortly afterwards, the Philistines arrived on the shores of Palestine, and they brought the first iron objects that are found in Palestine.

Under Philistine domination, perhaps taking a leaf from the Hittites, ironworking appears to have been maintained by the Philistines as a monopoly. During the period that Saul was preparing for the War of Liberation (from the Philistines), in *Samuel* we read: "Now there was no smith to be found throughout all the land of Israel; for the Philistines said, 'Lest the Hebrews make themselves swords or spears'; but every one of the Israelites went down to the Philistines to sharpen his ploughshare, his mattock, his axe, or his sickle; and a third of a shekel for sharpening the axes and setting the goads. So on the day of battle there was neither sword not spear found in the hand of any of the people with Saul and Jonathan; but Saul and Jonathan his son had them." (1 Sam. 12:19-22) From this we may infer that ironworking was unknown among the Israelites, at least until the time of Saul. The possession of iron weapons by Saul and Jonathan was so unusual as to excite admiration and comment.[2258]

Although several Israelite victories under Saul over the Philistines are recorded, they were not subdued until the time of David.[2259] The Philistines presumably remained quasi-independent

---

[2257] Keller, pp. 166-167.

[2258] Although not mentioned, the passage refers to iron; copper and bronze were of course already long known and in wide use throughout the Near East.

[2259] "After this David defeated the Philistines and subdued them, and David took Methegammah out of the hands of the Philistines." (2 Sam. 8:1) It is not known whether Methegammah is a place name, or a phrase meaning "the bridle of the mother city," being a metaphor for the suzerainty exercised by the Philistines.

vassals until the end of the reign of Solomon and the division of the kingdom under his son.

The first reference we have of Israelite use of iron occurs during the reign of David. After the conquest of Rabbah of the Ammonites,[2260] David looted the city and condemned the people to forced labor. "And he brought forth the people who were in (the city), and set them to labor with saws and iron picks and iron axes, and made them toil at the brick kilns; then David and all the people returned to Jerusalem." (2 Sam. 12:31)[2261]

These passages are evidence that iron had come into greater use during the reign of David. Although they are not specific proof that the Israelites were engaged in ironworking, they verify its spreading use during that period, in contrast with the passage describing the situation at the time of Saul that showed that the working of iron was unknown among the Israelites. In this respect, a passage in *Chronicles* relating to preparations for the building of the Temple at Jerusalem may be quoted. Even though it is probably unhistorical in itself (see below), its reference to metal working may be based upon a sound tradition: "David also provided great stores of iron for nails for the doors of the gates and for clamps, as well as bronze in quantities beyond weighing..." (1 Ch. 22:3)

As a warrior and a successful general who paid a great deal attention to the development of his army and its equipment, it is safe to assume that one of the first reforms David would have made would be to break the monopoly of ironworking that had heretofore been held by the Philistines. The superiority of iron weapons over bronze weapons would have been as evident as the superiority of a jet fighter to a propeller aircraft, or a modern repeating rifle to a muzzle-loading musket, is to us.

Archeological evidence also supports the slow introduction of iron among the Israelites, "being hindered by the Philistine iron monopoly."[2262] As vassals of David, the Philistines would have been forced to give up their secrets and probably train Israelites in their craft. By the time of the capture of Rabbah mentioned above, the monopoly seems to have become a thing of the past.

[2260] Modern Amman, the capital of Jordan.

[2261] There is a difficulty with the parallel Passage in *Chronicles* where the Hebrew (as translated in the KJV) appears to indicate that David had the Ammonites tortured with iron implements, reading: "And (David) brought forth the people that were in (the city), and cut them with saws, and with harrows of iron, and with axes." (1 Ch. 20:3) More modern translations, including the RSV and JB, have amended the text in conformity with *Samuel*.

[2262] Albright-Pal, p. 110.

It is quite possible that memory of the introduction of iron during the time of David lies behind the Arab tradition of David's smithery and the invention (or at least manufacture) of chain mail. For reasons now unknown, this fact made an impression among the Arabs and, suitably embroidered, it became the tradition attested by the pre-Islamic poets. It is even more extraordinary that this tradition, so famous among the Arabs, seems to have been unknown among the Jews (at least those outside of Arabia).

D. THE CHAIN OF DAVID

David, peace be upon him, used to judge among the people by means of a chain. (Surabadi, p. 363)

Surabadi relates a tradition that David judged the people by means of a chain which was let down from the sky. The hand of whoever's cause was just would be able to reach it; and whoever was guilty would be unable to do so. However, one day a man entrusted a jewel to another and went to retrieve it, but the latter denied knowledge of the jewel. Since he knew that their dispute would be judged by the chain, the man who had violated the other's trust fixed the jewel in a staff and went to David. The complainant touched the chain, then the other handed him the staff to hold while he was tested. Since he was the owner of the staff, he was able to touch the chain and went free. David was disturbed by this and from that day, the judgment by the chain was ended.[2263]

This story was supplied as a commentary on the Quranic verse: *We made (David's kingdom strong and gave him wisdom and decisive speech.* (Q. 38:20) As can be readily seen, Surabadi's story has no real connection with the general statement in the Quran, but it is supposed to illuminate for us the matter of David's wisdom and judgment. There is nothing in the Bible that parallels Surabadi's story of justice being meted out by a chain suspended form heaven. It is reminiscent of the story of the chain at King Anushirvan's palace of Mada'in (Ctesiphon). There is a story found in the *Yerushalmi Talmud* of David's committing judicial murder. A pious man was convicted of sodomy and executed on the testimony of two false witnesses;[2264] but the only similarity is that justice was not done in either case.

[2263] Surabadi, pp. 363-364.
[2264] LJ, VI, 261.

Although credited with wisdom and justice, David was not especially associated with those traits in the Bible and Jewish tradition, being overshadowed in those respects by his son Solomon. In fact, the Biblical account seems to suggest some popular dissatisfaction with David's administration of justice. At one point in his tumultuous career, his son Absalom seized the throne and forced his father to take refuge east of the Jordan. As part of his propaganda while preparing public sentiment in his favor, Absalom is reported as saying: "'Oh, that I were judge in the land! Then every man with a suit or cause might come to me, and I would give him justice.'" (2 Sam. 15:4)

Perhaps Surabadi's somewhat negative tradition about David's justice is a reflection of this situation. But all of this should set against the final verdict upon David and his stewardship in *Samuel* which is in accordance with above-cited verse from the Quran: "So David reigned over all Israel; and David administered justice and equity to all his people." (2 Sam. 8:15)

E. DAVID AND BATHSHEBA

This my brother had ninety-nine ewes whilst I had one (Q. 28:23)

Probably the most famous (or perhaps we should say notorious) episode in the life of David, after the combat with Goliath, is that of Bathsheba (Ar. *Batshāya^c* or *Batshaba^c*), the future mother of Solomon. This story is referred to obliquely in the Quran, by relating the parable of the ewes (Q. 38:21-24). In the Quran, this story is a warning to David and effectively prevents him from committing a sin. In the Bible, this warning comes, as we shall see, after the adultery had been committed. The Quran mentions David's repentance: *Be patient with what they say and remember Our servant David, the mighty; he was indeed a penitent.* (Q. 38:17) The Quran does not cite the reason for David's penitence. Since this verse is followed shortly by the parable of the ewes, it is reasonable to suppose that it may be connected with the Bathsheba affair.

Surabadi, in a more chaste variation of the Biblical story, makes David's crime simply looking upon Bathsheba, rather than an adulterous act: One day when David was sitting in his retreat with the Psalms a strange multihued bird flew by and David went to catch it for his son. The bird flew up to an aperture and David went after it. When he looked out of the opening, he saw Bathsheba, the wife of his general Uriah.[2265] In

---

[2265] Surabadi, p. 363.

another place, Surabadi depicts David asking what his punishment will on the Day of Judgment for gazing at Uriah's wife.[2266]

The story of David and Bathsheba is found in *Samuel* (2 Sam. 11:1-12:25), but it is absent in the parallel account in *Chronicles*. In *Samuel*, David appears in the unsavory light of adultery, trying to deceive the husband into thinking that the child David has fathered is the husband's, and finally committing murder by proxy. It is one of the most shocking crimes attributed to a major YHWH-fearing Hebrew in the Bible; no wonder the Chronicler shrank from repeating it.

Before turning to the actual Biblical account, it is perhaps appropriate to remind ourselves again that the text of *Samuel* is one of the most corrupt and poorly edited books of the entire Old Testament. Moreover, despite the work of a series of redactors and editors throughout several centuries, *Samuel* vacillates between pro- and anti-monarchical points of view. Consequently, we can perhaps ascribe the present version of this pericope to anti-monarchical factions, and since the story reflects upon the character of Solomon's mother, it is more likely aimed at besmirching Solomon than David. In other words, the story implies that Solomon is of ignoble lineage on his mother's side.[2267] The colorful story (it may be an invention in its present form) was simply too well known and salacious (a guarantee of wide circulation) for anyone to attempt to replace it with another, more benign invention.

And so it stands. As the Chronicler, with his special view of the House of David, had nothing to refute the story with, he simply ignored it and did not incorporate it into his work. Later Jewish tradition also exonerated David of the charge of adultery, and asserted that David's physical relationship with Bathsheba began only after their marriage. It also exonerated him of the charge of murder, a position that the Quran tacitly endorses.

Despite the silence of the Chronicler, or perhaps because of it, it is certain that David committed some sort of indiscretion involving Bathsheba. The most favorable reconstruction of the incident would be that David saw Bathsheba (bathing) accidentally and became enamored of her, as in Surabadi. (His marriage with Saul's daughter Michal was a difficult one.[2268]) Uriah, Bathsheba's husband, a brave soldier, fell in

---

[2266] Surabadi, p. 366.

[2267] The "double standard" for sexual behavior is, after all, based upon the assumption that few men, even honorable men, can resist the blandishments of a dishonorable woman and are therefore less culpable.

[2268] After David had danced before the Ark on its procession into Jerusalem, she (Michal) encountered him: "And David returned to bless his household. But Michal the daughter of Saul came out to meet David, and said, 'How the king honored himself today,

battle, and David naturally felt guilty for perhaps having a secret wish fulfilled. Nonetheless, his passion for Bathsheba overcame his good sense and he probably married her with indecent haste, occasioning the reproof of the prophet Nathan for lusting after Bathsheba whilst she was the wife of another man, and then hurriedly marrying her as soon as her husband was out of the way. (Opponents of David—and we know that there were such—could have seized upon the fortuitous death of Uriah to spread the scandalous story that David had contrived his death.)

This version would be sufficient to warrant the Quranic reference to David's indiscretion and God's forgiveness, and the parable of Nathan in Q. 38. The sin would have been coveting Bathsheba while she was still the wife of another. That would be the most favorable interpretation of the story consistent with the Quranic references. The least favorable would be the sordid account that we now find in *Samuel*.

In the Bible, the circumstances of David's first view of Bathsheba are somewhat different from those given to us by Surabadi. However, Talmudic tradition has a story similar to Surabadi's, which may be his ultimate source: "Once Satan appeared to (David) in the shape of a bird. David threw a dart at him. Instead of striking Satan, it glanced off and broke a wicker screen that hid Bathsheba combing her hair. The sight of her aroused passion in the king."[2269]

In *Samuel*, the story begins in a more ordinary way: "It happened, late one afternoon, when David arose from his couch and was walking upon the roof of the king's house, that he saw from the roof a woman bathing; and the woman was very beautiful. And David sent and inquired about the woman. And one said, 'Is not this Bathsheba, the daughter of Eliam,[2270] the wife of Uriah the Hittite?' So David sent messengers and took her; and she came to him, and he lay with her... Then she returned to her house. And the woman conceived; and she sent

---

uncovering himself today before the eyes of his servants' maids, as one of the vulgar fellows shamelessly uncovers himself' And David said to Michal, 'It was before the Lord, who chose me above thy father, and above all his house, to appoint me as prince over Israel, the people of the Lord—and I will make merry before the Lord. I will make myself yet more contemptible than this, and I will be abased in thy eyes; but by the maids of whom you have spoken, by them I shall be held in honor.' And Michal the daughter of Saul had no child to the day of her death." (2 Sam. 6:20-23) Their marriage started out more cordially with Michal behaving like a loyal wife and assisting David to escape her father's wrath, but it deteriorated in later years, as this last recorded exchange between them illustrates.

[2269] LJ, IV, 104.

[2270] Bathsheba was quite possibly the granddaughter of David's counsellor Ahithopel of Gilo, one of David's elite Thirty (2 Sam. 23:34). He was a Judahite, Gilo being located in the southern hills of Judah. (Gilo, DB, p. 331.)

to David, 'I am with child.'" (2 Sam. 11:2-5) Her husband, called a Hittite in *Samuel*, may have been an 'Adite (see Part Two, I).

Though this was bad enough, the worst was yet to come: David sent for Uriah and told him to go home, thinking he would lie with his wife and thus believe that the child was his own. However, since there was a war going on, Uriah had taken a vow not to lie with his wife. Frustrated, David tried to get him drunk so that he would break his vow, go home, and lie with his wife, but to no avail. One gets the impression that Bathsheba was no better than she should have been. She offers no conspicuous resistance to David's advances and is patently conniving with him (or at least privy to David's intentions) in the matter of Uriah's death that follows.

Finally, "in the morning David wrote a letter to Joab [David's army commander], and sent it by the hand of Uriah. In the letter he wrote, 'Set Uriah in the forefront of the hardest fighting, and then draw back from him, that he may be struck down, and die...' And the men of the city came out and fought with Joab; and some of the servants of David among the people fell. And Uriah the Hittite was slain also." (2 Sam. 11:14-15,17)

"When the wife of Uriah heard that Uriah her husband was dead, she made lamentation for her husband. And when the mourning was over, David sent and brought her to his house, and she became his wife, and bore him a son. But the thing that David had done displeased the Lord." (2 Sam. 11:26-27) And thus David took to wife a woman of dubious character, who was to become the mother of Solomon.

It is at this point, if we follow the text of *Samuel*, that the parable of the ewes belongs. In the Quran, we read: *And has the story of the litigants come unto thee? How they climbed the wall into the royal chamber! How they burst in upon David, and he was afraid of them! They said: Be not afraid! (We are) two litigants, one of whom has wronged the other, therefore judge aright between us; be not unjust; and show us the fair way. Lo, this my brother has ninety-nine ewes while I had one ewe; and he said: Entrust it to me, and he conquered me in speech. (David) said: "He has wronged thee in demanding thine ewe in addition to his ewes, and lo, many partners oppress one another, save such as believe and do good works, and they are few. And David guessed that We had tried him, and he sought forgiveness of this Lord, and he bowed himself and fell down prostrate and repented. So We forgave him that; and lo, he had access to Us and an excellent result.* (Q. 28:21-25)

In Surabadi's expansion of the Quranic references, he tells us that when David was sitting alone in his retreat, two enemies descended from the aperture. David was surprised because 33,000 warriors were guarding the palace.[2271] The two told him that they were disputants and wanted David to judge between them, but in reality, they were angels.[2272] One said that his brother had 99 ewes and he had one, and his brother had talked him out of that one. David understood that he had been tested, and the two men disappeared. David begged forgiveness from God, and God forgave him, but did not inform him, for God loves the repentance of man.[2273]

The Biblical version is somewhat different: "And the Lord sent Nathan to David. He came to him, and said to him, 'There were two men in a certain city, the one rich and the other poor. The rich man had very many flocks and herds; but the poor man had nothing but one little lamb, which he had bought... and it was like a daughter to him. Now there came a traveler to the rich man, and he was unwilling to take one of his own flock or herd to prepare for the wayfarer who had come to him.' Then David's anger was greatly kindled against the man; and he said to Nathan, 'As the Lord lives, the man who has done this deserves to die; and he shall restore the lamb fourfold, because he did this thing, and because he had no pity.'" (2 Sam. 12:1-6)

Then, Nathan uttered his damning accusation: "Nathan said to David, 'Thou art the man! Thus says the Lord, the God of Israel, 'I anointed thee king over Israel, and I delivered thee out of the hand of Saul; and I gave thee thy master's house, and thy master's wives in thy bosom, and gave thee the house of Israel and Judah: and if this were too little, I would add to thee as much more. Why hast thou despised the word of the Lord, to do what is evil in His sight? Thou hast smitten Uriah the Hittite with the sword, and hast taken his wife to be thy wife, and hast slain him with the sword of the Ammonites. Now therefore the sword shall never depart from thy house... Thus says the Lord, "Behold, I will raise up evil against thee out of thy own house; and I will take thy wives before thy eyes, and give them to thy neighbor, and he shall lie with thy wives in the sight of the sun. For thou didst it secretly; but I will do this thing before all Israel, and before the sun."'" (2 Sam. 12:7-12)

[2271] As we have seen above in the Introduction (Section A), David had an elite group of warriors known as the Thirty. There was also a small group of three mighty men who were especially close to him (2 Sam. 23:8-20). Surabadi seems to have multiplied them a thousandfold.

[2272] A parallel to this exists in the Haggadah where the two harlots who came to Solomon for judgment about the possession of a child (1 K. 2:16-18) become spirits sent to reveal Solomon's wisdom. (Solomon, EJ, XV, 106)

[2273] Surabadi, pp. 364-365.

These precise predictions of future calamities, as is often the case, were doubtless put in the mouth of Nathan long after the event. (Genuine prophecies are usually vaguer.) Since these calamities actually did occur later in David's reign, it is possible that later generations, troubled by the suffering of so righteous a man such as David, wondered how he could have been plagued by such events, including rebellion within his own family, and were persuaded to accept the gossip about David and Bathsheba as a suitable explanation.

"David said to Nathan, 'I have sinned against the Lord.' And Nathan said to David, 'The Lord also has put away thy sin; thou shalt not die. Nevertheless, because by this deed thou hast utterly scorned the Lord, the child that is born to thee shall die.' Then Nathan went to his house." (2 Sam. 12:13-15a)

When one contemplates that Saul was disinherited for sparing a life, one wonders at the Lord's forbearance in the case of David. The adulterers suffer no immediate punishment for their adultery and the murder by proxy that has been committed. As is frequently the case in the Bible, God's vengeance is visited upon the innocent:

"And the Lord struck the child that Uriah's wife bore to David, and it became sick. David therefore besought God for the child, and David fasted, and went in and lay all night upon the ground. And the elders of his house stood beside him, to raise him from the ground; he would not, nor did he eat food with them. On the seventh day the child died... Then David arose from the earth, and washed, and anointed himself, and changed his clothes; and he went into the house of the Lord, and worshipped; he then went to his own house; and when he asked, they set food before him, and he ate. Then his servants said to him. 'What is this thing that thou hast done? Thou didst fast and weep for the child while it was alive; but when the child died, thou didst arise and eat food.' He said, 'While the child was alive, I fasted and wept; for I said, 'Who knows whether the Lord will be gracious to me, that the child may live?' But now he is dead; why should I fast? Can I bring him back again? I shall go to him, but he will not return to me.'" (2 Sam. 12:15b-18, 20-23)

"Then David comforted his wife, Bathsheba, and went in to her, and lay with her; and she bore him a son, and he called his name Solomon. And the Lord loved him, and sent a message by Nathan the prophet; so he called his name Jedidiah, because of the Lord." (2 Sam. 12:24-25)

This story embarrassed later Jews who invented several explanations of the behavior of their national hero. Among them: they claimed that it was the custom for the warriors to divorce their wives before going into battle so that they would not leave them widows if they were killed. Upon return from battle, they would remarry their wives. This story is apparently based upon the very ancient custom of abstention from sexual intercourse while participating in a holy war. Therefore, the reason (although there is no textual justification for such a conclusion) that since Uriah was in a state of ritual purity befitting a warrior (as is attested by his refusal to obey David and lie with his wife), he had actually divorced her! In this reasoning, Bathsheba had no husband at the time of her liaison with David, and therefore David had not committed adultery! (But he would still be guilty of the lesser crime of fornication. What about the forgotten woman, David's lawful wife? Does she count for nothing?) As though to further enhance the acceptability of this ingenious evasion, the law requiring warriors to divorce their wives before going into battle was attributed to David himself!

One of the most conspicuous deficiencies in the *Samuel* narrative is that the punishment does not fit the crime. In acquiring Bathsheba, David is shown breaking at least three of the Ten Commandments: "Thou shalt not kill; thou shalt not commit adultery; thou shalt not covet thy neighbor's wife..." (Ex. 20:13,14,17) The punishment for premeditated murder was death (Ex. 21:12). Similarly the punishment for adultery was death to both parties: "If a man is found lying with the wife of another man, both of them shall die, the man who lay with the woman, and the woman; so thou shalt purge every evil from Israel." (Deut. 22:22)

According to the God's Own Law, death should have been the fate of both David and Bathsheba. Yet the punishment decreed by God by the mouth of Nathan is "the sword shall never depart from thy house," a phrase which is subject to open-ended interpretations and, if taken as a prediction of war and disturbances in his dynasty, would hardly be a fate exclusive to the House of David as it has been the fate of rulers from the beginning of recorded history until the present day. There is nothing, therefore, exemplary about this threat as a punishment. If is taken to mean the insurrection of Absalom, David's son, and later Sheba, and still later Adonijah, these too are hardly unusual occurrences in the reign of an ancient king or even a modern dictator. In any case, such punishments do not serve in any way to redress the wrong done to the unfortunate, trusting Uriah.

One of the threatened punishments was that of a usurper from David's own house lying with his wives. This actually occurred (according to the Bible) during the rebellion of Absalom. Absalom was

David's son by Maacah, the daughter of Talmai, the king of Geshur.[2274] During Absalom's rebellion, he occupied the capital Jerusalem took possession of those women of his father's harem remaining in the palace. This was the custom of the time, and taking possession of a former king's harem was a sign of the new king's authority.[2275] (This procedure was, of course, prohibited by Islam, at least in the case of certain close relatives.) However, in the era we are discussing this in itself was not viewed as a sin. When David regained his throne, he refused to touch those women who had been with Absalom, but he did provide for them. According to the rules of the day, Absalom's crime was rebellion, not incest.

The other part of the punishment, the death of the child he had fathered upon Bathsheba is again not commensurate with the enormity of David's (alleged) crime. The death of a child was hardly an unusual event in those times. Even if the required death penalty for murder and adultery were not executed in the case of the king, one would suppose that after the series of crimes and deceits of which David was accused (by his enemies?), YHWH—through Nathan—would have at least prohibited David from enjoying the fruits of those crimes and deceits, and would have prohibited him from approaching Bathsheba further, if the accusations had had a foundation of truth. But no, instead, we find her the honored mother of the future king Solomon. Bathsheba went on to bear for David four sons who survived: Shimea, Shobab, Nathan, and Solomon (1 Ch. 3:5). (Do we have still another instance of ultimogeniture here?)

When considering the story of David and Bathsheba and the appropriateness of the punishment, we may view the issue in two ways: Either the *punishment* was inadequate considering the gravity of the crimes, or that the punishment was just, but the *crimes* have been exaggerated. Perhaps, instead of being guilty of adultery and murder, David was guilty of covetousness. The graver charges could be considered anti-Davidic propaganda, perhaps occasioned by the conservative reaction to Solomon's rule, and more especially the acrimonious disputes that led to the splitting of the United Kingdom under Solomon's successor. As we have suggested above, the real target of these stories may have been Solomon rather than David. There was

---

[2274] Geshur was a small Aramaean kingdom northeast of the Sea of Galilee. Though part of the allocation to the half-tribe of Manasseh, the Geshurites were still in possession of their land at the time of David.

[2275] Note the reference in Nathan's speech (quoted above) to David's having assumed Saul's harem.

opposition to the building of the Temple, not just because of the expense, but because it symbolized the centralization of worship in Jerusalem, especially the important (and revenue-producing) sacrifices. The suspension of the sacrifices in the several local shrines, within easy reach of the people, in favor of distant Jerusalem would have occasioned considerable local resentment and anger, as we see clearly from the aftermath. It would have necessitated the worshippers' submitting themselves to both the costs and the dangers of the journey, as well as injuring local pride.

It is interesting to notice that the Quran shows David as repenting his lapses, but in the Biblical account, there is no such clear statement. David is shown pleading with God to spare the child, but he is not reported repenting for his sins of adultery and murder. Abject repentance and the putting away of Bathsheba would have been the least we should have expected from David—if he had actually committed the crimes attributed to him. But in the Bible, neither of these penances occurred. The story of David's adultery has been too good a story for scholars to seriously challenge it in most quarters, although Jewish tradition shows some reservations about it. So, has God simply forgotten those violations of His commandments in an era in which He seems to have been personally involved in every little thing? Was Nathan's speech a fiction, or was it redacted into its present catalogue of accusations?

Perhaps we may think that the most serious crimes had not occurred, but were the fabrications of struggles and hatreds long since dead, except in their perpetuation in the pages of *Samuel*.

Those of us who are cynical enough to do so may dismiss Nathan's speech as a retrospective fabrication, in part motivated by hostility to the House of David, and in part—the other side of the coin—to explain the disasters that befell David, in many respects an ideal, almost King Arthur-like figure, who also had problems with his wife's behavior. These personal and political crises must have had a cause; otherwise, God would not have inflicted them upon him. We have observed that the punishments do not fit the crimes. There is more agreement about the historicity of the punishments, so should we not be emboldened to question the severity and nature of the crimes? There is no *a priori* reason for us to accept the component accusations in *Samuel* and the speech of Nathan, except that they make a good read.

However, with respect to David's penitence, the Talmud, while not contradicting the text of *Samuel*, makes up for this deficiency: "David realized his transgression, and for twenty-two years he was a penitent. Daily he wept a whole hour and ate his bread with ashes. But he had to undergo still heavier penance. For a half-year he suffered with leprosy..."[2276] The pseudepigraphic *Apocalypse of Sedrach* says that David was saved by tears.[2277]

And Surabadi tells us (in a display of particularly extravagant hyperbole) that David was forgiven because he wept so much that plants grew from his tears. However, his breath was so hot from anguish that as soon as he raised his head, the plants would be scorched by his breath. He summoned 4,000 readers and he mourned and wept more tears than all mankind put together. He would wander into the desert, and people found that his voice was not so pleasant as it had formerly been. Revelation came that the beauty of his voice had been from his innocence. Then Gabriel came to David at night and told him to weep no more. David sent Gabriel to ask God for permission to speak with Him face to face. God replied that He already knew all that he would think, but Gabriel left him and he spoke with God alone. He asked what would happen between Uriah and himself on the Day of Judgment because of the look he had cast upon Uriah's wife. God said that he would exact retribution. David said he would be ashamed that day. God said that if one tree brushed against another, on that Day retribution would be expected; why would it not be exacted from him? But God forgave him, in both worlds.[2278]

The *Book of Samuel* gives us several examples of the sorrowing David. At the funeral of Saul's former commander-in-chief Abner, David "...lifted up his voice and wept... And the king lamented for Abner saying,

> "Should Abner die as a fool dies?
> Thy hands were not bound,
> Thy feet were not befettered;
> as one falls before the wicked
> Thou hast fallen."

And all the people wept again over him." (2 Sam. 3:33-34)

And the elegy attributed to David at the deaths of Saul and Jonathan:

> "Thy glory, O Israel, is slain upon thy high places!

[2276] LJ, IV, 104. How many people have we encountered thus far afflicted with leprosy as a punishment for misdeeds? The ancients' view was that sickness was often a punishment, if not for the individual afflicted, then for someone close to him or her.

[2277] LJ, VI, 266.

[2278] Surabadi, pp. 365-367. Surabadi's vision of the Day of Judgment does not properly belong to the Biblical period of David, as this concept did not enter Israelite theology until much later, probably under Persian influence.

> How are the mighty fallen!
> Tell it not in Gath.
>> publish it not in the streets of Ashkelon;
> lest the daughters of the Philistines rejoice,
>> lest the daughters of the uncircumcised exult.

> Ye daughters of Israel, weep over Saul,
>> who clothed you daintily in scarlet,
>> who put ornaments of gold upon your apparel.
> How are the mighty fallen
>> in the midst of battle!
> Jonathan lies slain upon thy high places.
> I am distressed for thee, my brother Jonathan;
> very pleasant hast thou been to me;
>> thy love to me was wonderful
>> passing the love of women." (2 Sam. 1:19-20, 24-26)

The above laments have the ring of the authentic voice of David. And at the death of his son Amnon: "And as soon as he had finished speaking, behold, the king's sons came, and lifted up their voices and wept; and the king also and all his servants wept very bitterly." (2 Sam. 13:36)

And we may hear again, we believe, the true voice of David in his heartfelt lament at the death of his rebellious son and would-be heir Absalom: "And the king was deeply moved, and went up to the chamber over the gate, and wept; and as he went, he said, 'O my son Absalom, my son, my son Absalom! Would I had died instead of thee, O Absalom, my son, my son!'" (2 Sam. 18:33)

II. SOLOMON

And God gave Solomon wisdom and understanding beyond measure...
(1 K. 4:29)

A. INTRODUCTORY REMARKS

No Biblical character has been surrounded—one might add obscured—by legendary and fanciful embellishments to the degree that Solomon has in Jewish, Christian, and Islamic literature. In general, Christians have been more unreservedly favorable to Solomon than Jews, but Muslims elevate him even more. His empire, from being a second-rate kingdom at the western end of the Fertile Crescent, has become magnified in legend and fable to include not only the earth, but the heavens as well.[2279] His prosperity has been exaggerated into a fabulous wealth such as has never been seen, and the magical powers attributed to him have become almost as proverbial as his wisdom. The slightest clue in the either the Bible of the Quran has been used to launch the most unrestrained flights of fancy and imagination.

The oldest extant documents about Solomon are those in *1 Kings* (chs. 1-11). The later parallel account in *Chronicles* (2 Ch., chs. 1-9) is considerably more restrained. Most of the themes that were developed by later legend can be traced to those texts: Solomon's wealth, his power, his building operations, his commercial enterprises, and his wisdom. At the beginning of his career, he is represented as possessing high ideals and striving after righteousness. This is the view of the Chronicler who, as he was with David, is silent about (or discounts) the unfavorable stories about Solomon we find in *Kings*. He was, after all, the builder of the Temple that had become the central shrine of Judaism.

As was the case with David in *Samuel*, *Kings* also preserves some highly unfavorable material about Solomon, one of Israel's greatest monarchs. The reasons for this were various, among them: a reaction against the burdens imposed upon the people by the monarchy, especially in the North; conservative reaction to Solomon's foreign marriages and alliances; the displeasure of the priests and followers of other shrines at being eclipsed in favor of the dynastic sanctuary at Jerusalem; discontent and fear caused by rapidly changing social and economic conditions; and attempts to attack those changes by casting suspicion upon the legitimacy of the House of David. This did not

---

[2279] Solomon, EJ, XV, 107.

originate in Solomon's reign. Instead, they were part of his inheritance from his father David.

Solomon's name (in Heb. *Shelomoh*; Ar. *Sulaymān*) is derived from the Hebrew cognate of the Arabic root *s-l-m*, and means "peaceful." Another of David's sons possessed a name using the same root, Absalom ("the father is peace"). This suggests that David may have been longing for peace when he bestowed such names upon his children.[2280]

In his own lifetime, David proclaimed Solomon his successor. Apparently, they were co-rulers for the period 967-965 BCE. Solomon's independent rule began upon the death of his father and lasted to about 923 BCE.[2281] Since he was one of David's younger sons, his selection would seem to be still another example of ultimogeniture in the Old Testament. Though he is referred to as a little child at his accession (1 K. 3:7), he was probably nearer 20 years of age than the traditional 12.[2282]

David's nomination of Solomon did not go uncontested, and another son of David, Adonijah, was acclaimed king with support of a section of the army. However, this was not a serious threat. After the conspiracy was quelled, Solomon spared Adonijah's life (temporarily); a demonstration of mercy he would have certainly not shown had his brother's claims had any wide support.[2283] Nevertheless, he soon found an excuse to put him out of the way.[2284] As David is depicted at the time as being old and virtually senile, that Solomon attained power through a coup d'état arranged possibly by his mother Bathsheba cannot be ruled out.[2285]

Solomon inherited the kingdom (enthusiasts refer to it as an "empire") created by David. It stretched from Elath at the head of the Gulf of Aqabah to middle Syria and possibly as far as the western Euphrates, and included most of western Syria and all of Palestine except Phoenicia and Philistia. Philistia still maintained a tenuous independence, proof of Philistine military prowess, although by this time, perhaps as the result of manpower losses in the wars with Saul and David, the Philistines were probably more or less completely mixed with the local Semitic population. The distinctive pottery styles brought with them from the Aegean world disappeared during this era.[2286]

[2280] Solomon, DB, p. 928; the form is analogous to the Phoenician *slmyn*. (Solomon, EJ, XV, 96.)

[2281] Solomon, EJ, XV, 98-99; the DB gives his reign as 969-922. (Solomon, DB, p. 928.)

[2282] Solomon, DB, p. 928.

[2283] 1 K. 1; Solomon, DB, p. 928.

[2284] See next section.

[2285] Anderson, p. 57.

[2286] Philistines, EJ, XIII, 402.

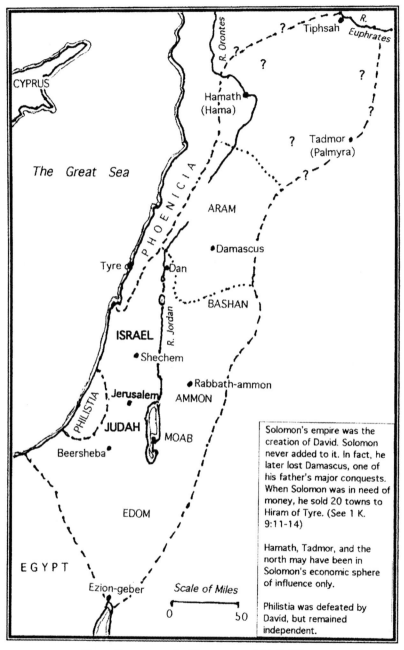

KING SOLOMON'S EMPIRE, C.950 BCE

Solomon's empire, described as stretching from Tiphsah in the north to Gaza in Philistia in the south (1 K. 4:24), was something of a flash in the pan. It was created by the energies of one man, David, who was favored by the accidents of history. Egypt was in the hands of the weak rulers of the XXIst Dynasty and preoccupied with its own internal problems.[2287] Assyria was just recovering from the Aramaean incursions of the previous century,[2288] and the Phoenicians were thriving, but looking westward towards the sea with its promise of commercial opportunities, rather than inland beyond the high, protecting walls of Mts. Lebanon and Anti-Lebanon.[2289] Thus, Solomon's inheritance was an extensive one and coincided with the exhaustion or disinterest of his more powerful neighbors. However, this state of affairs changed unfavorably later in his reign. Pharaoh Shishak of Egypt (rgd. c. 940-920 BCE), the founder of the XXIInd Dynasty caused Solomon some problems, and he attacked and plundered Jerusalem a few years after Solomon's death.[2290] The Aramaeans at Damascus also became increasingly independent during his reign.[2291]

Though there were no major military confrontations between his "empire" and its neighbors whilst he was on the throne, Solomon followed his father's policy of strengthening his standing army, paying particular attention to horses and chariotry in which Israel had formerly been weak.[2292] Solomon's friendship with Hiram, the king of Tyre in Phoenicia, carried with it commercial advantages to both parties, and also provided Solomon with the technical and engineering skill needed to carry out his grand building enterprises, projects that were conducted on a scale unprecedented in Canaan. These were not confined to the Palace and Temple at Jerusalem, but included fortifications throughout the kingdom.[2293] Another much-criticized aspect of Solomon's foreign policy was his marriages with women of Moab, Ammon, Edom, Sidon, the Hittites, and especially his marriage to a daughter of Pharaoh, an event that is recorded with mingled pride and repugnance in 1 K. 3:1; 11:1.[2294]

The geographical situation of Solomon's kingdom, astride the great land routes of the ancient East from Egypt to Mesopotamia and Arabia, and his partnership with Hiram of Tyre who similarly controlled

---

[2287] Breasted, pp. 439-440.
[2288] Saggs, pp. 103-104.
[2289] Solomon, DB, p. 929.
[2290] Solomon, DB, p. 928; Shishak, DB, p. 911.
[2291] Aramaeans, DB, p. 48.
[2292] Solomon, DB, p. 929.
[2293] Solomon, EJ, XV, 102-103.
[2294] Solomon, EJ, XV, 101.

the sea routes of the eastern Mediterranean world, brought a period of unparalleled wealth and prosperity to Israel and Judah (or at least its magnates and upper classes). Agriculture flourished[2295] and products and luxuries never before available to the Israelites became common in the markets, but (as has been the case with other imperial systems) the wealth probably did little to improve the lot of the common people very much. Great wealth brought higher taxes and prices.

Solomon ruled with a strong hand, and continued the centralizing policies of his father. With a more efficient administration, and an (expensive) standing army to back up its demands, the tax burden upon the peasantry gradually increased until it must have become oppressive. Conscription for the army and the corvée was introduced, reminding the people of the bondage of their ancestors in Egypt. It is a sign of the strength of Solomon that the resentment these burdens generated amongst a people shortly out of tribalism was not able to find expression until after his death.[2296] Even with the increased income from trade and improved agriculture, the expenses of Solomon's huge court and his construction projects must have put severe pressure on the mere 800,000 or so Israelites who formed the core of his kingdom.[2297]

Despite this underside of his reign, Solomon became famous for his wealth, wisdom, and justice (at least in the Biblical accounts). His wisdom and wealth attracted attention from as far away as southern Arabia, prompting (according to the Biblical tradition) the visit of the queen of Sheba. There can be little doubt but that he started his reign with high ideals. To some extent (to what extent is a matter of dispute), Solomon's inclination towards ostentation and display may have compromised those ideals. The author of the relevant tradition of *Kings* accuses Solomon of lapsing into apostasy and idolatry towards the end of his life. We shall examine these accusations in another place.[2298]

The Solomon whom we find in the Quran is another royal prophet, like David. And like his story, Solomon's story (to be found in five surahs[2299]) concentrates upon his positive virtues only: his wisdom, his wealth (symbolizing God's bounty), and several of the other rather

---

[2295] Solomon, EJ, XV, 102.
[2296] Solomon, DB, pp. 929-930.
[2297] Albright's population estimate. He gives Jerusalem and its environs in Solomon's reign a population of about 50,000. (Albright-Ab to Ez, pp. 56, 105-106.) Saggs proposes a figure of 700,000 for Palestine at that time. (Saggs, p. 251.) McEvedy and Jones suggest a much lower figure, about half a million. (McEvedy, p. 141.)
[2298] See Section K below.
[2299] Q. 2:102; 21:78-82; 27:15-44; 34:12-14; 38:30-40. Solomon is also mentioned in Q. 4:162 and 6:38, but only in passing.

marvelous traditions that had grown up about the historical figure (possibly influenced by the Iranian traditions of Jamshid[2300]) that were obviously circulating in the Arabia of the time. That the Solomonic cycle was known to the pre-Islamic Arabs is attested by the nature of the references to him and the marvels associated with him in pre-Islamic poetry.[2301]

In this brief survey of Solomon and his reign, of necessity we have concentrated upon the external events of his life. The Biblical writers were awed by Solomon's wealth and wisdom and do not give us many glimpses of the inner man. He seems to have been more remote than almost any other figure in the Old Testament, separated from the people by an Oriental court and temple ritual, as well as the administrative burdens imposed by a large kingdom and extensive commercial enterprises. Perhaps our lack of information about the inner man has permitted such divergent and contradictory traditions to form about him: the king who performed sacral functions in the temple and succumbed to his lusts with a thousand women; the devotee of YHWH who built the splendid Temple to glorify Him and who then supposedly apostatized and joined his foreign wives in the worship of idols; the possessor of unlimited power who lost his kingdom; the recipient of an incredible income who reduced his people to poverty through taxation and the corvée; the apostate and the penitent; the king who possessed more wisdom than any man who lived, but who never learned moderation.

Such is the contradictory figure of Solomon presented to us by the Bible and Jewish tradition. Let us see what the Quran and Surabadi made of this legend.

B. THE SUCCESSION

And Solomon was the heir of David... (Q. 27:16)

Thus the Quran declares Solomon's succession to the throne of David. *And We bestowed on David Solomon; how excellent a servant! Lo, he was ever turning (to God) in repentance.* (Q. 38:30) This establishes the close relationship of Solomon to David, in accordance with the Biblical history; although if one accepts the validity of the scandalous tales of Solomon's later years as recorded in *Kings,* one might question how excellent a servant Solomon really was. This aspect

---

[2300] Sulaiman, SEI, p. 551.
[2301] Solomon, EJ, XV, 108.

will be discussed below. Let us first look at Solomon's succession to the throne of David.

The Quran does not make any reference to the manner of Solomon's selection as David's heir from among his several surviving sons. Surabadi tells us that when David was about to die, Gabriel brought a scroll and told him that whichever of his sons could disclose the contents of the scroll without breaking the seal would be his successor. Solomon was twelve years old and the smallest of David's sons. He was able to read the scroll without breaking the seal and solve the ten riddles it contained. Having passed that test, Solomon received the Ring from David. Surabadi relates that it had inscriptions on its four facets: on one: *Sovereignty belongs to God,* on another: *Dominion belongs to God,* on the third: *Glory belongs to God,* and on the fourth: *Muhammad is the Messenger of God.*[2302]

In another place, Surabadi repeats much the same story of the scroll, but is closer to the Biblical narrative, as we shall see, when he adds a promise David had made to Bathsheba to make her son, among David's twenty sons, his successor.

After successfully passing the test of the scroll, David sent him to be tested further by the elders, the middle-aged, and the young. While being tested, he laughed, displeasing them. Later, when David asked whether they had found any fault with Solomon, the young mentioned his laughter. David asked Solomon about the laughter; he replied that while responding with inspired answers, he had heard two ants conversing on the ceiling, one cautioning the other not to cause dust to fall on the successor's head.[2303] Except for Solomon's understanding the communication of the ants,[2304] none of this is based upon anything in the Quran.

Surabadi speaks of David's twenty sons. A list of six sons born at Hebron is given in 1 Sam. 3:2-5, and another list of eleven sons born at Jerusalem is found in the same book (2 Sam. 5:14-16). The Chronicler gives a consolidated list of nineteen sons, but two of those appear to be duplicates, thereby reducing the number to seventeen (1 Ch. 3:1-9).[2305] In the two latter lists (Solomon's name naturally does not occur in the Hebron list), he appears fourth—the fourth son of Bathsheba—a position

---

[2302] Surabadi, p. 345.

[2303] Surabadi, pp. 277-278.

[2304] See below, Section G.

[2305] BC, III, 311. The Chronicler mentions additional progeny: "All these [nineteen] were David's sons, besides the sons of the concubines..." (1 Ch. 3:9.) Solomon would have been 13th son by David's wives, not counting his offspring by his concubines.

which is remarkable considering that he should have been the *eldest* surviving son of David by Bathsheba according to *Samuel*,[2306] still another probable inconsistency that weakens the reliability of the David-Bathsheba story. Incidentally, the Chronicler gives the name of Solomon's mother as Bathshua (Ar. *Batshāya^c*) (1 Ch. 3:5), which is the variant that has found its way into Islamic tradition. This suggests that *Chronicles* was the basis of much of the information about this Biblical period in the traditions of Arabia (before Muslim scholars had access to other sources after the Arab conquest of the Near East), rather than *Samuel-Kings* with its explicitly negative stories about both David and Solomon compromising the generally pro-Davidic narrative.

In the Bible, the Chronicler adopts the view that later is found in the Quran, and simply states: "When David was old and full of days, he made Solomon his son King over Israel." (1 Ch. 23:1) *Kings* paints a more complicated picture and Surabadi's references to David's promise to Bathsheba are based upon that. *Kings* agrees with *Chronicles* in that David nominated Solomon during his own lifetime. For the two years or so before the death of his father, Solomon probably ruled as a co-king.[2307]

The first chapter of *Kings* depicts David as an old, sick man, for whom his courtiers secure a beautiful virgin to lie with him and keep him warm.[2308] Seeing his father in this condition, Adonijah, who may have been David's first heir apparent, assumed the royal duties. He was the fourth of the sons born at Hebron, after Absalom, who had been David's heir until his rebellion and death. The first son, Amnon, had already been killed by Absalom for incest with his half-sister Tamar (2 Sam. 13). The Bible says nothing about the fate of the second, Chileab,[2309] but in Talmudic tradition he was noted for his piety,[2310] whilst Adonijah usurped royal prerogatives.

Another party, which included Nathan the prophet who had been earlier represented as condemning David for taking Bathsheba, supported Solomon: "Then Nathan said to Bathsheba, the mother of Solomon, 'Hast thou not heard that Adonijah the son of Haggith has become king

---

[2306] 2 Sam. 12:24-25: "Then David comforted his wife, Bathsheba [after the death of their first son], and went in to her, and lay with her; and she bore a son, and he called his name Solomon." He would thus have been her second and eldest surviving son by David. Whence came the others named before Solomon?

[2307] See above, Section A.

[2308] 1 K. 1:1-4. This was not done for carnal reasons, Biblical commentators assure us, but rather in the belief that her rejuvenating youth would flow from her body into his with her warmth. (Gaster, II, p. 489.)

[2309] Or "Daniel," as the Chronicler calls him in 1 Ch. 3:1.

[2310] LJ, IV, 118.

and David our lord does not know it? Now therefore come, let me give thee counsel that thou mayest save thy own life and the life of thy son Solomon. Go in at once to King David, and say unto him, "Didst thou not, my lord the king, swear unto thy maidservant, saying, 'Solomon thy son shall reign after me, and he shall sit upon my throne' When then is Adonijah king?" Then whilst thou art still speaking with the king, I also will come in after thee and confirm thy words.'" (1 K. 1:11-14)

Can this be the prophet Nathan, now treating Bathsheba with such solicitude, who had formerly condemned her husband (and by implication) herself for adultery? Has he forgotten the divinely inspired rebuke he delivered to David? Or is this further evidence that the whole episode was a malicious fiction against David? There has been no previous mention of such a promise made by David to Bathsheba in *Samuel-Kings*, and though some commentators take a charitable view of the affair and assume that there had been such an oath privately made and known only to David, Bathsheba, and Nathan.[2311] The text of *Kings* makes it sound suspiciously like a devious conspiracy to take advantage of the old and feeble David in order to secure the throne for Solomon by the unscrupulous means of reminding David of a forgotten "promise" he had never made.

In any event, Bathsheba did as Nathan proposed. In conclusion, she said to David: "'And now, my lord the king, the eyes of all Israel are upon thee, to tell them who shall sit on the throne of my lord the king after him. Otherwise it will come to pass when my lord the king sleeps with his fathers, that I and my son Solomon will be counted offenders.'" (1 K. 1:12-21)

Offenders? This does not refer to the alleged adultery and murder, as Solomon had not yet been born to be included in the term. In the game of palace intrigue and royal succession, the stakes were often life or death. Adonijah was surely aware of her ambitions for her son (and for herself, for the king's mother wielded considerable power in the hothouse atmosphere of a royal harem). So Bathsheba plays upon her dying husband's feelings artfully to ensure her own and her son's survival, for Adonijah would surely have disposed of them.

According to the prearranged plan, the pious prophet Nathan then entered the chamber of the king "while she was still speaking"[2312] and made a similar report about the usurpation of royal prerogatives by Adonijah. Then he asked David: "'Has this thing been brought about by

---

[2311] BC, III, 159.
[2312] 1 K. 1:22.

my lord the king and thou hast not told thy servants who should sit upon the throne of my lord the king after him?'" (1 K. 1:27)

"Then King David answered, 'Call Bathsheba to me.' So she came into the king's presence, and stood before the king. [Apparently, the conflater putting the pieces of this narrative together did not realize that Bathsheba was already present, so he gave her another entrance.] And the king swore, saying, 'As the Lord lives, Who has redeemed my soul out of every adversity, as I swore to thee by the Lord, the God of Israel,[2313] saying, "Solomon thy son shall reign after me, and he shall sit upon my throne in my stead"; even so will I do this day.' Then Bathsheba bowed with her face to the ground, and did obeisance to the king, and said, 'May my lord King David live for ever!'" (1 K. 1:28-31)

We would seem to have, once again a double account of the promise of David to Bathsheba, one unfavorable, showing Nathan and Bathsheba conspiring to put Solomon on the throne by putting one over on the old man, thereby making Solomon something of a usurper; and the other showing Nathan reporting to the king about the activities of Adonijah and not even mentioning Solomon as he should have done according to the conspiracy version. David himself is shown remembering his promise and summons Bathsheba from another place (she was already in the room when Nathan entered in the conspiracy version). He reiterated his promise, thus confirming Solomon's right to the throne. Since the conspiracy pericope (1 K. 1:11-22) presupposes the existence of the scene of Nathan's report and David's reaction to it, the confirmation of Solomon as his successor, it is clearly later than the surrounding text, and must be considered a slanderous interpolation to cast a shadow upon Solomon's right to the throne.

This interpolation is, therefore, anti-Davidic in character, as is the story of David's adultery and the affair of Uriah, and its authenticity is just as questionable. On the other hand, to be fair, we must admit that the older narrative may also be equally suspect as an invention of pro-Solomonic propaganda, as there is no earlier record of the promise made by David that is thrust rather suddenly into the Biblical narrative—unless it has been excised. In any event, we can see how ancient politics have influenced the shape and content of the text of the Bible as it grew. The Chronicler, with his religious concerns, dismissed these derogatory stories—perhaps because he had not discerned the two strata of tradition here and considered the whole tale to be one, and that unfavorable to his exalted idea of the House of David.

[2313] Notice again that God is always referred to restrictively as the God of Israel in this epoch, rather than as the God of the Universe (*rabb al-ᶜālamīn*).

The record in *Kings* continues with David's giving immediate orders for the anointing of Solomon and the proclamation of his kingship. "...Zadok the priests took the horn of oil from the tent, and anointed Solomon. Then they blew the trumpet; and all the people said, 'Long live King Solomon!' And all the people went up after him, playing on pipes, and rejoicing with great joy, so that the earth was split by their noise." (1 K. 1:39-40) Realizing that he could not compete with Solomon, Adonijah came and did obeisance to him. "Then David slept with his fathers, and was buried in the City of David. And the time that David reigned over Israel was forty years... So Solomon sat upon the throne of David his father; and his kingdom was firmly established." (1 K. 2:10-12)

Although both traditions of Solomon's accession, the original pro-Davidic story of David's promise, and its later expanded anti-Davidic form have the odor of propaganda, there may have been more to Adonijah's claims than *Kings* credits. Immediately after the coronation of Solomon, an incident occurred that suggests that Adonijah may genuinely have felt himself wronged, and his rights usurped. He is shown approaching Bathsheba and requesting her to ask Solomon to give him as wife Abishag (the young virgin who had warmed David's bed in his old age referred to above). He phrased his request thus: "'Thou knowest that the kingdom was mine, and that all Israel fully expected me to reign; however, the kingdom has turned about and become my brother's, for it was his from the Lord. And now I have a request...'" (1 K. 2:15-16)

In this view, Adonijah was saying that the crown was rightfully his, but circumstances and political machinations, gracefully attributed to divine intervention ("from the Lord"), had deprived him of it. So, was Solomon a usurper of Adonijah's rights through an unrecorded military action or, more likely, court intrigue, as is hinted? Oddly enough, Bathsheba, who must have been familiar with the implications of Adonijah's request, is reported as having taken it to Solomon. Solomon naturally interpreted this as an attempt by Adonijah to establish another claim to the throne or to strengthen an existing one, for "the right of the father's harem was a significant right of succession,"[2314] as we have already noted in the cases of David and Absalom. Adonijah paid for this audacity with his life, the inevitable fate of rival claimants to a throne, especially for those whose claims hold some validity.[2315]

[2314] BC, III, 164.

[2315] Despite the assertions of the Bible, perhaps Solomon did not yet feel himself powerful enough, or his position sufficiently consolidated, for him to take action against Adonijah immediately upon his accession to the throne.

Following the death of Adonijah, Abiathar the priest was banished because he had supported Adonijah. David's commander-in-chief Joab was assassinated (supposedly in fulfillment of a deathbed command given by David to Solomon), and Shimei, the last representative of the Benjaminite (Saulic) royal aspirations was put under house arrest and, shortly after, an excuse was found—an alleged violation of his house arrest—to put him to death (1 K. 2:36-46).

All of this suggests that Solomon's accession to the throne was not without the opposition and bloodshed typical of monarchical systems where primogeniture is not firmly established.[2316] As we have proposed, the oath that David was alleged to have sworn to Bathsheba may very well have been put into his mouth in later times to justify the realities of history. Alternatively, we may say that all of these intrigues and machinations were the means—the process—by which God achieved His end: the enthronement of Solomon.

There may also be some evidence of trouble in the accession of Solomon in *Chronicles*. Though the Chronicler apparently makes the transition from David to Solomon an orderly one, in one place we read of David, in a public assembly, charging his son to build the Temple,[2317] and then conducting a royal sacrifice in the presence of the people. At the conclusion of the passage, we find: "...they made Solomon the son of David king the second time, and they anointed him as prince for the Lord, and Zadok as priest. Then Solomon sat on the throne of the Lord as king instead of David his father; and he prospered, and all Israel obeyed him. All the leaders and the mighty men, and also the sons of David, pledged their allegiance to King Solomon, and bestowed upon him such royal majesty as had not been on any king before him in Israel." (1 Ch. 29:22-25)

The phrase "made Solomon... king the second time" catches our attention. It has not been satisfactorily explained. Although it probably refers to the ceremonies attendant upon the commencement of his reign as sole sovereign after his co-regency with David, it may also conceal a

---

[2316] Anderson states bluntly that Solomon's accession was the result of a coup d'état (Anderson, p. 57). Perhaps it would be more appropriate to consider it the fruit of palace (i.e., harem) intrigue, as one finds in the later Ottoman Empire.

[2317] In order to give the Jerusalem Temple greater authority, it seems, the Chronicler pushed back its establishment to David who is quoted as issuing detailed instructions to Solomon about the plan of the temple, its furnishings, the classes of priests, and the rites of worship and sacrifice to be established in it when Solomon has constructed it (1 Ch. 28:11-19). David had been deprived of the honor of constructing the Lord's House because of the blood he had shed (1 Ch. 28:1-8).

hint of dynastic troubles that necessitated a second public confirmation of his legitimacy.

Surabadi, following Jewish traditions,[2318] states that Solomon was twelve years old when he ascended the throne. The *Targum Sheni* makes him thirteen,[2319] and in Josephus we have: "So Solomon died when he was already an old man, having reigned 80 years, and lived 94"[2320]; thus he would have been 14 at the time of his (first?) accession.[2321] However, most authorities feel that Solomon was an adult when he became king.[2322] The tradition that he was a child is based upon his statement at Gibeon where he had gone to make a sacrifice at the high place there. During the night he dreamed that he was having a conversation with the Lord, in the course of which he is reported as saying, "'And now, O Lord my God, Thou hast made Thy servant king in place of David my father, although I am but a little child; I do not know how to go out or come in.'" (1 K. 3:7)

Since Solomon had, previous to this dream, already taken forceful action in putting to death Adonijah and other potential rivals, more befitting a man than a child of twelve, and he also had just married the daughter of Pharaoh, his statement is either out of place in the text, or perhaps to be regarded as a modest exaggeration. The prophet Jeremiah, when being called to preach used much the same language: "Then I said, 'Ah, Lord God! Behold, I do not know how to speak, for I am only a youth...'" (Jer. 1:6)

THE RING OF SOLOMON: Surabadi mentions the ring given to Solomon by David and accorded magical properties by tradition. This ring does not appear in either the Bible or the Quran. Surabadi relates that it had inscriptions (obviously of Islamic origin) on its four facets: *Sovereignty belongs to God, Dominion belongs to God, Glory belongs to God,* and *Muhammad is the Messenger of God.*[2323]

According to the *Testament of Solomon*, a pseudepigraphic work dating back to the 4th century BCE, but with later additions,[2324] the ring was given to Solomon by the angel Michael in answer to Solomon's prayer that he be granted victory over a malicious spirit who was stealing food and obstructing the construction of the Temple. "The archangel

---

[2318] LJ, IV, 125.
[2319] LJ, VI, 277.
[2320] Josephus, Antiquities, VIII.7.8, p. 183.
[2321] The Bible allots Solomon's reign 40 years (1 K. 11:42; 2 Ch. 9:30).
[2322] See preceding Section A.
[2323] Surabadi, p. 345.
[2324] Pseudepigrapha, DB, p. 823.

Michael appeared to him, and gave him a small ring having a seal consisting of an engraved stone, and he said to him: 'Take, O Solomon, king, son of David, the gift which the Lord God, the highest Zebaot,[2325] hath sent thee. With it thou shalt lock up all the demons of the earth, male and female; and with their help thou shalt build up Jerusalem. But thou must wear this seal of God; and this engraving of the seal of the ring sent thee is a Pentalpha.'"[2326] More will be said about this ring in other places.

C. SOLOMON THE BUILDER

Solomon in all his glory... (Mt. 6:29)

Solomon's building operations are mentioned in the Quran: *...and (We gave Solomon) certain of the jinn who worked before him by permission of his Lord. And such of them as deviated from Our command, them We caused to taste the chastisement of burning fire. They made for him what he willed: places of worship, statues, basins like water-troughs and boilers built into the ground. Give thanks, O house of David! Few of My servants are thankful.* (Q. 34:12-13) *And of the devils, some dived for him and did other work besides; and We were watching over them.* (Q. 21:82) More explicit references to Solomon as a builder are found in pre-Islamic poetry, especially concerning the castle of Al-Ablaq near Tayma, thought to have been one of Solomon's legacies.[2327] Ancient ruins in Iran, at Masjed-e Sulayman, near Pasargad, and at Takht-e Sulayman in western Iran are ascribed to him.[2328] A long, high mountain in the Alborz range west of Tehran is also called Takht-e Sulayman (Throne of Solomon).

Before proceeding to Surabadi's elaboration of these verses, we may pause briefly to consider the matter of the "jinn" and "devils" mentioned in these verses. We could content ourselves with the traditional explanations for these words, that they are other classes of beings existing in a kind of parallel world, but some of us may wish to explore other possible interpretations. As we shall see, the jinn and

---

[2325] Zebaot: Lord Zebaot, one of the names of God meaning "Lord of Hosts."

[2326] LJ, IV, 150. The Pentalpha is a five-pointed star made by the joining of five *alpha*s (the letter A) at their bases in the form of a circle.

[2327] SolSheba, p. 878.

[2328] The ruins near Masjed-e Sulayman are Parthian; those at Pasargad, *Zindān-e Sulaymān* (Prison of Sulayman) and *Takht-e Mādar-e Sulaymān* (Throne of the Mother of Solomon = Bathsheba) are Achaemenian. The ruins at Takht-e Sulayman (Throne of Solomon) are Parthian and Mongol.

demons here can be considered a substitution for the foreigners Solomon is recorded as having employed on his imperial constructions. The requisite building skills were not available among the Israelites, whose construction techniques were considerably cruder than those of the older, more established kingdoms around them. Maulana Muhammad Ali cites the authority of Lane to show that the term devils (*shayāṭīn*) can be applied to men, as well as the non-human beings who normally go by that name; and he extends this to include the jinn as well. He would interpret every reference in the Quran to jinn to mean a class of humans whose reported creation from fire symbolizes their rebellious nature, whilst those of dust are potentially obedient.[2329] He does not similarly expand the meaning of "devils/demons" to cover all references to them in the Quran. Muhajir mentions these views, but rejects them.[2330]

Nonetheless, we think they warrant further consideration, at least with reference to the story of Solomon. Numerous parallels, in addition to the metaphorical use for evil persons, exist: the Chinese frequently referred to foreigners as "devils"; the Greeks called all non-Greeks "barbarians," as did the Romans with non-Romans after them. The Jews clearly distinguished between themselves and the non-Jews (Gentiles): the *goyim* or nations, as opposed to the nation *par excellence* (the Jews). Muslims traditionally made a three-fold classification: Muslims, People of the Book, and the heathen. Amerindians often referred to their own tribe as "the people," distinct from other tribes of lesser beings. Therefore it would not be, *ipso facto*, unusual for an epithet such as *jinn* or *devil* to be applied to foreigners, particularly those following a different (or despised) religion, speaking a different dialect or language, or possessing strange customs.

A superficial similarity exists between the English "gentile" (the translation of the Hebrew *goyim*, both meaning in the Biblical context "non-Jew"), and the Arabic jinn. "Gentile" is derived from the Latin *gentil(is)* meaning "belonging to the same family." *Gentil(is)* is in turn a formation of which *gens*, meaning family or clan, is a part.[2331] A relationship between the Latin "gens" and the Arabic "jinn" has been proposed.[2332] The question arises, could this use in the Quran of the word

---

[2329] Quran-MMA, pp. 511, 639, 824, 872, 1108-1107.
[2330] Muhajir, p. 169.
[2331] RHD, entries for "gentile, gentle, gens," p. 551.
[2332] The possibility of words of foreign origin in the Quran should not surprise the reader, even from Latin. It has been suggested, for example, that the Arabic words *qaṣr* (castle) and *ṣirāṭ* (road) derive from Latin *castrum* and *strata* respectively, possessing approximately the same meaning. Many common Arabic words are Persian in origin; although, that said, the number of loan words in Arabic is far, far less than in English.

jinn, at least in the story of Solomon, be related to "goyim/gentile"? And, if it could be demonstrated that it was, how was it understood during the time of the Prophet? Could it be used as an epithet of a class of men as "devils" could be? Further examination of the problem is warranted.

Surabadi, along with the other classical commentators, regards the jinn as a species of non-humans. He tells us that Solomon wanted to build a mosque without pillars, so he called upon Sakhr,[2333] the jinni who lived on an island in the sea. Solomon told Sakhr that he wanted to build a mosque one league square.[2334] Sakhr devised a plan to construct it, by building a roof and then pouring the copper over it. When the copper had cooled and solidified, the frame could be removed from under the roof, and, lo! Solomon would have his Temple. Solomon asked Sakhr where he (Solomon) could get so much copper. Sakhr replied that Solomon himself knew. A spring of copper appeared[2335] and the devils, fairies, and men were ordered to collect it for this project. While they were still working, the king died.[2336] Thus, we see in Surabadi a continuation of the tradition that attributes the execution of Solomon's building projects to Sakhr and other non-humans, although Surabadi indicates that ordinary mortal men were also involved, as in his inclusion of men among the gatherers of the copper.

The Biblical account of the public works of Solomon is less colorful, although the scope of the projects he undertook was clearly a source of wonder and admiration for the writers of the traditions describing them. Let us look first at the question of the labor force.

It appears that David was the first to introduce the corvée (forced labor) among the Israelites. The forced labor of the Israelites in bondage in Egypt had been a form of corvée, so David's move could not have been popular. David had an officer, or minister, in charge of the corvée whose name was Adoram (2 Sam. 20:24; 1 K. 12:18), or Adoniram (1 K. 4:6; 5:14). The same man was in charge of the levy of 30,000 forced laborers that Solomon (who greatly expanded his father's use of the corvée for his grandiose building works) sent to Lebanon to cut timber for his palace and the Temple.

Adoram survived the death of Solomon, but his murder was the first act of violence that signaled the secession of the North (Israel),

---

[2333] Sakhr: the named appears to be derived from an Arabic root *(ṣ-kh-r)* referring to "stone." Does this have any connection with the "stone" *(ṣakhrah)*, which is the principle feature of the Dome of the Rock at the site of Solomon's Temple?

[2334] "one league [or parasang] square": about 3 miles square. Such a structure would have covered nearly 5800 acres.

[2335] ...*And We caused the fount of copper to gush forth for him...* (Q. 34:12)

[2336] Surabadi, pp. 345-346.

leaving the House of David to reign over Southern Judah. After Solomon's successor, his son Rehoboam, had rejected the pleas of the Northerners that their yoke be lightened, "King Rehoboam sent Adoram, who was taskmaster over the forced labor, and all Israel stoned him to death with stones. And King Rehoboam made haste to mount his chariot, to flee to Jerusalem." (1 K. 12:18-19) This corvée established by the House of David in imitation of neighboring monarchies such as Egypt was a source of profound resentment, especially among the Northern Israelites, who considered themselves free men. This recalls the theory that the Exodus from bondage in Egypt was an experience of the Northern Josephic tribes and perhaps not the Southern tribes (see "Moses" above).

It may be noted that in *Kings* we have contradictory statements about the participation of the Israelites in this corvée. In one place we read that Solomon raised a levy of forced corvée labor out of all Israel for the work in Lebanon (1 K. 5:13), and in another place: "The man Jeroboam was very able, and when Solomon saw that the young man was industrious, he gave him charge over all the forced labor of the house of Joseph [i.e., the Northerners]." (1 K. 11:28)[2337] Both verses clearly state that the Israelites were subjected to the corvée.

Against these explicit statements, in the same book we find another passage defending Solomon against this charge of raising a corvée from among the Israelites: "All the people who were left [in Canaan] of the Amorites, the Hittites, the Perizzites, the Hivites, and the Jebusites, who were not of the people of Israel—their descendants who were left after them in the land, whom the people of Israel were unable to destroy utterly—these Solomon made a forced levy of slaves, and so they are to this day. But of the people of Israel Solomon made no slaves; they were the soldiers, they were his officials, his commanders, his captains, his chariot commanders and his horsemen." (1 K. 9:20-22) [It would appear that the ancient Israelites had no qualms of conscience about inflicting upon others what the Egyptians had been inflicted upon them, even if the statement itself be unhistorical.]

[2337] The "house of Joseph" referred to the tribes of Ephraim and Manasseh, the principal components of the Israelite population of the north. It is one of the ironies of Biblical history that after the death of Solomon this same Jeroboam, who was responsible for implementing the corvée in the Josephic tribes, approached the new king Rehoboam saying: "'Thy father made our yoke heavy. Now therefore lighten the hard service of thy father and his heavy yoke upon us, and we will serve thee.'" (1 K. 12:4) Rehoboam unwisely refused, and the North seceded, selecting as its own king their former taskmaster, Jeroboam.

It is likely, in view of the repetition of the story about vengeance wreaked upon Adoram/Adoniram in several different places in the Biblical text, taken with its being a part of the story of the secession of the North, that the House of David did indeed institute a corvée, not just among the descendants of the former owners of the land before the Hebrew Conquest who plainly had a second-class social status, but also among the Israelites themselves. We owe the preservation of this tradition to the anti-Davidic feelings that we have noted elsewhere in parts of *Samuel-Kings*.

The second passage quoted above (1 K. 9:20-22) is probably an idealization: the forced laborers have become exclusively the former inhabitants of Canaan whom the occupying Israelites had not been able to dispossess or slay.[2338] The Israelites are depicted as overlords and Solomon is thus totally exonerated. The passage reeks of later pro-Davidic propaganda with a double purpose: the removal of the stain of oppressing Israel from the now-idealized House of David whilst at the same time elevating the status of the later Jews by showing them as rulers and exploiters of other races in their brief period of glory under David and Solomon, instead of being ruled and exploited themselves.

As would be expected, the Chronicler, writing his version of the history of the building of the Temple, does not mention any Israelite forced labor, and he also takes pains to repudiate this charge against Solomon: "Then Solomon took a census of all the aliens who were in the land of Israel, after the census which David his father had taken; there were found a hundred and fifty-three thousand six hundred. Seventy thousand of them he assigned to bear burdens, eighty thousand to quarry in the hill country, and three thousand six hundred as overseers to make the people work." (2 Ch. 2:17-18)[2339] However, when writing of the reign of Solomon's son Rehoboam (2 Ch. 10:1-5), the Chronicler follows *Kings*, inconsistently repeating the same complaints of hard service and a heavy yoke upon the people during the reign of Solomon, thereby tacitly giving the lie to his earlier statements.

It would appear that these contradictions must be resolved in favor of the position that Solomon, and presumably David as well, although he is not credited with such vast building projects, did use a

---

[2338] This may be an incomplete picture, because there are good reasons to believe (e.g., the references to sparing the women of the conquered during the Conquest) that a considerable degree of mixture of the races—which were in any case for the most part related to the Israelites—had already taken place. Ethnic purity had not yet assumed the importance it was to attain in Jewish thinking in later times.

[2339] Once again, we are in the realm of impossibly inflated figures. The "153,600" refers to men capable of working, implying an alien population of at least 400,000.

corvée of Israelites as well as labor drafted from the non-Israelite inhabitants of Palestine. Perhaps they did not make any real distinction between Israelite and non-Israelite; as such a concept was probably the product of a later, more racially conscious age. Regardless of our present-day views on such an issue, there is no doubt that Solomon, following the example of virtually all his neighbors in the ancient world and, considering himself not the least of the rulers of his era, would not have deemed the procedure inherently unjust. There was as yet no coined money of a standard weight and purity (not until the Persian period)[2340] and revenues were largely in the form of bullion, services, and kind. The court, the cult, the standing army all required expensive maintenance on a scale unprecedented for Palestine.

Solomon's empire, it should be remembered, was largely the product of fortuity. The temporary exhaustion of the traditional centers of power, Egypt and Mesopotamia, the lack of interest by the Phoenicians in a land empire, and the military skills of David had all facilitated the Israelite expansion. Yet, the average Israelite probably had no such visions of grandeur, and did not benefit much from them, if at all. When the opportunity arose after the death of Solomon, Israel chose a less important role in world affairs and a reduced burden of central government. (Many living in our own age can sympathize with such feelings, that less is more.)

In *Kings*, there is still more information about those involved in the construction of Solomon's palace and the adjoining Temple at Jerusalem: "So Solomon's builders and Hiram's builders and the men of Gebal[2341] did the hewing and prepared the timber and the stone to build the house." (1 K. 5:18) These skilled Phoenician workers could not have been from Solomon's levies, and we know that he paid King Hiram of Tyre[2342] for their services (1 K. 5:10-11). In addition, in the 20th year of his reign, Solomon was apparently still in debt to Hiram, because after the completion of the palace and the Temple, he repaid the debt by giving Hiram twenty cities in Galilee.[2343]

The belief that there was non-human participation in the construction of the Temple, though not directly based upon any Biblical

---

[2340] Money, DB, p. 670.

[2341] Gebal is the modern Jubayl, or Byblos, in Lebanon. (Gebal, DB, p. 318.) Jubayl was the port most convenient to the rich cedar forests of northern Mount Lebanon, a few groves of which still survive there.

[2342] The Phoenician port city of Tyre was the paramount city of the Phoenicians at that time. (Hiram, EJ, VIII, 500-501.)

[2343] Hiram, who visited the cities (read: villages) on an inspection tour, is reported as having felt that he got the short end of the bargain (1 K. 9:10-14).

statement, is found in Jewish rabbinical writings and in the pre-Islamic *Testament of Solomon*. According to the latter, after Solomon had received the Ring from the angel Michael (see above), Solomon summoned the demons and using the ring's power vanquished them one by one and compelled them to aid in the construction of the Temple.[2344] "Ornias, the vampire spirit who had maltreated Solomon's servant, was the first demon to appear, and he was set to the task of cutting stones near the Temple. And Solomon bade Ornias come, and he gave him the seal, saying: 'Away with thee, and bring me hither the prince of all the demons.'

"Ornias took the finger-ring, and went to Beelzeboul, who has kingship over the demons. He said to him: 'Hither! Solomon calls thee.' But Beelzeboul, having heard, said to him: 'Tell me, who is this Solomon of whom thou speakest to me?' Then Ornias threw the ring at the chest of Beezeboul, saying: Solomon the king calls thee.' But Beelzeboul cried aloud with a mighty voice, and shot out a great, burning flame of fire, and he arose and followed Ornias, and came to Solomon. Brought before the king, he promised him to gather all the unclean spirits unto him... Solomon bade them dig the foundations of the Temple, for the length of it was two hundred and fifty cubits.[2345] And he ordered them to be industrious, and with one united murmur of protest they began to perform the tasks enjoined..."

The demons also supplied skilled labor: "A hound-like spirit, whose name was Rabdos, followed, and he revealed to Solomon a green stone, useful for the adornment of the Temple. A number of other male and female demons appeared, among them the thirty-six world-rulers of darkness, whom Solomon commanded to fetch water to the Temple. Some of these demons he condemned to do the heavy work on the construction of the Temple, others he shut up in prison, and others, again, he ordered to wrestle with fire in the making of gold and silver, sitting down by lead and spoon, and to make ready places for the other demons, in which they should be confined."[2346]

A tradition in the pre-Islamic 6th-century *Songs Rabbah* limits Solomon's dominion over the demons to the period of the construction of the Temple.[2347] Obviously, such spectacular traditions were known in the

---

[2344] LJ, IV, 150.

[2345] About 375 ft., a substantial work, but a far cry from Surabadi's three miles.

[2346] LJ, IV, 151-152. The date of the *Testament of Solomon* is uncertain, but it is pre-Islamic. Internal evidence suggests that it was written between 100 and 300 CE. (Solomon, Testament of. EJ, XV, pp. 118-119.)

[2347] LJ, VI, 291.

pre-Islamic Age of Ignorance in Arabia and stand behind the more sober allusions in the Quran to the "devils" who participated in Solomon's works.[2348]

THE TEMPLE: Surabadi's reference to the mosque "three parasangs square" that Solomon ordered to be constructed is of course to be identified with the Temple at Jerusalem, his most famous building project (but not his largest; that was his own palace). It was not built of metal, although a prodigious amount of metal went into its furnishings, as we shall see.

Jerusalem was the last of the major sanctuaries of YHWH worship established in Palestine. It was destined from the very beginning to be the most important, because it combined the prestige of the Davidic monarchy with the zeal of the centralized cult of YHWH. In a sense, without this centralization, absolute monotheism may never have come to replace Israel's henotheism. Before its capture, Jerusalem housed a sanctuary to El Elyon (God Most High),[2349] but the exact location of that shrine is unknown. Under David, YHWH assimilated the attributes of El Elyon and perhaps the latter deity's priesthood as well.[2350] However, a new foundation story had to be provided to account for the association of YHWH with the Jerusalem sanctuary.

It is not known where David established the Ark and the Tabernacle when he brought them to Jerusalem, but it was certainly not the site of the future Temple of Solomon (the present Haram). That was purchased by David late in his reign in order to erect an altar. In the last chapter of *Samuel* (2 Sam. 24), we are given an account of the theophany that occasioned the sanctification of the spot. For some unexplained reason, God was angered by Israel, and in punishment, He ordered David to take a census of the people. This may seem a strange divine punishment, but apparently, the census carried with it the implications of compulsory military service, the corvée mentioned above, and (perhaps

---

[2348] Rationalist explanations for these references in the Quran cited earlier in this section, though of interest, are based upon the assumption that the stories in the Quran must be interpreted as literal truth, whereas the real purpose may be allegorical and parabolic, not historical. Such wonders and miracles were alluded to because they were in general part of the oral literature and belief system of the time, and even now, their lessons affect us. Notwithstanding a belief in the miraculous, people are not restrained from neglecting God and His justice in their behavior and dealings. They believe in God's power, but do they truly believe in His omniscience?

[2349] God, DB, p. 335.

[2350] de Vaux, II, p. 310.

even worse) taxation.[2351] The taking of this census apparently met with great resistance and possibly bloodshed.[2352]

Though God Himself had ordered the census (2 Sam. 24:1), He is inexplicably shown as punishing Israel for the arrogance of having conducted it (2 Sam. 24:10-15): "So the Lord sent a pestilence upon Israel from the morning until the appointed time; and there died of the people from Dan to Beersheba[2353] seventy thousand men. And when the angel stretched forth his hand toward Jerusalem to destroy it, the Lord repented of the evil, and said to the angel who was working destruction among the people, 'It is enough; now stay thy hand.' And the angel of the Lord was by the threshing floor Araunah the Jebusite. Then David spoke to the Lord when he saw the angel was smiting the people, and said, 'Lo, I have sinned, I have done wickedly; but these sheep, what have they done? Let thy hand, I pray thee, be against me and against my father's house.'" (2 Sam. 24:15-17)

This story of the stemming of YHWH's murderous rage established the sanctity of the site of the future Temple of Solomon. "And Gad[2354] came that day to David, and said to him, 'Go up, rear an altar to the Lord on the threshing floor of Araunah the Jebusite.'"[2355] (2 Sam. 24:18) After some negotiation—Araunah wanted to donate the site, but David insisted upon paying for it—"David bought the threshing floor and the oxen for fifty shekels of silver. And David built there an altar to the Lord, and offered burnt offerings and peace offerings. So the Lord heeded supplication for the land, and the plague was averted from Israel." (2 Sam. 24:24-25)

Once again, we seem to have *two* different foundation stories, this time concerning the sanctification of the threshing floor of Araunah. In one, the angel was restrained from destroying Jerusalem and David built the altar to commemorate this event on the spot where he saw God. In the other, the altar was erected in a place designated by the prophet Gad. Because of the sacrifices and worship there by David, the plague

---

[2351] Consider the effect of the *Domesday Book* ordered by William the Conqueror in England, 1085-6 CE.

[2352] BC, III, 143-144. The figures given as the result of this census, 800,000 fighting men in Israel and 500,000) in Judah (2 Sam. 24:9) are not considered reliable. (Trawick-OT, p. 110.)

[2353] "Dan to Beersheba": the traditional north-south extent of Biblical Israel.

[2354] Gad was a prophet or seer who advised David. Among other things, he brought the divine condemnation of the census that God *Himself* had ordered and recommended the construction of the altar on threshing floor of Araunah. This place was also called, possibly spuriously, Mount Moriah in the Bible. (Moriah, DB, pp. 674-675.)

[2355] It is interesting to note that though Jebus had been conquered, the Jebusites still survived in the new Jerusalem.

was averted from Jerusalem.[2356] In any event, when compared with other theophanies on mountains (Moses on Mount Horeb, Abraham's Sacrifice, Elijah on Mount Carmel) this foundation story is neither striking nor adequate. Since the place had no previous history as a shrine,[2357] it probably was not the shrine of El Elyon, unless this fact has been suppressed. Indeed, in later times, the sacrifice of Abraham was transferred there in order to create the impression of hoary sanctity and to enhance the authority of the Jerusalem Temple, thus adding the sacrifice to the dubious tradition linking Abraham with Jerusalem recorded in Gen. 14:18-20.[2358]

Considering the importance David gave to YHWH-worship, the establishment of its central shrine in Jerusalem, and its identification with his dynasty, the question naturally arises: Why did David himself not build a temple there? The Bible gives us three answers:

1. After bringing the Ark to Jerusalem and establishing his rule, David is shown contemplating the construction of a Temple for the Ark and YHWH's residence. "Now when the king dwelt in his house and the Lord had given him rest from all his enemies round about, the king said to Nathan the prophet, 'See now, I dwell in a house of cedar, but the ark of God dwells in a tent.'" (2 Sam. 7:1-2)

At first, Nathan agreed with this proposal to build a temple, "but that same night the word of the Lord came to Nathan, 'Go and tell my servant David, "Thus says the Lord: Wouldst thou build Me a house to dwell in? I have not dwelt in a house since the day I brought up the people of Israel from Egypt to this day, but I have been moving about in a tent for My dwelling. In all places were I have moved with the people of Israel, did I speak a word with any of the judges of Israel... saying, 'Why have ye not built Me a house of cedar?'" Now therefore thus thou shalt say to My servant David, "Thus says the Lord of Hosts, I took thee from the pasture... that thou shouldst be prince over My people Israel; and I have been with thee wherever thou didst go... When thy days are fulfilled and thou liest with thy fathers, I shall raise up thy offspring after thee, who shall come for thee from thy body, and I will establish his

---

[2356] There were other shrines in the immediate region of Jerusalem. Of them, Gihon and En-rogel were certainly older than that of the Temple Mount, although it would soon eclipse them all. (Smith, p. 489.)

[2357] Or perhaps that is what the ancient editors want us to believe.

[2358] In which Abraham is involved in a covenantal relationship with Melchizedek, the king and high priest of Salem (most probably to be identified with Jebus/Jerusalem; Salem, DB, pp. 877-878). Sarna feels that the story was invented in order to give the Temple site greater antiquity and an association with Abraham. (Sarna, p. 117.)

kingdom. He shall build a house for My Name, and I will establish the throne of his kingdom for ever.""" (2 Sam. 7:4-9,12-13)

Although this passage is frequently interpreted to mean that God's worship should not be restricted to one place and as a polemic against institutionalized religion, the text really does not justify such conclusions.[2359] God seems to be saying that before the Exodus and the choice of Israel as His people, He *did* live in a house (read: a temple, perhaps on Mount Horeb), and that in the future He would again. This, however, is ordained to be accomplished in the days of Solomon, not David—and the wording suggests that the passage dates from after the reign of Solomon, before the breakup of the kingdom under Rehoboam, because of the references to the establishment of the kingdom "for ever" would have been inappropriate at a later time. Scholars attribute the shape of this passage to the Deuteronomist (D) writing in the first half of the 6th century BCE. No reason is given for the postponement of the construction of the Temple, and the passage is probably an attempt to justify the historical reality that David had not built the Temple, citing a supposed divine prohibition, and not because of any deficiency in his zeal for YHWH.

2. In *Kings*, a different interpretation of David's inactivity is put into the mouth of Solomon: When planning to build the Temple, he said to Hiram of Tyre: "'Thou knowest that David my father could not build a house for the name of the Lord his God because of the warfare with which his enemies surrounded him, until the Lord put them under the soles of his feet'" (1 K. 5:3) In other words, David was too busy with wars and pacification to attend to the matter of building the Temple in Jerusalem, despite the statement quoted above that David had found rest from all his enemies.

3. In *Chronicles*, David is not allowed to build the Temple because of all the blood he had shed. "Then (David) called for Solomon his son and charged him to build a house for the Lord, the God of Israel... 'I had it in my heart to build a house to the name of the Lord my God. But the word of the Lord came to me, saying, "thou hast shed much blood and hast waged great wars; thou shalt not build a house to My name, because thou hast shed so much blood before Me upon the earth. Behold a son shall be born to thee; he shall be a man of peace from all his enemies round about; and his name shall be Solomon... He shall build a house for My name."'" (1 Ch. 22:6-10) In another place, the Chronicler relates: "But God said to me (David), 'Thou mayest not build

---

[2359] BC, III, 103.

a house for My name, for thou art a warrior and hast shed blood.'" (1 Ch. 28:3)

This last is a much later interpretation of why David did not build the Temple, and it ignores the fact that God's approval of David's military exploits, recorded in *Samuel*, was unequivocal. Nonetheless, apparently the Chronicler did not consider this excuse sufficient, and he also involved David further in the matter of Temple by writing that David had actually commenced the preparation of the building materials in order to assist his son, though he knew that he would not have the honor of completing the building himself:

"David commanded to gather together the aliens [non-Israelite indigenous Canaanites] who were in the land of Israel, and he set stonecutters to prepare dressed stones for building the house of God. David also provided great stores of iron for nails for the doors of the gates and for clamps, as well as bronze in quantities beyond weighing, and cedar timbers without number; for the Sidonians and the Tyrians brought great quantities of cedar to David. For David said, 'Solomon my son is young and inexperienced, and the house that is to be built for the Lord must be exceedingly magnificent, of fame and glory throughout all lands; I will therefore make preparations for it.' So David provided materials in great quantity before his death." (1 Ch. 22:2-5)

This tradition is certainly unhistorical, and is designed both to associate the prestige of David with the Temple, thereby enhancing its glory, and at the same time to answer the charge of inaction in such an important undertaking that would inevitably be brought by later generations (and probably was; hence the passage in *Chronicles*). In passing, it also exonerates David of instituting forced labor among the Israelites.

The real answer to our question is probably quite different. David was a divinely chosen leader, a poet, and a warrior. He was believed to have been divinely inspired, a kind of prophet in the sense that Muslims use this term. Regardless of any lapses or imperfections, his basic zeal for YHWH is unquestionable. That YHWH-worship was a useful tool in building a national identity, and therefore politically expedient, cannot be denied; but David's faith cannot be dismissed simply as realpolitik or opportunism. In our modern cynical era, we seem to expect too little from our leaders, whilst expecting too much from our heroes. The reason David did not build a Temple for YHWH was that he simply did not see the need for one.

David was from the pastoral tribe of Judah, it must be remembered. By the time of David, about two centuries after the

Conquest, the Northern tribes had already become a farming peasantry and were more influenced by the agriculturally-oriented religious practices of the earlier Canaanite agricultural cults, as well as their neighbors to the north and east. They had taken the anciently established shrines and usurped many of them for their own somewhat syncretistic YHWH-worship. Livestock and herding were secondary to the cultivation of the land.

On the other hand, settled agriculture was of secondary importance to herding in Judah, south of Jerusalem where the soil was poorer and rainfall scantier. The numerous references to David as a former shepherd cannot be ignored if we would understand the manner of his expression of his religious beliefs.[2360] Because of the migratory nature of pastoralism, fixed shrines have less importance than in farming communities, and they tend to be simpler and ruder, partly because the herdsmen are usually poorer and the population base supporting the shrines is smaller, and also because the shrines are left unguarded and untended for long periods of time. Portable shrines were a feature of the Semitic world, particularly in its less settled areas. The Ark of the Covenant was originally such a portable shrine. The conservatism of religious belief and custom is well known, and David would have seen no reason to change the traditional symbols of YHWH carried over from the time when He was worshipped by the wandering tribes: the portable Ark, and the tent Tabernacle.

However, once he had become king and established a fixed court, he erected a "house of cedar" for himself; an inevitable consequence of this change of the manner of living would be the urge to erect a Temple for the now-settled YHWH. Though David would have been content with the open-air worship of his ancestors, Solomon, born in the capital and far more exposed to the influences and practices of neighboring kingdoms such as Egypt and Phoenicia, as well as the growing sophistication of the court and priesthood, would have been far

---

[2360] The most famous of the Davidic psalms takes its beautiful imagery from the pastoral life:

"The Lord is my shepherd, I shall not want;
He maketh me to lie down in green pastures.
He leadeth me beside the still waters;
    He restoreth my soul.
He leadeth me in the paths of righteousness
    for His name's sake.
Yea, though I walk through the valley of the shadow of death,
    I will fear no evil;
For Thou art with me;
    Thy rod and Thy staff they comfort me." (Ps. 23:1-4)

more likely to conceive the plan to provide a home for the cult of YHWH comparable to the temples of Egypt, Syria, and Mesopotamia. It would also serve to advertise his power, taste, and wealth.

And so it happened. The writers of the Bible, perplexed by this strange omission in the career of David, tried to discover reasons for David's not building such a natural necessity as a Temple, as it would have seemed to them in a more settled age. They did not understand the environment in which David had lived and saw only their own idealization of him. The transformation of a semi-pastoral people from southern Palestine into a more settled population with more elaborate religious and administrative apparatus belonged to a vaguely understood past.

To the people of Judah at the time David, a permanent Temple was an exotic novelty, faintly improper because of the association of the idea with the heathen temples of the Egyptian and Canaanite deities. For the parvenu generation of Solomon, however, the question would be: Why should YHWH not have a dwelling commensurate with His status as the national God of the new Israelite kingdom? Did not YHWH, living in a mere tent, reflect adversely upon the splendor of the united Israelite kingdom when the gods of the rest of the world lived in great temples of stone? Solomon set about to remove this reproach from his kingdom.

Solomon, who had good relations with Hiram the king of Tyre, wrote to him, "'And now I purpose to build a house for the name of the Lord my God, as the Lord said to David my father, "Thy son, whom I will set upon thy throne in thy place, shall build the House for My name." Now therefore command that cedars of Lebanon be cut for me; and my servants will join thy servants, and I will pay thee for thy servants such wages as thou shalt set; for thou knowest that there is no one among us who knows how to cut timber like the Sidonians.'" (1 K. 5:5-6)

Hiram agreed to provide the cedar and cypress needed for the Temple and to send carpenters with the wood. Solomon raised a levy of labor from among his own subjects, numbering 30,000 men. "Solomon also had 70,000 burden-bearers and 80,000 hewers of stone in the hill country, beside Solomon's 3,300 chief officers who were over the work... At the king's command, they quarried out great, costly stones in order to lay the foundation of the house with dressed stones." (1 K. 5:15-17)

While Surabadi speaks of a mosque "one parasang square," a fantastic exaggeration, the size of the real Temple, despite its great fame, was considerably more modest: "The House which Solomon built for the

Lord was sixty cubits [90 ft.] long,[2361] twenty cubits [30 ft.] wide, and thirty cubits [45 ft.] high. The vestibule in front of the nave of the house was twenty cubits [30 ft.] long, equal to the width of the house, and ten cubits [15 ft.] deep in front of the house." (1 K .6:2-3)

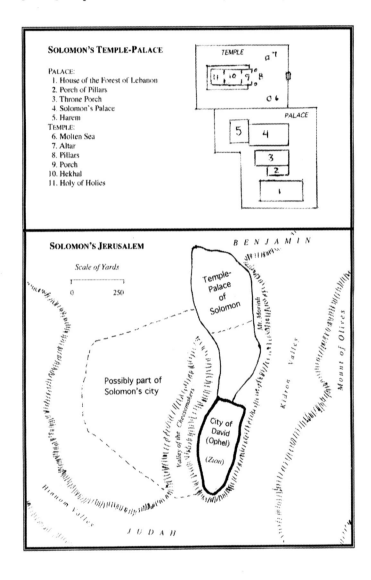

SOLOMON'S TEMPLE-PALACE

PALACE:
1. House of the Forest of Lebanon
2. Porch of Pillars
3. Throne Porch
4. Solomon's Palace
5. Harem
TEMPLE:
6. Molten Sea
7. Altar
8. Pillars
9. Porch
10. Hekhal
11. Holy of Holies

TEMPLE

PALACE

SOLOMON'S JERUSALEM

Scale of Yards

0   250

BENJAMIN

Temple-Palace of Solomon

Mt. Moriah

Kidron Valley

Mount of Olives

Possibly part of Solomon's city

Valley of the Cheesemakers

City of David (Ophel)

(Zion)

Hinnom Valley

JUDAH

[2361] These conversions from cubits to feet are approximate. By way of comparison, the Ka'bah at Makkah measures about 35' x 40' and is some 50' high (Ka'ba, SEI, p. 191).

Techniques of prefabrication were used in the construction, apparently for ritual reasons: "When the house was built, it was with the stone prepared at the quarry; so that neither hammer nor axes nor any tool of iron was heard in the temple, while it was being built." (1 K. 6:7)

The interior of the Temple was elaborately decorated and paneled with cedar wood. "The inner sanctuary was twenty cubits [30 ft.] long, twenty cubits [30 ft.] wide, and twenty cubits [30 ft.] high; and (Solomon overlaid it with pure gold, and he drew chains of gold across, in front of the inner sanctuary, and overlaid it with gold." (1 K. 6:20-21) It may be thus seen that the inner sanctuary, the Holy of Holies, was a cube. As the sacred Ka'bah at Makkah is also roughly a cube, we can only speculate upon a possible relationship in the use of this geometric form.[2362]

Two large cherubim were carved from olivewood and plated with gold, and the doors of the sanctuary were also of olivewood overlaid with gold. Though Surabadi says the construction was in progress when Solomon died, according to the Bible the Temple was completed in seven years (1 K. 6:37-38).[2363]

After the fabric of the building had been completed, "King Solomon sent and brought Hiram from Tyre. He was the son of a widow of the tribe of Naphtali, and his father was a man of Tyre, a worker in bronze; and he was full of wisdom, understanding, and skill, for making any kind of work in bronze. He came to King Solomon and did all his work." (1 K. 7:13-14) Hiram of Tyre (not to be confused with the king of Tyre of the same name) is thus at least a part of the Sakhr of Surabadi's commentary. In *Chronicles*, probably under the influence of the story of Bezalel who built the Tabernacle and its furnishings for Moses (Ex. 31:6), Hiram's role (in *Chronicles* he is called Huramabi) is expanded and his mother is from the tribe of Dan (as was Bezalel), instead of the tribe of Naphtali.[2364] The Chronicler, quoting a probably fabricated letter

---

[2362] A deity was worshipped in Petra by the Nabataeans (during the Roman era) in the form of a black cube-shaped rock. (Hachette, p. 565.)

[2363] By comparison, it took Solomon 13 years to complete his own palace (1 Kg. 7:1).

[2364] The Biblical insistence that his mother was an Israelite may be historical, or it may be explained by the desire of the ethnically motivated writers and redactors of the Hebrew scriptures to claim the artisan Hiram as a Jew, such status being determined by the race of the mother, not the father, in Jewish custom. The close connection of a non-believer and, what was just as bad or worse, a non-Israelite, with the construction and furnishing of the Temple may have seemed embarrassing in later times. The Israelites of the time of David and Solomon (as their many marriages to non-Israelites demonstrate) were probably not much concerned by such questions. One of David's ancestresses (his great-grandmother) was Ruth, a woman of Moab (Ruth 1:4)).

from King Hiram of Tyre to Solomon, gives us an enlarged catalogue of Hiram the artisan's skills: "'Now I have sent a skilled man, endued with understanding, Hurambi [Hiram in *Kings*], the son of a woman of the daughters of Dan, and his father was a man of Tyre. He is trained to work in gold, silver, bronze, iron, stone, and wood, and in purple, blue, and crimson fabrics and fine linen, and to do all sorts of engraving and execute any design that may be assigned him with thy craftsmen, the craftsmen of my lord, David thy father.'" (2 Ch. 2:13-14) In this, Hiram/Hurambi is beginning to approach the role Surabadi has given to Sakhr.

Although Hiram is not reporting building a mosque of copper for Solomon, his recorded accomplishments in metallurgy were sufficiently prodigious to give rise to such a legend. The interior of the temple was overlaid with gold, and presumably Hiram was in charge of the work.[2365] Among the more impressive of Hiram's artifacts were:

1. The Pillars of Bronze: "He cast two pillars of bronze. Eighteen cubits [27 ft.] was the height of one pillar, and a line of twelve cubits [18 ft.] measured the circumference[2366]; it was hollow, and its thickness was four fingers, and the second pillar was the same. He also made the tops of the pillars; the height of one capital was five cubits [7.5 ft.] and the height of the other capital was five cubits." (1 K.7: 15-16) The Chronicler gives the height of the pillars as an improbable 35 cubits (52.5 ft.) in 2 Ch. 3:35.

2. The altar: "He made an altar of bronze, twenty cubits [30 ft.] long, and twenty cubits [30 ft.] wide, and ten cubits [15 ft.] high." This is found only in the Chronicler (2 Ch. 4:1). The corresponding passage of in *Kings* appears to be missing. The altar was in the court outside of the shrine itself.

3. The molten sea: "then he made the molten sea; it was round, ten cubits [15 ft.] from brim to brim, and five cubits [7.5 ft.] high... It stood upon twelve oxen... Its thickness was a handbreadth; and its brim was made like the brim of a cup, like the flower of a lily; it held two thousand baths [18,000 gallons]." (1 K. 7:23-26) The Chronicler agrees with these figures, except that he gives the capacity as 3,000 baths [27,000 gallons] instead of 2,000 (2 Ch. 4:2-5). Some Muslim commentators, rejecting the story of a literal source of copper bubbling out of the earth that is frequently repeated by traditional commentaries, including Surabadi, suggest that this was the Fount of Molten Brass

---

[2365] The "he" in 2 Ch. 3:4-4:10 must refer to Hiram, not to Solomon, because 4:11 begins "Huram [Hiram] also made the pots..."

[2366] Or a diameter of something over 5.5 ft.

referred to in the Quran (Q. 34:12, quoted above). The following verse surely refers to these works (and others not enumerated) of Hiram/Sakhr. This view of Muhammad Ali and Yusuf Ali is the not at all unreasonable.[2367]

After an inventory of Hiram's work for Solomon in *Kings*, there is a note on their manufacture: "Now the pots, the shovels, and the basins, all these vessels of the house of the Lord, which Hiram made for King Solomon, were of burnished bronze. In the plain of the Jordan the king cast them, in the clay ground between Succoth and Zarethan. And Solomon left all these vessels unweighed, because there were so many of them; the weight of the bronze was not found out." (1 K. 7:45-47) Of course, Solomon did not personally cast them; he ordered them to be cast by Hiram.

Jewish tradition tells us that during the seven years the Temple was a-building, not a single workmen fell sick or died. After the dedication of the Temple, however, they all died off lest they build such a marvelous temple for the heathens and their gods. Hiram/Huramabi was rewarded by being allowed to enter paradise alive.[2368] The *Pesikta Rabbati* (8th or 9th century CE, but the same tradition is found in the pre-Islamic *Songs Rabbah*) says that the Temple built itself, with the stones breaking loose from the quarries and arranging themselves in courses at the construction site.[2369]

The splendor which Solomon bestowed upon the Temple and its furnishings was not destined to remain long undisturbed. Within five years of the death of its builder, it was looted by the Egyptians (1 K. 14:25). Nebuchadnezzar of Babylon 586 BCE finally demolished it, about 350 years after it had been built.

SOLOMON'S PALACE: Although there is no Quranic basis for his story, in order to enhance Solomon's reputation for opulence, Surabadi also relates the construction of a jeweled palace for Solomon. After Solomon had conquered the devils, he wanted to keep them busy with hard work such as building, warfare, weaving, pearling and diving for jewels. His household [read: womenfolk] wanted a palace, so Solomon ordered the devils to secure the necessary jewels. After they had done so, they built a jeweled palace 100 cubits (150 ft, or 15 storeys high), with

---

[2367] Quran-MMA, pp. 824-825; Quran-Yusuf Ali, pp. 1136-1137.
[2368] LJ, IV, 155.
[2369] LJ, VI, 295.

100 women to a storey. Like the carpet Shadurwan,[2370] it would also fly when the court was on the move.[2371]

The more fantastic features of this tale have no parallel in the Biblical sources about Solomon; however, the building of his palace is described. Though the Bible emphasizes the Temple (for religious reason), Solomon's personal residence was a considerably more impressive complex than that which he constructed to be YHWH's dwelling. When David made Jerusalem his capital, he built a royal residence of which no description remains for us, although *Samuel* states: "and Hiram king of Tyre sent messengers to David, and cedar trees, also carpenters and masons who built David's house." (2 Sam. 6:11) It must have been modest in comparison with the palace his son Solomon planned to build, again with the help of Hiram's skilled workmen.

Despite its fame, the City of David, or Jerusalem, during the reign of David (according to the best archeological estimates), had an area of only about 1500 ft. by 400 ft., that is, less than 15-17 acres.[2372] Considering the unsettled conditions of the times and the fact that Araunah's threshing floor was only about a 300 yds. north of the northern wall of the Davidic city, it is unlikely that there were densely populated suburbs around the city in David's time, but rather open farming, pasture, and orchards. The population within the walls probably did not exceed 2,000, the population of a large Near Eastern village of the present era.[2373]

Whilst there is general agreement about the approximate location of the walls of the City of David, there is considerably more dispute about the limits of Jerusalem during the reign of Solomon. Estimates vary from about 50 to 165 acres, indicating a population within the walls of between 5,000 and 18,000. Perhaps an even lower figure should be preferred because of the relatively large area of the city within the walls taken up by the Palace-Temple complex, which itself covered about 12.5 acres. Albright estimates that during the later monarchy, Jerusalem and

---

[2370] See Section F below.

[2371] Surabadi, pp. 369-370.

[2372] See OBA, p. 81; ABL, p. 30.

[2373] "The walled town of classical times covered 50-150 acres; a density of 100 inhabitants to the acre is a reasonable assumption though probably a slightly lower figure would be indicated for Western Europe and a slightly higher one for the Near East." In the 9th century BCE (a century after Solomon), the largest cities in the world were: Memphis (Egypt), Tyre (Phoenicia), and Babylon, Nimrud, and Nineveh (all in Mesopotamia). Despite the exaggerations of later writers, the largest—Nineveh—probably contained no more than 100,000 people in its 7th-century BCE heyday. Gaza, Sidon, Samaria, and Damascus were in the 10-15,000 range. (McEvedy-AH, p. 44.)

its suburbs had a population of about 50,000.[2374] This is probably too high, and it was certainly less at the time of Solomon.

Later ages delighted in recounting the splendors of Solomon's Temple, but his Palace was at best looked upon as a symbol of Israel's departed glory, and at worst a sinful vanity.[2375] Considering this disapproval, it is not surprising that the Chronicler, in his account of Solomon's reign, skips right over the building of the palace, with no mention of its construction. We must turn to the earlier writers of *Kings* for a description of the palace which, while not so tall and unable to fly, in other ways justifies many of Surabadi's extravagant traditions about it.

"Solomon was building his own house thirteen years, and he finished his house." (1 K. 7:1) Note that the palace took nearly twice as long to build as the Temple. "He built the House of the Forest of Lebanon; its length was a hundred cubits [150 ft.] and its breadth fifty cubits [75 ft.], and its height thirty cubits [45 ft.], and it was built upon three rows of cedar pillars, with cedar beams upon the pillars." (1 K. 7:2) They were arranged in three rows of 15 pillars each.[2376] The dimensions of the House of the Forest of Lebanon alone exceeded the Temple of YHWH by 50% and covered two and a half times its area.

"And he made the Hall of Pillars, its length was fifty cubits [75 ft.] and its breadth thirty cubits [45 ft.]; there was a porch in front with pillars, and a canopy before them. And he made the Hall of the Throne

---

[2374] Albright-Ab to Ez, p. 105.

[2375] Solomon's marriage to a daughter of Pharaoh does not seem to have influenced his palace project. Despite the popular impression to the contrary, Egyptian homes and even palaces were built largely of simple and perishable materials: mud brick, plaster, and wood. From the entire period of 3,000 years of pharaonic history, not one palace of stone (except those ceremonial structures built for the dead) remains. Permanent construction in stone and baked brick was reserved almost exclusively for temple and tombs, and the occasional public works where the strength and permanence of stone was necessary. The gods and the dead were housed magnificently, but the absolute despot of Upper and Lower Egypt, the god-king, lived in compounds which, except in a few cases where archeologists have been able to painstakingly trace their foundations of mud, have completely disappeared; melted back into the earth. In building his palace, Solomon was once again demonstrating the cultural affinity of Palestine with the western Fertile Crescent where housing of stone was common, and at the same time its curious obliviousness to the material and religious culture of Egypt.

[2376] This great 10th century BCE House of the Forest of Lebanon may be compared with the equally famous 5th century BCE Hall of a Hundred Columns (destroyed by Alexander the Great's vandalism) built by Xerxes and his successor Artaxerxes I, the ruins of which are still extant at Persepolis in Iran. It measured almost 250 ft. square (more than an acre), and the 100 columns are arranged in ten rows of ten columns each. Though Solomon's edifice was considerably smaller, it must have been similarly impressive.

where he was to pronounce judgment, even the Hall of Judgment; it was finished with cedar from floor to rafters. His own house where he was to dwell, in the other court back of the hall, was of like workmanship. Solomon also made a house like this hall for Pharaoh's daughter whom he had taken in marriage." (1 K. 7:6-8) This also was considerably larger than the Temple.

"All these were made of costly stones, hewn according to measure, sawn with saws, back and front, even from the foundation to the coping, and from the court of the house of the Lord to the great court. The foundation was of costly stones, huge stones, stones of eight and ten cubits [12 and 15 ft.]. And above were costly stones, hewn according to measurement, and cedar. The great court had three courses of hewn stones round about, and a course of cedar beams; so had the inner court of the house of the Lord, and the vestibule of the house." (1 K. 7:9-12) Thus, the Temple and the Palace were juxtaposed, and the Temple, though open to the public, had also the characteristics of a royal chapel. The palace occupied nearly 60% of the complex area on Mount Moriah north of the City of David.[2377]

Ezekiel, in his vision of the new temple, protests the proximity of the palace, and it has no part in his New Jerusalem. "And the house of Israel shall no longer defile My holy name, neither they, nor their kings, by their harlotry, and by the dead bodies of their kings, by setting their threshold by My threshold and their doorposts beside My doorposts, with only a wall between Me and them..." (Ezek. 43:7-8) This passage would seem to indicate that the kings of Judah were buried in the complex, although no trace of this has been found. In any case, "there is now no trace of the houses built by David and Solomon."[2378] YHWH has had His wish fulfilled and whole area is now dedicated to the worship of the One God.

Nonetheless, Solomon's palace must have been a truly impressive building. The visitor would first have entered the House of the Forest of Lebanon, a hall 150' wide and half as deep, its high ceiling

---

[2377] The present-day Haram al-Sharif in Jerusalem occupies roughly all of this area, but is extended to the north and northeast. The Temple was probably located just west of the Dome of the Rock. The al-Aqsa Mosque occupies the presumed site of the House of the Forest of Lebanon, the Hall of the Pillars, and the Hall of the Throne. The palace area covered about 10 acres, while the Temple and its courts took up about 5 acres of the site. There was direct access from the Palace to the Temple, and the Temple must have functioned (at least in part) as a royal chapel. For comparison, the (ritual?) complex of Persepolis (*Takht-e Jamshīd*) begun some 450 years later covers about 35 acres, roughly twice the size of the City of David.

[2378] Palace, DB, p. 717.

supported by 45 cedar columns, doubtless brightly painted and glowing with gilt. The walls were adorned with 500 shields of gold, 200 large and 300 small (1 K. 10:16-17). Passing through another hall, the Hall of Pillars, about half the size of the Hall of the Forest of Lebanon, one entered the throne room, the Hall of Judgment, paneled with carved and painted cedarwood and housing at one end Solomon's fabulous ivory throne, overlaid with gold. "The throne had six steps, and on each side of the seat were arm rests and two lions standing beside the arm rests, while twelve lions stood there, one on each end of a step on the six steps. The like of it was never made in any kingdom." (1 K. 10:18-20) It was doubtless in this hall that Solomon's famous encounter with the queen of Sheba took place. (See Section J below.) In addition to the Temple and the Palace, Solomon is also recorded as building and fortifying cities throughout his kingdom, including extensive works on the walls of Jerusalem (1 K. 9:15-19; 2 Ch. 8:3-6).

As in the case of the Temple, the splendor of Solomon's palace was short-lived. "In the fifth year of King Rehoboam, Shishak king of Egypt came up against Jerusalem; he took away the treasures of the house of the Lord and the treasures of the king's house; he took away everything. He also took away all the shields of gold which Solomon had made; and King Rehoboam made in their stead shields of bronze, and committed them to the hands of the officers of the guard, who kept the door of the king's house. And as often as the king went into the house of the Lord, the guard bore them and brought them back to the guardroom." (1 K. 14:25-28)

Though the descendants of David and Solomon were able to cling to their tiny kingdom for another several centuries, the glory of Solomon had flared but briefly, like a meteor, and then vanished forever. *Sic transit gloria mundi.*[2379]

D. SOLOMON'S WEALTH

Oh, the curse of being so rich! —Horace (65-8 BCE)

Quranic verses such as: *So when (the envoy) came unto Solomon, (Solomon) said: "What! Would ye help me with wealth? But that which God has given me is better than that which He has given you. But it is ye who exult in your gift."* (Q. 27:36) and: *This is Our gift, so bestow thou, or withhold, without reckoning,* (Q. 38:30) are usually taken to refer at least in part to Solomon's fabulous material wealth, although they are

---

[2379] *Sic transit gloria mundi* (Latin): *Thus passeth the glory of the world.*

capable of other more spiritual interpretations as well. In his stories of Solomon, Surabadi accepts the reports of Solomon's immense wealth and refers to it directly and indirectly in several places.[2380] The Talmud also notes it, though with a disapproval not unmixed with admiration (and exaggeration): "(Solomon) kept many horses, which a Jewish king ought not to do, and, what the law holds in equal abhorrence, he amassed much silver and gold. Under Solomon's rule silver and gold were so abundant among the people that their utensils were made of them instead of the baser metals." In another place we are told that Solomon's wealth came to him in a remarkable fashion: The sea cast up for Solomon everything of value that had ever been lost or thrown into it.[2381]

The unusual circumstances that permitted the expansion of the Israelite kingdom also gave it temporary control over much of the land commerce of the ancient world. Despite the political decline of Egypt and Mesopotamia, there was still considerable trade, and both the Phoenicians cities with their sea-trade and Solomon with his land-trade prospered greatly. That the Phoenicians and the Israelites were partners rather than rivals was profitable to both parties. Their energies and income were not exhausted in military adventures and posturing against each other. Given these conditions, Solomon was able to spend his unprecedented income in the maintenance of an extravagant court and vast public works.[2382]

Nevertheless, it would appear that even with the United Kingdom's greatly expanded revenues, Solomon's expenditures exceeded them. Despite his ambitions, the southwestern end of the Fertile Crescent could never have equaled Egypt and Mesopotamia in wealth, and Solomon's attempts to outdo his neighbors sowed the seeds of the domestic unrest which brought about the division of his kingdom after his death and the reduction of its influence to the limits of southern Palestine, a trivial piece of land of some strategic but little economic consequence. For us, its chief importance lies in that it preserved the idea of the One God in a sea of idolatry, an idea which would burst forth again in later Judaism, primitive Christianity, and Islam.

The Biblical accounts of Solomon's reign in *Kings* and *Chronicles* are replete with notes on his wealth, income, and

---

[2380] Surabadi, pp. 345,369-370, 282-283.

[2381] LJ, IV, 120; VI, 281.

[2382] As did the Roman emperors after the period of building the empire was over, and many other empires before and since. One is also reminded of the extravagance and conspicuous consumption of the rulers of certain Muslim lands, who use the national income as a kind of privy purse.

magnificence. Indeed, the land of the Palestine had never seen such a display of wealth, and was not to see anything approaching it again until the days of the Herods and the Roman Empire. "Thus King Solomon excelled all the kings of the earth in riches and in wisdom. And the whole earth sought the presence of Solomon to hear his wisdom, which God had put into his mind. Every one of them brought his present, articles of silver and gold, garments, myrrh, spices, horses, and mules, so much year by year." (1 K. 10:23-25)

"Now the weight of gold that came to Solomon in one year was 666 talents of gold, besides that which the traders and merchants brought; and all the kings of Arabia[2383] and the governors of the land brought gold and silver to Solomon." (2 Ch. 9:13-14) "Moreover the servant of Huram [i.e., Hiram the artisan] and the servants of Solomon, who brought gold from Ophir, brought algum wood[2384] and precious stones. And the king made of algum wooden steps for the house of the Lord and for the king's house, lyres also and harps for the singers; never was seen the like of them before in the land of Judah." (2 Ch. 9:10-11)

"King Solomon built a fleet of ships at Ezion-geber, which is near Eloth [modern Elath] on the shore of the Red Sea [actually, the Gulf of Aqabah], in the land of Edom. And Hiram sent with the fleet his servants, seamen who were familiar with the sea, together with the servants of Solomon; and they went to Ophir, and brought from there gold, to the amount of four hundred and twenty talents; and they brought it to King Solomon." (1 K. 9:26-28)[2385] The queen of Sheba is reported as having presented Solomon with "one hundred and twenty talents of gold,

---

[2383] "kings of Arabia": chiefly nomadic tribal leaders and shaykhs in the desert and semi-desert west, south, and east of Solomon's kingdom. (Arabia, DB, p. 47.)

[2384] "algum" (or "almug" in *Kings*): probably red sandalwood. (Almug, DB, p. 23.) It is native to India and Ceylon.

[2385] Phoenician sources, as reflected in the writings of the priest Sanchuniathon, give a somewhat different account of this partnership in shipping between Solomon and King Hiram of Tyre, though supporting the fact of its existence: "Hiram of Tyre offered to deliver to the prince of the Judaeans [Solomon] building materials for a new palace, if he would concede him a port on the Ethiopian [Red] Sea." Solomon "gave him the town and port of Eilotha." The priest continues with a description of Phoenician building activities at Elath: "Although there were great palm forests in the neighborhood of this place, there was no timber suitable for building purposes, so Joram (Hiram) had to transport the timber there on 8,000 camels. A fleet of ten ships was built from it." (Quoted in Keller, p. 222.) This has the ring of truth, and the version of the practical Phoenicians is more likely to be closer to the real nature of the deal between Hiram and Solomon than the sycophantic accounts in *Kings* and *Chronicles*. Interestingly, Solomon's palace is mentioned, but not his temple.

and a very great quantity of spices, and precious stones: there were no spices such as those the queen of Sheba gave to Solomon." (2 Ch. 9:9)[2386]

When describing the gold work of the Temple, the Chronicler notes: "The gold was gold of Parvaim." (2 Ch. 3:6) It is thought that Parvaim was located in the far south (see below), and is more evidence of Solomon's commercial enterprises in that region. These enterprises were not limited to the south: "For the king had a fleet of ships of Tarshish at sea with the fleet of Hiram. Once every three years the fleet of ships of Tarshish used to come bringing gold, silver, ivory, apes, and peacocks." (1 K. 10:22) The identification of Tarshish is not certain. It may be in Spain (or perhaps Sardinia), but it definitely refers to a location the access to which is by the Mediterranean Sea.[2387] Nonetheless, the products listed would be more appropriate to southern Arabia, East Africa, and India, sea access to which would have been via the Red Sea.

In Biblical accounts of Solomon's wealth, much space is given to luxury items that were obviously destined for the use of the Jerusalem court or as gifts to important local and foreign princes. Gold is reported as having come from Sheba, Ophir, Parvaim, as well as through Tyre. Sheba is known to be highland Yemen, but the locations of Ophir and Parvaim are disputed. Ophir may have been India, or East Africa, but it is more like a part of coastal South Arabia.[2388] Parvaim is probably also in South Arabia, the modern Farwa in Yemen.[2389] More recently, it has been proposed that a major source for Solomon's gold may have been in the Hejaz. Archaeology is in its infancy there, and more evidence may be forthcoming.

However, in the more skeptical 19th century CE, there was a considerable reaction to these statements in *Kings* and *Chronicles*, and Solomon was reduced to the status of little more than a petty prince. And, whilst it is certain that there is considerable exaggeration and inflation of figures in the Biblical accounts, it is relative to the ages in

---

[2386] In order to convert these weights of gold into modern terms, a talent contained (in Palestine) 3,000 shekels, and it is estimated that a talent was the equivalent of about 81 lbs. (1180 troy ounces). If the price of gold were, say, $300 an ounce, a talent of gold would be worth about $350,000. The queen of Sheba's gift would have amounted to a about $42,000,000, and Solomon's annual revenue would have been more than $230,000,000! (Weights and Measures, DB, p. 1035; Money, DB, p. 670; RHD entries "ounce" "gram.") Surely, these are vastly inflated figures. Not to be dismissed lightly today, in ancient times these would have been incredibly immense sums.

[2387] Tarshish: the identification of this place is not certain, but most probably it refers to Tartessus or Tarseion in southern Spain, a source silver, iron, tin, and lead. Less probable is the identification with Sardinia. (Tarshish, DB, pp. 958-959; BC, III, 189.)

[2388] Ophir, DB, p. 713; BA, Vol. 39, No. 3, p. 85.

[2389] Parvaim, DB, p. 729.

which the writers and editors of those books lived. They looked back upon the visible evidence of Solomon's reign in astonished regret and inevitably compared it with the yardstick of their own reduced circumstances—the shrunken kingdom of Judah, a virtually impotent strategic pawn between Assyria and Egypt in *Kings*, and the helplessness of the post-Exilic community in *Chronicles*. Inevitably, and perhaps forgivably, they dwelt upon exaggerated memories of the riches and power of a vanished Golden Age.

The diligence of the archeologists working in Palestine has come to rescue Solomon's reputation from the denigrations of the 19th century scholars. Evidence supporting the general tenor of the Hebrew imperial claims has begun to be uncovered. "The age of Solomon," writes Albright conservatively, "was certainly one of the most flourishing periods of material civilization in the history of Palestine. Archeology, after a long silence, has finally corroborated the biblical tradition in no uncertain way."[2390] The discovery in 1928 of the stables built by Solomon at Megiddo with room for 450 horses is well known.[2391] And, confirming the Biblical statement that Solomon imported skilled stonemasons from Phoenicia: "Solomonic masonry shows clear indications of having been borrowed from the Phoenicians..."[2392]

Despite the silence of the Bible about the sources of the more prosaic copper and bronze, it is for these metals that Solomon is famous in tradition. The Quran mentions the Fount of Molten Brass made to flow for Solomon (Q. 34:12), and if this is not to be taken as a reference to the Molten Sea in front of the Temple, then it must be about the sources of the metals which go into bronze and brass, especially copper.[2393] Though the Temple was not built of copper as Surabadi would have it (see above), vast quantities of the metal (not found in Palestine) were used in

---

[2390] Albright-Pal, pp. 123-124.

[2391] Megiddo is mentioned in *Kings* as one of the cities enjoying Solomon's building activities: "...and all the store-cities that Solomon had, and the cities for his chariots, and the cities for his horsemen..." (1 K. 9:19) More recently the Israeli archeologist Yigael Yadin has claimed that these stables were built by King Ahab (rgd. c. 874-853 BCE) rather than Solomon. However, a Solomonic gate and palace have been discovered there. (ArchHL, p. 168.)

[2392] Albright-Pal, p. 125.

[2393] The Quranic sentence is: *wa asalnā lahu ʿayna-l-qiṭr*; literally, "and We caused to flow (*wa asalnā*) for him (*lahu*) a spring/fountain (*ʿayna*) of molten bronze/brass (*al-qiṭr*)." Although the Temple vessel is an attractive explanation and by no means impossible, we feel that the phrase better fits the description of a large-scale smelting operation, a source of metal as a spring is a source of water. This would have been a cause of pride and wonder in a land where little smelting was carried on because of the lack of native ore deposits.

the manufacture of its furnishings, as noted earlier. The existence of the foundries in the Jordan valley established or used by Hiram for casting metal objects has been verified by archeological excavation.[2394]

A generation or so ago it was thought that the source of Solomon's copper had been found with Glueck's discovery of the refineries of Ezion-geber in 1938. "Much smaller installations of similar type for smelting iron had been discovered by Petrie at Jemmeh, but nothing remotely comparable to the copper refineries of Ezion-geber has been found anywhere in the ancient world."[2395] These were thought by Glueck to belong to the period of Solomon. However, more recent investigations by Rothenberg in the same region seem to have established that these workings belong to the Egyptians of the XIXth and XXth Dynasties, being operated from the end of the 14th century BCE to the middle of the 12th century BCE, several centuries earlier than Solomon.[2396]

There are other copper sources in the area which have not yet been explored thoroughly by archeologists, including those in Midian in northwestern Arabia. They are thought to hold richer deposits than those in Edom investigated by Rothenberg and Glueck.[2397] Does the statement in *Deuteronomy* that God would give the Israelites a land "in which ye will lack nothing, a land whose stones are iron, and out of whose hills ye can dig copper" (Deut. 8:9) refer to Midian? There was certainly no such abundant mineral wealth in the traditional "Promised Land" from "Dan to Beersheba." Or did Solomon's fleets go to Oman, which is thought to have been another major source of copper in ancient times?[2398]

At present, it does not seem possible to go beyond this in our quest for the sources of King Solomon's copper. Perhaps the late tradition recorded in *Chronicles* is true after all, that Solomon's copper for the Temple came from the loot won by David from the Aramaeans: "And David took the shields of gold which were carried by the servants of Hadadezer, and brought them to Jerusalem. And from Tibbath and from Cun, cities of Hadadezer, David took very much bronze; with it Solomon made the bronze sea and the pillars and the vessels of bronze." (1 Ch. 18:7-8) However, the older parallel passage in (2 Sam. 8:7-8), aside from giving the cities different names, does not mention Solomon's making use of the bronze. In another place (1 Ch. 22:2-5), David is also

---

[2394] BC, III, 178.

[2395] Albright-Pal, p. 127.

[2396] Rothenberg, p. 180.

[2397] Albright-Stone Age, p. 257.

[2398] Bibby, p. 67.

associated with the preparations for the construction of the Temple involving great quantities of iron and bronze, but the tradition is almost certainly unhistorical as it stands and probably is, as we have noted, an attempt to associate the prestige of David to the Temple.

Despite the fact that the sources of Solomon's metals have not yet been identified, their known importation, preparation and use would be ample justification for the Quranic reference to the Fount of Molten Brass. Palestine was and is still a country relatively poor in minerals. The foundation of Solomon's wealth clearly was the result of trade and the prosperity that the transitory Pax Solomonica brought to his empire.

E. SOLOMON'S FEAST

At that time Solomon held the feast for seven days... (2 Ch. 7:7)

There is no specific Quranic verse attached to the description of the feast given by Solomon of which Surabadi writes. In his version: Solomon wanted to invite the entire population of the earth. God said that this was beyond even the power of Solomon, but he begged God's help and permission. Messengers were sent out and vast amounts of food prepared. The entire world came to the feast. God told the beast upon which the earth rests to come up from the bottom of the sea and join in the repast. He looked at all the food and opening his mouth like a Bedouin [!], ate it all in one gulp, then clicked his tongue, belched, and asked Solomon for more. Solomon was astonished and asked the beast how many of his kind there were. The beast replied that they were 700 nations, and all the food he had eaten was only one-third of the morning meal of each one of them.[2399]

This tradition of Solomon's feast can be traced to reports of the dedication ceremonies of the Temple upon its completion. At the conclusion, Solomon hosted a huge feast described in *Kings* and *Chronicles*: "So Solomon held a feast at that time, and all Israel with him, a great assembly, from the entrance of Hamath[2400] to the Brook of Egypt[2401] before the Lord our God, seven days. On the eighth day he sent the people away; and they blessed the king, and went to their homes

---

[2399] Surabadi, pp. 347-348. Jewish tradition also mentions the beast upon which the world rests. The *Apocalypse of Abraham* tells us that the world rests upon Leviathan, and rabbinic writings inform us that the world rests upon pillars, which in turn are resting on one fin of Leviathan. (LJ, V, 45.) His prodigious appetite and thirst are also attested in Jewish tradition. (LJ, I, 27.)

[2400] Hamath: the modern Hama in west-central Syria.

[2401] The Brook of Egypt: not the Nile, but Wadi al-'Arish in the northern Sinai.

joyful and glad of heart for all the goodness that the Lord had shown David his servant and to Israel his people." (1 K. 8:65-66) The parallel account in *Chronicles* (2 Ch. 7:8-10) is in substantial agreement with the above. Both accounts agree that Solomon offered 22,000 oxen and 120,000 sheep as sacrifice to the Lord, most of which was consumed by the assembly (1 K. 8:63; 2 Ch. 7:5). Perhaps 700,000 people attended the dedicatory feast,[2402] an immense gathering in any period of history, and more than enough to give rise to the even more extravagant elaborations of tradition.

Ginzberg does not cite any important traditions about Solomon's feast, but presumably, it became known to the Muslim commentators through Jewish sources and developed in the retelling in the usual way with medieval amplifications. Whereas the purpose of the Biblical story is to display Solomon's magnificence and to impress the reader with the importance and scale of the Temple dedicatory ceremonies in which the entire nation participated, Surabadi's story is a lesson in humility and the limitations of human power when compared with divine providence.

F. THE CARPET OF SOLOMON

(We made) the wind (subservient) to Solomon... (Q. 34:12)

Although the Quran does not mention it, Islamic tradition has credited Solomon with the possession of a fabulous carpet that could carry him from Estakhr to Damascus on the morning breeze, and back again on the evening breeze, and to Babylon in one hour.[2403] Surabadi calls it *Shadurwan*, a name borrowed from the famous curtain woven like a rug that once hung in the Sassanian palace of Mada'in.[2404] In another place he gives more details about it: The carpet was 100 leagues [300 miles!] square, upon which was a tent one league square [3 miles on each side] of a material thinner than egg shell. Within the tent was a dais a mile square; on its right were 10,000 golden chairs for the religious scholars and on the left 10,000 silver chairs for the courtiers. Solomon sat enthroned and mankind stood before him, the fairies behind them, the demons surrounding them, and the angels with maces of fire chastising the demons, the fairies, and the disobedient. The birds wove a canopy

---

[2402] Saggs, p. 250. This figure is probably much too high.

[2403] Surabadi, p. 345. Estakhr was an important medieval city, now in ruins, near Persepolis in southern Iran.

[2404] Burhan, III, 1223. Dr. Mo'in notes that the name is derived from Pahlavi *Shāturvān* meaning "carpet."

over him with their wings. The wind[2405] would carry the carpet gently, but with a noise that caused the people to look up at it traveling seven miles above their heads. If Solomon had had one particle of pride, the whole would have plunged crashing to the earth.[2406]

This apocalyptic vision of Solomon and his court assembled upon his magical transport—a mirror image of the medieval concept of the heavenly court of God Himself—is composed of a number of elements, including the medieval Muslim's conception of society, with the king at the top, advised and guided by the next class, the religious scholars, who had more honor and influence than the courtiers. The resplendent state of these, the virtuous, is contrasted with the scene from hell surrounding them, with the sinners and devils being punished before their eyes.

This story of Solomon's magic carpet seems to be found only in later Jewish writings where it is probably a borrowing from Islamic legends. These traditions in turn would seem of have Iranian origins, as is betrayed by the Persian name of the carpet itself. Solomon's throne, which was borne in the air on the carpet Shadurwan, has a parallel in Jamshid's flying throne, as described by Firdawsi:

> "By his royal glory he made a throne
> With the essence of spirituality and understanding—
> what did he not make?
> When he desired, a demon lifted it up
> And raised it from the plain to the firmament;
> Like the shining sun amidst the sky,
> The sovereign king was seated upon it,
> The world became a congregation on his throne
> From that arose the splendor of his good fortune
> And jewels were showered upon Jamshid."[2407]

This throne legend of Jamshid appears to have been coupled with the tradition of the marvelous carpet and conflated with the traditions of

---

[2405] Both the Quran (Q. 21:81) and pre-Islamic poetry mention Solomon's command of the winds, which stands behind the legends of his ability to fly. Ginzberg considers this story to be of Arab origin (LJ, VI, p. 298). If he means that it is an Islamic invention, he would be wrong. W. Montgomery Watt points out in an article (*The Queen of Sheba in Islamic Tradition*) that the evidence of pre-Islamic poetry, now generally accepted, indicates it was known to the pre-Islamic pagan Arabs (SolSheba, p. 87). Ginzberg, of course, did not assert that it was Islamic.

[2406] Surabadi, pp. 282-283.

[2407] Firdawsi, p. 28.

Solomon's famous throne from Jewish sources in pre-Islamic times, as it was plainly familiar to the Arabs of the time of the Prophet.

Compare Surabadi's description of Solomon's regal dais above with this one from the 6th-century *Targum Sheni*: "On the upper part of the throne stood seventy golden chairs for the members of the Sanhedrin,[2408] and two more for the high priest and his vicar. When the high priest came to do homage to the king, the members of the Sanhedrin also appeared, to judge the people, and they took their seats to the right and left of the king. At the approach of the witnesses, the machinery of the throne rumbled—the lamb bleated, the leopard growled, the goat cried, the falcon screamed, the peacock gobbled, the cock crowed, the hawk screeched, the sparrow chirped—all to terrify the witnesses and keep them from giving false testimony. These animals were made of gold and flanked the steps of the throne.[2409]

About the Throne itself, the *Targum Sheni* declares: "Next to the Temple in its magnificence, it is the throne of Solomon that perpetuates the name and fame of the wise king. None before him and none after him could produce a like work of art, and when the kings, his vassals, saw the magnificence of the throne they fell down and praised God. The throne was covered with fine gold from Ophir, studded with beryls, inlaid with marble, and jewelled with emeralds, and rubies, and pearls, and all manner of gems. On each of its six steps there were two golden lions and two golden eagles, a lion and an eagle to the left, and a lion and an eagle to the right, the pairs standing face to face, so that the right paw of the lion was opposite to the left wing of the eagle, and his left paw was opposite to the right wing of the eagle. The royal seat was at the top, which was round."[2410]

"Above the throne twenty-four vines interlaced, forming a shady arbor over the head of the kings, and sweet aromatic perfumes exhaled from two golden lions, while Solomon made the ascent to his seat upon the throne."[2411]

Elements from the traditions represented in the above have doubtless contributed to Surabadi's pageant of Solomon and his court on the throne, the throne itself resting on Shadurwan. Another, the birds sheltering Solomon, can be seen in the tradition of the birds sheltering

---

[2408] Sanhedrin: the Jewish religious council. See *The New Testament: An Islamic Perspective* for more about it.
[2409] LJ, IV, 158.
[2410] LJ, IV, 157.
[2411] LJ, IV, 159.

the corpse of David from the sun at the command of Solomon.[2412] These elements and others, largely from extra-Biblical sources have been combined by the early Muslim commentators and historians into a new and marvelous creation, not to be found in early Judaeo-Christian writings. But in a medieval Jewish Midrash we find the following description of the carpet: "Solomon had a precious piece of tapestry, sixty miles square, on which he flew through the air so swiftly that he could eat breakfast in Damascus and supper in Media.[2413] To carry out his orders he had at his beck and call Asaph ben Berechiah[2414] among men, Ramirat among demons, the lion among beasts, and the eagle among birds. Once it happened that pride possessed Solomon while he was sailing through the air on his carpet, and he said: 'There is none like unto me in the world, upon whom God has bestowed sagacity, wisdom, intelligence, and knowledge, besides making me the ruler of the world.' The same instant the air stirred, and 40,000 men dropped from the magic carpet. The king ordered the wind to cease from blowing, with the word: 'Return!' Whereupon the wind: 'If thou wilt return to God, and subdue thy pride, I, too, will return.' The king realized his transgression."[2415] The dependence of this story, with its mention of Asaph, upon Islamic stories of Solomon similar to the one summarized from Surabadi above, is obvious.

G. SOLOMON'S KNOWLEDGE OF THE SPEECH OF BIRDS AND ANIMALS

And Solomon was David's heir. And he said: "O mankind! Lo, we have been taught the language of birds..." (Q. 27:16)

In another place in the same surah cited above, Solomon is depicted as conversing with ants.[2416] Surabadi does not give us a story of how Solomon acquired this knowledge of the languages of birds and animals, but simply states it as a fact.[2417] Dr. J. Walker[2418] thinks that this story arose from the report of a passage in *Kings*: "And God gave Solomon wisdom and understanding beyond measure, and largeness of

---

[2412] LJ, IV, 114. The source for this, the *Ruth Rabbah*, is pre-Islamic.

[2413] Media: west-central Iran.

[2414] See section K below for more about Asaph ben Berechiah.

[2415] LJ, IV, 162-163. Nothing further is said about the 40,000 who perished because of Solomon's seizure of pride.

[2416] See the following Section, H, below.

[2417] Surabadi, p. 278.

[2418] Sulaiman, SEI, pp. 549-550.

mind like the sand on the seashore, so that Solomon's wisdom surpassed the wisdom of all the people of the east, and all the wisdom of Egypt... He also uttered three thousand proverbs; and his songs were a thousand and five. He spoke of trees, from the cedar that is in Lebanon to the hyssop that grows out of the wall; *he spoke also of beasts, and of birds, and of reptiles, and of fish* [our italics]. And men came from all peoples to hear the wisdom of Solomon, and from all the kings of the earth, who had heard of his wisdom." (1 K. 4:29-30, 32-34)

There is a passage in the *Wisdom of Solomon* that may be relevant. This apocryphal work—included in the Old Testament Apocrypha—is purported to be the work of Solomon, who is represented as writing in the first person, although scholars feel that it was written originally in Greek by an unknown person some time in the period between 100 BCE and 50 CE.[2419] In one place, this pseudo-Solomon writes: "May God grant me to speak as He would wish and express thoughts worthy of his gifts, since he himself is the guide of Wisdom, since he directs the sages... It was he who gave me true knowledge of all that is, who taught me the structure of the world and the properties of the elements, the beginning, end and middle of the times, the alternation of the solstices and the succession of the seasons, the revolution of the year and the positions of the stars, the natures of animals and the instincts of wild beasts, the powers of spirits and the mental processes of man, the varieties of plants, and the medical properties of roots. All that is hidden, all that is plain, I have come to know, instructed by Wisdom who designed them all." (Wis. 7:15,17-21)

This passage would seem to have been suggested by the one from *Kings* quoted above, although the claims it makes are far more sweeping and exhaustive than those in *Kings* are. For our purposes the question is, do passages such as this stand behind the Islamic tradition of Solomon's knowledge of the language of birds and animals, a story doubtless already in circulation in Arabia before the Call of the Prophet as the nature of the Quranic references show?

Dr. Walker implies that there was a direct dependence of the Arab/Islamic story upon *Kings*. This is possible, but Islamic tradition shows much more affinity to *Chronicles* than it does to *Kings*, as we have seen in several stories. There are versions of the story in Jewish Midrashim probably earlier than the promulgation of the Quran, although the dating is close.[2420] The traditions incorporate Persian themes as well. Such stories were doubtless already a part of campfire lore and gave

---

[2419] Apocrypha, DB, pp. 40-41.
[2420] See LJ, VI, 287-288.

leave to the Muslims commentators to further embellish them with new material invented or borrowed from other sources.

Surabadi takes the opportunity of this verse to regale his audience with wisdom and proverbial material put in the mouths, or rather beaks, of a variety of birds. Some of these are also aetiological in nature, such as the explanation of why the owl does not eat crops or drink water; or how the special characteristics of the bat developed.[2421] None of these stories have close parallels in the Bible.

The last of Surabadi's birds who conversed with Solomon in this dialogue was the phoenix who told him that he, the phoenix, could not accept Fate. Solomon told him that the night before a daughter had been born to the King of the West and a son to the King of the East, and they were foreordained to be married. In order to confound this decree of God, the phoenix seized the girl and placed her on the world's highest mountain in the middle of the sea. She was placed in a nest on one of the branches of an immense tree on the top of that mountain and there taken care of. When the boy grew to manhood, he developed a passion for hunting. One day he decided to go fishing.[2422] With some courtiers, he set out in a ship that was suddenly blown off course till it reached that mountain. The youth saw the girl who thought that she was the daughter of the phoenix. He succeeded in tricking the bird by hiding himself in a hollowed horse and having the phoenix carry it up to her. The youth came out of the horse and slept with her. She became pregnant, and the Wind carried the news to Solomon. Solomon told the phoenix who denied that it was possible. Solomon told him to bring the hollow horse to him. When this had been done, it was opened and they found the two inside together. Then the phoenix accepted the rule of Fate.[2423]

This story, the popular princess in a tower theme, with parallels in folklore around the world, is, of course, not based upon anything in the Bible or the Quran. Parallels to it exist in Jewish literature. This is one Jewish version;[2424] in it Solomon himself attempts to thwart Fate: Solomon had a daughter of extraordinary beauty, "and in the stars he read that she was to marry an extremely poor youth. To prevent the undesirable union, Solomon had a high tower erected in the sea, and to this he sent his daughter. Seventy eunuchs were to guard her, and a huge quantity of food was stored in the tower for her use.

[2421] Surabadi, pp. 279-281.

[2422] In Arabic, fishing is considered a form of hunting; to be specific it is called "the hunting of fish" (ṣayd al-samak).

[2423] Surabadi, pp. 281-282.

[2424] As told in LJ, IV, 175-176.

"The poor youth whom fate had appointed to be her husband was travelling one cold night. He did not know where to rest his head, when he espied the rent carcass of an ox lying in the field. In this he lay down to keep warm. When he was ensconced in it, there came a large bird, which took the carcass, bore it, together with the youth stretched out in it, to the roof of the tower in which the princess lived, and, settling down there, began to devour the flesh of the ox. In the morning, the princess, according to her wont, ascended to the roof to look out upon the sea, and she caught sight of the youth. She asked him who he was, and who had brought him thither." The closeness to Surabadi's story is obvious, though Surabadi's suitor contrives to get to the princess, whilst the Jewish version has it accidental. Then:

"He told her that he was a Jew from Accho [modern Acre], and had been carried to the tower by a bird. She showed him to a chamber, where he could wash and anoint himself, and array himself in fresh garb. Then it appeared that he possessed unusual beauty. Besides, he was a scholar of great attainments and of acute mind. So it came about that the princess fell in love with him. She asked him whether he would have her to wife, and he assented gladly. He opened one of his veins, and wrote the marriage contract with his own blood. Then he pronounced the formula of betrothal, taking God and the two archangels Michael and Gabriel as witnesses, and she became his wife, legally married to him.

"After some time the eunuchs noticed that she was pregnant. Their questions elicited the suspected truth from the princess, and they sent for Solomon. His daughter admitted her marriage, and the king, though he recognized in her husband the poor man predicted in the constellations, yet he thanked God for his son-in-law, distinguished no less for learning than for his handsome person."[2425]

That this story and Surabadi's are versions of the same tale is apparent, although the scale of Surabadi's version is both vaster and more fantastic. At the same time, it is kinder to Solomon, who is not put in the position of challenging the degree of God. The means by which the predestined husband reaches his predestined bride is the same in both stories, in the body of an animal, although Surabadi's version contains an echo of the Trojan horse of Homer's *Iliad*.[2426]

[2425] LJ, IV, 175-176.

[2426] In the ancient Greek story, the Greeks had been besieging Troy unsuccessfully for ten years, when they finally resorted to the stratagem of the horse. They pretended to give up the siege and withdrew to their ships as though making ready for departure, leaving behind on the shore a huge wooden horse. The Trojans, joyfully thinking that the war was over at last, decided to pull the horse into the city and place it in the citadel. After they had done this, at night, Greek soldiers, who had been hiding in the belly of the hollow

H. SOLOMON AND THE ANTS

Distress not the ant that toils hauling a seed!
For it has life, and a sweet life is happiness.
(Sa'di, *Bustan*)

*And there were gathered together unto Solomon his armies of the
jinn and humankind, and of the birds, and they were set in battle order;
till, when they reached the Valley of the Ants, an ant exclaimed: "O ants!
Enter your dwellings lest Solomon and his armies crush you,
unperceiving." And (Solomon) smiled, laughing at her speech, and said:
"My Lord, arouse me to be thankful for Thy favor wherewith Thou hast
favored me and my parents, and to do good that shall be pleasing unto
Thee, and include me amongst Thy righteous servants." (Q. 27:17-19)*

The point of this story is to remind those who possess power
over others to exercise such power with care and responsibility. Surabadi
understands it as a lesson in humility. In his version, one day while
Solomon was passing overhead, the wind carried the voice of an ant
called Mundhirah, telling the other ants to hide in their burrows in the
Valley of the Ants. Solomon summoned Mundhirah[2427] to ask her why
she had ordered the ants to hide while he was flying overhead.
Mundhirah replied that worldly sovereignty is perishable, and it might
come to an end over their heads, causing the carpet to crash down upon
them, crushing them. Mundhirah informed Solomon that she was the
ruler of the ants, and that she was their shield; she had 40,000[2428]
commanders, each of which had 40,000 standard bearers and each
standard had 40,000 troops, and each troop had 40,000 ants. She showed
her armies to Solomon.[2429] Surabadi seems to mean by this that power is
relative, and the queen of the ants in her own world was fully as
powerful as Solomon was in his.

Surabadi then continues with a wisdom dialogue between
Solomon and Mundhirah, in which the latter, in his hand, appears to be

---

horse, climbed out stealthily and threw open the city gates, letting their comrades in to
sack the city and slaughter its unfortunate inhabitants. (Graves, II, pp. 330-345.)

[2427] For grammatical reasons, an unpersonified single ant is construed as feminine in
Arabic, although the ant in question may not be female. However, Surabadi, gives the ant
a feminine name, and we shall treat her here as a queen. The name Surabadi gives her,
Mundhirah, means "warner, cautioner" in Arabic and is feminine in form. In the Quran,
only "an ant" is mentioned, and we do not know its sex or rank. Of course, like bees, ants
have queens.

[2428] Or 40,000 times 40,000.

[2429] Surabadi, pp. 283-284.

the wiser. When Solomon asked her what she thought of the carpet, Mundhirah replied that it was better to be in the hand of Solomon, for his carpet was the work of demons (an allusion to the jinn and demons who had labored for Solomon and produced the material signs of his splendor). Then Solomon asked Mundhirah what she thought of his kingdom, the demons and the wind at his command, and the birds that were his allies. Mundhirah scorned them all, and when Solomon asked her to name a boon for herself, Mundhirah asked to be made young and whole (she was old and had one leg, one arm, and one eye), but Solomon replied that that was beyond his power.[2430]

This parable of Solomon and the ants has no parallel in the Bible, and is only found in medieval Jewish literature, a borrowing from Islamic sources: "On one occasion he strayed into the valley of the ants in the course of his wanderings. He heard one ant order all the others to withdraw, to avoid being crushed by the armies of Solomon. The king halted and summoned the ant that had spoken. She told him that she was the queen of the ants, and she gave her reasons for the order of withdrawal. Solomon wanted to put a question to the ant queen, but she refused to answer unless the king took her up and placed her on his hand. He acquiesced, and then he put his question: 'Is there any one greater that I am in all the world?' 'Yes,' said the ant. Solomon: 'Who?' Ant: 'I am.' Solomon: 'How is that possible?' Ant: 'Were I not greater than thou, God would not have led thee hither to put me on thy hand.'"[2431]

The Jewish story is dependent upon the Islamic story, but upon what is the Islamic story dependent? Apparently oral tradition, the oral tradition of Arabia, and we can only speculate upon the ultimate origins of the story. However, Muhammad Ali's rationalist theory that the story may be about a tribe called the Namlah in the valley of Naml which he locates, on the authority of *Tāj al- ʿArūs*,[2432] between Jibrīn and Ashkelon in southwestern Palestine,[2433] deserves consideration. Animal totems in ancient Arabia still survive in tribal and clan names.

[2430] Surabadi, pp. 284-285.

[2431] LJ, IV, 163.

[2432] *Tāj al-ʿArūs min Jawāhir al-Qāmūs*, by the Yemeni scholar Murtaḍā Zabīdī (1732-1790 CE), a philological commentary on Firuzabadhi's great dictionary.

[2433] "Many of the fables regarding Solomon have been due to a misconception of the word *naml*. It should be noted that *wādi-l-Naml* cannot be properly translated as the *valley of the ants*, for *Naml* is a proper noun, and according to *Tāj al-ʿArūs* (see under the root *wady*), the valley of the Naml is situated between Jibrīn and ʿAsqalān [Ashkelon]. And *Namlah* is the name of a tribe, like *Māzin*, which literally signifies *the eggs of the ants*. *Namil* means *a clever man* (Tāj al-ʿArūs). The name Namlah used also to be given to a child in whose hands an ant was placed at its birth, because it was said such a child would be wise and intelligent (Tāj al-ʿArūs). And the Namlah are plainly spoken of as

In this respect, one bit of evidence has come to light recently which further strengthens the possibility of Naml's being used as a name: "One recently discovered seal from the 8th or 7th century [BCE] has the figure of a locust on it, and above that the inscription 'belonging to Azaryaw (son of) Haggobeb.' Since Haggobeb is closely related to one of the Hebrew words for locust, it looks as though the locust in this case was the family emblem. Insects as family names are not unknown elsewhere in the Old Testament."[2434]

Although these instances are not proof that there was a clan of Namlah or Naml during the reign of Solomon, it is no longer beyond the realm of possibility. In any event, no documentation has thus far been found (if ever there was any) supporting an association of Solomon with the Namlah, and we are still confronted by the wall of silence created by the paucity of surviving extra-Biblical writings of the Old Testament period with which we are concerned. The earliest written testimony of the orally transmitted tradition is in the Quran—pending new discoveries. *And God knows best.*

I. THE WISDOM OF SOLOMON

And We did give knowledge unto David and Solomon... (Q. 27:15)

Despite the extent of his kingdom, the prosperity of his country, the wealth and splendor of his court, Solomon was most remembered in later ages for his wisdom. "As David was the patron of psalms and music in Israel, so Solomon was the traditional founder of the wisdom movement."[2435] According to the Bible, shortly after he had secured his possession of the throne, Solomon went to Gibeon to offer sacrifice at the high place there. At night, he had a vision in which he met with God.[2436] Solomon prayed loftily for divine guidance: "Give Thy servant therefore an understanding mind to govern Thy people, that I may discern between good and evil; for who is able to govern this Thy great people?'" (1 K. 3:9) "It pleased the Lord that Solomon had asked this.

---

tribe in the Qāmūs, which says under the word *barq, Abriqah is of the waters of Namlah.*" (Quran-MMA, Note 1847, p. 731.)

[2434] Biblical Criticism, pp. 61-62. Other insect names include: Flea (Parosh), Ezra 10:25; and Locust (Hagaba), Neh. 7:48. Animal totems are common tribal names in the Arabian Peninsula, even to this day.

[2435] Wright, p. 196.

[2436] Note that this theophany occurred not at the newly established Jerusalem shrine but at the more ancient (and reliable?) shrine at Gibeon some 10 miles to the NNW of Jerusalem.

And God said to him... 'Behold I give thee a wise and discerning mind, so that none like thee has been before thee and none like thee shall arise after thee.'" (1 K. 3:10-12)

The Biblical and extra-Biblical wisdom literature is extensive, though most of the latter is relatively late (after the 3rd century BCE). The "wisdom" movement came to personify and virtually deify Wisdom and led to (or became mixed with) Hellenistic and later Christian Sophism. But the wisdom of Solomon was of the more traditional sort: pithy sayings and ironic truths. There are sayings and proverbs, often in little collections, scattered throughout the books of the Old Testament. A number can be found associated with Biblical personages, beginning with Joseph. However, among the Israelites, as the above passages—and many others not cited—show, wisdom was associated with Solomon more than any other person.

It is difficult to say whether any of the material attributed to him was actually based upon his words. Perhaps he sponsored several collections of court wisdom that form the core sections of *Proverbs* and other books.[2437] Certainly, much of this material reflects the conditions of Solomon's reign.[2438] The proverbs ascribed to Solomon may be found in the *Book of Proverbs* (Prbs. 1:1-9:18; 10:1-22:16; 25:1-29:27). Additionally, *Ecclesiastes* (actually composed in the 3rd century BCE), the *Wisdom of Solomon* (written in the c. first half of the 1st century BCE), two psalms (Pss. 72 & 127), the *Song of Songs* (c.350-250 BCE) and several other pseudepigraphic works are all ascribed to him, but either erroneously or falsely. Nonetheless, the tendency for this type of literature to take shelter in the reputation of Solomon is itself an indication that the strong and persistent traditions of Solomon's wisdom probably have a core of historical truth.

In addition to the type of wisdom that found expression in proverbs and sayings, Solomon's wisdom was also noted for its practical implementation in the administration of justice. Surabadi gives five examples of this, although only one of them can be found in the Bible, and that one is not associated with Solomon. Oddly enough, the famous judgment of the two harlots claiming motherhood of a child found in *Kings* (1 K. 3:16-28) is not cited by Surabadi.

The first given by Surabadi is also alluded to in the Quran, presupposing that the audience would recognize it, again the effect of oral transmission: *And David and Solomon, when they gave judgment concerning the field, when people's sheep had strayed and browsed*

[2437] JB, pp. 931-932.
[2438] Trawick-OT, p. 339.

therein by night; and We were witnesses to their judgment. And We made Solomon to understand (the case); and unto each of them We gave judgment and knowledge... (Q. 21:78-79) The well-known story was not repeated in the Quran, but it is mentioned to inform us that both David and Solomon possessed divinely bestowed wisdom, Solomon excelled David in that respect.

In Surabadi, the circumstances are more fully explained: The owner of an orchard complained to David that a neighbor's flock of sheep had despoiled it. David ordered that the sheep be given to the owner of the orchard. The 11-year old Solomon suggested a different judgment: that the sheep be given to the owner of the orchard so that he might live by them until the owner of the sheep had restored the garden and the property of each would be restored to its original owner. This judgment was considered more equitable.[2439] The nature of the allusion makes it clear that the story was a familiar among the Makkans and, though it is not in the Bible, a version of it can be found in the c. 10th century CE Jewish Midrash, the *Exodus Rabbah*,[2440] perhaps under Islamic influence.

Surabadi's second story is found in the Bible, although not in connection with Solomon. A virtuous woman refused the advances of a lewd man and was in reprisal accused by him of adultery, with the support of false witnesses. David condemned her, but Solomon requested a respite and questioned the witnesses separately and found their testimony contradictory. Thus, the woman was proved innocent and the false accuser punished.[2441]

This incident is so similar to the one told in the short story *Daniel and Susanna* that there can be little question but that Surabadi's anecdote is dependent upon it.[2442] The Biblical version is included in the Old Testament Apocrypha, and in the LXX was placed at the beginning of *Daniel*. It is excluded from the Protestant canon, but is included in Roman Catholic Bibles as ch. 13 of *Daniel*. The original language and its sources are unknown (it has come down to us in Greek), but it is believed to have been set down in its present form in the 1st century BCE:[2443]

"There once lived in Babylon a man named Joakim. He married Susanna daughter of Kilkiah, a very beautiful and devout woman... Now

---

[2439] Surabadi, pp. 262-263.

[2440] Jellinek, pp. 145-146.

[2441] Surabadi, p. 263.

[2442] The early Christian writer Hippolytus made Susannah the sister of the prophet Jeremiah, as the names of the fathers of Susannah and Jeremiah are identical (LJ, VI, 384), but this is erroneous, as is the attribution of the tale to Solomon.

[2443] Trawick-OT, p. 322.

two elders of the community were appointed that year as judges." (Dan. 13:1-2,5)[2444] Joakim was a wealthy man, and the Jews used his house as a court, so the judges were constantly there. "When the people went away at noon, Susanna used to go and walk in her husband's garden. Every day the two elders saw her entering the garden and taking her walk, and they were obsessed with lust for her... They were both infatuated with her; but they did not tell each other what pangs they suffered, because they were ashamed to confess that they wanted to seduce her. Day after day they watched eagerly to see her." (Dan. 13:7-12)

Finally, they made their passions known to each other and plotted to accomplish their desire. One day they hid in the garden, and Susanna, thinking she was alone, began to bathe. The elders came out and told her that the garden doors were locked and she had no choice but to yield to them. "'If you refuse, we shall give evidence against you that there was a young man with you and that was why you sent your maids away.'" (Dan. 13:21) Susanna refused and cried out for help. When the household rushed into the garden through another door, the elders told their pre-arranged tale.

The following day the community assembled to try the case. The elders repeated their accusation that Susanna had arranged a tryst with a young man who had fled when they discovered him. "As they were elders of the people and judges, the assembly believed them and condemned her to death. Then Susanna cried out loudly: 'Eternal God, Who dost know all secrets and foresee all things, Thou knowest that their evidence against me is false. And now I am to die, innocent though I am of all the wicked things these men have said against me.'" (Dan. 13:41-43)

"Just as she was being led off to execution, God inspired a devout young man named Daniel to protest," (Dan. 13:44-46) and he demanded that the trial be re-opened. "Daniel said to them, 'Separate these men and keep them at a distance from each other, and I shall examine them.'" (Dan. 13:51) Then he called each one separately and asked him under which tree he had seen the supposed lovers. One said a clove-tree, and the other a yew. "Then the whole assembly gave a great shout and praised God, the savior of those who trust in him. They turned on the two elders, for out of their own mouths Daniel had convicted them of giving false evidence; they dealt with them according to the law of Moses, and put them to death, as they in their wickedness had tried to do their neighbor. And so an innocent life was saved that day. And from that day forward Daniel was a great man among his people." (Dan. 13:60-64)

[2444] For purposes of reference, we are considering the story as Dan. 13.

It is evident that this story from the Daniel cycle stands behind Surabadi's story ascribed to Solomon. It would have been well known among the Jews, and was probably borrowed by the commentators from them. It may be pointed out, however, that the story itself doubtless has an even longer history, as the theme of the slandered innocent wife and false accusations against her chastity is an ancient and common one. Modern scholars consider it a moral tale and a didactic fiction.[2445]

In Surabadi's third story, a man, who had prayed for lawful sustenance, killed a cow which had strayed into his yard. The cow's owner complained to David that the man had stolen his cow. David ordered that the accused pay compensation for the cow and that his hand should be cut for the theft. Solomon considered the matter and said that the plaintiff was actually the slave of the father of the accused. He had extorted the cow from his master and killed him. Now that the cow has returned to her master, (under the law of indemnification) blood money should be paid by the plaintiff to the accused.[2446]

This story would seem to be an Islamized relative of a story with a similar theme in medieval Jewish writings: "A wealthy man had sent his son on a protracted business trip to Africa. On his return he found that his father had died in the meantime, and his treasures had passed into the possession of a crafty slave, who had succeeded in ridding himself of all the other slaves, or intimidating them. In vain the rightful heir urged his claim before King David. As he could not bring witnesses to testify for him, there was no way of dispossessing the slave, who likewise called himself the son of the deceased. The child Solomon heard the case and he devised a method of arriving at the truth. He had the father's corpse exhumed, and he dyed one of the bones with blood first of one of the claimants, and then of the other. The blood of the slave showed no affinity with the bone, while the blood of true heir permeated it. So the real son secured his inheritance."[2447] (A medieval DNA test, it would seem.)

The linking of David and Solomon, common in the Quran, suggests a strong Islamic—perhaps indirect—influence upon the Jewish story. In any event, despite the differences of setting and circumstance, the stories show independent development, but are clearly related, either by using a common source, or in some other manner. "The earlier Jewish literature hardly knows of this rivalry between father and son, though we find there some remarks to the effect that certain views expressed by

---

[2445] As does George Knight, writing in the Introduction to *Susanna* in Laymon, p. 583.
[2446] Surabadi, pp. 263-264.
[2447] LJ, IV, 131.

Solomon in his writings do not always agree with those of his father..."[2448]

Surabadi's fourth story, the wicked man who was jealous of a virtuous man and plotted to humiliate him, does not seem to have any parallels in the Davidic-Solomonic literature we have consulted. There are no direct parallels in the Bible itself. In this story the wicked man gave the virtuous man seven large jugs of juice for safekeeping and when he collected them he said that one was only half full, and he went to David. David ordered compensation be paid and reproved the virtuous man. Then Solomon suggested that the dregs be weighed and compared with the full jugs. They were found to be only half as much, and thus the plot of the wicked man was exposed.[2449]

Surabadi's fifth instance of Solomonic wisdom and justice is a rather elaborate fable in which a woman was carrying a basket of flour on her head and three pieces of bread in her hand. She gave the bread to a beggar and then a wind blew the flour out of the basket. She went to David to lodge a complaint against the wind. David said he did not know which wind was guilty and he gave the woman 1,000 dirhams. Solomon told her to come back because she deserved more. David gave her another thousand. At Solomon's advice she kept came back, collected 10,000 dirhams, and continued to return.

David called Solomon and asked him why he was doing this. Solomon told his father to summon the wind. It came, and David asked it why it had blown the flour away. The wind replied that it was by order of the Keeper of the Wind. They summoned the Keeper who told them that Gabriel had ordered him to do thus. Gabriel said Michael had told him, and Michael said that Israfil had passed the order to him. Israfil explained that a ship had sprung leaks and the flour was needed to stop them up. Then God commanded the value of the ship and the cargo be ascertained, as one third of it belonged to the woman. The ship was worth 900,000 dirhams, and her share was thus 300,000. David asked the woman what she had done to deserve such a reward. She said that she had given three pieces of bread to a poor man. He said: "Know that this was the reward of that."[2450]

Almost the identical story may be found in Jewish writings: In the version cited by Ginzberg,[2451] the recipient of the reward is a poor man rather than a woman, and there is no mention of his charity earning

---

[2448] Ginzberg, writing in LJ, VI, 285.

[2449] Surabadi, p. 264.

[2450] Surabadi, pp. 264-265.

[2451] LJ, Vol. VI, pp. 285-286.

such a reward; it would seem to be simply a repayment for the use of the flour. In other respects, the stories are close. In the absence of chronological data, it is not clear which version influenced which, but the Islamic story has all the characteristics of a developed Muslim medieval moral parable, yet it is not impossible that some version of the more restrained Jewish story preceded it.

J. SOLOMON AND THE QUEEN OF SHEBA

She came to Jerusalem with a very great retinue. (1 K. 10:2)

This is the only Biblical story that draws far Arabia beyond Midian into the main orbit of Hebraic tradition. Despite the obvious potential of the Solomon-Sheba story, the earlier Jews made little of it.[2452] The main Jewish source, other than the Bible, is the *Targum Sheni* (c. 6th century CE), almost certainly written in Palestine when it was dominated by Christians, that is to say, before Islam.[2453] The Biblical story is a testament to the fame and glory of Solomon. The Quran has taken this encounter and given it an entirely new direction: It is the story of the conversion of the queen of Sheba to the religion of Solomon as a result of the impact of her meeting with Solomon, the royal prophet. Surabadi combines both motifs, but emphasizes the fantastic and the marvelous in medieval fashion.

In the Quran, the story of the queen of Sheba (*Sabā*) is one of its longest narrative episodes. All that is said about her is found in the Makkan surah al-Naml. The story, one of a string of parabolic pericopes, immediately follows Solomon's encounter with the ants, and begins with Solomon noting the absence of the hoopoe from his assembly: *And he sought among the birds and said: "How is it that I see not the hoopoe, or is he among the absent? I will indeed punish him with a hard punishment or I will slay him, or he must bring me a clear excuse."* (Q. 27:20-21)

Surabadi, in his version, tells us why the absence of the hoopoe was of such importance (this is not explained in the Quran). The hoopoe possessed the faculty of locating water underground, as it could see water 60 ft. beneath the surface. It was the time for prayer, and there was no water for ablutions. Presumably, it was the hoopoe's responsibility to

---

[2452] SolSheba, p. 65.

[2453] SolSheba, pp. 65-66. The uncertainties of Jewish chronology are exemplified by the wide range of estimates for the dating of this document, from the 3rd to the 13th century CE, although a majority are of the opinion that it belongs to the environment of pre-Islamic Christian Palestine.

locate water at such times, and when Solomon found the bird absent and himself in need of water, he was irritated. But his irritation was not untempered by justice, for he had qualified it by saying he would spare the negligent bird if it had a good excuse.[2454]

The Bible does not mention the episode with the hoopoe, but the story of Solomon and the queen of Sheba in the *Targum Sheni* begins in much the same way. Solomon was giving a great feast for all the kings of the East and the West. As a part of the festivities, the wild animals, birds, reptiles, devils, demons, and spirits danced before him to show his greatness. [This is the prevailing theme of the pericope in both the *Targum* and the Bible. It is quite worldly and secular, unlike the Quranic version in which religious concerns dominate.] During a roll call, it was found that the hoopoe was absent. Considering himself insulted, Solomon ordered that the bird be brought before him on pain of death.[2455]

In the Quran, the bird arrived late and told Solomon (by way of explanation for his tardiness), that he had been to a place of which Solomon had no knowledge, to Sheba where he had found a kingdom ruled by a woman: *But he was not long in coming, he said: I have found out (a thing) that thou apprehendest not, and I come unto thee from Sheba with sure tidings. Lo! I found a woman ruling over them, and she has been given (an abundance) of all things, and hers is a mighty throne.* (Q. 27:21-22) The real point of the story comes to the fore as the hoopoe says: *I found her and her people worshipping the sun instead of God; and Satan makes their works fair-seeming unto them, and debars them from the Way, so that they go not aright; so that they worship not God Who brings forth the hidden in the heavens and the earth, and knows what ye hide and what ye proclaim, God! There is no god but He, the Lord of the tremendous Throne.* (Q, 27:24-26) The real thrust of the story may be seen by comparing the amount of space the hoopoe gives to her material prosperity (one verse: 23) to the description of her religious practices (3 verses 24-26).

Solomon appeared to be a bit skeptical of the hoopoe's story but gave the bird a letter to take to the queen (Q. 27:27-28). Surabadi expands upon this section considerably. A more detailed version of the cause of the hoopoe's trip to Sheba is given: "'Afira (Solomon's hoopoe) was visited by a hoopoe from Sheba, one 'Afir, who, after commenting upon Solomon's kingdom, invited 'Afira to see Sheba for himself. When he arrived there, he found that the queen, Bilqis (Ar. *Bilqīs*), was very beautiful. Her mother was a fairy, they said, and her father Sharahil,

---

[2454] Surabadi, p. 285.
[2455] SolSheba, p. 66; LJ, IV, 142.

whose ancestors had been kings for forty generations. He could find no suitable mate among mankind, so he married Rayhanah, whose parents had been rulers of the fairies for forty generations. Bilqis was born to them. Her name was Maqqad or Maqqeh, and her nickname (*kunyah*) Bilqis in their own language.[2456]

The hoopoe is not given a name in the *Targum Sheni*, nor is there any mention of a second hoopoe. As in the Quran, the bird returned from his trip with a report about Sheba, where silver lay about like dung in the streets [again the lure of wealth] and whose gardens were watered by waters from the Garden of Eden.[2457] The capital city was Kitor,[2458] and it was ruled by a woman whose name in the *Targum* was Malkath (= queen) Sheba. Josephus gives her name as Nikaulis or Nikaule.[2459] The origin of her name in Islamic literature, Bilqis, has not yet been determined. Neither the Bible not the Quran mentions her name. The Maqqad of Surabadi is doubtless connected with the name given to her by the Ethiopians, Makeda.[2460] It has been suggested that Bilqis is a corruption of the Greek *pallakis* ("concubine"), perhaps through a Hebraized intermediate form such as *pilegesh* or *pilgesh*, or that it is a misreading [or a distortion through oral transmission] of the Nikaulis of Josephus.[2461] Neither explanation is totally satisfactory. The name may have an entirely different etymology, perhaps from South Arabia.

Continuing with Surabadi's version: When the bird arrived at Sheba, he found that she was seated on a jeweled throne, 45 cubits [67.5 ft.] high and 60 cubits [90 ft.] wide, in a palace with golden parapets and rubies so arranged as to reflect the rising sun. The people worshipped the sun at sunrise, and the abode of Bilqis was their direction of prayer (*qiblah*), so that it was as though they worshipped Bilqis. After seeing this, the hoopoe returned to Solomon. He reported to the king that she had 1,000 chiefs, each with 100,000 men [i.e., one hundred million men!], all sun-worshippers. Thereupon Solomon wrote a letter 60 cubits [90 ft.] long on silver[2462] and gave it to the hoopoe to carry to Sheba. The bird fluttered about flirtatiously, because "I have the name of the

---

[2456] Surabadi, pp. 285-286.
[2457] SolSheba, pp. 66-67; LJ, IV, 143.
[2458] Kitor: a word related to the Hebrew *ketoret*, "the smoke of incense," a reference to the incense trade associated with Sheba that was located in Yemen.
[2459] SolSheba, p. 67.
[2460] Queen of Sheba, EJ, XIII, 1424.
[2461] SolSheba, pp. 100-101; LJ, VI 389.
[2462] The letter was in the form of a scroll.

beloved, and the letter of the beloved to the beloved."[2463] The hoopoe had understood that Solomon had written a love letter.

In the *Targum Sheni*, the shape of the narrative is closer to that of the Quran than Surabadi and the differences are of detail rather than of substance. In the *Targum*, the bird offered to go to Kitor himself and bring back the rulers in chains to Solomon. Solomon agreed, and with a letter demanding submission, he sent a vast flock of birds which, when they reached Sheba, obscured the sun and caused darkness, throwing the queen into consternation: "And they came to Kitor in the land of Sheba. It was morning, and the queen had gone forth to pay worship to the sun. Suddenly the birds darkened his light. The queen raised her hand, and rent her garment, and was sore astonished. Then the hoopoe alighted near her. Seeing that a letter was tied to his wing, she loosed it and read it."[2464]

The text of the letter is given briefly in the Quran, and Surabadi follows that: *"In the name of God, the Beneficent, the Merciful; exalt not yourselves against me, but come unto me as those who surrender."* (Q. 27:30-31)[2465] The letter, as given in the *Targum Sheni*, is considerably longer and more threatening: "From me, King Solomon! Know that God has appointed me king over the beasts of the field, the birds of the air, the demons, the spirits, and the specters. All the kings of the East and the West come to bring me greetings. If thou wilt come and salute me, I shall show thee great honor, more than to any of the kings that attend me. But if thou wilt not pay homage to me, I shall send out kings, legions, and riders against thee. Thou askest, who are these kings, legions, and riders of King Solomon: The beasts of the field are my kings, the birds my riders, the demons, spirits, and shades of the night my legions. The demons will throttle you in your beds at night, while the beasts will slay you in the field, and the birds will consume your flesh."[2466]

In the Quranic narrative, the letter, when read by the queen to her council, evoked a reaction of defiance from the councilors: *They said: "We are lords of might and lords of great prowess...* (Q. 27:33), but they agreed to abide by the queen's decision. Surabadi takes this as a cue to describe the strength of the Shebans: They had 360 prelates,[2467] and each one had under him 100,000 men.[2468] But Bilqis thought of the suffering caused by war, as the Quran puts it: *She said: "When kings enter a*

[2463] Surabadi, pp. 286-288.

[2464] LJ, IV, 143-144; SolSheba, p. 70.

[2465] Surabadi, p. 288.

[2466] LJ, IV, 144.

[2467] Surabadi uses the word *jālathīq* which usually refers to a Christian patriarch, but it clearly has a different meaning here, perhaps a soldier-bishop of the sun-worshippers.

[2468] Surabadi, p. 288. An army of 36,000,000 men!

township, they ruin it, and make the honor of the people its shame. Thus they will do." (Q. 27:34) She decided to send messengers with presents and wait to see what Solomon's response would be. (It is unfortunate that more leaders do not reflect upon her words before they launch their ruinous aggressions.)

The reaction to Solomon's letter in the *Targum* is similar to that depicted in the Quran. The princes and elders, having been called in conclave, said to her: "'We know nothing of King Solomon, and his dominion we regard as naught.' But their words did not reassure the queen. She assembled all the ships of the sea, and laded them with the finest kinds of wood, and with pearls and precious stones. Together with these she sent Solomon 6,000 youths and maidens, born in the same years, in the same month, on the same day, in the same hour—all of equal stature and size, all clothed in purple garments. They bore a letter to King Solomon as follows: 'From the city of Kitor to the land of Israel is a journey of seven years. As it thy wish and behest that I visit thee, I shall hasten and be in Jerusalem at the end of three years.'"[2469]

Surabadi at this point introduces the first of the tests of Solomon's wisdom by the queen. In the letter her messengers are bearing, Bilqis challenges Solomon to separate the 10 female slaves from the 10 male (who were pretending to be girls for the occasion) without causing them to undress or touching them. In addition, a pierced jewel was to be threaded and the unpierced jewel with it to be made like the first (the hole was twisted). He was also to separate mares from their foals, and to fill the cup she was sending him with water not of the heavens or of the earth.[2470]

Since the Quran does not mention these tests, and the Bible does not specify them, these riddles proposed in Surabadi come from another source (not directly from the *Targum* as the three riddles posed in that text are quite different and are placed during the actual meeting of Solomon and the queen). Their place here in Surabadi may have been suggested by the mention of the 6,000 youths and maidens at this point in the *Targum*, the sets of riddles in both texts both possibly influenced by an earlier tradition. The shape of the Quranic story is related to the form of the narrative in the *Targum*.

At this point, the Quran introduces a variation not found in the *Targum Sheni*. In the *Targum*, the messengers and presents were sent to announce the queen's impending visit three years later. In the Quran, however, an interview between Solomon and the messengers is reported:

[2469] LJ, IV, 144-145; SolSheba, p. 70. The distance is about 1300 miles.
[2470] Surabadi, p. 289.

So when (the envoy) came unto Solomon, (the King) said: "What! Would ye help me with wealth? But that which God has given me is better than that which He has given you. Nay, it is ye who exult in your gift. Return unto them. We shall surely come unto them with hosts that they cannot resist, and we shall drive them out from thence with shame, and they will be humbled." (Q. 27:36-37) This speech has parallels in the letter of Solomon found in the *Targum*.

The reception of the messengers of the queen of Sheba was a scene too potentially marvelous not to be seized upon by Muslim commentators. In Surabadi's version, Solomon ordered 200,000 armed men to be borne by the wind. They stood in two lines fighting each other, whilst in another direction there were similar lines of devils making a like display with standards of fire. The fairies, too, were on the throne with drums, horns, and cymbals. The messengers were terrified. They arrived at a place where their road was paved with bricks of gold and silver, but two spots were left empty. When the messengers saw the empty places, they set the two bricks of precious metal they were carrying into them, lest they should be accused of stealing them from the road. Jewels were poured at the hooves of their mounts. After this display of power and wealth, Solomon rejected the presents brought by the stunned messengers, and instead ordered the items of the trials be brought in.[2471]

Solomon solved the first riddle, that of separating the boys from the girls, by observing the manner in which they washed their hands before eating.[2472] This riddle is also found in the *Proverbs Midrash* of the 7th or 8th century CE.[2473]

To solve the riddle of the horses, Solomon had them brought to a manger and the mares nosed their colts and thus were made known.[2474] This rather dull riddle does not correspond with any of the twenty-two cited in Jewish writings in connection with Solomon and the queen.[2475]

The third task, that of threading the jewel was accomplished by tying it to a worm which passed through the jewel and then bored the other one in the same way.[2476] This trial also has no parallel among the Jewish riddles, but is probably connected with the Jewish legend of the

---

[2471] Surabadi, pp. 289-290. In the solutions, the order of the second and third riddles is reversed.

[2472] Surabadi, p. 290.

[2473] LJ, IV, 146; SolSheba, p. 75.

[2474] Surabadi, p. 290.

[2475] See LJ, IV, 145-149.

[2476] Surabadi, pp. 290-291.

shamir, a creature sometimes thought of as a worm which possessed miraculous powers, especially with regard to cutting stone.[2477]

The last of the tests, the filling of the cup with water neither from the heavens nor from the earth, was done by filling it with the sweat of exercised horses. This test is also not to be found among the riddles given by the Jewish writings. When the last task was completed, Solomon told the messengers to return to Sheba and inform the queen that they must submit or fight.[2478]

Though the Quran does not mention the departure of the messengers, we assume that in the tradition it was following, it occurred before Solomon addressed his hosts and asked which one of them would bring him the throne of Sheba.[2479] Apparently, one of the jinn volunteered to do so, but was anticipated in this by *one with whom was knowledge of the Book...*[2480] and the throne was present in an instant (Q. 27:38-40). To this, Surabadi adds that Solomon already knew that Bilqis would come to him with her court. The one having the *knowledge of the Book* is identified as Asaph son of Berechiah (see following section). He brought the throne a month's journey away in the wink of an eye.[2481]

When the throne arrived, Solomon ordered: *"Disguise her throne for her that we may see whether she will go aright or be of those not rightly guided."* (Q. 27:41)[2482] This was a recognition test. The incident of the bringing of the throne does not seem to be found in Jewish versions of the story, at least in those unaffected by Islamic traditions, and probably belongs to the form the oral story had acquired in Arabia. After all, Sheba in the south of the peninsula was a part of local lore, as was its queen. Indeed, even though the story in *Targum Sheni* has priority in time as a text, it itself was probably in part dependent upon oral traditions from Arabia where there would have been greater interest in the story and hence, a greater tendency to elaborate it,

---

[2477] LJ, I, 34.

[2478] Surabadi, p. 291.

[2479] Such narrative gaps are further indications that once again a familiar tradition, well known amongst the Arabs of the time, was being reshaped in the Quran for its own didactic purposes.

[2480] A possible reference to the miraculous power of the knowledge of the Divine Name, much reported in Jewish tradition.

[2481] Surabadi, p. 291.

[2482] Maulana Muhammad Ali interprets this bringing of the throne to mean that the throne had been included among the presents the queen had sent to Solomon, and was thus already at his court. (Quran-MMA, p. 733.) This is an interesting rational explanation, but the Quranic text seems to imply that the arrival of throne was accomplished in some unusual fashion.

rather than in the Fertile Crescent where, as we have observed above, there was not much interest in it in earlier times.

It is only at this point that the actual meeting of Solomon and the queen of Sheba begins in the Quran, the *Targum*, and Surabadi. None of the above (except the riddles which in Surabadi are placed before the meeting rather than during it as in the Bible and the Targum) can be found in the Bible. It introduces the story with the words: "Now when the queen of Sheba heard of the fame of Solomon concerning the name of the Lord, she came to test him with hard questions. She came to Jerusalem with a very great retinue, with camels bearing spices, and very much gold, and precious stones; and when she came to Solomon, she told him all that was on her mind. And Solomon answered all her questions; there was nothing hidden from the king which he could not explain to her." (1 K. 10:1-3)

Thus, in the Biblical version, the queen took the initiative and there is no mention of a diplomatic exchange or ultimatum. The queen, attracted by Solomon's fame, came to him on a visit. Biblical commentators have suggested that this had commercial implications as well, as Sheba is mentioned in connection with trade in several places in the Bible.[2483] Nonetheless, it is hard to believe that even three thousand years ago, a matter as important as a peaceful state visit by one sovereign to another would not have been preceded by negotiations and arrangements of some sort, as in the Quran and elsewhere.

After the queen had seen all of Solomon's palace and wealth, "there was no more spirit in her." (1 K. 10:5) "And she said to the king, 'the report was true which I heard in my own land of thy affairs and of thy wisdom, but I did not believe the reports until I came and my own eyes had seen it; and, behold, the half was not told me; thy wisdom and prosperity surpass the report which I heard. Happy are thy wives! Happy are these thy servants, who continually stand before thee and hear thy wisdom! Blessed be the Lord thy God, Who has delighted in thee and set thee on the throne of Israel! Because the Lord loved Israel forever, He has made thee king, that thou may execute justice and righteousness.' Then she gave the king a hundred and twenty talents of gold, and a very great quantity of spices, and precious stones; never again came such an abundance of spices as these which the queen of Sheba gave unto King Solomon." (1 K. 10:6-10)

Up to this point, the narratives in *Kings* and in the parallel passage in *Chronicles* (2 Ch. 9:1-9) are virtually the same word for word. The conclusions, however, are slightly different, a difference which is of

---

[2483] Sheba, DB, p. 902.

some significance when considering some aspects of the Quranic story. The Quran may contain a hint of a tradition of some discord in the matter of the presents sent by the queen of Sheba: *"Would ye help me with wealth? But that which God has given me is better than that which He has given you. Nay, it is ye who exult in your gift."* (Q. 27:36) Solomon is shown annoyed and in the following verse he threatens Sheba. (This incident has just a followed a war council in Sheba where they councilors had assessed their strength with respect to that of Solomon.) The queen decided on a peaceful course, and sent presents in accordance with the custom of the ancient world, which were in fact a kind of tribute, and a token of partial submission, or at the very least, peaceful intentions.

Solomon was displeased by her gifts for unstated reasons (were the presents inadequate or, on the other hand, insultingly lavish?) and, in a rationalist interpretation, he therefore dispatched an expedition that succeeded in stealing the queen's throne. The audacity of this gesture and the threatening diplomatic exchange combine with feminine curiosity (not to say that men are not also curious) generated by reports of Solomon's wisdom and splendor, prompted her state visit to the court at Jerusalem. Although we can read considerations of trade and diplomacy into the Biblical account, there is no reference to a dispute over the "presents." Or is there?

In *Kings*, the account of the queen's visit is concluded with: "And Solomon gave to the queen of Sheba all that she desired, *whatever she asked besides what was given her by the bounty of King Solomon* [our italics]." (1 K. 10:13) This would seem to be the record of a commercial transaction disguised as an exchange of gifts, as was frequently the practice in the pre-monetary ancient world. However, the parallel passage in *Chronicles* (2 Ch. 9:12) has: "whatever she asked besides what she brought the king" instead of the clause from *Kings* in italics above.

The difference suggests that there may have been another version of the relations between the queen and Solomon in circulation. In the version adopted by the Chronicler, Solomon is shown returning the gifts she brought him. This very closely parallels the Quranic verse cited above. The returning of the gifts, unless it was genuinely a gesture of munificence, was a serious matter (as it is today socially), and we have no other clue to the circumstances save this single difference between the narratives of *Kings* and *Chronicles*. Further deductions may be made, assuming the difference is real. We know that the gifts the queen brought with her were accepted by Solomon as the wonder expressed in *Kings* at quantity the spices is too genuine to be rejected under the hypothesis that

Solomon returned the presents listed. The returned gifts must refer to a different (and unrecorded in the present Biblical text) stage of negotiations between the two rulers.

This is, of course, speculation and it must be admitted that the passage lends itself to other interpretations. Nonetheless, the text is obscure, and the difference between the two versions, though slight, may have some basis. The words "in return for" are omitted in the Hebrew text. The translators of the New English Bible note that "*besides his gifts in return for* what she brought him" is a probable reading.[2484] Francisco, writing in the Broadman Commentary, remarks on the difference between the two versions and adds: "What is meant is that she brought gifts that were matched by presents from Solomon. Then she was given gifts above that official interchange."[2485] Perhaps the Chronicler had access to a version of the story unknown to or rejected by the author of that portion of *Kings*.

There is one other curious feature about the concluding verse in the Biblical story of the visit of the queen of Sheba that merits comment. In both *Kings* and *Chronicles*, the final verse appears out of place. Instead of following the main part of the story directly, in both books (*Chronicles* probably following *Kings*) two verses about Solomon's trading activities are inserted which have nothing to do with the queen, her country, or her visits (1 K. 10:11-12; 2 Ch. 9:10-11), and it may very well be that the original story ended without mention of her departure, as does the story in the Quran (and the *Targum Sheni*). Perhaps the last verse was a gloss that crept into the text of *Kings* from the margin, but in the wrong place. Since the Chronicler usually follows the order of *Kings* when there is no particular reason—theological or other—not to do so, in his version the verse is out of place, too.[2486]

To continue with the Quranic version: *So, when she came, it was said (unto her): "Is thy throne like this?" She said: "(It is) as though it were the very one." And (Solomon said): "We were given the knowledge before her and we had surrendered (to God)." And (all) that she was wont to worship instead of God hindered her, for she came of a disbelieving people.* (Q. 27:42-43) These verses are difficult, but the sense seems to be that the queen was barred by her sun worship from

---

[2484] NEB, p. 459.

[2485] Clyde T. Francisco, writing in BC, III, 375.

[2486] We should note that, if the hint contained in the Chronicler's variation of the concluding verse is correctly taken, once again we see the Quran following the Chronicler rather than *Samuel-Kings*. The moral attitude of *Chronicles* is much closer to that of the Quran than is *Samuel-Kings*.

attaining true perspicacity, the recognition of a reality even though it has been superficially altered to another form. Maulana Muhammad Ali suggests that the submission referred to is not to the religion of Solomon, but a temporal submission to his worldly might, and the knowledge is the knowledge that her gift had displeased Solomon because of its idolatrous adornments.[2487] Our discussion above of the variant concluding verses to the story in the Bible would fit neatly here. Yusuf Ali supposes that she had already become a Muslim, a rendering that would blunt the climax of the story. The queen's acceptance of Islam is in its last verse.[2488]

Surabadi does not add much to the Quran in this place, but the *Targum*, which does not know of the throne incident, has the queen arriving at the court of Solomon and greeted by Benaiah, whom she mistakenly takes for Solomon himself.[2489] Then, in the Quran, we read the conclusion of the story: *It was said unto her: "Enter the hall." And when she saw it she deemed it a pool and bared her legs. (Solomon) said: "Lo! It is a hall, made smooth, of glass." She said" "My Lord! I have indeed wronged myself, and I have submitted with Solomon to God, the Lord of the Worlds."* (Q. 27:44) The point of this verse is a parallel of that about the throne; that she had been deceived by appearances. She had mistaken an illusion for reality, and this discovery set on her the Straight Path. The experience had suddenly given her an insight into the true nature of the one invisible God, rather that the visible sun which she had been worshipping. The verse is rich with spiritual implications.

The *Targum* describes the same scene: "Benaiah conducted the queen to Solomon, who had gone to sit in a house of glass to receive her. The queen was deceived by an illusion. She thought the king was sitting in water, and as she stepped across to him she raised her garment to keep it dry. On her bared feet the kings noticed hair, and he said to her: 'Thy beauty is the beauty of a woman, but the hair is masculine; hair is an ornament on a man, but it disfigures a woman.'"[2490]

This matter of the hair on the queen's legs is not alluded to in the Quran. In later Jewish writings, this incident provided an excuse to credit Solomon with the invention of depilatories. Islamic tradition also credits Solomon with the discovery of depilatories in order to remedy Bilqis' hairy legs.[2491] In Surabadi, the shape of her leg is mentioned: Bilqis was invited into the palace. They had heard that her foot was like that of an

---

[2487] Quran-MMA, pp. 734-745.
[2488] Quran-Yusuf Ali, p. 988.
[2489] LJ, IV, 145; SolSheba, p. 70.
[2490] LJ, IV, 145; SolSheba, p. 71.
[2491] SolSheba, p. 99.

ass, and in order to learn the truth, the pool was covered with glass and Solomon seated in the center. When she approached and lifted her skirt so as not to wet it, it was learned that the rumor was false. And, as in the Quran, Surabadi's story concludes with Bilqis, struck with wonder that the pavement was glass rather than stone, repenting of her sun worship and entering the religion of Solomon (Islam).

These stories of her hirsuteness and the rumors about the form of her foot because of her non-human descent seem to be related to another strain in the tradition of the queen of Sheba which identified her, in Jewish legend at least, with Lilith the queen of the demons.[2492] The Quran, Surabadi, and the *Targum Sheni* end their accounts without any mention of a further relationship between Solomon and the queen. However, Jewish tradition also describes an intimate relationship between Solomon and the queen, the fruit of which was Nebuchadnezzar, the oppressor of the Jews and the destroyer of Jerusalem and the Temple, 586 BCE.[2493] This rather negative version is countered by the Ethiopian claim that the former royal family of Ethiopia were descendants of the union of Solomon and the queen.[2494]

As we have suggested, the purposes of this narrative in the Quran are to show Solomon as a proselytizer and to demonstrate the superiority of the worship of the one invisible God over the adoration of illusory material symbols. Solomon uses his opulent wealth and piercing wisdom to convert people to the true faith of the One God, that which we call Islam. This is not the case in the Bible or the *Targum*, both of which concentrate upon the material aspects of the visit as a validation of Solomon's worldly magnificence and power. There is little space given to Invitation (*da^cwah*) in the Islamic sense. The close correspondence of the Quranic story (or rather, the Quranic excerpts from and allusions to the well-known story) to the *Targum Sheni* cannot be a coincidence and is indicative of the form in which the story was known to the Arabs.

The lack of interest displayed by the Jews in the exegesis of this pericope in *Kings*, as well as the general flavor of the story, cause us to suspect that it is a Judaized Arabian tradition rather than an Arabized Jewish tradition. With the link provided by the Bible between Solomon and the queen of Sheba, the main development of the story in oral tradition probably occurred in Arabia where there was a meeting of both Jewish and Arab traditions in the Hejaz and in Yemen. In the Quran, it becomes a parable of the awakening of perception, shedding the

---

[2492] SolSheba, pp. 78-84.
[2493] SolSheba, pp. 76-78.
[2494] SolSheba, p. 104.

distractions of the material world, and coming to the truth of the One God.

Before ending this section, we may enquire whether there is any other evidence supporting the story of the meeting of Solomon and the queen of Sheba. There seems to be no literary confirmation from other nations. Unfortunately, archeological work has been too scant to warrant any conclusions about the state of culture in Sheba.[2495] The Shebans are thought to have settled in the region of Yemen between 1600 and 1200 BCE,[2496] in ample time for the queen's visit which would have taken place during Solomon's reign (965-928 BCE). However, most of the more substantial material remains in highland Yemen belong to a period several centuries or more later than the period of the queen.[2497]

Scholarship seems divided on the question of the historicity of the meeting.[2498] Sheba was inhabited in the 10th century BCE and in later centuries, a high civilization flourished there. That it was possible for a woman to rule is established from Assyrian inscriptions of the second half of the 8th century BCE (only two hundred years later than our queen) which name two Arabian queens, Zabibe and Samsi.[2499] Indeed, the region certainly had a reputation for great wealth later on. We hope that archaeology will produce more evidence to fill in the gaps our knowledge and we pray that Muslims will take more interest in their own past before all is lost to the vicissitudes of time, history and indifference. In the absence of such interest, quite possibly we may never obtain any more evidence of the meeting of Solomon and the queen of Sheba (and much else in Islamic history).

K. THE SEDITION OF SOLOMON

For when Solomon was old, his wives turned away his heart after other gods. (1. K. 11:5)

As was the case with David, some event in the history of Solomon is alluded to in the Quran (but not further described) that caused him to lose divine favor, favor that was restored after his repentance: *And We did indeed try Solomon, and set upon his throne a (mere) body. Then he repented. He said: "My Lord! Forgive me and*

[2495] SolSheba, p. 40
[2496] SolSheba, p. 43.
[2497] SolSheba, pp. 48-56.
[2498] SolSheba, p. 148.
[2499] SolSheba, p. 40.

bestow upon me sovereignty such as shall not belong to any after me. Verily Thou art the Bestower." (Q. 38:34-35)

Surabadi takes these verses as the occasion for relating stories concerned with Solomon's life.[2500] Plainly, he is influenced here by the story of Solomon' apostasy found in *Kings*, even though it is explicitly denied in the Quran: *And they follow that which the devils falsely related against the kingdom of Solomon. Solomon disbelieved not; but the devils disbelieved, teaching mankind sorcery...* (Q. 2:102) Let us first consider the Biblical references to Solomon and his family, as well as his alleged apostasy, before looking at Surabadi's stories that are, in part, related in their shadow. These passages are to be found in *Kings*, the Chronicler having ignored them, as they are ignored or refuted in the Quran.

According to *Kings*, soon after his reign began, but before the building operations that he had undertaken in Jerusalem had been completed and occupancy of his new palace possible, Solomon "made a marriage alliance with Pharaoh king of Egypt; he took Pharaoh's daughter and brought her into the city of David..." (1 K. 3:1) Solomon received the city of Gezer from Pharaoh as part of her dowry.[2501] This seems to have been the most important of Solomon's foreign marriage alliances, for there are several more notices in the Bible about her. She had sufficient status to warrant an apartment in the palace equal to that of Solomon himself (1 K. 7:8). Her taking up residence in those quarters was worthy of another notice (1 K. 9:24).

During the Solomonic period, Egypt was in a state of decline and civil disturbance. His father-in-law must have been either the last or the next to the last pharaoh of the XXIst Dynasty. That dynasty was replaced by the Libyans under Shishak, the founder of the XXIInd Dynasty c. 940 BCE, in the middle of Solomon's reign. Since at the time Jeroboam was in rebellion against Solomon, he took refuge in the Egyptian court (1 K. 11:40), it is not likely that Shishak was Solomon's father-in-law. The Pharaoh would have been motivated by a desire to secure his eastern flank in order to turn his energies toward the problems of the Libyans in the west and the priests of Amon who had usurped his authority in Upper Egypt. In all the notices about the Pharaoh's daughter (except in 1 K. 11 which was broadly critical of Solomon), there is not the slightest hint of disapproval of this marriage. These charges in ch. 11 bear investigation:

The allegations of profligacy and apostasy in *Kings* begin: "Now Solomon loved many foreign women; the daughter of Pharaoh, and

---

[2500] Surabadi, pp. 367-368.

[2501] Gezer, located on the frontier between Philistia and Judah was under Egyptian influence, and this deeding of the city suggests that Philistia was also at that time.

Moabite, Ammonite, Edomite, Sidonian, and Hittite women, from the nations concerning which the Lord had said to the people of Israel, 'Ye shall not enter into marriage with them, neither shall they with you, for surely they will turn away your heart after their gods'; Solomon clung to these in love." (1 K. 11:1-2)

"He had seven hundred wives, princesses, and three hundred concubines; and his wives turned away his heart.[2502] For when Solomon was old his wives turned away his heart after other gods; and his heart was not wholly true to the lord his God, as was the heart of David his father." (1 K. 11:3-4) This unfavorable comparison with David is somewhat astonishing considering what had already been reported of David in *Samuel* about the Bathsheba affair.

Now the charges of idolatry become more explicit: "For Solomon went after Ashtoreth the goddess of the Sidonians, and after Milcom the abomination of the Ammonites. So Solomon did what was evil in the sight of the Lord, and did not wholly follow the Lord, as David his father had done. Then Solomon built a high place for Chemosh the abomination of Moab, and for Molech, the abomination of the Ammonites, on the mountain east of Jerusalem. And so he did for all his foreign wives, who burned incense and sacrificed to their gods." (1 K. 11:5-8)

The passages quoted above reek of angry disapproval. This disapproval was noticeably absent in the earlier chapters concerning his reign, and it intrudes itself into the text quite abruptly. It cannot be denied that by all accounts Solomon had a love for ostentation and display, the cost of which eventually sank the kingdom he ruled. Yet, his devotion to YHWH and the cult of YHWH can hardly be questioned. Solomon doubtless contracted many foreign, politically expedient, marriages in the interest of both diplomacy and status, a phenomenon not unknown among the ruling families of most of the world, including those of the modern West. That some or all of these women imported their own beliefs with them is certain. Solomon's tolerance of their religious practices in private may have alarmed the more conservative and militant YHWH-worshippers during his lifetime and after. They thought it a reproach upon Israel that its king should tolerate these foreign religious practices in (newly) holy Jerusalem itself.[2503]

We believe that at worst, Solomon was guilty of tolerating a potential danger to the purity of YHWH-worship, but the enemies of the

---

[2502] Surabadi has these figures reversed. See below.

[2503] The concept of the centralized YHWH-worship of the Temple itself was a novelty indicating the influence of foreign religious ideas.

House of David and its pretensions probably enlarged the charges considerably, as zealots will, until they had involved Solomon in apostasy as well. This was clearly too much for the Chronicler with his concern for the Temple as the center of Judaism. He could not have it founded by an apostate, so he rejected the story entirely. The Quran joins him in this rejection. It is quite probable that the instincts of the Chronicler and the statement of the Quran are correct: Solomon himself, despite the accusations leveled against him by the Deuteronomist writing in the middle of the 6th century BCE and the author of this chapter,[2504] is not likely to have become an idolator, although he may have been imprudently lenient in acceding to the importunities of his wives. His sacral status as the founder of the Temple continued to the end of the Judahite monarchy.

As in the case of David's alleged adultery, the punishments to be brought down upon Solomon do not suit the charges brought against him. The first punishment is that Solomon's kingdom will be divided, really a punishment of his successors and the people. This is announced by God Himself to Solomon in a vision vouchsafed him, but even the appearance of the Creator of the Universe does not seem to lead to repentance in the Bible. No such reaction to this theophany is credited to Solomon here. At the end, God says: "'Yet for the sake of David thy father I will not do it in thy days, but I will tear it out of the hand of thy sons.'" (1 K. 11:12) In other words, the first portion of Solomon's punishment is the knowledge that his kingdom will be divided in the reign of his son, a punishment that would have suited ancient ideas of justice (which did not consider the afterlife), but is singularly unjust in the modern view. Of course, this (retrospective) prophecy (and indeed the whole history of Solomon) was compiled after the division of the kingdom had ben accomplished.

The second punishment was the raising up of rebellions against Solomon. Three adversaries are named: Hadad, a scion of the royal house of Edom, now subject to Solomon; Rezon, a rebel who had established himself in the region of Damascus; and the third, the Ephraimite Jeroboam, who eventually founded the Northern Kingdom of Israel after the death of Solomon and thus implemented the first of the punishments promised by God earlier: the division of the kingdom in the reign of his son. Yet of the three, only one, Jeroboam, fits the conditions of the punishment. The activities of the others (despite the position of the present account in *Kings*) are said to have begun at the beginning of Solomon's reign,[2505] that is, long before the alleged apostasy of his old

---

[2504] Laymon, pp. 182, 190.
[2505] See 1 K. 11:15-17, 24-25.

age. We have become familiar with such inconsistencies in the Old Testament historical books, and while they make fascinating subjects for study and speculation, they do not add to our confidence in their historicity.

Though Surabadi's story was obviously influenced by the Biblical pericope of Solomon's apostasy, it does not go so far as *Kings*. Surabadi refrains from accusing Solomon of idolatry. In relating the stories, he gives different reasons for the reproof contained in the Quran. The number of these disparate stories suggests that no standard version had been accepted as the prevailing explanation for the reproof by the medieval traditionalists.

In one, Solomon had a handsome son whom he loved. He ordered a cloud to protect him from devils and fairies. He relied upon the cloud instead of God, and as a result, the boy was found dead on his bed.[2506] This story does not seem to have a parallel in the Jewish Solomonic cycle. Once again, an innocent is depicting paying for a perpetrator's sin.

In Surabadi's next explanation, he states that Solomon had 700 concubines and 300 wives, but no children. Then one of the concubines became pregnant and gave birth to a half-boy. Solomon realized the he should have trusted in God for progeny (instead of a multitude of women).[2507] Although the Bible states that Solomon had 700 wives and 300 concubines, the reverse of Surabadi's allotments, the total is the same (probably exaggerations in both case). The rest of the story is also absent from the Bible, as it is from Jewish legend. Still another innocent suffers for his father's lapse.

In the third story, Surabadi introduces the motif of the worship of idols. Solomon had conquered an island and taken the beautiful daughter of the king for himself. She became lonesome, and since her father had died, a picture of her father was made which she worshipped after her customs. Solomon ignored that.[2508] Once again this is without a Biblical parallel, although it is reminiscent of the notice in the Bible that Solomon permitted his wives to worship the gods and idols of their own peoples, as recorded in *Kings*. The other, the story of the origin of idol worship by making representations of deceased loved ones that has been discussed in another place (see Noah, in Part One, V). However, here it seems more allied to the strong prohibition against making pictures of human beings.

[2506] Surabadi, p. 367.

[2507] Surabadi, p. 367.

[2508] Surabadi, p. 367.

Surabadi continues the third story, introducing Asaph, who became aware of what was occurring. He told Solomon that he wished to hold an assembly before he died. Solomon agreed and the nobles of the kingdom assembled. Asaph began praising all the prophets, from Adam to Solomon, in their infancy and at the end of their lives, but when he came to Solomon, he mentioned Solomon's youth but not his old age.[2509] Solomon was astonished and after the guests had departed, he reproved Asaph. Asaph told him that he had said that because there were idolators in Solomon's household, but he ignored that. Solomon went in and destroyed the idols, but God punished him for his neglect. His kingdom was taken away from him and a devil sat on his throne for forty days and forty nights.[2510]

This would be a later Islamic response to the story in *Kings*, because of the firm insistence of the Jews on the correctness of their traditions. It is an incomplete acceptance of the story of the apostasy, but by replacing the king with a demon for that period, it cleverly absolves Solomon from the blasphemy of idol-worship.

ASAPH: Surabadi has already mentioned Asaph (Ar. *Āṣaf*), the minister of Solomon, above.[2511] Several Asaphs are mentioned in the Old Testament, but the one found in Islamic tradition is undoubtedly Asaph, the son of Berechiah.[2512] We may eliminate Asaph the father of Joah, who was a recorder in the reign of Hezekiah (2 K. 18:18,37) and Asaph, the keeper of the king's forest (Neh.2:8) on chronological grounds; neither could have been alive during the time of Solomon or his father David. Another Asaph (1 Ch. 26:1) is a scribal error for Abisaph, the son of Korah (Ex. 6:24).[2513]

The Asaph whom we are discussing is not mentioned in *Samuel-Kings* at all, but is found in *Chronicles*[2514] with the Chronicler's interest in Temple rites. In *Chronicles* we read: "David also commanded the chiefs of the Levites to appoint their brethren as the singers who should play loudly on musical instruments on harps and lyres and cymbals, to raise sounds of joy. So the Levites appointed Heman the son of Joel: and of his brethren Asaph the son of Berechiah; and of the sons or Merari, their brethren, Ethan the son of Kushaiah..." (1 Ch. 15:16-17) Later on

---

[2509] "For when Solomon was old, his wives turned away his heart after other gods." (1 K. 11:4)

[2510] Surabadi, pp. 367-368.

[2511] See preceding Section, J, above.

[2512] There are also several Berechiahs in the Old Testament.

[2513] Asaph, DB, p. 60; Asaph, EJ, III, 672-673.

[2514] Once again we note the Islamic preference for *Chronicles* over *Samuel-Kings*.

in the same chapter, a Berechiah is mentioned as one of the two gatekeepers for the Ark (1 Ch. 15:23), although he is probably not the father of our Asaph.

Asaph, in these passages, is thus a founder of one of the three Temple musical guilds (along with Heman and Ethan, also known as Jeduthun, who founded the other two), and does not seem possessed of those characteristics — the wise minister of the king — that we find in Islamic tradition. He is not mentioned in the Quran, although the commentators usually tell us that the *one with whom was knowledge of the Book* (Q. 27:40) and brought the throne of Sheba to Solomon by invoking the Divine Name was Asaph.

The Bible does give us another clue. During the reign of Hezekiah (715-687 BCE), one of two kings after the time of Solomon who earned the unqualified approval of later generations,[2515] the Temple was repaired, cleansed, and rededicated. The Levite musicians were commanded to play music and sing. "And Hezekiah the king and the princes commanded the Levites to sing praises to the Lord with the words of David and Asaph the seer." (2 Ch. 29:30)

This may be a reference to the psalms credited to Asaph in the Psalter, of which there are twelve: Pss. 50, 73-83; and therefore this Asaph must be Asaph the musician, the Asaph son of Berechiah of *Chronicles*.[2516] We should take special note of the epithet appended to his name in the verse quote: "seer." This shows that in addition to the role of Levite Temple musician and founder of a musician's guild, there were other traditions about Asaph that justified the use of the word "seer."

Now, a "seer" is one who sees what others fail to perceive. Seers were often sought out for political advice, the assumption being that their advice would be delivered under divine inspiration. The seer was closely connected with ecstatic prophecy. When referred to as a seer, he seems to have functioned as the leader of a group of devotees, similar to the Muslim communities of dervishes.[2517] Saul, when looking for his lost asses, approached Samuel, who was described as a seer, for aid in finding them (1 Sam. 9:11). A gloss in the same incident indicates the close connection between seer and prophet: "Formerly in Israel, when a man went to inquire of God, he said, 'Come, let us go to the seer' for he who is now called a prophet was formerly called a seer." (1 Sam. 9:9) The "formerly" seems to indicate that at the time of the writer the institution had lapsed, but the prophet-seer was an important functionary

---

[2515] The other was Josiah, rgd. 640-609 BCE.

[2516] Asaph, DB, p. 60 and Asaph, EJ, III, 673 agree with this assumption.

[2517] Prophecy, DB, p.802.

in ancient Israel. We know that Nathan (2 Sam. 7:1-17) and Gad (2 Sam. 24:11) performed this function for David. The latter is specifically called "David's seer."

Ahijah, a prophet who flourished during and after the reign of Solomon, but was attached to the Northern shrine of Shiloh, was a critic of Solomon and his son Rehoboam (1 K. 11:29-40; 2 Ch. 10:15). There is no mention of a pro-Solomonic seer specifically connected with Solomon, but at the end of David's reign, when Solomon had been proclaimed co-king, according to the Chronicler, David established the duties of the Levites and the Temple service. At this point, it is said of Asaph that he "prophesied under the direction of the king." (1 Ch. 25:2) The king is presumably David, but as Solomon was co-king, a link between him and Asaph may be assumed.

We know from the Bible that Asaph was alive during the reign of David, and there is nothing improbable in his being active during the reign of Solomon. We have the evidence of the Chronicler that Asaph was also remembered as a seer, even though the Chronicler gives no further details of what lay behind this statement, while *Samuel-Kings* is completely silent. We can only guess at the reasons for this silence, as few contemporary early extra-Biblical writings have come down to us. A minor figure in our present records may have had far more important role in some other record no longer extant. Possibly, rivalry among the Levitical choirs in later times may have led to the excision of information which may have tended to exalt the status of the ancestor of one group over another.

Nevertheless, Jewish tradition is not entirely silent about Asaph son Berechiah. There was uncertainty about the identification of the Asaph the psalmist with Asaph ben Berechiah,[2518] but he was also known as the father of medicine, the Jewish Hippocrates and Galen.[2519] Asaph as the implementer of Solomon's commands in Jewish tradition appears to be a late borrowing from the Islamic stories.[2520]

THE USURPER: Surabadi continues with the story of the passing of the kingdom from Solomon, which is based upon the Quranic statement that God *set upon his throne a (mere) body* (Q. 38:34), after

---

[2518] LJ, VI, 105.

[2519] LJ, I, 174.

[2520] LJ, IV, 162. The role assigned by Islamic tradition to Asaph is given to Benaiah, the son of Jehoiada (LJ, IV, 145, 166, etc.). In the Bible, he was a brave soldier of David and later a supporter of Solomon (Benaiah, DB, p. 96). According to *Kings*, Solomon made Benaiah his commander-in-chief (1 K. 2:35).

which Solomon repented and regained his throne. Solomon's power, Surabadi tells us, resided in his signet ring; without it, he was like any other mortal. [2521] With it, if anyone looked askance at him, a thunderbolt would strike the ill-wisher dead. When Solomon went to the privy, he would not take the ring with him, out of respect for the Name of God that was written on it. At such times it was kept by a concubine named Jawwadah. [2522]

One day when Solomon was in the bath, a devil came to Jawwadah in the form of Solomon and, securing the ring, then sat upon Solomon's throne. When Solomon realized what had happened, he fled to the seashore and prayed that his kingdom might be restored to him. This absence lasted forty days. After that, the devil became afraid as the people were murmuring against his judgments and decrees. Finally, the devil fled, throwing the ring into the sea. At the direction of God, a fish swallowed the ring and fishermen caught that fish. Solomon had spent forty days in prayer and fasting, whilst also helping the fishermen, who would give him some fish for his trouble; they thought he was a foreigner. One of the fish given to him had the ring in its stomach; thus, Solomon got it back and returned to his court. [2523]

Though not in the Bible, a similar story is found in the *Babylonian Talmud* and other Jewish sources. In the Talmudic version, Solomon had captured Asmodeus, the ruler of the demons, in order to get the shamir, [2524] which he needed for his building works... However, after the shamir had been obtained, Solomon kept Asmodeus until the Temple was completed. "One day the king told Asmodeus that he did not understand wherein the greatness of the demons lay, if their king could be kept in bonds by a mortal. Asmodeus replied, that if Solomon would remove his chains and lend him the magic ring, he would prove his greatness. Solomon agreed. The demon stood before him with one wing touching heaven and the other reaching to the earth. Snatching up Solomon, who had parted with his protecting ring, he flung him 400 parasangs [1200 miles] away from Jerusalem, and then palmed himself off as king." [2525]

The similarity to Surabadi's story is obvious. However, in the Jewish sources, Solomon's absence from the throne seems to have been

---

[2521] Cf. Samson (above, Part Four, I), whose great strength lay in his uncut hair. When shorn, his strength became that of an ordinary man.

[2522] Surabadi, p. 369.

[2523] Surabadi, pp. 368-369.

[2524] See above, Section J.

[2525] LJ, IV, 168-169.

three years rather than a mere forty days (the Quran mentions no period of time), and he spent his exile as a wandering mendicant: "Banished from his home, deprived of his realm, Solomon wandered about in far-off lands, among strangers, begging his daily bread. Nor did his humiliation end there; people thought him a lunatic, because he never tired of assuring them that he was Solomon, Judah's great and mighty king."[2526] Another version, in the *Midrash Proverbs*, contradicts this and makes Solomon hide his identity. "The lowest despair he reached, however, when he met some one who recognized him. The recollections and associations that stirred within him then made his present misery almost unbearable."[2527]

The Jewish version of the finding of the ring is also similar to the Islamic story, though with the preamble of a love story: After three years of wandering, "Solomon took service as an underling with the cook in the royal household (of Ammon),[2528] and he proved himself so proficient in the culinary art that the king of Ammon raised him to the post of chief cook. Thus he came under the notice of the king's daughter Naamah, who fell in love with her father's cook. In vain her parents endeavored to persuade her to choose a husband befitting her rank. Not even the king's threat to have her and her beloved executed availed to turn her thoughts away from Solomon. The Ammonite king had the lovers taken to a barren desert, in the hope that they would die of starvation there. Solomon and his wife wandered through the desert until they came to the seashore. They purchased a fish to stave off death. When Naamah prepared the fish, she found in its belly the magic ring belonging to her husband, which he had given to Asmodeus, and which, thrown into the sea by the demons, had been swallowed by a fish. Solomon recognized his ring, put it on his finger, and in the twinkling of an eye he transported himself to Jerusalem. Asmodeus, who had been posing as King Solomon during the three years, he drove out, and he himself ascended the throne again.

"Later on he cited the king of Ammon before his tribunal, and called him to account for the disappearance of the cook and the cook's wife, accusing him of having killed them. The king of Ammon protested that he had not killed, but only banished them. Then Solomon had the

---

[2526] LJ, IV, 169.

[2527] LJ, IV, 169.

[2528] Ammon: the modern Amman in Jordan and the region around it.

queen appear, and to his great astonishment and still greater joy the king of Ammon recognized his daughter."[2529]

This story of Solomon and Naamah and the finding of the ring in the fish, sharing common elements with the Islamic tradition is relatively late, and is probably dependent upon Arabic sources, rather than the other way round.[2530] The story of the loss of the kingdom alluded to in the Quran is, however, much older, antedating Islam. The Quranic allusion is evidence that it was already in circulation in Arabia. In the *Babylonian Talmud*, it is the devil that seizes the throne, whilst in the *Palestinian Talmud*, it is an angel that rules in Solomon's stead. The derogatory nature of the reference to the usurper in the Quranic verse suggests that it was the Babylonian version that was known in Arabia. It has been proposed that the form of the story in the *Babylonian Talmud* is itself ultimately based upon Persian legends of Jamshid, who sinned and lost his kingdom to the Zahhak; Jamshid/Solomon was replaced by Zahhak/Asmodeus.

Different endings of the story are given in Jewish writings, in addition to the happy ending of the tale quote above. In one Talmudic version, Solomon never regained his throne,[2531] and this makes the parallel with the Jamshid story even closer. According to Ferdawsi, Jamshid was ultimately sawn in two by Zahhak:

> "When Zahhak suddenly got hold of him
> All at once, he did not waste any time;
> He cut him in half with a saw,
> The world was cleansed of fear and awe of him."[2532]

In another version, alarmed by reports of the strange behavior of Asmodeus who was pretending to be Solomon, the council decided to give the magic ring (which had not been lost) to a wandering beggar who called himself King Solomon. "As soon as Asmodeus caught sight of the true king protected by his magic ring, he flew away precipitately." Thus, Solomon was restored to his throne.[2533]

These stories of Solomon losing his kingdom (but not the incident of the ring) would appear to lie behind the tradition mentioned

---

[2529] LJ, IV, 170-171. Naamah was to become the mother of Solomon's successor, Rehoboam, whose imprudence caused the North to secede.
[2530] LJ, VI, 300.
[2531] LJ, VI, 301.
[2532] Firdawsi, p.29.
[2533] LJ, IV, 172.

in the Quran. Whether the tradition was related to the *Palestinian Talmud* (an angel replacing Solomon) or the *Babylonian Talmud* (the devil replacing Solomon) would appear to depend upon a close examination of the meaning of the term "body" (*jasad*) in the Quranic text. If it is to be taken disparagingly (which is our opinion), then it too, like the *Babylonian Talmud* story, might be based upon traditions originating in Iran. On the other hand, it might be based upon a third tradition of the absence of Solomon from his throne not reflected in either of the Talmudic versions. However, Surabadi's expansion is clearly influenced by the Babylonian tradition.

L. THE DEATH OF SOLOMON

And Solomon slept with his fathers... and Rehoboam
his son reigned in his stead. (1 K. 11:43)

The Quran rarely comments upon the death of a prophet. Solomon is one of the few exceptions: *And when We decreed death for him, nothing showed his death to them save a creeping creature of the earth which gnawed away his staff. And when he fell the jinn saw clearly how, it they had known the unseen, they would not have continued in humbling chastisement.* (Q. 34:14) The purpose of the citation of this little legend in the Quran is once again to stress the difference between two kinds of truth: the apparent and the genuine. However, inevitably, Muslim commentators seized upon the fabulous aspect of the parable and embellished it.

In Surabadi's account, when Solomon's time came he saw a plant which told him that its name was Kharnub, meaning that his kingship had come to an end that it was another's turn.[2534] When the Angel of Death came to him, as was his custom, he found Solomon grieving. Solomon asked to see him in the form he appeared when taking a soul. Azrail (the angel of death) got permission from God to do so, and when Solomon saw him in this form, he fainted. Then he asked whether there were any angels more fearsome. Azrail replied that near him was an angel whose neck was at the Throne of God and whose foot was 500 years' journey below the seventh earth, and he could lift the seven worlds and heavens without difficulty. This angel was near another whose head was near the Throne and whose feet were 1000 years' journey below the earth, and if God were to order him, he could put the

---

[2534] This is distantly reminiscent of the handwriting on the wall in *Daniel*, and that incident may have played some part in the formation of the tradition of this encounter.

seven heavens and worlds in his mouth. And near to him was another angel whose upper lip was near the Throne and his upper lip was below the foundations of the firmament. If God were to order him, he would suck the heavens and the worlds into his mouth without knowing it.[2535]

Here Surabadi has used the occasion of Solomon's contemplation of his mortality as an excuse for an awesome angelology. The fearsome appearance of the Angel of Death is also noted in Jewish tradition. In one place, he is described as showing two heads, one with the face of a serpent, the other like a sword.[2536] In another place, he is described as being like a serpent, but with the hands and feet of a man and twelve wings.[2537] The huge angels described about the Throne of God do not seem to have parallels in early Jewish tradition, where angels are seen on a more human scale; however, their great height is mentioned.[2538] Surabadi's towering angels would seem to have more in common with the Titans of classical Greek mythology, one of whom, Atlas, supported the world on his shoulders.[2539]

Surabadi then proceeds to the story of Solomon's death. When Solomon died, he was standing in the niche of prayer. He had ordered that he should not be buried quickly, as the demons would cease their labors on the mosque. When the Angel of Death came, Solomon asked to be allowed to return home and bless his family, but this request was not granted. Surabadi observes that death came to five prophets unexpectedly: Abraham, Moses, Aaron, David, and Solomon.

After his death, Solomon remained standing, supported by his staff, and the demons continued to work, afraid to look at him, but commenting that they had never witnessed such a long prayer. Then they sent the Beast of the Earth to see if Solomon were dead. The Beast gnawed at the staff until collapsed, and the body of Solomon fell. All mankind then knew that the fairies and demons had lied in their claims of knowledge of the unseen.[2540]

The Biblical account of the death of Solomon has nothing in common with Surabadi or the Quran. Towards the end of his reign, Solomon was beset with increasing troubles, especially the rebellion of Jeroboam (1 K. 11:26-40). The Biblical notice of his death is quite simple, with no hint of the traditions that later developed around that

---

[2535] Surabadi, p. 348.
[2536] LJ, I, 306.
[2537] LJ, V, 123.
[2538] LJ, V, 155.
[2539] Graves, I, pp. 4041.
[2540] Surabadi, pp. 348-349.

event: "Now the rest of the acts of Solomon, and all that he did, and his wisdom, are they not written in the *Book of the Acts of Solomon*? And the time that Solomon reigned in Jerusalem over all Israel was forty years. And Solomon slept with his fathers, and was buried in the city of David with his fathers; and Rehoboam his son reigned in his stead." (1 K. 11:41-43)

The account in Chronicles (2 Ch. 9:29-31) is the same as to the details of the length of his reign and his burial place, but it quotes different sources: *The History of Nathan the Prophet*, *The Prophecy of Ahijah the Shilonite*, and *The Vision of Iddo the Seer*. These sources mentioned in *Kings* and *Chronicles* are all lost to us today, unless some of their material was incorporated in *Kings* or *Chronicles* by D, the Chronicler, or another redactor. We have no way of knowing what additional material these lost books may have contained to supplement our knowledge or what light they would have shed upon the extra-Biblical traditions about Solomon found both in Judaism and Islam.

The story of Solomon's death and his body resting on his staff until eaten away, does not seem to be found in any old Jewish traditions uninfluenced by the Islamic story. It is possibly related to the tradition recorded in the Talmud (*Sanhedrin*) that Solomon gradually lost his kingdom because of his sins. "At first he ruled over the inhabitants of the upper world as well as over those of the lower; then only over the inhabitants of earth; later over Israel alone; then he retained only his bed and staff; and finally only his staff was left to him."[2541] The Beast of the Earth, gnawing at the staff reminds us of the worm-like shamir which was employed by Solomon to cut stone, according to Jewish legend; but the staff and the shamir do not seem to have been linked in Jewish traditions.

The dramatic end of Solomon's life in Islamic tradition is a fitting conclusion to the story of the prophet-king about whom more marvels have collected than any other figure in Old Testament. Jewish commentators began the process, but in the hands of the Muslims, the marvelous took upon itself a life of its own, spawning wonder after wonder. While the Jews were not so concerned about Solomon's theological role, except as the builder of the Temple, these Jewish enhancements to the Biblical story focus on Solomon's splendor and temporal power. The Muslim commentators went further, as was frequently the case when they retold and added to Jewish legends. In the case of Solomon this extravagant enhancement proceeded further than

---

[2541] Quoted from *Sanhedrin* in Solomon, EJ, XIV, 107.

with any other Biblical personality. Solomon's story has become more an entertainment than an edification.

Yet, perhaps the instincts of the commentators were not wrong; for the Solomon of Surabadi and the other commentators is marvelous and unforgettable, and his power is tempered by just enough wisdom and humility—and occasional misfortune—to make him profoundly human. His ability to fly to the farthest lands has led to a trend to identify ruins and natural wonders in far-flung places with his local adventures. The Solomonic legend, perhaps more than any other in Islam, has provided a basis for cultural unity among the widely separated parts of the Islamic world through the ready identification of episodes of his life with local legendary history, a role also played in folklore by Ali, the son -in-law of the Prophet.

PART SIX: FROM MONARCHY TO HELLENISM

I. ELIJAH

...probably the strangest figure among the prophets of Israel...[2542]

INTRODUCTORY REMARKS: Though the title of this Part encompasses a period of more than eight centuries and is replete with colorful and famous Biblical personages (such as Hezekiah, Josiah, Jeremiah, and Nehemiah) in addition to the selection represented here, alas, they are not mentioned or alluded to in the Quran and have, therefore, not earned a place in the *Commentary* of Surabadi. Therefore, we must pass over them and discuss those who are known to Islamic tradition. First, a short review of the historical setting:

From the death of Solomon and the division of his kingdom with the secession of the Northern tribes under Jeroboam c. 925 BCE, the Northern kingdom Israel embarked upon a history of frequent, destabilizing changes of rulers. Furthermore, it was more exposed than Judah to the aggressive nations of the north and east: Syria, Babylon, and Assyria. The North also seems to have been subject to foreign religious influences, though the Temple at Jerusalem still retained an importance for the Northerners. They still regarded it as a place of pilgrimage,[2543] but not Palestine's sole shrine. Judah in southern Palestine, continuing under the descendants of David and Solomon, enjoyed comparative security, although in much reduced circumstances. The Jerusalem Temple, still flourishing in the South, eventually found its claims to paramountcy unopposed after the destruction of the Northern kingdom by the Assyrians 721 BCE.

The House of David managed to hang on to its rule over the small kingdom of Judah—usually an area smaller the State of Delaware, much of it sparsely inhabited desert—until the Babylonians blinded Judah's last king and destroyed Jerusalem together with its Temple in 586 BCE. The craftsmen and the religious and secular leaders of Judah were carried off to Babylonia to begin the Exile that lasted almost five decades, until the Edict of Cyrus in 538 BCE permitted them to return.

Not all the exiles returned, but the experience of the Exile had converted the Judahite YHWH-worshippers into Jews. Judaism as we know it may be said to have been born in this period. Jerusalem was later

---

[2542] Elijah, DB, p. 242.
[2543] Anderson, p. 132.

reinhabited and the Temple rebuilt (c. 520-515 BCE) and its claims to be the sole center of YHWH-worship vigorously revived, causing the schism that gave birth to the Samaritans as an independent sect. Yet, the fundamental shift from the Temple ritual and sacrifices to the Torah was not forgotten.

Judah continued as a province of the Persian Empire until it became part of the empire of Alexander and the successor Hellenistic Ptolemaic Empire based in Alexandria, Egypt. The comparatively light hand of the Ptolemids ruled from about 301 to 200 BCE. It then passed to the Seleucids whose rule was harsh and hostile to the Jews. This precipitated the Maccabee insurrection in 167 BCE and the establishment of an independent Jewish kingdom (not of the House of David). This last managed to survive for more than a century, until direct Roman control began in 63 BCE with the expedition of Pompey.

During these eight an one-half centuries, YHWH-worship slowly evolved. After the experience of the Exile, great theological and cultic changes took place in the religion of the Israelites that warranted giving it a new name: Judaism. It was largely an ethnic religion rather than a universal one, as it has remained to this day, with significant but rarely discussed exceptions. However, during the Exile, the stern YHWH-worship received a leavening of Mesopotamian ideas. During the Persian period, as a parallel, some say, to the universal kingdom of the Persian King of Kings (*Shahanshah*), the Israelites came to perceive that their unique and invisible God, who was not to be worshipped by means of symbols or idols, was truly universal. He was not simply one national deity among the many national gods of other nations; He was the One God and all other gods were false and non-existent. [2544]

[2544] This post-Exilic universalism may be compared with the older belief that God could not be worshipped except upon His own soil. In a conversation between David and Saul, after David had fled from Saul's court and become an exile, David is represented as saying to Saul: "If it is the Lord Who has stirred thee up against me, may He accept an offering; but if it is men, may they be cursed before the Lord, for they have driven me out this day that I should have no share in the inheritance of the Lord, saying, 'Go serve other gods.'" (1 Sam. 26:19) That is, leaving the territory of YHWH, David would have entered the territory belonging to other gods whom he would be obliged to placate because he was no longer under the jurisdiction of YHWH. Similarly, in the story of the acceptance of YHWH-worship by Naaman the Syrian commander at the hands of Elisha, Naaman had to request that the be given two mules' burden of earth from the land of Israel to carry home with him to Syria "for henceforth thy servant will not offer burnt offering or sacrifice to any god but the Lord." (2 K. 5:17) In other words, the rites of YHWH-worship could not be performed except on soil belonging to YHWH, that is, from the land of Israel.

This was a great theological stride forward in the evolution of monotheism, perhaps adumbrated by the Egyptian pharaoh Akhenaton's short-lived monotheism which was also universal but required a material symbol, the solar disk. Among the Jews, this realization retained a corollary from the past; that though God was One and Universal, He had chosen one people among many, Israel, as His own. It was as though the Jews, having survived so many calamities, felt threatened by their new realization, and so they gradually hedged themselves with rules forbidding inter-marriage with foreigners and tests of racial purity retrospectively attributed to the their ancient prophets. The fabrication of genealogies, and the development of a double set of standards and ethics, one for dealing amongst themselves, and another for dealing with the Gentiles, was a part of this movement. This exclusivity was inconsistently applied and there are frequent reports of conversions to Judaism in the early centuries and in the Classical era. Ethnocentricity did not become the norm until medieval times and the persecutions suffered by the Jews, principally in Europe.

It was during the religious renewal of this post-Exilic period that belief in an afterlife, the nature of which was determined by behavior in this life, and a judgment after death entered Judaism (causing still another schism of belief, as we shall see when we discuss the New Testament stories[2545]). It was an idea that the Israelites had heard in Egypt, but rejected; now it had become acceptable from the hands of the more benign Persians.

Another major theme of Jewish thought was gaining strength, especially during the last centuries of the period we are discussing. It has persisted to the present day and played a large part in the events leading up to Christianity: the belief in a promised Messiah who would arise from the House of David and restore the kingdom of Israel, defeating and humbling its enemies. In the form in which we now know it, this belief can also be traced to the destruction of Jerusalem by Nebuchadnezzar and the fall of the House of David, although the concept was implicit in the Israelite idea of kingship from the very beginning, starting with Saul and David.

There is not space to given even a brief survey of all the developments this remarkable people underwent in the period from

---

[2545] Even during the lifetime of Jesus, not all Jews accepted this innovation. The Pharisees did, but the Sadducees held to the older belief that there was no judgment after death and therefore no reward or punishment. Jesus, of course, made this belief a central doctrine in his teachings.

Solomon to Pompey,[2546] but it is important to remember that the fall of Jerusalem (586 BCE) is the most significant date in those centuries. It marks a clear separation from their slowly evolving YHWH-worship that survived the destruction of its central shrine and then they returned to rebuild it as Judaism.

ELIJAH: The judgment of the Bible on the kings of the Israel and Judah who followed Solomon was a harsh one. All of Israel's nineteen kings were condemned as bad, with rarely a good word said about any of them. The kings of Judah fared somewhat better; of the twenty rulers, eight are mentioned with approbation, the rest rejected as unworthy or worse. This obviously reflects the Southern bias of the Bible, edited primarily under the influence of the Jerusalem cult. The two pre-Exilic prophets to be discussed in this Part, Elijah and Jonah, belong to the Northern tradition, although only Elijah (Ar. *Ilyās*) is concerned with events in Israel itself. He was active during the reigns of Ahab (c. 874-853 BCE) and Ahaziah (c, 853-852 BCE), that is, during the middle of the 9th century BCE.

In the Quran, a list of righteous men is found in Surah al-An'am (Q. 6:85), with a fuller notice in Surah al-Saffat: *And lo! Elias [Elijah] was of those sent (to warn), when he said unto his people: "Will ye not ward off evil? Do you call upon Baal and forsake the Best of the Creators, God, your Lord and the Lord of your forefathers?" But they denied him, so they surely will be summoned (for judgment), save the sincere servants of God. And We left for him among the later generations (the greeting): "Peace be unto Elias!" Verily, thus We reward the doers of good.* (Q. 37:123-132)

Elijah, in Islamic tradition, is called Elias (Ar. *Ilyās*), the Greek form of his name, and the form used in the New Testament and Apocrypha. Since this form is attested in the Quran itself,[2547] Elijah must have been known as Elias in Arabia in pre-Islamic times. The frequency of Greek forms in the Quran suggests that many traditions coming to Arabia were transmitted through Greek (Hellenistic) sources rather than directly from Hebrew.

[2546] See *The New Testament: An Islamic Perspective*, Introduction and Stories for about this later period of Judaism.

[2547] "Ilyāsīn" in Q. 37:130 is simply a variant of Ilyās (Elias). (Quran-MMA, pp. 862-863.) Some commentators have construed this variant to mean "son of Yasin." (Elias, Hughes, p. 108.) A. Yusuf Ali, while noting the variant, also suggests that it may a plural of Ilyas meaning "such as Elias."

The Canaanite god Baal is mentioned in the Quran only in this passage (Q. 37:125).[2548] Baal is used with meaning of "lord" (*rabb*) in Yemeni dialects and has been found in Nabataean inscriptions.[2549] In Hebrew, *baal* is used in a general sense to mean possessor, inhabitant, or controller, and—by extension—husband.[2550] In Canaan, Baal, was also used as the proper name of a god associated with fertility. His cult, which apparently involved orgiastic rites, was in competition with YHWH-worship in Canaan until post-Exilic times, and was especially influential in the North where the population seems to have contained larger non-Israelite elements retaining the old worship. There was also a tendency towards syncretism in the North with YHWH-worship and Baal-worship accommodating each other, a kind of accommodation tolerated by some modern Christian missionaries in Africa and elsewhere. It was against this threat to the purity of YHWH worship that the Northern prophets spoke out. The first of these major prophets was Elijah.

Surabadi tells us that Elijah called the people of Baalbek to the Unity of God, but they rejected him. In that country, there was a tyrannical king, Ahab, whose wicked wife was called Jezebel. It was she who had killed John the Baptist. Ahab and Jezebel wanted to kill Elijah, but he fled and took shelter in a cave.[2551]

The identification of Elijah with Baalbek seems to have been suggested by the mention of Baal in the Quran; the scene of the Biblical story is of course northern Palestine, some 150 miles south of Syrian Baalbek, now located in eastern Lebanon. The Bible states that Elijah was from Tishbe in the Gilead, east of the Jordan (1 K. 17:1). Tishbe has been identified as the modern Kh. Lisdib on Wādī al-Yābis, some 6 miles northwest of modern 'Ajlun in Jordan.[2552] Although Jezebel may have been guilty of many crimes in the eyes of the compilers of *Kings*, she could not have had anything to do with the death of John the Baptist, as Surabadi states. John was born more than eight centuries after the time of Ahab and Jezebel. The confusion was caused by anachronistically identifying Jezebel with queen Herodias who, according to Christian tradition, instigated John's murder.[2553] However, the association of Elijah with Ahab and Jezebel is, according to *Kings*, historical.

[2548] The word *baˁal* is used in two other places (Q. 4:128; 11:72) but with the meaning of "husband" or "lord."

[2549] Jeffrey, p. 81.

[2550] Baal, DB, p. 82.

[2551] Surabadi, p. 359.

[2552] Tishbe, DB, p. 1005; OBA, pp. 62, 69.

[2553] John, DB, p. 510. See also John the Baptist in the Stories (I.C) in *The New Testament: An Islamic Perspective*.

The story of Elijah is told in *Kings* (1 K. 17-19, 21 and 2 K. 1-2:11). Ahab, the seventh king of Israel, had married Jezebel, the daughter of Ethbaal, king of Sidon. Ethbaal was a usurper and had previously been the high priest of the cult of the goddess Astarte.[2554] According to Josephus, Ethbaal had seized the throne after murdering Phales, the last king of the line of Hiram the great, the friend of Solomon.[2555] Jezebel's devotion to the religion of her homeland appears to have been genuine, and she promoted Baal-worship in her adopted country, Israel. It must not be supposed the Baal-worship was introduced into Israel by Jezebel; it was older in Canaan than YHWH-worship and it survived alongside the newer creed the Hebrews had brought with them. Indeed, a century after Ahab and the events of this story, Baal-worshippers (based on epigraphic evidence of theophoric names) still constituted a third of the Northern kingdom's population. In Judah, the situation was different, and the population was almost entirely composed of YHWH-worshippers.[2556]

In the eyes of the YHWH-worshippers, Jezebel was a deadly enemy to the purity of their faith and to its survival in Israel. It is little wonder that she became the prototype of the wicked woman in Judaeo-Christian tradition. According to the Bible, she oppressed the followers of YHWH and was a propagandist (missionary) for her own faith. Her measures created great tensions in Israel, and it was at this critical point that Elijah appeared from the eastern part of the kingdom, warning Ahab of a punishing drought. After delivering his message, Elijah was commanded by God to withdraw to the Wadi Cherith where there was water and he was fed miraculously by ravens (1 K. 17:1-7). There is no indication in the text that Elijah was threatened by either Ahab or Jezebel, as Surabadi would have it, but it is not impossible.

Surabadi continues his story, telling us that Ahab had a sick son and he finally sent for Elijah to come and pray for him. Elijah replied that Ahab should return to God. Angered by Elijah's presumption, Ahab sent fifty soldiers after him. They were destroyed by fire from heaven. Another fifty met the same fate. (This incident is mistakenly connected by Surabadi with Ahab; in the Bible it occurred during the brief reign of Ahab's son. See below.)

Jezebel had a scribe, a believer, who was the secret friend of Elijah. He went to the prophet and told him that the royal couple wanted to kill him. Elijah went into the city and hid with a woman for six

---

[2554] Astarte (a.k.a. Ashtoreth) was the consort of Baal, and both were prominent in fertility rites. (Ashtoreth, DB, p. 64: Baal, DB, p. 82.)

[2555] Harden, p. 48.

[2556] Albright-Ab to Ez, pp. 70-71.

months. She had a son named Elisha (Ar. *Alyasa*^{c}; Surabadi, deeming the *al* the Arabic akin to the Arabic definite article *al*, simply writes *Yasa*^{c}) whom Elijah converted.

Elijah became discouraged and prayed that seven years famine would afflict the kingdom. God said that He was more merciful and He allowed two years for them to reform. Elijah asked that the clouds be put under his control to make sure that they did not drop rain. God sent a bird to feed him, whilst the rest of the people were dying of hunger. The people repented and the famine ended.[2557]

The Biblical Elijah can be seen in Surabadi's story, but the events are in a different order, and the most spectacular event of his mission, the contest with the priests of Baal and Ashtoreth, is not mentioned, though it would seem to have been alluded to in the Quran. The feeding by the birds, which with the drought, Surabadi puts towards the end of Elijah's mission, occurs at the beginning of it in the Biblical record. After the drought had begun, the stream upon which Elijah depended for water dried up. Elijah went to Sidon where he took refuge in the town of Zarephath[2558] in the home of a widow, whose jar of flour and flask of oil were miraculously refilled no matter how much she used to feed herself, her son, and Elijah. However, the son sickened and died. Elijah resurrected him, and the widow was converted (1 K. 17:8-24).[2559]

In Surabadi, the story of the sick son of the widow has been transferred to Ahab. However, Surabadi's widow does have a son who becomes a prophet: Elisha. In Jewish tradition, the son also became a prophet, though not Elisha. The son was identified with Jonah.[2560] Elisha was Elijah's successor (1 K. 19:19-21), and was born in the same region of the Gilead whence Elijah had appeared.[2561]

The narrative in *Kings* continues: In the third year, Elijah was commanded to go to Ahab as God was planning to send rain. In the meantime, Ahab had summoned Obadiah, a devout worshipper of YHWH and steward of the royal household, to divide the task with him of searching the land for grazing and water during the drought. Obadiah

---

[2557] Surabadi, pp. 359-360. This drought during the reign of Ahab is independently attested by the Phoenician historian Menander of Ephesus who mentions a catastrophic drought during the reign of Ittobaal (Ahab's father-in-law Ethbaal) in Palestine and Syria that lasted a whole year. (Keller, p. 261.)

[2558] The modern Sarafand, about 8 miles south of Sidon. (Zarephath, DB, p. 1051.)

[2559] These miracles of provision and resurrection probably suggested the stories of similar miracles attributed to Jesus. See the Story of Jesus in *The New Testament: An Islamic Perspective*.

[2560] LJ, IV, 197. See the story of Jonah in the following section.

[2561] Elisha, DB, p. 244.

saved one hundred of the prophets during the massacre organized by Jezebel by hiding them in caves, fifty in each, and supplying them with food and drink. In the course of his search, Obadiah met Elijah and was commanded by him to return to Ahab and tell where he, Elijah, was. Obadiah was afraid, because Elijah was a fugitive whom Ahab had sought at home and abroad. He was also afraid that Elijah would leave the place and Ahab, angered at not finding him, would kill him (Obadiah). Elijah assured him that he would remain where he was. Thus, the king came to see Elijah (1 K. 18:1-16).

Here we have Surabadi's meeting of Elijah with Ahab. It has nothing to do with a sick son. Though there is a similarity in figures, the two parties of fifty each hidden by Obadiah, this incident is not that of the war parties of fifty men each destroyed by celestial fire in Surabadi's account. That belongs to another part of Elijah's remarkable story.

At the meeting, Elijah told Ahab to summon the people of Israel and the 450 prophets of Baal and the 400 prophets of Asherah[2562] to Mount Carmel. The king did so, and Elijah issued a challenge: Two bulls were to be sacrificed on separate altars, one in the name of Baal and Asherah, and the other in the name of YHWH. The prophets of Baal and Asherah were to call upon their gods, and Elijah upon YHWH to ignite their sacrifices. "The god who answers by fire, he is God." (1 K. 18:17-24)

The prophets of Baal invoked their god futilely and Elijah mocked them.[2563] Then Elijah called the people to him and they repaired the altar, using twelve stones to symbolize the twelve sons of Jacob. To further emphasize the power of God (and perhaps sympathetically to encourage the end of the drought) twelve jars of water were poured on the bull and the wood, soaking them. Then Elijah called on God and the fire fell upon the sacrifice, consuming the bull, the wood, the stones of the altar, and the water in the trench around it. The people were convinced and Elijah commanded them to seize the priests of Baal and take them to the valley of Kishon to be slaughtered. Elijah told Ahab to go back as rain would be coming. He himself went up Carmel and sent his servant out seven times to look for clouds in the west (over the sea). Soon rain was pouring down and Elijah ran before the chariot of Ahab

---

[2562] Asherah: understandably sometimes confused with Ashtoreth/Astarte, even in the Old Testament. She was another Canaanite fertility goddess, originally the mother of the gods. (Asherah, DB, p. 62.)

[2563] Nothing is said about the prophets of Asherah, but presumably, they were included in the prophets of Baal, the more prominent deity. The Quran only mentions Baal.

(indicating a willingness to serve him and work with him) to Jezreel (1 K. 18:30-37)

This was the famous test of Elijah. It should be pointed out that once again the victory of YHWH here is not a categorical negation of other gods, but rather an assertion that YHWH alone shall rule in Israel.[2564] As we have noted, Surabadi does not seem to know of this test, although the Quran alludes to it (Q. 37:125ff, quoted above). The summoning of the clouds after the sacrifice is, of course, the source of the request that Elijah in Surabadi made to God to give him control over the clouds.

In the Bible, despite this dramatic demonstration of YHWH's power, plus the breaking of the drought, when Ahab described to Jezebel all that had happened, instead of being converted, she sent a messenger to Elijah threatening his life! And despite this recent evidence of firm divine support, Elijah "was afraid, and he arose and went for his life, and came to Beersheba, which belongs to Judah, and left his servant there." (1 K. 19:3) So, Elijah had taken refuge in the Southern kingdom of Judah.

Sitting under a broom tree, Elijah prayed for his own death, and then fell asleep. An angel awakened him with food and drink, and Elijah traveled to the sacred mountain Horeb, in forty days and forty nights (1 K. 19:4-8) "And there he came to a cave, and lodged there; and behold, the word of the Lord came to him, and He said to him, 'What art thou doing here, Elijah?' He said, 'I have been very jealous for the Lord, the God of hosts; for the people of Israel have forsaken the covenant, thrown down Thy altars, and slain Thy prophets with the sword; and I, even I only, am left; and they seek my life, to take it away.'" (1 K. 19:9-10)

Something is missing in the Biblical narrative here. How did this glorious triumph culminating in the ending of the drought and the slaughter of hundreds of pagan priests suddenly become a defeat for Elijah and his fellow prophets? Perhaps to set the scene for a theophany:

Elijah was commanded to stand on the mountain. "And behold, the Lord passed by, and a great and strong wind rent the mountains, and broke in pieces the rocks before the Lord, but the Lord was not in the wind; and after the wind an earthquake, but the Lord was not in the earthquake; and after the earthquake a fire, but the Lord was not in the fire; and after the fire a still small voice. And when Elijah heard it, he wrapped his face in his mantle and went out and stood at the entrance of the cave." (1 K. 19:11-13) From this, we see that distant Horeb was still

---

[2564] Anderson, p. 34.

thought of by the Israelites as the home or principal residence of YHWH, and associated with volcanic phenomena.

The question that began the theophany ("What art thou doing here?") was repeated thrice, then God commanded Elijah to do three things: 1. go to Damascus via the desert road (avoiding Israel) and anoint Hazael to be king of Aram, 2. anoint Jehu son of Nimshi to be king of Israel, and, 3. anoint Elisha son of Shaphat of Abel-moloch to be prophet in his stead (1 K. 19:14-18). Elijah left Horeb and, coming upon Elisha ploughing, cast his mantle upon him, and Elisha followed him and became his disciple (1 K. 19:20-21). Many Christians believe there is a prefiguring of Christ in this.

Very little of this portion of Elijah's career is found in Surabadi, except a notice of Elisha, who is mentioned twice in the Quran (Q. 6:87 and 38:48) as a righteous man, although no more is said about him.

The next Biblical notice about Elijah has no parallel in Surabadi, although it does shed light upon the characters of Ahab and Jezebel and why they were censured by later generations as well as in Islamic tradition. It is the story of the vineyard of Naboth of Jezreel, which was located near Ahab's palace in Samaria. Ahab wanted to buy or exchange it so that he could make it into a garden for his palace. Naboth refused, and Ahab became angry and sulked. Jezebel enquired as to the cause of his demeanor. Learning it, she said that she would arrange matters. She told Ahab to proclaim a feast and to give Naboth the seat of honor. This was done, and two false witnesses were brought during the feast. They accused Naboth of blasphemy against God and king. Naboth was taken out and stoned to death. Ahab took possession of the vineyard (1 K. 21:1-16).

At God's command, Elijah went to Ahab and rebuked him for this deed. Elijah prophesied that Ahab and his house would be destroyed, and Jezebel would be eaten by dogs by the rampart of Jezreel. Ahab repented, and God told Elijah that because of Ahab's repentance, the destruction would come in the reign of his son rather than in his own reign.[2565] After this, Ahab was killed in a battle with the Syrians and his son Ahaziah succeeded him to the throne, reigning for only two years, but following the tyrannical example of his parents.

Ahaziah suffered a fall in his palace, and sent messengers to ask of Baalzebub—a pagan god—at Ekron whether he would recover. Elijah came to the messengers and asked them why they had been sent to enquire of an idol instead of God, and he told them that Ahaziah would

---

[2565] Note that this is still another instance of delayed, or perhaps it would be better to say, deflected punishment, as in the cases of David and Solomon. See Part Five above.

die. The messengers returned to Samaria with Elijah's prediction (2 K. 1:2-8). Outraged by Elijah's message, Ahaziah sent a captain with fifty men to bring Elijah to him. "Then fire came down from heaven, and consumed him and his fifty." (2 K. 1:10) A second company of fifty was sent to bring him in, and met with a like fate. A third company was sent, and the captain begged Elijah to spare them. Elijah was commanded by God to go with them. In Samaria at the court of Ahaziah, he repeated his prophecy in the presence of the king. And so the king died (2 K. 1:9-18). As we have noted above, this story of the destruction by heavenly fire of two companies of fifty men each sent by Ahaziah to arrest Elijah is erroneously attached to Ahab in Surabadi's story.[2566]

In concluding his story, Surabadi says that Elijah asked for a delay in his death and was taken up to heaven on a fiery steed.[2567] This end of Elijah is similar to that reported in *Kings*: Elijah and Elisha, who accompanied him despite repeated admonitions, went from Gilgal to the Jordan, followed by fifty prophets (disciples). Elijah rolled up his cloak and struck the waters with it. The waters parted and Elijah and Elisha crossed the river on dry land.[2568] "Suddenly there appeared chariots of fire and horses of fire, which separated them one from the other, and Elijah was carried up in the whirlwind to heaven." (2 K. 2:11)

The notorious Jezebel, instead of dying promptly, survived until the reign of Jehu (rgd. 841-814 BCE) and would seem to have attained a ripe old age. *Kings* describes how Elisha anointed Jehu king of Israel (2 K. 9), thus encouraging him to rebel against Jehoram (rgd. 852-841 BCE) of the house of Ahab, and charged him with vengeance on Jezebel. Jehu acted immediately and rushed to Jezreel where he killed both Jehoram the king of Israel and Ahaziah, the king of Judah,[2569] before the walls. When Jezebel heard of this, she knew what was in store for her. The old woman "painted her eyes and dressed her hair." (2 K. 9:30) When Jehu entered Jezreel, she stood at a window and taunted him. Jehu ordered the eunuchs standing by her to cast her down. They did so, and she was trampled by the hoofs of the horses. Later, when he sent to have her buried, they found nothing but her skull, feet, and the palms of her hands. Dogs had eaten the rest of her, thus fulfilling Elijah's prophecy (2 K. 9:30-37).

[2566] As mentioned elsewhere, there is in fact no real evidence in his commentary that Surabadi had access to the received text of the Bible itself, as such confusions demonstrate. His information seems to us to be second- or third-hand.

[2567] Surabadi, p. 360.

[2568] Another echo of the story of Moses in the story of Elijah. The theophany on Mount Horeb was similarly an echo of that of Moses.

[2569] This Ahaziah of Judah is not son of Ahab having the same name.

Surabadi remarks that Elijah is still alive in the desert, as Khidr is in the sea. Elijah helps whomever God wants to save in the desert as Khidr does at sea. They meet once a year at Arafat, they say, in the same mountain of the Companions of the Cave.[2570]

Elijah is a unique figure in the Bible, the parallels of his story with that of Moses are obvious. There is an extensive rabbinic and legendary literature about him. He is particularly connected with Israel's sufferings and exile, and is pictured as a precursor of the Messiah.[2571] In Jewish folklore, he is the agent of God's justice and is especially concerned with rewarding the poor and punishing the rich.[2572] He is a special antagonist of the Angel of Death, repeatedly saving the young who are fated to die,[2573] and this theme may be echoed in Surabadi's statement that Elijah asked that his death be delayed.

These Jewish ideas about Elijah obviously presuppose that he did not die as a mortal dies. He was translated to heaven without undergoing death, and God has given him power over death. In heaven, he records the deeds of men and guides the pious to their places in Paradise; he also leads the sinners into Paradise after their appointed punishments have been completed.[2574] Though he is in a sense the patron saint of Israel, he does not seem to be particularly identified with the guiding of the lost on land, although the Islamic tradition could easily have been developed from some of the other components of the Elijah cycle in Jewish tradition. One such tradition states that Elijah and the righteous will flee into the desert from which they will return after forty-five days, led by the Messiah.[2575] Some scholars identify Elijah with the mysterious companion of Moses on his journey in the Quran, and with Khidr.[2576] By making Elijah the patron saint of all the sojourners by land rather than just the patron saint of Israel, Islam has universalized him.

[2570] Surabadi, p. 360. Of course, the scene of the story of Companions of the Cave was not Makkah. See *The New Testament: An Islamic Perspective* about the New Testament.

[2571] Elijah, EJ, VI, 636,637.

[2572] Elijah, EJ, VI, 638.

[2573] Elijah, EJ, VI, 639.

[2574] LJ, IV, 200-201.

[2575] LJ, VI, 340.

[2576] See the "Journey of Moses" I.L in Part Three.

II. JONAH

The word of the Lord... (spoken) to his servant Jonah. (2 K. 14:25)

Jonah (Ar. Ar. *Yūnus*) is the only one of the twelve Minor Prophets[2577] to be mentioned by name in the Quran. The Hebrew Bible, it will be recalled, is divided into three sections: *The Law* (the Pentateuch); *the Prophets*, which are further subdivided into the Former Prophets (*Joshua, Judges, Samuel, Kings*) and the *Latter Prophets* (Isaiah, Jeremiah, Ezekiel, and the *Twelve*: *Hosea, Joel, Amos, Obadiah, Jonah, Micah, Nahum, Habakkuk, Zephaniah, Haggai, Zechariah,* and *Malachi*); and the *Writings*. It was customary to write the Latter Prophets on four separate scrolls: *Isaiah, Jeremiah, Ezekiel,* and the *Twelve Prophets.*[2578] The Quranic citation of Jonah is doubtless because his is the only book of the Twelve containing a memorable story in addition to the psalms, preaching, oracles, and visions found in them. Such a marvelous tale was widely circulated in the Semitic world and would have certainly been known to the trading Arabs of the Hejaz. Among early Christians, *Jonah* was highly regarded because of the allusions they saw in it to Christ and Christianity. It became a favorite theme for Christian artists.[2579]

Since Jonah is presumed to have lived before the Exile, this story of God's judgment and mercy on non-Israelite foreigners, the Assyrians, might seem to disprove the theory that the Israelite pre-Exilic view of YHWH's sphere of action was limited to the land of Israel and its immediate environs. However, based upon internal historical and linguistic evidence, scholars have concluded that the *Book of Jonah* was not written earlier than 400 BCE (nearly a century and one half after the return from the Exile) and no later than 200 BCE.[2580] Consequently, it represents the post-Exilic point of view, not that of the 8th-century BCE pre-Exilic Israelites, who would have been the contemporaries of the real prophet Jonah.

Outside of the book bearing his name, Jonah is mentioned in the Old Testament in one other place, in *Kings*: King Jeroboam II of Israel (rgd. c. 782-753 BCE) "restored the border of Israel from the entrance of Hamath as far as the Sea of Arabah, according to the word of the Lord,

---

[2577] The term Minor Prophets refers to the relatively short length of the twelve writings ascribed to them, not to their importance.

[2578] Bible, DB, p. 102; Bible, EJ, IV, 820-822. See also Introduction, III.C.

[2579] Jonah, DB, p. 525.

[2580] Jonah, DB, p. 524.

the God of Israel, which he spoke by his servant Jonah the son of Amittai, the prophet, who was from Gath-hepher." (2 K. 14:25) Jonah's hometown, Gath-hepher, was located in the tribal territory of Zebulon. It is identified with the modern Kh. Ez-Zurra', about six miles northeast of modern Nazareth in the Galilee, where a tomb of Jonah is shown, much more likely to be authentic than the one in Mosul, Iraq.[2581] He is not mentioned in the parallel history of *Chronicles*. The reign of Jeroboam II witnessed a temporary revival of Israelite power, this time from the Northern capital of Samaria.

Though Judah had its own king and was nominally independent, it was at that time within Jeroboam's sphere of influence. Israel-Judah in this period had restored the boundaries of David's kingdom from Damascus to the Gulf of Aqabah. According to *Kings*, this was done in fulfillment of a prophecy given by Jonah. It is thought that Jonah's prophecy was delivered in the early part of the reign of Jeroboam, or perhaps even earlier; making Jonah active about the beginning or during the first quarter of the 8th century BCE. There is nothing in this brief notice to connect him Nineveh or Assyria.[2582]

In the Quran, like Elijah, Jonah was known among the Arabs by a version (*Yūnus*) of the Greek form of his name, Ionas. He is mentioned several times: *If only there had been a community that believed and profited by its belief, as did the folk of Jonah! When they believed, We drew away from them the punishment of disgrace in the life of the world and gave them comfort for a while.* (Q. 10:98) This verse stresses the averted fate of the (unnamed) city to which Jonah had been sent, but the respite would not be forever. In other places, the story of Jonah himself is briefly told, as it was known amongst the Arabs:

[2581] OBA, p. 62; Jonah, DB, p. 524; Gath-hepher, DB, p. 317.

[2582] Jonah, DB, p. 524. Although their art is (often gruesomely) impressive and found in most of the major museums of the world, the Assyrians rarely evoke feelings of admiration except from very aggressive and disciplined societies. The Assyrians rampaged through the Fertile Crescent like storm troopers and few wept when the Medes and the Babylonians ended their militaristic empire in 612 BCE. Even by harsh ancient standards, they were a brutal people and gloried in their brutality, as their bas-reliefs amply display. Taking the Biblical notice at face value, Jonah was sent to Nineveh some time between c. 786 and 746 BCE. He had the good fortune to miss the reign of the cruelest of all Assyrian kings, Ashurnazirpal, by a century. His grandfather had founded the New Assyrian Empire c. 900 BCE. Jonah would have visited Nineveh before Tiglath-Pileser III converted it into a world empire in the latter half of the 8th century BCE. The chief city, Nineveh was reaching its peak of glory; even the conservative McEvedy thinks its population may have been in the vicinity of 100,000, an enormous city in ancient times. (McEvedy-AH, p. 44)

Verily, Jonah was of those sent (to warn) when he fled to the laden ship. And they drew lots and he was of those rejected; and the sea animal swallowed him while he was blameworthy; and had he not been one of those who glorify (God), he would have tarried in its belly until the day they shall be raised. Then We cast him on a desert shore while he was sick, and We caused a tree of gourd to grow above him; and We sent him to a hundred thousand (people) or more and they believed, therefore We gave them comfort for a while. (Q. 37:139-148)

These verses are a summary of the story of Jonah, although there is a slight difference in the order of events from that of the Biblical version, as we shall see. The destination of his mission is not mentioned, but, as stated in the Bible, it was surely the large city of Nineveh, the capital of Assyria. The respite given to the Assyrians was indeed temporary,[2583] as the Quranic text implies, and Nineveh was eventually so thoroughly destroyed by the Medes and the Babylonians in 612 BCE (about 150 years after the mission of Jonah) that its site was forgotten.

In two other passages, where the name Jonah is not used, there is greater emphasis on his reluctance to undertake the mission entrusted to him: *And Dhul-Nun,[2584] when he went forth enraged and thought that We would have no power over him; then he called out in the darkness: "There is no god but Thou!" So We answered him, and delivered him out of grief. Even so do We deliver the believers.* (Q. 27:87-88) And: *But wait thou for thy Lord's decree, and be not like him of the sea animal, who cried out in despair. Had it not been that favor from his Lord reached him, he surely had been cast into the wilderness while he was blameworthy. But his Lord chose him and placed him among the righteous.* (Q. 68:48-50)

Maulana Muhammad Ali argues that the Quranic text does not actually state that Jonah was swallowed by the fish, but rather that he was in danger of being swallowed; that is to say, the passage could be construed to mean that Jonah was threatened by a fish, such as a shark, but escaped from it through God's providence.[2585] The root of the Arabic verb *iltaqama* is *l-q-m* meaning "block" or "bite." *Luqmah* means a "a bite, a mouthful." The usual meaning of the verb is "to bite and (eventually) swallow," The more common root associated with

---

[2583] "the comfort for a while" lasted about a century and a half, before Nineveh's final destruction.

[2584] *Dhūl-Nūn*: an epithet meaning "he of the fish" for Jonah (*Yūnus*). (Jonah, Hughes, p. 249.

[2585] This is the interpretation given Maulana Muhammad Ali, Quran-MMA, p. 863; also Muhajir, p. 121.

swallowing is *b-l-'*, as opposed to the taking a bite with the intention of swallowing, of *l-q-m*. So there is something to be said for M. Ali's argument that Quranic verses can be construed to mean that the sea animal took Jonah in its mouth as though to take a bite, but was prevented from doing so. It must also be pointed out that the Arabic word we have translated "sea animal" (*ḥūt*) includes the whale and sea mammals that, as they do not possess gills, are not technically fish.[2586]

However, one suspects that original audience of the parable would have taken it to refer to the well-known version in which Jonah actually lands in the belly of the beast. The story was included in the Quran was as a parable to recommend patience and obedience to God, and to illustrate vividly that the certainty of responsibility cannot be avoided by flight. Without doubt, in our opinion, it was intended to call to the mind the story in its traditional form, albeit the traditional form, as it was known in Arabia.

That the story was taken quite literally in ancient and medieval times is attested by the importance Jonah's three-day sojourn in the belly of the beast assumed in Christian thinking. The early Christians felt it to be a parabolic prophecy of the passion and resurrection of Jesus. Jesus was (as they believed) crucified and entombed for three days prior to his resurrection, the argument went, just as Jonah was swallowed by the fish and remained in its belly three days before being cast out.

Clearly, the Muslim commentators also took the story literally, as witness Surabadi's version. He tells us that Jonah, the son of Amittai, was a prophet. A prophet was inspired by God to tell Hezekiah the king to send a messenger (prophet) to Nineveh to invite the people to the Divine Unity. Jonah was chosen, but refused because he did not desire to mix with mankind. The king was angered, so Jonah boarded a ship to flee the country.[2587]

The Biblical *Book of Jonah* does not offer much assistance in establishing a chronology for these events. The only individual named in it is Jonah himself, the son of Amittai. No kings are named, either Assyrian or Israelite. Consequently, we are forced to rely upon the verse in *Kings* cited above to establish an approximate time frame for the story. We have seen that this seems to place him in the first half of the 8th century BCE, during the reign of Jeroboam II or perhaps his immediate

---

[2586] The modern common Arabic word for "fish" (*samak*) is not found in the Quran. (A word from the same trilateral root *s-m-k*, *samk*, is found in Q. 79:28 with the meaning of "roof" or "ceiling.") Considering the possibilities, it is preferable to use "sea animal," which would also include true fish, in our translations of the Quran, rather than "fish."

[2587] Surabadi, pp. 360-361.

predecessors. Hezekiah, mentioned by Surabadi, was a king of Judah who reigned from 715 to 687 BCE, nearly three quarters of a century after Jeroboam II of Israel.[2588] Since Jonah was a Northerner, it is unlikely that a prophet would have been commissioned to deliver his message to a Southern king, though not impossible. This anachronism in Surabadi is preceded by another: naming Isaiah,[2589] who was active about half a century after Jonah, as the prophet inspired to inform Hezekiah of the Lord's wish to give Nineveh a chance for salvation.

Jewish tradition says that Jonah was a disciple of Elisha.[2590] This Jewish tradition also gives a reason for Jonah's reluctance to undertake the mission entrusted to him: Elisha had ordered Jonah to anoint Jehu (rgd. 841-814 BCE).[2591] After doing so, he was sent to Jerusalem to proclaim the imminent destruction of the city. Because the people repented and God had mercy upon them, the doom did not come, so the people of Israel called Jonah a false prophet. Therefore, when he was commanded to go to Nineveh to warn the inhabitants there to repent lest they be destroyed, he decided to disobey and flee.[2592]

The Bible knows nothing of these preliminary events. *Jonah* begins: "Now the word of the Lord came to Jonah the son of Amittai, saying, 'Arise, go to Nineveh, that great city, and cry against it; for their wickedness has come up before me.'[2593] But Jonah rose to flee to Tarshish from the presence of the Lord. He went down to Joppa and found a ship going to Tarshish, away from the presence of the Lord." (Jonah 1:1-3)[2594]

When they were in the middle of the sea, Surabadi continues, a storm arose and the sailors repented and prayed for salvation. The storm grew worse, and they decided that it was because of the presence of a sinner. Jonah said that he was the sinner, but the sailors only reproved him for saying this. Jonah told them to cast lots, and the lot fell upon him

---

[2588] BC, III, 151.

[2589] One manuscript has Shu'ayb instead of Isaiah. It is quite possible that Surabadi is referring to this tradition and that a copyist has mistaken Shu'ayb for the less familiar Isaiah to which, in Arabic script, it bears some similarity. (Surabadi, p. 360 note,)

[2590] LJ, IV, 246.

[2591] If this tradition be historical, then Jonah's period of activity would be more than half a century earlier than that which we have suggested above based on the notice in *Kings*. All things considered, it is probably better to accept the verse in *Kings* as the stronger evidence.

[2592] LJ, VI, 246-247.

[2593] This phrasing reminds us of the ancient Sumerian god Enlil who was annoyed by the noise mankind was making and so decided to destroy them. See Part One, V.B.

[2594] More than a hint of the territoriality of YHWH's authority is contained in this passage.

no less than seventy times. Jonah put his prayer rug on his head and went to the side of the ship. He saw a huge fish, longer than the ship, which had opened its mouth. Jonah entered the mouth of the fish and was swallowed. The fish thought Jonah was his daily food, but a voice told it that the man was only to be a prisoner in his stomach. After Jonah had left the ship, it sailed on safely.[2595]

This part of Surabadi's tale corresponds to the Biblical story rather closely: At sea, a violent storm arose and the ship was in danger of foundering. The prayers of the pagan mariners were of no avail, and the sailors went below and were astonished to find Jonah asleep through the tempest. They woke him and asked him to call upon his god to save them (Jonah 1:4-6). Then: "And they said to one another, 'Come, let us cast lots, that we may know on whose account this evil has come upon us.' So they cast lots, and the lot fell upon Jonah." (Jonah 1:7) The sailors asked Jonah for particulars about himself; they already knew that he was fleeing from the presence of the Lord, but not the reason why. They asked him what should be done, and Jonah told them to throw him overboard. At first, they were reluctant, but as the storm grew worse, they agreed to do so (Jonah 1:8-14). "So they took up Jonah and threw him into the sea; and the sea ceased from its raging." (Jonah 1:15) "And the Lord appointed a great fish to swallow up Jonah; and Jonah was in the belly of the fish three days and three nights." (Jonah 1:17)

According to Surabadi, Jonah was in the fish not three days but forty. (The Quran does not specify a length of time.) The stomach of the fish became transparent so that he was able to see the wonders of the sea.[2596] This is not mentioned in the Bible or the Quran, but it has a parallel in Jewish tradition: "The fish carried Jonah whithersoever there was a sight to be seen. He showed him the river from which the ocean flows, showed him the spot at which the Israelites crossed the Red Sea, showed him Gehenna and Sheol, and many other mysterious and wonderful places."[2597]

Then, Surabadi tells us, at the end of forty days and nights, God caused the prayers of Jonah to reach the angels, who interceded for him. Surabadi quotes a tradition that the fish himself was an ascetic who had requested conversation with a saint, and Jonah was God's response to his prayer.[2598] While this bizarre piscine conduct is not found in the Midrash *Jonah*, that document offers something even more marvelous: "three

---

[2595] Surabadi, p. 361.
[2596] Surabadi, p. 361.
[2597] LJ, IV, 249. Gehenna and Sheol are names for hell.
[2598] Surabadi, p. 361-362.

days Jonah spent in the belly of the fish, and he still felt so comfortable that he did not think of imploring God to change his condition. But God sent a female fish big with three hundred and sixty-five thousand little fish to Jonah's host, to demand the surrender of the prophet, else she would swallow both him and the guest he harbored. The message was received with incredulity, and leviathan had to come to corroborate it; he himself had heard God dispatch the female fish on her errand. So it came about that Jonah was transferred to another abode. His new quarters, which he had to share will all the little fish, were far from comfortable, and from the bottom of his heart a prayer for deliverance arose to God on high."[2599]

In the Bible, after remaining in the stomach of the fish for three days and three nights: "Jonah prayed to the Lord his God from the belly of the fish, saying, 'I called to the Lord, out of my distress, and He answered me; out of the belly of Sheol I cried, and Thou didst hear my voice. For Thou didst cast me into the deep, in the heart of the seas, and the flood was round about me; all Thy waves and Thy billows passed over me. Then I said, "I am cast out from Thy presence; how shall I again look upon Thy holy temple?"'" (Jonah 2:1-3) At the end of this fine prayer, Jonah said: "'Deliverance belongs to the Lord.' And the Lord spoke to the fish, and it vomited out Jonah upon the dry land." (Jonah 2:9-10)[2600]

Following the Quranic sequence of events, Surabadi writes that Jonah, ill, thin, and tired, was cast up on a plain. A gourd plant grew up to shade him, and a gazelle gave him milk for forty days. Then Jonah grew fond of the tree; God caused it to wither, and Jonah became sad. Revelation came upon him: "O Jonah, thou art saddened because of the tree, but not saddened for the people I would destroy?" So Jonah went to the 120,000 people of Nineveh and warned them to worship the One God, but they were stubborn. Then Jonah told them in thirty-five days they would be punished by a black cloud.[2601] He went into a cave in a mountain as the cloud appeared to wait and watch. The people realized that destruction was about to come upon them. They all went out into the plain and repented, confessing their faith in the One God, and they were saved.[2602]

[2599] LJ, IV, 249-250. The father of a brood of pestering children must have penned those words.

[2600] According to Jewish tradition, the sea animal spewed him out and Jonah landed 965 leagues [c. 2900 miles] away from it.

[2601] This detail seems to have been borrowed from the story of the destruction of the people of 'Ad. See Part Two, I.

[2602] Surabadi, p. 362.

In the Biblical account, after being cast up on the shore, Jonah proceeded to Nineveh, "a vast city, three day's journey across" (Jonah 3:3), where he proclaimed that in forty days it would be overthrown. When the king heard this, he repented and ordered the people and even the animals to partake in a public fast of repentance (Jonah 3:4-9). "When God saw what they did, how they turned away from their evil way, God repented of the evil which He had said He would do to them; and He did not do it." (Jonah 3:10)

The Quranic story ends at this point, but in the Bible, it is only now that the episode of the gourd occurs. In the Quranic list of signs, it comes between Jonah's being cast into the wilderness sick and his being sent to the city (Q. 37:145-147 quoted above). If these are not random references, then it doubtless reflects the sequence of events in the version of the story, as it was known in the Arabia of the Prophet's time. However, in the Bible it is part of the story's denouement:

"But it displeased Jonah exceedingly, and he was angry... Then Jonah went out of the city, and made a booth for himself there. He sat under it in the shade, till he should see what would become of the city. And the Lord God appointed a plant, and made it come up over Jonah, that it might be a shade over his head, to save him from his discomfort. So Jonah was exceedingly glad because of the plant. But when dawn came up the next day, God appointed a worm which attacked the plant, so that it withered." (Jonah 4:1,5-7) The day became hot and Jonah suffered from the heat, and was angry because the plant no longer gave shade (Jonah 4:8-9) "And the Lord said, 'Thou pitiest the plant, for which thou didst not labor, nor didst thou make it grow, which came into being in a night, and perished in a night. And should not I pity Nineveh, that great city, in which there are more than a hundred and twenty thousand persons who do not know their right hand from their left, and also much cattle?'" (Jonah 4:10-11)

Interestingly, Surabadi follows the Biblical tradition rather than the Quranic by giving the city's population as 120,000 instead of the "100,000 or more" mentioned in the Quran (Q. 37:147). However, the principal question here is: Why is the episode of the shading tree displaced in the Quranic version? Is it, as a critic might suggest, a case of confusion? Not likely, for with the transposition the thrust of the story is altered, and Jonah is shown in a more favorable light. Since the story is almost certainly a moral fiction (see below), there is no compelling reason not to reshape the material to fit the Quranic view of prophethood. In the Biblical version, Jonah is shown to be vindictive and pouty, angry because the city was not destroyed. Is this the way a prophet should behave? It is particularly discordant, because his mission had been to warn them to repent lest they be destroyed. When they repented, his mission had been successfully accomplished (as it would have been, presumably, had they not repented and been destroyed). Why, then, was he angry? Did he want to see the pyrotechnics of the destruction of Nineveh? Jonah's reaction strikes the reader as being mean and unworthy. Although the lesson of the tree in the Bible, a parable within a parable, has its point, we are still left with a rather unfavorable opinion of Jonah's behavior and attitude.

By shifting the material around, this unfavorable portrait is redeemed, and Jonah's story becomes morally edifying. In the Quran, the example of tree teaches the nature of God's mercy and it spurs Jonah to assume the burden of the message given him and to deliver it to the people of the city, which he does successfully. End of story. By fleeing in the ship and disobeying God by not warning Nineveh, he was condemning them to certain destruction, and destroying himself in the process. After he had been saved from the sea and cast up on the shore, God demonstrated His mercy by growing the shade tree for him. When Jonah had become attached to it and it withered, as in the Bible, God made the telling point of His concern for all people, for God's mercy encompasses all mankind, even those who are not yet enlightened. As a sign of His mercy, God had commissioned the Israelite Jonah to deliver this message to the non-Israelite Ninevites and it became the cause of their salvation, at least for a few generations.

In the Bible, this result initially displeased Jonah, but in the Quran, it is the logical and hoped-for consequence of Jonah's mission. Since Jonah had already learned the importance of his responsibility, there was no need for him to behave petulantly after the city was saved. From the Islamic version, we may assume that he rejoiced in their salvation. As we have noted above, it is also quite possible that this was the more or less the outline of the tale as it was circulated in pre-Islamic Arabia, or perhaps divine revelation simply improved it.

Jonah delivered the warning and the people listened. Alas, the later excesses of the Assyrian empire earned the total obliteration of the city something over 150 years later.

The *Book of Jonah* really belongs to the class of writings known as Pseudepigrapha, though its place in the canon of the Old Testament has shielded it from that epithet. Since the short book was written in the 4th or 3rd centuries BCE, centuries after the historical Jonah (and long after the destruction of the historical Nineveh by the Medes and the

Babylonians in 612 BCE), it could not possibly be from his hand, or even his school. Modern critics tend to regard it as a piece of fiction, quite possibly a reaction to the ethnic and religious exclusivism which characterized post-Exilic Judaism,[2603] and advocating proselytization, as did a similar tale, *Ruth*.[2604]

As to whether *Jonah* is based upon any traditions associated with the prophet Jonah, we do not know. Aside from the short mention in *Kings*, we have no further information of Jonah's life and deeds in the other years of life. Living on the northern fringes of Israel, he made have indeed undertaken a mission to Nineveh. We cannot prove that he did, but neither can we prove that he did not. Those who believe in the general historicity of the story may take comfort in that uncertainty. *And God knows best.*

Parallels to the Jonah story (or parts of it) exist in other literatures. A Buddhist story tells of a merchant's son from Benares (India), one Mittavindaka, who was put off a ship at sea because he had been disobedient to his mother, and might bring disaster upon the ship.[2605] In another Indian story, Saktideva was swallowed by a great fish after a storm had capsized his ship. Fisherman caught the fish, and after they had slit his belly, Saktideva emerged unharmed.[2606] An ancient Egyptian story tells of a shipwrecked traveler swallowed by a serpent and brought safely to land.[2607] And in Greek mythology we read: "With Athene's help, the Trojans then built Herakles a high wall which served to protect him from the monster as it poked its head out of the sea and advanced across the plain. On reaching the wall, it opened its great jaws and Herakles leaped full-armed down its throat. He spent three days in the monster's belly, and emerged victorious, although the struggle cost him every hair on his head."[2608] This is supposed to have happened near Joppa (modern Jaffa in Palestine), the port from which Jonah departed.[2609] It is possible that these legends are connected and were added to an old tradition by the writer of *Jonah* for his own purposes.

In any event, this parable of divine mercy for all, thereby attacking ethnic and religious exclusivism, represents another step in the

---

[2603] Trawick-OT, pp. 297, 301.

[2604] Weber, p. 418. The rather beautiful pastoral romance of *Ruth* was probably written in the 4th century BCE. (See Note 173 in Vol. 1, above.)

[2605] Gaster, II, p. 653.

[2606] Gaster, II, p. 653-654.

[2607] Jonah, DB, p, 525.

[2608] Graves, II, p. 169)

[2609] Gaster, II, p. 654.

universalization of YHWH, from a tribal god to the One God of all mankind. Because the Quran proclaimed the One God from the outset, there is no surprise at this extension of God's mercy to other nations and other peoples. The story has been used in Islam as a lesson of obedience, humility, and responsibility, none of which may be shirked without moral loss.

III. NEBUCHADNEZZAR

It is unnecessary to emphasize Nebuchadrezzar's ability
as a statesman and military commander... (Saggs, p. 147)

From the Quran: *And We decreed for the Children of Israel in the Scripture: Ye verily will work corruption in the earth twice, and ye will become great tyrants. So when the time for the first of the two came, We roused against you servants of Ours, men of great might, and they went through the habitations, and it was a promise implemented. Then We gave you once again your turn against them, and We aided you with wealth and children, and made you a greater host.* (Q. 17:4-6) These Quranic verses have traditionally been taken to refer to the destruction of Jerusalem by Nebuchadnezzar in 586 BCE. The second of the destructions is described in the following verse: *...So when the time of the (fulfillment of the) latter promise came to discountenance you, they did enter the Temple as they entered it the first time and they laid waste to all they conquered.* (Q. 17:7) This would be a reference to the destruction of Jerusalem and the Second Temple by the Romans in 70 CE.[2610]

Although other explanations are possible because Jerusalem was captured and violated more than two times, the heart of the city, the Temple, was famously destroyed twice: first by Nebuchadnezzar and later by the Romans. There is little reason to discount the traditional exegesis out of hand. During Jerusalem's history as an Israelite city, from about 990 BCE to 135 CE when the Romans expelled the Jews entirely, the destructions wrought by Nebuchadnezzar the Chaldean and Titus the Roman were the most memorable. It is the first destruction of Jerusalem in 586 BCE with which we are concerned here.

Surabadi takes the opportunity of these verses to give us a rather fanciful account of Nebuchadnezzar. He gives the name as Bukht-nassar (*Bukht-naṣṣar*). Tabari and Bal'ami use the same form. The name was actually *Nabū-kudur-uṣur*, meaning "O Nabu,[2611] guard my border!" in Akkadian.[2612] Surabadi relates that Nebuchadnezzar was the son of Kay-

---

[2610] See *The New Testament: An Islamic Perspective* for a discussion of these events.

[2611] Nabu was a god of the Babylonians, the son of Marduk. He was the god of the city of Borshippa southwest of Babylon, and was the patron of the scribal art and wisdom. He seems to have been supplanting Marduk as the principal deity of the Mesopotamians when the Babylonian religion was transformed by new ideas from Persia, Greece, and Palestine (Saggs, p. 327).

[2612] Nebuchadrezzar, DB, p. 693; Nebuchadnessar, EJ, XII, 912. Through a scribal error (Hebrew *n* and *r* are very similar), Nabukudurusur became Nebuchadnezzar; hence, the

Qubad and his name was Kay-Kurosh. As a child, his mother and nurses could not manage him, so they placed him under a tree. A bitch came to him and gave him her milk, and Nebuchadnezzar grew up to be handsome, clever, and fearless.[2613]

This would seem to identify Nebuchadnezzar with the historical Anushirvan (Khusraw I, rgd. 531-579 CE), the son of Qubad I, the Sassanian monarch; or more likely, the Kay-Kavus and Kay Khusraw of Persian mythology. Khusraw was brought up in wild surroundings, albeit by shepherds, not a dog. This intrusion of the bitch is probably an echo of the famous story of Romulus and Remus, the twins who were brought up by a wolf in the foundation myth of ancient Rome, itself probably influenced by the Greek tale of the hero Miletus who was suckled by wild animals.[2614] In Jewish tradition, one of the ancestors of Nebuchadnezzar, the father of Baladan, had the face of a dog.[2615] Nebuchadnezzar was also reputedly a descendant of Nimrod.[2616] Another tradition makes him the offspring of the liaison of Solomon with the queen of Sheba.[2617]

Surabadi says that the People of the Book had read of Nebuchadnezzar in their books and knew that he had come to reduce the Israelites, destroy the Temple of Solomon at Jerusalem, pry out the Sakhrah,[2618] and massacre the citizenry. An Israelite saw him playing when he was seven years old and, recognizing him, sent someone to kill him. The assassin seized him and took him to the desert to perform the deed, but Gabriel seized him.[2619] This was because he was to be God's instrument in the punishment of a sinful people.

It may be noted that the Biblical view of Nebuchadnezzar is not so harsh as that of the rabbis and the later Midrashim.[2620] Later Jews painted him in barbarous colors—he was supposed to have eaten a hare by tearing flesh from the living animal, and to have forcibly sodomized his royal prisoners, except—of course—the Judaean king and his family

---

Arabic form *Bukht-naṣṣar* rather than *Bukht-raṣṣar*. Though Nebuchadrezzar is more accurate, Nebuchadnezzar is still more common in English.

[2613] Surabadi, p. 208.

[2614] Roman Myths, p. 115.

[2615] LJ, IV, 275.

[2616] LJ, IV, 334.

[2617] LJ, IV, 300; See also Part Five, II.J.

[2618] The Sakhrah, the stone around which the Temple was built, now covered by the Dome of the Rock at Jerusalem. In Islamic stories about the Prophet's Night Journey, it is said that he ascended to heaven from it.

[2619] Surabadi, p. 209.

[2620] Nebuchadnezzar, LJ, XII, 914.

who escaped such an indignity.[2621] Surabadi's view is apparently closer to that of the Bible than to the rabbis. He shows Nebuchadnezzar under divine protection.

That Nebuchadnezzar was destined to destroy the Temple was also foreseen by another Israelite wise man, says Surabadi, who had seen him drawing pictures of the Temple before he had laid eyes upon it.[2622] This theme of the predestination of Nebuchadnezzar's role is not prominent in the Jewish legends. However, Nebuchadnezzar is prominent in the Biblical book of *Daniel*, but the references to him there are also largely unhistorical.

Surabadi continues with more breathtaking anachronisms: During the period of these predictions, Solomon was king. After Solomon died, Persia placed Nebuchadnezzar on the throne, and God put hatred for the Israelites in his heart, because of their killing of John the Baptist and Zechariah![2623]

Nebuchadnezzar would have had to live 1000 years to take part in all of those events. The historical Nebuchadnezzar reigned from 605 to 562 BCE, more than three centuries after Solomon. Solomon's influence never reached the Mesopotamian heartland, and during his era, Persia was not in existence as an organized state. Iranian power during Nebuchadnezzar's era was represented by the pre-Achaemenian Medes, upon whose throne he never sat. Similarly, John the Baptist is an anachronism as he belongs to the period of the New Testament, that is Rome, some five centuries later. As for Zechariah, there is one who belonged to the Roman era and was killed by the Zealots during the turmoil that led up to the destruction of Jerusalem and the Second Temple in 70 CE.[2624] However, Surabadi's reference is doubtless to the priest Zechariah who lived during the reign of Joash, king of Judah from 835 to 796 BCE,[2625] and therefore about two centuries earlier than Nebuchadnezzar.

[2621] LJ, IV, 291, 336.

[2622] Surabadi, p. 209.

[2623] Surabadi, p. 209.

[2624] Josephus, Jewish War, IV.5.4, PP. 534-535.

[2625] "Then the spirit of God took possession of Zechariah the son of Jehoiada the priest; and he stood above the people, and said to them, 'Thus says God, "Why do ye transgress the commandments of the Lord, so that ye cannot prosper? Because ye have forsaken the Lord, He has forsaken you.' But they conspired against him, and by command of the king they stoned him with stones in the court of the house of the Lord. Thus Joash the king did not remember the kindness which Jehoiada, Zechariah's father, had shown him, but killed his son. And when he was dying, he said. 'May the Lord see and avenge!'" (2 Ch. 24:20-22)

Jewish tradition, too, makes a connection between this tragedy and the destruction of the Temple. "Still more horrible was the carnage among the people by Nebuzaradan,[2626] spurred on as he was by the sight of the blood of the murdered prophet Zechariah seething on the floor of the Temple. At first, the Jews sought to conceal the true story connected with the blood. At length they had to confess that it was the blood of a prophet who had prophesied the destruction of the Temple, and for his candor he had been slain by the people. Nebuzaradan, to appease the prophet, ordered the scholars of the kingdom to be executed first on the bloody spot, then the school children, and at last the young priests, more than a million [!] souls in all. But the blood of the prophet went on seething and reeking, until Nebuzaradan exclaimed: 'Zechariah, Zechariah, the good in Israel I have slaughtered. Dost thou desire the destruction of the whole people?" Then the blood ceased to seethe."[2627]

Though Zechariah is not mentioned in the account of the last days of Jerusalem, to the writers of the Bible, Nebuchadnezzar's attack upon Judah was seen as divine vengeance: "Jehoiakim was twenty-five years old when he began to reign, and he reigned eleven years in Jerusalem... And he did what was evil in the sight of the Lord, according to all that his fathers had done. In his days Nebuchadnezzar king of Babylon came up, and Jehoiakim became his servant three years; then he turned and rebelled against him. And the Lord sent against him bands of Chaldeans, and bands of Syrians, and bands of Moabites, and bands of Ammonites, and set them against Judah to destroy it, according to the word of the Lord which He spoke by His servants the prophets." (2 K. 23:36-37; 24:1-2)

In Surabadi's story, Nebuchadnezzar attacked Jerusalem for seven years and slaughtered the inhabitants, except for a few who were dispersed throughout the world. He had 600,000 standards, and under each standard 10,000 men.[2628] He destroyed the Temple and seized the Treasure of Solomon.[2629] It is possible that Surabadi's mention of Zechariah is a mistake for Zedekiah, the last king of Judah (see below).

Judah, after the loss of the Northern kingdom of Israel, did not have the power to pursue so aggressive a foreign policy as did Israel. In

---

[2626] Nebuzaradan was Nebuchadnezzar's captain of the guard. According to the tradition, the blood of the martyred priest had remained on the floor for two centuries.

[2627] LJ, IV, 304.

[2628] This would make Nebuchadnezzar's army total some 6,000,000,000 men! According to an expert estimate, the population of the entire world did not exceed 100,000,000 at the time of Nebuchadnezzar. Mesopotamia, the home base of Nebuchadnezzar, had a population probably somewhat in excess of a million. (McEvedy, p. 343;149.)

[2629] Surabadi, p. 209.

addition to successfully defending itself from Israel, Judah made some minor incursions into Edom, had dealings—both friendly and unfriendly—with the Philistines, and suffered from the expedition of the Egyptian pharaoh Shishak, who despoiled the Temple. However, in general, its relative unimportance,[2630] its geographical isolation (the barriers of the Dead Sea and the escarpment of the Jordan valley to the east, the desert of Edom to the south), the existence of alternative routes between Syria and Egypt through the plains of the Philistines to the west, and the acquired wisdom that the prolonged continuity a single dynasty often provides enabled the kings of Judah to retain a semblance of independence even after the catastrophic destruction of the kingdom of Israel[2631] by the Assyrians in 721 BCE. Though usually paying some form of tribute to one powerful neighbor or another, Judah lived on until Nebuchadnezzar put an end to it in 586 BCE.

Nebuchadnezzar and his Chaldeans were of East Arabian origin and continued to retain an interest in Arabia, as his and later Nabonidus' expeditions into Arabia demonstrate.[2632] The father of Nebuchadnezzar, Nabopolassar (rgd. 626-605 BCE), had founded the Neo-Babylonian Empire on the wreckage of the Assyrian Empire. This had been brought about by an attack upon Assyria in coordination with the Iranian Medes, bringing the Assyrian Empire to an abrupt and stunning end in 612 BCE while still at the height of its power. Under Nebuchadnezzar, this Neo-Babylonian Empire, as it is called by historians, reached its greatest extent and splendor, ruling the entire Fertile Crescent from the borders of Egypt on the southwest to the frontiers of Media and Elam on the east, from the Mediterranean Sea to the head of the Persian Gulf.

In the last decades of its existence, Judah was caught between the expansionist ambitions of the Neo-Babylonians on the north and east, and a reviving Egyptian power under Pharaoh Necho (rgd. 610-595

[2630] Though Jerusalem and Judah loom large in the Biblically based Western view of the Near East, at the end the remnant of Solomon's empire governed an area of about 3,000 square miles, three quarters of which was sparsely inhabited semi-desert and desert. The population did not exceed 125,000 (Albright-Ab to Ez, p. 84). One hundred years earlier, Judah's population was probably twice as much and its area somewhat greater.

[2631] It is ironic that when the Zionist state was established in Palestine, the name of the ill-fated Israel was chosen rather than Judaea or Judah, for Israel and Judaea were generally rivals and often hostile to each other. Modern Judaism, as its name indicates, traces its history to the Judahite House of David at Jerusalem, against whom Israel rebelled, rejecting the exclusivity of the Jerusalem cult. If anything, the tiny present-day minority of Samaritans has more right to claim the heritage of ancient Israel, than does Zionist Israel, a quasi-restoration of ancient Judah, unsanctified by the messiah.

[2632] Albright-Ab to Ez, p. 109. About Nabonidus' expedition, see "The Origin of the Jews of Hejaz" in the Introduction, I.C.

BCE) to the southwest. Josiah, perhaps the finest of the kings of Judah, was tragically killed in a battle with the Egyptians at Megiddo[2633] in 606 BCE. His son Jehoahaz was made king at Jerusalem, but Necho managed to imprison and replace him with another son of Josiah, Jehoiakim, who was in fact an Egyptian vassal. But in 605 BCE, Necho was defeated by then crown prince Nebuchadnezzar at Carchemish (in northern Syria).[2634] As a result, Judah passed from the Egyptian to the Babylonian sphere of influence. Almost immediately after the battle, Nebuchadnezzar succeeded his father on the throne of Babylon. At the beginning of his reign, he seems have had some difficulty in establishing his rule in the western part of the Fertile Crescent, which included Judah. Jehoiakim seized the opportunity to assert his independence and withhold tribute to Babylon—a bad decision, as it turned out. But before Nebuchadnezzar could attend to this upstart, Jehoiakim died. When the Babylonians finally laid siege to Jerusalem in 597 BCE, the new king, Jehoiakim's son Jehoiachin, was forced to submit after three months.

As a result: "The king of Babylon took (Jehoiachin) prisoner in the eighth year of (Nebuchadnezzar's) reign,[2635] and carried off all the treasures of the king's house, and cut in pieces all the vessels of gold in the temple of the Lord, which Solomon king of Israel had made, as the Lord foretold. He carried away all Jerusalem, and all the princes, and all the mighty men of valor, ten thousand captives, and all the craftsmen and the smiths; none remained, except the poorest people of the land. And he carried away Jehoiachin to Babylon; the king's mother, the king's wives, his officials, and the chief men of the land, he took into captivity from Jerusalem to Babylon. And the king of Babylon brought captive to Babylon all men of valor, seven thousand, and the craftsmen and the smiths, one thousand, all of them strong and fit for war." (2 K. 24:12b-16)

Despite the tenor of this passage, which probably had later events in mind, Jerusalem was not destroyed, merely looted. Only certain classes of her people were carried off, not the entire population. Nebuchadnezzar placed Zedekiah, an uncle of the deposed king on the throne of Judah as a vassal and returned to Babylon. By good fortune, a cuneiform tablet of the *Babylonian Chronicle* has survived giving the Babylonian version of the capture of Jerusalem: "In the seventh years, in the month of Kislev [Nov-Dec], the Babylonian king mustered his

---

[2633] Megiddo: in northern Palestine, in the region that the apocalyptic battle of Armageddon is expected to take place.

[2634] The ruins of Carchemish are now in Turkey, close to the Syrian border.

[2635] It was actually the seventh year of his reign; see below.

troops, and, having marched to the land of Hatti [Syria], besieged the city of Judah [Jerusalem], and on the second day of the month of Adar [Feb-Mar] took the city and captured the king. He appointed therein a king of his own choice, received its heavy tribute and sent (them) to Babylon."[2636]

Zedekiah, the "king of (Nebuchadnezzar's) own choice," was the last king of Judah. Despite the terrifying power of the Babylonian king that he must have witnessed, the imprudent Zedekiah was persuaded to conspire with Pharaoh Neccho's successor Hophra (rgd. 595-570 BCE) to rebel against Nebuchadnezzar. The outcome was catastrophe:

"And in the ninth year of (Zedekiah's) reign, in the tenth month, on the tenth day of the month, Nebuchadnezzar king of Babylon came with all his army against Jerusalem, and laid siege to it; and they built siege works against it round about. So the city was besieged till the eleventh year of King Zedekiah. On the ninth day of the fourth month,[2637] the famine was so severe in the city that there was no food for the people of the land. Then a breach was made in the city; the king with all the men of war fled by night by way of the gate between the two walls, by the king's garden, though the Chaldeans were around the city. And they went in the direction of the Arabah.[2638] But the army of the Chaldeans pursued the king, and overtook him in the plains of Jericho; and all his army was scattered from him. Then they captured the king, and brought him up to the king of Babylon at Riblah,[2639] who passed sentence upon him. They slew the sons of Zedekiah before his eyes, and put out the eyes of Zedekiah, and bound him in fetters, and took him to Babylon." (2 K. 25:1-7)

Jerusalem was put to the torch. The Temple, the palace, and "every great house" were looted, burned, and demolished. The walls around the city were torn down. "And the rest of the people who were left in the city and the deserters who had deserted to the king of Babylon, together with the rest of the multitude, Nebuzaradan the captain of the guard carried into exile. But the captain of the guard left some of the poorest of the land to be vine-dressers and ploughmen." (2 K. 25:11-12)

"And the pillars of bronze that were in the house of the Lord, and the stands and the bronze sea that were in the house of the Lord, the

---

[2636] Thomas, p. 80.

[2637] That is after 19 months of siege, in 586 BCE.

[2638] The great valley containing the Jordan valley and the Dead Sea that stretches from north of the Sea of Galilee to the Gulf of Aqabah,

[2639] The same as modern Riblah just north of the Lebanese-Syrian border in Syria. It was probably the chief center for Nebuchadnezzar's control of the western Fertile Crescent. (Riblah, DB, p. 852.0

Chaldeans broke in pieces, and carried away the bronze to Babylon. And they took away the pots, and the shovels, and the snuffers, and the dishes for incense and all the vessels of bronze used in the temple service, the firepans also, and the bowls. What was of gold the captain of the guard took away as gold, and what was silver, as silver. As for the two pillars, the one sea, and the stands, which Solomon had made for the house of the Lord, the bronze of all these vessels was beyond weight." (2 K. 25:13-16) Alas, *sic transit gloria mundi* indeed!

This is the disaster to which the Quran and Surabadi were referring, although the long siege lasted nineteen months instead of Surabadi's seven years, and the hosts brought up against Jerusalem could not have been so vast as Surabadi records, as the population of the entire Fertile Crescent did not exceed three millions. As we have seen, this was the calamitous second—not the first—capture of Jerusalem by Nebuchadnezzar. The exasperated king was determined that Jerusalem would cause him no further trouble. After the fall of the city, a number of captives were taken to his camp at Riblah where they were put to death, probably as a warning to the other Jews. "So Judah was taken into exile out of its land." (2 K. 35:21)

Despite the finality in those words, we know that Jerusalem was still not completely deserted. In the final chapter of *Jeremiah* (Jeremiah lived during these events), there is a summary of the captives carried off by Nebuchadnezzar: "In the seventh year [597 BCE] 3023 Jews; in the eighteenth year of Nebuchadnezzar [586 BCE, the year of the destruction and depopulation quoted above] he carried off 832 persons; in the 23rd year of Nebuchadnezzar [581 BCE], Nebuzaradan the captain of the guard carried away captive of Jews 745 persons; all the persons were 4,600." (Jer. 52:28-30)

Thus, the captivity was carried out in three phases, of which the first witnessed widespread looting and the largest deportation and the second, the destruction of the Temple and the city, and the end of the Judahite monarchy. The third phase, carried out in 581 BCE, is not mentioned in *Kings* or *Chronicles*, but seems to indicate that Jerusalem either was not totally depopulated in the calamity of 586 BCE, or had been to some extent repopulated soon after the armies had departed. Probably the destruction of the Temple and the symbols of Davidic glory were the psychological equivalent of total destruction to the scribes who recorded the story of those tragic events. [2640]

[2640] Stanley Brice Frost, writing in Laymon, notes that the last chapter of Jeremiah (ch. 52) is an historical appendix added possibly by the Deuteronomist, and regards the tradition and the figures given for the threefold captivity as more reliable than those of

Since the destruction of Assyria and the rise of the Neo-Babylonian Empire were made possible by the cooperation of the Iranian Medes, it is perhaps not an exaggeration to say with Surabadi that the Persians (*'Ajam*) were responsible for Nebuchadnezzar's power. Despite his military exploits, Nebuchadnezzar (like Solomon and Ramses II) wanted to be remembered as a builder, and most of the inscriptions that have been recovered from his reign deal with his building activities. Archaeological evidence supports his claims, as Babylon reached the apogee of its material splendor under his rule, and the effect upon the rather provincial Jewish exiles there was incalculable.

Surabadi concludes his story by relating that Cyrus of Hamadan [the first Achaemenian king, Cyrus the Great] arose and defeated Nebuchadnezzar and seized his kingdom. In a battle with him, Nebuchadnezzar shot an arrow that turned back upon him and struck his own horse. He fell from the animal and was killed. The Israelites recovered, but within forty years they were again corrupt and ignoring the commandments of God. Then Natwas the Roman conquered them.[2641]

This, too, is largely unhistorical. Nebuchadnezzar died in 562 BCE, apparently peacefully. Cyrus did not capture Babylon until 539 BCE when Nabu-na'id (Nabonidus) was king. Nabu-na'id was not of Nebuchadnezzar's family, but was the son of a nobleman who ascended

---

Kings-Chronicles. Since these figures considerable reduce the image of the massive deportation of tens of thousands, then who were the exiled? The elite and craftsmen. If only 4600 were deported, what happened to the rest of the population? "The answer is that most of them were the *poorest in the land* (vs.16) left to till their little plots and struggle as best they could." In other words, the bulk of the population, many of whom later (voluntarily) emigrated to Babylon and Egypt in search of a better life. "The idea of forced mass deportation... is historically as well as practically unsound." Laymon, pp. 374, 403-404.)

Archeological evidence certifies that the Babylonian conquest caused an almost complete break in urban life, and a mass depopulation of Judah. (Albright-Ab to Ez, p. 110.) Not a single town in Judah thus far excavated escaped the depopulation. (Keller, p. 329.) On the surface, this would appear to contradict Frost's opinion, but in reality, it does not. Remove the leadership and the craftsmen and there would certainly follow a radical change in material life. The depopulation could be explained by a voluntary depopulation that follows defeat, as happened in Ireland in the 19th century after the horrors of the potato famines.

[2641] Surabadi, pp. 209-210. Surabadi associates the second destruction with the Roman "Natwas" As Dr. Mahdavi says in his note (Surabadi, p. 210), this was probably meant to be "Tatyus" (the difference between N and T is a single dot in Perso-Arabic script); that is, the Roman emperor Titus who destroyed Jerusalem in 70 CE. Titus, the son of emperor Vespasian, was born c. 40 CE, and was co-ruler with his father after 71 CE, then sole emperor after his father's death from 79 to 81 CE. Thus he was only about 30 years old when he crushed the Jewish revolt. (See *The New Testament: An Islamic Perspective* for about these events in Roman times.)

the throne in 555 BCE. Nabu-na'id's connection with Arabia has already been described. He seems to have been sincerely interested in religious reform, and while so engaged, Cyrus, by means of his agents, was busily spreading propaganda that skillfully played up the religious tensions created by Nabu-na'id's reforms and the fear of the power of Persia.[2642] In such conditions, the conquest of Babylon by Cyrus was relatively easy, though it was of tremendous symbolic importance to the Persians.

In 538 BCE, Cyrus issued the edict permitting the return of the Jews to Jerusalem. The Jews hailed him as a Messiah.[2643] The Temple was rebuilt by 515 BCE. The Babylonian Captivity had lasted 48 years, although its impact on Judaism was much greater than a mere two generations suggest. Prosperity slowly returned to Jerusalem and Judah.

HABAKKUK: As a postscript to the story of Nebuchadnezzar, we take the opportunity to mention the prophet Habakkuk, the reputed author of a small book bearing his name in the Old Testament about whom there is an almost certainly unhistorical story in the 2nd-century BCE apocryphal book *Bel and the Dragon* found in some Bibles. Our only excuse for mentioning Habakkuk is the existence of a tomb reported to be his near the Iranian town of Tuysirkan in the Zagros Mountains, not far from Hamadan (where the patently unhistorical tombs of Esther and Mordecai are shown). The present building is a tomb tower with a fluted conical roof standing in a field a short distance from town. Stylistically, the present structure apparently belongs to the Mongol period (13th to early 14th century CE), but the inscription inside is in Hebrew. Rebuilt shrines are frequently encountered in the Near East; it is, after all, the site that is sanctified. Sylvia Matheson mentions it and the Hebrew inscription in her archaeological guide to Iran, but does not link it to Habakkuk.[2644] However, locally this link is firmly established. We have had occasion to visit this little tomb several times.

Little is known about Habakkuk.[2645] The oracles in the Biblical book bearing his name refer to an oppressor. The introduction to the book in the *Jerusalem Bible* notes that an identification of this "oppressor" with the Chaldeans during the years between the battle of

---

[2642] Saggs, pp. 155-156.

[2643] In Is. 45:1, attributed to the possibly 2nd century BCE "Second" Isaiah. This will be discussed in the *The New Testament: An Islamic Perspective*, in connection with the messianic movement and Jesus.

[2644] Matheson, p. 121.

[2645] Noeldeke suggests that his name was of Arabic derivation: *hibhkatun* (sic) meaning "dwarf." (The Arabic *hibiqqah* does have a meaning of "short man.") Noth offers an Akkadian derivation, *hambaqūku*, the name of a plant. (Habakkuk, IDB, Vol. 2, 503.)

Carchemish (605 BCE) and the first siege of Jerusalem by Nebuchadnezzar in 597 BCE has been made,[2646] our excuse for appending these paragraphs here. *The Interpreter's Dictionary of the Bible* states that he was a cultic prophet of Judah from the last days of the reforming King Josiah (rgd. 640-609 BCE) through the disappointing reign of his successor, Jehoiakim (rgd. 609-598 BCE); that is, a contemporary of Nebuchadnezzar of Babylon (lived c. 630-562 BCE).

The aforementioned story in *Bel and the Dragon* is this: "Now there was in Jewry the prophet Habakkuk, who had made pottage, and had broken bread into a bowl, and was going into the field, for to bring it to the reapers. But the angel of the Lord said unto Habakkuk, 'Go carry the dinner that thou hast into Babylon unto Daniel, in the lions' den.' And Habakkuk said, 'Lord, I never saw Babylon; neither do I know where the den is.' Then the angel of the Lord took him by the crown, and lifted him up by the hair of his head, and with the blast of his breath set him in Babylon over the den. And Habakkuk cried, saying, 'O Daniel, Daniel, Daniel, take the dinner which God hath sent thee.' So Daniel arose, and did eat: and the angel of God set Habakkuk in his own place immediately."[2647]

The high Zagros Mountains of western Iran were the core of the Median Empire and not a part of Nebuchadnezzar's extensive realm, so how Habakkuk came to be buried in Tuysirkan—if indeed he was—can only be guessed. We know that the prophets of that period frequently went off into the desert, far away from the iniquities they were lamenting. Perhaps the pericope in *Bel and the Dragon* is based on a tradition of Habakkuk's removal from Judah to Babylon, and perhaps he fled the corruption of Babylon for the safety of the Median Empire centered about Hamadan.

We would not be speculating about these things were it not for the little, seemingly out-of-place tomb, and the curious tradition it represents, on a dusty field outside a small, pleasant town—so far from Jerusalem.

[2646] JB, p. 1138.
[2647] Apocrypha, (Bel and the Dragon) p. 308.

IV. EZRA

He was a scribe skilled in the Law of Moses... (Ezra 7:6)

EZRA OR EZEKIEL? Surabadi's story of Ezra (*'Uzayr*) will be discussed in two parts. In the first, about resurrection, Surabadi tells us that when Ezra was traveling and had come to the village of Dir Hirqul,[2648] he had two skins of juice and two baskets of figs, and a donkey. He walked thoughtfully among the ruins of that place, tethered his ass, and sat down upon a platform. He asked God how could the dead be revived. God caused him to die for a hundred years and then revived him. "God asked him: 'How long hast thou tarried here?' He answered: 'A day or a part of a day.' God said: "Thou has tarried here a hundred years.'"

God told him to look at his food and then at the dead ass, which God had also resurrected. First, the eyes came back to life and he looked at the bones, and then the bones came together and were clothed in flesh as before, and the food was also restored. After this miraculous proof, Ezra loaded his ass and went home.[2649]

This parable is based upon a verse of Surah al-Baqarah in a passage discussing how the resurrection of the dead would be achieved. It is immediately followed by the parable of Abraham and the birds[2650] that treats the same theme. Except in a few details, Surabadi's version follows the Quranic text rather closely: *Or it is like him who, passing by a city that had fallen into utter ruin, exclaimed: "How shall God give this city[2651] life after its death?" And God made him die for a hundred years, then brought him back to life. (God) said: "How long hast thou tarried?" (The man) said: "I have tarried a day or part of a day." (God) said: "Nay, but thou hast tarried for a hundred years. Look thou at thy food and drink which have not aged! Look at thine ass! And, that We may make thee a token unto mankind, look at the bones, how We adjust them and then cover them with flesh!" And when the matter became clear unto him, he said: "I know now that God is able to do all things."* (Q. 2:259)[2652]

[2648] Dīr Hirqūl: the name means "Monastery (or Cloister) of Hercules."

[2649] Surabadi, pp. 21-22.

[2650] See III.J above.

[2651] Most Muslim commentators hold that the city was Jerusalem (Quran-Pickthall, p. 41), most probably after its destruction by Nebuchadnezzar.

[2652] There is some disagreement about the condition of the food and drink, as well as the ass. Maulana Muhammad Ali takes the view that they were not affected by the passage of time. A. Yusuf Ali writes that the food and drink were fresh, but the animal had been

This verse describes a miracle not unlike that of the Companions of the Cave in Surah al-Kahf.[2653] Although the forms of the stories are quite different, both are in a sense concerned with resurrection, parables of the second life.

This was particularly important, for the pagan Arabs had only a vague notion of the afterlife, sharing the earlier Semitic beliefs in which behavior was rewarded or punished by the gods in this life.[2654] They accepted the immortality of the soul, but had difficulty comprehending judgment with reward and punishment according to the character of one's life in this world. Physical resurrection, disquieting to some, makes this comprehensible. If one accepts the thesis of a kind of resurrection after death, then reward and punishment, based upon moral behavior will determine the starting point for further spiritual progress, perhaps dispensing with even the shadow of this mortal life's physical being. The idea that the soul survived death in some manner was not foreign to the pagan Arabs, but resurrection and judgment was, as it was to the Jews throughout most of the Old Testament period.

The Quran does not name the prophet of the parable. Surabadi identifies him as Ezra, but there is no such story associated with Ezra in the Bible. There is, however, a similar story in *Ezekiel*. Ezekiel[2655] writes: "The hand of the Lord was upon me, and He brought me out by the Spirit of the Lord, and set me down in the midst of the valley; it was full of bones... And He said to me, 'Son of man, can these bones live?' And I answered, 'O Lord God, Thou knowest.' Again He said to me, 'Prophesy to these bones, and say to them, O dry bones, hear the word of the Lord. Thus says the Lord God to these bones: Behold, I will cause breath to enter you and ye shall live. And I will lay sinews upon you, and will cause flesh to come upon you, and cover you with skin, and put breath into you, and ye shall live; and ye shall know that I am the Lord.'" (Ezek. 37:1,3-6)

---

reduced to bones that were the subject of the revivification, and Maududi agrees with him, as does Ibn Kathir. Pickthall construes the text to mean that the food and drink had rotted. (Quran-MMA, pp. 113-114; Quran-Yusuf Ali, p. 105; Quran-Maududi, I, pp. 175-176; Kathir, p. 656; Quran-Pickthall, p. 41.) We follow the majority here.

[2653] See the story of the Companions of the Cave in *The New Testament: An Islamic Perspective*, Stories, IV.A.

[2654] Arabs, ERE, I, 671-673.

[2655] The prophet Ezekiel was active from 593 to 571 BCE (Ezekiel, DB, 283), and thus during the period of the fall of Jerusalem to Nebuchadnezzar and the Exile. He himself was carried off to Babylon where he exercised leadership among the community of displaced Jews. The text of the *Book of Ezekiel* is both difficult and corrupt, and the numerous duplications and variants indicate that it is conflated (Ezekiel, EJ, VI, 1089-1090).

"So I prophesied as I was commanded; and as I prophesied, there was a noise, and behold, a rattling; and the bones came together, bone to its bone. And as I looked, there were sinews on them, and flesh had come upon them, and skin had covered them; but there was no breath in them. Then He said to me, 'Prophesy to the breath,' ...So I prophesied as He commanded me, and the breath came into them. And they lived, stood upon their feet, an exceedingly great host." (Ezek. 37:7-10)

Then God said to Ezekiel: "'Son of man, these bones are the whole house of Israel. Behold, they say, "Our bones are dried up, and our hope is lost; we are clean cut off." Therefore prophesy, and say to them, Thus says the Lord god: Behold, I will open your graves, and raise you from your graves, O my people; and I will bring you home into the land of Israel. And ye shall know that I am the Lord, when I open your graves, O my people. And I will put My Spirit within you, and ye shall live, and I will place you in your own land; then ye shall know that I, the Lord, have spoken, and I have done it, says the Lord'" (Ezek. 37:11-14)

Despite appearances, this is *not* a prophecy of personal resurrection, but rather foresees the return of Israel to Palestine from the "death" that is Babylonian Exile. The return of Jews from Babylon to Judah is meant, the resurrection or rebirth of a nation, as a careful reading of the text will show.[2656] Assuming that this passage from *Ezekiel* is the ultimate basis of the Quranic reference, once again the Quran has transformed a popular miracle-story into a different and broader parable promising the resurrection of all mankind. Ezekiel's parable of the future revival of Israel (actually the kingdom of Judah here) in this world has become a demonstration of the nature of individual resurrection and accountability.

This passage from *Ezekiel*, however, accounts for only a part of the material in the Quranic parable; the death and resurrection of the prophet is not mentioned. Parallels with the Christian story of the Seven Sleepers (the Companions of the Cave) have already been noted, but another Jewish tradition seems to lie behind these elements. It is found in the pseudepigraphic *Rest of the Words of Baruch*:

"The sons of Moses were not the only ones to escape from under the heavy hand of Nebuchadnezzar. Still more miraculous was the deliverance of the pious Ethiopian Ebed-melech from the hands of the Babylonians. He was saved as a reward for rescuing Jeremiah when the prophet's life was jeopardized. On the day before the destruction of the Temple, shortly before the enemy forced his way into the city, the

---

[2656] Trawick-OT, p. 208; Ezekiel, EJ, VI, 1088.

Ethiopian was sent, by the prophet Jeremiah acting under divine instruction, to a certain place in front of the gates of the city, to dole out refreshments to the poor from a little basket of figs he was to carry with him. Ebed-melech reached the spot, but the heat was so intense that he fell asleep under a tree, and there he slept for sixty-six years. When he woke up, the figs were still fresh and juicy, but all the surroundings had so changed, he could not make out where he was. His confusion increased when he entered the city to see Jeremiah, and found nothing as it had been. He accosted an old man, and asked him the name of the place. When he was told it was Jerusalem, Ebed-melech cried out in amazement..."[2657]

It appears fairly obvious that the tradition represented in the story of Ebed-Melech also entered Arabian oral literature and stands behind two elements of the Quranic parable: the death and revival of the prophet a century later, and the mention of the freshness of the food. However, whilst these elements serve in the Islamic parable to illustrate the concept of the resurrection of the dead, in the Ebed-melech story the point is quite different: a reward in this world for a pious act: not witnessing the terrible destruction of the Temple and not participating in the sorrows of the Exile.

Whether these elements were combined in pre-Islamic tradition is difficult to say. The fullness of the Quranic text here as well as the novelty of the concept being illustrated suggest that it may have been a new parable for its audience, at least in its Quranic form. It was obviously in answer to the complaint that after a great passage time the flesh would turn to dust and the bones would become scattered and their material reused by other creatures, so how could they be reassembled and reclothed for the Day of Judgment? From the materials of the Ezekiel vision and the Ebed-melech story a striking parable of physical resurrection was created to answer this question. A long time had passed, a hundred years in the Quran, in the normal course of which the physical body would have become dust. By reviving this disintegrated corpse after such a time and demonstrating to the incredulous, similarly revived man how he himself had been reconstituted, the parable's point is forcefully made.

EZRA: The second part of Surabadi's story is based upon the story of Ezra as found in the Bible, although he links it with the preceding Quranic parable by beginning this section with the return of

---

[2657] LJ, IV, 318-319. Washington Irving's famous 1819 story *Rip Van Winkle* uses the same device to great effect.

the revived prophet to his home. Ezra was forty years old when he left, and he had had a twenty-year old son. When he returned, he was still forty, however, his son was one hundred and twenty years old![2658] This is the rather amusing consequence of cold mathematics when applied to a parable. Undaunted, Surabadi continues:

At first, the people did not believe him, but they tested him, saying that Ezra knew the Torah by heart. They searched for a copy, but Nebuchadnezzar had destroyed them all. Finally, some one said he had a copy that he had hidden in a jug and buried. They brought it, and when they followed the written text as Ezra recited it flawlessly, the people believed his story and accepted him as Ezra.[2659] None of this has anything to do with the Quranic text, and rather little with the Bible. But it probably refers to something of much greater significance than is at first apparent:

The books of and *Nehemiah* are believed to be the work of the same compiler who wrote *Chronicles*. In *Ezra*, the Chronicler used official Aramaic reports, a memoir written by Ezra himself, and oral tradition. In *Nehemiah*, he used a similar memoir by Nehemiah with other additions.[2660] These books, *Chronicles-Ezra-Nehemiah*, constitute the Chronicler's history of the Jewish nation from Adam to his own era, about 300 BCE, or perhaps somewhat later.[2661] His emphasis, as discussed in the Introduction (III.E), was on the religious history of Israel and Israel's status as God's chosen people and the importance of the Temple as Judaism's central shrine. The Chronicler has given us a Judahite history, as opposed to the Israelite history of *Samuel-Kings*. Josephus, oddly, does not mention Ezra, although he does Nehemiah.

The present text of *Ezra-Nehemiah*, despite its relative lateness, is in great disorder and creates the impression that the prophet Ezra preceded Nehemiah, whereas a majority of scholars today feels that the reverse is true.[2662] In the more generally accepted reconstruction of events, after the Edict of Cyrus in 536 BCE permitting the Jews to return to Jerusalem, a number of them actually did so and they rebuilt the Temple between 520 and 515 BCE, but the community remained small and dispirited. Nehemiah received permission from the Persian king

---

[2658] Surabadi, p. 22.

[2659] Surabadi, p. 22.

[2660] Trawick-OT, p. 142; Ezra, DB, p. 286; Nehemiah, DB, pp. 695-696.

[2661] There is another view which makes the Chronicler active earlier, about 400 BCE, and therefore, as we shall see, a contemporary of Ezra. Some have suggested that the Chronicler *is* Ezra. (Ezra-Nehemiah, EJ, VI, 1121-1122. See also Introduction, V.E.10 "The Chronicler.")

[2662] Trawick-OT, p. 143.

Artaxerxes I (rgd. 464-423 BCE) to rebuild the walls of Jerusalem and the work commenced in 444 BCE.[2663] However, it still lacked definitive spiritual leadership. In the seventh year of the reign of Artaxerxes (II?),[2664] Ezra the scribe, son of Seraiah, of the priestly line of Aaron, secured permission from the Persian king to go from Babylon to Jerusalem in order to restore the Temple service and the Law (Ezra 7). In a company of priests and Temple servants, Ezra's journey to Jerusalem lasted four months. Arriving at the holy city, the Temple furniture was replaced, the service renewed, and the sacrifices begun.

After accomplishing this, Ezra learned that many of the returnees, including the priests, had taken non-Jewish wives. Horrified, Ezra convinced them that they must repudiate those wives and their offspring by them, in order to purify the Jewish race from association with idolators and render the nation once again worthy of worshipping YHWH. This was actually done, or at least that is what *Ezra* tells us in chs. 9 and 10 of the Biblical book bearing his name.[2665] There is considerable evidence that this emphasis upon extreme racial purity was something of an innovation, although tendencies towards it were inherent in earlier practices. The fact that there were many references in the Bible to marriage of Israelites to non-Israelites, beginning with Moses himself, became a later embarrassment. To explain this, in the view of some, Moses did so before the promulgation of the Law; but what about David and Solomon? They had no such excuse.

In any event, this traumatic purification was followed by a rededication of the people in a great law-reading ceremony wherein Ezra read the Torah[2666] to the assembled people in seven days.[2667] This was the

---

[2663] Trawick-OT, pp. 143, 144. Nehemiah, DB, pp. 694-695 gives the date as 445 BCE. Albright suggests that instead of "seventh year" we should read "37th year", which would be about 428 BCE (Albright-Ab to Ez, p.93). Though there is no proof for it, such a date would resolve virtually all of the chronological problems of *Ezra-Nehemiah*. (Ezra-Nehemiah, EJ, VI, 1106.)

[2664] Which Artaxerxes is not specified. Modern scholars believe that Artaxerxes II, who reigned from 404 to 358 BCE, is meant; and thus the year indicated is 398 BCE. See also Introduction, V.E.

[2665] After a long list of names, Ezra 10 ends: "And these had married foreign women, and they put them away with their children." (Ezra 10:44) One may wish to pause and contemplate the breathtaking enormity implicit in Ezra's satisfaction.

[2666] Scholars are not sure exactly what document it was that Ezra read to the people. It could have been the Pentateuch, the Priestly Code, or *Deuteronomy*. (Anderson, p. 163.)

[2667] This public reading of the Law was greeted with dismay: "And Nehemiah, who was the governor, and Ezra the priest and scribe, and the Levites who taught the people said to all the people, 'this day is holy to the Lord your God; do not mourn or weep.' For all the people wept when they heard the words of the law." (Neh. 8:9)

occasion for a great revival of religious enthusiasm and the reinstitution of the provisions of the Law and the feasts. In an impassioned speech, Ezra reminded the people of their unique history and their Covenant with God (Neh. 7:73-9:38).

It is this public reading of the Law which forms the core of the tradition reported by Surabadi that Ezra was required to recite the Law in order to prove his identity. Different Jewish stories are told about the copy of the Law from which Ezra read. In one tradition, the copy was that written by Eli at Shiloh. It had been buried in the Temple and was rescued by Ezekiel, who took it with him to Babylon. This was the copy that Ezra brought back to Jerusalem to read to the people.[2668] While the stories Surabadi associates with him are not negative, Ezra's association with the text of the Torah has led many Muslims commentators to accuse him of being responsible for the corruption of the Torah mentioned in the Quran. In this view, Ezra plays a role somewhat akin to that of Paul in the New Testament: the corrupter of the Message. This attitude may have been influenced by a non-traditional interpretation of the name 'Uzayr (see below).

In another tradition, recorded in the *Apocalypse of Ezra* (also called *2 Esdras* and *IV Ezra*),[2669] chs. 3 to 14 of which were written by a Jew c. 95-100 CE, Ezra is associated with the renewal of the scriptures: "I took with me the five men as I had been told, and we went away to the field, and there we stayed. On the next day I heard a voice calling me, which said: 'Ezra, open your mouth and drink what I give you.' So I opened my mouth, and was handed a cup full of what seemed like water, except that its color was the color of fire. I took it, and drank, and as soon as I had done so my mind began to pour forth a flood of understanding, and wisdom grew greater and greater within me, for I retained my memory unimpaired. I opened my mouth to speak, and I continued to speak unceasingly.

"The Most High gave understanding to the five men, who took turns at writing down what was said, using characters which they had not known before. [Ezra is credited with the introduction of the square Aramaic script now used in Hebrew, replacing the Canaanite script previously employed.] They remained at work through the forty days, writing all day, and taking food only at night. But as for me, I spoke all through the day; even at night I was not silent. In the forty days ninety-four books were written. At the end of the forty days the Most High spoke to me. 'Make public the books you wrote first,' He said, 'to be

---

[2668] LJ, VI, 220.
[2669] Ezra, Apocalypse of, EJ, VI, 1108.

read by good and bad alike. But the last seventy books are to be kept back, and given to none but the wise among your people. They contain a stream of understanding, a fountain of wisdom, a flood of knowledge.' And I did so." (2 Esdras 14:37-48)[2670]

Of the ninety-four books, seventy were esoteric apocalypses not for circulation amongst the general public; only the first twenty-four were suitable for general dissemination. They were, of course, the twenty-four books of the present Hebrew Bible. Elements of these traditions seem to be echoed in Surabadi's story.

In point of fact, Ezra may have been the last major redactor of the present text of the Old Testament.

Oddly, our text of Surabadi does not mention the only explicit reference to Ezra in the Quran: *And the Jews say: "Ezra is the son of God,"...* (Q. 9:30) This assertion has caused a storm of controversy, with Jewish scholars flatly denying such an allegation. Mawlana Muhammad Ali cites only Islamic references when writing that a sect among the Jews held such a belief, and Yusuf Ali does the same:[2671] "Al-Baizawi says that during the Babylonian Captivity the *tawrat* (the law) was lost, and that as there was no one who remembered the law when the Jews returned from captivity, God raised up Ezra from the dead, although he had been buried a hundred years. And that when the Jews saw him thus raised from the dead, they said he must be the son of God."[2672]

This tradition may well explain the use of the phrase in the Quran, but without further evidence it will not satisfy Jewish critics who consistently deny such an allegation. It is possible that we have a situation here similar to the interpretation of some verses in the Quran asserting that Mary was the third person of the Trinity, taking the place of the Holy Ghost. Whilst this is not a mainstream Christian position, from early (pre-Islamic) documents we have learned that a sect with Mesopotamian and East Arabian associations worshipped Mary as a deity in the 4th century CE. The Quranic citation could easily be a

---

[2670] NEB translation.

[2671] Quran-Yusuf Ali, p. 448. Muhammad Ali writes: "That there was a sect among the Jews who raised Ezra to the dignity of godhead, or son of God, is shown by Muslim historians. Qaṣṭallānī says, in the *Kitāb al-Nikāḥ*, that there was a party of Jews who held this belief. Nor did the Jews deny this allegation. The Qur'an, too, mentions it only here in connection with Christian doctrine, never blaming the Jews directly in the many controversies with them in the earlier chapters, and this shows that the Jewish nation as a whole was not guilty of entertaining this belief." (Quran-MMA, p. 391.) While Muslims may be convinced by this, non-Muslims would probably require more proof.

[2672] Ezra, SEI, p. 114.

reference to this.[2673] However, we have no equivalent extra-Biblical pre-Islamic testimony to Ezra's being called "a son of God." Oral tradition may be proposed, but cannot be proven, so we shall cast our net a little further out to see what other possibilities we may catch.

The term "son of God" is used in several senses in the Old Testament. We have already noted the "sons of God" who married the daughters of men (Gen. 6:2).[2674] In *Job*, the "sons of God" (Job 38:7) seem to be a kind of heavenly court. These texts both refer to concepts no longer held by orthodox Judaism after the Exile and were explained by the later rabbis as referring to angels, or as metaphors.

In another usage, Israel is said to be the son of God: "'Thus says the Lord, Israel is my first-born son, and I say unto thee, 'Let My son go that he may serve Me.'" (Ex. 4:22) The prophet Hosea repeats the same usage: "When Israel was a child, I loved him, and out of Egypt I called My son." (Hos. 11:1) And in the *Wisdom of Solomon*: "They who, thanks to their sorceries, had been wholly incredulous, at the destruction of their first-born now acknowledged this people to be the son of God." (Wis. 18:13)

Ezra himself is greatly glorified in the apocryphal *IV Ezra (2 Esdras)*: "You are more blessed than most other men, and few have such a name with the Most High as you have." (2 Esdras 10:57) And at the end: "Ezra was caught away, and taken up into the place of such as were like him after having written all these things. And he is called the Scribe of the knowledge of the Most High forever and ever." (IV Ezra 14:49-50) The phrase "such as were like him" is explained as meaning the Messiah and his companions.[2675]

It used to be thought that *2 Esdras* attested to a Jewish belief that the Messiah was the "son of God" because of such statements such as "My son the Messiah shall appear with his companions and bring four hundred years of happiness to all who survive." (2 Esdras 7:28) However, recent research has shown that the phrase "son of God" really represents an Aramaic original "servant of God."[2676] This would seem to have laid to rest the interpretation of the epithet as a reference to the Messiah before Christian influence.

However, there is the new evidence form the Dead Sea Scrolls that demonstrates that the Messiah was indeed called the son of God in a

---

[2673] See *The Quranic View of Jesus: Trinity and Mariolatry*, V.D in the Introduction to *The New Testament: An Islamic Perspective*.
[2674] See "Harut and Marut," Part One, IV.
[2675] A&P, p. 624.
[2676] Fuller, p. 32.

Jewish environment. In one text God is represented as saying: "I will be his father, and he shall be My son."[2677] Hebrew kings were also called "sons of God" in an adoptive sense.[2678] In the 1st century BCE *Wisdom of Solomon*, the virtuous man is said to call himself "a son of the Lord." (Wis. 2:13) and "boasts of having God for his father." (Wis. 2:16) These texts attest to a more widespread use of the term, albeit in a metaphorical, adoptive sense, among the Jews than is commonly thought. There is no specific association of the phrase with Ezra here, but its use in such an adoptive fashion would not have been so unusual as we have been accustomed to suppose.[2679]

There is yet another possibility. Azariah[2680] was the name used by the archangel Raphael when he introduced himself to the blind Tobit (Tob. 5). This was also his first appearance in Jewish writings, in the Apocrypha in this case. In the succeeding centuries, he became one of the most important archangels in literature. Being an angel, he could easily have been called a "son of God," in the *Genesis* usage. The concept of "son of God" is not foreign to ancient Jewish thinking, though it should not normally be equated with the use of that term in Christianity.[2681]

The Arabic form 'Uzayr, taken to be a diminutive of Ezra (*Ezra* means *help* in Hebrew, perhaps a shortening of Azariah, *Yahweh helps*[2682]), has perplexed scholars. There does not seem to be any pre-Islamic evidence for such a diminutive's being applied to the name "Ezra." If 'Uzayr equals 'Uzayl, from 'Azael (see below), then it would be an import and not necessarily a diminutive, but if we equate 'Uzayr with Ezra, we must admit that, aside from oral tradition—and the Quranic citation seems to imply a well-known truth among the Arabs of that era—as yet no non-Islamic literary evidence has come to light from

---

[2677] Fuller, p. 32.

[2678] Fuller, p. 24.

[2679] It is not impossible that in the Quranic verse Ezra represents the nation of Israel, which, as we have seen, did claim to be the "son of God," that is the chosen of God; or as the type of the virtuous man as in *Wisdom*. The use of the epithet would easily suggest Christian claims concerning the sonship of Jesus. Parallelism would require that Jesus be contrasted with Ezra, although in the case of Jesus, the usage is meant to be individual and literal, while in the case of Ezra, the "founder" of revived (modern) Judaism, the usage would be typical and metaphorical. In either case, such hyperbole would be rejected by Islam.

[2680] Azariah, Davidson, p. 63.

[2681] For more about the Christian use of "son of God," see the Introduction to the New Testament Stories, II.D.2, in *The New Testament: An Islamic Perspective*

[2682] Ezra, DB, p. 285.

amongst the scant literary survivors of Old Testament times substantiating that Ezra was called the son of God.

However, there may yet be a better explanation. Casanova has suggested that Ezra, 'Uzayr in Arabic, should be identified with "'Uzail-Azael, Azazel"[2683] [through the well-known consonantal interchange between *l* and *r*], a fallen angel and one of the "sons of God," as that phrase was used in *Genesis* (Gen. 6:2). Though Islamic tradition is almost uniform in identifying 'Uzayr with Ezra, there is no reason why we should not pursue the enquiry afresh. Jewish tradition equated the fallen angels with "the sons of God" mentioned in the Bible.[2684] Azazel was identified with Azzael;[2685] indeed, they are forms of the same root. Azazel was the prince of the fallen angels[2686] and he taught man magic arts,[2687] and how to make weapons of war and utilize beauty aids.[2688] In rabbinic literature he was the scapegoat referred to in Lev. 16:8.[2689]

It is not at all improbable (since the Enoch literature was well known in the Near East of that period) that the Quranic verse in question is using the device of contrast rather similarity. The Jewish belief that Azazel, the fallen angel, was a son of God (as used in *Genesis*), is contrasted with the Christian belief that Jesus was the son of God. This would also fit nicely with the Muslim opinion that Ezra was involved in the corruption of the Scriptures (perhaps innocently if he had a faulty memory).

If this exegesis be correct, then the juxtaposition of the two "sons of God" is even more striking. The Quranic protest would be against the ascription of even adoptive paternity to God of beings as disparate as Azazel[2690] and Jesus. Despite the weight of centuries of commentary and exegesis in favor of identifying 'Uzayr with Ezra, it would do us no harm to explore other identifications with an open mind. Is the Muslim story of

---

[2683] Cited in 'Uzair, SEI, 617. Casanova also suggested that Ezra should be identified with Idris (ibid.), instead of Enoch.

[2684] See "Harut and Marut," Part One, IV.

[2685] LJ, V, 152.

[2686] Azazel, DB, p. 81.

[2687] LJ, V, 124.

[2688] Enoch 8 in A&P, p. 192.

[2689] Azazel, Davidson, p. 63. Azazel was the chief of the Watchers, whom God blamed for coming to earth and teaching mankind the secrets of heaven. Raphael had to tie him up and throw him into an abyss. In Jewish tradition, it was he who refused to bow down to Adam. (Azaz'el, Briggs, p. 36.)

[2690] Tisdall notes that Azazel in Jewish tradition is probably the equivalent of and derived from the Persian Ahriman (Tisdall, p. 242). For a discussion of another fallen angel, Samael, in connection with the identity of al-Samiri, see Part Three, I, I.

Ezra really a conflation of Ezekiel, Ezra, and perhaps a fallen angel? *And God knows best.*

V. DHUL-QARNAYN

The Old Testament stories in Surabadi's *Commentary* end properly with Ezra. Why do we continue? The story of Dhul-Qarnayn has no obvious connections with either Jewish or Christian tradition; neither is it about an ancient Arab prophet or figure. It is included in this collection because his mention in the Quran has exercised commentators such as Surabadi and because of the indirect impact of the person with whom Dhul-Qarnayn is most frequently identified upon later Judaism and early Christianity. Because his empire bridged east *and* west, even more than did the great Persian kings who founded the vast, multi-cultural Persian Empire, his gave mankind the idea of one world-embracing civilization and one universal government. It was this empire, with its unity amidst diversity, as short lived as it was, followed by the more successful empire that of the Romans, that accelerated the rise and the acceptance of the great supranational monotheistic cultures: first, Christianity that soon shrank back from the implications of absolute monotheism, and afterwards Islam which reasserted the uncompromising monotheistic ideal.

With the revelation of Islam, the One God swept aside all the idols of the mind that would divert us from that simple reality. At some moment before history came to be recorded, a biped animal had been infused with an immortal soul and gifted (or burdened) with a conscience and the knowledge of good and evil. Since that time, we have been on a journey of material and spiritual development. On our way, we have witnessed the aborted monotheisms of Akhenaton of Egypt and the Greek philosophers, and the hesitations of ethnocentric Judaism and Trinitarian Christianity.[2691]

[2691] The monotheistic experiment of Akhenaton is discussed in the Story of Moses. In Greece, too, quite possibly as a result of contact with Persian thought, philosophers were also perceiving the essential unity of the world and its implications for theology, perhaps. Plato (c. 427-347 BCE) was groping towards a kind of monotheism with an afterlife dependent upon out actions in this life. "(W)hen he speaks most seriously. He expresses theological principles which are of permanent value. God is the author of all good, but never of evil. If He chastises men, it is that He may make them better... God is the measure of truth, not man... The world is ordered not by chance, but according to the mind of God... Yet above and beyond all such rules of [pagan] worship, there are unmistakable indications of a true monotheism. God is virtually identical with the good mind or soul, which in the end prevails over the evil or imperfect soul. That is the prime cause of motion and becoming—itself eternal, unchanging, and unmoved. The unity of the supreme will is expressly recognized in the *Statesman*." Lewis Campbell. God (Greek) ERE. Vol. VI, p. 282.

God did not neglect to send us guides and guidebooks from time to time to aid us, according to the level of our ability and understanding, to find our way through the labyrinth of illusion on that journey to the sublime realization of the ultimate Truth: the Unity of God. Guidance is needed if we would avoid the noisome distractions and enticements of the material world in order to perceive our goal that is the spiritual unity that glows softly behind it. Its light is so subtle that we may not see or comprehend it, though we are in its midst, without God's Grace and our complete submission to His Unity, that which we call Islam.

In the Quran, Dhul-Qarnayn is mentioned only in Surah al-Kahf. In that place, we find allusions to several episodes of his life: *They will ask thee of Dhul-Qarnayn. Say: I shall recite unto you a remembrance of him. Lo! We made him strong in the land and gave him unto everything a road. And he followed a road till, when he reached the setting place of the sun, he found it setting in a muddy spring, and found a people hereabout; We said: O Dhul-Qarnayn! Either punish them or show them kindness.* (Q. 18:83-86) Having established justice among the people there, he traveled eastwards until he found *the rising-place of the sun, he found it rising on a people for whom We had appointed no shelter therefrom. Thus! And We knew all concerning him.* (Q. 18:90-91) *Then he followed a road till, when he came between the two mountains, he found upon their far side a folk that could hardly understand a saying. They said: O Dhul-Qarnayn! Lo! Gog and Magog are spoiling the land. So, may we pay thee tribute on condition that thou set a barrier between us and them?* (Q. 18:92-94) He agreed, but required their labor and assistance: *Give me pieces of iron—till, when he had leveled up (the gap) between the cliffs, he said: Blow!—till, when he had made a fire, he said: Bring me molten copper to pour thereon.* (Q. 18:96) Gog and Magog

---

The monotheism of Judaism was not absolute until relatively late in the Old Testament era. Perhaps the example of the Persian Empire with its single worldly ruler made possible the idea of a single God for the entire universe. Early Hebrew monotheism began as henotheism. The Israelites worshipped one god—Yahweh—but the existence of other gods was not denied. Yahweh was simply stronger than the pantheons of other nations and cults. The contest between Moses and the Egyptian sorcerers, for example, does not deny the reality of the Egyptian gods; it just shows that Yahweh is stronger than they, even when He is in their territory. (See the Story of Moses, Part Three). It was as though God were revealing His Uniqueness and his Unity progressively, as though it were a concept too great for man to bear without preparation. As Christianity shrank away from the full meaning of God's Oneness by taking refuge in the diluted polytheism of the Trinity, so Judaism shrank away from the burden of spreading the message of true monotheism to the world. After a few centuries of proselytizing, Judaism reverted to an ethnocentrism, like Hinduism. Converts, while accepted, are not actively sought, unlike Christianity, Islam, and Buddhism, which encourage them.

were shut off behind the barrier and then Dhul-Qarnayn addressed the people: *He said: This is a mercy from my Lord; but when the promise of my Lord cometh to pass, He will lay it low, for the promise of my Lord is True.* (Q. 18:98) With that somber warning of the Last Day, the pericope concludes.

This is all the Quran tells us about Dhul-Qarnayn, although from the opening of the story it is evident that Dhul-Qarnayn was already well known to the first hearers of these verses, but they were somewhat puzzled by what they knew of him. The passage is thought to date from the Madinan period.[2692] It follows directly upon a similar wide-ranging story, that of Moses and the servant of God.[2693] Whereas that story of Moses was a parable of a quest for knowledge that can be achieved only through patience and obedience, the adventures of Dhul-Qarnayn have more to do with the active establishment of justice and the righting of wrongs. It is the complement of the passivity of the Mosaic episode, an active quest for deeds and justice benefiting mankind, in the manner of a medieval knight errant.

The name Dhul-Qarnayn (Ar. *Dhū-l-Qarnayn*) is usually taken to mean "he of the two horns." As the number of identifications of Dhul-Qarnayn by the commentators of later times with various historical figures indicates, no firm tradition has come down about this. Perhaps the epithet perplexed them. In the SEI article, Mittwoch lists four identifications: (1) Al-Mundhir al-Akbar bin Māᵓ al-Samāᶜ the grandfather of al-Nuᶜmān bin al-Mundhir; he is said to have worn two long curled locks on his forehead and for that reason was called Dhul-Qarnayn; (2) the South Arabian king Tubba' al-Aqran (*Tubbaᶜ al-Aqrān*), an identification which is supported (quite naturally) by South Arabians; (3) Alexander the Great, about whom more below; and (4) 'Ali bin Abi Talib (*ᶜAlī bin Abī Ṭālib*, the son-in-law of the Prophet and the Fourth Caliph), a rare view and, for our purposes to be dismissed now.[2694] Among these, Alexander is the clear favorite of the commentators, and Surabadi assumes such an identification.

ALEXANDER THE GREAT: According to Surabadi, Dhul-Qarnayn was Alexander, the son of the Roman Caesar, or alternatively the son of Qalīsūn the Egyptian.[2695] Alexander the Great (we must assume that, although there other historical figures by that name, this is

---

[2692] According to the Egyptian edition. Watt-Bell, pp. 59, 207.
[2693] See "The Journey of Moses" Stories, Part three, L.
[2694] Dhu'l-Karnain, SEI, p. 76.
[2695] Surabadi, p. 220.

the Alexander meant) was a Macedonian. The Macedonians were close relatives of the Greeks, but regarded by them as being somewhat rude and uncivilized. Surabadi calls him a Roman, in accordance with the Arab practice of referring to the Greeks as Romans.[2696] The title Caesar is an anachronism, as it originated in classical Rome with Julius Caesar during the first century BCE. It became the dynastic name of the first emperors and then, later, was synonymous with "emperor"; hence, the German *kaiser*, the Russian *tsar*, and the Perso-Arabic *qayṣar*. The tradition of Alexander as the son of Qalisun the Egyptian may be related to the adoption of Alexander as his son by the god Jupiter Ammon in Egypt. More probably, it is an element borrowed from the *Alexander Romance*, a fanciful work written in the 2nd century CE in which Alexander was fathered on Olympias, his mother, by the Egyptian Pharaoh Nectanebus.[2697]

Historically, his father was king Philip II of Macedonia, although there was a nasty episode between father and son in which the jealous father Philip, apparently disliking the imperial ambitions of his son and heir, wanted to sire a new heir by a new wife (named Cleopatra, appropriately enough). He broadly suggested at his wedding feast that Alexander, who had just recently distinguished himself in the decisive defeat of the massed Greeks at Chaeronea (338 BCE), had been fathered by someone other than he, that is, he was a bastard and would be barred from the succession. In the resulting uproar, Alexander fled from Macedonia with his mother, leaving her with her relatives in Epirus and continuing on himself to Illyria.[2698] Two years later Philip was dead, sordidly murdered by a guard named Pausanias of good family, supposedly out of homosexual jealousy. Philip had not sired a son and so was succeeded by Alexander III: Alexander the Great.[2699]

Surabadi gives several explanations for the title Dhul-Qarnayn: Alexander was wounded on one side of his head, died and was resurrected, was wounded on the other side, again died and was again

---

[2696] When the Arabs first came into contact with the Greeks, during the period of the Byzantine Empire, that empire was also known as the Eastern *Roman* Empire, the western half together with Rome itself having succumbed to the barbarian invasions more than a century and a half before the rise of Islam.

[2697] Green, pp. 478-79.

[2698] Green, pp. 88-90. Illyria was the coastal region and its hinterland lying east of the Adriatic Sea, corresponding roughly to parts of Croatia, Bosnia, Montenegro, Serbia, and Albania. In other words, Alexander fled to the north and west.

[2699] Green, pp. 105-110. This explanation is not satisfactory and it did not satisfy the ancients. Green advances the theory that Pausanias was incited by Olympias, and from what is known of her character and ambitions for her son, the theory has a strong degree of probability.

resurrected. The scars were the horns.[2700] History tells us that Alexander was wounded several times, at least three times seriously: at Tyre, in Central Asia, and most serious of all in India, where he very nearly died. There seems to be no report of any remarkable scars on the sides of his head that could give rise to the story.[2701]

Another explanation was that he wore two jeweled locks of hair.[2702] This is more suggestive of the Mundhir mentioned above than of Alexander. That Alexander dreamt that he had seized the two sides of the sun at sunrise and sunset, perhaps suggested by the Quranic verses, is in keeping with some of Alexander's extravagant claims, but is unhistorical. The last explanation given by Surabadi is the simplest of all: that he had two horns on his head.[2703] Unfortunately, this is also fanciful and unhistorical. However, if the identification of Alexander with Dhul-Qarnayn be correct, the origin of the epithet is probably to found in the representation on coins of Alexander wearing a horned helmet. These coins were quite common and widely circulated and copied in later times, about which more below. Alexander was by no means the only ancient to be depicted with two horns. Moses is sometimes so represented, as may be seen on Michelangelo's famous statute of him in the church of San Pietro in Vincoli at Rome.[2704]

[2700] Surabadi, pp. 220-1.

[2701] Green, pp. 266, 357, 420-23.

[2702] Surabadi, p. 221.

[2703] Surabadi, p. 221.

[2704] We have in our possession a copy of the Holy Bible in Hebrew (the Old Testament of Christian Bibles), the frontispiece of which is a portrait of Moses holding the Decalogue in his left hand, his rod in his right hand, and with two horn-like projections from the top of his head, possibly rays of light. An article in *Bible Review* by William H. Propp is accompanied by illustrations of medieval Christian art showing the horned Moses, the oldest being mid-11th century CE. Scholars believe that this idea arose from a misreading of Ex. 34.29-35 which states that after Moses had had his vision of God and came down from Mount Sinai with the two tablets of the covenant, "...he did not know that skin of his face *qāran* from his conversing with Him. When Aaron and all the Israelites saw the skin of Moses' face *qāran*, they were too afraid to approach him." (Ex. 34:29-30) KJ and RSV translate *qaran* as "shone"; the JB has "radiant." The Hebrew root *q-r-n* may also mean "horn." The Arabic cognate has a principal verbal meaning of "linking, joining," and the specialized usage of *qarn* to mean "horn" and "century, age" may be a borrowing. Although substituting "horn" for "shone" does not make complete sense in the passage, it was popular in the Middle Ages and thus appears in Christian art. Propp notes that both horns and radiance were attributes of gods and godlike kings in the ancient Near East. In other places in the Bible, "horn" is connected with "light" (Hab. 3:3-4; Ps. 123:17; etc.). Propp also tells of the Jewish heretic Hiwi (Hayyawayh) of Balkh who had written that Moses' skin had dried up "until it was as hard as horn," perhaps giving it a glossy and unhealthy (and thus frightening) appearance. (William H. Propp, "Did Moses Have Horns?" BR, Vol. IV, No. 1 (February, 1988), pp. 30-37.) The article

3RD-CENTURY BCE COIN SHOWING THE HORNED ALEXANDER

Alexander's putative father, the god Jupiter Ammon, was also depicted with two horns. Perhaps to reinforce this claim of divine origin, Alexander had himself so shown on his coinage.[2705] The Mesopotamian ruler Naram-Sin (rgd. 2224-2187 BCE) was similarly depicted as having two horns. [2706]

Surabadi continues: "He seized the kingdom of the all the world. In the Traditions it is related that of Muslims, there were two who ruled the entire world: one was Solomon the son of David and the other was Dhul-Qarnayn."[2707] This statement seems to be related to Jewish traditions of world-rulers. Different lists are given. In the *Targum Yerushalmi,* we find a list of four, two Jews (Solomon and Ahab) and two Gentiles (Nebuchadnezzar and Ahasuerus). The *Esther Rabbah* lists David, Solomon, Ahab, Nebuchadnezzar, Cyrus, and Darius. The *Pirke de Rabbi Eliezer* lists God, Nimrod, Joseph, Solomon, Ahab, Nebuchadnezzar, Cyrus, Alexander, and in the future, the Messiah, and ultimately again God.[2708] Historically, Solomon's kingdom was hardly

---

also has a photograph of a Naram-Sin victory stela showing him wearing a horned helmet, the *agū,* the crown of the gods. (Ibid., p. 32.)

[2705] "Alexander appears on coins as Jupiter [Zeus]-Ammon incarnate." (*Dhul'l-Karnain,* SEI, p. 26.) When Alexander visited the Oracle of Zeus-Ammon at the oasis of Siwa in Egypt in 331 BCE, the oracle confirmed that Alexander was indeed the son of Zeus, whom the Egyptians identified with their own chief god Amen-Ra (Greek *Ammon*). (Plutarch, pp. 283-284.) The modern tourist may still see the long avenues of horned ram-headed sphinxes sacred to Amun-Ra at Luxor and other places in Egypt. Amun-Ra was created by an identification of the southern god Amun with the northern sun-god Ra.

[2706] Dhul-Karnain, SEI, p. 76.

[2707] Surabadi, p. 221.

[2708] LJ, V, pp. 199-200.

worldwide; it stretched from the borders of Egypt to central Syria, far from world rule. The exact nature of his control over large parts of that territory is disputed.[2709] The empire of Alexander stretched from India to middle of the Mediterranean lands. He died before he could conquer Rome, Italy, and the West.

Next, Surabadi relates a story of Alexander's youth: When he first inherited the throne, a boon companion invited him to the True Religion. This angered Alexander and he threw his erstwhile friend into prison. Angels broke open the roof and brought him back to his own home. Then Alexander pursued the companion with an army in order to capture him. He found the companion praying. Heaven-sent lightning destroyed the army and Alexander was enlightened, his companion becoming his teacher.[2710] In this pericope, we may have a reference to Alexander's relationship with his teacher, the famous Greek philosopher Aristotle that turned from warm to a complete break. There was no final reconciliation. There are even suggestions that Aristotle was implicated in Alexander's death at Babylon.[2711]

The escape through the intervention of the angels reminds us of two incidents found in *Acts*. In the first, the apostles of Jesus had been arrested at the instigation of the high priest of Jerusalem and the Sadducees: "But at night an angel of the Lord opened the prison doors and brought them out..." (Acts 5:19) and the incident recorded in Acts 12:6-10, discussed in the Story of Paul.[2712]

Surabadi continues, informing us that the first king Alexander vanquished was Dara (*Dārā*), or Darnush (*Dārnūsh*). Alexander wrote a letter to him inviting him to the Unity, but Darnush treated it contemptuously beginning his reply with: "I, Darnush the King of the World to Dhul-Qarnayn the thief." With the letter, he sent a whip, a colt, a ruby, a sack of sesame seed, and a coffer of gold. When the messengers arrived, Alexander had them stripped and said: "If I am a thief as the king has written, this is the act of thieves." However, he treated them well afterwards and interpreted the meaning of the gifts in his own favor: "The whip is the whip of punishment which he has placed in my hand; the colt is the sign that the kingdom of the world will come to me on such a colt; the ruby signifies the bright radiance of my affair; the golden coffer is his treasuries which shall all be mine; the bag of sesame seed signifies (the number) of his troops. My army is the help of God; what

---

[2709] See the Story of Solomon, Part Five, II.

[2710] Surabadi, p. 221.

[2711] Green, p. 460.

[2712] See III.C, Peter in *The New Testament: An Islamic Perspective*.

danger is there in the number of seeds in the sack when placed beside the help of God?"[2713]

Dara/Darnush is of course Darius III (rgd. 336-330 BCE), the last of the Achaemenian kings of Persia, *not* Darius the Great (rgd. 522-486 BCE; see below). There were diplomatic exchanges between him and Alexander, although in the Surabadi version there is a strong echo of the Prophet's letters to the four sovereigns inviting them to Islam. (Darius' reaction to Alexander's call to faith is the same as that of the Sassanian king Chosroes[2714] to the letter of the Prophet.)

After the battle of Issus[2715] (333 BCE) in which Alexander defeated the Persians, Darius succeeded in escaping, but Alexander captured the Persian king's family. Darius entered into negotiations, offering Alexander Asia Minor west of the Halys River[2716] and a ransom for his family. Alexander's reply has the tone of Darnush's letter in Surabadi. According to Arrian,[2717] Alexander wrote: "Your ancestors invaded Macedonia and Greece and caused havoc in our country, though we had done nothing to provoke them. As supreme commander of all Greece, I invaded Asia because I wished to punish Persia for this act—an act which must be laid wholly to your charge... Come to me, therefore, as you would come to the lord of the continent of Asia... Come, then, and ask me for your mother, your wife, and your children and anything else you please; for you shall have them, and whatever besides you can persuade me to give you. And in the future let any communication you wish to make with be addressed to the King of all Asia. Do not write to me as an equal. Everything you possess is now mine; so, if you should want anything, let me know in the proper terms, or I shall take steps to deal with you as a criminal. If, on the other hand, you wish to dispute

---

[2713] Surabadi, pp. 221-22.

[2714] Chosroes: Persian Khusraw II surnamed Parwiz, rgd. 590-628 CE. Although unlike Darius, Khusraw did not lose his kingdom, at his death it descended into dynastic chaos during which no less than a dozen kings reigned briefly until the Arab victory at Nahavand in 642 CE that effectively ended the Sassanian Empire.

[2715] The battle of Issus was fought near modern Iskanderun in Turkey, near the northeastern corner of the Mediterranean Sea. The actual site of the battle is a large plain at the head of the Gulf of Alexandretta approximately 25 miles north of Iskanderun.

[2716] That is, Darius was offering Alexander the western third of modern Turkey, west of the Kizilirmak River. (Actually, the word Kizilirmak itself means "Red River" in Turkish, so adding "River" is redundant.)

[2717] Arrian (Flavius Arrianus Xenophon) (c.90-c.175 CE) was the author *The Campaigns of Alexander*, the most reliable account of Alexander's quest for empire to survive from ancient times. (See *Arrian* in the Bibliographies.)

your throne, stand and fight for it and do not run away. Wherever you may hide yourself, be sure I shall seek you out."[2718]

After this, Surabadi relates, Alexander made to attack Dara and fought him in Iraq for seven days and nights, defeating him (again).[2719] This is a reference to the battle of Gaugamela (331 BCE)[2720] in which Darius made his last attempt to save his empire from Alexander's grasp. The battle was preceded by still another effort by Darius to negotiate with Alexander. He offered him all of the Persian Empire west of the Euphrates, a 30,000-talent ransom[2721] for his mother and daughters, and one of his daughters in marriage. Alexander rejected this proposal.[2722]

According to Greek historians, the actual battle of Gaugamela lasted but one day, 30 Sept. 331 BCE, although Alexander had crossed the Tigris twelve days earlier and soon sighted Persian military units. He sighted them again on the 24th, but he did not see the assembled Persian army until the day before the battle. The odds were about five to one, approximately 250,000 Persian troops against Alexander's 47,000.[2723] When Alexander outgeneraled him, Darius fled once again. A little later, he was treacherously murdered by Bessus and Nabarzanes.[2724] Bessus, the usurper, was eventually captured, tried by Alexander for regicide, his nose and ears cut off and then executed at Ecbatana.[2725]

After seizing Iraq and Khorasan, Surabadi continues, Alexander made for India. There he was opposed by Porus (Per. *Fūr*)[2726] who met him with a huge army, including 20,000 elephants. On the advice of his wise men, Alexander made copper horses filled with oil and mounted on wheels. They were ignited and pulled forward. The elephants came to attack and burned their trunks. They then ran wild, trampling Porus' troops. Porus surrendered, and Alexander made use of Porus and his advisors in the capture of other cities.[2727]

[2718] Arrian, pp. 127-28.

[2719] Surabadi, p. 222.

[2720] Sometimes called the battle of Arbela, though it was actually fought at Gaugamela some 60 miles north of Arbela in northeastern modern Iraq.

[2721] The weight of the talent varied. By one calculation, it would weight about 23.4 lbs. If silver be intended, say at $10 an ounce, it would have been something over $100,000,000. If gold were intended, the sum would have been in the billions.

[2722] Green, p. 287.

[2723] Green, pp. 285, 286, 288, 292-95.

[2724] Bessus, presumably the instigator of Darius' murder, paid with his life, but Nabarzanes, who was also involved in the affair, escaped with a pardon (Green, p. 333).

[2725] Green, pp. 328-29, 355. Ecbatana is the modern Hamadan in west-central Iran.

[2726] Surabadi gives us the Arabicized form of Porus, *Fūr*. (Arabic does not have a *p*, so *b* or *f* are the usual substitutes.) Porus was a king in the Indo-Pakistani Punjab.

[2727] Surabadi, p. 222.

This rough history generally agrees with the outline of the progress of Alexander's career. After consolidating his rule in Persia,[2728] he struck out for the east and brought Khorasan, Central Asia, and modern Afghanistan under his rule. He then invaded India and in 326 BCE fought a decisive battle with Porus, the local king, on the banks of the Jhelum in modern Pakistan. Porus' army consisted of from three to four thousand cavalry, up to 50,000 infantry, 300 war chariots, and 200 elephants, not Surabadi's impossible figure of 20,000.[2729] Alexander's horses were terrified by the elephants and this caused a considerable problem, but continuous pressure on the elephants, rather than any remarkable mechanical devices, gradually forced them into a narrow space in their own lines where the elephants began to trample the Indian troops as viciously as the had Alexander's men.[2730] Porus was indeed captured, and thereafter did assist Alexander in his campaigns.[2731]

After this, Surabadi's story becomes even more fabulous. He writes that Dhul-Qarnayn had two armies, one of light going before and the other of darkness following. Dhul-Qarnayn went to Rome, to the farthest east and the farthest west. He conquered a city made of wood by erecting a tower and placing a mirror on the top it. The mirror reflected the sunlight on the city causing it to catch fire. The city surrendered and gave Dhul-Qarnayn three things: a wise man, a horse that could travel 300 leagues in a day, and a blade that could cut granite. The wise man wished to demonstrate his wisdom to Dhul-Qarnayn and sent him a jar of oil. Dhul-Qarnayn returned it filled with needles. The wise man made a mirror of them, and Dhul-Qarnayn returned the mirror polished on both sides. The wise man accepted Islam.[2732]

[2728] And avenging the burning of the Acropolis of Athens by Xerxes. After entering it in 330 BCE, Alexander torched the immense palace of Persepolis, destroying among many other priceless works of art and artifacts the archives written on combustible materials. Whether any of these valuable documents, which would have told us much about the workings of the Persian Empire and its literary achievements, would otherwise have survived the vagaries of history is a moot question. It was an uncharacteristic act of wanton barbarism by Alexander and may have been the result of a drunken orgy, but the consensus is that it was deliberate. As a result, we must rely principally upon the Greek historians, representing after all the enemy, for information about the Achaemenians. (See Green, pp. 314-16.)

[2729] Green, p. 289.

[2730] Green, p. 400. Alexander's men would encircle the elephants, kill the mahouts riding them, and then discharge volleys of spears and javelins into their most vulnerable parts, while infantrymen slashed through their trunks or chopped at their feet with scimitars. (Green, p. 399.)

[2731] Arrian, pp. 280-1, 290.

[2732] Surabadi, pp. 222-23.

There are a number of elements here, some of which can be found in the history of Alexander. The two armies may refer to the division of forces in India, when Alexander decided to return to Babylon after his troops refused to go any further east. He divided his troops near modern Shikarpur in middle Pakistan, and led his portion by land through Baluchistan and southern Iran whilst his commander Craterus led another potion northwest to Kandahar (in modern Afghanistan) and then west and southwest by way of Sistan into eastern Iran. Meanwhile, at the port of Pattala near the mouth of the Indus, Alexander divided his forces again. He continued by land, but the other group boarded ships and followed the coast to the head of the Persian Gulf. The land forces rendezvoused in Carmania (the Iranian region of Kerman). Alexander, leading the reunited land troops, proceeded to Susa,[2733] whilst his admiral Nearchus and his forces reached the same destination traveling by sea.[2734]

With respect to the tower, during the sieges of Tyre and Gaza on the Mediterranean coast where Alexander had met stiff resistance, he made use of massive engineering works. Tyre was built on an offshore island. Alexander had his engineers construct a mole outward from the shore to reach the island and placed wooden towers on it to attack the walls. The Tyrians were successful in burning these once, and Alexander was forced to rebuild them. After an horrendous siege lasting seven months, he succeeded in reducing the city. At Gaza too, Alexander was forced to surround the city with a mound to the height of the city walls in order to force it into submission. [2735]

However Surabadi's story is more likely to refer to the famous Tower or Lighthouse of Pharos at Alexandria—counted as one of the seven wonders of the ancient world—which, however, was not built until half a century after Alexander's death in the city he had founded and named after himself. It was constructed by Ptolemy II about 280 BCE.[2736] The Pharos was a lighthouse with mirrors and fires on the top which were supposedly also used to set enemy ships at sea on fire.[2737] The horse may have been suggested by Alexander's beloved steed Bucephalas,

---

[2733] Susa: modern Shush (Pers. *Shūsh*) at the edge of the alluvial Mesopotamian plain in southwestern Iran.

[2734] Green, pp. 440, 444. Alexander's routes are shown in many historical atlases as well as in Green pp. 298 and 352.

[2735] Green, pp. 253, 266-67.

[2736] Pharos, CE, p. 1647. The Pharos survived until a severe earthquake finally toppled the structure already weakened by previous tremors in 1307 CE. It had stood nearly 16 centuries.

[2737] Scientific American, June 1977, pp. 64ff.

although in Surabadi it seems to have acquired the attributes of Pegasus, Perseus' famous flying horse of Greek mythology.[2738]

Alexander enjoyed the company of learned men. In addition to his ultimately unhappy association with Aristotle, he had a number of philosophers in his entourage (as did Napoleon 2,000 years later when he invaded Egypt in 1798 CE, perhaps in imitation of Alexander). However, the encounter with the ten Indian wise men recorded by Plutarch and others, or something similar, is probably behind the incident Surabadi gives us.[2739] Alexander had other meetings with Indian ascetics, one of whom asked: "Why did Alexander come all this way to India?"[2740]

[2738] Graves, Vol. 1, p. 253.

[2739] Plutarch's version: "(Alexander) captured ten of the Indian philosophers who had played the most active part in persuading Sabbas [another Indian king] to revolt and had stirred up [the] most trouble for the Macedonians. These philosophers enjoyed a great reputation for their ingenuity in devising short pithy answers to questions, and so Alexander confronted them with a series of conundrums. He had previously announced that he would put to death the first man who gave a wrong answer, and the rest of them in order according to their performance, and he ordered one of them, the eldest, to act as judge in the contest."

This is Plutarch's record of the questioning:

"First Philosopher, Question: Which are more numerous the living or the dead? Answer: The living, since the dead no longer exist.

"Second Philosopher, Question: Which breeds the larger creatures, the land or the sea. Answer: The land, since the sea is only a part of it.

"Third Philosopher, Question: Which is the most cunning of animals? Answer: The animal which man has not yet discovered.

"Fourth Philosopher, Question: Why did you incite Sabbas to revolt? Answer: Because I wished him either to live or to die with honor.

"Fifth Philosopher, Question: Which was created first, the day or the night? Answer: the day, by one day. When the philosopher saw that the king was astonished by this reply, he added, 'Abstruse questions will necessarily produce abstruse answers.'

"Sixth Philosopher, Question: How can a man make himself most beloved? Answer: If he possesses supreme power, and yet does not inspire fear.

"Seventh Philosopher, Question: How can a man become a god? Answer: By doing something a man cannot do.

"Eighth Philosopher, Question: Which is stronger: life or death? Answer: Life, since it endures so many evils.

"Ninth philosopher, Question: How long is it good for a man to live? Answer: So long as he does not regard death as better than life."

With the questioning ended, Alexander asked the judge for his opinion. He replied that each was worse than the one preceding him. Alexander said:

"'In that case,' Alexander replied, 'you shall be executed first yourself for having given such a verdict.' 'That is not right, you majesty,' returned the judge, 'unless you did not mean what you said when you announced that you would put to death first the man who gave the worst answer.' Alexander distributed presents to all ten and sent them away unharmed." (Plutarch, pp. 321-22.)

[2740] Plutarch p. 323.

Perhaps the most famous is the ascetic Calanus who accompanied Alexander from India to Persia. At Pasargad,[2741] according to Strabo, Calanus, who had been weakening, felt that it was time to die. At his request, Alexander reluctantly commanded that a funeral pyre be erected for him. With military honors, Calanus mounted his pyre and was immolated.[2742]

There does not seem, to be any special association of Alexander with a sword; this motif is reminiscent of the famous sword of Ali bin Abi Talib, Dhul-Fiqar, and has other parallels in history and legend such as King Arthur's Excalibur. Perhaps the mentioning of the sword was prompted by Alexander's slicing of the Gordian knot with his sword, one of the most well-known incidents of his early career.[2743]

The last section of Surabadi's story of Alexander is clearly influenced by the *Alexander Romance*. Alexander was saddened as he thought of death and wanted to know whether there was any way to escape it. The wise men told him that by drinking the Water of Life found in the darkness he could secure immortality. Only virgin mares could see it. Alexander assembled 20,000 mares and sent Khidr ahead. Khidr found it and became immortal, but Alexander did not and he returned home. Then the angels brought him a jewel and told him to weigh it; but nothing could lift it. Finally, the angel told him to take a handful of earth and put it in the scales, and the handful of earth proved heavier, demonstrating that only the earth (the grave) can satisfy greed. Thus, Alexander died.[2744]

This part of Surabadi's story is dependent upon the *Alexander Romance*, itself dependent upon the Sumerian *Epic of Gilgamesh*. The link of Khidr with Alexander supports the theory that elements of this story have entered the story of the journey of Moses.[2745]

[2741] Pasargad was the original capital of Cyrus who founded the Persian Empire. Its ruins lie some 50 miles northeast of Shiraz in Iran.

[2742] Arrian, pp. 351-52.

[2743] Green, pp. 213-14. Plutarch tells the story in this fashion: "When he captured Gordium, which is reputed to have been the home of the ancient king Midas, he saw the celebrated chariot which was fastened to its yoke by the bark of the cornel-tree, and heard the legend which was believed by all the barbarians, that the fates had decreed that the man who untied the knot was destined to become the ruler of the whole world. According to most writers the fastenings were so elaborately intertwined and coiled upon one another that their ends were hidden; in consequence Alexander did not know what to do, and in the end loosened the knot by cutting through it with his sword, whereupon the many ends sprang into view." Plutarch, p. 271.

[2744] Surabadi, pp. 223-34.

[2745] The story of Gilgamesh is discussed in Part One, I. It concerns the search for the Water of Life. Some aspects of these popular Khidr stories show the persistence of this

GOG AND MAGOG: In his story of Dhul-Qarnayn, Surabadi does not mention Gog and Magog, though he had done so earlier in a story about Noah. However, as they figure prominently in the Dhul-Qarnayn story, they will be discussed here.

Gog and Magog (Ar. *Yajūj* and *Majūj*) are mentioned twice in the Quran. In Q. 21:96, their being set loose upon the rest of mankind will be one of the signs of Judgment Day, a role they have in *Ezekiel* and *Revelation* (see text below).[2746] In the other place (Q. 18:94-97), much of which has been quoted above, they are connected with the activities of Dhul-Qarnayn. In this story, the people offer Dhul-Qarnayn tribute if he will erect a barrier to keep Gog and Magog from raiding them. Surabadi's added details are in keeping with the picture of a savage people. Gog and Magog are shown as peoples rather than individuals.

In the Bible, the terms Gog and Magog are used in *Ezekiel* in connection with an apocalyptic battle with Gog (Ezek. 38, 39). In Ezekiel's vision, God will do battle against "Gog, of the land of Magog, the chief prince of Meshech and Tubal" (Ezek. 38:2), who will be allied with Persia, Cush (Ethiopia), Put (Somalia?), Gomer and his hordes (the Cimmerians), and Togarmah (Armenia). (Ezek. 38:5-6) A two-pronged assault upon Palestine seems envisioned, one from the south (Cush and Put, and the main force from the north under the leadership of Gog. Gog is a person and Magog a land or people.

In Surabadi's version, Gog appears as an individual, or at least a personification, the leader of the forces who set out to destroy the civilized world and the restored Israel. From Assyrian records, we know that Meshech and Tubal, called by them Mushki and Tabali, are lands located to the northeast of Cilicia[2747] and therefore would appear to be located in the eastern half of modern Turkey or beyond. Magog is placed in the steppes around the north of the Caspian Sea.[2748] One is tempted to speculate that Tubal or Tabali may be identified with Tabar or Tepur, that is *Tabaristan*, the mountainous region in Iran bordering on the southern shores of the Caspian Sea.[2749]

Josephus connected Magog with the Scythians: "Magog founded those that from him were named Magogites, but who are by the Greeks

---

theme, See especially the stories of Adam (Part One, II), Moses (Part Three, I.L), St. George in *The New Testament: An Islamic Perspective*, V.G), Elijah (above, I), and Luqman (below, VI).

[2746] See comment on Muslim hostility to Gog and Magog, in Part One, V.D.

[2747] Magog, DB, 612; Meshech, DB, 645-6.

[2748] ABL, p. 4.

[2749] Burhan, III, 1347.

called Scythians."[2750] Proposed identifications of Meshech with Moscovy and Tubal with the Tartars do not have much in their favor.[2751] It has also been suggested that Magog refers to the Macedonians.[2752]

In the Table of Nations in *Genesis,* ch. 10, the sons of Japheth (traditionally the ancestor of the Indo-Europeans) are given: Gomer, Magog, Madai (the Medes), Javan (Ionians), Tubal, Meshech, and Tiras (Gen. 10:2). Togarmah is listed as a son of Gomer in the following verse. Thus, all of the northern peoples listed in the vision of Ezekiel are Japhethites. This rather derogatory association of the Japhethites with the enemies of Israel would appear to be unconsciously reflected in Islamic tradition about Gog and Magog.

Among the identifications proposed for Gog, that with Gaga, a corruption of Gasga, a wild region in eastern Turkey appears the most probable. Even after the people had disappeared or had been absorbed by others, the name persisted with the meaning of "barbarian."[2753] In *Revelation* (c. 96 AD), Ezekiel's "Gog of the land of Magog" has become "Gog and Magog" in the same sense that the coupled names are used in Islamic tradition: "And when the thousand years are ended, Satan will be loosed from his prison and will come out to deceive the nations which are at the four corners of the earth, that is, Gog and Magog, to gather them for battle; their number is like the sand of the sea. And they marched up over the broad earth and surrounded the camp of the saints and the beloved city; but fire came down from heaven and consumed them."[2754]

Jewish tradition does not add much more to this picture, but of course elaborates upon it. It recognizes that Gog is a Japhethite[2755] and dwells upon the sufferings that Gog and Magog cause and the magnitude of God's triumph over them.[2756] God will appear in person to combat Gog,[2757] a blasphemous image in Muslim eyes. The second Psalm is

---

[2750] Josephus, Ant., pp. 30-31.

[2751] Notes to Quran-MMA, p. 589.

[2752] Magog, DB, 612.

[2753] Gog, DB, 338. The Reubenite Gog mentioned in I Ch. 5:4 as a son of Joel has nothing to do with the Gog of *Ezekiel* and later tradition.

[2754] Rev. 20:7-9. See also III.D in the Stories of *The New Testament: An Islamic Perspective.*

[2755] LJ, I, 170.

[2756] LJ, III, 47; II, 356-7.

[2757] LJ, III, 455; VI, 154.

sometimes interpreted as a reference to the rebellion that will be led by Gog.[2758,]

The idea that Gog is different in status or nature from Magog persists throughout Jewish literature, whereas in the Christian *Revelation* and later, Gog and Magog are linked together as though complementary and of an equivalent nature. Since this is the apparent Quranic use of the term, it would seem that this is the form of the tradition that had reached Arabia.

The image of the savage northerners from the mountainous north was not an unnatural one for the Semitic peoples living in the ancient Near East, and indeed until recent times. Repeatedly, warlike peoples have swept out of the mountains north and east to descend upon the rich plains and cities of Mesopotamia and Syria. These peoples were generally more vigorous but more uncivilized than the settled agrarian peoples of the lands they conquered were. At the dawn of recorded history, the Sumerians came out of the Iranian mountains and occupied Mesopotamia, where they invented civilization. After a thousand years, they were gradually absorbed by Semites from the west and south. They, in turn, were conquered by the Aryan Kassites in the middle of the second millennium BC.

During the same period the Hurrians, a people who, like the Sumerians, were of unknown linguistic affiliation, moved in from the north, and so it went throughout history. When powerful Semitic empires based in Babylonia and Assyria tried to extend their influence into those mountains, they were usually successful for short periods, but as soon as their armies had returned to the plains, the mountaineers pursued their own independent ways. No empire with Mesopotamia as its power base was successful in controlling those mountainous hinterlands in ancient times. New peoples periodically swarmed out of them to conquer and infiltrate the older civilizations of the lowlands.[2759]

In much wider arena of the Persian and Hellenistic periods, with the spread of the arts of civilization into those neighboring areas, the threat changed its character and moved to new frontiers further north — the steppes of Eurasia. The Japhethites of *Genesis* were now within the circle of the civilized world and the hostile feelings about them became

---

[2758] LJ, VI, 266. "Why do the nations conspire, and the people plot in vain? The kings of the earth set themselves, and the rulers take counsel together, against the Lord and his anointed, saying, 'Let us burst their bonds asunder, and cast their ropes from us.'" (Ps. 2:1-3.)

[2759] Of course, empires such as the Persian, Sassanian, and Abbasid had winter capitals in Mesopotamia, but their power bases were often elsewhere.

transferred in later times to the Turkic peoples who were moving in upon their heels from Central and East Asia. Yusuf Ali states: "It is practically agreed that they [Gog and Magog] were the wild tribes of Central Asia which have made inroads on settled kingdoms and Empires at various stages of the world's history... These tribes were known vaguely to the Greeks and the Romans as 'Scythians,' but that term does not help us very much, either ethnically or geographically."[2760]

Modern exegetes even identify Gog and Magog with the Russians or the Chinese.[2761] All of these identifications share one thing: they all lie to the north of whatever was the then civilized world. As in the case of the mountain upon which Noah's ark came to rest,[2762] as the boundaries of civilization expanded northward and regions unknown became known, these mysterious places and peoples receded northward, usually just beyond the limits of civilized regions. While the region of Gaga in eastern Turkey may have given its name to Gog, it seems probable that in later times—as the evidence of Josephus shows—they were in some way identified with the tribes that inhabited the steppes of Russian and Central Asia.

ALEXANDER'S DAM: Returning to the Quranic references, the incident of Alexander's building a wall or dam against the wild tribes of the north is also found in the *Alexander Romance*. This was thought by de Goeje to have been suggested by reports of the Great Wall of China that possessed a gate, the Jasper Gate.[2763] However, Yusuf Ali, who supports the identification of Dhul-Qarnayn with Alexander, cites two other possible origins of the story. One is the 50-mile long wall between the Caucasus Mountains and the Caspian Sea at Derbend in Daghistan, now part of Russia. Local tradition associates it with Alexander, but history tells us of no campaigns or travels by Alexander in the area, and the association would appear to have no known historical foundation. The second, the one that Yusuf Ali favors, fits the Quranic description better. It is located in a narrow defile and is in an area southwest of Samarqand where Alexander is known to have campaigned. It is no longer in existence, but was mentioned by the 7th century CE Chinese traveler Hiouen Tsiang. Muqaddasi, writing c. AH 375/985 CE cites a report by a caliphal commission which visited the wall about 140 years before Hiouen Tsiang and left a description: the defile was about 150

[2760] Quran-Yusuf Ali, p. 761.
[2761] Halley, pp. 333-4.
[2762] See "Noah" in Part One, V.C.
[2763] Yadjudj wa-Madjudj, SEI, p. 637,

yards wide and was blocked by a wall into which two gates had been let with jambs made of blocks of iron welded with lead. We can only speculate now about the accuracy of that report and the antiquity of the gates those visitors saw.[2764]

That Alexander campaigned in the East, India, and the north— that is, Central Asia—is well established and confirms his presence in the second and third places mentioned in the Quranic verse (Q. 18:86). But what of the first, the West?[2765] As we have observed, Alexander never campaigned very far to the west of his home base, Macedonia. The tradition may be based upon Alexander's 335 BCE expedition to the Danube in which he defeated the Thracians and then crossed the Danube and routed some 4,000 Setae nomads. Another troublesome tribe, the Triballians, also submitted to him.[2766] This expedition into a marshy, riverine country, which can be very muddy and dismal at times, may be that to which the Quran is referring.

However, Yusuf Ali suggests that vv. 86-87 refer to a different location. This is his translation of the passage in question: *One (such) way he followed until, when he reached the setting of the sun, he found it set in a spring of murky water: Near it he found a people: We said: "O Dhul-Qarnayn! (Thou hast authority), either to punish them, or to treat them with kindness.' He said: 'Whoever doth wrong, him shall we punish; then shall he be sent back to his Lord; and He will punish him with a punishment unheard-of (before).* (Q. 18:85-87)

He then describes the setting, Lake Ochrida, now lying between Albania and Macedonia just north of Greece: "The water is so dark that the river which forms the outlet of the lake to the north is called the Black Drin. Looking at the sunset from town [Ochrida], the observer would see the sun set in a pool of murky water ([Q.] 18:86)." During an expedition in this region the youthful Alexander had to decide what to do with some captured Illyricans [Illyrians]. Yusuf Ali says: "It was a question before the boy Alexander... whether he would put the barbarous Illyricans to the sword or show them mercy. He showed true discrimination and statesmanship. He punished the guilty but showed kindness to the innocent, and thus consolidated his power in the

---

[2764] Quran-Yusuf Ali, p. 762.
[2765] Quoted above at the beginning of this section.
[2766] Green, pp. 125-30.

west."[2767] The incident certainly fits the circumstances implied by the verses.

Alexander's father Philip defeated the Illyrians at Lake Ochrida in 359/8 BCE when he was 23;[2768] Alexander was not yet born. Alexander also fought at Chaeronea, but there is no conspicuous act of generosity associated with him in the aftermath of that victory, although he did display extraordinary leadership and daring for one so young.

[2767] Quran-Yusuf Ali, pp. 764-65. If this be a reference to an incident in Alexander's expedition to the Danube shortly after he became king at the age of 18, we have not yet been able to substantiate Alexander's generous behavior at Pelium from sources available to us. Although Alexander was capable of dramatic generosity in victory, none is mentioned by his ancient biographers Arrian, Plutarch, or Diodorus in this instance. Alexander did battle in the Lake Ochrida region on his return from the Danube. According to Green (pp. 132-35), the battle at Pelium (335 BCE), near Lake Ochrida, ended with the slaughter of thousands of Alexander's enemies with little display of clemency. The ancients praised his generalship in the campaign but make no mention, in this context, of the incident Yusuf Ali describes. Unfortunately, he does not mention his source for the story.

However, Ridpath does write: "Alexander next directed his course against the revolted Illyrians. Marching [southwest from the Danube] with great rapidity into their country, he penetrated to the capital Pellion [Pelium], which he seized before the insurgents were well aroused to a sense of their danger. The Illyrians, however, and the Taulantians, who had joined them, trusted rather to the defensible position which they had chosen among the hills than to the risks of a battle. They therefore waited to be attacked, and it was some time before Alexander could bring them to an engagement. At last, however, he assaulted them in their position, and they were quickly dispersed. The leaders of the revolt thereupon made overtures of peace, which were readily accepted by the king. News had already been carried to him of a troublous state of affairs in Greece, whereat Alexander was so greatly disturbed that he speedily withdrew from Illyria and returned to Macedon." (Ridpath, Vol. II, p. 631.)

In the situation described by Ridpath, there may very well have been some conspicuous generosity on Alexander's part, as he needed urgently to return to Macedonia and Greece, a return which led to the destruction of the city of Thebes with great slaughter; there was little clemency or generosity displayed there. It may also be pointed out that the Quranic verse in question—*We said: O Dhul-Qarnayn! Either punish or show them kindness. He said: As for him who doth wrong, we shall punish him, and then he will be brought back unto the Lord, who will punish him with awful punishment! But as for him who believeth and doth right, good will be his reward, and We shall speak unto him a mild command.* (Q. 18:86-88)—quotes God's command to Dhul-Qarnayn, and his determination to punish wrongdoers, whom God will also punish or reward. This does not necessarily mean that some sort of judgment was executed on the spot. It could also be interpreted as a decisive oath by Dhul-Qarnayn to do justice in his reign to follow. In Alexander's case, these incidents occurred at the beginning of his reign and before he set out to do battle with the Persian Empire. Incidentally, Dhul-Qarnayn visited the land of the setting sun (Q. 18:86-88) before that of the rising sun (Q. 18:90), which was also the sequence of the expeditions of the historical Alexander, first the west (Illyria) and then the east (Persia and India).

[2768] Green, pp. 24-25.

DARIUS THE GREAT: Though Yusuf Ali accepts the identification of Dhul-Qarnayn with Alexander,[2769] Maulana Muhammad Ali advocates an identification with Darius the Great,[2770] largely on the basis of the Persian king's expedition to the same region of the lower Danube in 514/513 BCE. Since Darius' base was in Fars, in the heart of his empire, the references to traveling west (to the Danube) and east (to India) are perhaps more appropriate to Darius. He also conducted campaigns against the Scythians in Central Asia.[2771] Our information about those eastern and central Asian campaigns is rather vague, because most of our fuller sources are Greek,[2772] primarily concerned with the Mediterranean world and the Near East. Too, there seems to have been more purpose in Darius than in Alexander. Alexander, it is true, extended the frontiers of the classical world, making possible the acceleration of the Hellenization that was already taking place in Western Asia, but he seems to have been in many ways an inadvertent instrument in this process.

On the other hand, Darius, who had the advantage of a much longer reign,[2773] created the organized, mature Persian Empire with its administration, institutions, and laws. However attractive the character and life of Alexander may have been, and his charismatic personality certainly made a tremendous impression upon his contemporaries and later ages, the rule of Darius with its stability, security, and system of justice was undoubtedly more beneficial to the people of southwestern Asia. What we can glimpse of the personality of Darius, as seen through the eyes of a people who feared him, is impressive although he has not had the propagandists with whom Alexander had been favored.

[2769] Quran-Yusuf Ali, p. 761.

[2770] Quran-MMA, pp. 586-87. Muhajir, for similar reason makes Dhul-Qarnayn Cyrus the Great. He explains the epithet "Dhul-Qarnayn" not as "he who possesses two horns," but as "lord of the two epochs. Muhajir, pp. 207-8. There is something to be said for his reasoning: *qarnayn* may mean "two horns," but it also may mean "two centuries" or "two epochs." It could be applied in that sense to a man who influenced or affected two eras. Indeed, Maulana Muhammad Ali uses the same explanation in defending his thesis that Darius is meant.

[2771] The founder of the Achaemenian dynasty, Cyrus the Great, had been killed in battle in the Caucasus region or the northern steppes in 530 BCE.

[2772] See Note 2728 above.

[2773] Alexander was born 356 BCE. He ascended the throne 336 BCE and died at Babylon in 323 BCE; thus, he was only thirty-three years old at the time of his death and had reigned about thirteen years. Darius was probably born some time about the middle of the 6th century BCE. He became the king 521 BCE and died 486 BCE after a reign of 35 years.

This discussion has so far not had anything to do with the Bible. As his period was too late, Alexander is not mentioned by name in the canonical books of the Old Testament, but several late passages in *Daniel* are thought to refer to him. *Daniel*, written or brought into its present form about 164 BCE,[2774] is a comparatively late work containing many anachronisms and historical errors in describing the time in which the hero Daniel is supposed to have lived. According to the story, Daniel was carried away to Babylon as a youth in the first group of captives in 598 BCE.[2775] He also witnessed the capture of Babylon by "Darius the Mede" in 529 BCE.[2776] A Jewish exilic hero, Daniel is depicted as possessed of the ideal qualities of steadfastness, reliance upon God, judgment, and wisdom. In *Daniel*, chs. 1 through 6, Daniel narrates his story in the third person. Chs. 7 through 12 relate four visions, largely in the first person. The second of these visions, found in ch. 8, is thought to refer to Alexander the Great and the Persian Empire:

"In the third year of the reign of King Belshazzar a vision appeared to me, Daniel, after that which appeared to me at the first. And I saw in the vision; and when I saw, I was in Susa the capital,[2777] which is in the province of Elam;[2778] and I saw in the vision, and I was at the river Ulai.[2779] I raised my eyes and saw, and behold, a ram standing on the bank of the river. It had two horns; and both horns were high, but one was higher than the other, and the higher one came up last. I saw a ram charging westward and northward and southward; no beast could stand before him, and there was no one who could rescue from his power; he did as he pleased and magnified himself." (Dan. 8:1-4)

"As I was considering, behold, a he-goat came from the west across the face of the whole earth, without touching the ground; and the goat had a conspicuous horn between his eyes. He came to the ram with the two horns, which I had seen standing on the bank of the river, and he ran at him in his mighty wrath. I saw him come close to the ram, and he was enraged against him and struck the ram and broke his two horns; and the ram had no power to stand before him, but he cast him down to the

---

[2774] Daniel, Book of, DB, p. 200.

[2775] See the story of Nebuchadnessar. The sack of Jerusalem by Nebuchadnessar occurred in 598 BCE. (See 2 K. 24:10-17.)

[2776] Babylon was captured by Cyrus the Great who, as was Darius, a Persian, not a Mede.

[2777] Susa was actually one of several capitals as the Persian court moved about seasonally. In the summer, it was at Ecbatana (Hamadan) and in the winter at Susa (Shush), whilst in the spring it was at Persepolis. A tomb, purported to be that of Daniel, is a place of local pilgrimage near the ruins of Susa.

[2778] Elam: an ancient kingdom most of which is now in Iran's province of Khuzestan.

[2779] Probably either the Karkhah or the Karun in southwestern Iran.

ground and trampled him; and there was no one who could rescue the ram from his power. Then the he-goat magnified himself exceedingly; but when he was strong, the great horn was broken, and instead of it there came up four conspicuous horns toward the four winds of heaven." (Dan. 8:5-8)

In this vision, the ram with the two horns is supposed to represent Media and Persia, the higher horn (Persia) appearing after the lesser one (Media). This reflects the history of Iran: first the Medes formed a kingdom centered in the west and northwest of Iran which was soon overthrown by the Persians from southern Iran who established the first true world-empire, the Persian empire under the Achaemenian dynasty which lasted nearly two centuries.

The he-goat, with one-horn between his eyes (not one on each side of his head), is presumed to be Alexander the Great who destroyed the Persian Empire, but was cut off at the height of his power. The four "conspicuous horns" would represent the division of his empire among his four generals: Seleucus, Ptolemy, Cassander, and Lysimachus. It is possible that the writer of *Daniel* had the situation contemporary to him in mind, in which case, the four would have been the Ptolemids in Egypt, the Seleucids in Syria and the East, the Antigonids in Macedonia, and the Attalids in western Anatolia (Turkey).[2780]

The use of the image of the horn in this passage has led some to try to connect Daniel's vision with the Dhul-Qarnayn of the Quran. However, in *Daniel*, Alexander has only one horn, whilst it is Persia that has two. We may stretch the intent of the text and say that this could represent Darius as the rule of Media and Persia, but it is not clear in *Daniel* that an individual is meant. However, the theory that Darius stands behind the Dhul-Qarnayn story cannot be dismissed out of hand.

CYRUS THE GREAT: Still another Persian king has been proposed as the original of Dhul-Qarnayn: Cyrus the Great (*Kūrush-i kabīr*). A Quranic commentator, in his note to verse 18:84, argues that Dhul-Qarnayn and Gog and Magog "are inseparably linked with each other." He then states that Dhul-Qarnayn is the king who founded the Medeo-Persian Empire, represented by the two-horned ram in the passage from Daniel cited above. "And of all kings of Media and Persia, the description given in the Quran most fitly applies to Cyrus." He possessed "the four distinctive marks of Dhul-Qarnayn: (a) He was a powerful monarch and a kind and just ruler (18:85,89); (b) He was a righteous servant of God and was blessed with divine revelation

---

[2780] Trawick-OT, pp. 317-18; Daniel, Book of, DB, pp. 199-200; Guthrie, pp. 697-98.

(18:92,99); (c) He marched to the West and made great conquests till he came to a place where he found the sun setting, as it were, in a pool of murky water and then he turned to the East and conquered and subdued vast territories (18:87,88); (d) He went to a midway region where a savage people lived and where Gog and Magog made great inroads; and he built a wall there to stop their inroads (18:94-98). Of the great rulers and famous military captains of ancient times, Cyrus possesses, in the greatest measure, the four above-mentioned qualities. He, therefore, rightly deserves to be considered the Dhul-Qarnayn of the Quran."[2781]

In his note, the annotator points to several Biblical references referring to Cyrus. In *Isaiah*, we find: "Thus says the Lord to his anointed, to Cyrus, whose right hand I have grasped, to subdue nations before him and ungird the loins of kings to open doors before him that gates may not be closed." (Is. 45:1) Thus, God has chosen Cyrus and made him His anointed one; that is, His Messiah.[2782] In *Ezra* we read: "… the Lord stirred up the spirit of Cyrus king of Persia so that he made a proclamation throughout all his kingdom…" (Ezek. 1:1) The proclamation ended the Babylonian Exile of the Jews and allowed them to return to Jerusalem and rebuild the Temple. Not only that, he provided them with treasure for the work. This is a formidable endorsement by God of Cyrus. He was certainly tolerant of religions other than is own. There is no cloud over his coming to power (he became king in the old-fashioned way by inheritance and military genius), as there is over Darius where trickery is supposedly involved. Frye says about him: "Herodotus says (III.89) the Persians remembered his mildness and called him father. We also have the 'Cyrus Saga' with variations. All of this indicates the esteem and affection in which the founder of the dynasty was held by his people."[2783] Says Lamb: "He had brought into being the novel concept of a ruler responsible to all his subjects… The Iranians said: 'Cyrus was a father, Cambyses a master, and Darius a penny pincher… Without Cyrus there could have been no Alexander."[2784] In addition, there are the traditions associating Cyrus with Zoroaster, but they are probably unhistorical.

Considering the parallels with the *Alexander Romance* and the known events of Alexander's extraordinary, meteoric career, the identification of Dhul-Qarnayn with Alexander accepted by a majority of Muslim commentators is *probably* the one intended by the Quran, but we

---

[2781] Quran-Farid, pp. 632-33.

[2782] Messiah, Metzger, p. 195.

[2783] Frye, p. 111.

[2784] Lamb-Cyrus, pp. 272, 273, 291.

should not dismiss competing candidates out of hand. Certainly, the case for Alexander is formidable, but we must confess our personal preference for Cyrus the Great.

VI. LUQMAN

Wisdom literature was produced in every part of the ancient East. Every linguistic and cultural group produced its own collections of folk wisdom enshrined in easily remembered proverbs, maxims, and short fables. Among the ancient Israelites, Solomon was especially revered for his wisdom. Several of the wisdom works in the Bible the Apocrypha are attributed to him, either wholly or in part.[2785]

The wisdom of other nations was also assimilated into the Bible. The Egyptian *Instruction of Amen-em-ope* (1000-900 BCE) provided the material found in Proverbs 22:17-24:22.[2786] The Aramaic *Wisdom of Aḥikār*, Assyrian in origin, with a manuscript tradition going back to the 6th century BCE, influenced the apocryphal *Book of Tobit*.[2787] *The Book of Job* contains blocks of wisdom literature, and its associations with

---

[2785] Pr. 1-9, 10-22:16, 25-29; Ecc.; *The Wisdom of Solomon*; and other examples scattered throughout various books such as *1 Kings* and *Psalms*. The *Song of Songs* (*Song of Solomon*) is also ascribed to him, although it is not strictly speaking wisdom literature.

[2786] Wisdom, DB, 1040. This view has not been without its opponents among scholars defending the primacy of the Hebrew text over the Egyptian. However, the majority admits that the chapters in *Proverbs* must be dependent upon *The Insruction of Amen-em-ope*. This is the view of William K. Simpson writing in the Introduction to Erman, pp. xii-xiii. The reader may judge for himself. Compare:

> "Incline thine ear, and hear the words of the wise
>   and apply thy mind to my knowledge;
> for it will be pleasant if thou keep them within thee,
>   if all of them are ready on thy lips." (Pr. 22:17-18)

> "Give thy ears, hear what is said,
> Give thy heart to understand them,
> To put them in thy heart is worth while,
> (But) it is damaging to him who neglects them." ANE, Vol. 1, p. 237.

The above are the beginning of the borrowing by *Proverbs* from the *Instruction of Amen-em-ope*. The entire text of the Egyptian document (called the *Teaching of Amen-em-ope* in the above DB reference) may be found on pp. 237-243 of ANE Vol. I. While the texts are not exactly the same, there are numerous parallels with the text of *Proverbs* indicated in the margins.

[2787] The *Book of Tobit* is included in the Apocrypha of the Old Testament, but not usually printed in Protestant editions of the Bible. It exists in a number of different versions of Hebrew, Greek, Latin, and Syriac. An Aramaic text has also been found at Qumran. DB states that it is earlier than the 1st century BCE, JB believes that it was written among the Jews of the Diaspora, "possibly in Egypt, between the 4th and 5th centuries" BCE. (JB, p. 724; A&P, II, 719.) In addition to textual influence, Ahikar is mentioned and described in Tob. 1:21-22, and mentioned elsewhere.

Edom have already been noted.[2788] North Arabia and Edom produced other sages of considerable fame, some of whose names have been preserved for us in the Bible and Apocrypha. Several passages attest the prestige of Arabian wise men:

> "Concerning Edom.
> Thus says the Lord of Hosts:
> 'Is wisdom no more in Teman?[2789]
> 　　　　Has counsel perished from the prudent?
> 　　　　Has their wisdom vanished?'' (Jer. 49:7)

> "Will I not on that day, says the Lord,
> 　　　　destroy the wise men out of Edom,
> 　　　　and understanding out of Mount Esau?" (Ob. 8)

> "Nothing has been heard of her [wisdom] in Canaan,
> nothing has been seen of her in Teman;
> the sons of Hagar in search of worldly wisdom,
> the merchants of Midian and Tema,
> the tale-spinners and the philosophers
> have none of them found the way of wisdom,
> or discovered the paths she treads." [2790] (Bar. 3:22-23)

In the present edition of *Proverbs*, two sections are attributed to men from the North Arabian tribe of Massa, which seems to have at one time inhabited the region to the east of Palestine.[2791] Chapter 30 has this heading: "The words of Agur son of Jakeh of Massa"; ch. 31:1-9 is entitled "the words of Lemuel, king of Massa, which his mother taught him."

The Biblical knowledge of Arabia was largely confined to the areas proximate to Palestine, so we may not expect to have many names of personalities farther afield preserved in the Biblical texts. Wisdom is especially ascribed to several prophets in the Quran, but the one

---

[2788] Wisdom, DB, 1040. See also the discussion of Job in Part Three, II.

[2789] Teman was a district inhabited by a tribe of the same name in Edom, probably located in the southern half of modern Jordan. (Teman, DB, 961.) Not to be confused with Tayma, in northwestern Saudi Arabia.

[2790] Note that wisdom is personified as a woman, as was the custom in Classical writings. Tema: modern Tayma in Hejaz, in northwestern Saudi Arabia. Baruch is saying that wisdom will not be found in such places with a reputation for sagacity (Laymon, p. 578)

[2791] Massa, DB, 630.

character to whom the epithet "the wise" is most commonly applied is Luqman (Q. 31:12), who is not identified there more specifically.

There is no doubt that Luqman the sage was well known to the pre-Islamic Arabs, and that the Quranic reference is to a body of traditions, probably oral, associated with him. He was called Luqman bin 'Ad (Ar. *Luqmān bin ᶜĀd* that is, Luqman of the tribe of 'Ad) and he was noted for his wisdom and longevity. He is also credited with a role in the design of the famous dam of Ma'rib in Yemen. Because of his longevity, he was given the epithet "*muᶜammar*" (long-lived).[2792] The Arab traditions about him are diffuse and often conflicting. The development of the Luqman literature among Muslims did not stop with Quran, and later biographies and collections of proverbs and fables attributed to him are clearly influenced by reports of other wise men, such as Aesop.

In their efforts to establish Luqman's credentials more firmly, the commentators gave him several genealogical connections with Biblical characters, although the weight of opinion seems to be against his having been a prophet.[2793] In some traditions he is linked with the people of Hud, in others he is identified with Balaam.[2794] He was a nephew of Job, or a nephew of Abraham, or he was born in the time of David.[2795] Surabadi says that David envied him his wisdom[2796] and that, as he was a slave, he was liberated during the time of David.[2797] In view of this uncertain chronology, we shall leave the question of his era open.

All that the Quran authentically tells us about Luqman may be found in six verses in the Surah bearing his name: Q. 31:12-13, 16-19. (Vv. 14 and 15 are a parenthetical statement by God, suggested by the preceding verse about Luqman, but are not part of his tradition.) The Luqmanid verses read: *And verily We gave Luqman wisdom, saying: Give thanks unto God; and whosoever giveth thanks, he giveth thanks for his soul. And whosoever refuseth—Lo! God is Absolute, Owner of Praise. And (remember) when Luqman said unto his son, when he was exhorting him: O my dear son! Ascribe no partners unto God. Lo! To ascribe partners (unto Him) is a tremendous wrong.* (Q. 31:12-13)

[2792] Lukman, EI, Vol. V, p. 811. The *muᶜammarūn*, were persons, either legendary or historical, who had exceptionally long lives. In Islamic tradition, the age of seventy is the starting point. See Muᶜammar, EI, Vol. VI, pp. 258-9.

[2793] Lukman, SEI, p. 289.

[2794] Lukman, SEI, p. 290.

[2795] Luqman, Hughes, pp. 301-3.

[2796] Surabadi, p. 319.

[2797] Surabadi, p. 317.

O my dear son! Lo! Though it be but the weight of a grain of mustard-seed, and though it be in a rock, or in the heavens, or in the earth, God will bring it forth. Lo! God is Subtle, Aware. O my dear son! Establish worship and enjoin kindness and forbid iniquity, and persevere whatever may befall thee. Lo! That is of the steadfast heart of things. Turn not thy cheek in scorn toward folk, nor walk insolently in the land. Lo! God loveth not each braggart boaster. Be modest in the bearing and subdue thy voice; surely the harshest of all voices is the voice of the ass. (Q. 31:16-19)

This is the Quranic record of Luqman. Luqman directs his son, and by extension, mankind, to be grateful to God and not to compromise His Unity. The totality of His knowledge is emphasized and we are to enjoin the good and forbid the bad. The braggarts are condemned and the humble exalted. The statements are of a kind that would arise in any proverbial folk literature, and the scattered parallels that exist in other literatures including the Bible cannot be considered as a necessary source or "borrowing" in the absence of stronger indications of similarity.

"The identification with Bal'am is old," states Heller in the SEI article. "Arabic legend gives the following genealogy: Lukman b. Ba'ur b. Nahur b. Tarikh (= Azar, father of Ibrahim). It is evident that the Kur'an exegetes sought for something corresponding to Lukman in the Bible. They found this in Bal'am, as the roots *bala'* and *laqama* both mean the same: 'to swallow.'" Though this identification received wide acceptance and even entered Jewish tradition, it is improbable that the Prophet made such an identification himself. "In no other instance did Muhammad translate a biblical name into Arabic." Heller goes on to say that pre-Quranic tradition of Luqman among the Arabs shows reverence, while Balaam is a hated and despised character in the Bible and the Haggada.[2798] Overall, the argument that the commentators erred in making this identification is quite persuasive.

A case has been made for the identification of Luqman with Ahikar on the basis of the close resemblance of one of Ahikar's proverbs with v. 19 quoted above: "Son, incline thine eyes and soften the utterances of thy mouth, and look under things eyes; that thou mayst not appear senseless to men, for if a temple were built by hallooings, an ass would build seven palaces every day..."[2799] In the Syriac version, the proverb is given thus: "My son, cast down thine eyes, and lower thy voice, and look from beneath thine eyelids: for if a house could be built by a high voice, the ass would build two houses in one day: and if by

---

[2798] Lukman, SEI, p. 290. See the discussion of the Balaam cycle in Stories III.N.

[2799] A&P, II, p. 735. Armenian version of Ahikar, dated c. 450 CE.

sheer force the plough was guided, its share would never be loosed from the shoulder of the camel."[2800]

The similarity between these versions of the Ahikar proverb to the Quranic verse cannot be denied, although the bray of an ass evokes similar comments worldwide. However, since we do not know the prior history of the Ahikar proverbs—and proverbs are notorious vagabonds—it is still too much to assert "the Koran knows Ahikar by the name of Loqman."[2801] *The Story of Ahikar* doubtless has its own history of accretion from other sources, and the great diversity of texts cited in the Ahikar portion of the Pseudepigrapha certainly makes the provenance of any particular proverb a matter of debate. However, the identification is attractive and it should be remembered the Quranic statements do not localize Luqman in Arabia, although he was known in Arabia by that name.

Many passages of the Bible offer parallels to the wisdom sayings of the five verses of the Quran quoted above. A few will be cited below, although no theory of dependence is necessary, because the general nature of the material would permit, for the most part, independent development in any reflective society.

Giving thanks to God (Q. 31:12) is one of the more recurrent themes of the Bible:
"O give thanks to the Lord, call on his name,
and make known his deeds among the peoples!
Sing to him, sing praises to him,
tell of his wonderful works!" (1 Ch. 16:8-9)
"At that time Jesus declared, 'I thank thee, Father, Lord of Heaven and earth, that thou hast hidden these things from the wise and understanding and revealed them to babes...'" (Mt. 11:25)
"I will give thanks to thee, Lord and King
and praise thee, God, my saviour,
I give thanks to thy name;
for thou hast been protector and support to me,
and redeemed my body from destruction..."
(Eccs. 51:1-2)

The warning to Luqman's son not to associate any other deity with God (Q. 31:13) immediately calls to mind the First of the Ten Commandments: "Thou shalt have no other gods before Me." (Ex. 20:3) And in *Deuteronomy* we read: "To thee it was shown, that thou mightest know that the Lord is God; there is no other beside Him." (Deut. 4:35)

[2800] A&P, II, pp. 728, 730.
[2801] A&P, II, p. 719.

Again: "Hear, O Israel: The Lord our God is one Lord; and thou shalt love the Lord thy God with all thy heart, and will all thy soul, and with all thy might." (Deut. 6:4-5)

The verse about the mustard seed (Q. 31:16) brings to mind the parable attributed to Jesus, although the point is different: "Another parable he put before them saying, 'The kingdom of heaven is like a grain of mustard seed which a man took and sowed in his field; it is the smallest of all seeds, but when it has grown it is the greatest of shrubs and becomes a tree, so that the birds of the air come and make nests in its branches." (Mt. 13:31-32)

The command to prayer and action for both the establishment of good and the prevention of evil, together with patience in adversity is a summary of the ethics of the Quran and one of its most noteworthy and distinctive moral statements (Q. 31:17). It is a commandment to righteous action and inner strength.

Exhortations to prayer (private supplication) are more common in the New Testament than in the Old. "Rejoice in your hope, be patient in tribulation, be constant in prayer." (Rom. 12:12) "And he told them a parable, to the effect that they ought always to pray and not lose heart." (Lk. 18:1) "Continue steadfastly in prayer, being watchful in it with thanksgiving..." (Col. 4:2)

A passage in *1 Thessalonians* gives several of the elements of the Quranic verse: "See that none of you repays evil for evil, but always seek to do good to one another and to all. Rejoice always, pray constantly, give thanks in all circumstances..." (1 Th. 5:15-18)

Parallels to the injunctions to enjoin good and forbid evil may be seen in the following passages:

"Seek good, and not evil that ye may live;
and so the Lord, the God of hosts will be with you
    as ye have said.
Hate evil, and love good and establish justice in the gate..."
                        (Amos 5:14-15)

"Thus sayeth the Lord God: Enough, O princes of Israel! Put away violence and oppression, and execute justice and righteousness; cease your evictions of my people, sayeth the Lord God." (Ezek. 45:9) "Therefore, O king, let my counsel be acceptable to thee; break off thy sins by practicing righteousness, and thy iniquities by showing mercy to the oppressed, that there may perhaps be a lengthening of thy tranquility." (Dan. 4:27)

"So shun youthful passions and aim at righteousness, faith, love, and peace, along with those who call upon the Lord from a pure heart."

(2 Tim. 2:22) "Beloved, do not imitate evil but imitate good. He who does good is of God; he who does evil has not seen God." (3 Jn. 11) "So whatever you wish that men would do to you, do so to them; for this is the Law and the prophets." (Mt. 7:12)

The above is a sampling of the parallels that can be found in Biblical literature, and are cited to show how similar ideas and moral impulses were treated in the Bible and do not imply any direct dependence. People of all faiths and cultures recognize the duality of human nature and its propensities for good and evil. Although there are numerous calls to righteous behavior and the avoidance of evil in the Bible, they are rarely couched in such succinct and unequivocal terms of social action as we find in the Quranic verse.

With regard to the Quranic recommendation of humility and the eschewal of pride (Q. 31:18) there are again many Biblical parallels:
"The fear of the Lord is hatred of evil.
Pride and arrogance and the way of evil
   and perverted speech I hate." (Pr. 8:13)
"Whoever humbles himself like this child, he is the greatest in the kingdom of heaven." (Mt .18:4) "Clothe yourselves, all of you, with humility towards one another, for 'God opposes the proud, but gives grace to the humble.' Humble yourselves therefore under the mighty hand of God, that in due time He may exalt you." (1 P. 5:5-6) "Humble yourselves before the Lord and he will exalt you." (Jas. 4:10)

The last of the Luqmanid verses in the Quran, about lowering the voice (Q. 31:19), has already been commented upon above.

As in so many instances in the Quran, the brief references therein refer to bodies of (oral) tradition no longer known to us in the form in which they were circulating during the period of the revelation, and so are perhaps lost forever. The whole point of wisdom literature is that it is universal and encapsulates truths in pithy sayings, truths that are valid for all climes and times. We still derive instruction from them, even though the historical context has been lost to us, at least in the form it was understood by those hearing them in the revelations for the first time from the lips of the Prophet.

The commentators, in their zeal to recover this contextual material in answer to the questions of later generations about the context and the meaning of the verses were sometimes not very discriminating, as we have seen. Much unsuitable, confusing, and fabulous material has been imported into the stories in an effort to convert them into spiritual romances, according to the medieval taste for such things. The Luqman cycle has not been spared this development, and the material brought forward by the commentators has hardly helped us to identify him with any historical character, if such an identification be necessary, or even desirable. Surabadi tells us several stories about him that occasionally refer to Biblical characters.

To begin, after informing us that Luqman was an Ethiopian slave who was freed by an Israelite master during the time of David, he gives us four different versions of the occasion of that manumission:

1. Luqman was freed because his master had once slaughtered a sheep and asked him to bring him the best parts. Luqman brought him the heart and the tongue. When asked to bring the worst parts, be brought the same heart and tongue. When asked by his master about this, Luqman replied: "There is nothing better or worse than these two things in the body of a person." Astonished at his slave's wisdom, his master set him free.

2. Luqman was told by his master to plant certain crops in certain fields. Luqman did not follow the instructions and when the master came to the field expecting to see wheat, he saw barley instead. Master: "Didst thou not know that if thou plantest barley it will not grow into wheat?" Luqman: "Didst thou not know that if thou sinnest today thou shalt not go to heaven tomorrow?" Deeply affected, the master freed Luqman.

3. Luqman's master was a gambler who once bet a friend that if he lost, he would drink all the water of the river beside which they were playing. He lost and was given three days to drink all the water. He returned home frantic. Luqman asked him why he was so upset. Master: "What business is it of yours?" Luqman: "Tell me; perhaps your salvation is in my hands. *In every head there is wisdom.*" The master told Luqman about his bet and the consequences of his losing the gamble. Luqman: "O master, this is simple! Tell the man: 'I was talking about the water that was flowing in the river that day and at that time. You bring back that water and I shall drink it.' He cannot bring it back and nothing can happen to you." His master was so delighted by this stratagem that he freed Luqman.

4. Once Luqman's master was eating cucumbers and came upon one that was extremely bitter. He passed it to Luqman who ate it without making a face. Astonished, the master asked how he could eat anything so bitter without making a face. Luqman replied that he had received so many good things from him that it would be ungenerous to complain

because for once something was bitter. His master was pleased and manumitted him.[2802]

None of these stories has a direct parallel in the Bible. Some of the ideas expressed in them may, however, be found there. For example, in Surabadi's first anecdote, the symbolism of the heart and the tongue is echoed here and there: "Death and life are in the power of the tongue, and those who love it will eat its fruits." (Pr. 18:21) "The tongue of the righteous is choice silver; the mind of the wicked is of little worth." (Pr. 10:20) "A gentle tongue is a tree of life, but perverseness in it breaks the spirit." (Pr. 14:4)

The theme of planting and reaping in the second pericope has many Biblical parallels: "Do not be deceived; God is not mocked, for whatever a man sows, that he will also reap. For he who sows to his own flesh will from the flesh reap corruption; but he who sows to the Spirit will from the Spirit reap eternal life." (Gal. 6:7-8) "For they sow the wind, and they shall reap the whirlwind." (Hos. 8:7) "He who sows injustice will reap calamity, and the rod of his fury will fall." (Pr. 22:8) "As I have seen, those who plough iniquity and sow trouble reap the same." (Job 4:8)

When Surabadi speaks of Luqman as an Ethiopian slave, he is apparently implicitly identifying him with the Aesop of Classical literature. The earliest reference to Aesop in Greek writings is to be found in the *Histories* of Herodotus (5th century BCE): "(Rhodophis the courtesan) was by birth a Thracian,[2803] the slave of Iadmon, the son of Hephaestopolis of Samos, and fellow-slave of Aesop the fable-writer. The clearest proof that Aesop was the slave of Iadmon is the fact that when the Delphians, in obedience to the oracle's command,[2804] repeatedly advertised for someone to claim compensation for Aesop's murder, the only person to come forward was the grandson of Iadmon (a man of the same name)."[2805]

We can further deduce from Herodotus that Aesop was believed to have lived in the time of the Egyptian pharaoh Amasis (mid-6th century BCE), that is, about a century before Herodotus. Later authors

---

[2802] Surabadi, pp. 317-18. Mayhani uses the same story in connection with the great 11th-century CE Sufi saint Abū Saʿīd Abī Khayr. (Mayhani, p. 86.)

[2803] Thracian: a native of Thrace, the southeastern corner of the Balkan Peninsula, now shared amongst Bulgaria, Greece, and Turkey in Europe.

[2804] A reference to the Oracle of Delphi, the most famous of the classical world.

[2805] Herodotus, p. 182.

tell us that he was a Phrygian[2806] or a Thracian.[2807] Greek tradition, as exemplified by Herodotus, seems to indicate that Aesop did not die a natural death, but this is not reflected in the story of Luqman that Surabadi offers us. A biography of Aesop from the 1st century CE associates him with the island of Samos, and states that Aesop was a slave who, after gaining his freedom, went to Babylon where he solved riddles for King Lycurgus, and finally met his death at Delphi.[2808]

Writing about the same time, Plutarch states: "That he was captured young and brought a slave to Athens, and after several changes of ownership enfranchised by Iadmon; that during Pisistratus' usurpation he visited Athens and composed the fable *King Log and King Stork* for the edification of the citizens; that, going to the Lydian court, he became Croesus' favorite, was sent by him as envoy to Delphi to distribute money to the people [c. 546 BCE], and, refusing to do so on account of a quarrel among them, was thrown from a cliff by them."[2809] A commentator on the classical Greek playwright Aristophanes tells us that the cause of Aesop's death was the finding of a temple cup deliberately planted in his baggage by his enemies. The story is suspiciously similar to that of Joseph and Benjamin in *Genesis*[2810] and supports the thesis that many elements of the Aesop legend were borrowed from the East over a lengthy period.

In all of these references, he is seen to be from the world of the eastern Aegean. The idea that he was an Ethiopian seems to have arisen because of a similarity between his name Aesop and the word "Ethiopia" (Ethiopian) in the Greek language. The later traditions that Aesop was a misshapen black are of medieval origin. A 13th century CE manuscript in Florence, Italy, mentions them,[2811] but they gained wide circulation through the work of a scholarly monk, Maximus Planudes,[2812] who in 1301 CE produced an edition of such stories called the *Greek Anthology*, prefacing it with a romantic biography in which the above elements are present.[2813] The stories in Maximus' work were culled from 1700 years of Greek literature, from the 7th century BCE to the 10th CE. Some of the stories are quite probably the result of the influence of the Islamic stories

---

[2806] Phrygia: an ancient kingdom in west-central Anatolia.

[2807] Aesop, xv.

[2808] Aesop, EB, Mic, I, 115.

[2809] Quoted in Aesop, EA, I, 198.

[2810] The Biblical story is found in Gen.44. It is discussed in Part Two, VI, of the Old Testament stories.

[2811] Aesop, EB, I, 263, 1960 ed.

[2812] Planudes, Maximus, EB, Mic., VIII, 28.

[2813] Aesop, EA, I, 198.

of Luqman on the growth of the Aesop legend rather than the other way around.[2814]

The story of Ahikar may also have influenced the development of the Greek Aesop legend, especially with regard to the story of Aesop's journey (see below). A minister of the Assyrian king Sennacherib (rgd. 704-681 BCE), Ahikar gave a book of proverbs and fables to his adopted son, Nadan, for his edification. Nadan was able to replace his adopted father as minister and Ahikar retired; however, Nadan falsely accused Ahikar of plotting against the king, and the king ordered Ahikar's execution. Ahikar managed to save himself from the executions and was later proved innocent.[2815]

Returning to Surabadi's narrative, after securing his freedom Luqman sought knowledge from 1,700 teachers and was wise, pious, ascetic, kind, and truthful. God gave him the choice of prophethood or wisdom. Luqman chose wisdom and became the wise man *par excellence* of the world. He lived for 1,000 years. David approved of him for his wisdom, and Khidr envied him. When asked about the source of his wisdom, he replied: "Three things: truth, fulfillment of trust, and the abandonment of that which preoccupies me."

Luqman had one thousand sons whose birth did not give him joy, nor did their deaths cause him sorrow. He advised his sons to fear God and to try to please Him (Q. 31:13-14). One of his sons was named Nu'man (*Nuʿmān*). He would not listen to his father's advice. Luqman filled a sac with millet and for each grain he gave his son instruction, but to no avail. Finally, Luqman had one grain left and said: "If it be the weight of a grain of mustard-seed" (Q. 31:16). Luqman's son was suddenly enlightened and died on the spot in ecstasy.[2816]

Although not mentioned in the Quran, Luqman's journey, his search for knowledge is a common enough theme not to demand a literary antecedent. However, there is a parallel in the life of Aesop, his journey to Babylon mentioned in sources cited above. Ahikar also went on a journey (which may be the source of the journey by Aesop), but his was not for knowledge, but rather to save his life; a parallel to the story of Apollonius discussed in Story of Jesus, in *The New testament: An Islamic Perspective*.

[2814] Sale also takes this view. See Quran-Sale, p. 401; also quoted in Hughes, "Luqman," p. 302.

[2815] Ahikar, Book of, DB, 17.

[2816] Surabadi, pp. 318-20.

That Luqman was a freed slave seems to be derived from the Aesop cycle, as this tradition can be traced to the classical Greek writings of Plutarch and others.[2817] Heller is probably correct when he suggests that the story of Luqman's being offered the choice of prophethood or wisdom is a Muslim invention to explain why Luqman was not considered a prophet.[2818]

Luqman's phenomenal life span reminds us of the identification of Luqman with the Mu'ammar of the story of Hud.[2819] In that place, he was credited with a life of 2,100 years. Surabadi seems to suggest that the two are different individuals bearing the same name, the Luqman in the story of Hud being called Luqman bin 'Ad. Nonetheless, there is some mixing of traditions here.

Surabadi tells us that Luqman had a prodigious number of sons. In this he differs from both Ahikar and Aesop, neither of whom seems to have had any offspring. Indeed, it was because he had no offspring that Ahikar adopted the ungrateful Nadan. There is a similar incident in the story of Aesop: "Now as Aesop himself had no children, he annexed a certain young man of noble birth named Ennus, and brought him to the king, with commendation as his proper son. And when, not long after, Ennus played false with the concubine of his adoptive father, Aesop, becoming aware of it, would have banished him (from) the house."[2820] The results of this betrayal of trust in the Aesop story were the same as in *Ahikar*; the young man tried to save himself by falsifying evidence that Aesop was in correspondence with the king's enemies. Aesop was sentenced to death, but managed to escape, and his "son" in the meantime took over his affairs. This pericope would seem to be clearly derived from the Assyrian story of Ahikar.

On the surface, Surabadi's Luqman would appear to have nothing in common with this episode; however, the mention of Luqman's rebellious and unreceptive son Nu'man is suggestive of Nadan. In Surabadi's story, Luqman relentlessly continues to teach his son until suddenly he is enlightened and dies in ecstasy. This is close to the end of Nadan in the story of Ahikar: Following the Armenian version, after Nadan's treachery had been exposed, and Ahikar's

---

[2817] Herodotus does not appear to know of Aesop's achieving his freedom; perhaps this element entered the story after his time.

[2818] Lukman, SEI, p. 289.

[2819] See the Story of the Destruction of the People of Hud in Part Two, I. {In this series, in *Abraham*.}

[2820] Cited in *The Story of Ahikar*, A&P, II, p. 780. The Greek story of Aesop is given in sections that show the coincidence with the *Ahikar*. Here the identification of the two characters is virtually complete.

property and honors had been restored to him, he tells us in (in the first person): "And the king gave Nathan[2821] my sister's son into my hands, and I bound him with a single chain of iron, which was the weight of seven talents,[2822] at the door of my portico; and I entrusted him to Beliar my servant. And I ordered him to scourge him on his back and belly. And I said to him in my coming and going forth: 'Whatsoever I speak in proverbs with him, do thou write on paper and keep it with thee; and I gave to (Nathan) a little bread and a little water. I began to speak and said as follows: 'Son, him that with his ears heareth not they make to hear through his back.'"

In a lengthy dialogue, presumably recorded for posterity by Beliar, Nathan pleas and Ahikar continues to utter precepts and reproaches. Finally, Nathan admits his error. "And I spake to Nathan thus: 'Son, thou has been to me like a palm-tree which was growing with roots on the bank of the river. When the fruit ripened, it fell into the river. The lord of the tree came to cut it down, and the tree said: Leave me in this place, that in the next year I may bear fruit. The lord of the tree said: Up to this day hast thou been to me useless, in the future thou wilt not become useful.

"'Son, God hath rescued me because of my innocence, but hath destroyed thee because of thy lawlessness. God passes judgment between me and thee. For the tail of the dog gives bread and his mouth a cudgel.' In the same hour Nathan swelled up and all his body swelled up and all his body burst asunder, and I said: 'Son, he that doeth good winneth good; and he that digs a pit for others, himself falls into the pit. The good endeth in good and the evil in evil.'"[2823]

In other words, Ahikar may have talked Nathan to death. In any case, the end of Nathan strikingly parallels the end of Nu'man in Surabadi, with the difference that Nathan was unable to achieve enlightenment.

Finally, after these speculative identifications of Luqman with Balaam, Aesop, and Ahikar, we may take note of one more, this one proposed by Spenger: that Luqman is identical to Elxai of the Ebionites.[2824] Elkesai (Elxai)[2825] was the founder of a Jewish sect of

---

[2821] Nadan is so called in the Syriac version; in the Armenian version, he is called Nathan, another form of the same name.

[2822] According to Smith, a talent was a weight of 75.5 lbs. Weights, BD-Smith, p. 605. This would make the chain weigh about 528.5 lbs., something over a quarter of a ton. Let us hope that this is an exaggeration.

[2823] A&P, II, pp. 768, 775-76.

[2824] Cited in Hughes, p. 302.

Baptists called by the Arabs *al-mughtasilah*. Elkesai founded the sect early in the reign of Trajan (rgd. 98-117 CE). The central feature of his cult was the remission of sins through baptism by total immersion of the clothed body. From the beginning of his career, Elkesai possessed a revealed book, of which a few fragments have been preserved in the writings of his Christian critics. He seems to have been a charismatic speaker and an ecstatic, but he was not learned and there appears to be no particular ascription of wisdom literature to him. He apparently died naturally.[2826]

It has been suggested that the Elkesaites are the Sabians of the Quran (Q. 2:62; 5:69; 22:17).[2827] Whether or not this be true, it is difficult to see Luqman in Elkesai; more difficult than in the cases of Balaam, Aesop, and Ahikar. Though the identification of Quranic characters with personages otherwise known from other sources is always attractive because of its neatness, the possibility that there are not such identifications to be made must not be excluded. The Luqman tradition may be a genuine memory of some local sage about whom stories collected, known to the Arabs, but not to the literatures of the rest of the ancient world. The collection of proverbs in Ahikar is just that, a collection from sources either oral or written, much of which is now lost to us. It cannot be expected to have originated at one time and, as we have noted above, proverbs are notorious vagabonds.

Unfortunately, the history of their oral transmission is lost to us forever. The ancient sages of various nations seem to have always been magnets, attracting the wisdom and proverbs of their neighbors to their names, as in the cases of Solomon and Aesop. We can only speculate upon the relationship between the Luqman and Ahikar traditions in the pre-Islamic past; that there was such a contact is attested by the Quran.

The introduction of Aesop is the work of later Muslim writers. With that step, more elements of the Ahikar story entered the Luqmanic corpus through the medium of Aesop. The identification with Balaam is also the work of later Muslims.[2828] That such divergent traditions could appear in later times is the result of brevity of the Quranic references, the scantiness of relevant Traditions, and the loss of the oral context.

[2825] The Arabic form of founder's name is ʾlḥsyh, probably vowelized something like Al-Ḥasīh (Elkesaites, ERE, V, 262-63).

[2826] Elkesaites, ERE, V, 263-66. They are also mentioned in the discussion of the *Gospel of John* in the Introduction to the *The New Testament: An Islamic Perspective*, q.v.

[2827] Al-Sabia, SEI, p. 477; Elksaites, ERE, V, 268. There is some confusion about their relationship to the Mandaeans.

[2828] Lukman, SEI, p. 9290.

AFTERWORD TO THE OLD TESTAMENT

We have now arrived at the end of our journey through the Old Testament stories found in the Quran and the Commentary of Surabadi. After our tour, though restricted to those things that touch upon the Islamic stories in the Quran and Commentary, we may find ourselves a little bewildered by what we have encountered on our way. Let us pause for a moment before commencing the next journey through the world of the New Testament to reflect upon what we have observed in the Old.

We have identified many instances of textual conflation, corruption and alteration in the Biblical narratives that seriously damage the assumption that the Biblical form of a story must be taken as the standard by which the intrinsic merit of differing versions, including those in the Quran, are assessed. The frequent use of the devices of ultimogeniture and barren, elderly women miraculously bearing children to enhance the status of a character is so common as to have become a Biblical cliché. And then, there are the disturbing anecdotes of immoral or unethical behavior ascribed to some of the most revered figures in the Biblical tradition

Ironically, it is precisely among these textual problems—the garblings, duplications, contradictions, and defamations—that we may find clues in our search for the true state of affairs. Sometimes we encounter contrary versions of long-received truths hidden amidst the patchwork text left to us by the variously motivated multiple redactions. It is in these confused and spliced narratives that we may discover pieces of the puzzle, aiding us in understanding the Bible and in the reconstruction of the transmission of the Biblical pericopes into the Arabian oral literature of the Prophet's lifetime, the context of the revelation of the Quran.

For our purposes, one of the principal differences between the Old Testament and the New is that in this part we have had to rely primarily on the Biblical text for our comparison. Extra-Biblical material, especially about the historical books (which are our chief concern) is relatively scanty and random. Most dissenting sources seem to have perished, if they ever existed in writing. As we have seen, with the exception the stories in Part One from *Genesis* that have a number of Mesopotamian parallels and antecedents (recovered in large part by the hard work of archeologists and linguistic scholars), for most of the stories that we are considering, we must argue almost entirely from the (fortunately) heterogeneous text of the Bible, as there are comparatively few extra-Biblical contemporary materials extant.

The Apocrypha and Pseudepigrapha, the Talmuds and the Midrashim preserve many probably oral traditions, and we have relied upon them when they exist, but they are all products of a much later age, often composed a thousand years after the fact. We are faced with a paucity of early alternative traditions, except those we find in the Bible itself. Consequently, there are more unresolved questions, more lacunae, than we find in the New Testament stories, although they have their share of problems.

In such a situation we have laid out as much information for the reader as we could muster and encourage him to use his own judgment, but not to miss the forest for the trees, as the saying goes. Such questions that we have posed here about the text have their own importance, but the real questions of life are more often moral dilemmas, not historical puzzles. Intellectual disputation must give way at some point to inward search, meditation, prayer, and faith.

In the New Testament, as we shall see in the next volume, the text is much more homogeneous and coherent, for the most part maintaining a consistently Pauline point of view. Fortunately, there exists also a large corpus of extra-Biblical material we can turn to so that we may get behind that Pauline façade. However, in the Old Testament stories, we have to rely upon much more upon the hypothetical oral transmission of variants. The Midrashim and other Jewish writings of the Hellenistic and early Christian eras demonstrate the existence of such material. The Quran, a most carefully preserved text of the early 7th century CE, testifies to the shape of the stories at the time of its revelation in Makkah and Madinah. References that cause us problems today, such as to al-Samiri, the water test, and the like evidently spawned no criticism or discussion, or we would probably have heard about it from early Arab sources. When one reads *Sahih al-Bukhari* or *Mishkat al-Masabih*, one is frequently astonished by the detailed material that is preserved in them. Whatever the truth of matter is, the answer lies in the now vanished oral literature that was its context. What was important is what is still important: the purpose of the parable, the moral of the lesson, the guidance it gives.

This is true of the Quran and it is true for the inspired portions of the Bible or any other sacred writing. We do not understand what happened to the Prophet—or to any prophet for that matter—when the Supreme Being elected to communicate His message to him. In some manner, the messenger is granted a wondrous vision of the Eternal. To relieve himself of that burden, he is compelled to convey it to us, if those be his instructions. The ineffable is transmuted into human language.

Even divine messages are not imperishable. Not every prophet was given a scripture to deliver. For those who were, that scripture is left as a trust to succeeding generations. They must preserve the integrity of its text so that others may benefit from it and live by it through the ages. Few would deny that Muslim scholars and teachers have done a superb job of maintaining that trust. With respect to the integrity of text, there can be no challenge to the basic integrity of the text of the Quran.

The Quranic charge that the Biblical text has been altered has been amply proven, as our review of what scholarship has revealed about it over the past two and one-half centuries. However, we should qualify our sense of triumph by remembering that the idea of a sacred scripture came late to Judaism, after most of the damage to the text had been done. Once Jewish scholars realized what was being lost, they worked diligently to preserve what was left. As Muslims, we should not rejoice, nor experience any schadenfreude, in being right. How much more might we have had to examine, discuss, and profit from? Alas, many books live on only in their names. Except for the fragments preserved in the Bible, they are as vanished into thin air as is the Arabian oral context of the Quran.

Throughout our discussion, we have pointed out some of the consistencies, contradictions, and crudities that litter the historical books of the Old Testament, but at the same time, these passages testify to a laudable attempt to preserve all that could be preserved. We have seen the largely unacknowledged debt to the older civilizations of Egypt and Mesopotamia at the beginning; towards the end we get hints of the changes taking place in the Fertile Crescent that would soon herald the assault of Alexander and Hellenism upon its ancient culture. We have seen that Israel was really founded by Moses, not Abraham who should be a focus of unity instead of rivalry among his spiritual descendants, Jew, Christian, and Muslim alike. We have seen the beginnings of apocalyptic literature in *Daniel* and some of the other late writings that have spawned passions and ideas that haunt us to this day.

The story of the Israelites in the Bible is a very human story. We see mankind at its most exalted and at its most depraved. Through the struggles, personal fortunes and misfortunes of the various players in the millennia-long epic, we watch monotheism develop and evolve. It starts with the idea of a single Deity, invisible, rejecting idolatry, in direct contact with His creation. At first, He is henotheistically perceived as the god of a single people. Having revealed Himself on a mountain, He is thought of as a god of the mountain and He is thought to dwell there. Then we witness, through the Old Testament stories, the awful step-by-step realization dawning upon His worshippers that this God is in fact the Creator of all mankind and the entire Universe.

And parallel to this growing recognition of God's essential Unity, we have also watched the moral evolution of a people. At first, it was thought that justice would be done and wrongs righted in this life. The soul was in some manner eternal, but the afterlife held no promise. Then Job cried out: "Why do the innocent suffer?" The cruel answer was that there is no perfect justice in this life, a judgment echoed by Plato. The answer to Job's question was not to be found in this world, but in another when the Lord of the Worlds would rectify our imperfect justice.

Thus, at the end of this our first journey we have arrived at the doorway of universality. In the intervening centuries, between the end of the Old Testament era and the beginning of the New, Palestine was once again an incubator of religious ideas. The last great prophet to come out of Israel was soon to appear and teach the kingdom of heaven in which all mankind had a share. This concept would be too much for many to bear and so his simple message was diluted and compromised. In His mercy, God called another Messenger... but that is after the end of the next journey, through the New Testament.

GLOSSARY

Abbasid: pertaining to the Abbasid dynasty (rgd. AH132-656/750-1258 CE) based in Mesopotamia, principally Baghdad.

Achaemenian: the dynasty that ruled history's first great world empire, that of the Persians (559 to 330 BCE).

Adventist/Adventism (*Second Adventist/Second Adventism*): as used here, refers to any of several evangelical Christian sects and factions, past and present, whose beliefs are largely concentrated upon the expected Second Coming of Christ (the Second Advent) and the Last Days which, in their belief, are inextricably linked with those cataclysms. The terms are general and are not specific to any particular sect or group (such as the Seventh-Day Adventists) that may use the word or words in its name.

Aetiology: adj. *aetiological*: the study of causes. Also, *etiology*, *etiological*.

Antichrist: one who rejects or opposes Christ; also, the anticipated opponent of Christ in the Second Coming.

Antinomian: a doctrine that disregards human and moral law, asserting that faith justifies all.

Amphictyony: a confederation established around a shrine or religious center.

Apocalypse: revelation; later a writing or vision about the catastrophic events accompanying the end of the world.

Apocrypha: non-canonical religious writings.

Apology: in literary language it signifies a defence, rather than an admission of regret for an error as it is more frequently used in modern speech.

Aramaic: the Semitic language spoken by the people of the New Testament Near East. It replaced several other Semitic languages, including Hebrew among the Jews.

Assyria: a Semitic empire based in northern Iraq. In its imperial phase (883-626 BCE), Assyria was a world power.

Babylon: the chief city of Semitic peoples of southern Iraq in ancient times. Its ruins lie some 70 miles south of Baghdad.

Babylonian Captivity (*Exile*): the period that the Jews of Jerusalem spent in Babylon after being carried off by Nebuchadnezzar in 586 BCE. The Edict of Cyrus (538 BCE) permitted the Jews to return and officially ended the "Captivity" or "Exile."

Baptism: an initiatory rite (and Christian sacrament) using water either by immersion or in some other manner.

Canon: the list of books officially accepted for inclusion in the Bible. It varies according to the faith. The Jews, for example, only recognize the books of the Old Testament as canonical.

Cherubim (sing. *cherub*): an order of angels, usually depicted as winged children.

Christology: a theological interpretation of the life and mission of Jesus.

Corvée: a kind of labor tax upon the peasantry in kind in a non-monetary society; forced labor, often in the form of a stated number of days during the year, due a feudal lord or ruler.

Daniel: an Old Testament prophet; the Biblical book (Dan.) bearing his name.

Disappearance, The: In this book, the Disappearance of Jesus after the events of the Passion and the end of his public ministry in Palestine.

Diaspora: the dispersion of the Jews from Palestine and the areas in which they settled. Also used in a general sense for any such dispersal of population from its homeland, as in the Palestinian Diaspora.

Eastern Church: the churches and denominations of Christians originating in the Eastern Roman Empire, including the Greek and Russian Orthodox Churches amongst others.

Ebionite, Ebionism: a Jewish-Christian sect of the early Christian centuries. They have been divided into two factions: those following the Jewish Law, regarding Jesus as a prophet and Paul an apostate; and the Gnostic Ebionites who more esoterically regarded Jesus as a spirit. The Ebionites were considered heretical by the Pauline Church. (Ebionites, CE, p. 620; Ebionism, ERE, Vol. V, pp. 139-141.)

Elohist: also designated E; the second earliest strand in the Pentateuch representing Northern traditions, and its writer.

Ephod: priestly vestment, often adorned with precious stones.

Epiphanius: a bishop of Salamis in Cyprus (d. 403 CE) whose writings preserve many valuable quotations from otherwise lost books that he was refuting.

Eschatology: the study of the last things, that is, the final events of the world and mankind.

Esoteric: knowledge or ideas restricted to a special or initiated group; not for the commons; the opposite of *exoteric*, q.v.

Eucharist: the sacrament in which bread and wine (or grape juice) are consumed in commemoration of the sacrifice of Christ. Some churches believe that the bread and wine miraculously become the flesh and blood of Jesus at the time they are consumed.

Exile, the: see *Babylonian Captivity*.

Exoteric: knowledge or ideas considered suitable for the general public; the opposite of *esoteric*, q.v.

Ezekiel: an Old Testament prophet; the Biblical book (Ezek.) bearing his name.

Fertile Crescent: a term applied to the agricultural lands that arch around the northern deserts of Arabia; modern Palestine, Syria, and Iraq.

Firdawsi: Hakim Abul-Qasim Firdawsi (c. 940-1020 CE), the author of the *Shāhnāmah*, q.v., one of the greatest poets of world literature.

Form Criticism: a method of analyzing the historicity and sources of documents, especially Biblical writings, employed in the higher criticism.

Fourfold Gospel: the first four books of the New Testament dealing with the life of Christ (the gospels of *Matthew, Mark, Luke,* and *John*) are often collectively referred to as the *Fourfold Gospel*.

Gentile: non-Jewish persons or practices.

Gnostic: the adjective from *gnosis,* the belief held by early and pre-Christian sects that matter is evil and freedom comes through spiritual knowledge.

God-fearers: Gentiles sympathetic to Judaism, participants in some rites, but not fully Jews under the Law.

Gog and Magog: Ar. *Jūj wa Mājūj*. In *Revelation,* they represent the nations at the four corners of the world whom Satan will trick into participating in the final battle of the Apocalypse. (Rev. 20: 7-8)

Graven image: an idol carved of wood or stone.

Haggada(h): that part of the Talmud containing the stories, legends, parables, and tales that illustrate the Halakah (the legal part of the Talmud).

Hagiography: the biography of a saint, often replete with miracles and wonders, usually laudatory and edifying in nature.

Hasmonean: roughly synonymous with "Maccabean" derived from the ancestor of the Maccabees.

Hellenization: an ancient parallel to modern Westernization or Europeanization; the adoption of Greek modes of thought, customs, dress, culture, and worldview—sometimes by force and sometimes voluntarily.

Henotheism: the worship of one god while recognizing the reality of other gods; adj., *henotheistic.*

Hexateuch: the Pentateuch plus *Joshua*; the first six books of the Jewish Bible and the Christian Old Testament.

Higher Criticism: in Biblical studies, the discipline that examines the text produced by the lower criticism in order to answer questions of authorship, date, the circumstances of composition, historicity, literary sources, relationships to other writings, theological development, the influence of other factors, types, forms, etc.

Injīl: the message or gospel that God gave to Jesus to deliver to mankind but which, in the Islamic view, as been corrupted or lost.

Isaiah: an Old Testament prophet and the Biblical book (Is.) bearing his name.

Israelite: adj., related to the descendants of Abraham through Jacob in Canaan (Palestine); also applied particularly to the people of the Northern Kingdom of Israel (the ten northern tribes).

Jeremiah: an Old Testament prophet active from c. 627 to some time after 586 BCE, and the Biblical book (Jer.) bearing his name.

Jewish Christians: followers of Jesus, especially after his Disappearance, who were also practicing Jews. Also called Nazarenes.

Jesus people: followers of Jesus, especially after the Disappearance. Mainly Jews, but perhaps with some Gentiles.

Johannine: pertaining to the writings ascribed to John, the *Gospel of John* and the three letters (*1 John, 2 John, 3 John*).

Judah (*Judaea*): the southern part of Palestine, usually not including the Negev desert to the south. Jerusalem is its chief city.

Kerygma: the apostolic proclamation of salvation through Jesus Christ (Webster).

Lacuna, pl., lacunae: a gap or missing part, often of a manuscript or chain of transmission.

Lower Criticism: in Biblical studies, the discipline that strives to achieve the best possible text in the original languages of composition.

Lucan: pertaining to writings ascribed to Luke (*Gospel of Luke, Acts of the Apostles*).

LXX: an abbreviation for the Greek Bible, the *Septuagint*.

Maccabean: also called *Hasmonean*, describing the reformist Jewish dynasty that maintained a relative independence from its much larger neighbors from 167 to 63 BCE.

Mahdi, Mahdism: a leader expected by several Islamic sects to come in the future to establish peace throughout the world and whose preaching will lead to the conversion of all mankind to Islam.

Marcan: pertaining to the *Gospel of Mark*.

Matthean: pertaining to the *Gospel of Matthew*.

Mesopotamia: the Land Between the Rivers, the name given by the Greeks to the plains of the eastern end of the *Fertile Crescent* (q.v.) between the Tigris and Euphrates Rivers, roughly coterminous with modern Iraq.

Micah: an 8th-century BCE Old Testament prophet and the Biblical book (Mic.) bearing his name.

Millenarianism: belief in the millennium of Christian prophecy (Webster).

Mishnah: that part of the Talmud containing the Oral Law, secondary in importance only to the Mosaic Torah. Sometimes written *Mishna*.

Molten image: an idol cast of bronze or some other metal.

Monophysite: one who holds that Christ is one nature (divine) not of two natures (human and divine). Monophysitism was one of the controversies that greatly weakened the unity of the church.

Mount of Olives: the mountain to the east of ancient of Jerusalem.

Mustafa: (*Muṣṭafā*) a byname of the Prophet Muhammad.

Mystery, Mystery cult/religion: secret or semi-secret sects centered upon a god or demigod such as Isis, Herakles, Adonis, or Mithras, offering the initiate eternal happiness in a future life. The most famous in ancient times were the mysteries celebrated at Eleusis, near Athens, Greece.

Nazarenes: Jews who, after the Disappearance, followed Jesus as the Christ with an as yet to be fulfilled mission, perhaps a faction of the Pharisees; also called Jewish Christians.

Nazirite: one who had separated himself by a special vow to Yahweh (God). This could be lifelong or for a limited period.

Nebuchadnezzar: 6th century BCE Babylonian king who carried off the Jews from Jerusalem and Judaea to Babylon. Sometimes written *Nebuchadrezzar*, (See *Babylonian Captivity* above.)

Noahic (Noachian) Precepts (Laws): the rules, based upon several passages in *Genesis*, which governed relations between Jews and Gentiles in Old Testament times.

Non-canonical: writings (religious in this context) not included in the canon and not regarded as authoritative.

Numen: a spiritual force or influence often identified with a natural object or phenomenon.

Oracle: a divinely inspired utterance, usually of a prophetic nature.

Oral Law: the traditional legal teachings now found in that part of the Talmud called the Mishna(h).

Palindrome: a phrase or sentence that reads the same backward or forward.

Parousia: the Second Coming. The awaited return of Christ to this world in triumph.

Parthian: describing Parthia, the second great but loosely organized Persian Empir (247 BCE to 227 CE) based in Central Asia and northeastern Iran, and the rival of Roman power with which it was roughly contemporaneous.

Passion, The: used in the older sense of "suffering"; the events of the last of Jesus' journeys to Jerusalem, his arrest, trial, the (alleged) crucifixion, and his resurrection or reappearance before the final Disappearance.

Pauline: pertaining to Paul and his doctrines.

Pentateuch: the first five books of the Jewish Bible and the Christian Old Testament: *Genesis, Exodus Leviticus, Numbers, and Deuteronomy*. They are traditionally ascribed to Moses.

Pericope: a selection from a longer text, often a brief narrative or incident.

Pronouncement Story: a short dialogue or exchange in which the principal figure, Jesus in the case of the New Testament, and the Prophet in the case of the Traditions, has the last word or makes some usually pithy pronouncement about an issue.

Provenance: origin, source; pedigree.

Psalms: (Ps.) the "hymnal" of the Old Testament, perhaps containing the Quranic *Zabūr*.

Pseudepigrapha: writings falsely or spuriously attributed to personages significant in religious history, especially Biblical characters.

Ptolemaic: concerning the dynasty (305-31 BCE) founded in Egypt by the Macedonian general Ptolemy.

Sassanians: the rulers and peoples of the Sassanian Empire based in Iran. It flourished from the 3rd to 7th centuries CE until overthrown by the Arabs. Adj. also *Sassanid*.

Second Coming: in Christianity, the return of Christ. See *Parousia*.

Seraphim (sing. *seraph*): 6-winged angels standing in the presence of God.

Shahādah: the Muslim Testimony of Faith.

Shāhnāmah: the *Book of Kings*, Firdawsi's (q.v.) national Persian epic chronicling the history of Iran from ancient times to the time of Islam, completed c. 1010 CE.

Soteriology: the theology of salvation, especially through Jesus.

Sumeria: the seat of the world's oldest civilization; roughly, the Tigris-Euphrates plain below Baghdad in modern Iraq. The ethnic and linguistic affinities of the Sumerians are still unknown.

Surah: Ar., a chapter of the Quran. The Quran contains 114 chapters, or *surah*s.

Synoptics: the first three gospels (*Matthew*, *Mark*, and *Luke*) share sources and themes. The fourth, *John*, is quite different from them.

Talmud: "The principal literary production of post-Biblical Judaism," divided into two parts: the *Mishnah* ("second law") and the *Gemara* ("completion). (DB, p. 954)

Targum: an Aramaic paraphrase of the Jewish Bible (the Old Testament), made necessary by the change of the Jewish vernacular from Hebrew to Aramaic in the centuries before the beginning of the Common Era.

The Temple: the Temple of Jerusalem, reconstructed by Herod the Great in the 1st century BCE and destroyed by the Romans in 70 CE after a Jewish insurrection.

Teraphim (sing. *teraph*): household gods, often associated with fertility.

Tetrateuch: the first four books of the *Pentateuch*; i.e., *Genesis*, *Exodus*, *Leviticus*, and *Numbers*.

Theodicy: the defense of God's goodness and omnipotence in view of the existence of evil. (Webster)

Theophany: the visible manifestation of a deity to a human being.

Theophorous, theophoric: adj., describing a name compounded with the name of God or a god.

Traditionist: (*muhaddith*), capitalized to distinguish it from "traditionist" or "traditionalist" used in the general sense of a supporter of tradition and custom; a student or narrator of religious traditions and stories, especially the Traditions of the Prophet.

Tribulation: the time of confusion and disorder. It is during this period that, according to Lindsey, 144,000 Jews in Israel will miraculously come to believe that Jesus is indeed the Messiah.

Ugaritic: the language (Semitic related to Canaanite) and culture of the ancient Syrian city of Ugarit, flourishing in the 15th and 14th centuries BCE.

Umayyad: pertaining to the Umayyad dynasty based at Damascus in Syria, rgd. AH 41-132/661-750 CE. Overthrown by the Abbasid revolution.

Way, the: usually in the context of the early Christians, the Way of Jesus.

Wisdom literature: collections of proverbs and aphorisms, usually of a practical nature, represented in the Bible by *Proverbs*, portions of *Job*, etc.; pre-Christian philosophical Jewish literature.

Yahwist: also designated J; the writer of the earliest of the component documents of the historical books of the Bible. Scholars believe the J document is a combination of and earlier J (J1) and another of the same tradition about a century later (J2).

YHWH: the Tetragrammaton; the four consonants of the unutterable name of God in the Old Testament. Now vowelized as *Yahweh*, usually translated as "the Lord." It may mean, "I am Who I am," or "O He!" (God, DB, pp. 334-335.)

Zechariah: the name of the father of John the Baptist, not to be confused with an Old Testament prophet of the same name (active late 6th century BCE) and the Biblical book (Zech.) bearing his name.

Ziggurat: a Mesopotamian pyramidal temple, usually constructed in steps or platforms.

Zoomorphic: concerning a deity conceived of as an animal.

BIBLIOGRAPHY (CODED)

(A&P) Charles, R.H., ed. *Apocrypha and Pseudepigrapha of the Old Testament*. Volume Two. London: Oxford Univ. Press, 1968; reprint of 1913 edition.

(AAWH) Kinder, Herman & Hilgeman, Werner. *The Anchor Atlas of World History*. 2 vols. New York: Bantam, Doubleday, Dell Publishing Group, 1974.

(ABD) Freedman, David Noel, ed. *The Anchor Bible Dictionary*, 5 vols. New York: Doubleday, 1992-.

(ABL) *Atlas of the Bible Lands*. Maplewood: Hammond, 1959.

(Abot) Goldin, Judah. *The Living Talmud: The Wisdom of the Fathers* (Pirke Abot). New York: New American Library, 1957.

(Ackroyd) Ackroyd, Peter R. *Israel under Babylon and Persia*. New Clarendon Bible, Old Testament, Vol. 4. London: Oxford Univ. Press, 1970.

(Acts) *Acts of the Apostles, The*. Trans. E.V. Rieu. Harmondsworth: Penguin Books, 1957.

(Aesop) Aesop. *Fables*. Trans. S. A. Handford. New edition. Harmondsworth: Penguin Books, 1964.

(Aesop-Jones) Aesop. *Fables*. Trans. V.S. Vernon Jones. London: Pan Books, 1975.

(Afarinash) Muqaddasi, Mutahhir bin. *Afarinash wa Tarikh*. Trans. From Arabic by Muhammad Rida Shafi'i Kadkani (Persian) Tehran: Bunyad-i Farhang-i Iran, AHS1349-1352.

(Ahmed) Ahmed, Syed Magbool. "Supernaturalism of al-Quran VI: Biblical Names I the Quran." *Islamic Review*, XVIII, No. 12 (Dec. 1930), pp. 436-445.

(Albright-Ab to Ez) Albright, William F. *The Biblical Period From Abraham to Ezra*. New York: Harper Torchbooks, Harper & Row, 1963.

(Albright-Arch) Albright, William F. *Archaeology, Historical Analysis, and Early Biblical Tradition*. Baton Rouge: Louisiana State Univ. Press, 1966.

(Albright-Pal) Albright, William F. *The Archaeology of Palestine*. Revised edition. Harmondsworth: Penguin Books, 1960.

(Albright-Stone Age) Albright, William F. *From Stone Age to Christianity*. Second edition. Garden City: Doubleday Anchor Books, 1957.

(Allegro-Chosen) Allegro, John M. *The Chosen People*. St. Albans: Panther Books, 1973.

(Allegro-Sacred) Allegro, John M. *The Sacred Mushroom and the Cross*. Revised edition. London: Sphere Books, 1973.

(Allegro-Scrolls) Allegro, John M. *The Dead Sea Scrolls*. Harmondsworth: Penguin Books, 1958, 1959.

(Ameer Ali) Ali, Syed Ameer. *The Spirit of Islam*. London: Christophers, 1922.

(Anderson) Anderson, G.W. *The History and Religion of Israel*. New Clarendon Bible, Vol. I. London: Oxford Univ. Press, 1966.

(ANE) Pritchard, James B., ed. *The Ancient Near East*. 2 vols. Princeton: Princeton Univ. Press, 1958, 1975.

(Angus) Angus, S. *The Mystery Religions*. New York: Dover Publications, 1975. Reprint of 1928 edition.

(Ansari) Ansari, Khwajah 'Abd Allah. *Tafsir-i Adabi wa 'Irfani Quran-i Majid*. 2 vols. Abridged by Habib Allah Amuzgar. (Persian) Tehran: Iqbal, AHS1347-8.

(ANW) Wilson, A.N. *Paul—The Mind of the Apostle*. New York: Norton, 1997.

(AO) *Archaeology Odyssey* (periodical).

(Apocrypha) *Apocrypha, The*. 1894 revised edition. London: Oxford Univ. Press, 1926.

(Arberry-Mutanabbi) Arberry, A.J. *Poems of Mutanabbi*. London: Cambridge Univ. Press, 1967.

(ArchHL) *Archaeology of the Holy Land*. Compiled from material in the EJ. Israel Pocket Library series. Jerusalem: Keter Publ. House, 1974.

(Arden) Arden, Harvey. "In the Steps of Moses." *National Geographic Magazine*. Vol. 149, No. 1, Jan. 1976, pp. 21.

(Arnold) Arnold, T.W. *The Preaching of Islam*. Lahore: Sh. Muhammad Ashraf, 1961. Reprint of 1896 edition.

(Arrian) Arrian: *the Campaigns of Alexander*. Revised edition. Trans. Aubrey de Selincourt. Harmondsworth: Penguin Books, 1971.

(Asad) Asad, Muhammad. *The Road to Mecca*. London: Max Reinhardt, 1954.

(Asatir) Bahar, Mihrdad. *Asatir-i Iran*. (Persian) Tehran: Bunyad-i Farhang-i Iran, AHS1352.

(Ashe) Ashe, Geoffrey. *King Arthur's Avalon*. London: Fontana Books, 1973.

(Asimov-NT) Asimov, Isaac. *Asimov's Guide to the Bible: The New Testament*. New York: Avon, 1971.

(Asimov-OT) Asimov, Isaac. *Asimov's Guide to the Bible: The Old Testament*. New York: Avon Books, 1971.

(Atiyah) Atiyah, Edward. *The Arabs*. Harmondsworth: Penguin Books, 1955.

(Attridge) Attridge, Harold W. & Oden, Robert A., eds. *De Dea Syria*. Texts and Translations. Society of Biblical Literature. Missoula: Scholars Press, 1976.

(BA) *Biblical Archeologist*. Magazine.

(BA1) Wright, G. Ernest & Freedman, David Noel, eds. *The Biblical Archaeologist Reader 1*. Reprints from BA magazine. Missoula: Scholars Press, 1975.

(BA2) Freedman, David Noel & Campbell, Edward F., Jr., eds. *The Biblical Archaeologist Reader 2*. Reprints from BA magazine. Missoula: Scholars Press, 1977.

(BA3) Campbell, Edward F., Jr. & Freedman, David N., eds. *The Biblical Archaeologist Reader 3*. Reprints from BA magazine. Garden City: Anchor Books, 1970.

(Bainton) Bainton, Roland. *The Penguin History of Christianity*. 2 vols. Harmondsworth: Penguin Books, 1967.

(Bal'ami) Bal'ami, Abu 'Ali Muhammad bin Muhammad bin. *Tarikh-i Bal'ami*. 2 vols. Dr. Muhammad Taqi Bahar, ed. (Persian) Tehran: Kitabfurushi-yi Zawwar, 1353.

(Balaghi) Balaghi, Sadr al-Din. *Qisas-i Quran*. (Persian) Tehran: Amir Kabir, AHS 1349.

(BAR) *Biblical Archaeology Review* (periodical)

(Baring-Gould) Baring-Gould, Sabine. *Curious Myths of the Middle Ages*. New Hyde Park: University Books, 1967 (reprint of the 1866-8 edition).

(Barnabas) Barnabas. *The Gospel of Barnabas*. Trans Lonsdale and Laura Ragg. Oxford: Clarendon Press, 1907. Reprinted with introduction: Karachi: Quran Council of Pakistan, 1973.

(Barnstone) Barnstone, Willis, ed. *The Other Bible*. San Francisco: Harper & Row, 1984.

(Barrett) Barrett, C.K., ed. *The New Testament Background*. New York: Harper & Row, 1961.

(Barrow) Barrow, R.H. *Slavery in the Roman Empire*. (Reprint of 1928 edition.) New York: Barnes & Noble Bks., 1996.

(Baskin) Baskin, Wade. *Dictionary of Satanism*. New York: Bonanza Books, 1972.

(BC) Allen, Clifton J., gen. ed. *Broadman Bible Commentary, The.* 12 vols. London: Marshall, Morgan & Scott, 1970-72.

(BD-Smith) Smith, William. *Bible Dictionary*. New York: Family Library, 1975.

(Bell) Bell, Richard. *The Origin of Islam in Its Christian Environment*. London: F. Cass & Co., 1968, reprint of 1926 edition.

(Bibby) Bibby, Geoffrey. *Four Thousand Years Ago*. Harmondsworth: Penguin Books, 1961.

(Bibby-Dilmun) Bibby, Geoffrey. *Looking for Dilmun*. New York: New American Library, 1974

(Bible Key) Harrington, Wilfrid J., O.P. *Key to the Bible*, 3 vols. Garden City: Image Books, 1976.

(Bible Myths) *Bible Myths and Their Parallels in Other Religions*. (Author unknown; anonymous?). New York: J.W. Bouton, 1883.

(Biblical Criticism) Davidson, Robert & Leaney, A.R.C. *Biblical Criticism*, Vol. 3 of the Pelican Guide to Modern Theology. Harmondsworth: Penguin Books, 1970.

(Bickerman) Bickerman, Elias. *From Ezra to the Last of the Maccabees*. New York: Schocken Books, 1962.

(Bierlein) Bierlein, J.F. *Parallel Myths*. New York: Ballantine Books, 1994.

(Bishop) Bishop, E.F.F. "The Qumran Scrolls and the Quran." *Muslim World*, XLVIII (1958) No. 3, 223-236.

(Bornkamm) Bornkamm, Gunther. *The New Testament: A Guide to Its Writings*. Trans. Reginald H. Fuller and Ilse Fuller. London: SPCK, 1974.

(Bosworth) Bosworth, C.E. *The Islamic Dynasties*. Islamic Surveys, Vol. 5. Edinburgh: Edinburgh Univ. Pres., 1967.

(Bowra) Bowra, C.E. *The Greek Experience*. London: Cardinal, 1957.

(BR) *Review* (periodical)

(Brauer) Brauer, Jr., George C. *Judaea Weeping*. New York: Crowell, 1970.

(Brauer-YE) Brauer, Jr., George C. *The Decadent Emperors* (original title: The Young Emperors: Rome, A.D. 193-244). New York: Barnes & Noble, 1995 (1967).

(Breasted) Breasted, James Henry. *A History of Egypt*. New York: Bantam Books, 1964; reprint of revised edition of 1909.

(Breasted-Religion) Breasted, J.H. *Development of Religion and Thought in Ancient Egypt*. New York: Harper & Row, 1959. Orig. Edition Scribner's, 1912.

(Briggs) Briggs, Constance Victoria. *The Encylopedia of Angels*. New York: Penguin Books Inc., 1977.

(Brodie) Brodie, Thomas L. *The Quest for the Origin of John's Gospel*. New York: Oxford Univ. Press, 1993.

(Buber) Buber, Martin. *Moses*. New York: Harper & Row, 1958.

(Bucaille) Bucaille, Maurice. *The Bible, the Quran and Science*. Trans. Alastair D. Pannell & author. Paris: Seghers (French edition), 1977.

(Budd) Budd, Philip J. *The New Century Bible Commentaries: Leviticus*. London: Marshall Pickering, 1996.

(Budge-Bk) Budge, E. Wallis, trans. & ed. *The Egyptian Book of the Dead*. New York: Dover Publications, 1967. Reprint of 1895 edition.

(Budge-Cave) Budge, Sir E.A. Wallis, ed. *The Book of the Cave of Treasures*. Trans. Sir E. A. Wallis Budge. London: Religious Tract Society, 1927.

(Budge-Gods) Budge, E.A. Wallis. *The Gods of the Egyptians*. 2 vols. New York: Dover Publications, 1969. Reprint of 1904 edition.

(Budge-Osiris) Budge, E.A. Wallis. *Osiris and the Egyptian Resurrection*. 2 vols. New York: Dover Publications, 1973. Reprint of 1911 editon.

(Bukhara) Al-Narshakhī, Abū Bakr Muḥammad. *Tārīkh-i Bukhārā* (History of Bukhara). Abū Naṣr Aḥmad bin Muḥammad al-Qibāwī, trans. from Arabic into Persian. Ed. & notes by Mudarris Ridawi. (Persian) Tehran: Bunyad-i Farhang-i Iran, AHS1351/1972 CE.

(Bukhari) Bukhari, Imam. *Sahih al-Bukhari*. Dr. Muhammad Muhsin Khan, translator. Nine volumes. Lahore: Kazi Publications, 1979.

(Bultmann) Bultmann, Rudolph. *Primitive Christianity*. Trans. Rev. R.H. Fuller. New York: New American Library, 1974.

(Burhan) Bidokht, Nahid, *Burhan-i Qati'*, Muhammad Husayn ibn Khalaf Tabrizi 'Burhan,' dtd AH 1062, ed. Dr. Muhammad Mu'in Tehran: Ibn Sina, 2nd printing, AHS 1342.

(Butler) Butler, Alban. *Butler's Lives of the Saints*, 4 vols. Herbert Thurston, S.J. & Donald Attwater, eds. Rev. & supp. New York: P.J. Kenedy & Sons, 1956.

(Caird) Caird, G.B. *Saint Luke*. Pelican New Testament Commentaries. Harmondsworth, 1963.

(Cambridge Commentary) Matini, Dr. Jalal, ed. *Commentary on the Glorious Quran* (Cambridge), 2 vols. Tehran: Bunyad-i Farhang-i Iran, AHS 1349.

(Cambridge) Ackroyd, P.R., et al, eds. *Cambridge History of the Bible, The*. Three vols. Cambridge Univ. Press, 1970, 1969, 1963.

(Campbell) Campbell, Joseph: *The Masks of God*. 4 vols. New York: Viking Press, 1970.

(Campbell, A) Campbell, Antony F. *The Ark Narrative*, Dissertation Series No. 16. Missoula: Society of Biblical Literature, 1975.

(Carmichael) Carmichael, Joel. *The Death of Jesus*. Harmondsworth: Penguin Books, 1966)

(Carnegie) Carnegie, Dale. *Little Known Facts About Well Known People*. New York: Blue Ribbon Books, 1934.

(Carpenter) Carpenter, Edward. *The Origins of Pagan and Christian Beliefs*. First published 1920 as *Pagan and Christian Creeds: Their Origin & Meaning*. London: Senate, 1996.

(CE) *Columbia Encyclopedia, The*. Wm. Bridgwater and Seymour Kurtz, eds. New York: Columbia Univ. Press, 1968.

(Chadwick) Chadwick, Henry. *The Early Church*. Harmondsworth: Penguin Books, 1967.

(Church Doc) Bettenson, Henry, ed. *Documents of the Christian Church*. 2nd edition. London: Oxford Univ. Press, 1967.

(Churton) Churton, Tobias. *The Gnostics*. Reprint of 1987 ed. New York: Barnes & Noble, 1997.

(Cirlot) Cirlot, J.E. *A Dictionary of Symbolism*. Reprint of trans. from Spanish by Jack Sage, 1971. New York: Barnes & Noble, 1995.

(Clifton) Clifton, Chas. S. *Encyclopedia of Heresies and Heretics*, (reprint of 1992 edition), New York: Barnes & Noble, 1998.

(Clow) Clow, Rev. W.M. *The Bible Reader's Encyclopædia and Concordance* (based on The Bible Reader's Manual by Rec. C.H. Wright). London: Collin's Clear-Type Press, undated.

(Coats) Coats, George W. "From Canaan to Egypt: Structural and Theological Context for the Joseph Story." *The Catholic Biblical Quarterly Monograph Series 4*. Washington: The Catholic Biblical Assoc. of America, 1976.

(Comay) Comay, Joan. *The Hebrew Kings*. New York: William Morrow, 1977.

(ComGospels) Miller, Robert J., ed. The Complete Gospels: Annotated Scholars Version. Sonoma: HarperSanFrancisco, 1994.

(Cooper) Cooper, David.L. *Messiah: His Glorious Appearance Imminent.* Messianic Series No. 6. Los Angeles: Biblical Research Society, 1961.

(Cottrell) Cottrell, Leonard. *The Land of Shinar.* London: Souvenir Press, 1965.

(Cruden) Cruden, Alexander. *Concordance of the Holy Scriptures.* New York: Family Library, 1974.

(Cumont) Cumont, Franz. *The Mysteries of Mithra.* Thomas J. McCormack, trans. New York: Dover Publications, 1956; reprint of 1903 edition.

(CV) Bridgwater, William, ed.-in chief. *The Columbia-Viking Desk Encyclopedia.* New York: Dell Publishing Co., 1966.

(Davies) Davies, W.D. *Invitation to the New Testament.* Garden City: Anchor Books, Doubleday & Co., 1969.

(Davies, E) Davies, Eryl W. *The New Century Bible Commentaries: Numbers.* London: Marshall Pickering, 1995.

(Davidson) Davidson, Gustav. *A Dictionary of Angels.* New York: The Free Press, 1967.

(DB) Hastings, James, ed. *Dictionary of the Bible*, rev. Ed. Frederick C. Grant & H.H. Rowley. New York: Charles Scribner's Sons, 1963.

(DB-1900) Smith, William. *A Dictionary of the Bible.* New York: Bible House, 1900.

(DB5) Hastings, James, ed. *A Dictionary of the Bible*, 5 vols. NY: Scribners, 1908-9.

(de Camp) de Camp, Sprague. *The Ancient Engineers.* New York: Ballantine, 1974.

(de Lange) de Lange, Nicholas. *Apocrypha: Jewish Literature of the Hellenistic Age.* New York: Viking Press, 1978

(de Vaux) de Vaux, Roland. *Ancient Israel*, 2 vols. New York: McGraw-Hill, 1965.

(Dead Sea) Gaster, Theodor H., ed. *The Dead Sea Scriptures.* Garden City: Anchor Books, 1964.

(Delaney) Delaney, John J. *Dictionary of Saints.* Garden City: Image Books, 1983.

(Delehaye) Delehaye, Hippolyte. *The Legends of the Saints.* Trans. D. Attwater. New York: Fordham Univ. Press, 1962.

(Dibelius) Dibelius, Martin. *From Tradition to Gospel.* Trans. From revised 2nd edition Bertram Lee Wolff in collaboration with author. New York: Scribner's, undated.

(Dimont) Dimont, Max I. *Jews, God and History.* New York: New American Library, 1962.

(Doresse) Doresse, Jean. *Secret Books of the Egyptian Gnostics.* Trans. P. Mairet. London: Hillis & Carter, 1960.

(Doughty) Doughty, Charles M. Passages from *Arabia Deserta*, selected by Edward Garnett. Harmondsworth: Penguin Bks, 1956 (1931).

(Dudley) Dudley, D.R. & Lang, D.M., eds. *The Penguin Companion to Literature*: Vol. 4, Classical & Byzantine, Oriental & African Literature. Harmondsworth: Penguin Books, 1969.

(Dunkerley) Dunkerley, Roderic. *Beyond the Gospels*. Harmondsworth: Penguin Books, 1957.

(Dunkling) Dunkling, Leslie and William Gosling. *The New American Dictionary of First Names*. New York: New American Library, 1983.

(Durant-2) Durant, Will. *The Life of Greece*, The Story of Civilization, Vol. 2. New York: Simon & Schuster, 1939.

(Durant-3) Durant, Will. *Caesar and Christ*, The Story of Civilization, Vol. 3. New York: Simon & Schuster, 1944.

(Durant-4) Durant, Will. *The Age of Faith*, The Story of Civilization, Vol. 4. New York: MJF Books, 1950.

(EA) *Encyclopedia Americana*. New York: Americana Corp., 1962 ed.

(Early Fathers) Bettenson, Henry, ed & trans. *The Early Christian Fathers*. London: Oxford Univ. Press, 1969.

(Eaton) Eaton, Charles Le Gai. *Remembering God: Reflections on Islam*. ABC International Group, distributed by Kazi Publications, Inc., Chicago, 2000.

(EB) *Encyclopædia Britannica*. Chicago: Encyclopædia Britannica, 1960 ed.

(EB-CD) *Encyclopædia Britannica, Inc.* 1994-1999 Edition (on CD).

(EBSE-04) *Encyclopædia Britannica Standard Edition, 2004, C- ROM*, Copyright © 1994-2003 Encyclopædia Britannica, Inc. May 30, 2003.

(EB, EB-Mac, EB Mic) *New Encyclopædia Britannica*. Univ. of Chicago. 15th edition. Chicago: Enc. Britannica, 1967. Micropædia and Macropædia.

(ECF) *Early Church Fathers, The*. All 38 volumes of the series originally published by Scribner's (New York), 1900, on CD-ROM produced by Harmony Media, 2000, of Salem OR.

(ECW) *Early Christian Writings*. Trans. Maxwell Staniforth. Harmondsworth: Penguin Books, 1968.

(Egypt-BG) Seton-Williams, Veronica & Peter Socks. *Blue Guide Egypt*. London: Ernest Benn, 1983.

(EI) *Encyclopædia of Islam, The*. 11 vols. + indices. Leiden: E.J. Brill, 1960-2002.

(Eisenman) Eisenman, Robert. *James the Brother of Jesus*. New York: Penguin Books, 1997.

(Eisenman-Wise) Eisenman, Robert & Wise, Michael. *The Dead Sea Scrolls Uncovered*. New York: Barnes & Noble, 1994.

(Eissfeldt) Eissfeldt, Otto. *The Old Testament: an Introduction*. Trans. P.R. Ackroyd. New York: Harper & Row, 1965.

(EJ) *Encyclopædia Judaica*. 16 vols. New York: Macmillan & Co, 1971.

(Eliade) Eliade, Mircea. *From Primitive to Zen*. 4 volumes. New York: Harper & Row, 1974.

(Enslin) Enslin, Morton Scott. *Christian Beginnings: Parts I and II*. New York: Harper & Row, 1956 (1938).

(Epstein) Epstein, Isidore. *Judaism*. Harmondsworth: Penguin Books, 1959.

(ERE) Hastings, James, ed. *The Encyclopædia of Religion and Ethics*. 12 vols. + Index. New York: Scribner's, 1961.

(Erman) Erman, Adolf, ed. *The Ancient Egyptians*. Trans. Aylward M. Blackman. New York: Harper Torchbooks, 1966. Orig. Ed. 1923.

(Eusebius) Eusebius. *Ecclesiastical History*. Trans. C.F. Cruse. Grand Rapids: Baker Book House, 1955. Reprint of 1850 edition.

(Eusebius-NY) Eusebius. *The History of the Church From Christ to Constantine*. Trans. G.A. Williamson. New York: New York Univ. Press, 1966.

(Explorers) Cary, M. & Warmington, E.H. *The Ancient Explorers*. Revised edition. Harmondsworth: Penguin Books, 1963. Reprint of Methuen edition, 1929.

(Faber-Kaiser) Faber-Kaiser, A. *Jesus Died in Kashmir*. London: Abacus, 1978.

(Faharis) Ramya, Muhammad. Faharis al-Quran. (Arabic) Tehran: Amir Kabir, AHS 1345.

(Fairservis) Fairservis, Walter A., Jr. *The Ancient Kingdoms of the Nile*. New York: Mentor Books, 1962.

(Fathers) Roberts, Rev. Alexander and Donaldson, James, eds. *The Apostolic Fathers*. Vol. 1 of the Anti-Nicene Christian Library. Edinburgh: T. and T. Clark, 1879.

(Fenton) Fenton, J.C. *Saint Matthew*. Pelican New Testament Commentaries. Harmondsworth: Penguin Books, 1963.

(Ferdowsi) Ferdowsi. *The Epic of the Kings* (Shahnamah). Trans. Reuben Levy. London: Routledge & Kegan Paul, 1967.

(Finbert) Finbert, Elian, ed. *Israel*. Hachette World Guides. Paris: Hachette, 1956.

(Finkelstein) Finkelstein, Israel and Neil Asher Silberman. *The Bible Unearthed*. New York: The Free Press, 2001.

(Finley) Finley, M.I. *Aspects of Antiquity*. Harmondsworth: Penguin Books, 1972.

(Firdawsi) Firdawsi, Hakim Abu al-Qasim. *Shahnamah*. (Persian) Tehran: Amir Kabir, AHS 1343.

(FourGos) *The Four Gospels*. Trans. E.V. Rieu. Harmondsworth: Penguin Books, 1952.

(FRA) Ansari, F.R. *Islam and Christianity in the Modern World*. Karachi: World Federation of Islamic Missions, 1965.

(Frankfort) Frankfort, Henri, et al. *Before Philosophy*. Harmondsworth: Penguin Books, 1949.

(Frazer) Frazer. Sir James George. *The Golden Bough*. Abridged edition. New York: Macmillan Pub., 1963

(Frazer-Folklore) Frazer, James George. *Folklore in the Old Testament.* New York: Hart Publishing Co., 1975.

(Frend) Frend, W.H.C. *The Early Church.* Philadelphia: Lippincott, 1965.

(Freud) Freud, Sigmund. *Moses and Monotheism.* Trans. Katherine Jones. New York: Vintage Books, 1939.

(Friedman) Friedman, Richard Elliot. *Who Wrote the Bible?* New York: Harper Collins, 1989.

(Frye) Frye, Richard N. *The Heritage of Persia.* New York: The New American Library, 1966.

(Fuller) Fuller, R.H. *The Foundations of New Testament Christology.* London: Fontana, 1969.

(Funk) Funk, Robert W. et al. *The Five Gospels.* New York: Scribner, 1993.

(Gabrieli) Gabrieli, Francesco. *Muhammad and the Conquests of Islam.* Trans. Virginia Luling and Rosamund Linell. London: Weidenfeld and Nicolson, World Univ. Library, 1968.

(Gager) Gager, John G. *Moses in Greco-Roman Paganism.* Society of Biblical Literature Monograph Series, Vol. 16, Robt. A. Kraft, ed. Nashville, Abdingdon Press, 1972.

(Galvin) Galvin, John. "Egypt's First Pharaohs." *National Geographic Magazine.* Vol. 207, No. 4, Apr. 2005, pp. 106-121.

(Gaster) Gaster, Theodor H. *Myth, Legend, and Custom in the Old Testament.* 2 vols. New York: Harper & Row, 1975.

(Geo HL) Smith, George Adam. *The Historical Geography of the Holy Land.* London: Fontana Library, 1966 (1931).

(Ghazzali) Ghazzali. *The Alchemy of Happiness.*

(Gibbon) Gibbon, Edward. *Decline and Fall of the Roman Empire.* 6 vols. London: Everyman's Library, J.M. Dent & Sons, 1910.

(Gilgamesh) Sandars, N.K., trans. *The Epic of Gilgamesh.* Harmondsworth: Penguin Books, 1964, revised ed.

(Goodspeed) Goodspeed, Edgar J. *A History of Early Christian Literature.* Revised and enlarged by R.M. Grant. Chicago: Univ. of Chicago Press, 1966.

(Gordon-Scripts) Gordon, Cyrus H. *Forgotten Scripts.* Harmondsworth, revised edition, 1971.

(Graham) Graham, Lloyd A. Deceptions and Myths of the Bible. New York: Bell Publishing, 1979.

(Grant) Grant, Robert M. *A Historical Introduction to the New Testament.* New York: Simon & Schuster, 1972.

(Grant-Peter) Grant, Michael. *Saint Peter.* New York: Barnes & Noble, 1998 (1994).

(Graves) Graves, Robert. *The Greek Myths.* Two volumes. Harmondsworth: Penguin Books, revised edition, 1960.

(Graves-Jesus) Graves, Robert. *King Jesus.* New York?: Minerva Press, 1946.

(GreekNT) Wilson, Benjamin, trans. & ed. *The Emphatic Diaglott of What Is Commonly Called the New Testament.* New York: Fowler & Wells, 1864.

(Greeley) Greeley, Andrew M. *The Sinai Myth.* Garden City: Doubleday, 1972.

(Green) Green, Peter. *Alexander of Macedon.* Harmondsworth: Penguin Books, 1974.

(Grierson) Grierson, Roderick & Munro-Hay, Stuart. *The Ark of the Covenant.* London: Weidenfeld & Nicholson, 1999.

(Grimal) Grimal, Pierre. *The Penguin Dictionary of Classical Mythology.* Stephen Kershaw, ed. Trans., A.R. Maxwell-Hyslop. Harmondsworth: Penguin Books, Ltd., 1991.

(Gunkel) Gunkel, Herman. *The Legends of Genesis.* Trans. W.H. Carutth. New York: Shocken Books, 1964.

(Gurney) Gurney, O.R. *The Hittites,* rev. 2nd edition. Harmondsworth: Penguin Books, 1961.

(Guthrie) Guthrie, D. et al. *The New Bible Commentary* revised. London: New Varsity Press, 1970.

(Hachette) Hachette World Guides: *The Middle East.* Paris: Librairie Hachette, 1966.

(Haggith) Haggith, David. *End-Time Prophecies of the Bible.* New York: Perigree, 2000 (1999).

(Hallet) Hallet, Jean-Pierre. *Pygmy Kitabu.* Greenwich: Fawcett Pub., 1973.

(Halley) Halley, Henry H. *Bible Handbook.* 24th edition. Grand Rapids: Zondervan Publishing House, 1965.

(Halsell) Halsell, Grace. *Forcing God's Hand.* Washington: Crossroads International Publishing, 1999.

(Hanson) Hanson, R.P.C., commentator. *The Acts,* The New Clarendon Bible. Oxford: Oxford Univ. Press, 1967.

(Harden) Harden, Donald. *The Phoenicians.* Harmondsworth: Penguin Books, 1971.

(Hardy) Baring-Gould, Sabine. Edited and shortened by Edward Hardy. *Curious Myths of the Middle Ages.* Orig. Published 1866. New York: Barnes & Noble Books, 1994.

(Harrington) Harrington, Daniel J., ed. & trans. *The Hebrew Fragments of Pseudo-Philo Texts and Translations 3*, Pseudepigrapha Series 3. Missoula: Society of Biblical Literature, 1974.

(Hassnain) Hassnain, Fida. *A Quest for the Historical Jesus.* Bath: Gateway Books, 1994.

(Hayes) Hayes, Christine Elizabeth. *Between the Babylonian and Palestinian Talmuds.* New York: Oxford Univ. Press, 1997.

(Hebrew Bible) *Holy Bible, The.* (Hebrew and English) Trans. Isaac Leeser. New York: Hebrew Publishing Co., undated.

(Hebrew) Ben-Yehuda, Ehud & Weinstein, David. *English-Hebrew/Hebrew-English Dictionary.* New York: Pocket Books, 1961.

(Heidel) Heidel, Alexander. *The Babylonian Genesis.* 2nd edition. Chicago: The Univ. of Chicago Press, 1963.

(Hellenistic) Schalit, Abraham, ed. *The Hellenistic Age.* Vol. VI, The World History of the Jewish People. Israel: Jewish History Publications, 1972.

(Hennecke) Hennecke, E. *New Testament Apocrypha:* 2 vols. Trans R. McL. Wilson. London?: SCM Press, 1973, 1974.

(Herodian) Avi-Yonah, Michael & Baras, Zvi, eds. *The Herodian Period.* The World History of the Jewish People, Vol. VII. Israel: Jewish History Publications, 1975.

(Herodotus) Herodotus. *The Histories.* Trans. Aubrey de Selincourt. Harmondsworth: Penguin Books, 1972.

(Herschel) Herschel, Abraham J. *The Prophets.* 2 vols. New York: Harper Torchbooks, 1969, 1971.

(Heston) Heston, E.W. *The Hebrew Kingdoms.* New Clarendon Bible, Old Testament, Vol. 3. London: Oxford Univ. Press, 1968.

(Herzl) Herzl, Theodor. *The Jewish State.* Intro. by Louis Lipsky. New York: American Zionist Emergency Council, 1946.

(Hijazi) Hijazi, Abu Tariq. *Islam 01 AH-250 AH: A Chronology of Events.* New York: The Message Publications, 1994.

(Hinnells) Hinnells, John R. *Persian Mythology.* London: Hamlyn Publishing Group, 1973.

(Hist Theo) Danielou, J., Couratin, A.H. & Kent, John. *Historical Theology,* Vol. 2 of the Pelican Guide to Modern Theology. Harmondsworth: Penguin Books, 1969.

(History Atlas-1) Kinder, Herman, & Hilgemann, Werner. *The Penguin Atlas of World* History, Vol. 1. Trans. Ernest A. Menze with maps designed by Harald and Ruth Bakor. Harmondsworth: Penguin Books, 1974.

(Hooke) Hooke, S.H. *Middle Eastern Mythology.* Harmondsworth: Penguin Books, 1963.

(Hotchkiss) Hotchkiss, Robert B., ed. & trans. *A Pseudo-Epiphanius Testimony Book.* Texts & Translations 9. Early Christian Literature 1. Missoula: Society of Biblical Literature, 1974.

(Hudson) Hudson, D.F. *New Testament Greek* (Teach Yourself Series). Sevenoaks: Hodder and Stoughton, 1960.

(Hughes) Hughes, Thomas Patrick. *A Dictionary of Islam.* Chicago: Kazi Publications, 1994 reprint of 1886 edition.

(Humber) Humber, Thomas. *The Fifth Gospel: the Miracle of the Holy Shroud.* New York: Pocket Books, 1974.

[Husaini] Husaini, Moulavi S.A.Q., *Ibn al-'Arabi,* Muhammad Ashraf, Lahore, undated.

(Huxley) Huxley, Francis. *The Way of the Sacred.* New York: Dell Publishing, 1976.

(Huxley, A.) Huxley, Aldous. *Island.* Reprint of 1952 Harper & Row edition. New York: Bantam Books, 1963.

(IB) *Bible, The Interpreter's.* 12 volumes. Nashville: Abington Press, 1951-57.

(Ibn Ishaq) Ibn Ishaq. *The Life of Muhammad.* Trans. A. Guillaume. Karachi: Oxford Univ. Press, 1955.

(Ibn Sa'd) Ibn Sa'd. *Kitab al-Tabaqat al-Kabir,* 2 vols. Trans. S. Moinul Haq. Karachi: Pakistan Historical Society, 1967, 1972.

(IDB) Buttrick, George Arthur, ed. *The Interpreter's Dictionary of the Bible,* 4 vols. plus Supplementary volume. Nashville: Abdingdon Press, 1962, 1976.

(Israel Gospel) Greenlees, Duncan. *The Gospel of Israel* (World Gospel Series, Vol. 11). Adyar: Theosophical Publishing House, 1955.

(Israel Land) *History of the Land of Israel until 1880.* Compiled from material in the EJ. Israel Pocket Library series. Jerusalem: Keter Publ. House, 1973.

(Jalalayn) *Tafsir al-Jalalayn.* (The Commentary by the Two Jalals: Jalal al-Din al-Mahalli and Jalal al-Din al-Suyuti). Eighth edition (Arabic). Beirut: Dar al-Jil, AH1415/1995 CE.

(James) James, Montague Rhodes. *The Apocryphal New Testament.* London: Oxford Univ. Press, 1953.

(JB) *Bible, The Jerusalem.* Jones, Alexander, gen. ed. Standard edition. London: Barton, Longman & Todd, 1966.

(Jeffrey) Jeffrey, Arthur. *The Foreign Vocabulary of the Quran.* Baroda: Oriental Institute, 1938.

(Jeffrey, G) Jeffrey, Grant R. *Armageddon Appointment With Destiny.* Reprint with supplement of 1988 edition. New York: Bantam Books, 1990.

(Jellinek) Jellinek, A. *Beit-ha-Midrash* 4, 1967.

(Jenks) Jenks, Alan W. *The Elohist and North Israelite Traditions.* Society of Biblical Literature Monographs Series, Vol. 22. Missoula: Scholars Press, 1977.

(Jeremiou) Kraft, Robert A. & Purintun, Ann-Elizabeth, eds. & trans. *Paraleipomena Jeremiou.* Texts and Translations 1, Pseudepigrapha Series 1. Missoula: Society of Biblical Literature, 1972.

(Jonas) Jonas, Hans. *The Gnostic Religion,* 2nd edition. Boston: Beacon Press, 1963.

(Jones) Jones, A.H.M. *Constantine and the Conversion of Europe.* Harmondsworth: Penguin Books, 1972.

(Jormier) Jormier, Jacques. *The Bible and the Koran.* New York: Descless Co., 1964.

(Josephus) Josephus. *Complete Works.* Trans. William Whiston. Grand Rapids: Kregel Publications, 1967; orig. Published in Edinburgh, 1867.

(Josephus-War) Josephus. *The Jewish War.* Trans. G.A. Williamson. Harmondsworth: Penguin Books, 1959.

(Joyce) Joyce, Donovan. *The Jesus Scroll.* New York: New American Library, 1974.

(Judges) Mazar, Benjamin, ed. *Judges,* Vol. III, The World History of the Jewish People. Israel: Jewish History Publications, 1971.

(Juwayri) Juwayri, Mawlana Muhammad. *Qisas al-Anbiya* (Stories of the Prophets). Tehran: 'Ali Akbar 'Ilmi, undated.

(Kapelrud) Kapelrud, A.S. *The Ras Shamra Discoveries and the Old Testament*. Oxford: Blackwell, 1965.

(Kathir) Ibn Kathir, 'Imad al-Din Abu al-Fida Isma'il (d. AH774/1372-3CE). *Qisas al-Anbiya'* (Stories of the Prophets) (Arabic). Riyadh: Dar al-Qiblatayn, AH1412/1992 CE.

(Keler) von Keler, Theodore M.R. *The Esssence of the Koran*. Ten-Cent Pocket Series, No. 428. Girard: Haldeman-Julius Co., 1923.

(Keller) Keller, Werner. *The Bible as History*. Trans. William Neil. New York: Bantam Books, 1974.

(Kenyon) Kenyon, Kathleen. *Royal Cities of the Old Testament*. New York: Schocken Books, 1971.

(Kersten) Kersten, Holger & Elmar R. Gruber. *The Jesus Conspiracy*. Brisbane: Element Books, 1995.

(Khanlari) Khanlari, Dr. Parviz Natel. *Yusef-o Zulaykha* (Masterpieces of Persian Literature, No. 1) (Persian). Tehran: Amir Kabir, AHS 1352.

(Kisa'i) Kisa'i, Muhammad ibn 'Abd Allah. *Tales of the Prophets*. Trans. Wheeler M. Thackston, Jr. Chicago: Great Books of the Islamic World, 1997.

(Kitchen) Kitchen, K.A. *Ancient Orient and Old Testament*. Chicago: Inter-Varsity Press, 1966.

(Kitto) Kitto, H.D.F. *The Greeks*. Harmondsworth: Penguin Books Ltd., 1951.

(KJV) *Bible, The Holy (King James Version)*. Cleveland: World Publishing Co., undated, but conforming to edition of 1611.

(Kramer-Myth) Kramer. Samuel Noah, ed. *Mythologies of the Ancient World*. Garden City: Doubleday & Co., 1961.

(Kramer-Sumer) Kramer, Samuel Noah. *History Begins at Sumer*. Garden City: Doubleday & Co., 1959.

(Kritzeck) Kritzeck, James. *Peter the Venerable and Islam*. Princeton: Princeton University Press, 1964.

(Kuhan) *Bakhshi az Tafsiri Kuhan*. Annotated by Dr. Mujtaba Minawi, edited by Muhammad Rawshan. (Persian) Tehran: Bunyad-i Farhang-i Iran, AHS 1351.

(Lamb-Cyrus) Lamb, Harold. *Cyrus the Great*. Garden City: Doubleday & Co., 1960.

(Later Fathers) Bettenson, Henry, ed. & trans. *The Later Christian Fathers*. London: Oxford Univ. Press, 1974.

(Laymon) Laymon, Charles M., ed. *The Interpreter's One-Volume Commentary on the Bible*. Nashville: Abingdon Press, 1971.

(Lazarus) Lazarus, Rabbi Dayan H.M. *Mo'ed Katan*. London: Soncino Press, 1938.

(Legge) Legge, Francis. *Forerunners and Rivals of Christianity: From 330 B.C. to 330 A.D.* 2 vols. bound as one. New Hyde Park: University Books, 1964.

(Lemprière) Lemprière, John. *Classical Dictionary*. Orig. Edition, 1788; revised, 1850. London: Bracken Bks., 1994.

(Léon-Dufour) Léon-Dufour, Xavier. *The Gospels and the Jesus of History.* Trans. John McHugh. London: Collins, 1968.

(Lindsey-80s) Lindsey, Hal. *The 1980's: Countdown to Armageddon.* New York: Bantam, 1981.

(Lindsey-LGPE) Lindsey, Hal. *The Late Great Planet Earth.* New York: Bantam, 1973; reprint of the Zondervan edition of 1970.

(Lindsey-R) Lindsey, Hal. *The Rapture: Truth or Consequences.* New York: Bantam, 1983.

(Littman) Littman, E. "Jesus in a Pre-Islamic Arabic Inscription." *Moslem World,* XL, 1950, 16-18.

(LJ) Ginzberg, Louis. *The Legends of the Jews.* 7 volumes. Philadelphia: Jewish Publication Society of America, 1909-1938.

(Lost Bks) *Lost Books of the Bible, The.* No. Ed. Cited. New York: New American Library, 1974; reprint of 1926 Alpha House edition.

(LXX) *Bible: The Septuagint,* Greek &English Old Testament with the Apocrypha. Trans. Sir Launcelot Lee Brenton. London: Samuel Bagster & Sons, 1976.

(Maccoby) Maccoby, Hyam. *The Mythmaker: Paul and the Invention of Christianity.* New York: Barnes & Noble, 1986.

(Mack) Mack, Burton L. *Who Wrote the New Testament?* New York: Harper Collins, 1995.

(Mackenzie-Egypt) Mackenzie, Donald A. *Egyptian Myth and Legend.* (Reprint of 1907 edition.) New York: Bell Publishing, 1978.

(Mackenzie-Myth) Mackenzie, Donald A. *Mythology of the Babylonian People.* (Reprint of 1915 edition originally titled *Myths of Babylonia and Assyria.*) London: Bracken Books, 1996.

(Mani) Greenless, Duncan. *The Gospel of the Prophet Mani* (World Gospel Series, Vol. 12) Adyar: Theosophical Publishing House, 1956.

(Margoliouth) Margoliouth, D.S. *The Relations Between Arabs and Israelites Prior to the Rise of Islam.* London: the British Academy, 1924.

(Marsh) Marsh, John. *Saint John.* Pelican New Testament Commentaries. Harmondsworth: Penguin Books, 1968.

(Matarasso) Matarrasso, P.M., trans. *The Quest of the Holy Grail.* Harmondsworth: Penguin Books, 1969.

(Matheson) Matheson, Sylvia A. *Persia: an Archaeological Guide.* London: Faber and Faber, 1972.

(Maududi-TUI) Maududi, Sayyid AbulAla. *Towards Understanding Islam.* Dr. Abdul Ghani, trans. Lahore: Tarjumanul Quran, 5th edition, 1954.

(Mayhani) Mayhani, Muhammad bin Munawwar. *Asrar al-Tawhid* (Secrets of Divine Unity). Persian. Tehran: Amir Kabir, AHS1348.

(McEvedy) McEvedy and Richard Jones. *Atlas of World Population History.* Harmondsworth: Penguin Books, 1978.

(McEvedy-AH) McEvedy, Colin. *Penguin Atlas of Ancient History.* Harmondsworth: Penguin Books, 1967.

(Mercatante) Mercatante, Anthony S. *Who's Who in Egyptian Mythology.* New York: Potter, 1978.

(Metzger) Metzger, Bruce and Coogan, Michael D., eds. *The Oxford Essential Guide to People and Places of the Bible* (American Edition). New York: Berkley Books, 2001.

(Meyer) Meyer, Marvin W., ed. & trans. *The Mithras Liturgy.* Texts and Translations 10, Graeco-Roman Religion 2. Missoula: Society of Biblical Literature, 1976.

(Mishkat) Baghawi (Al-), Abu Muhammad. *Mishkat al-Masabih.* (Revised and retitled by Wali al-Din al-Tabrizi. 4 vols. Trans. James Robson. Lahore: Sh. Muhammad Ashraf, 1963-6.

(Mitchell) Mitchell, Stephen. *Genesis: A New Translation of the Classical Biblical Stories.* New York: Harper-Collins, 1996.

(Mommsen) Mommsen, Theodor. *The Provinces of the Roman Empire.* (Reprint of 1909 edition, two volumes in one.) New York: Barnes & Noble Bks., 1996.

(Morison) Morison, Frank. *Who Moved the Stone?* London: Faber and Faber, 1958 (1930).

(Mowry) Mowry, Lucetta. *The Dead Sea Scrolls and the Early Church.* Notre Dame: Univ. of Notre Dame Press, 1966.

(Muhajir) Muhajir, Ali Musa Raza. *Lessons From the Stories of the Quran.* Lahore: Sh. Muhammad Ashraf, 1965.

(Muhit) Bustani, Butrus. *Muhit al-Muhit.* (Arabic-Arabic dictionary). Beirut: Maktabah Lubnan, 1983.

(Munjid) Ma'luf, Louis, ed. *Al-Munjid.* (Arabic) Beirut: Catholic Press, 1956.

(MW) *Muslim World.* Periodical.

(NADE) *New American Desk Encyclopedia*, 4th edition. New York: Signet, 1997.

(Nadvi) Nadvi, Syed Muzaffer-ud-Din. *A Geographical History of the Quran.* Lahore: Sh. Muhammad Ashraf, 1936.

(Nasafi) Nasafi, Abu Hafs Najmuddin 'Umar. *Tafsir-i Nasafi.* 2 vols. Dr. 'Aziz Allah Juwayni, ed. (Persian) Tehran: Bunyad-i Farhang-i Iran, AHS1353-1354.

(Nathan) Nathan, Rabbi. *The Fathers According to Rabbi Nathan.* Trans. Judah Goldin. New York: Shocken Books, 1974.

(NCBD) *New Compact Bible Dictionary, The.* T. Alton Bryant, ed. Grand Rapids: Zondervan, 1967.

(NCE) *New Catholic Encyclopedia*, 18 vols., incl. supplements 1967-1988. Catholic Univ. of America, Washington, DC. New York: McGraw-Hill, 1967.

(NEB) *Bible with the Apocrypha, The New English.* Oxford study edition. New York: Oxford Univ. Press. 1976.

(NIB) *New Interpreter's Bible, The.* 12 vols. Nashville: Abdingdon Press, 1994-8.

(Nicholson) Nicholson, Reynold A. *A Literary History of the Arabs,* first edition 1907; reprinted, Cambridge: Cambridge Univ. Press, 1969.

(Nineham) Nineham, D.E. *Saint Mark.* Pelican New Testament Commentaries. Harmondsworth: Penguin Books, revised 1969.

(Nordhoff) Nordhoff, Charles. *The Communistic Societies of the United States.* Reprint of 1875 edition. New York: Dover Publications, 1966.

(NT4) *New Testament in Four Versions, The.* The versions are: King James, Revised Standard, Phillips Modern English, and New English Bible. Washington: Canon Press, 1963.

(O'Grady) O'Grady, Joan. *Early Christian Heresies.* Reprint of 1985 ed. New York: Barnes & Noble, 1994.

(O'Neill) O'Neill, J.C. *Paul's Letter to the Romans.* Pelican New Testament Commentaries. Harmondsworth: Penguin Books, 1975.

(O'Shea) O'Shea, Stephen. *The Perfect Heresy.* New York: Walker & Co., 2000.

(OBA) May, Herbert G., ed. *Oxford Bible Atlas,* 2nd edition. London: Oxford Univ. Press, 1974.

(Olmstead) Olmstead, A.T. *History of the Persian Empire.* Chicago: Univ. of Chicago Press, 1948.

(Orations) Akbar, Maulana Muhammad Ubaidul. *The Orations of Muhammad.* Shaikh Muhammad Ashraf: Lahore, 1954.

(Ovid) Ovid. *Metamorphoses.* Trans. Mary M. Innes. Harmondsworth: Penguin Books, 1955.

(OxBible) *Bible, The Oxford Annotated.* Revised Standard Version— College edition. H.G. May and B.M. Metzger, eds. New York: Oxford Univ. Press, 1962.

(Pagels) Pagels, Elaine. *The Gnostic Gospels.* New York: Vintage, 1981.

(Panati) Panati, Charles. *Extraordinary Origins of Everyday Things.* New York: Harper & Row, Perennial Library, 1987.

(Passover) Schonfield, Hugh J. *The Passover Plot.* New York: Bantam Books, 1967.

(Pastoral) Houlden, J.L. *The Pastoral Epistles.* Harmondsworth: Penguin Books, 1976.

(Patai) Patai, Raphael. *The Hebrew Goddess.* New York: Avon Books, 1978.

(Patriarchs) Mazar, Benjamin, ed. *Patriarchs,* Vol. II, The World History of the Jewish People. Israel: Jewish History Publications, 1970.

(Penrice) Penrice, John. *A Dictionary and Glossary of the Koran.* (Reprint of the 1873 edition.) Mineola: Dover Publications, 2004.

(Pesikta) *Pesikta Rabbati.* Trans. W. C. Braude. New Haven: Yale Univ., 1968.

(Petrie) Petrie, W.M. Flinders, trans. *Egyptian Tales.* First series, IVth to XIIth Dynasty. New York: Benjamin Blom, 1971. Reprint of 1899 edition.

(Philostratus) Philostratus the Elder. *Life and Times of Apollonius of Tyana.* Charles P. Eells, trans. University Series. Language and Literature, Vol. II, No. 1. Stanford: Stanford Univ., 1923.

(Phipps) Phipps, William E. *Muhammad and Jesus.* New York: Continuum, 1996.

(Pickering) Pickering, David. *Cassell Dictionary of Superstitions.* London: Cassell, 1995.

(Platt) Platt, Rutherford H., ed. *Forgotten Books of Eden, The.* New York: New American Library, 1974; reprint of 1927 Alpha House edition.

(Pliny) Pliny the Younger (C. Plinius Caecilius Secundus). *The Letters of the Younger Pliny.* Betty Radice, trans. Harmondsworth: Penguin Books, 1969.

(Plutarch) Plutarch. *The Age of Alexander.* Trans. Ian Scott-Kilvert. Harmondsworth: Penguin Books, 1973.

(Pope) Pope, Arthur Upham. *Persian Architecture.* London: Tames & Hudson, 1965.

(Potter) Potter, Rev. Dr. Charles Francis. *The Lost Years of Jesus Revealed.* Greenwich: Fawcett Pub., 1962.

(Powell) Powell, Evan. *The Unfinished Gospel.* Westlake Village: Symposium Books, 1994.

(PRE) Eliezer ben Hyrkanos, Rabbi. *Pirke de Rabbi Eliezer.* Trans. & ed. Gerald Friedlander. New York: Harmon Press, 1970; from London 1916 edition.

(Prison Letters) Houlden, J.L. *Paul's Letters From Prison.* Hardmondsworth: Penguin Books, 1970.

(PseudoCal) Pseudo-Callistenes. *The Romance of Alexander the Great.* Trans. Albert M. Wolohokian. New York: Columbia Univ. Press, 1969.

(Quran-Arberry) *Quran:* Arberry, Arthur J. The Koran Interpreted. London: Oxford Univ. Press, 1964.

(Quran-Dawood) *Quran:* The Koran. Trans. N.J. Dawood. Harmondsworth: Penguin Books, 1966.

(Quran-Farid) *Holy Quran, The.* Malik Ghulam Farid, ed. (and trans.?). Orig. publication by The Oriental and Religious Publishing Corp., Ltd., of Pakistan 1969. Present edition: Tilford: Islam International Publications, 1994.

(Quran-Maududi) *Quran:* Maududi, S. Abul A'la, commentator. The Meaning of the Quran. Trans. Muhammad Akbar Muradpuri. First 17 surahs in 6 vols. Lahore: Islamic Publications, 1971-73.

(Quran-MMA) *Quran:* The Holy Quran. Trans. & commentary by Maulana Muhammad Ali. 5th edition. Lahore: Ahmadiyyah Anjuman Isha'at Islam, 1963.

(Quran-Pickthall) *Quran:* The Meaning of the Glorious Koran. Trans. Mohammed Marmaduke Pickthall. New York: Mentor Books, 1953.

(Quran-Sale) The Koran. Trans. & annotated by George Sale. London: Frederick Warne and Co, undated.

(Quran-Yusuf Ali) *Quran:* The Holy Quran. Trans. & commentary by Abdullah Yusuf Ali, 2 vols., continuous pagination. Lahore: Sh. Muhammad Ashraf, 1969.

(Rabin) Rabin, Chaim. *Qumran Studies.* New York: Schocken, 1975. Reprint of Oxford 1957 edition.

(Rahman) Rahman, H.U. *A Chronology of Islamic History.* Boston: G.K. Hall & Co., 1989.

(Randi) Randi, James. *An Encyclopedia of Claims, Frauds, and Hoaxes of the Occult and Supernatural.* New York: St. Martin's Press, 1995.

(Randolph) Randolph, Vance. *Religious Philosophers.* Ten-Cent Pocket Series, No. 614. Girard: Haldeman-Julius Co., 1924.

(Rappoport) Rappoport, Angelo S. *Ancient Israel: Myths and Legends.* 3 vols. London: Senate, 1995.

(Rawwaqi) Rawwaqi, 'Ali, ed. *Tafsir-i Quran-i Pak.* (Arabic-Persian) Tehran: Bunyad-i Farhang-i Iran, AHS 1348.

(RHD) *Random House Dictionary of the English Language, The.* (College Edition). Laurence Urdang, ed. NY: Random House, 1968.

(Rice) Rice, Michael. *Who's Who in Ancient Egypt.* London: Routledge, 1999.

(Ridpath) Ridpath, John Clark. *Ridpath's History of the World*, 9 vols. Cincinnati: Jones Bros. Publishing Co., 1923.

(Robinson) Robinson, James, general ed. *The Nag Hammadi Library.* New York: Harper & Row, 1977.

(Rodinson) Rodinson, Maxime. *Mohammed.* Trans. Anne Carter. Harmondsworth: Penguin Books, 1971 (1961).

(Rodinson-Israel) Rodinson, Maxime. David Thorstad, tr. *Israel: A Colonial-Settler State?* New York: Monad Press, 1973.

(Roman Myths) Grant, Michael. *Roman Myths.* Harmondsworth: Penguin Books, 1973.

(Rosenberg) Rosenberg, David & Bloom, Harold. *The Book of J.* New York: Grove Weidenfeld, 1990.

(Rosenthal) Rosenthal, Erwin I.J. *Judaism and Islam.* Popular Jewish Library. London: Thomas Yoseloff, 1961.

(Rothenberg) Rothenberg, Beno. *Were These King Solomon's Mines?* Excavations in the Timna Valley. New York: Stein & Day, 1972.

(RSV) *Bible, The Holy (Revised Standard Edition).* Revised 1952. London: Oxford Univ. Press, 1952.

(Ruef) Ruef, John. *Paul's First Letter to Corinth.* Pelican New Testament Commentaries. Harmondsworth: Penguin Books, 1971.

(Runes) Runes, Dagobert, ed. *Dictionary of Philosophy.* 15th edition. New York: Philosophical Library, Inc., 1960.

(Russell) Russell, D.S. *The Jews From Alexander to Herod.* The New Clarendon Bible, Old Testament, Vol. V. London: Oxford Univ. Press, 1967.

(Saggs) Saggs, H.W.F. *The Greatness That was Babylon.* New York: The New American Library, 1968.

(Saglam) Saglam, Bahaeddin. *The Torah.* Trans. Selahattin Ayaz. Istanbul: Tabligh, 1999.

(Sarna) Sarna, Nahum M. *Understanding Genesis.* New York: Schocken Books, 1970.

(Sayers) Sayers, Dorothy L., trans. *The Song of Roland.* Harmondsworth: Penguin Books, Ltd., 1937.

(Schauss) Schauss, Hayyim. *Guide to Jewish Holy Days: History and Observance*. New York: Schocken Books, 1962.

(Schurer) Schurer, Emil. *A History of the Jewish People in the Time of Jesus*. New York: Schocken Books, 1961, Reprint of 1886-1890 Eng. Trans.

(Scofield) *Scofield Bible, The*. Rev. C.I. Scofield, ed. New York: Oxford Univ. Press, 1917.

(Segal) Segal, Moses H. *The Pentateuch: Its Composition and Its Authorship and Other Biblical Studies*. Jerusalem: The Magnes Press, Hebrew Univ., 1967.

(SEI) Gibb, H.A.R. & Kramers, J.H., eds. *The Shorter Encyclopædia of Islam*. Leiden: E.J. Brill; London: Luzac & Co., 1961.

(Shams) Shams, J.D. *Where Did Jesus Die?* Qadian: Nazir Dawat-o-Tabligh, 1973.

(Shanks) Shanks, Hershel, ed. *Ancient Israel: From Abraham to the Roman Destruction of the Temple*, rev. & expanded ed. Washington: Biblical Archaeological Society, 1999.

(Shanks-City) Shanks, Hershel. *The City of David: A Guide to Biblical Jerusalem*. Washington: Biblical Archaeological Society, 1973.

(Shinnie) Shinnie, P.L. *Meroe: A Civilization of the Sudan*. London: Thames and Hudson, 1967.

(Shonfield) Schonfield, Hugh J. *Those Incredible Christians*. New York: Bantam Books, 1969.

(Shulvass) Shulvass, Moses A. *The History of the Jewish People: Vol. I, The Antiquity*. Chicago: Regener Gateway, 1982.

(Siddiqui) Siddiqui, Abdul Hameed. *The Life of Muhammad*, 10th edition. Lahore: Islamic Publications, 1993.

(Silver) Silver, Abba Hillel. *Moses and the Original Torah*. New York: Macmillan Co., 1961.

(Simon) Simon, Edith. *The Saints*. Harmondsworth: Penguin Books, 1972.

(Smelik) Smelik, Klass A.D. *Writings From Ancient Israel*. Edinburgh: T&T Clark, 1991.

(Smith) Smith, W. Robertson. *The Religion of the Semites*. New York: Schocken Books, 1972 (1889)

(Smith-Jesus) Smith, Morton. Jesus the Magician. New York: Barnes & Noble, 1993. Reprint of 1978 ed.

(SolSheba) Pritchard, J.B., ed. *Solomon and Sheba*. London: Phaidon, 1974.

(Sox) Sox, David. *The Gospel of Barnabas*. London: George Allen & Unwin, 1981.

(Speiser) Speiser, E.A., ed. At the Dawn of Civilization. Vol. I, The World History of the Jewish People. Israel: Jewish History Publications, 1963.

(Spence) Spence, Lewis. *The History of Atlantis*. Reprint of 1926/1968 edition. Mineola: Dover Publications, 2003.

(Stanley) Stanley, Arthur Penrhyn. *The Eastern Church*. London: John Murray, 1861.

(Stanley-Sinai) Stanley, Arthur Penrhyn. *Sinai and Palestine.* New York: 1895.

(Stedman) *Stedman's Medical Dictionary,* 22nd edition. Baltimore: Williams & Wilkins, 1972.

(Stone) Stone, Jon R., ed. *Expecting Armageddon—Essential Readings in Failed Prophecy.* New York: Routledge, 2000.

(Storey) Storey, C.A. *Persian Literature.* Vol. 1, Part I. Royal Asiatic Society. London: Luzac & Co., 1970, first published 1927-39.

(Stott) Stott, John R.W. *Basic Christianity,* 2nd edition. London: Inter-Varsity Press, 1971.

(Suetonius) Suetonius, Gaius. *The Twelve Caesars.* Trans. Robert Graves. Baltimore: Penguin Books, 1957.

(Surabadi) Surabadi, Abu Bakr 'Atiq Nishaburi. *Stories From the Holy Quran.* Dr. Mahdavi, ed. Persian. No. 66 in Iranian Texts Series. Tehran: Tehran Univ., AHS1347.

(Surabadi-Photo) Surabadi. *Tafsir.* Vol. 1. Photographic reproduction. (Persian) Tehran: Bunyad-i Farhang-i Iran, AHS 1353.

(Surabadi-Photo2) Surabadi. *Tafsir.* Photographic reproduction of AH523 copy. (Persian-Arabic) Tehran: Bunyad-Farhang, AHS 1345.

(Tabari) Tabari, Muhammad bin Jarir. *Tarikh-i Tabari.* 16 vols. Persian trans. Abu al-Qasim Payandah. Tehran: Bunyad-i Farhang- Iran, AHS 1352-54.

(Tacitus) Tacitus, Cornelius. *The Annals of Imperial Rome.* Trans. Michael Grant. Harmondsworth: Penguin Books, 1959.

(Taylor) Taylor, Vincent. *The Text of the New Testament.* London: St. Martin's Press, 1961.

(Test Abraham) *The Testament of Abraham.* Trans. Michael E. Stone. Texts and Translations 2. Society of Biblical Literature. Missoula: Scholars Press, 1972.

(Test Job) Kraft, Robert A., ed. *The Testament of Job.* Texts and Translations 5. Society of Biblical Literature. Missoula: Scholars Press, 1974.

(Thapar) Thapar, Romila. *A History of India,* Vol. 1. Harmondsworth: Penguin Books Ltd., 1966.

(Thesiger) Thesiger, Wilfred. *Arabian Sands.* Harmondsworth: Penguin Books, 1964.

(Thomas) Thomas, D. Winston, ed. *Documents From Old Testament Times.* New York: Harper Torchbooks, 1961.

(Tichenor-Primitive) Tichenor, H.M. *Primitive Beliefs.* Ten-Cent Pocket Series, No. 184, Girard: Haldeman-Julius Co., 1921.

(Tichenor-Sun) Tichenor, H.M. *Sun-Worship and Later Beliefs.* Ten-Cent Pocket Series, No. 204. Girard: Haldeman-Julius Co., 1921.

(Tisdall) Tisdall, Rev. Wm. St. Clair. *The Original Sources of the Quran.* London: 1905.

(Torrey) Torrey, C.C. *The Jewish Foundation of Islam.* New York: Ktav Publishing House, 1967; reprint of 1933 edition.

(Trawick-NT) Trawick, Buckner B. *The Bible as Literature: The New Testament.* Second edition. New York: Barnes & Noble, 1968.

(Trawick-OT) Trawick, Buckner B. *The Bible as Literature: The Old Testament and the Apocrypha*. Second edition. New York: Barnes & Noble, 1970.

(Treece) Treece, Henry. *The Crusades*. New York: Mentor Books, 1964.

(Ulansey) Ulansey, David. The Origins of the Mithraic Mysteries. New York: Oxford University Press, 1989.

(Ushri) *Tafsiri bar 'Ushri az Quran Majid* (British Museum). Dr. Jalal Matini, ed. (Persian) Tehran: Bunyad-i Farhang-i Iran, AHS1352.

(Vermes) Vermes, G. *The Dead Sea Scrolls in*. Harmondsworth: Penguin Books, 1962.

(Vermes-97) Vermes, Geza. *The Complete Dead Sea Scrolls in English*. New York: Penguin Books, 1997.

(Voorst) Van Voorst, Robert E. *Jesus Outside the New Testament*. Grand Rapids: Wm. B. Eerdmans, 2000.

(Ware) Ware, Timothy. *The Orthodox Church*. Harmondsworth, Penguin Books, 1969.

(Waterfield) Waterfield, Robin E. *Christians in Persia*. London: George Allen & Unwin, 1973.

(Watt-Bell) Watt, W. Montgomery. *Bell's Introduction to the Quran*. Revised and enlarged by W.M. Watt. Islamic Surveys, Vol. 8. Edinburgh University Press, 1970.

(Watt-Influence) Watt, W.Montgomery. *The Influence of Islam on Medieval Europe*. Islamic Surveys, Vol. 9. Edinburgh University Press, 1972.

(Watt-Md) Watt, W. Montgomery. *Muhammad: Prophet and Statesman*. New York: Oxford Univ. Press, 1964.

(Watts-Hands) Watts, Alan W. *The Two Hands of God*. New York: College Books, 1969.

(Watts-Myth) Watts, Alan W. *Myth and Ritual in Christianity*. Boston: Beacon Press, 1968.

(Weber) Weber, Max. *Ancient Judaism*. Trans. & ed. Hans H. Gerth & Don Martindale. New York: The Free Press, 1952.

(Webster) *Webster's Ninth New Collegiate Dictionary*, Springfield: Merriam-Webster, Inc., 1991.

(Wehr) Wehr, Hans. *Arabic-English Dictionary*. Trans. J.M. Cowan. Beirut: Librairie du Liban, 1980.

(Wells) Wells, G.A. *The Jesus Legend*. Chicago: Open Court, 1996.

(White) White, Ellen G. *Cosmic Conflict*. (First published 1888.) Boise: Pacific Press Publishing Assoc., 1971.

(Williams) Williams, Jay G. *Understanding the Old Testament*. New York: Barron's Educational Series, 1972.

(Wilson) Wilson, Colin. *A History of the Devil*. St. Albans: Panther Books, 1975.

(Wolff) Wolff, Hans Walter. *The Old Testament: A Guide to Its Writings*. Trans. Keith R. Crim. London: SPCK, 1974.

(Woodward) Woodward, Kenneth L. *The Book of Miracles*. New York: Simon & Schuster, 2000.

(Woolley) Woolley, Sir Leonard. *Ur of the Chaldees*. Harmondsworth: Penguin Books, revised ed., 1952.

(World Almanac) *The World Almanac and Book of Facts*. 2002 edition. New York: World Almanac Bks, 2002.

(Wright) Wright, G. Ernest & Fuller, Reginald. *The Book of the Acts of God*. Harmondsworth: Penguin Books, 1965.

(WRMEA) *Washington Report on Middle East Affairs*, periodical.

(Wunderlich) Wunderlich, Hans Georg. *The Secret of Crete*. Trans. Richard Winston. Glasgow: Fontana/Collins, 1976.

(Young) Young, William G. *Patriarch, Shah and Caliph*. Rawalpindi: Christian Study Centre, 1974.

BIBLIOGRAPHY (ALPHABETICAL)

Ackroyd, P.R., et al, eds. *Cambridge History of the Bible, The.* Three vols. Cambridge Univ. Press, 1970. 1969, 1963. (Cambridge)

Ackroyd, Peter R. *Israel under Babylon and Persia.* New Clarendon Bible, Old Testament, Vol. 4. London: Oxford Univ. Press, 1970. (Ackroyd)

Acts of the Apostles, The. Trans. E.V. Rieu. Harmondsworth: Penguin Books, 1957. (Acts)

Aesop. *Fables.* Trans. V.S. Vernon Jones. London: Pan Books, 1975. (Aesop-Jones)

Aesop. *Fables.* Trans. S. A. Handford. New edition. Harmondsworth: Penguin Books, 1964. (Aesop)

Ahmed, Syed Magbool. "Supernaturalism of al-Quran VI: Biblical Names I the Quran." *Islamic Review*, XVIII, No. 12 (Dec. 1930), pp. 436-445. (Ahmed)

Akbar. Maulana Muhammad Ubaidul. *The Orations of Muhammad.* Shaikh Muhammad Ashraf: Lahore, 1954. (Orations)

Albright, William F. *Archaeology, Historical Analysis, and Early Biblical Tradition.* Baton Rouge: Louisiana State Univ. Press, 1966. (Albright-Arch)

Albright, William F. *From Stone Age to Christianity.* Second edition. Garden City: Doubleday Anchor Books, 1957. (Albright-Stone Age)

Albright, William F. *The Archaeology of Palestine.* Revised edition. Harmondsworth: Penguin Books, 1960. (Albright-Pal)

Albright, William F. *The Biblical Period From to Ezra.* New York: Harper Torchbooks, Harper & Row, 1963. (Albright-Ab to Ez)

Ali, Syed Ameer. *The Spirit of Islam.* London: Christophers, 1922. (Ameer Ali)

Allegro, John M. *The Chosen People.* St. Albans: Panther Books, 1973. (Allegro-People)

Allegro, John M. *The Dead Sea Scrolls.* Harmondsworth: Penguin Books, 1958, 1959. (Allegro-Scrolls)

Allegro, John M. *The Sacred Mushroom and the Cross.* Revised edition. London: Sphere Books, 1973. (Allegro-Sacred)

Allen, Clifton J., gen. ed. *Broadman Bible Commentary, The.* 12 vols. London: Marshall, Morgan & Scott, 1970-72. (BC)

Anderson, G.W. *The History and Religion of Israel.* New Clarendon Bible, Vol. I. London: Oxford Univ. Press, 1966. (Anderson)

Angus, S. *The Mystery Religions.* New York: Dover Publications, 1975. Reprint of 1928 edition. (Angus)

Ansari, F.R. *Islam and Christianity in the Modern World.* Karachi: World Federation of Islamic Missions, 1965. (FRA)

Ansari, Khwajah 'Abd Allah. *Tafsir-i Adabi wa 'Irfani Quran-i Majid.* 2 vols. Abridged by Habib Allah Amuzgar. (Persian) Tehran: Iqbal, AHS1347-8. (Ansari)

Apocrypha, The. 1894 revised edition. London: Oxford Univ. Press, 1926. (Apocrypha)

Arberry, A.J. *Poems of Mutanabbi.* London: Cambridge Univ. Press, 1967. (Arberry-Mutanabbi)

Arberry, Arthur J. *The Koran Interpreted.* London: Oxford Univ. Press, 1964. (Quran-Arberry)

Archaeology of the Holy Land. Compiled from material in the EJ. Israel Pocket Library series. Jerusalem: Keter Publ. House, 1974. (ArchHL)

Archaeology Odyssey (periodical). (AO)

Arden, Harvey. "In the Steps of Moses." *National Geographic Magazine.* Vol. 149, No. 1, Jan. 1976, pp. 21. (Arden)

Arnold, T.W. *The Preaching of Islam.* Lahore: Sh. Muhammad Ashraf, 1961. Reprint of 1896 edition. (Arnold)

Arrian: the Campaigns of Alexander. Revised edition. Trans. Aubrey de Selincourt. Harmondsworth: Penguin Books, 1971. (Arrian)

Asad, Muhammad. *The Road to Mecca.* London: Max Reinhardt, 1954. (Asad)

Ashe, Geoffrey. *King Arthur's Avalon.* London: Fontana Books, 1973. (Ashe)

Asimov, Isaac. *Asimov's Guide to the Bible: The New Testament.* New York: Avon, 1971. (Asimov-NT)

Asimov, Isaac. *Asimov's Guide to the Bible: The Old Testament.* New York: Avon Books, 1971. (Asimov-OT)

Atiyah, Edward. *The Arabs.* Harmondsworth: Penguin Books, 1955. (Atiyah)

Atlas of the Bible Lands. Maplewood: Hammond, 1959. (ABL)

Attridge, Harold W. & Oden, Robert A., eds. *De Dea Syria.* Texts and Translations. Society of Biblical Literature. Missoula: Scholars Press, 1976. (Attridge)

Avi-Yonah, Michael & Baras, Zvi, eds. *The Herodian Period.* The World History of the Jewish People, Vol. VII. Israel: Jewish History Publications, 1975. (Herodian)

Baghawi (Al-), Abu Muhammad. *Mishkat al-Masabih.* (Revised and retitled by Wali al-Din al-Tabrizi. 4 vols. Trans. James Robson. Lahore: Sh. Muhammad Ashraf, 1963-6. (Mishkat)

Bahar, Mihrdad. *Asatir-i Iran.* (Persian) Tehran: Bunyad-i Farhang-i Iran, AHS1352. (Asatir)

Bainton, Roland. *The Penguin History of Christianity.* 2 vols. Harmondsworth: Penguin Books, 1967. (Bainton)

Bakhshi az Tafsiri Kuhan. Annotated by Dr. Mujtaba Minawi, edited by Muhammad Rawshan. (Persian) Tehran: Bunyad-i Farhang-i Iran, AHS 1351. (Kuhan)

Bal'ami, Abu 'Ali Muhammad bin Muhammad bin. *Tarikh-i Bal'ami.* 2 vols. Dr. Muhammad Taqi Bahar, ed. (Persian) Tehran: Kitabfurushi-yi Zawwar, 1353. (Bal'ami)

Balaghi, Sadr al-Din. *Qisas-i Quran*. (Persian) Tehran: Amir Kabir, AHS 1349. (Balaghi)

Baring-Gould, Sabine. *Curious Myths of the Middle Ages*. New Hyde Park: University Books, 1967 (reprint of the 1866-8 edition). (Baring-Gould)

Baring-Gould, Sabine. Edited and shortened by Edward Hardy. *Curious Myths of the Middle Ages*. Orig. Published 1866. New York: Barnes & Noble Books, 1994. (Hardy)

Barnabas. *The Gospel of Barnabas*. Trans Lonsdale and Laura Ragg. Oxford: Clarendon Press, 1907. Reprinted with introduction: Karachi: Quran Council of Pakistan, 1973. (Barnabas)

Barnstone, Willis, ed. *The Other Bible*. San Francisco: Harper & Row, 1984. (Barnstone)

Barrett, C.K., ed. *The New Testament Background*. New York: Harper & Row, 1961. (Barrett)

Barrow, R.H. *Slavery in the Roman Empire*. (Reprint of 1928 edition.) New York: Barnes & Noble Bks., 1996. (Barrow)

Baskin, Wade. *Dictionary of Satanism*. New York: Bonanza Books, 1972. (Baskin)

Bell, Richard. *The Origin of Islam in Its Christian Environment*. London: F. Cass & Co., 1968, reprint of 1926 edition. (Bell)

Ben-Yehuda, Ehud & Weinstein, David. *English-Hebrew/Hebrew-English Dictionary*. New York: Pocket Books, 1961. (Hebrew)

Bettenson, Henry, ed & trans. *The Early Christian Fathers*. London: Oxford Univ. Press, 1969. (Early Fathers)

Bettenson, Henry, ed. & trans. *The Later Christian Fathers*. London: Oxford Univ. Press, 1974. (Later Fathers)

Bettenson, Henry, ed. *Documents of the Christian Church*. 2nd edition. London: Oxford Univ. Press, 1967. (Church Doc)

Bibby, Geoffrey. *Four Thousand Years Ago*. Harmondsworth: Penguin Books, 1961. (Bibby)

Bibby, Geoffrey. *Looking for Dilmun*. New York: New American Library, 1974 (Bibby-Dilmun)

Bible Myths and Their Parallels in Other Religions. (Author unknown; anonymous?). New York: J.W. Bouton, 1883. (Bible Myths)

Bible Review (periodical) (BR)

Bible with the Apocrypha, The New English. Oxford study edition. New York: Oxford Univ. Press. 1976. (NEB)

Bible, The Holy (King James Version). Cleveland: World Publishing Co., undated, but conforming to edition of 1611. (KJV)

Bible, The Holy (Revised Standard Edition). Revised 1952. London: Oxford Univ. Press, 1952. (RSV)

Bible, The Interpreter's. 12 volumes. Nashville: Abington Press, 1951-57. (IB)

Bible, The Jerusalem. Jones, Alexander, gen. ed. Standard edition. London: Barton, Longman & Todd, 1966. (JB)

Bible, The Oxford Annotated. Revised Standard Version—College edition. H.G. May and B.M. Metzger, eds. New York: Oxford Univ. Press, 1962. (OxBible)

Bible: The Septuagint, Greek &English Old Testament with the Apocrypha. Trans. Sir Launcelot Lee Brenton. London: Samuel Bagster & Sons, 1976. (LXX)

Biblical Archaeology Review (periodical) (BAR)

Biblical Archeologist. Magazine. (BA)

Bickerman, Elias. *From Ezra to the Last of the Maccabees.* New York: Schocken Books, 1962. (Bickerman)

Bidokht, Nahid, *Burhan-i Qati',* Muhammad Husayn ibn Khalaf Tabrizi 'Burhan,' dtd AH 1062, ed. Dr. Muhammad Mu'in Tehran: Ibn Sina, 2nd printing, 1342. (Burhan)

Bierlein, J.F. *Parallel Myths.* New York: Ballantine Books, 1994. (Bierlein)

Bishop, E.F.F. "The Qumran Scrolls and the Quran." *Muslim World,* XLVIII (1958) No. 3, 223-236. (Bishop)

Bornkamm, Gunther. *The New Testament: A Guide to Its Writings.* Trans. Reginald H. Fuller and Ilse Fuller. London: SPCK, 1974. (Bornkamm)

Bosworth, C.E. *The Islamic Dynasties.* Islamic Surveys, Vol. 5. Edinburgh: Edinburgh Univ. Pres., 1967. (Bosworth)

Bowra, C.E. *The Greek Experience.* London: Cardinal, 1957. (Bowra)

Brauer, Jr., George C. *Judaea Weeping.* New York: Crowell, 1970. (Brauer)

Brauer, Jr., George C. *The Decadent Emperors* (original title: The Young Emperors: Rome, A.D. 193-244). New York: Barnes & Noble, 1995 (1967). (Brauer-YE)

Breasted, J.H. *Development of Religion and Thought in Ancient Egypt.* New York: Harper & Row, 1959. Orig. Edition Scribner's, 1912. (Breasted-Religion)

Breasted, James Henry. *A History of Egypt.* New York: Bantam Books, 1964; reprint of revised edition of 1909. (Breasted)

Bridgwater, William, ed.-in chief. *The Columbia-Viking Desk Encyclopedia.* New York: Dell Publishing Co., 1966. (CV)

Briggs, Constance Victoria. *The Encylopedia of Angels.* New York: Penguin Books Inc., 1977. (Briggs)

Brodie, Thomas L. *The Quest for the Origin of John's Gospel.* New York: Oxford Univ. Press, 1993. (Brodie)

Buber, Martin. *Moses.* New York: Harper & Row, 1958. (Buber)

Bucaille, Maurice. *The Bible, the Quran and Science.* Trans. Alastair D. Pannell & author. Paris: Seghers (French edition), 1977. (Bucaille)

Budd, Philip J. *The New Century Bible Commentaries: Leviticus.* London: Marshall Pickering, 1996. (Budd)

Budge, E. Wallis, trans. & ed. *The Egyptian Book of the Dead.* New York: Dover Publications, 1967. Reprint of 1895 edition. (Budge-Bk)

Budge, E.A. Wallis. *Osiris and the Egyptian Resurrection.* 2 vols. New York: Dover Publications, 1973. Reprint of 1911 editon. (Budge-Osiris)

Budge, E.A. Wallis. *The Gods of the Egyptians.* 2 vols. New York: Dover Publications, 1969. Reprint of 1904 edition. (Budge-Gods)

Budge, Sir E.A. Wallis, ed. *The Book of the Cave of Treasures.* Trans. Sir E. A. Wallis Budge. London: Religious Tract Society, 1927. (Budge-Cave)

Bukhari, Imam. *Sahih al-Bukhari.* Dr. Muhammad Muhsin Khan, translator. Nine volumes. Lahore: Kazi Publications, 1979. (Bukhari)

Bultmann, Rudolph. *Primitive Christianity.* Trans. Rev. R.H. Fuller. New York: New American Library, 1974. (Bultmann)

Bustani, Butrus. *Muhit al-Muhit.* (Arabic-Arabic dictionary). Beirut: Maktabah Lubnan, 1983. (Muhit)

Butler, Alban. *Butler's Lives of the Saints,* 4 vols. Herbert Thurston, S.J. & Donald Attwater, eds. Rev. & supp. New York: P.J. Kenedy & Sons, 1956. (Butler)

Buttrick, George Arthur, ed. *The Interpreter's Dictionary of the Bible,* 4 vols. plus Supplementary volume. Nashville: Abdingdon Press, 1962, 1976. (IDB)

Caird, G.B. *Saint Luke.* Pelican New Testament Commentaries. Harmondsworth, 1963. (Caird)

Campbell, Antony F. *The Ark Narrative,* Dissertation Series No. 16. Missoula: Society of Biblical Literature, 1975. (Campbell, A)

Campbell, Edward F., Jr. & Freedman, David N., eds. *The Biblical Archaeologist Reader 3.* Reprints from BA magazine. Garden City: Anchor Books, 1970. (BA3)

Campbell, Joseph: *The Masks of God.* 4 vols. New York: Viking Press, 1970. (Campbell)

Carmichael, Joel. *The Death of Jesus.* Harmondsworth: Penguin Books, 1966) (Carmichael)

Carnegie, Dale. *Little Known Facts About Well Known People.* New York: Blue Ribbon Books, 1934. (Carnegie)

Carpenter, Edward. *The Origins of Pagan and Christian Beliefs.* First published 1920 as *Pagan and Christian Creeds: Their Origin & Meaning.* London: Senate, 1996. (Carpenter)

Cary, M. & Warmington, E.H. *The Ancient Explorers.* Revised edition. Harmondsworth: Penguin Books, 1963. Reprint of Methuen edition, 1929. (Explorers)

Chadwick, Henry. *The Early Church.* Harmondsworth: Penguin Books, 1967. (Chadwick)

Charles, R.H., ed. *Apocrypha and Pseudepigrapha of the Old Testament.* Volume Two. London: Oxford Univ. Press, 1968; reprint of 1913 edition. (A&P)

Churton, Tobias. *The Gnostics.* Reprint of 1987 ed. New York: Barnes & Noble, 1997. (Churton)

Cirlot, J.E. *A Dictionary of Symbolism.* Reprint of trans. from Spanish by Jack Sage, 1971. New York: Barnes & Noble, 1995. (Cirlot)

Clifton, Chas. S. *Encyclopedia of Heresies and Heretics*, (reprint of 1992 edition), New York: Barnes & Noble, 1998. (Clifton)

Clow, Rev. W.M. *The Bible Reader's Encyclopædia and Concordance* (based on The Bible Reader's Manual by Rec. C.H. Wright). London: Collin's Clear-Type Press, undated. (Clow)

Coats, George W. "From Canaan to Egypt: Structural and Theological Colntext for the Joseph Story." *The Catholic Biblical Quarterly Monograph Series 4*. Washington: The Catholic Biblical Assoc. of America, 1976. (Coats)

Columbia Encyclopedia, The. Wm. Bridgwater and Seymour Kurtz, eds. New York: Columbia Univ. Press, 1968. (CE)

Comay, Joan. *The Hebrew Kings*. New York: William Morrow, 1977. (Comay)

Cooper, David L. *Messiah: His Glorious Appearance Imminent.* Messianic Series No. 6. Los Angeles: Biblical Research Society, 1961. (Cooper)

Cottrell, Leonard. *The Land of Shinar*. London: Souvenir Press, 1965. (Cottrell)

Cruden, Alexander. *Concordance of the Holy Scriptures*. New York: Family Library, 1974. (Cruden)

Cumont, Franz. *The Mysteries of Mithra*. Thomas J. McCormack, trans. New York: Dover Publications, 1956; reprint of 1903 edition. (Cumont)

Danielou, J., Couratin, A.H. & Kent, John. *Historical Theology*, Vol. 2 of the Pelican Guide to Modern Theology. Harmondsworth: Penguin Books, 1969. (Hist Theo)

Davidson, Robert & Leaney, A.R.C. *Biblical Criticism*, Vol. 3 of the Pelican Guide to Modern Theology. Harmondsworth: Penguin Books, 1970. (Biblical Criticism)

Davies, Eryl W. *The New Century Bible Commentaries: Numbers.* London: Marshall Pickering, 1995. (Davies, E)

Davies, W.D. *Invitation to the New Testament*. Garden City: Anchor Books, Doubleday & Co., 1969. (Davies)

Davidson, Gustav. *A Dictionary of Angels*. New York: The Free Press, 1967. (Davidson)

de Camp, Sprague. *The Ancient Engineers*. New York: Ballantine, 1974. (de Camp)

de Lange, Nicholas. *Apocrypha: Jewish Literature of the Hellenistic Age*. New York: Viking Press, 1978 (de Lange)

de Vaux, Roland. *Ancient Israel*, 2 vols. New York: McGraw-Hill, 1965. (de Vaux)

Delaney, John J. *Dictionary of Saints*. Garden City: Image Books, 1983. (Delaney)

Delehaye, Hippolyte. *The Legends of the Saints*. Trans. D. Attwater. New York: Fordham Univ. Press, 1962. (Delehaye)

Dibelius, Martin. *From Tradition to Gospel*. Trans. From revised 2nd edition Bertram Lee Wolff in collaboration with author. New York: Scribner's, undated. (Dibelius)

Dimont, Max I. *Jews, God and History.* New York: New American Library, 1962. (Dimont)

Doresse, Jean. *Secret Books of the Egyptian Gnostics.* Trans. P. Mairet. London: Hillis & Carter, 1960. (Doresse)

Doughty, Charles M. Passages from *Arabia Deserta*, selected by Edward Garnett. Harmondsworth: Penguin Bks, 1956 (1931). (Doughty)

Dudley, D.R. & Lang, D.M., eds. *The Penguin Companion to Literature: Vol. 4, Classical & Byzantine, Oriental & African Literature.* Harmondsworth: Penguin Books, 1969. (Dudley)

Dunkerley, Roderic. *Beyond the Gospels.* Harmondsworth: Penguin Books, 1957. (Dunkerley)

Dunkling, Leslie and William Gosling. *The New American Dictionary of First Names.* New York: New American Library, 1983. (Dunkling)

Durant, Will. *Caesar and Christ*, The Story of Civilization, Vol. 3. New York: Simon & Schuster, 1944. (Durant-3)

Durant, Will. *The Age of Faith*, The Story of Civilization, Vol. 4. New York: MJF Books, 1950. (Durant-4)

Durant, Will. *The Life of Greece*, The Story of Civilization, Vol. 2. New York: Simon & Schuster, 1939. (Durant-2)

Early Christian Writings. Trans. Maxwell Staniforth. Harmondsworth: Penguin Books, 1968. (ECW)

Early Church Fathers, The. All 38 volumes of the series originally published by Scribner's (New York), 1900, on CD-ROM produced by Harmony Media, 2000, of Salem OR. (ECF)

Eaton, Charles Le Gai. *Remembering God: Reflections on Islam.* ABC International Group, distributed by Kazi Publications, Inc., Chicago, 2000. (Eaton)

Eisenman, Robert & Wise, Michael. *The Dead Sea Scrolls Uncovered.* New York: Barnes & Noble, 1994. (Eisenman-Wise)

Eisenman, Robert. *James the Brother of Jesus.* New York: Penguin Books, 1997. (Eisenman)

Eissfeldt, Otto. *The Old Testament: an Introduction.* Trans. P.R. Ackroyd. New York: Harper & Row, 1965. (Eissfeldt)

Eliade, Mircea. *From Primitive to Zen.* 4 volumes. New York: Harper & Row, 1974. (Eliade)

Eliezer ben Hyrkanos, Rabbi. *Pirke de Rabbi Eliezer.* Trans. & ed. Gerald Friedlander. New York: Harmon Press, 1970; from London 1916 edition. (PRE)

Encyclopædia Britannica, Inc. 1994-1999 Edition (on CD). (EB-CD)

Encyclopædia Britannica Standard Edition, 2004, C- ROM, Copyright © 1994-2003 Encyclopædia Britannica, Inc. May 30, 2003. (EBSE-04)

Encyclopædia Britannica. Chicago: Encyclopædia Britannica, 1960 ed. (EB)

Encyclopædia Judaica. 16 vols. New York: Macmillan & Co, 1971. (EJ)

Encyclopædia of Islam, The. 11 vols. + indices. Leiden: E.J. Brill, 1960-2002. (EI)

Encyclopedia Americana. New York: Americana Corp., 1962 ed. (EA)

Enslin, Morton Scott. *Christian Beginnings: Parts I and II.* New York: Harper & Row, 1956 (1938). (Enslin)

Epstein, Isidore. *Judaism.* Harmondsworth: Penguin Books, 1959. (Epstein)

Erman, Adolf, ed. *The Ancient Egyptians.* Trans. Aylward M. Blackman. New York: Harper Torchbooks, 1966. Orig. Ed. 1923. (Erman)

Eusebius. *The History of the Church From Christ to Constantine.* Trans. G.A. Williamson. New York: New York Univ. Press, 1966. (Eusebius-NY)

Eusebius. *Ecclesiastical History.* Trans. C.F. Cruse. Grand Rapids: Baker Book House, 1955. Reprint of 1850 edition. (Eusebius)

Faber-Kaiser, A. *Jesus Died in Kashmir.* London: Abacus, 1978. (Faber-Kaiser)

Fairservis, Walter A., Jr. *The Ancient Kingdoms of the Nile.* New York: Mentor Books, 1962. (Fairservis)

Fenton, J.C. *Saint Matthew.* Pelican New Testament Commentaries. Harmondsworth: Penguin Books, 1963. (Fenton)

Ferdowsi. *The Epic of the Kings* (Shahnamah). Trans. Reuben Levy. London: Routledge & Kegan Paul, 1967. (Ferdowsi)

Finbert, Elian, ed. *Israel.* Hachette World Guides. Paris: Hachette, 1956. (Finbert)

Finkelstein, Israel and Neil Asher Silberman. *The Bible Unearthed.* New York: The Free Press, 2001. (Finkelstein)

Finley, M.I. *Aspects of Antiquity.* Harmondsworth: Penguin Books, 1972. (Finley)

Firdawsi, Hakim Abu al-Qasim. *Shahnamah.* (Persian) Tehran: Amir Kabir, AHS 1343. (Firdawsi)

Frankfort, Henri, et al. *Before Philosophy.* Harmondsworth: Penguin Books, 1949. (Frankfort)

Frazer, James George. *Folklore in the Old Testament.* New York: Hart Publishing Co., 1975. (Frazer-Folklore)

Frazer. Sir James George. *The Golden Bough.* Abridged edition. New York: Macmillan Pub., 1963 (Frazer)

Freedman, David Noel & Campbell, Edward F., Jr., eds. *The Biblical Archaeologist Reader 2.* Reprints from BA magazine. Missoula: Scholars Press, 1977. (BA2)

Freedman, David Noel, ed. *The Anchor Bible Dictionary,* 5 vols. New York: Doubleday, 1992-. (ABD)

Frend, W.H.C. *The Early Church.* Philadelphia: Lippincott, 1965. (Frend)

Freud, Sigmund. Moses and Monotheism. Trans. Katherine Jones. New York: Vintage Books, 1939. (Freud)

Friedman, Richard Elliot. *Who Wrote the Bible?* New York: Harper Collins, 1989. (Friedman)

Frye, Richard N. *The Heritage of Persia.* New York: The New American Library, 1966. (Frye)

Fuller, R.H. *The Foundations of New Testament Christology.* London: Fontana, 1969. (Fuller)

Funk, Robert W. et al. *The Five Gospels.* New York: Scribner, 1993. (Funk)

Gabrieli, Francesco. *Muhammad and the Conquests of Islam.* Trans. Virginia Luling and Rosamund Linell. London: Weidenfeld and Nicolson, World Univ. Library, 1968. (Gabrieli)

Gager, John G. *Moses in Greco-Roman Paganism.* Society of Biblical Literature Monograph Series, Vol. 16, Robt. A. Kraft, ed. Nashville, Abdingdon Press, 1972. (Gager)

Galvin, John. "Egypt's First Pharaohs." *National Geographic Magazine.* Vol. 207, No. 4, Apr. 2005, pp. 106-121. (Galvin)

Gaster, Theodor H. *Myth, Legend, and Custom in the Old Testament.* 2 vols. New York: Harper & Row, 1975. (Gaster)

Gaster, Theodor H., ed. *The Dead Sea Scriptures.* Garden City: Anchor Books, 1964. (Dead Sea)

Ghazzali. *The Alchemy of Happiness.* (Ghazzali)

Gibb, H.A.R. & Kramers, J.H., eds. *The Shorter Encyclopædia of Islam.* Leiden: E.J. Brill; London: Luzac & Co., 1961. (SEI)

Gibbon, Edward. *Decline and Fall of the Roman Empire.* 6 vols. London: Everyman's Library, J.M. Dent & Sons, 1910. (Gibbon)

Ginzberg, Louis. *The Legends of the Jews.* 7 volumes. Philadelphia: Jewish Publication Society of America, 1909-1938. (LJ)

Goldin, Judah. *The Living Talmud*: The Wisdom of the Fathers (Pirke Abot). New York New American Library, 1957. (Abot)

Goodspeed, Edgar J. *A History of Early Christian Literature.* Revised and enlarged by R.M. Grant. Chicago: Univ. of Chicago Press, 1966. (Goodspeed)

Gordon, Cyrus H. *Forgotten Scripts.* Harmondsworth, revised edition, 1971. (Gordon-Scripts)

Graham, Lloyd A. *Deceptions and Myths of the Bible.* New York: Bell Publishing, 1979. (Graham)

Grant, Michael. *Roman Myths.* Harmondsworth: Penguin Books, 1973. (Roman Myths)

Grant, Michael. *Saint Peter.* New York: Barnes & Noble, 1998. (Grant-Peter)

Grant, Robert M. *A Historical Introduction to the New Testament.* New York: Simon & Schuster, 1972. (Grant)

Graves, Robert. *King Jesus.* New York?: Minerva Press, 1946. (Graves-Jesus)

Graves, Robert. *The Greek Myths.* Two volumes. Harmondsworth: Penguin Books, revised edition, 1960. (Graves)

Greeley, Andrew M. *The Sinai Myth.* Garden City: Doubleday, 1972. (Greeley)

Green, Peter. Alexander of Macedon. Harmondsworth: Penguin Books, 1974. (Green)

Greenlees, Duncan. *The Gospel of Israel* (World Gospel Series, Vol. 11). Adyar: Theosophical Publishing House, 1955. (Israel Gospel)

Greenless, Duncan. *The Gospel of the Prophet Mani* (World Gospel Series, Vol. 12) Adyar: Theosophical Publishing House, 1956. (Mani)

Grierson, Roderick & Munro-Hay, Stuart. *The Ark of the Covenant.* London: Weidenfeld & Nicholson, 1999. (Grierson)

Grimal, Pierre. *The Penguin Dictionary of Classical Mythology.* Stephen Kershaw, ed. Trans., A.R. Maxwell-Hyslop. Harmondsworth: Penguin Books, Ltd., 1991. (Grimal)

Gunkel, Herman. *The Legends of Genesis.* Trans. W.H. Carutth. New York: Shocken Books, 1964. (Gunkel)

Gurney, O.R. *The Hittites,* rev. 2nd edition. Harmondsworth: Penguin Books, 1961. (Gurney)

Guthrie, D. et al. *The New Bible Commentary* revised. London: New Varsity Press, 1970. (Guthrie)

Hachette World Guides: *The Middle East.* Paris: Librairie Hachette, 1966. (Hachette)

Haggith, David. *End-Time Prophecies of the Bible.* New York: Perigree, 2000. (Haggith)

Hallet, Jean-Pierre. *Pygmy Kitabu.* Greenwich: Fawcett Pub., 1973. (Hallet)

Halley, Henry H. *Bible Handbook.* 24th edition. Grand Rapids: Zondervan Publishing House, 1965. (Halley)

Halsell, Grace. *Forcing God's Hand.* Washington: Crossroads International Publishing, 1999. (Halsell)

Hanson, R.P.C., commentator. *The Acts,* The New Clarendon Bible. Oxford: Oxford Univ. Press, 1967. (Hanson)

Harden, Donald. *The Phoenicians.* Harmondsworth: Penguin Books, 1971. (Harden)

Harrington, Daniel J., ed. & trans. *The Hebrew Fragments of Pseudo-Philo Texts and Translations 3,* Pseudepigrapha Series 3. Missoula: Society of Biblical Literature, 1974. (Harrington)

Harrington, Wilfrid J., O.P. *Key to the Bible,* 3 vols. Garden City: Image Books, 1976. (Bible Key)

Hassnain, Fida. *A Quest for the Historical Jesus.* Bath: Gateway Books, 1994. (Hassnain)

Hastings, James, ed. *A Dictionary of the Bible,* 5 vols. NY: Scribners, 1908-9. (DB5)

Hastings, James, ed. *Dictionary of the Bible,* rev. Ed. Frederick C. Grant & H.H. Rowley. New York: Charles Scribner's Sons, 1963. (DB)

Hastings, James, ed. *The Encyclopædia of Religion and Ethics.* 12 vols. + Index. New York: Scribner's, 1961. (ERE)

Hayes, Christine Elizabeth. *Between the Babylonian and Palestinian Talmuds*. New York: Oxford Univ. Press, 1997. (Hayes)

Heidel, Alexander. *The Babylonian Genesis*. 2nd edition. Chicago: The Univ. of Chicago Press, 1963. (Heidel)

Hennecke, E. *New Testament Apocrypha*: 2 vols. Trans R. McL. Wilson. London?: SCM Press, 1973, 1974. (Hennecke)

Herodotus. *The Histories*. Trans. Aubrey de Selincourt. Harmondsworth: Penguin Books, 1972. (Herodotus)

Herschel, Abraham J. *The Prophets*. 2 vols. New York: Harper Torchbooks, 1969, 1971. (Herschel)

Herzl, Theodor. *The Jewish State*. Intro. by Louis Lipsky. New York: American Zionist Emergency Council, 1946. (Herzl)

Heston, E.W. *The Hebrew Kingdoms*. New Clarendon Bible, Old Testament, Vol. 3. London: Oxford Univ. Press, 1968. (Heston)

Hijazi, Abu Tariq. *Islam 01 AH-250 AH: A Chronology of Events*. New York: The Message Publications, 1994. (Hijazi)

Hinnells, John R. *Persian Mythology*. London: Hamlyn Publishing Group, 1973. (Hinnells)

History of the Land of Israel until 1880. Compiled from material in the EJ. Israel Pocket Library series. Jerusalem: Keter Publ. House, 1973. (Israel Land)

Holy Bible, The. (Hebrew and English) Trans. Isaac Leeser. New York: Hebrew Publishing Co., undated. (Hebrew Bible)

Holy Quran, The. Malik Ghulam Farid, ed. (and trans.?). Orig. publication by The Oriental and Religious Publishing Corp., Ltd., of Pakistan 1969. Present edition: Tilford: Islam International Publications, 1994. (Quran-Farid)

Hooke, S.H. *Middle Eastern Mythology*. Harmondsworth: Penguin Books, 1963. (Hooke)

Hotchkiss, Robert B., ed. & trans. *A Pseudo-Epiphanius Testimony Book*. Texts & Translations 9. Early Christian Literature 1. Missoula: Society of Biblical Literature, 1974. (Hotchkiss)

Houlden, J.L. *Paul's Letters From Prison*. Harmondsworth: Penguin Books, 1970. (Prison Letters)

Houlden, J.L. *The Pastoral Epistles*. Harmondsworth: Penguin Books, 1976. (Pastoral)

Hudson, D.F. *New Testament Greek* (Teach Yourself Series). Sevenoaks: Hodder and Stoughton, 1960. (Hudson)

Hughes, Thomas Patrick. *A Dictionary of Islam*. Chicago: Kazi Publications, 1994 reprint of 1886 edition. (Hughes)

Humber, Thomas. *The Fifth Gospel: the Miracle of the Holy Shroud*. New York: Pocket Books, 1974. (Humber)

Husaini, Moulavi S.A.Q., *Ibn al-'Arabi*, Muhammad Ashraf, Lahore, undated. [Husaini]

Huxley, Aldous. *Island*. Reprint of 1952 Harper & Row edition. New York: Bantam Books, 1963. (Huxley, A.)

Huxley, Francis. *The Way of the Sacred*. New York: Dell Publishing, 1976. (Huxley)

Ibn Ishaq. *The Life of Muhammad*. Trans. A. Guillaume. Karachi: Oxford Univ. Press, 1955. (Ibn Ishaq)

Ibn Kathir, 'Imad al-Din Abu al-Fida Isma'il (d. AH774/1372-3CE). *Qisas al-Anbiya'* (Stories of the Prophets) (Arabic). Riyadh: Dar al-Qiblatayn, AH1412/1992 CE. (Kathir)

Ibn Sa'd. *Kitab al-Tabaqat al-Kabir*, 2 vols. Trans. S. Moinul Haq. Karachi: Pakistan Historical Society, 1967, 1972. (Ibn Sa'd)

James, Montague Rhodes. *The Apocryphal New Testament*. London: Oxford Univ. Press, 1953. (James)

Jeffrey, Arthur. *The Foreign Vocabulary of the Quran*. Baroda: Oriental Institute, 1938. (Jeffrey)

Jeffrey, Grant R. *Armageddon Appointment With Destiny*. Reprint with supplement of 1988 edition. New York: Bantam Books, 1990. (Jeffrey, G)

Jellinek, A. *Beit-ha-Midrash 4*. 1967. (Jellinek)

Jenks, Alan W. *The Elohist and North Israelite Traditions*. Society of Biblical Literature Monographs Series, Vol. 22. Missoula: Scholars Press, 1977. (Jenks)

Jonas, Hans. *The Gnostic Religion*, 2nd edition. Boston: Beacon Press, 1963. (Jonas)

Jones, A.H.M. *Constantine and the Conversion of Europe*. Harmondsworth: Penguin Books, 1972. (Jones)

Jormier, Jacques. *The Bible and the Koran*. New York: Descless Co., 1964. (Jormier)

Josephus. *Complete Works*. Trans. William Whiston. Grand Rapids: Kregel Publications, 1967; orig. Published in Edinburgh, 1867. (Josephus)

Josephus. *The Jewish War*. Trans. G.A. Williamson. Harmondsworth: Penguin Books, 1959. (Josephus-War)

Joyce, Donovan. *The Jesus Scroll*. New York: New American Library, 1974. (Joyce)

Juwayri, Mawlana Muhammad. *Qisas al-Anbiya* (Stories of the Prophets). Tehran: 'Ali Akbar 'Ilmi, undated. (Juwayri)

Kapelrud, A.S. *The Ras Shamra Discoveries and the Old Testament*. Oxford: Blackwell, 1965. (Kapelrud)

Keller, Werner. *The Bible as History*. Trans. William Neil. New York: Bantam Books, 1974. (Keller)

Kenyon, Kathleen. *Royal Cities of the Old Testament*. New York: Schocken Books, 1971. (Kenyon)

Kersten, Holger & Elmar R. Gruber. *The Jesus Conspiracy*. Brisbane: Element Books, 1995. (Kersten)

Khanlari, Dr. Parviz Natel. *Yusef-o Zulaykha* (Masterpieces of Persian Literature, No. 1) (Persian). Tehran: Amir Kabir, AHS 1352. (Khanlari)

Kinder, Herman & Hilgeman, Werner. *The Anchor Atlas of World History*. 2 vols. New York: Bantam, Doubleday, Dell Publishing Group, 1974. (AAWH)

Kinder, Herman, & Hilgemann, Werner. *The Penguin Atlas of World History*, Vol. 1. Trans. Ernest A. Menze with maps designed by Harald and Ruth Bakor. Harmondsworth: Penguin Books, 1974. (History Atlas-1)

Kisa'i, Muhammad ibn 'Abd Allah. *Tales of the Prophets*. Trans. Wheeler M. Thackston, Jr. Chicago: Great Books of the Islamic World, 1997. (Kisa'i)

Kitchen, K.A. *Ancient Orient and Old Testament*. Chicago: Inter-Varsity Press, 1966. (Kitchen)

Kitto, H.D.F. *The Greeks*. Harmondsworth: Penguin Books Ltd., 1951. (Kitto)

Kraft, Robert A. & Purintun, Ann-Elizabeth, eds. & trans. *Paraleipomena Jeremiou*. Texts and Translations 1, Pseudepigrapha Series 1. Missoula: Society of Biblical Literature, 1972. (Jeremiou)

Kraft, Robert A., ed. *The Testament of Job*. Texts and Translations 5. Society of Biblical Literature. Missoula: Scholars Press, 1974. (Test Job)

Kramer, Samuel Noah. *History Begins at Sumer*. Garden City: Doubleday & Co., 1959. (Kramer-Sumer)

Kramer. Samuel Noah, ed. *Mythologies of the Ancient World*. Garden City: Doubleday & Co., 1961. (Kramer-Myth)

Kritzeck, James. *Peter the Venerable and Islam*. Princeton: Princeton University Press, 1964. (Kritzeck)

Lamb, Harold. *Cyrus the Great*. Garden City: Doubleday & Co., 1960. (Lamb-Cyrus)

Laymon, Charles M., ed. *The Interpreter's One-Volume Commentary on the Bible*. Nashville: Abingdon Press, 1971. (Laymon)

Lazarus, Rabbi Dayan H.M. *Mo'ed Katan*. London: Soncino Press, 1938. (Lazarus)

Legge, Francis. *Forerunners and Rivals of Christianity*: From 330 B.C. to 330 A.D. 2 vols. bound as one. Mew Hyde Park: University Books, 1964. (Legge)

Lemprière, John. *Classical Dictionary*. Orig. Edition, 1788; revised, 1850. London: Bracken Bks., 1994. (Lemprière)

Léon-Dufour, Xavier. *The Gospels and the Jesus of History*. Trans. John McHugh. London: Collins, 1968. (Léon-Dufour)

Lindsey, Hal. *The 1980's: Countdown to Armageddon*. New York: Bantam, 1981. (Lindsey-80s)

Lindsey, Hal. *The Late Great Planet Earth*. New York: Bantam, 1973; reprint of the Zondervan edition of 1970. (Lindsey-LGPE)

Lindsey, Hal. *The Rapture: Truth or Consequences*. New York: Bantam, 1983. (Lindsey-R)

Littman, E. "Jesus in a Pre-Islamic Arabic Inscription." *Moslem World*, XL, 1950, 16-18. (Littman)

Lost Books of the Bible, The. No. Ed. Cited. New York: New American Library, 1974; reprint of 1926 Alpha House edition. (Lost Bks)

Ma'luf, Louis, ed. *Al-Munjid*. (Arabic) Beirut: Catholic Press, 1956. (Munjid)

Maccoby, Hyam. *The Mythmaker: Paul and the Invention of Christianity.* New York: Barnes & Noble, 1986. (Maccoby)

Mack, Burton L. *Who Wrote the New Testament?* New York: Harper Collins, 1995. (Mack)

Mackenzie, Donald A. *Egyptian Myth and Legend.* (Reprint of 1907 edition.) New York: Bell Publishing, 1978. (Mackenzie-Egypt)

Mackenzie, Donald A. *Mythology of the Babylonian People.* (Reprint of 1915 edition originally titled *Myths of Babylonia and Assyria.*) London: Bracken Books, 1996. (Mackenzie-Myth)

Margoliouth, D.S. *The Relations Between Arabs and Israelites Prior to the Rise of Islam.* London: the British Academy, 1924. (Margoliouth)

Marsh, John. *Saint John.* Pelican New Testament Commentaries. Harmondsworth: Penguin Books, 1968. (Marsh)

Matarrasso, P.M., trans. *The Quest of the Holy Grail.* Harmondsworth: Penguin Books, 1969. (Matarasso)

Matheson, Sylvia A. *Persia: an Archaeological Guide.* London: Faber and Faber, 1972. (Matheson)

Matini, Dr. Jalal, ed. *Commentary on the Glorious Quran* (Cambridge), 2 vols. Tehran: Bunyad-i Farhang-i Iran, AHS 1349. (Cambridge Commentary)

Maududi, Sayyid AbulAla. *Towards Understanding Islam.* Dr. Abdul Ghani, trans. Lahore: Tarjumanul Quran, 5th edition, 1954. (Maududi-TUI)

May, Herbert G., ed. *Oxford Bible Atlas*, 2nd edition. London: Oxford Univ. Press, 1974. (OBA)

Mayhani, Muhammad bin Munawwar. *Asrar al-Tawhid* (Secrets of Divine Unity). Persian. Tehran: Amir Kabir, AHS1348. (Mayhani)

Mazar, Benjamin, ed. *Judges*, Vol. III, The World History of the Jewish People. Israel: Jewish History Publications, 1971. (Judges)

Mazar, Benjamin, ed. *Patriarchs*, Vol. II, The World History of the Jewish People. Israel: Jewish History Publications, 1970. (Patriarchs)

McEvedy and Richard Jones. *Atlas of World Population History.* Harmondsworth: Penguin Books, 1978. (McEvedy)

McEvedy, Colin. *Penguin Atlas of Ancient History.* Harmondsworth: Penguin Books, 1967. (McEvedy-AH)

Mercatante, Anthony S. *Who's Who in Egyptian Mythology.* New York: Potter, 1978. (Mercatante)

Metzger, Bruce and Coogan, Michael D., eds. *The Oxford Essential Guide to People and Places of the Bible* (American Edition). New York: Berkley Books, 2001. (Metzger)

Meyer, Marvin W., ed. & trans. *The Mithras Liturgy.* Texts and Translations 10, Graeco-Roman Religion 2. Missoula: Society of Biblical Literature, 1976. (Meyer)

Miller, Robert J., ed. *The Complete Gospels*: Annotated Scholars Version. Sonoma: HarperSanFrancisco, 1994. (ComGospels)

Mitchell, Stephen. *Genesis: A New Translation of the Classical Biblical Stories.* New York: Harper-Collins, 1996. (Mitchell)

Mommsen, Theodor. *The Provinces of the Roman Empire.* (Reprint of 1909 edition, two volumes in one.) New York: Barnes & Noble Bks., 1996. (Mommsen)

Morison, Frank. *Who Moved the Stone?* London: Faber and Faber, 1958 (1930). (Morison)

Mowry, Lucetta. *The Dead Sea Scrolls and the Early Church.* Notre Dame: Univ. of Notre Dame Press, 1966. (Mowry)

Muhajir, Ali Musa Raza. *Lessons From the Stories of the Quran.* Lahore: Sh. Muhammad Ashraf, 1965. (Muhajir)

Muqaddasi, Mutahhir bin. *Afarinash wa Tarikh.* Trans. From Arabic by Muhammad Rida Shafi'i Kadkani (Persian) Tehran: Bunyad-i Farhang-i Iran, AHS1349-1352. (Afarinash)

Muslim World. Periodical. (MW)

Nadvi, Syed Muzaffer-ud-Din. *A Geographical History of the Quran.* Lahore: Sh. Muhammad Ashraf, 1936. (Nadvi)

Narshakhī (Al-), Abū Bakr Muḥammad. *Tārīkh-i Bukhārā* (History of Bukhara). Abū Naṣr Aḥmad bin Muḥammad al-Qibāwī, trans. from Arabic into Persian. Ed. & notes by Mudarris Ridawi. (Persian) Tehran: Bunyad-i Farhang-i Iran, AHS1351/1972 CE. (Bukhara)

Nasafi, Abu Hafs Najmuddin 'Umar. *Tafsir-i Nasafi.* 2 vols. Dr. 'Aziz Allah Juwayni, ed. (Persian) Tehran: Bunyad-i Farhang-i Iran, AHS1353-1354. (Nasafi)

Nathan, Rabbi. *The Fathers According to Rabbi Nathan.* Trans. Judah Goldin. New York: Shocken Books, 1974. (Nathan)

New American Desk Encyclopedia, 4th edition. New York: Signet, 1997. (NADE)

New Catholic Encyclopedia, 18 vols., incl. supplements 1967-1988. Catholic Univ. of America, Washington, DC. New York: McGraw-Hill, 1967. (NCE)

New Compact Bible Dictionary, The. T. Alton Bryant, ed. Grand Rapids: Zondervan, 1967. (NCBD)

New Encyclopædia Britannica. Univ. of Chicago. 15th edition. Chicago: Enc. Britannica, 1967. Micropædia and Macropædia. (EB, EB-Macro, EB Micro)

New Interpreter's Bible, The. 12 vols. Nashville: Abdingdon Press, 1994-8. (NIB)

New Testament in Four Versions, The. The versions are: King James, Revised Standard, Phillips Modern English, and New English Bible. Washington: Canon Press, 1963. (New Testament4)

Nicholson, Reynold A. *A Literary History of the Arabs*, first edition 1907; reprinted, Cambridge: Cambridge Univ. Press, 1969. (Nicholson)

Nineham, D.E. *Saint Mark.* Pelican New Testament Commentaries. Harmondsworth: Penguin Books, revised 1969. (Nineham)

Nordhoff, Charles. *The Communistic Societies of the United States.* Reprint of 1875 edition. New York: Dover Publications, 1966. (Nordhoff)

O'Grady, Joan. *Early Christian Heresies*. Reprint of 1985 ed. New York: Barnes & Noble, 1994. (O'Grady)

O'Neill, J.C. *Paul's Letter to the Romans*. Pelican New Testament Commentaries. Harmondsworth: Penguin Books, 1975. (O'Neill)

O'Shea, Stephen. *The Perfect Heresy*. New York: Walker & Co., 2000. (O'Shea)

Olmstead, A.T. *History of the Persian Empire*. Chicago: Univ. of Chicago Press, 1948. (Olmstead)

Ovid. *Metamorphoses*. Trans. Mary M. Innes. Harmondsworth: Penguin Books, 1955. (Ovid)

Pagels, Elaine. *The Gnostic Gospels*. New York: Vintage, 1981. (Pagels)

Panati, Charles. *Extraordinary Origins of Everyday Things*. New York: Harper & Row, Perennial Library, 1987. (Panati)

Patai, Raphael. *The Hebrew Goddess*. New York: Avon Books, 1978. (Patai)

Penrice, John. *A Dictionary and Glossary of the Koran*. (Reprint of the 1873 edition.) Mineola: Dover Publications, 2004. (Penrice)

Pesikta Rabbati. Trans. W. C. Braude. New Haven: Yale Univ., 1968. (Pesikta)

Petrie, W.M. Flinders, trans. *Egyptian Tales*. First series, IVth to XIIth Dynasty. New York: Benjamin Blom, 1971. Reprint of 1899 edition. (Petrie)

Philostratus the Elder. *Life and Times of Apollonius of Tyana*. Charles P. Eells, trans. University Series. Language and Literature, Vol. II, No. 1. Stanford: Stanford Univ., 1923. (Philostratus)

Phipps, William E. *Muhammad and Jesus*. New York: Continuum, 1996. (Phipps)

Pickering, David. *Cassell Dictionary of Superstitions*. London: Cassell, 1995. (Pickering)

Platt, Rutherford H., ed. *Forgotten Books of Eden, The*. New York: New American Library, 1974; reprint of 1927 Alpha House edition. (Platt)

Pliny the Younger (C. Plinius Caecilius Secundus). *The Letters of the Younger Pliny*. Betty Radice, trans. Harmondsworth: Penguin Books, 1969. (Pliny)

Plutarch. *The Age of Alexander*. Trans. Ian Scott-Kilvert. Harmondsworth: Penguin Books, 1973. (Plutarch)

Pope, Arthur Upham. *Persian Architecture*. London: Tames & Hudson, 1965. (Pope)

Potter, Rev. Dr. Charles Francis. *The Lost Years of Jesus Revealed*. Greenwich: Fawcett Pub., 1962. (Potter)

Powell, Evan. *The Unfinished Gospel*. Westlake Village: Symposium Books, 1994. (Powell)

Pritchard, J.B., ed. *Solomon and Sheba*. London: Phaidon, 1974. (SolSheba)

Pritchard, James B., ed. *The Ancient Near East*. 2 vols. Princeton: Princeton Univ. Press, 1958, 1975. (ANE)

Pseudo-Callistenes. *The Romance of Alexander the Great.* Trans. Albert M. Wolohokian. New York: Columbia Univ. Press, 1969. (PseudoCal)

Quran: Arberry, Arthur J. *The Koran Interpreted.* London: Oxford Univ. Press, 1964. (Quran-Arberry)

Quran: Maududi, S. Abul A'la, commentator. *The Meaning of the Quran.* Trans. Muhammad Akbar Muradpuri. First 17 surahs in 6 vols. Lahore: Islamic Publications, 1971-73. (Quran-Maududi)

Quran: The Holy Quran. Trans. & commentary by Abdullah Yusuf Ali, 2 vols., continuous pagination. Lahore: Sh. Muhammad Ashraf, 1969. (Quran-Yusuf Ali)

Quran: The Holy Quran. Trans. & commentary by Maulana Muhammad Ali. 5th edition. Lahore: Ahmadiyyah Anjuman Isha'at Islam, 1963. (Quran-MMA)

Quran: The Koran. Trans. & annotated by George Sale. London: Frederick Warne and Co, undated. (Quran-Sale)

Quran: The Koran. Trans. N.J. Dawood. Harmondsworth: Penguin Books, 1966. (Quran-Dawood)

Quran: The Meaning of the Glorious Koran. Trans. Mohammed Marmaduke Pickthall. New York: Mentor Books, 1953. (Quran-Pickthall)

Rabin, Chaim. *Qumran Studies.* New York: Schocken, 1975. Reprint of Oxford 1957 edition. (Rabin)

Rahman, H.U. *A Chronology of Islamic History.* Boston: G.K. Hall & Co., 1989. (Rahman)

Ramya, Muhammad. *Faharis al-Quran.* (Arabic) Tehran: Amir Kabir, AHS 1345. (Faharis)

Randi, James. *An Encyclopedia of Claims, Frauds, and Hoaxes of the Occult and Supernatural.* New York: St. Martin's Press, 1995. (Randi)

Randolph, Vance. *Religious Philosophers.* Ten-Cent Pocket Series, No. 614. Girard: Haldeman-Julius Co., 1924. (Randolph)

Random House Dictionary of the English Language, The. (College Edition). Laurence Urdang, ed. NY: Random House, 1968. (RHD)

Rappoport, Angelo S. *Ancient Israel: Myths and Legends.* 3 vols. London: Senate, 1995. (Rappoport)

Rawwaqi, 'Ali, ed. *Tafsir-i Quran-i Pak.* (Arabic-Persian) Tehran: Bunyad-i Farhang-i Iran, AHS 1348. (Rawwaqi)

Rice, Michael. *Who's Who in Ancient Egypt.* London: Routledge, 1999. (Rice)

Ridpath, John Clark. *Ridpath's History of the World,* 9 vols. Cincinnati: Jones Bros. Publishing Co., 1923. (Ridpath)

Roberts, Rev. Alexander and Donaldson, James, eds. *The Apostolic Fathers.* Vol. 1 of the Anti-Nicene Christian Library. Edinburgh: T. and T. Clark, 1879. (Fathers)

Robinson, James, general ed. *The Nag Hammadi Library.* New York: Harper & Row, 1977. (Robinson)

Rodinson, Maxime. David Thorstad, tr. *Israel: A Colonial-Settler State?* New York: Monad Press, 1973. (Rodinson-Israel)

Rodinson, Maxime. *Mohammed.* Trans. Anne Carter. Harmondsworth: Penguin Books, 1971 (1961). (Rodinson)

Rosenberg, David & Bloom, Harold. *The Book of J.* New York: Grove Weidenfeld, 1990. (Rosenberg)

Rosenthal, Erwin I.J. *Judaism and Islam.* Popular Jewish Library. London: Thomas Yoseloff, 1961. (Rosenthal)

Rothenberg, Beno. *Were These King Solomon's Mines?* Excavations in the Timna Valley. New York: Stein & Day, 1972. (Rothenberg)

Ruef, John. *Paul's First Letter to Corinth.* Pelican New Testament Commentaries. Harmondsworth: Penguin Books, 1971. (Ruef)

Runes, Dagobert, ed. *Dictionary of Philosophy.* 15th edition. New York: Philosophical Library, Inc., 1960. (Runes)

Russell, D.S. *The Jews From Alexander to Herod.* The New Clarendon Bible, Old Testament, Vol. V. London: Oxford Univ. Press, 1967. (Russell)

Saggs, H.W.F. *The Greatness That was Babylon.* New York: The New American Library, 1968. (Saggs)

Saglam, Bahaeddin. *The Torah.* Trans. Selahattin Ayaz. Istanbul: Tabligh, 1999. (Saglam)

Sandars, N.K., trans. *The Epic of Gilgamesh.* Harmondsworth: Penguin Books, 1964, revised ed. (Gilgamesh)

Sarna, Nahum M. *Understanding Genesis.* New York: Schocken Books, 1970. (Sarna)

Sayers, Dorothy L., trans. *The Song of Roland.* Harmondsworth: Penguin Books, Ltd., 1937. (Sayers)

Schalit, Abraham, ed. *The Hellenistic Age.* Vol. VI, The World History of the Jewish People. Israel: Jewish History Publications, 1972. (Hellenistic)

Schauss, Hayyim. *Guide to Jewish Holy Days: History and Observance.* New York: Schocken Books, 1962. (Schauss)

Schonfield, Hugh J. *The Passover Plot.* New York: Bantam Books, 1967. (Passover)

Schonfield, Hugh J. *Those Incredible Christians.* New York: Bantam Books, 1969. (Shonfield)

Schurer, Emil. *A History of the Jewish People in the Time of Jesus.* New York: Schocken Books, 1961, Reprint of 1886-1890 Eng. Trans. (Schurer)

Scofield Bible, The. Rev. C.I. Scofield, ed. New York: Oxford Univ. Press, 1917. (Scofield)

Segal, Moses H. *The Pentateuch: Its Composition and Its Authorship and Other Biblical Studies.* Jerusalem: The Magnes Press, Hebrew Univ., 1967. (Segal)

Seton-Williams, Veronica & Peter Socks. *Blue Guide Egypt.* London: Ernest Benn, 1983. (Egypt-BG)

Shams, J.D. *Where Did Jesus Die?* Qadian: Nazir Dawat-o-Tabligh, 1973. (Shams)

Shanks, Hershel, ed. *Ancient Israel: From Abraham to the Roman Destruction of the Temple*, rev. & expanded ed. Washington: Biblical Archaeological Society, 1999. (Shanks)

Shanks, Hershel. *The City of David: A Guide to Biblical Jerusalem.* Washington: Biblical Archaeological Society, 1973. (Shanks-City)

Shinnie, P.L. *Meroe: A Civilization of the Sudan.* London: Thames and Hudson, 1967. (Shinnie)

Shulvass, Moses A. *The History of the Jewish People: Vol. I, The Antiquity.* Chicago: Regener Gateway, 1982. (Shulvass)

Siddiqui, Abdul Hameed. *The Life of Muhammad*, 10th edition. Lahore: Islamic Publications, 1993. (Siddiqui)

Silver, Abba Hillel. *Moses and the Original Torah.* New York: Macmillan Co., 1961. (Silver)

Simon, Edith. *The Saints.* Harmondsworth: Penguin Books, 1972. (Simon)

Smelik, Klass A.D. *Writings From Ancient Israel.* Edinburgh: T&T Clark, 1991. (Smelik)

Smith, George Adam. *The Historical Geography of the Holy Land.* London: Fontana Library, 1966 (1931). (Geo HL)

Smith, Morton. *Jesus the Magician.* New York: Barnes & Noble, 1993. Reprint of 1978 ed. (Smith-Jesus)

Smith, W. Robertson. *The Religion of the Semites.* New York: Schocken Books, 1972 (1889) (Smith)

Smith, William. *A Dictionary of the Bible.* New York: Bible House, 1900. (DB-1900)

Smith, William. *Bible Dictionary.* New York: Family Library, 1975. (BD-Smith)

Sox, David. *The Gospel of Barnabas.* London: George Allen & Unwin, 1981. (Sox)

Speiser, E.A., ed. *At the Dawn of Civilization.* Vol. I, The World History of the Jewish People. Israel: Jewish History Publications, 1963. (Speiser)

Spence, Lewis. *The History of Atlantis.* Reprint of 1926/1968 edition. Mineola: Dover Publications, 2003. (Spence)

Stanley, Arthur Penrhyn. *Sinai and Palestine.* New York: 1895. (Stanley-Sinai)

Stanley, Arthur Penrhyn. *The Eastern Church.* London: John Murray, 1861. (Stanley)

Stedman's Medical Dictionary, 22nd edition. Baltimore: Williams & Wilkins, 1972. (Stedman)

Stone, Jon R., ed. *Expecting Armageddon—Essential Readings in Failed Prophecy.* New York: Routledge, 2000. (Stone)

Storey, C.A. *Persian Literature.* Vol. 1, Part I. Royal Asiatic Society. London: Luzac & Co., 1970, first published 1927-39. (Storey)

Stott, John R.W. *Basic Christianity*, 2nd edition. London: Inter-Varsity Press, 1971. (Stott)

Suetonius, Gaius. *The Twelve Caesars.* Trans. Robert Graves. Baltimore: Penguin Books, 1957. (Suetonius)

Surabadi, Abu Bakr 'Atiq Nishaburi. *Stories From the Holy Quran*. Dr. Mahdavi, ed. Persian. No. 66 in Iranian Texts Series. Tehran: Tehran Univ., AHS1347. (Surabadi)

Surabadi. *Tafsir*. Photographic reproduction of AH523 copy. (Persian-Arabic) Tehran: Bunyad-i Farhang, AHS 1345. (Surabadi-Photo2)

Surabadi. *Tafsir*. Vol. 1. Photographic reproduction. (Persian) Tehran: Bunyad-i Farhang-i Iran, AHS 1353. (Surabadi-Photo)

Tabari, Muhammad bin Jarir. *Tarikh-i Tabari*. 16 vols. Persian trans. Abu al-Qasim Payandah. Tehran: Bunyad-i Farhang- Iran, AHS 1352-54. (Tabari)

Tacitus, Cornelius. *The Annals of Imperial Rome*. Trans. Michael Grant. Harmondsworth: Penguin Books, 1959. (Tacitus)

Tafsir al-Jalalayn. (The Commentary by the Two Jalals: Jalal al-Din al-Mahalli and Jalal al-Din al-Suyuti). Eighth edition (Arabic). Beirut: Dar al-Jil, AH1415/1995 CE. (Jalalayn)

Tafsiri bar 'Ushri az Quran Majid (British Museum). Dr. Jalal Matini, ed. (Persian) Tehran: Bunyad-i Farhang-i Iran, AHS1352. (Ushri)

Taylor, Vincent. *The Text of the New Testament*. London: St. Martin's Press, 1961. (Taylor)

Thapar, Romila. *A History of India*, Vol. 1. Harmondsworth: Penguin Books Ltd., 1966. (Thapar)

The Four Gospels. Trans. E.V. Rieu. Harmondsworth: Penguin Books, 1952. (FourGos)

The Testament of Abraham. Trans. Michael E. Stone. Texts and Translations 2. Society of Biblical Literature. Missoula: Scholars Press, 1972. (Test Abraham)

The World Almanac and Book of Facts. 2002 edition. New York: World Almanac Bks, 2002. (World Almanac)

Thesiger, Wilfred. *Arabian Sands*. Harmondsworth: Penguin Books, 1964. (Thesiger)

Thomas, D. Winston, ed. *Documents From Old Testament Times*. New York: Harper Torchbooks, 1961. (Thomas)

Tichenor, H.M. *Primitive Beliefs*. Ten-Cent Pocket Series, No. 184, Girard: Haldeman-Julius Co., 1921. (Tichenor-Primitive)

Tichenor, H.M. *Sun-Worship and Later Beliefs*. Ten-Cent Pocket Series, No. 204. Girard: Haldeman-Julius Co., 1921. (Tichenor-Sun)

Tisdall, Rev. Wm. St. Clair. *The Original Sources of the Quran*. London: 1905. (Tisdall)

Torrey, C.C. *The Jewish Foundation of Islam*. New York: Ktav Publishing House, 1967; reprint of 1933 edition. (Torrey)

Trawick, Buckner B. *The Bible as Literature: The New Testament*. Second edition. New York: Barnes & Noble, 1968. (Trawick-NT)

Trawick, Buckner B. *The Bible as Literature: The Old Testament and the Apocrypha*. Second edition. New York: Barnes & Noble, 1970. (Trawick-OT)

Treece, Henry. *The Crusades.* New York: Mentor Books, 1964. (Treece)

Ulansey, David. *The Origins of the Mithraic Mysteries.* New York: Oxford University Press, 1989. (Ulansey)

Van Voorst, Robert E. *Jesus Outside the New Testament.* Grand Rapids: Wm. B. Eerdmans, 2000. (Voorst)

Vermes, G. *The Dead Sea Scrolls in English.* Harmondsworth: Penguin Books, 1962. (Vermes)

Vermes, Geza. *The Complete Dead Sea Scrolls in English.* New York: Penguin Books, 1997. (Vermes-97)

von Keler, Theodore M.R. *The Essence of the Koran.* Ten-Cent Pocket Series, No. 428. Girard: Haldeman-Julius Co., 1923. (Keler)

Ware, Timothy. *The Orthodox Church.* Harmondsworth, Penguin Books, 1969. (Ware)

Washington Report on Middle East Affairs, periodical. (WRMEA)

Waterfield, Robin E. *Christians in Persia.* London: George Allen & Unwin, 1973. (Waterfield)

Watt, W. Montgomery. *Bell's Introduction to the Quran.* Revised and enlarged by W.M. Watt. Islamic Surveys, Vol. 8. Edinburgh University Press, 1970. (Watt-Bell)

Watt, W. Montgomery. *Muhammad: Prophet and Statesman.* New York: Oxford Univ. Press, 1964. (Watt-Md)

Watt, W. Montgomery. *The Influence of Islam on Medieval Europe.* Islamic Surveys, Vol. 9. Edinburgh University Press, 1972. (Watt-Influence)

Watts, Alan W. *The Two Hands of God.* New York: College Books, 1969. (Watts-Hands)

Watts, Alan W. *Myth and Ritual in Christianity.* Boston: Beacon Press, 1968. (Watts-Myth)

Weber, Max. *Ancient Judaism.* Trans. & ed. Hans H. Gerth & Don Martindale. New York: The Free Press, 1952. (Weber)

Webster's Ninth New Collegiate Dictionary. Springfield: Merriam-Webster, Inc., 1991. (Webster)

Wehr, Hans. *Arabic-English Dictionary.* Trans. J.M. Cowan. Beirut: Librairie du Liban, 1980. (Wehr)

Wells, G.A. *The Jesus Legend.* Chicago: Open Court, 1996. (Wells)

White, Ellen G. *Cosmic Conflict.* Reprint of 1911? edition. Boise: Pacific Press Publishing Assoc., 1971. (White)

Williams, Jay G. *Understanding the Old Testament.* New York: Barron's Educational Series, 1972. (Williams)

Wilson, A.N. *Paul—The Mind of the Apostle.* New York: Norton, 1997. (ANW)

Wilson, Benjamin, trans. & ed. *The Emphatic Diaglott of What Is Commonly Called the New Testament.* New York: Fowler & Wells, 1864. (GreekNT)

Wilson, Colin. *A History of the Devil.* St. Albans: Panther Books, 1975. (Wilson)

Wolff, Hans Walter. *The Old Testament: A Guide to Its Writings.* Trans. Keith R. Crim. London: SPCK, 1974. (Wolff)

Woodward, Kenneth L. *The Book of Miracles.* New York: Simon & Schuster, 2000. (Woodward)

Woolley, Sir Leonard. *Ur of the Chaldees.* Harmondsworth: Penguin Books, revised ed., 1952. (Woolley)

Wright, G. Ernest & Freedman, David Noel, eds. *The Biblical Archaeologist Reader 1.* Reprints from BA magazine. Missoula: Scholars Press, 1975. (BA1)

Wright, G. Ernest & Fuller, Reginald. *The Book of the Acts of God.* Harmondsworth: Penguin Books, 1965. (Wright)

Wunderlich, Hans Georg. *The Secret of Crete.* Trans. Richard Winston. Glasgow: Fontana/Collins, 1976. (Wunderlich)

Young, William G. *Patriarch, Shah and Caliph.* Rawalpindi: Christian Study Centre, 1974. (Young)

INDEX

This index is to the text and notes. The Table of Contents, Glossary, Bibliographies, maps, charts, and tables are not indexed. The reader should refer to the Table of Contents for the general location of broader topics; the Glossary also contains relevant information. *Bible, Islam, God, Quran,* and *Surabadi* are not listed (except topically), as the words occur too frequently throughout the text to be indexed usefully. References to the 66 books of the Bible (see list on p. xiii) and the Quran are not indexed. The names of Biblical books are in italics.

H

CPSIA information can be obtained
at www.ICGtesting.com
Printed in the USA
FFOW04n2306260715
15368FF